Years of Division
Europe Since 1945

Contributors
JOHN LAVER, CHRIS ROWE AND
DAVID WILLIAMSON

Edited by
JOHN LAVER

Hodder & Stoughton

A MEMBER OF THE HODDER HEADLINE GROUP

Orders: please contact Bookpoint Ltd, 39 Milton Park, Abingdon, Oxon OX14 4TD.
Telephone: (44) 01235 400414, Fax: (44) 01235 400454. Lines are open from 9.00–
6.00pm, Monday to Saturday, with a 24-hour message answering service. E-mail address:
orders@bookpoint.co.uk

British Library Cataloguing in Publication Data
A catalogue record for this title is available from The British Library

ISBN 0 340 69726 1

First published 1999
Impression number   10   9   8   7   6   5   4   3   2   1
Year   2004   2003   2002   2001   2000   1999

The front cover shows the Berlin Wall, December 1989, reproduced courtesy of Corbis/
Owen Franken.
Produced by Gray Publishing, Tunbridge Wells, Kent.

Printed in Great Britain for Hodder & Stoughton Educational, a division of Hodder
Headline Plc, 338 Euston Road, London NW1 3BH by J. W. Arrowsmith Ltd, Bristol.

Contents

✺ LIST OF TABLES ✺

⤹ LIST OF MAPS ⤸

⤹ LIST OF DIAGRAMS ⤸

LIST OF ILLUSTRATIONS

∾ LIST OF PROFILES ∾

∾ LIST OF ANALYSES ∾

ACKNOWLEDGEMENTS

The publisher would like to thank the following for permission to reproduce material in
this book:
Allen Lane, for an extract from *A History of Twentieth-century Russia* by R. Service (1997)
used on page 127; Arnold, for extracts from *Twentieth-century France* by J.F. McMillan
and J. Lacouture (1992) used on page 69; and *Franco's Spain* by J. Grugel and T. Rees
(1997) used on page 247; Bantam Press, for an extract from *The Road Ahead* by Christabel
Bielenberg (1992) used on page 454; the BBC, for an extract from the radio documentary
World Powers in the Twentieth Century by Philip Windsor (1982) used on page 391; BBC
Publications, for an extract quoted in *The Unsettled Peace* by R. Morgan (1974) used on
page 3; Berg, for extracts from 'Denazification in the British zone' by I. Turner and
'Pruning the past of German democracy' by David Welch, in *Reconstruction in Post-War*

Germany, ed. I. Turner (1989) used on page 12; Berghahn, for extracts from *Konrad Adenauer*, Vol. 1 by H.-P. Schwarz (1995) used on page 34 and *Documents and Debates, 1944–1993*, ed. Jarausch and Gransow (1994) used on page 561; Bertelsmann Verlag, for an extract from *Untergang auf Raten* by A. Mitter and S. Wolle (1993) used on page 42; Blackwells, for extracts quoted in *A History of West Germany*, Vol. 1 by D. Bark and D. Gress (1993) used on pages 5 and 38; *Blatter für deutsche und internationale Politik* (1989) for an extract taken from Jarausch and Gransow (1894) used on page 57; Cambridge University Press, for an extract from *The Fading Miracle* by Giesch, Paque and Schmieding (1992) used on page 30; Cape, for extracts from *Europe's Name: Germany and the Divided Continent* by Timothy Garton Ash (1993) used on pages 39 and 49; Cornell, for an extract from *American Policy and the Division of Germany* by B. Kuklick (1972) used on page 15; Deutsch Verlags-Anstalt/Brockhaus, for an extract translated by the author from *Jahre der Besetzung, 1945–49*, Vol. 1, *Geschichte der Bundesrepublik Deutschland* by D.T. Eschenburg (1983) used on page 15; Dunker and Humbolt for an extract translated by the author from *Student zür Deutschlandfrage*, Vol. 12 by S. Suckut (1993) used on page 12; *Ein Erfolg der Politik der Vermunft und des Realisms* (1987) for an extract taken by Jarausch and Gransow (1994) used on page 57; H. Evans, for an extract from *Meeting at Potsdam* by Charles Mee (1975) used on page 424; Fischer, for an extract from *Entnaziferung in Bayern* by L. Niethammer (1972) used on page 12; Fourth Estate, for extracts from *The Cold War* by M. Walker (1993) used on pages 403 and 405; FRG, for an extract from *Dokument über die Mabuahmeu zür Gesundung der politischen Lage . . . Naclab Grotewohl* 90/699, a report by the Central Committee of the Soviet Communist Party in the *Siftung Archiv der Parteien und Massen Organisationen der DDR im Bundesarchiv (Potsdam)* used on page 41; HarperCollins, for extracts from *De Gaulle; the Ruler* by J. Lacouture (1991) used on pages 101 and 102; and *Franco* by Paul Preston (1993) used on page 235; *Historical Journal*, for an extract from 'Stalin and German reunification' by G. Wethig in Vol. 37, no. 2 (1994) used on page 37; the Institut für Geschichte der Arbeiterbewegung, for an extract from the *Parteiarchiv* (ref. NL 36/735 Blatt 55) used on page 17; the Institute of World Economics and International Relations (Moscow), for an extract from *Seventeen Theses on the Common Market* (1957) used on page 371; the *Journal for Contemporary History*, for an extract from 'Cold War misinterpretations: the Communist and Western responses to the East German refugee crisis in 1953'in Vo. 29, by V. Ingimundaison (1994) used on page 41; Longman, for extracts from *the Bonn Republik* by A.J. Nicholls (1997) used on pages 26, 30, 31, 36 and 38; 'Domestic political developments II: 1969–90' by Siekmuer and Larres in *The Federal Republic of Germany*, ed. Larres and Panay (1986) used on page 30; *Gorbachev* by Martin McCauley (1998) used on page 127; *Modern Italy* (2nd ed.) by Martin Clark (1996) used on page 223; and *Italy since 1800* by Roger Absalom (1995) used on page 224; Macmillan, for extracts from *The Two Germanies, 1945–90: Problems of Interpretation* by M. Fulbrook (1992) used on page 111; *The Rise and Fall of the Soviet Empire* by R. Pearson (1998) used on page 167; and *Eastern Europe Since 1945* by G. and N. Swain (1993) used on page 187; Michael Joseph, for extracts from *Age of Extremes –The Twentieth Century 1914–1991* and *The Age of Extremes* by Eric Hobsbawm (1994) used on pages xxi, xxv, xxvi and 460; the *New York Times* (25/10/89), for an extract taken from Jarausch and Gransow (1994) used on page 57; Opus, for extracts taken from *Modern France* by R. Gildea (1996) used on page 31; Oxford University Press, for extracts from *German Politics, 1945–95* by P. Pulzer (1995) used on pages 18 and 28; *Germany Since 1945* by L. Kettenacker (1997) used on page 25; *Anatomy of a Dictatorship* by M. Fulbrook (1997) used on pages 41 and 56; *Last of the Empires* by J. Keep (1997) used on page 127; *Modern Spain* by R. Carr (1980) used on page 248; *The Sixties* by Arthur Marwick (1998) used on page 455; and *The Oxford History of Modern Europe* by Richard Bessel (1996) used on page 455; Penguin, for extracts from *An Economic History of the USSR* by A. Nove (1998) used on page 127; *Franco and the Politics of Spain* by Edouard de Blay (1976) used on page 239; *Shattered Peace* by Daniel Yergin (1980) used on page 383; and *A Guide to Central Europe* by Richard Bassett (1987) used on page 421; Progress, for extracts from *History of the USSR* by Y. Kukushkin (1981) used on page 154; The Royal Institute of International Affairs (London), for an extract from *East Central Europe from Reform to Transformation* by J. Batt (1991) used on page 184; Routledge, for an extract from *The Triumph of Democracy in Spain* by Paul Preston (1982) used on page 248; Secker and Warburg, for an extract from *The Locust Years* by F. Giles (1991) used on page 71; Stanford, for an extract from *The French in Germany* by F. Willis (1962) used on page 8; Thames Television, for an extract from *Stalin: Generalissimo* by Stephen Cohen (1990) used on page 315; Harvard University Press, for extracts from *The Russians in Germany* by N. Naimark (1995) used on pages 3, 7 and 10; Vandenhoeck and Ruprecht, for extracts translated from *Die Doppelte Staatsgundung* by C. Klessmann (1988), used on pages 8 and 42; and BasisBruck Verlag, for an extract taken by Jarausch and Gransow (1994) from *Ich Liebre euch doch alle Behehle und lagebenchte des MFS*, ed. A. Mitter and S. Wolle used on page 57.

The publisher would like to thank the following for permission to reproduce the following copyright illustrations in this book:
AKG pages 10, 39, 41, 453; PD Allan page 293; Archiv für Kunst und Geschichte pages 1, 10, 39, 41 and 453; Arnold page 293; Battle of Britain Prints International Limited page 401; Bloomsbury pages 462 and 463; Bundesbildstell, Bonn, page 51; Cambridge University Press page, 457; Camera Press Limited page 117; Cartier Bresson page 62; Corbis pages 212, 213, 214 and 215; Colour Library Books pages 449; and 450; The Guardian page 354; Hulton Getty Picture Gallery pages 377, 388, 435, 450 and 451; Hulton Deutsche Collection page 450; The Independent page 78; Life File page 435; London Evening Standard and Blower page 373; New Liberty Productions page 453; Krokadil pages 156, 157, 158, 159 and 160; Magnum Photos pages 166, 170, 214, 273, 287, 288 and 462; Paul Popper Ltd pages 227, 401 and 449; Gerald Scarfe page 409; Topham Picturepoint page 463.

Every effort has been made to trace and acknowledge ownership of copyright. The Publishers will be glad to make any suitable arrangements with copyright holders whom it has not been possible to contact.

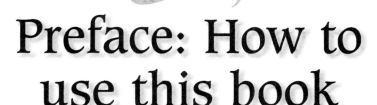

Preface: How to use this book

We approached the preparation and writing of this book with a mixture of enthusiasm and trepidation. The enthusiasm was sparked by several factors. We felt that there was a distinct gap in the provision of material written for students studying recent and contemporary European history. There are many books written on European topics, both general and very specific. However, as experienced teachers, examiners and authors, we were also aware that there was very little to compare with the wealth of material available on the European history of the first half of this century. There are books on European history which take an earlier period as their starting point, and include material on the post-1945 era. However, all too often the later material seems to be added almost as an afterthought to what are essentially studies of the period from around 1900 to 1945. We believe that the period from 1945 is worth studying in its own right; the end of war in 1945 is a natural starting point, whilst the momentous changes in Central and Eastern Europe and the ending of the Cold War at the end of the 1980s give the period from 1945 to 1990 a coherence which was not evident until recently.

The trepidation on our part arose because there is always an extra difficulty in studying recent events. There is certainly a lot of information available. However, the events have taken place within recent memory, and it is notoriously difficult to formulate a clear perspective on contemporary happenings. We are quite certain that interpretations, if not the facts, will continue to change, as indeed they do from time to time for all periods of history. Nevertheless, we also believe that as more and more students study this period of European history, they will welcome a book which treats the period 1945–90 as a coherent whole – even if they and their teachers do not agree with all the interpretations.

The implications of the title should be emphasised. It is a book about European history. It seeks to give an appropriate balance to different geographical regions, topics and themes, whilst recognising that certain subjects deserve fuller treatment than others, if their wider significance merits it. We have concentrated on political and economic themes, but have also covered social and cultural topics where appropriate or where space permits. Inevitably, since the different constituencies of the twentieth-century world have become more interdependent, world events have increasingly impinged upon European ones. Therefore, for example, the USA will frequently be mentioned in this book, and the impact of Europe on the wider world will be addressed, although the main focus is very much upon Europe itself.

The book is deliberately structured in a similar way to earlier volumes in the *Years Of* ... series. It seeks to combine a substantial narrative and analysis of those events which have shaped European history, in this case between 1945 and the early 1990s. Some chapters will focus upon individual countries, some on particular regions or groups of countries, and some upon more general themes or topics, such as supranational organisations or broader cultural issues. Where the history of individual countries is addressed, the text is divided as far as possible into sections on political history, economic history and foreign policy. We would be the first to acknowledge that this division is often artificial: history is a complex web of interwoven themes, even if at certain times particular factors or events seem more prominent than others. However, we have retained the division between political, economic and foreign affairs where possible because students generally find books divided into sections easier to handle than a more 'thematic' approach, even if the latter is equally valid for studying contemporary history.

There will inevitably be overlapping. For example, some of the political and economic policies of individual countries will overlap with the history of the European Union, which, in view of its importance, is the main focus of a separate chapter. This is an additional reason for using the index!

Whilst we have attempted to give a balanced coverage of Europe as a whole, it has to be recognised that some countries have experienced changes of apparently greater significance than others, or have exerted considerable influence outside their own frontiers. These considerations affect the content of individual chapters and the amount of space devoted to individual countries. Within these constraints, we have attempted to do justice to topics which usually receive less attention than others. This helps to explain, for example, why we have included a chapter somewhat loosely called 'Northern Europe', comprising the Scandinavian countries and the Baltic States. Books on European history rarely devote much space to this region, probably because these countries have rarely had a great impact on their southern neighbours. Nevertheless, Scandinavia is an important part of the new Europe, and the Baltic States have a recent turbulent history bound up with the collapse of the once-great Soviet Empire.

Other areas appeared to us to cry out for significant treatment. For example Yugoslavia, although a relatively small state, has had a dramatic and bloody history in the late twentieth century, one which made it a focus of European attention. Therefore, the origins of the break-up of Yugoslavia and its subsequent civil war are examined in some detail.

Inevitably, some readers may quarrel not only with our interpretations, but also with our emphases. We acknowledge also that Britain, despite being very much part of the new Europe, does not receive detailed treatment on its own account. This is partly for reasons of space, and partly because examination syllabuses, always slow to change, still tend to separate Britain artificially from continental Europe. However, in a book such as this, difficult decisions had to be made, and we can only hope that our selection and treatment of content accords with the needs of most teachers and students.

We are also very conscious of the practical needs of students studying for higher level examinations. Additional material at the end of each chapter is designed to further develop students' knowledge and understanding of the contents and to give opportunities for practice, particularly in meeting examination requirements. We have drawn on our own experience as teachers and examiners to provide this material. It includes bibliographies helpful to further study of the topics, suggested essay titles, source exercises, and advice on how to write essays and examination answers, including structured questions.

No student studying history at this level should rely upon one textbook alone. Nevertheless, we hope that *Years of Division* will serve as a core textbook for those studying this exciting period in contemporary history.

A ∾ SOURCE–ANALYSIS SKILLS

Students are frequently required to answer questions on sources and documentary extracts, both primary and secondary. You need to be aware of the types of questions usually asked and the best ways in which to respond.

It is important not to make *stock responses* to source questions. For example, a statement such as 'All sources are biased' is not particularly helpful unless the source is treated in context; that is, the answer is specifically related to the particular source being considered. Also, *avoid generalisations*, which imply that one particular type of source, for example primary documentary sources, is automatically more reliable or useful than others. When answering questions, use the *mark allocations* as a guide: a question carrying two or three marks requires a short response; one carrying six or seven marks probably requires a response of one or two paragraphs; one carrying 9–12 marks probably requires a 'mini-essay'.

Make sure that you *read* both the sources and questions thoroughly before answering: self-evident perhaps, but many students make errors or miss obvious points, especially in examinations. Sources usually carry their *attribution*, that is, information about when they were produced, who produced them, sometimes for whom they were produced, and perhaps other information. Use this information when available – it is part of the evidence and may help you to answer the questions. Sources questions usually fall into one of several categories:

(**i**) Short introductory questions may ask you to explain a word, phrase or historical reference. Such questions usually test *recall*, and you will either know the answer or you will not, but the topic is not likely to be an obscure one.

(**ii**) Questions relating to one or more sources may ask you a variety of things – for example, why a source was significant in the history of a particular event. You may be required to *summarise* the contents. You will probably be required to show *comprehension* of the source; that is, an understanding of what you have read, and possibly the ability to précis or summarise the source. In doing this, you should avoid regurgitating the actual source or quoting large chunks of it wholesale – a fairly meaningless activity.

(**iii**) Some questions will ask you to *compare and/or contrast* particular sources for a particular reason. Make sure that you use all the sources to which the question refers, and make some conclusions, as well as describing each particular source.

(**iv**) Some questions will ask you about the *reliability* of sources. Always ask, 'reliable for what?'. Relate your answer to the particular source or sources, not to sources in general.

(**v**) Some questions will ask about the *value*, or the *uses and limitations* of sources. This is not the same thing as reliability: an 'unreliable' source may be useful to an historian; for example, a propaganda source may not be 'truthful', but may tell us a lot about the person who produced it, or the society in which it appeared.

(**vi**) Some important questions will require a *synthesis*. You may be asked to query a particular statement, making use of all the sources, or using the sources *plus* your own knowledge of the topic. If helpful, go through each source in turn, before coming to a conclusion.

In Chapters 4 and 7, there is specific advice on how to interpret photographs and cartoons. But remember, there are some similarities between answering sources questions and writing essays. It is just that sources questions tend to be broken down so that each one is testing a particular skill. This does not make them necessarily easier than essays and good answers require careful thought, preparation and practice.

Introduction

Eric Hobsbawm wrote in 1994 that 'there can be no serious doubt that in the late 1980s and early 1990s an era in world history ended and a new one began'. (E. Hobsbawm, *Age of Extremes – The Short Twentieth Century, 1914–1991*, Michael Joseph, 1994, p. 5). What is true of world history is certainly true of European history. The period 1945–*c*. 1990 appears now to be a coherent period of study, beginning with the end of the most destructive war in history – the Second World War – in 1945, and ending some forty-five years later with the collapse of the Soviet Empire and its satellite regimes. With that collapse came the end of the Cold War, in which East and West Europe had been major protagonists.

In order to understand any historical period properly it is necessary to put it into context. Nobody can hope to understand the post-1945 period without understanding what went before. What were the main political features of pre-Second World War Europe?

Hobsbawm called the period from 1914 to the mid-1940s an 'age of catastrophe'. The First World War of 1914–18 was a shattering experience: shattering not just for the huge numbers of combatants and civilians who were killed, but for the brutal ending of cosy assumptions that history was a story of human progress, in moral as well as material terms. A common assumption in 1914 was that war, if it broke out at all, would be a relatively short affair. The grinding attrition of the First World War instead proved the resilience of modern industrial powers, as well as the destructive potential of modern total war. Great powers with the ability to mobilise large numbers of civilian and military personnel, supported by huge industrial muscle, could both inflict upon and absorb great punishment from each other. Governments utilised propaganda, appeals to patriotism, compulsion, and whatever else was necessary to sustain national effort. Great European powers such as Britain, France and Germany were brought almost to a state of collapse by the war; some powers, notably Russia and Austria–Hungary, less efficient in their military and economic organisation, actually went under, although only after several years of all-out war.

Even the victorious European powers – chiefly Britain, France and Italy – were shattered and scarred by the war for a long time. Belief in economic progress, liberal or democratic political structures, and the superiority of European civilisation, was challenged, or even destroyed in some quarters. What was less evident at the time was the fact that the war hastened the process, which had already begun before 1914, by which Europe was ceasing to be the centre of the world in terms of political and economic importance. The USA, a late entry to the war and relatively unscathed by the experience, was already more powerful industrially than any European rival. America's potential was enormous but not fully recognised, partly because it retreated into its traditional isolation once the war was over. Europeans could thus continue to fancy themselves as the leading world powers. Despite growing nationalist pressures, the overseas empires of the victorious European powers remained intact.

However, confidence was in short supply. Liberal politicians were appalled at the possibility of another major war. There were new uncertainties. Russia's defeat in the First World War paved the way for Communist revolution. Through a mixture of exhortation, national fervour and force, the new Soviet State embarked on an economic transformation which produced Europe's first centrally-planned economy and a new great power, at ideological odds with the rest of Europe.

World economic collapse in 1929 plunged Europe into depression and more uncertainty. Two powers shattered by the First World War – Germany in defeat and Italy in victory – underwent political revolutions (several years earlier in Italy's case) that brought to power aggressive, nationalist, one-party regimes which openly proclaimed nationalist ambitions. The liberal democracies of Britain and France faced the prospect of renewed war in Europe with alarm, and were also unsure of their ability to defend their overseas interests. Nevertheless, after several years of appeasing the Fascist dictators Hitler and Mussolini, Britain and France went to war in 1939, ostensibly to support the independence of Poland when it was attacked by Germany, although most people were aware that far wider ideological issues and matters of national survival were ultimately at stake.

The Second World War was even more devastating than the first had been. Civilian as well as military casualties were enormous, both as a direct result of war and of deliberate policies of genocide. Material damage was also immense. The USSR survived invasion by Germany at enormous cost. All countries participating in the war, victors and vanquished, were exhausted by it, with the exception of the USA. The American homeland was untouched by war, and American industrial power not only met the demands that were placed upon it but was boosted by them.

The Second World War had profound physical and psychological consequences in Europe, and confirmed some trends that had already been present before the war. German power and hegemony in Central Europe was destroyed, at least temporarily. Although Britain, alone of the Allied Powers, had stood against Germany for the entire period of the war and derived moral prestige from this fact, Germany's defeat had been brought about by two factors: the productive capacity of the USA, and the resistance of the massive Red Army on the Eastern Front. By the end of the war the USA and USSR had emerged as the two superpowers. The USA had to face up to its international responsibilities, abandon its traditional isolationism, adopt a leading role in enforcing the peace settlement and resist the perceived threat of the advance of Communism. The Americans also had a monopoly of nuclear power in 1945. Although the USSR had been devastated by the war, its resilience was such that not only did it recover and replace much of the damage within five years, but the Soviets were also able to establish their influence or direct control over most of Central and Eastern Europe, and turn the states there into buffers against the possibility of renewed aggression from the West.

With one power on the periphery of Europe, the USSR, now emerging as the dominant force in Europe, and the USA adopting a world role, the era of European great power dominance in the world was over, although it was not until the Suez crisis of 1956 that the British came to accept the reality of this change. The liberal democracies of Western Europe, Britain and France, were not only struggling to adapt to a post-war climate of austerity in the second half of the 1940s; the war had stimulated nationalist movements in other parts of the world, and the British and French governments were forced

MAP 1
Europe in 1945

to witness the beginnings of a dismantling of empires. The granting of independence to India, the 'Jewel in the English Crown', was only an early stage in this process.

After the First World War many people in Europe hoped that they had experienced the 'war to end all wars', and that a period of lasting peace would ensue. Such idealistic hopes, enshrined in the League of Nations, were killed off by economic depression, the emergence of Fascist states, and the patent inability of the League to prevent aggression. The aftermath of the Second World War also witnessed idealism. There were those who thought that the experience of war, which had loosened class barriers amongst civilian populations, if not destroyed them, might lead to more social justice. There was a sense that justice had triumphed in that the aggressor states had clearly paid for their crimes. Hopes for peace were now transferred from the League of Nations to the United Nations, which had a far wider membership. However, despondency and a cold realism soon replaced much of the optimism. In 1945 there were millions of displaced civilians in Europe. In the countries of Central and Eastern Europe liberal democracy, which had never existed or had only shallow roots, was quickly snuffed out by Communist advances between 1945 and 1948. Hopes of preserving the wartime alliance of the USA and USSR were soon dashed; their political, economic and social systems were so different. Each was convinced that the other was bent on world domination, either by military or economic means. Suspicion turned into Cold War, a state of armed antagonism marked by the erection of the Iron Curtain across Europe, separating two mutually antagonistic philosophies. Tension was heightened by the stationing of large numbers of conventional and nuclear forces in Europe. If a Third World War were to break out, Europe was likely to be a key battleground.

There were to be crises, notably in Berlin in 1948–49, and some wars fought by great powers by proxy elsewhere, notably in Korea between 1950 and 1953. However, all-out war was averted. Europe, or at least Western, Northern and parts of Southern Europe, quickly recovered from the war. Hobsbawm's 'age of catastrophe' gave way to a 'Golden Age', which lasted from about 1947 to the early 1970s. The period was characterised by the triumph of capitalism and free-market enterprise, the backbone of American society. The world economy was increasingly interdependent, and economic institutions took less account of national boundaries. The European Community, which was based upon a free-market ethos amongst its members, symbolised a belief in the benefits of cooperation and integration.

The success of capitalism in this period was in some ways ironic. At the time of the world economic depression of 1929, many commentators believed they were witnessing the end of capitalism, which was under threat from the planned Soviet economy and the 'controlled capitalism' of the emerging Fascist states. Looking back from the 1990s, with a perspective denied to contemporaries, Hobsbawm concluded that the threat had been exaggerated. Although a Socialist himself, he conceded that the Communists had only achieved power in Russia because of the problems in capitalist countries preoccupied with the First World War. He also pointed out the irony that it was the Socialist regime which emerged in Russia in the 1920s and 30s that played a key role in assisting the liberal capitalist states to defeat Fascism between 1939 and 1945. And yet, once capitalism began to regenerate itself after the Second World War, it brought about, according to Hobsbawm, 'the greatest, most rapid and most fundamental' transformation in history. Soviet attempts to match the global strength of capitalism exacerbated strains already evident in the Soviet system, which in turn led to economic crisis in the USSR, belated attempts at reform, and eventual political collapse in the late 1980s.

And yet even the capitalist world could not be complacent. The era of economic expansion – characterised pithily by British Prime Minister Macmillan's pronouncement in 1957 that 'You've never had it so good' – came to an unexpected end in the early 1970s. War in the Middle East, an embargo on oil supplies to the West and a drastic increase in oil prices were part of a number of crises to afflict the

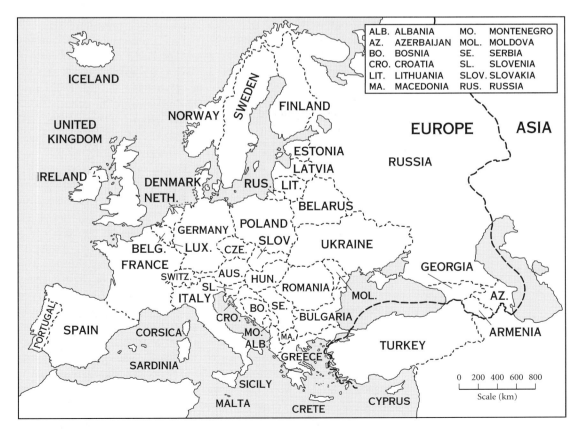

ALB.	ALBANIA	MO.	MONTENEGRO
AZ.	AZERBAIJAN	MOL.	MOLDOVA
BO.	BOSNIA	SE.	SERBIA
CRO.	CROATIA	SL.	SLOVENIA
LIT.	LITHUANIA	SLOV.	SLOVAKIA
MA.	MACEDONIA	RUS.	RUSSIA

MAP 2
Europe in 1994

capitalist world. Confidence came to a sudden end. Recession struck, and with it the problems reminiscent to some extent of the 1930s and earlier, but which were thought to have disappeared in an age of more sophisticated economies: slumps, large-scale unemployment, and a widening gap between haves and have-nots.

During the late 1970s and 1980s, European countries, whatever their political systems, sought ways out of recession. Some Western European governments, notably the British one led by Prime Minister Thatcher, adopted a radical policy of having fewer government controls, less public spending, deregulation, and a generally smaller role for government. Some Eastern European economies also experienced radical changes, but their planned economies were relatively cumbersome and ineffectual, and one-party regimes were reluctant to make reforms which might threaten their own monopoly of power. When Gorbachev finally launched policies of 'openness' and 'restructuring' in the USSR in the 1980s, he opened a can of worms and provoked confusion and discontent, rather than reversing economic stagnation. In any case, governments found themselves increasingly less able to control their own destinies. Economies of more advanced states had become too interlinked.

By the latter half of the 1980s there was a prevailing sense of pessimism in Europe. As Hobsbawm put it, 'The last part of the century was a new era of decomposition, uncertainty and crisis – and indeed, for large parts of the world such as Africa, the former USSR and the formerly Socialist parts of Europe, of catastrophe. As the 1980s gave way to the 1990s, the mood of those who reflected on the century's past

fin-de-siécle 'end of the century'

and future was a growing ***fin-de-siècle*** gloom.' This gloom was symbolised in Europe by the renewal of ethnic and nationalist tensions, most noticeably in Yugoslavia, which disintegrated into civil war.

However, it was not all gloom. Although towards the end of the period covered by this book there were millions of unemployed in Europe, and many uncertainties about the future, there were also some positive signs. Advances in science and technology continued. In emerging states or states such as those throwing off the relics of a Stalinist past in Central and Eastern Europe there were hopes of political, economic and social progress. The fact that Europe was increasingly part of the 'global village' – a world of transnational economics and rapid communications – posed its own problems, but interdependence also made war less likely (with the notable exception of Yugoslavia). Above all, the ending of the Cold War appeared to have lifted a major threat to Europe's peace, a threat which, although perhaps lessened over the years by familiarity with crises and crisis resolution, had nevertheless remained in the background as a dangerous fact of life. The years of division marking the period between 1945 and 1990 gave way to different uncertainties: about the environment, about the future of European union, about the restoration of full employment, about the stability of Eastern Europe and the Balkans, to name but some.

This book will examine how the constituent parts of a divided continent developed, interrelated and posed challenges for two generations of Europeans. These two generations had to survive a period between the ending of the greatest war in history and the last years of a century which had seen more rapid changes in people's lives than any previous era.

Germany 1945–95

INTRODUCTION

In May 1945 it seemed as if Germany would never recover. Its cities were piles of rubble. Large areas in the east were handed over permanently to the Poles and Russians, while the rest of the country was divided into four zones controlled by the victorious Allies. The Germans themselves called May 1945 'zero hour'. Germany's prospects were further threatened by the lack of agreement between the Allies over how a future German state should be run. By 1948 their disagreements had become so polarised that a unified Germany was no longer possible. Under American pressure, the Western Allies decided to set up the Federal Republic of Germany (FRG) at the London

PICTURE 1

Nuremberg in 1945. Over 50 per cent of the city was destroyed. Other cities, such as Cologne, were over 70 per cent destroyed.

See pages 18, 389–90

Conference in June 1948. In September 1949 Chancellor Adenauer formed the first West German government in Bonn. The Russians at first tried to halt the creation of the FRG by blockading West Berlin. When this failed, they too set up a separate German state, the German Democratic Republic (GDR).

When studying the complicated history of divided Germany it might be helpful to keep in mind the following key factors which influenced the development of German history from 1945–95:

- The overwhelming importance of the Cold War. This caused the division of Germany into two states in 1948–49 and influenced their development up to the end of the Cold War in 1989–90;
- Thanks to economic demand created by the Korean War (1950–53) and the ability to trade with America and Western Europe, the FRG was rapidly able to develop its huge economic potential and become the richest state in Europe;
- The GDR, on the other hand, still had to pay reparations to Russia until 1954 and was forced to trade with the much poorer Eastern Bloc;
- Both German states claimed to act in the name of a united Germany. The GDR believed that it could unite Germany on the basis of Socialism, whereas the FRG was convinced that its economic strength and prosperity would act as a magnet that would gradually draw the GDR into unity with itself;
- Throughout the 1950s, the GDR was constantly weakened by the flight westwards through Berlin of large numbers of skilled workers, doctors, teachers, engineers, etc. Only in 1961, with the building of the Berlin Wall, did the GDR become more stable and have a better chance of developing its economy;
- The 1960s was also a decisive decade for the FRG. When faced with a slow down in economic growth and the rise of extremist parties on the Right and Left, the government did not become more authoritarian, as many observers expected. On the contrary, democracy became stronger;
- Between 1970 and 1973, the FRG adopted a new and less hostile policy towards the GDR – *Ostpolitik* ('East policy'). This marked a complete break with the Cold War policies of Chancellor Adenauer;
- The dramatic rise in oil prices immediately after the Yom Kippur War of October 1973 had a profound impact on both Germanies, as it tripled the price of oil. By 1983 the GDR was virtually bankrupt and only kept solvent by loans from West Germany;
- With the collapse in oil prices in 1985, the FRG's economic position strengthened, as it was able to build up a large trade surplus with the rest of the world. It was this immense economic strength above all that enabled Chancellor Kohl in effect to purchase Russian agreement to German unity in 1990;
- The fall of the GDR occurred quickly and unexpectedly in the winter and spring of 1989–90. Once Russia, under President Gorbachev, was no longer ready to support the GDR, its failure to

win the loyalty of its citizens and its financial bankruptcy ensured that it could not withstand the magnet-like effect of the FRG. Germany was re-united on 3 October 1990;

● Germany was now unified politically, but economically and socially divisions between the two Germanies remained.

1 ◇ THE ALLIED OCCUPATION OF GERMANY, 1945–48

A *Initial plans and aims*

After the German defeats in North Africa and at Stalingrad in 1943, there was little doubt that Germany would eventually lose the war. As the Allies insisted on a total and unconditional German surrender, they drew up plans for the occupation and administration of post-war Germany, which were approved at Yalta. Germany and its capital, Berlin, were to be divided into four zones, each controlled by one of the victorious powers, and an Allied Control Council was to be set up to oversee the administration of Germany. It was also agreed that the northern half of East Prussia was to be annexed by the USSR and German territory to the east of the Oder and Neisse rivers was to be handed over to the Poles. The German population was simply to be pushed out and forced to migrate westwards. The Allies were unsure what they were going to do about Germany in the long term. The Americans and the British had initially decided to implement the **Morgenthau Plan**, but by the Spring of 1945 the USA was coming round to accept that a democratic united Germany would have an important role to play in a free global economy. Russian aims were equally contradictory. In 1943 Stalin had agreed that the Allies should eliminate 'forever' Germany's 'ability to function as a single state in the centre of Europe', yet by the Spring of 1945, he had accepted the possibility of a united Germany. This state would, of course, have to be neutral and disarmed, but it is far from clear whether he believed that it would be Communist. The USSR's most immediate demand was for reparations to help rebuild its shattered economy. The strongest opponents of German unity at this stage were the French, who were determined to break off the Rhineland and put the Ruhr under international control.

(side panel)

See page 383

Morgenthau was the USA Treasury Secretary. His plan was to divide Germany into a series of small states in which all the heavy industries would have been closed down.

KEY ISSUE

Did the USSR aim to create a Communist Germany in 1945?

B *The German surrender and the early months of the Occupation*

By the time Hitler had committed suicide on 30 April 1945, British troops had already crossed the Elbe and further south at Torgau Russian and American soldiers had already met up. Grand Admiral

MAP 3
The zonal division of Germany, 1945–49

Doenitz, who very briefly succeeded Hitler as Chancellor, had no alternative but to agree to the unconditional surrender of Germany on 8 May. Two weeks later, his government was dissolved and its members arrested. On 5 June the Allied Commanders-in-Chief announced in Berlin that 'supreme authority with respect to Germany' had been transferred jointly to the four victorious powers and that Germany was to be divided into the four zones agreed upon at Yalta and administered by an inter-Allied Control Council in Berlin. The Russians refused to allow the Western Allies to occupy their zones in Berlin until all British and American troops who were still in the areas designated at Yalta as belonging to the Soviet Zone, had been pulled

The four zones

The four zones of occupation were very different from each other in size, population and economic structure. The British Zone had the largest population of 22.3 million and as the Ruhr lay within its borders, it controlled 87 per cent of Germany's coal production and 70 per cent of its steel industry. It was, however, dependent on food imports from the other zones. The Soviet Zone, with a population of 17.3 million, was largely an agricultural area in the north, but it did possess the highly developed industrial region of Saxony. Apart from some lignite mines the Zone was dependent on Ruhr coal. The American Zone, with 17.2 million inhabitants, was a similar mix of predominantly rural regions with some modern manufacturing industries in Hessen and Württemberg. Again, it was completely dependent on the Ruhr for its coal and steel, and in the absence of adequate supplies was to become an expensive burden on the American economy. The French Zone, with a small population of 5.9 million, could be run at a profit, temporarily at least, thanks to the Saar coal fields and the timber supplies of the Black Forest, but in the end it also suffered from being cut off from its markets and suppliers in the other zones.

back into their own zones. It was not until 5 July that the Western Allies moved into West Berlin and the Control Council did not meet until the end of the month.

When the Allies first occupied Germany they were faced with what one German described in her diary as 'indescribable, impenetrable chaos'. The immediate problem for the occupying forces was to restore the basic services of water, gas, electricity and sewerage, to repair the transport infrastructure and to ensure that the population was provided with a minimum of rations. Confronted with emergencies on this scale the Allies had little option but to rely on experienced German local government officials, even if they had been former Nazis.

C *The Potsdam Conference and the Occupation*

As the Potsdam Conference could barely paper over the growing disagreements between the four great powers, only the most general guidelines on German policy could be issued to the Control Council and the Commanders-in-Chief:

● There was eventually to be a united but decentralised Germany. There would at first be no German government, but some central German departments dealing with trade, finance, etc., would be set up;

ANALYSIS

KEY ISSUE

What was the influence of the zonal economies on the German policies of the occupying powers?

TIMELINE

Occupied Germany, 1945–47

8 May 1945	Unconditional surrender of German armed forces
June	Anti-Fascist democratic parties allowed in Soviet Zone
July–Aug	Potsdam Conference
Nov	Nuremberg trials began
Jan 1946	Adenauer elected chairman of CDU in British Zone
April	SED formed in Soviet Zone
April–July	Paris Conference
Jan 1947	Bizonia created
Feb	State of Prussia dissolved
Oct	Trade unions in Soviet Zone made responsible for raising labour productivity
Dec	Jakob Kaiser, CDU leader in Soviet Zone, fled to the West

See pages 383–4

- Germany was to pay $20 billion reparations, half of which was to go to Russia. Failing agreement as to how or over what length of time this sum should be paid, a compromise was negotiated whereby both the USSR and the Western powers would take their portion of reparations from their own zones. However, Britain and America would allocate 10 per cent of the reparations gathered in their zones to the Soviets and a further 15 per cent in exchange for the supply of food and materials from the Soviet Zone;
- The Council of Foreign Ministers would be set up to prepare for a peace treaty with Germany;
- In the meantime, the four Commanders-in Chief would implement what was to become known as the 'four D's': denazification, democratisation, demilitarization and **decartelisation**.

decartelisation
breaking up the great industrial and business cartels or trusts – that is associations of industries, etc. – which fixed prices and prevented competition

The four Allied Commanders on the Control Council in Berlin were supposed to apply these guidelines jointly to occupied Germany as a whole, but as their governments at home could not agree on any detailed plan for the future of Germany, each occupying power interpreted the Potsdam Agreement in its own way. The Soviets, the Americans, the British and even the French, despite their defeat in 1940, all believed that victory had proved the superiority of their own political and social systems, features of which they then tried to introduce into their zones.

D *Denazification*

capitalism an economic system which is dominated by private capital (invested money) and businesses, all of which aim for profit

In each zone denazification was carried out with varying degrees of thoroughness. The Soviets believed that Nazism was a product of German **capitalism**, and so they not only removed from their posts Nazi judges, teachers and industrialists, but they also changed the whole economic structure of their zone. The estates of the big landowners, seen as breeding grounds for reactionaries, were broken up and the factories of the great industrialists who had profited from the war were nationalised. The Americans pursued denazification with an almost missionary-like zeal and by December 1945 they had interned nearly double the number of Nazis arrested by the British and more even than the Russians. Denazification inevitably quickly encountered major problems. Allied officials frequently arrested key administrators and managers without whose help Germany simply could not be run. After a major pit disaster in the Ruhr in which 402 miners were killed, the British tolerated Nazis in key positions, provided they were effective managers who could produce the coal. The Russians, too, turned a blind eye to Nazis if they were economically indispensable.

KEY ISSUE

How effective was denazification?

The Allied Military Governments also found that they had neither the time nor the staff to supervise the denazifiation of the millions of minor Nazis. By October 1946 German tribunals were increasingly entrusted with this task. A year later, with the onset of the Cold War, both the Soviets and the Western powers lost interest in denazification.

The Nuremberg Trials

In June 1945 the Allies agreed that the surviving Nazi leaders were to be put on trial. In November 1945 twenty-two top Nazis were brought before the International Military Tribunal at Nuremberg, which was seen as the spiritual home of Nazism. After an eleven-month trial, twelve were condemned to death, seven to varying terms of imprisonment and only three were acquitted. The trials were controversial. Many lawyers argued that they were in effect 'show trials', which were thinly disguised acts of revenge and often based on very shaky legal arguments. Nevertheless, they did succeed in destroying the Nazi political leadership and, through the immense amount of documentation that had to be provided as evidence, made clear to the German people the sheer scale of the Nazi atrocities. Later the Bonn government used this material for further prosecution of Nazi war criminals.

ANALYSIS

E *Re-education*

To be effective, denazification had to be backed up by educational reforms which aimed to eliminate the teaching of Nazism and militarism and, in the words of the Potsdam Agreement, to 'make possible the development of democratic ideas'. Nazi teachers were purged, the old textbooks destroyed and new teachers trained in crash courses. Again, it was the Russians who introduced the most radical reforms. Comprehensive schools were introduced, although a selective sixth form was kept on for those going to university, and the teaching of religion was dropped from the syllabus. They turned the universities into 'instruments of the party' by positively discriminating in favour of the children of workers and peasants, forcing the students to attend compulsory lessons in Marxism–Leninism and Russian. The loyalty of the student unions was achieved by making sure that the Communist members dominated their organisations. The Western powers, on the other hand, failed to change the basic structure of the German education system. In January 1947 the Americans did produce elaborate plans for a fully comprehensive school system at a time when they were also giving their zone greater powers of self-government. Consequently, it was hardly surprising that they were unable to force the Germans to accept them. The universities in the Western zones managed to survive the occupation with virtually no changes at all.

KEY ISSUE

What were the later consequences in the FRG of this failure to reform the education system? (See pages 12–13)

F *Democratisation and decentralisation*

By the Potsdam Agreement the occupying powers agreed to decentralise the political structure of Germany and to restore democratic local government 'as rapidly as is consistent with military security'. An important step in this process was the decision taken by the Control Council in January 1947 to break up the Prussian State, which before the War had consisted of nearly two-thirds of the whole German Reich. Not only did this liberate the smaller states from Prussian influence, but several new states or *Länder*, such as Rhineland–Westphalia in the British Zone or Brandenburg in the Soviet Zone had to be set up. Freed from Prussian domination, first West Germany and then in 1990 the whole of Germany was able to become a genuinely **federal** country.

See pages 18–19

federal a system of government in which several states unify but keep the power to regulate their own internal affairs

Each occupying power approached the problem of rebuilding a democratic local government system differently. Although at first the Americans moved more quickly than either the British or the French, who believed that political power should be given, as the historian F.R. Willis has put it, in 'small doses' from the bottom up, by the end of 1947 the *Länder* in the three Western zones all had their own local parliaments or *Landtage* and the outline of a future federal system could already be discerned. The Soviets, like the Western Allies, allowed *Länder* elections to take place in the winter of 1946–47, but essentially they distrusted federalism as they feared that it might make it more difficult for them to dominate a unified Germany. In 1952 the East German government dissolved the *Länder* in the GDR with their backing and created a centralised, rather than a federal state.

G *The formation of political parties and revival of politics*

To the surprise of the Western powers it was in the Russian Zone that German political parties first emerged. As early as 11 June 1945 four non-Nazi parties were permitted there and by December 1945 these four main party groupings were allowed in the Western zones as well. They were:

- the Communists (KPD);
- the Socialists (SPD);
- the Christian Democrats (CDU);
- the Liberals (LDPD).

Optimistically, the USSR hoped to be able to dominate them and use them to project Communist influence throughout Germany. Party leaders and activists were determined not to repeat the history of the Weimar Republic, whose large number of small, weak and mutually hostile parties had made it easier for the Nazis to seize power in January 1933. Thus the Christian Democratic Union aimed to appeal to both North German Protestants and South German and Rhineland Catholics. A French newspaper described it as being 'socialist and radical in Berlin, clerical [Catholic] and conservative in Cologne, capitalist and reactionary in Hamburg and counter-revolutionary and particularist [separatist] in Munich'. Not surprisingly, many observers

PROFILE

KONRAD ADENAUER (1876–1967) EMERGES AS LEADER OF THE CDU

Konrad Adenauer began his career as a local government official in Cologne. In 1917 he was elected Lord Mayor of Cologne, but was dismissed by the Nazis in 1933. After the failure of the July 1944 conspiracy against Hitler he was arrested as a suspect, although innocent of involvement. In March 1945 the Americans re-appointed him Lord Mayor, but he was dismissed by the British in October for discussing with the French the possibility of setting up an independent Rhineland state. This then enabled Adenauer to begin a new career as a professional politician at the age of seventy and he rapidly became leader of the CDU in the British Zone. Adenauer was a practical politican who believed that the main point of party programmes was to win elections. For example, although he was hostile to Socialism, he did agree to the Ahlen Programme in 1947, which proposed the nationalisation of some key industries, as a compromise with the more left-wing members of the party, who were influenced particularly by Jakob Kaiser, the leader of the CDU in the Soviet Zone. When Kaiser fled to the West in December 1947, Adenauer had little trouble in steering the CDU back to the right again.

thought that the CDU would fall apart as a result of its own inner contradictions, but they underestimated the skills of that formidable politician, Konrad Adenauer, who eventually took over the leadership of the party.

The Liberals also attempted to overcome the old divisions of the Weimar period by setting up a single German Liberal Democratic Party at Eisenach under the joint chairmanship of Theodor Heuss and Wilhelm Külz, who were the leaders of the Liberal parties in West and East Germany respectively, but it collapsed when Külz supported the Communist-dominated People's Congress in December 1947. A few months later the Liberals in the Western zones set up the Free Democratic Party under Heuss, with the aim of appealing to supporters of both the pre-1933 liberal parties.

At first, workers throughout Germany wanted the SPD and KPD to form a new working-class party, which would create a strong barrier against any revival of Fascism. In June 1945 Stalin rejected this demand as it did not fit in with his ideas for forming an anti-Fascist bloc of Liberal, Christian Democrat and Socialist parties right across Germany, dominated by the KPD. By the Autumn this policy was failing. The KPD was unpopular in the Eastern zone and its leaders were seen as puppets of the Soviets, while in the British Zone the SPD increasingly fell under the influence of Kurt Schumacher, a strongly anti-Communist leader. Belatedly then, Stalin decided on the forced

See biography box on page 21

amalgamation of the SPD and KPD in the Soviet Zone. After being subjected to several months of alternating bribery and intimidation by the Russians, the Central Executive of the SPD in the Soviet Zone agreed to the formation of a new united party, the Socialist Unity Party, by a vote of eight to three in February 1946. Embarassingly for the Russians, the lack of grass root support for this amalgamation was made very obvious when the SPD leadership agreed to hold a referendum on the question in Berlin. Although the Soviets managed to close down the polling stations in East Berlin just half an hour after they had opened, the voting went ahead in West Berlin, where 82 per cent of the party members voted against the union, but this massive rejection was partly contradicted by a second vote on the question of whether they supported 'an alliance ... which will guarantee continued cooperation and exclude fraternal strife'. This was answered positively by some 62 per cent of the membership. The creation of the SED effectively destroyed the claims of the SPD to be the strongest political movement in Germany, which could act as a bridge between East and West, and reduced it to a party drawing most of its support from the industrialised areas in the British Zone.

> **KEY ISSUE**
>
> *What was the significance of the amalgamation of the SPD/KPD in the Soviet Zone?*

H *The trade unions*

At Potsdam the Allies recognised the Germans' right to form unions, but once again the details of this policy were left to the individual occupying powers to work out. The French and Americans were convinced that the best approach was to create small local unions. In January 1946, for example, there were some 163 different local unions in the French Zone alone. It was, however, in the Soviet and British Zones, where there was the greatest concentration of industry and therefore of workers, that the future patterns of German trade unionism were to be created. The USSR strongly supported a unified and centralised trade union movement, because it believed that the SED would be able to dominate it. In February 1946 the Soviets set up the Free German Trade Union Association (FDGB) to represent all the German workers. In the British Zone, German trade unionists at first also wanted one large general union for all the workers, but both British trade unionists and the Military Government feared that such a centralised organisation would be vulnerable to a Communist take-over and insisted that separate unions should be set up under the general umbrella of a federation of trade unions. This principle was gradually accepted by the Americans and the French and by December 1948 the trade union movements in the three zones had amalgamated. At first there was considerable contact between the trade unions in West and East Germany, but the Cold War made the creation of a single all-German trade union movement an impossibility.

I *The Economy: demilitarisation and reparations*

At Potsdam the Allies had agreed to treat Germany as an economic whole, but there was little evidence of this in the winter of 1945–46. Interzonal trade was virtually non-existent and transport, if it was working at all, was subject to strict control by the Military Governments. Further problems were caused by the disastrous decline in coal production in the Ruhr and the collapse in the value of the *Reichsmark* as a result of inflation.

In March 1946 the occupying powers did agree on an overall plan for the level of production of the post-war German economy, which, if put into operation, would have kept post-war production at the level of 1932. As part of the demilitarisation measures the manufacture of armaments, aircraft, ships, synthetic fuels and light metals and radioactive substances were banned. All surplus plant was either to be destroyed or dismantled and handed over as reparations. However, disagreements between the four occupying powers over the future of Germany prevented the plan from being effectively put into operation. The Soviets, and to a lesser extent the French, ruthlessly exploited their zones in the interests of their home economies. The Soviets set up special companies (SAGs) which controlled 30 per cent of their zone's industrial production by the end of 1946 and ensured that it went directly to the USSR. For the British and the Americans, on the other hand, reparations rapidly became a secondary consideration, as they were more concerned to make their zones economically self-supporting and therefore less of a financial burden on their taxpayers.

J *Decartelisation*

As the Ruhr was in the British Zone, the initial responsibility for restructuring the coal and steel industries fell to the British. These industries were first put under the control of the Military Government and the original eight large steel cartels were broken up into twenty-four new companies, in the running of which the trade unions and the management had an equal say. However, further plans to nationalise the heavy industries in the Ruhr could never be realised because the creation of Bizonia increased American influence, which was hostile to all forms of nationalisation, over the British Zone. Eventually, decartelisation was left to the FRG to complete, which it did on a very limited scale.

See page 15

ANALYSIS

Was the Occupation a 'missed opportunity'?

This question was raised frequently in the 1960s. Many historians argued that the Western Allies should have been much more thorough in their attempts to cleanse their zones of Nazism and to create a new democratic society. Lutz Niethammer, for instance, has shown that there were more officials in the *Länder* administrations in the American Zone in 1949 who had been members of the Nazi party than there were actual Nazis in 1939. He argues that denazification only superficially removed the stain of Nazism from Germany's past and in fact allowed former Nazis to regain their positions 'with a fresh white waistcoat'. There were similar arguments about the failure to reform the education system, particularly the universities. David Welch believes that a major opportunity 'to break with the past was lost'. Other historians regret the failure to insist on a radical reform of the civil service (Schmidt) or total destruction of the cartels (Abelshauser). How accurate is this criticism? It is undeniable that many ex-Nazis regained positions of responsibility, but they returned to a society in which the appeal of Nazism had been permanently shattered through defeat and where, thanks to the Nuremberg trials, the atrocities of Nazism were well known. Certainly, the failure to reform the universities meant that they remained overcrowded and outdated structures, which helped to fuel the student revolt in the 1960s. There were, however, attempts made by the Western occupying powers to depoliticise the civil service by banning civil servants from standing for elected political posts, but in 1951 Adenauer restored to the civil service all its former privileges. It can also be argued that the process of decartelisation was very slow and by no means thorough, as it was not until 1957 that the Adenauer government passed anti-trust legislation and even this had loopholes in it. The

See pages 26–27

situation in the GDR was, of course, very different. The old social
and economic structures were swept away and Nazism was more
thoroughly eliminated, only to be replaced by Stalinism,
complete with secret police and labour camps.

2 ⇝ THE DIVISION OF GERMANY, 1948–49

A *Introduction*

The division of Germany can only be understood within the context of
the Cold War, but historians are still divided on whether or not it was
inevitable and which power was the most responsible for bringing it
about. Perhaps all that can be said with any accuracy is that Germany's
defeat and occupation by the Allies, who all had very different aims in
1945, made partition a possibility. With the exception of France, the
occupying powers at first wanted a united Germany, but one which was
united on their own terms. Stalin hoped that the new SED and the
formation of central German ministries in Berlin would enable the
Communist Party to permeate Germany as a whole. The British and
Americans, on the other hand, were working for a united federal
Germany integrated into the world economic system. When this proved
impossible to achieve, they were ready to settle for a divided Germany,
whilst hoping that their section of Germany would eventually act as a

See Chapter 9

TIMELINE

April 1946	General Clay halted transfer of reparations from the American to the USSR Zone
April–July	Paris Conference
Jan 1947	Creation of the Bizonia
March–April	Moscow Conference
June	German Economic Commission set up
	Marshall Plan announced
Dec	Break-up of London Foreign Ministers Conference
	German People's Congress met in Berlin
Feb 1948	Both Bizonia and Economic Commission given greater powers
June	London Six Power Conference recommended setting up West German state
	Currency reforms in Western Zones
	Berlin blockade
Sept	Parliamentary Council met in Bonn
May 1949	USSR lifted Berlin blockade
	Basic Law approved in FRG
Sept	Adenauer appointed Chancellor
	Occupation Statute came into force
Oct	GDR Provisional Government set up under Grotewohl

magnet to attract the Soviet Zone. Historians are less sure about Soviet intentions in 1948. Once the USSR knew that it had lost the struggle to win over the West Germans, there is some evidence that it was ready to tolerate a neutral and even non-Communist Germany rather than see West Germany, with its massive industrial potential, integrated into the West. General Robertson, the Military Governor of the British Zone, believed that a deal along these lines on German unity could have been negotiated in the summer of 1948, but by this time it was too late. The Western powers were not ready to sacrifice their plans for creating a Western Germany for the uncertainties of a weak, demilitarised Germany that could be overrun by the USSR.

Gradually, the majority of Germans in the Western zones began to share this view. Konrad Adenauer particularly supported an independent West Germany integrated into western Europe, which would in time become so wealthy that it would become an irresistible magnet for Eastern Germany. In the East the leaders of the SED and indeed many Communists were also quite prepared to accept a divided Germany because they realised only too well that Communism had little chance of success in West Germany.

KEY ISSUE

Was the 'magnet theory' realistic?

B *The actions of the Western powers, 1946–49*

At the height of the Cold War there was little doubt in the West that the USSR and the USSR alone was responsible for the partition of Germany, yet, as Mary Fulbrook argued in 1992 in her book, *The Two Germanies*, an actual analysis of the way in which the division of Germany took place shows that the Western powers 'repeatedly took initiatives to which Soviet measures came largely in response'. In the period 1946–48 Britain and America took the following key actions:

- the stopping of German reparation payments to the USSR;
- the creation of the Anglo–American Bizonia in January 1947;
- the drawing up of the Bevin Plan of February 1947 by the British government;
- the Marshall Plan;
- the decision to create an independent West Germany taken at the six Power London Conference in June 1948;
- the introduction of a new currency into West Germany, the *Deutsche Mark*, on 20 June 1948.

In retrospect, the failure to agree on a joint reparation policy at Potsdam was a step towards the division of Germany. Although the four occupying powers managed to agree to the Level of Industry Plan in March 1946, the Soviets rejected American arguments that Germany should only start to pay reparations once it had become economically self-supporting and that what they had already seized in their own zone should be deducted from the total amount owing to them. In May General Clay, the American Military Governor, announced that no further reparations would be delivered from the American to the Soviet

Zone until Germany was treated as a single economic unit. The Americans were signalling that they were ending what the American historian Kuklick has called their 'strategy of delay' and beginning to push hard for a revived German economy within an **international capitalist system**. Without adequate compensation the USSR could hardly agree to Germany becoming part of what would inevitably be an American-dominated economic system. At the Paris Conference in 1946 the Americans proposed a four-power pact to guarantee the demilitarisation of Germany and also offered to form an economic union between their zone and the three other zones of occupation, but they stood firm by their decision on reparations. Only the British accepted this offer, as they saw it as a way of sharing the massive expenses of running their zone with the Americans. On 6 September American policy on the future of Germany became clearer still when Byrnes, in a major speech in Stuttgart, stressed that German reconstruction should start immediately and that the Germans should be given responsibility for 'running their own affairs'. The economic merger of the British and American Zones to form Bizonia on 1 January 1947 marked the beginning of this process.

Recent work by historians has highlighted the role the British played in the division of Germany. By early February 1946 Bevin, the British Foreign Secretary, had come to the conclusion that the Soviets would never agree to a united Germany unless it was Communist. Therefore, in the interests of a Western European economic recovery an independent West German state must be set up as soon as possible. This came to be known as 'the Bevin Plan'. At the Moscow Conference the British skilfully isolated the USSR and managed to persuade the Americans to drop a proposal that would have allowed the Russians to take some reparations from the current production of coal and iron in

international capitalist system a system of global free trade where industry would be owned by private investors

Bizonia

Although the British and Americans argued that Bizonia was an economic organisation and not a blueprint for a new West German state, over the next eighteen months it did become what the West German historian, Theodor Eschenburg, had called 'the germ cell' of the later Federal Republic. With the failure of the Moscow and London Conferences in April and November 1947, Bizonia was given greater political powers by the Western Allies. By February 1948 it had a central bank, a supreme court and an Economic Council, which was given permission to raise money by taxation. When the Organisation for European Economic Cooperation was set up in April 1948 to administer the Marshall Plan funds, Bizonia was represented on it with sixteen other West European states.

ANALYSIS

See page 333

West Germany. By the time the next Foreign Ministers Conference met in London in November 1947 the momentum towards partition was accelerating. The Marshall Plan had been announced and Bizonia was beginning to look like a West German state. The USSR accused the Western Allies of breaking the Potsdam Agreement, while the latter rejected Soviet plans for setting up a central government on the grounds that it would lead to the formation of a satellite Communist regime. When the Conference broke up without any results, Marshall and Bevin drew up an ambitious programme for the setting up of an independent West German state where:

- the French Zone would have to be amalgamated with Bizonia;
- failing agreement with the Soviets on a single German currency, West Germany would be given a new currency;
- a democratic constitution for a new West German state would be drawn up.

From February to June 1948 Britain, France, the USA and the Benelux states (Belgium, Holland and Luxemburg) met in London to work out how this programme should be carried out. The proceedings were given an added note of urgency by the Communist seizure of power in Czechoslovakia at the end of February. The British and Americans secured French cooperation by signing an agreement which endorsed their policy of integrating the Saar economically into France. Thus on 2 June the six states were able to announce the decision to set up a federal West German state. On 20 June a new currency, the *Deutsche Mark* (DM) was introduced into Bizonia and the French Zone and, three days later, into West Berlin.

ANALYSIS

What did the currency reforms of June 1948 involve?

Before the *Deutsche Mark* was introduced in the Western zones the old currency, the *Reichsmark*, was virtually valueless and most deals were paid for on the black market, often by packets of American cigarettes. The new banknotes had been printed in the USA in November 1948. Only 60 *Reichsmarks* could be exchanged on a one-to-one basis. Above this total the old currency had to be exchanged at a ratio of 100 *Reichsmarks* to DM 6.50. This hit the small saver, as opposed to the industrialists and the owners of property or shares. The suffering this caused was partly alleviated by an emergency law in 1949, but it was not until 1952 that those who had lost their savings (either as a result of the currency exchange or the consequences of the war) were given more effective compensation by the Equalization of Burdens Act. In the Soviet Zone the introduction of the new East Mark was, as in the Western zones, aimed at squeezing out

See page 17

inflation and establishing a sound currency, but it was intended to weaken not just the small saver, but also the remaining independent industrialists and businessmen, whose financial assets were converted at a rate of 10 old marks to one new mark. Funds belonging to nationalised factories, the State and the SED were converted at a rate of 1:1. The DM was introduced into West Berlin on 23 June, where both new currencies were allowed to circulate by the Western Allies until the Spring of 1949, when the DM became the only valid currency. The introduction of the two currencies showed very clearly that Germany had already been divided into two different parts, which in the words of Tyulpanov, the Information Officer on the Soviet Military Government, 'were each developing according to different rules'.

C *The Soviet reaction, 1946–49*

The Soviets and East Germans responded to these Anglo–American initiatives in the following ways:

- In June 1947, in reply to Bizonia, they set up the German Economic Commission, which was composed of the heads of the zonal central ministries and leaders of such key groups as the Free Federation of German Trade Unions. Like the Bizonia administration, it was progressively given more powers;
- In September 1947, Stalin set up the Cominform, a new Communist coordinating agency to mastermind the fight against the Marshall Plan;
- To counter Western determination to build up West Germany, the Soviets allowed the SED to call two 'German People's Congresses for Unity and Just Peace', essentially as a propaganda exercise, which met in December 1947 and March 1948. Their task was to mobilise public opinion right across the zonal divisions against the impending partition of Germany. In March the second Congress elected the People's Council (*Volksrat*) to prepare for a national referendum on German unity and an all-German constitution. In reality, the SED and the Soviets knew that they would fail to unite Germany and that the constitution would be an East German one only;
- On 23 June the Soviets responded to the currency reform in the West by introducing the new East Mark;
- They also imposed a blockade on Berlin which lasted from 24 June 1948 to 12 May 1949, in an attempt to force the Allies to stop the creation of a West German state, which, with its massive industrial potential, would become aligned with the Western powers in the Cold War.

See pages 389–91

D *The creation of the Federal Republic*

On 1 July 1948, the three Western Military Governors presented the minister-presidents (prime ministers) of the West German *Länder* with the decisions of the Six Power London Conference:

- A **constituent assembly** was to be elected which would then draft a federal constitution. This would have to be approved later by a referendum.
- The Military Governors were to draw up an occupation statute, which would define what powers were still held by the occupiers.
- The International Ruhr Authority was to be set up, which would allocate the steel and coal production of the Ruhr throughout Western Europe.

> **constituent assembly**
> an elected body whose task is to draw up a constitution

Despite the reluctance of the minister-presidents to see their country divided, the Communist takeover of Czechoslovakia and the Soviet blockade of Berlin seemed to indicate that there was no alternative if they were to avoid a Communist Germany. To prevent East German propaganda from influencing public opinion during an election campaign, they rejected the proposal for an elected constituent assembly and instead recommended a parliamentary council composed of sixty-five delegates, chosen by the *Länder*. This was accepted and it began its work on the constitution in August. The constitution, which with a few amendments was approved by the Military Governors in the Spring of 1949, was as Pulzer has stressed, inspired by the overriding aim of 'disaster avoidance'. As the Western Allies had demanded it was a democratic federal constitution. The *Länder* were represented in the *Bundesrat* (the Upper House) on the basis of their population. At all costs, the West Germans were determined to prevent the emergence of another Hitler. Thus, great care was taken to create the conditions for stable parliamentary government. The Parliamentary Council therefore recommended that:

- the Chancellor could only be forced to resign if there was already a majority in the lower house (*Bundestag*) for his successor;
- the President had only a ceremonial role;
- to be represented in the *Bundestag*, political parties had to gain a minimum of 5 per cent of the vote;
- anti-democratic parties were banned;
- the voting system combined proportional representation with constituency representatives.

Again, to avoid the possibility of a Communist propaganda campaign the Parliamentary Council avoided a referendum on the constitution and instead set the date for the election to the *Bundestag* for 14 August 1949. The election campaign was a duel between Schumacher, the leader of the SPD and Adenauer, who had outmanoeuvered the left-wing of his party and made the main theme of his campaign a crusade against Socialism. He was supported by

Ludwig Erhard, who had taken the opportunities provided by the introduction of the new DM currency to sweep away price controls and establish a more competitive economy. The CDU and its ally in Bavaria, the Christian Social Union (CSU), won 139 seats as opposed to 131 by the SPD, while the FDP secured fifty-two. When the *Bundestag* met in Bonn in September Adenauer was elected Chancellor and Theodore Heuss, the leader of the FDP, as part of a political trade-off for the FDP's readiness to form a coalition with Adenauer, became the first President of the FRG.

KEY ISSUE

To what extent was the constitution of the FRG designed to prevent unstable coalition governments that could lead to the collapse of democracy?

E *The creation of the GDR*

While the West German politicians were drawing up a constitution for the FRG and the Berlin Blockade was still in force, the Soviets attempted to keep their options open. They allowed the East German SED leadership to draw up a constitution for a future East German state, but as long as there seemed even the slightest chance of stopping the setting up of the FRG, Stalin delayed the formation of an East German government. However, once it became clear that this was impossible, the GDR was formally set up on 7 October 1948 and the People's Council was turned into a provisional parliament. On 12 October Grotewohl became Prime Minister.

Links between the FRG and GDR

ANALYSIS

Although for the sake of clarity the histories of the FRG and GDR are dealt with separately in this chapter, it is important to remember that the two states shared common roots: each claimed to be the legal successor to the *Reich* Bismarck had created in 1871 and right up to 1990 they constantly interacted on each other.

Both states were the products of the Cold War. The GDR was a satellite of the USSR, while the FRG was slowly integrated militarily, politically and economically into the Western world, which was dominated by America. Although the two Germanies followed diametrically opposed policies, they faced similar economic and social problems – the rebuilding of their shattered countries, the integration of the refugees from the eastern territories – and each of them had to come to terms with their recent Nazi past. Religious links also remained in place until 1969: the Lutheran Churches in the two states were both members of the Evangelical Church of Germany. The two states were also influenced, although in different ways, by global developments, such as *détente* in the 1960s and 1970s and the world economic crisis caused by the rise in oil prices after 1973.

See pages 411–13

3 ～ THE DEVELOPMENT OF THE FRG, 1949–89

A *Political history*

THE ADENAUER ERA, 1949–63

In the Autumn of 1949 the problems facing Adenauer were formidable and most observers did not believe that his government would last long.

- The economy was in trouble and there were over two million unemployed. Prices were also rising;
- The FRG was distrusted by its neighbours. Through the **Occupation Statute** and the International Ruhr Authority, the Western Allies still had an iron grip on Western Germany;
- There were between about 12 million refugees from Germany's former eastern territories who had to be integrated into the FRG;
- Millions of houses and flats had to be built to provide homes;
- If the West Germans were not offered any hope of economic and social improvements, they might move either to the far right again or be attracted by the propaganda coming from the GDR;
- Adenauer had no absolute majority and was kept in power by the Liberals.

Adenauer soon showed that he was a subtle politician who could unite the CDU/CSU and turn it into a highly effective party that could

The Occupation Statute laid down that a High Commission composed of American, British and French officials would still have ultimate control over a wide range of areas, such as foreign affairs, trade, internal security and matters affecting the safety of the Western Allied troops still in Germany. They also had to approve all West German legislation.

TIMELINE

The Adenauer era, 1949–63

Sept 1949	Adenauer appointed Chancellor
Nov	Petersberg Agreement
Winter 1949–50	Unemployment over two million
June 1950	Korean War
April 1951	Law on co-determination in the iron and steel industries
	European Coal and Steel Community (ECSC) created
August 1952	Equalisation of Burdens Act
	Death of Schumacher
May	EDC Treaty signed
Sept 1953	Adenauer re-elected
Feb 1954	Basic Law amended to permit creation of Federal Army
May 1955	FRG became a sovereign state
Feb 1956	Majority of Free Democrats left coalition with CDU
March 1957	Treaty of Rome signed
Sept	Adenauer re-elected for third term
Nov 1959	SPD's Godesberg Programme
Aug 1960	Willy Brandt nominated to lead SPD in election campaign
Aug 1961	Berlin Wall constructed
Sept	Adenauer elected with reduced majority
Oct–Nov 1962	Spiegel Affair
Oct 1963	Adenauer resigned

attract a wide cross-section of support in the FRG. Adenauer attracted both Protestants and Catholics in the north, who wanted to rebuild the new Germany in a Christian spirit, the supporters of the social market economy, many younger voters who were inspired by the idea of European integration and finally a more diverse group of politicians and voters who were united by a hatred of the USSR and a desire to win back the eastern territories lost at Potsdam. He was also helped by the failures of the SPD. Under the uncompromising leadership of Schumacher, the SPD bitterly opposed Adenauer's economic and foreign policies, even when they began to work.

Adenauer laid the foundations for his later successes in his first government. By working closely with France and America he was able to persuade the Western Allies to revise drastically the Occupation Statute and agree to West German re-armament within the structure of the Pleven Plan. The great economic boom triggered by the Korean War also benefited the FRG enormously, despite initially causing a serious balance of payments crisis. By the Autumn of 1951 the West German economy was beginning to settle down to a period of sustained expansion that did not really come to a halt until the 1970s. Adenauer was therefore able to get on with the challenging task of turning the FRG into a socially united and prosperous state.

The upturn in the economy helped to stop labour unrest, but the good labour relations which lasted right up to the 1970s were also a product of a deliberate policy by the Adenauer government to create social peace. In 1950, when the codetermination scheme in the steel industry, agreed to by the British Military Government in 1947, was about to come to an end, Adenauer decided to continue it in a slightly modified form and even to extend it to the coal industry, despite

See page 31

See page 31

KURT SCHUMACHER (1895–1952)

PROFILE

Kurt Schümacher was elected as an SPD candidate to the *Reichstag* in 1930 where he was a strong opponent of both the Communists and Nazis, who interned him in Dachau concentration camp when they came to power. In 1945, from his base in Hanover, he rebuilt the SPD in the Western zones and refused to follow the policy of Otto Grotewohl in Berlin, who merged the SPD in the Soviet Zone with the KPD. However, he failed to modernise the party, which remained lumbered with the out-of-date Heidelberg programme of 1924. He supported the creation of a temporary West German state and believed that it would act as a magnet to attract the GDR, provided that it implemented social democratic reforms. He accused Adenauer of supporting big business and of working too closely with the Western Allies. Thus, he bitterly opposed the European Coal and Steel Community and the Pleven Plan.

See pages 333 and 337

See page 32

In the coal and steel industries full equality was not quite given to the unions. On the supervisory boards the shareholders and employees each had five representatives and the eleventh was nominated by the directors. Adenauer lived up to his reputation for cunning!

In 1950, for example, the extreme right-wing Bloc of Expellees and Disenfranchised which was led by ex-Nazis won 23.4 per cent of the vote in the Schleswig-Holstein *Land* election.

See page 35

opposition from the FDP and Big Business. At the height of the Cold War Adenauer did not want to antagonise the coal and steel workers, who might then be driven into the arms of the Communists. By agreeing to codetermination he was also able to gain trade union support for the ECSC (European Coal and Steel Community). In 1952 the Works Constitution Law was passed, which set up workers' consultative councils throughout industry. Although these two acts did not go as far as some trade unionists wanted, they did contribute greatly towards creating the framework for constructive labour relations.

The economic recovery also helped Adenauer to make a decisive start with an ambitious house and flat building programme. The Construction Law of April 1950 cleared the way for generous grants to be made by the central government to the cities and the *Länder* for house building. In 1952 some 430 000 housing units were built and by 1957 well over 4 million had been constructed. The visible success of this programme at last offered the West German people hope of gaining a flat or house of their own. Adenauer followed this up in 1952 with the Equalisation of Burdens Act, which aimed to ensure that the refugees and victims of the Allied bombing campaigns who had lost all their property, received compensation from those who had been more fortunate. The new leader of the SPD, Ollenhauer, had wanted to seize this chance to create a more equal and just society, whereas the CDU and FDP were opposed to any threats to the existing property structure. The Act was thus inevitably something of a compromise. On the one hand all property, buildings and shares were to be subjected to a 50 per cent tax on their value as estimated on 21 June 1948, to be paid over the course of thirty years. The profits would be paid out as compensation to the refugees and other casualties of war after their claims had been sifted by special committees. On the other hand, the long-term impact of the Act was blunted because the value of property, shares, etc. increased enormously over the next thirty years as a result of economic growth and inflation. Nevertheless, by 1978 over 110 billion marks had been raised and the refugees who otherwise might have moved dangerously to the far right were integrated into the FRG.

Not surprisingly, Adenauer became increasingly popular and consequently in the 1953 election the CDU/CSU was able to improve its share of the vote by nearly 15 per cent. During his second government Adenauer at last achieved West German sovereignty when in May 1955 the Western powers recognised the FRG as an independent state. The West Germans welcomed independence, but they were less happy about joining NATO and the decision to set up a new Federal Army so soon after the end of the war. Nevertheless, Adenauer's government was skilfully able to avoid the mistakes of the 1920s and to create an army that was subject to parliamentary control and loyal to the Federal Republic. Its soldiers were 'citizens in uniform' who were trained to think for themselves, rather than to obey orders like robots.

	CDU/CSU	SPD	FDP	Other parties	Greens
1949	31.0	29.2	11.9	7.5	
1953	45.2	28.8	9.5	3.3	
1957	50.2	31.8	7.7	1.0	
1961	45.3	36.2	12.8	0.8	
1965	47.6	39.3	9.5	2.0	
1969	46.1	42.7	5.8	9.3	
1972	44.9	45.8	8.4	0.6	
1976	48.6	42.6	7.9	0.3	
1980	44.5	42.9	10.6	0.2	1.5
1983	48.8	38.2	6.9	0.2	5.6
1987	44.3	37.0	9.1	0.6	8.3

TABLE 1
FRG general election results, 1949–87 (% of votes cast)

In the eight years since 1949 the FRG had achieved an extraordinary success. Its towns were largely rebuilt, its economy booming and its security assured by its position within NATO. Adenauer was rewarded for these impressive achievements in the general election of September 1957, when the CDU/CSU won an absolue majority of 50.2 per cent of the vote. The Chancellor had hit the right note in his campaign with his call for no experiments.

At the age of eighty-one, Adenauer seemed immune to the weaknesses of old age and was at the height of his power politically, but gradually over the next six years his luck and formidable political skills began to desert him. Both the general public, the FDP and the majority of his own party became increasingly impatient for his retirement in favour of Erhard, as the following events show:

KEY ISSUE

Why did the FRG recover so rapidly from the War?

- In 1956 the FDP split and the majority, led by Thomas Dehler, who was highly critical of Adenauer's rigid and uncompromising policy towards the USSR and the GDR, left the coalition and began to consider cooperation with the SPD. At the local level this did indeed happen when an SPD–FDP coalition brought down a CDU-led government in North Rhine–Westphalia. In 1957 Adenauer won an absolute majority in the election and thus was independent of the FDP, but nevertheless it had served notice on him that it would not follow the CDU blindly;
- Adenauer was in many ways an authoritarian figure impatient of parliament and politicians when they stood in his way. In 1959, for example, he played with the idea of becoming President of the FRG when Heuss retired, believing that he could still dominate politics as General de Gaulle did in France. When he discovered this was not so, he rapidly dropped the idea and pushed his Minister of Agriculture, the nondescript Heinrich Lübke, into the post;
- Adenauer began to be challenged by a modernised and more effective SPD which, in reaction to its defeat in 1957, produced the Godesberg Programme. This marked the acceptance by the Party of Erhard's economic policy. The SPD also dropped opposition to the FRG's membership of NATO and in August 1960 appointed a young dynamic politician, Willy Brandt, the Lord Mayor of Berlin, to lead the Party in the election campaign of 1961;

See pages 43–44

- This campaign was dominated by the building of the Berlin Wall on 13 August 1961. Adenauer made a serious mistake when he appeared to play down this momentous event and delayed visiting West Berlin until 22 August. Although the CDU/CSU still won 45 per cent of the vote, the FDP, by increasing its support from 7.7 per cent to 12.8 per cent, again held the balance. This time it insisted that Adenauer should step down in favour of Erhard after two years;

- What finally made his retirement inevitable was the *Spiegel* Affair. When the weekly news magazine, the *Spiegel*, published an article on the inefficiencies of the West German army, the Minister of Defence, Franz-Josef Strauss, immediately had the editors arrested, an action which Adenauer supported. The whole incident awoke memories of the Third Reich and led to widespread condemnation of Adenauer and student demonstrations in several universities;

- The FDP resigned and then only rejoined the coalition after insisting that Strauss should resign and that Adenauer himself should retire in favour of Erhard not later than October 1963;

- Adenauer never recovered from the *Spiegel* Affair. His support amongst the West Germans dropped dramatically and he had little option but to retire on 15 October 1963.

ANALYSIS

Did Adenauer create a New Germany?

Historians are divided as to whether Adenauer simply reconstructed an old traditional Germany or whether the FRG was really a new modern state. Those like Werner Abelshauser, who support the former argument, point out the lack of reform of the civil service and of the educational system and stress the conservative attitudes of the FRG. For instance, women were encouraged by the government to remain at home and to leave the labour market free for men. In the early years of the FRG the population did not want to get involved in politics and wished to retreat into family and private life. (This was called the '*ohne mich*' or 'without me' attitude.) There was also still some admiration for Hitler and a refusal to accept Germany's responsibility for the war. Other historians, such as Ralph Willett, point out that by the end of the decade Germany was increasingly becoming a consumer society on the American model, in which American industrial techniques were adopted to produce mass prosperity. They also stress that the West Germans were more liberal in their attitudes than before the war. Most of them approved of European integration, liked foreign films and recipes and travelled abroad when they had the money. Certainly, by the early 1960s the rigid conservativism of the 1950s was beginning to fade, as the reaction to the *Spiegel* Affair showed.

THE LAST YEARS OF CDU/CSU DOMINATION: ERHARD AND THE GREAT COALITION, 1963–69

By 1963 the FRG appeared to be a prosperous and democratic state, but many people still feared that the West Germans were only 'fair weather democrats' who would very quickly abandon democracy again if they faced a major political or economic crisis. In the Sixties the FRG faced, in Lothar Kettenacker's words, its 'first acid test'. Erhard, after winning an impressive election victory in 1964, was soon confronted with what by West German standards was a major economic crisis, which destroyed his reputation as an economic genius in the eyes of many voters. In July 1966 the CDU/CSU lost the important *Land* election in Westphalia and he himself was forced to resign in November, when the FDP quit the coalition in protest against his economic policy, which they felt was not cutting government expenditure sufficiently.

He was replaced by Kurt-Georg Kiesinger, the former Prime Minister of Baden-Württemberg, who made the controversial decision to form 'the Great Coalition' with the SDP. Kiesinger wanted to isolate the Liberals and stop them from influencing government policy, while the SPD hoped to show the electorate that it too was a responsible party which could effectively exercise power. The 'silent majority' of Germans welcomed the coalition as a reassuring sign of unity in the face of the growing economic problems, but there were others, particularly students, left-wing journalists, writers and intellectuals, who were convinced that Germany was turning into a one-party state. The SPD Students Federation set up the APO, the Extra-Parliamentary Opposition, to an opposition which they thought the *Bundestag* was no longer capable of providing.

At the opposite end of the spectrum, the Great Coalition was also opposed by the right-wing National Democratic Party, which campaigned for a strong Germany independent of NATO and the West.

It was against this background of often noisy and violent protest, mostly from the APO and other student groups, that the Great Coalition set about stabilising the economy by increasing the powers of the central government to raise taxation and to control extravagant expenditure by the *Länder*. It also filled a dangerous gap in the constitution in May 1968 when the Emergency Law was passed which at last gave the FRG the legal means to take emergency measures in the event of civil unrest or war. Theoretically, up to this point only the former occupying powers could declare a state of emergency. The law, however, was bitterly contested by a campaign group called the 'Emergency of Democracy'; it feared that the law would be similar to Article 48 of the Weimar Constitution, which had helped Hitler into power.

By 1969 the leaders of the SPD were becoming increasingly impatient of the coalition with the CDU/CSU. They felt that it was too conservative and was preventing them both from implementing further welfare reforms and pushing on more quickly with the new policy of *détente* with Eastern Europe. In the meantime the FDP, which had moved to the left under a new leader, Walther Scheel, had become a

TIMELINE

Sept 1964	West German elections Erhard continued in power
Dec 1966	Formation of the Great Coalition
April 1968	Rudi Dutschke shot
May	Emergency Laws passed
Oct 1969	Brandt elected Chancellor

See page 32

détente policy of reducing national tension

ANALYSIS

The student revolt and urban terrorism, 1968–92

The student revolt has been called by Nichols 'the greatest trauma of the entire history of the Federal Republic'. The revolt was caused by a number of factors. The trial in 1963–65 of seventeen former overseers and guards of Auschwitz concentration camp re-opened the whole question of Germany's past and inspired the most politically active amongst the students to attempt to force their parents' generation to face up to its Nazi past. The formation of the Great Coalition and the passing of the Emergency Laws appeared to indicate that West Germany was sliding back into the authoritarian habits of the late Weimar Republic. Protests against the war in Vietnam helped to mobilise the New Left and led to violent anti-American demonstrations. The students were also protesting against the overcrowded, outdated and authoritarian universities, which had not been reformed after 1945. The unrest reached its peak when one of the student leaders, Rudi Dutschke, was severely wounded by a right-wing assassin in April 1968. This led to the worst rioting in West Germany since 1932, with disturbances in twenty-seven cities.

Although the APO and the student protest movements soon fragmented, their impact on West German politics was considerable. Many of their members joined the SPD in due course, where they formed a strong passivist and anti-capitalist bloc, which pushed the party further to the left. Others did not join a conventional political party but launched various ecological protest groups, which gradually came together to form the Green Party in 1980. A very small number set up groups of urban terrorists, of which the Red Army faction (RAF) led by Andreas Baader and Ulrike Meinhof was the best known. Its aim was to inspire what it regarded as the intimidated and exploited masses, through arson and the murder of businessmen and state officials, especially judges, to rise up and free themselves from oppression by the State and the great industrialists. The wave of terrorism that swept the FRG from 1970–72 forced the government to strengthen the powers of the police and take greater care that only state employees loyal to the ideals of the Basic Law could be recruited. In June 1972 Baader and Meinhof were arrested after bomb attacks on the offices of the Springer press in Hamburg and the headquarters of the American army in Heidelberg. In the Autumn of 1977, the Red Army Group made an attempt to secure its leader's release by kidnapping a prominent businessman and persuading an Arab terrorist group to hijack a Lufthansa Boeing 737 and fly it to Mogadishu in Somalia. Chancellor Schmidt refused to make any concessions and, with the permission of the Somalian Government, sent a force of élite West German border guards, who successfully rescued the passengers on 17 October. Although this was a severe defeat for the terrorists – three key members of the RAF committed suicide in prison when they heard the news – sporadic assassinations and incidents continued to occur. Only when the fall of the GDR cut off financial and logistical support did the incidents end. In 1992 the Red Army Front at last declared a 'ceasefire'.

possible coalition partner. Consequently, when in the election of September 1969 the SPD and FDP won 48.5 per cent of the vote as compared to 46.1 per cent of the CDU/CSU, Willy Brandt decided to form a new Social Democratic–Liberal Coalition.

THE BRANDT–SCHMIDT ERA, 1969–82

Brandt was the first SPD Chancellor since 1930 and his electoral victory awakened huge expectations for reform which a combination of increasingly adverse economic conditions, his own failures in leadership and entrenched CDU opposition in the *Länder* stopped him from fulfilling. Nevertheless his achievements were considerable:

- He did expand the provisions of the welfare state by reforming the pension system and health and accident insurance;
- The criminal law was also made less harsh;
- Action was also taken to create greater equality between the sexes;
- Grants were made available for students from poorer backgrounds to study;
- He also increased the powers of the workers councils set up by Adenauer;
- His greatest success was to implement the new *Ostpolitik* with the GDR and the Soviet Bloc.

The cost of the welfare reforms, however, led to considerable tension within the party. The finance ministers, Möller and then Schiller, insisted on spending cuts in an effort to control inflation, which the left-wing of the party bitterly opposed. The opposition began to accuse the government of drifting to the left and by the summer of 1972, as a result of defections from both the FDP and the SDP, Brandt had lost his overall majority in the *Bundestag*. He only survived a vote of no confidence in his *Ostpolitik* by two votes, one of which was bribed. There was little doubt that the SPD was unpopular, but Brandt himself and *Ostpolitik* were not. He therefore decided to risk an election in November, which was in effect a referendum on his handling of *Ostpolitik*. The gamble paid off and thanks to Brandt the SPD won the biggest victory in its history.

However, Brandt failed to build on this success. At the very beginning illness prevented him from dominating his cabinet effectively. Within the SPD the New Left, made up of many former

TIMELINE

Oct 1969	Brandt elected Chancellor
1970 –72	The new Ostpolitik put into action
April 1972	Failure of vote of no confidence
Nov 1972	Brandt's second electoral victory
Nov 1973	Oil crisis began
May 1974	Brandt's resignation Schmidt appointed Chancellor
Oct 1977	Mogadishu Incident
Jan 1979	NATO's Twin-Track decision
Sept 1982	Resignation of FDP ministers from coalition
Oct 1982	Kohl appointed Chancellor

See pages 37–39

Ostpolitik literally means 'Eastern policy'. It improved relations between the FRG and the Soviet Bloc states, including the GDR.

See page 33

KEY ISSUE

What did Willy Brandt achieve?

monetarism the theory that the best way of stabilising the economy is to control the amount of money that circulates. This inevitably means that there is less money for banks to lend and for the state to spend.

APO members, was determined to press for a more radical left-wing programme, while they were opposed by the more conservative wing, led by the formidable Helmut Schmidt. Brandt's problems were made worse by the rising rate of inflation, the oil crisis and demands from the unions for large wage increases. His fate was finally sealed when it was discovered that his personal assistant, Günter Guillaume, was an East German agent. He had no option but to resign and was replaced by Schmidt.

Schmidt was essentially a man of action who had no time for the ecological and passivist concerns of his party's left wing. Over the next eight years his economic and defence policies were attacked more bitterly by the left wing of his own party than by the opposition. According to Pulzer, the borderline between Left and Right in German politics at this period ran 'not between the parties but down the middle of the SPD'. A greater potential threat to Schmidt's position came from the FDP under its new and more conservative leader, Genscher, who would really have preferred to have worked with the CDU, now led by Helmuth Kohl. He was increasingly worried about the rising influence of the New Left within the SPD and in March 1976 it seemed as if the FDP would leave the coalition. However, Schmidt was saved by Genscher's determination to make the new *Ostpolitik* work. There were still deep divisions within the CDU/CSU over *Ostpolitik* as both Strauss and Hans Filbinger, the CDU Minister-President of Baden, were strongly opposed to it, even though Kohl supported it. In the general election of October 1976 the Schmidt–Genscher coalition just scraped back into power with a two-vote majority. Strauss's continued hostility to *Ostpolitik* and return to the language of the Cold War almost certainly cost the CDU/CSU its victory.

By the late 1970s Schmidt had emerged as an impressive leader both within the European Community, the wider world and at home, as his refusal to give in to terrorism showed. As the 1980 election approached, the SPD/FDP coalition was helped by the divisions within the CDU/CSU and the rivalry between Kohl and Strauss which came to a head when Strauss replaced Kohl as the leader of the party. In the election campaign Strauss again frightened away many potential voters and Schmidt and Genscher were able to defeat the CDU/CSU for the fourth time.

Yet Schmidt's position still remained precarious and his fall was only a matter of time for the following reasons:

● Much of his party, including the trade unions, opposed the **monetarist** policies of the FDP Economics Minister, Count Otto von Lambsdorff;
● Schmidt's decision in 1979 to agree to having medium-range missiles based in Western Germany, if no disarmament agreement could be negotiated with the USSR, was met with deep hostility from the left wing of his party;
● The SPD also faced a growing challenge from the **Greens**, who had at last grouped together as a party in 1980. They had the potential

to attract many of the more left-wing SPD voters who, like them, were interested in ecological issues and wanted to ban nuclear power and weapons;

● After Strauss's failure to win the 1980 election his influence in the CDU declined and Kohl once again took over the leadership. Thus the way was open for a future CDU/FDP coalition led by Kohl.

Finally, in the autumn of 1982 Genscher pulled the FDP out of the coalition and the new CDU/FDP coalition was formed under Kohl the following month.

THE KOHL–GENSCHER COALITION, 1982–89

West German society had changed a lot since the collapse of the last CDU/CSU–FDP coalition in 1966. Personal attitudes had become more relaxed and less authoritarian. The ideas of the New Left had dominated the political debate and pushed German Conservatives on to the defensive. Although most of the population had grown more prosperous by the early 1980s, a new factor which had hardly been present in the 1960s was the growth of mass unemployment to over two million. Sociologists were beginning to talk about the two-thirds society, meaning that while most Germans enjoyed a prosperous life, a significant number formed a poor 'underclass', amongst whom were a disproportionate number of the four million immigrants, or 'guest-workers' who had come to work in Germany since the late 1950s.

At first it seemed that Kohl might try to turn the clock back to the social and economic policies of the early 1950s, but when he called an election in March 1983 it was clear that for all his talk about the need for 'spiritual, moral change' he was in reality going to continue the main policies of the Schmidt government. There were going to be no changes to *Ostpolitik* and NATO's decision to site nuclear missiles in the FRG would be carried out. Even his economic policy was not really so different from Schmidt's. The SPD suffered its worst defeat since 1961. It was in no position to defeat Kohl. Schmidt had resigned and its new leader, Hans-Jochen Vogel, inherited a party deeply split over the whole missile question. Many of its former voters turned to the Greens, who just managed to win sufficient votes to gain representation in the *Bundestag* for the first time. The new Coalition seemed set for a period of almost effortless domination of German politics. However, despite the fall in inflation and an impressive industrial recovery, the Kohl government failed to maintain its popularity for a number of reasons:

● Unemployment stubbornly remained over two million;
● There was considerable in-fighting in the coalition between Strauss and Genscher;
● The CSU itself was split when two of its members broke away to found the right-wing Republican party;
● 'Sleaze' also damaged Kohl. It was discovered that over a long period of time industry had secretly been making illegal donations to both coalition parties. In 1984 the FDP Finance Minister had to resign because he had exempted one of the largest businesses in

The Greens combined a programme for protecting the environment with demands for grassroots democracy, human (and especially women's) rights and pacifism

KEY ISSUE

What did Helmut Schmidt achieve and why did his cabinet fall in 1982?

TIMELINE

March 1983	Kohl's electoral victory
Nov	Medium-range missiles installed in FRG
May 1985	The Bitburg Affair
Jan 1987	Kohl won second victory
Sept 1987	Honecker visited FRG

Germany, the Flick Concern, from tax payments in return for money it had given to the FDP;

● The Bitburg Affair put into question Kohl's reputation for moderation. During President Reagan's visit to the FRG he had planned to mark the fortieth anniversary of the Second World War by staging a symbolic gesture of reconciliation at a military ceremony at Bitburg. When it emerged that SS troops were buried there he defiantly refused to stop the ceremony, despite the discomfort of Reagan and the anger of many Germans.

See page 23

KEY ISSUE

How true is it to say that only the unification of Germany in 1990 saved the Kohl government from defeat?

In the election of January 1987 the electorate showed its disillusion with the two major parties. The CDU/CSU vote declined to its lowest level since 1949 (44 per cent) while the SPD also failed to improve its position. It was the FDP and the Greens who made impressive gains. Thanks to Genscher's backing, Kohl managed to retain power, but over the next three years the splits in the coalition deepened. The results of the *Länder* elections confirmed the steady decline of the CDU. By 1989 it seemed likely that Kohl would soon be forced to resign, but the unexpected collapse of the GDR threw him, to quote Siekmeier and Larres, 'a much needed life-line'.

B *Economic history*

Few in 1945 would have foreseen the phenomenal success of the West German economy. It was so great that the term 'economic miracle' was used to describe it. Yet looking back the historian can see clearly, as Overy has expressed it, that it was not a miracle 'in the sense that defied explanation'. Western Germany possessed a series of 'inherited advantages' which helped it to take advantage of the great economic upturn of the 1950s:

● A high proportion of the German workforce was skilled and Germany had a strong scientific and technical tradition;
● Despite the bombing much of its industrial equipment survived. In May 1945, for instance, Germany possessed double the number of machine tools to be found in Britain;
● The future FRG possessed the great industrial power-house of the Ruhr.

Ludwig Erhard played a key role in the FRG's economic recovery. He was determined to create a free economy with the introduction of the new currency in June 1948 and to abolish most economic price controls and rationing, which he felt had made large-scale industrial production unprofitable and encouraged the black market. Thus from now on the prices for some foodstuffs and the majority of industrial goods were to be determined by market forces, that is by what people would pay for them in the shops. It suddenly became worthwhile for factories to produce the goods people wanted and the workers had every incentive to earn as much as possible. Although the shops rapidly filled up with consumer goods which had not been seen for years, Erhard's economic

Erhard and the social market economy

The term 'Social Market Economy' became 'the brand name' for the economic system of West Germany. Essentially it was a 'third way' between a completely free market and a state-controlled economy as in the GDR. It was the brainchild of Erhard and a group of economists teaching at the University of Freiburg, who were working on plans for replacing the central planning system of the Nazi economy once Hitler had been defeated, with a more liberal economy in which businessmen and industrialists had a bigger say. Their aim, as Nicolls has put it, was 'to wed free price mechanism and market competition to a socially responsible policy'. What this meant was that the state would still have a role in regulating the economy so that competition would be fair and that welfare benefits would protect those most in need. First as Economics Director of Bizonia and then as Economics Minister under Adenauer, Erhard was in a key position for implementing these ideas, although inevitably he had to make many compromises. Under Adenauer agriculture, for instance, continued to be as heavily subsidised as it was in the Third Reich.

liberalisation did at first cause considerable hardship, even though basic food stuffs continued to be rationed. Prices for most goods inevitably rose and as factories now had to make a profit to survive, many workers were made redundant.

At first it did not look as if West Germany's economy would take off. In the winter of 1948–49 there were still over two million out of work and exports were not paying for the imports the economy needed. By early 1950 pressure was growing on Erhard from the SPD, the Unions and the Allied High Commission to abandon the Social Market Economy and reintroduce state controls. The situation was temporarily eased by the outbreak of the Korean War, which forced the West to start re-arming and created a huge demand for Ruhr steel and high-tech exports, but by early 1951 the West German economy was again faced with a serious balance of payments deficit caused by the import of large amounts of raw materials, particularly coal. Erhard was put under pressure by the Western Allies to ration raw materials, so that the steel industry would have priority, but he cleverly avoided this by entrusting the industrialists themselves to allocate the raw materials through their own trade associations. By the autumn of 1951 the economic boom created by the Korean War at last began to work in favour of the FRG and the years 1952–60 saw a period of rapid and sustained growth, with unemployment quickly falling.

See pages 21–2

TABLE 2

Annual economic growth rates and unemployment in the FRG

	Growth rates (%)	Un-employment (%)
1952	8.9	8.5
1953	8.2	7.6
1954	7.4	7.1
1955	12.0	5.2
1956	7.2	4.2
1957	5.7	3.5
1958	3.7	3.6
1959	7.3	2.5
1960	9.0	1.3
1961	4.1	0.9
1962	4.7	1.2
1963	2.8	1.5

THE ECONOMY OF THE FRG, 1948–66

A number of factors explain the enormous success of the FRG's economy in the 1950s:

● The terms of world trade favoured the FRG: raw materials were cheap. The DM in the early 1950s was undervalued against other currencies and therefore German exports could undercut rivals;
● Thanks to the careful monetary policies of the *Bundesbank* (the FRG's central bank) inflation was avoided in Germany and therefore the prices of German exports remained stable;
● Under American influence barriers to trade were coming down in the Western world. Within Europe the creation of the European Coal and Steel Community in 1951 and the European Economic Community in 1958 also made it easier for the West Germans to export;
● The West Germans did not have to spend huge sums on re-armament like their competitors. Only in 1956 did they have an army;
● The trade unions exercised moderation because they did not want to harm the growth prospects of the FRG. Adenauer's co-determination policies also increased their sense of responsibility;
● There was a steady flow of refugees from the GDR to fill the growing number of job vacancies.

By 1958 the period of post-war reconstruction was over and the FRG began to face the problems of being a mature industrial economy. Both the economic growth rate and the trade surplus slowed down and there was an increasing scarcity of workers, which led to the immigration of foreign labour from Italy, Turkey, Greece and Yugoslavia. Wages began to rise more quickly than productivity, which once more raised fears of inflation. In early 1966 the inflation rate was creeping up to an annual rate of 4 per cent. By international standards the FRG's economic problems were minor, but memories of the hyperinflation of 1923 and the slump of 1929–33 were still fresh in the minds of many Germans. Erhard overreacted. Interest rates were raised and government spending cut. This plunged the FRG into recession and led to Erhard's resignation.

THE END OF THE MARKET ECONOMY AND THE IMPACT OF THE VIETNAM WAR AND THE OIL CRISIS, 1967–82

Both Kiesinger and Brandt were convinced that the State needed to intervene much more in the economy if the twin evils of inflation and unemployment were to be avoided. In 1967 the Great Coalition significantly increased the government's power to intervene through two important measures. Firstly, it gained the power through the Stabilisation Law to 'steer' the economy in times of recession by raising loans, increasing taxes and investing money in job creation projects. Secondly, in December a further law was passed in the *Bundestag* which gave the central government the power to plan financially five years ahead and to coordinate the spending of the *Länder* and the cities with the overall federal budget. These reforms managed to restore confidence and in 1969 the economy of the FRG grew by 5.6 per cent and inflation dropped to 1.5 per cent.

However, this improvement was only temporary. In the early 1970s the economy of the FRG was again hit by inflationary pressures triggered by the Vietnam War and the weakening of the exchange rate of the American dollar. Then in October 1973 the Arab States organised into **OPEC** decided to triple the price of oil. This meant that the FRG would now have to pay DM 17 billion more on oil imports in 1974 than in 1973. Inevitably this caused inflation to rise and by the spring of 1974 the economists were forecasting 8 per cent inflation and rising unemployment. By 1975 unemployment had risen to one million and domestic output (GDP) had sunk to 1.6 per cent. Despite demands from the left wing of the SPD for the government to pump large sums of money into the economy, Chancellor Schmidt cautiously began to cut government expenditure. He was above all determined that the oil crisis should not push the industrial nations of the West into adopting protectionist policies which would seriously damage international trade. Consequently he worked hard with the French President, Giscard d'Estaing, to create the European Monetary System, in which members of the European Community would coordinate their financial and trade policies. He also strongly supported such international economic institutions as the International Monetary Fund and the **G7**. In 1978 at the Bonn Economic Summit it was agreed that the FRG should begin to reflate its economy and act as a 'locomotive' for pulling the world economy out of recession, but before this really took effect, in the winter of 1979/80 OPEC once again drastically raised the price of oil and the FRG had plunged back into recession by late 1980.

OPEC the Organisation of Petroleum Exporting Countries

The G7 or Group of Seven was composed of the seven states with the world's leading economies

PARTIAL RETURN TO THE SOCIAL MARKET ECONOMY, 1982–90

Kohl was only partly successful in his efforts to restore the market economy. He announced a new policy which he called an economic 'turning point' or a moving away from the high spending policies of the previous governments since 1966. This involved tax cuts spread over seven years and a determined attempt to keep annual budget increases down to 3 per cent, but for electoral reasons he continued to subsidise farming, coal, steel and the aerospace industry. With the collapse in oil prices in 1985 world trading conditions again moved in favour of the FRG and over the next five years West German exporters built up a large trade surplus, but unemployment still stubbornly remained at over two million.

C *Foreign policy*

INTRODUCTION

A series of interlocking issues dominated the foreign policy of the FRG in the 1950s:

- In 1949 the FRG was still an occupied country subject to wide-ranging controls from the Allied High Commission. It needed to regain its independence from London, Paris and Washington;
- At the same time it was in the frontline of the Cold War and was entirely dependent for its defence on NATO and the USA;
- It needed to convince France that it was no longer a threat so that a way would be open for an agreement on the Ruhr and the Saar;
- The two Germanies could only be united with the agreement of the four occupying powers. Yet Adenauer wanted to prevent them doing a deal over the head of the FRG, which would create a neutral disarmed Germany that might be at the mercy of the USSR at a later date.

WESTERN INTEGRATION, 1949–58

The key to solving these interlocking problems was Western integration, which Hans-Peter Schwarz has called 'the great hope of the 1950s'. It offered the FRG both partnership with the Western European democracies and security within the international community. Gradually this partnership could be used as a means for securing greater independence for the FRG. Adenauer set about achieving this step by step:

- In November 1949 he signed the Petersberg Agreement with the High Commissioners. This enabled the FRG, as Adenauer himself observed, to re-enter 'the international sphere'. The FRG joined the Council of Europe and the OEEC and was also permitted to set up consulates abroad;
- Adenauer had already proposed plans to the Americans and French for joint Franco–German ownership of the Ruhr in the Autumn of 1949. He therefore responded positively to Schuman's proposals for a European Coal and Steel Community, even though he realised that it was a subtle plan to maximise French influence on the Ruhr. The advantage of the ECSC for the FRG was that it broke the vicious circle of Franco–German hostility and replaced the Ruhr Statute;
- Adenauer responded equally quickly to the French Pleven Plan for a European army in October 1950. He immediately saw that if Germany was providing troops and weapons to defend the West, then the occupying powers would have to restore German independence. Through the **General Treaty** negotiated with the High Commissioners it seemed that this would happen;
- However, all these plans collapsed like a pack of cards when the French Assembly rejected the EDC in August 1954. By consenting to keep the future size of the West German army to what had been

The General Treaty
The terms were that the Western powers recognised the FRG as an independent state, promised to work for a united Germany which would be integrated into the Western community and retained their rights to negotiate a peace treaty with a united Germany at some future date.

See page 337

agreed in the EDC treaty and by voluntarily renouncing nuclear weapons, Adenauer ensured that a new German treaty was rapidly negotiated in October 1954. France was also persuaded to allow the FRG to join NATO. On 5 May 1955 the treaty came into force and the FRG achieved its independence, although Berlin remained under four power control;

- Two years later Adenauer signed the Treaty of Rome, which created the EEC. He told Erhard that this was an historic event almost comparable to the unification of Germany. By operating within the context of the EEC West Germany was able to gain considerable influence in Western Europe and to begin the process of integration with its neighbours as an equal.

See pages 338–9

RELATIONS WITH FRANCE AND THE USA

Adenauer's foreign policy was based on Western integration and a close alliance with America. This worked very well as long as the Americans were ready to keep a large number of troops in West Germany and make absolutely no concessions to the USSR about the status of the GDR and East Berlin. Once America began to adopt a more flexible policy towards the USSR, Adenauer was driven towards following a more independent European policy. In the autumn of 1956 he responded to American plans for cutting the number of their troops in Western Germany by moving closer to France. The growing Franco–German friendship even survived the coming to power of General de Gaulle in May 1958, although both statesmen had fundamentally different visions of Europe. While de Gaulle wanted a Europe of independent nation states, which would be only very loosely linked through the EEC, Adenauer wanted an ever more integrated Europe and an alliance with America. What brought Adenauer closer to Gaullist France was his growing disillusionment with Britain and the USA during the Berlin crisis of 1958–61, when it became clear to him that they were ready to accept the division of Germany and negotiate a long-term settlement with Moscow. Consequently he raised no objections to the French veto on Britain's application to join the EEC in January 1963 and then shortly afterwards signed the Franco–

The solution of the Saar problem

Originally, the French intended to set up the Saar as an independent state with close economic connections to France. However, when the plebiscite was held in October 1955 to see whether the population approved this, 67 per cent voted against it, but in 1957 relations were so good between Bonn and Paris that the Saar was able to become the eleventh federal state of the FRG on the basis of Article 23 of the Basic Law. In 1990 this Article also enabled the states of the GDR to join the FRG.

ANALYSIS

See page 95

German treaty of friendship. The treaty triggered bitter rows in the cabinets of both Adenauer and Erhard between the Gaullists and the Atlanticists, who supported close links with Washington. Although the Gaullists never won the argument, good relations with France remained the cornerstone of the FRG's foreign policy. Both Brandt and Kohl got on well with their French counterparts. As Nicholls has written, Franco–German relationships took on 'the character of a well-established marriage in which quarrels would be expected but not taken as disastrous'.

As long as the Cold War lasted the FRG could not afford a major quarrel with the USA. Nevertheless, there were often quite sharp disagreements between the two powers. Willy Brandt was critical of the Vietnam War and of America's failure to control inflation, while during the Yom Kippur War with Israel in October 1973 and the subsequent oil crisis, Washington often accused Bonn of being too pro-Arab. Essentially, however, these were minor quarrels between allies. In the late 1960s and early 1970s both states believed in *détente* with the Soviet Bloc, and after some initial suspicions Washington fully backed Bonn's *Ostpolitik*. By the mid-1970s the FRG was seen as America's most reliable ally in Europe.

See pages 411–13

The Bonn–Washington special relationship came under renewed pressure after 1977. Not only did the USSR abandon its *détente* policy by building a new generation of middle-range nuclear missiles, which were a direct threat to Western Europe, but it also invaded Afghanistan in December 1979. Schmidt agreed that the Soviet missile threat should be countered by deploying Pershing II and Cruise missiles in Western Germany, if no compromise could be reached with the USSR. However, independently of both Washington and London he worked hard to defuse the growing crisis between the superpowers as he feared its impact on inter-German relations and *Ostpolitik*. He thus refused to join Britain and the USA in criticising the Soviet invasion of Afghanistan and the declaration of martial law in Poland in 1981. Yet when it became clear in 1983 that no agreement could be negotiated with the USSR, the new CDU/FDP coalition showed itself to be a loyal ally of Washington and deployed the missiles in the FRG.

See page 415

THE FRG'S POLICY TOWARDS THE GDR AND THE SOVIET BLOC

Adenauer was convinced that in the long term the USSR would not be able to afford the arms race with the West and that consequently the Western powers could only achieve better relations with the USSR through a policy of overwhelming economic and military strength. He was sure that German re-unification would occur on the FRG's terms, as the economic power of West Germany would in the end wrench the GDR out of the Soviet orbit. He was therefore hostile to any of the schemes which the USSR and the GDR kept on proposing in the early 1950s for creating a united but neutral Germany. Adenauer, with the support of his Western allies, insisted that the FRG was the legal successor state to the German Reich of 1871 and refused point blank to

Was German reunification possible in 1952–53?

In 1952 Stalin put forward plans for a united Germany. It would be neutral but would not have to pay reparations and it would be free to have any government that its voters wanted. It could also have its own army. Adenauer and the Americans rejected the proposal, which they believed was aimed at stopping the FRG's integration into the European Defence Community. Many Germans at the time thought that Adenauer had missed an historic opportunity to re-unify Germany. Were they right? Modern historians are divided about this: Steininger is convinced that Adenauer deliberately ignored Stalin's offer because he did not want to see his policy of Western integration unravel. Yet others, like Wethig, believed that it was not made in good faith and that Stalin simply wanted to 'oust Adenauer's government' and to force the Western powers out of Germany. Adenauer did not believe that Stalin could really give up the GDR as this would have a 'domino effect' on all the other Soviet satellite states in Eastern Europe.

ANALYSIS

recognise the GDR as an independent state. To him it was just the 'Soviet occupied zone'.

THE HALLSTEIN DOCTRINE

Adenauer could not, however, ignore the Soviet Union, and in September 1955 he visited Moscow where, in return for the repatriation of the remaining German prisoners of war, the USSR and FRG agreed to exchange ambassadors. Adenauer was determined that this would not lead to a recognition of the GDR and he announced in the *Bundestag* on his return that his government would regard the recognition of the GDR by any state other than the USSR as a hostile act which could only lead to a break in diplomatic relations. This become known as the Hallstein Doctrine. Throughout the developing world Bonn made financial assistance dependent on the non-recognition of the GDR. Until the early 1960s this 'diplomatic blockade' worked well enough. Only two states outside the Soviet Bloc – Cuba and Yugoslavia – had recognised the GDR by 1962.

Walther Hallstein ran the FRG's foreign office for Adenauer, who was, however, officially the Foreign Minister

KEY ISSUE

Did Adenauer prolong the division of Germany?

OSTPOLITIK AND *DÉTENTE*, 1963–87

In 1963, after the Berlin and Cuban missile crises, once it became clear that both Moscow and Washington wanted a *détente* and were therefore ready to recognise the reality of the division of Europe, the Hallstein Doctrine increasingly became an out-of-date policy unfitted for the realities of the 1960s. The construction of the Berlin Wall in

See pages 43–44

August 1961 had also given a new lease of life to the GDR and the hope that the state would collapse in the foreseeable future was too optimistic. If the misery that the Wall inflicted on divided Berlin were to be alleviated, some sort of agreement would have to be negotiated between the two Germanies. Out of these considerations, the FRG slowly began to develop a new policy towards the GDR and the whole Soviet Bloc.

An early example of a new approach to the GDR was at Christmas 1963 when Willy Brandt, then Lord Mayor of West Berlin, directly negotiated with the City Council of East Berlin. By agreeing to refer to East Berlin as the GDR capital, he managed to secure a period of eighteen days when West Berliners could visit their relatives across the Wall.

When Willy Brandt became Foreign Minister in the Great Coalition in December 1966 he had already made up his mind that Bonn would have to negotiate with the GDR, but it was not until he won the election three years later that he was in a position to put into action the new *Ostpolitik*. This was a major turning point in the foreign policy of the FRG and consisted of the following treaties:

- The Moscow Treaty, August 1970. Nicholls has called this 'the foundation stone of *Ostpolitik*'. The FRG recognised Poland's western frontier and gave up its claim to represent the whole of Germany. It also agreed that the GDR as well as itself should join the United Nations;
- The Warsaw Treaty, December 1970. Both the FRG and Poland recognised the Oder–Neisse Line as Poland's western frontier. Trade and financial assistance from Bonn was to be increased, while the remaining ethnic Germans in Poland would be allowed to emigrate to the FRG;
- The Prague Treaty, December 1973. This recognised Czechoslovakia's post-1945 frontiers, made the Munich Treaty of 1938, which had handed over the Sudetenland to Germany, 'void' and arranged for the emigration to the FRG of the remaining ethnic Germans in Czechoslovakia;
- The four former occupying powers also became what Barbara Marshall has called the 'guarantors of *Ostpolitik*' when they signed the Berlin Agreement of September 1971. The Soviets recognised West Berlin's ties with the FRG, and the right of West Berliners to visit the FRG. They also promised not to impede the flow of traffic along the corridors into West Berlin. This agreement has rightly been called a 'milestone in the history of divided Berlin and divided Germany' by Bark and Gress;
- The Berlin Agreement led to a series of further agreements between the two Germanies on transit traffic, postal communications and the rights of West Berliners to visit the East. Finally, in December 1972 the Basic Treaty was signed between the FRG and GDR. In it the FRG recognised the GDR as an equal and independent state, but made it clear that it still considered GDR citizens to be German

citizens and in a 'Letter concerning German Unity' which it sent to the GDR government, it stressed its determination to work for German re-unification.

HOW DID *OSTPOLITIK* WORK IN PRACTICE?

By 1973 most West Germans assumed that Germany would remain divided for generations. Thus the point of *Ostpolitik* in Chancellor Kohl's words was to 'ease the painful consequences of the division of our fatherland [and] to strengthen the consciousness of belonging together among all Germans...'. Gradually it was hoped in Bonn that this would lead to ever closer links between the two Germanies. On one level *Ostpolitik* was successful. The number of telephone calls and visits from West Germany to East Germany increased dramatically. In the years to 1989, Bonn was also able to buy the freedom of some 34 000 political prisoners in the GDR. At another level it can be argued that through *Ostpolitik* the FRG actually propped up the GDR. For instance, in 1983–84 a loan of DM one billion, 950 million was granted on generous terms to the GDR and stopped a possible terminal economic crisis. On the other hand, these loans did gradually make the GDR financially dependent on the FRG. By 1988 some East German financial

PICTURE 3
Schmidt and Honecker converse in the GDR, December 1981

confederation a loose
union in which member
states retain most of
their independence

Walther Ulbricht,
1893–1974 was a
trained cabinet maker.
He joined the German
Communist Party in
1919. He fled to
Moscow in 1933 and
returned in April 1945.

TIMELINE

Oct 1949	Provisional Government set up under Grotewohl
Feb 1950	Ministry of State security set up
Oct	GDR elections
March 1953	Stalin's death
June	Strikes and riots in GDR
Sept 1955	USSR recognised GDR sovereignty
Feb 1956	Khrushchev's secret speech on Stalin's crimes
Nov 1958	Khrushchev's Berlin ultimatum
Jan 1960	Collectivisation of remaining independent farms
Aug 1961	Border between East and Berlin sealed off
June 1963	New Economic System started in GDR
May 1971	Ulbricht resigned as First Secretary of SED. Succeeded by Honecker
Nov	Start of Unity of Social and Economic policy
Dec 1972	Basic Law signed
March 1978	Church–State Agreement
Sept 1987	Honecker visited FRG

officials were beginning to think that only a **confederation** with the FRG could save their state from bankruptcy.

4 ⌐ THE DEVELOPMENT OF THE GERMAN DEMOCRATIC REPUBLIC

A *Political history, 1949–89*

THE ESTABLISHMENT OF ONE-PARTY RULE

The Socialist Unity Party (SED) modelled itself on the Communist Party of the USSR and lost little time in creating a system of 'democratic centralism' which was virtually identical with the pattern of Communist rule in the USSR. The key decisions were usually taken by a small core of members in the Secretariat of the *Politburo*, of whom the most important was the Party's General Secretary, **Walther Ulbricht.** The SED, with the ultimate backing of the USSR, had effectively consolidated its power by the autumn of 1950 through the following measures:

- All cultural activities were controlled by the State. The Lutheran Church, with its links to the West, was subjected to considerable persecution;
- The SED set up the Ministry of State Security (*Stasi*) in February 1950;
- The SED was able to turn the mass organisations such as the trade unions into 'conveyor belts' for transmission of its policies;
- The two non-Communist parties, the East German CDU and the Liberal Democratic Party (LDP), were forced by threats and appeals for unity in face of the great problems facing the GDR to become part of the National Front, a huge national organisation which had developed from the Peoples Congress Movement (*Volkskongress*) and claimed to represent every organisation interested in national unity;
- For the elections of 15 October 1950 the National Front drew up a single list of candidates, who all supported the same policies. They were held in an atmosphere of considerable intimidation and the Party was able to claim that 99.72 per cent of the voters had voted for the unity list. The SED itself only won 25 per cent of the vote outright but its position was secured by the fact that most of the other parties and groups were all dominated by Communists.

THE DISTURBANCES OF 17 JUNE 1953

The unpopularity of the Stalinist regime which Ulbricht had set up was clearly displayed by the widespread disturbances that flared up across the GDR on 17 and 18 June 1953. Ulbricht had succeeded in uniting almost the whole of East Germany against his regime by the ruthlessness with which he had attempted to impose an Eastern European pattern of Socialism on a highly developed industrial society, which until 1945 had been essentially capitalist. The farmers were bitter about the low prices paid for their produce and the high fines they had to pay if they were late with their food deliveries. They also feared the constant threat of collectivisation. The remaining independent businessmen, shopkeepers and artisans were equally worried that their livelihoods would be nationalised by the state. Above all, the workers resented the State's control of their wages, high taxation and rising food prices which were necessary to pay for the five-year plan and creation of the new armed frontier police.

See page 42

When Stalin died in March 1953 Ulbricht came under increasing pressure to modify his policies. In early June he and Grotewohl were summoned to Moscow and told point blank that if there were no changes in the GDR, there would be a 'catastrophe'. They were then ordered by Malenkov to stop any further moves toward collectivising agriculture, to encourage independent businessmen and to stop persecuting the churches. The Russians, however, overlooked one vital thing: in May Ulbricht had increased the work norms for the workers by 10 per cent. Ulbricht's stubborn refusal to modify this policy caused an explosion of rage amongst the workers, and triggered the riots. When on 16 June a demonstration of building workers gained no concessions from the government, calls for a general strike, 'butter instead of cannon', the restoration of works councils and the re-legalisation of the SPD began. On 17 June East Berlin was at a standstill and right across the GDR a series of strikes and demonstrations erupted. Crowds collected outside prisons and party offices and called for the resignation of the government. Ulbricht, distrusting the loyalty of his own police forces, called on the USSR to intervene, and the situation was brought under control by the following day.

PICTURE 4
Two East Berliners throw stones at Soviet tanks. Contrary to impressions at the time, the Soviets were reluctant to intervene. Nevertheless, at least twenty-five Germans were killed.

ANALYSIS

How do historians assess 17 June 1953?

At the time Western observers saw it as an uprising against Stalinist tyranny, but in the Soviet Bloc it was dismissed as a reactionary conspiracy. Klessmann describes it as a 'workers uprising', while Mitter and Wolle, in a recent study argue that it was the first stage in the collapse of the GDR, although in fact after the Berlin Wall was built the GDR appeared to experience something of revival. Pritchard, a British historian, sees the revolt as a complex movement made up of many different factors: a revival of Nazism, a desire for re-unification with the West, a workers' revolt against the State as an employer and finally a youth protest movement.

The crushing of the riots by Soviet troops showed how dependent the GDR was on the USSR. Ulbricht's immediate reaction was to try to make sure that such a revolt would never happen again. Thus the *Stasi* was made more efficient and over 6000 suspects were rounded up. On Moscow's insistence, however, further concessions were also made to the East German population: pensions were increased, food prices made cheaper and more consumer goods were to be produced. As a gesture of goodwill the USSR also returned the last 33 SAGs – the companies it had set up in 1946 to produce German goods for the USSR – to GDR ownership.

See page 46

ULBRICHT'S SURVIVAL, 1953–58

In the immediate aftermath of the riots Ulbricht's dismissal seemed inevitable. He had no allies in Moscow and within the GDR *Politburo* he had only two supporters, Honecker and Matern, but he was saved by the fall of his main critic in Moscow, Beria. Once it became clear that Ulbricht's removal was no longer a priority in Moscow, the majority of his critics within the *Politburo* drew back from a confrontation and he was able to hang on to power and defeat his main critics individually. By the time of the Fourth Party Congress in 1954 he had sufficient backing to be re-elected as Party Secretary.

See pages 112–13

Two years later Ulbricht faced another crisis of confidence when Khrushchev's revelations of Stalin's crimes set off shock waves throughout the Soviet Bloc. In the GDR they caused growing criticism of the SED leadership. The late summer and autumn of 1956 was a particularly tense period. In August and September there were a series of strikes throughout the GDR and the Hungarian Revolt in October led to further unrest. One miner in Saxony observed, for example, that 'a small spark would be sufficient to begin an uprising amongst us'. Ironically, these crises were again to save Ulbricht. Khrushchev was planning to replace him with Karl Schirdewann, the Chief of the *Stasi*, but the unrest in Hungary and Poland, Ulbricht's skill in defusing the

See page 188

discontents through a combination of political and economic concessions and the effective use of the new factory defence forces caused him to have second thoughts. This reprieve gave Ulbricht the chance to get rid of his rivals. One group was arrested in early 1957 and by cleverly dividing his opponents Ulbricht managed to make a clean sweep of them by 1958.

THE CONSTRUCTION OF THE BERLIN WALL

For a short time in 1958–59 the GDR appeared to become stable. The economy grew by 12 per cent per annum, ration cards were at last abolished and wages rose. The number of refugees fleeing westwards declined to the lowest point for a decade, but the GDR was plunged into crisis again by several factors:

- the prolonged crisis triggered by Khrushchev's Berlin ultimatum of November 1958;
- the new labour law code which banned strikes and tightened up on factory discipline;
- the decision to force the remaining independent farmers into collective farms.

In January 1960 Party agents, backed up by special police forces, moved into the countryside to enforce collectivisation. This caused so

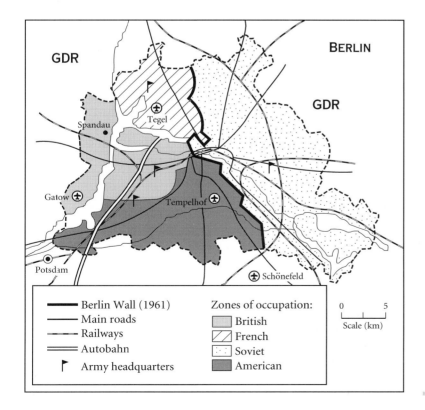

MAP 4
Divided Berlin

much chaos that yields in butter, meat and grain sank and food prices inevitably rose. All this led to a massive increase in the numbers of refugees fleeing westwards through the open frontier in Berlin. In 1960, 199 000 fled and in the six months up to June 1961 a further 103 000 followed. By July an increasing number of reports were coming in from the *Stasi* of mounting unrest in the factories. Khrushchev was faced with the stark choice of either allowing Ulbricht to close the open frontier in Berlin or of seeing the GDR collapse. At a meeting of the Warsaw Pact states on 3–5 August 1961 Ulbricht finally received the go-ahead to seal off East Berlin. In the early hours of 13 August Honecker, the minister in charge of security, set up the 'anti-Fascist protective wall'. At first this was a barbed wire barrier, but it was rapidly replaced by a more permanent structure. The security forces prevented any repetition of the disturbances of 17 June 1953.

Some historians, Staritz and Klessmann, for example, are convinced that Ulbricht deliberately caused chaos in the GDR by ordering collectivisation so that he could put pressure on Khruschchev to build the Wall. Others, like Mitter and Wolle, argue that collectivisation was merely intended to elimiate the private sector in agriculture, which still accounted for 67 per cent of the GDR's farms. Collectivisation would thus bring the agrarian sector into line with the industrial sector which was state run and there was no ulterior motive of putting pressure on Moscow.

THE GDR HAS A SECOND CHANCE

The closing of the border turned the GDR into a large prison from which the population could not escape, but at the same time it gave the government a second chance to get the economy right and perhaps by doing so to win over the people. Ulbricht was convinced that the GDR now had the chance to compete equally with the FRG and launched a series of ambitious economic reforms. To make these work however, he had to win the cooperation of the population by replacing the crude policy of terror and suppression with a more flexible and sophisticated approach, which he did by the following means:

See pages 46–7

- The trade union movement was actually encouraged to defend the rights of the workers more effectively;
- There was a more sensitive approach to young people. For a time they did not all have to join the FDJ (the Free German Youth);
- The legal code which dated back to the 1870s was brought up to date;
- In local elections voters were allowed to reject individual candidates on the single list.

All these reforms stopped far short of turning the GDR into a liberal democracy. The key positions in the trade union movement, for instance, were still held by the SED and in the new legal code the definition of crimes against the State was made so wide that it could be applied to almost any criticism of the regime. By 1969 the regime was again in trouble. Ulbricht's reforms had not achieved an East German 'economic miracle' and the hostile reaction of the population to the invasion of Czechoslovakia in 1968 by Warsaw Pact troops showed that there was still little sympathy for Communism in the GDR. In September 1970 Honecker and his allies on the *Politburo* managed to force Ulbricht to abandon his economic reforms and a few months later he was made to resign as Party Secretary by Brezhnev, who resented his independent attitude and criticism of Soviet policy over Berlin. He was replaced by Honecker.

THE HONECKER ERA, 1971–89

See page 48

In his radical attempt to modernise the economy Ulbricht had moved too quickly and plunged the GDR back into a major economic and social crisis . Honecker embarked on a strategy which in the long term was just as risky. He abandoned Ulbricht's reform programme and bought off unrest with a more generous welfare policy and an increase in consumer goods such as cars, fridges and televisions. In the end this bankrupted the GDR, but in the shorter term it did enable him to neutralise potential opposition amongst the workers and win a degree of acceptance for the regime. The majority of the population came to terms with the regime and people tried to live their lives as best they could.

In March 1978 the Lutheran Church itself recognised that it had to work within a Socialist society and negotiated an agreement with the State which allowed it some freedom to organise discussion on church premises of controversial issues. Honecker felt sufficiently secure to think that this would allow dissidents the chance to let off steam without damaging the Party, but this was to be a miscalculation. By the early 1980s, under the protection of the Church, peace and human rights groups were growing up, which began to criticise the regime openly. The mid-1980s also saw the emergence of the Environmentalist Movement.

When Gorbachev came to power in 1985 in the USSR, it seemed at first as if Honecker would follow his example and begin to liberalise the GDR. On the Olaf Palme Peace March in September 1987, for example, the unofficial peace groups were allowed to march alongside official

See pages 119–21

The niche society

ANALYSIS

Gunter Gaus, who was the FRG's first representative in East Berlin, described the GDR as a 'niche society'. By this he meant that most East Germans found a niche or refuge for themselves with their family, friends or hobbies and were happy to tolerate the SED's monopoly of political power. Now that the archives of the *Stasi* have been opened it is possible to see that the idea of the niche society was somewhat exaggerated. Workers' unrest and criticism of the regime were much more widespread than was imagined at the time.

State representatives. By the late autumn, however, it became clear that the government was reverting to repression. The *Stasi* raided the Environmental Library in Berlin and smashed its printing press. Even the Soviet magazine *Sputnik* was censored as it was too liberal for the GDR!

B *The economy*

In 1949 the East Germans, like the West Germans, had to face the challenge of post-war reconstruction. To achieve any degree of recovery, however, their economy had, in Mary Fulbrook's words, to 'run something of an obstacle course':

- Soviet reparation policy had stripped the Zone of much of its industrial plant. In 1950 some 25 per cent of the industrial goods produced in the GDR still went to the USSR;
- The GDR was cut off from its markets and suppliers in the West – above all from Ruhr coal and steel;
- It had to re-orientate its economy towards the more backward Soviet Bloc. In September 1950 it joined COMECON, the Commission for Mutual Economic Aid, and by 1951 76 per cent of German trade was with the Soviet Bloc;
- Its agricultural output was severely hit by the break-up of the larger farms over 100 hectares.

See pages 366–8

In its post-war reconstruction policy the Party leaders followed the Stalinist model of State Socialism as far as the conditions of the GDR allowed. By 1950 76 per cent of the total industrial production was accounted for by the nationalised enterprises and the banking and insurance sectors had been taken over by the State. The independent sector was harried by high taxation and fines if production targets were not met. The GDR had to follow the Soviet model of five-year plans and investment in heavy industry at the expense of consumer goods. To achieve its often impractical targets, wages were kept at a low level; such basic foodstuffs as butter, milk and sugar were still rationed, while pensions were kept to the barest minimum. The first five-year plan recorded some impressive results in the production of iron, steel and chemicals, but only at the cost of keeping down wages and living standards, which was to result in the revolts of June 1953.

See pages 40–1

Only after these traumatic events were successful efforts made to improve the standard of living of the population. By 1954 real wages were higher than in 1939 and consumption in eggs, butter and meat had now recovered to pre-war levels. Certainly the standard of living in the GDR was much better than in other Soviet Bloc states, but the East Germans were not impressed with such a comparison. It was inevitably with the 'economic miracle' of the West that the East Germans compared their situation. Each year it tempted some 200 000 people to flee westwards.

The leadership of the GDR attempted to counter this by desperately trying to create an East German 'economic miracle'. The second five-year plan was launched in 1956, which on Soviet insistence was replaced by a seven-year plan in 1959, but a decisive economic breakthrough was not achieved. By 1960–61 it was clear that the GDR had overreached itself and lacked the resources to expand to a high level both the industrial and consumer sectors of the economy simultaneously. On top of this, Ulbricht also embarked on the costly operation of collectivising the small farms! Only the construction of the Berlin Wall in August 1961 stopped the economic collapse of the GDR.

See pages 43–4

The Wall did, however give Ulbricht a second chance to get the GDR's economy right. Much to the surprise of many observers he introduced a radical new plan, the so-called 'New Economic System', which, to the horror of the old school Marxists, seemed to flirt with the free market economy by introducing the following reforms:

- A less rigid five-year plan where factory managers would be given greater independence;
- A more flexible pricing system, which acknowledged the need for profits;
- The linking of wages to profits;
- Limited worker participation in management decisions;
- No harassment of remaining private businesses by the State;
- The use of non-party experts in industry.

Once again, impressive production figures were achieved at first, but by 1968 it was clear that East German productivity was again falling in relation to the FRG. In one last gamble to reverse this Ulbricht invested a large amount of money, which had not been fully budgeted for, in

The consequences of the failure of the new economic system

ANALYSIS

The American historian Charles Maier has recently argued that Ulbricht's economic reforms were moving towards creating a more flexible economy which would have stood a better chance of dealing with the impact of the oil price rises of the 1970s and early 1980s. Given time, they would also have greatly increased the demand for a further liberalisation of the political system. But just how far would Ulbricht have been able to go? Could any GDR leader have allowed the creation of an East German democracy? Would the people have simply voted for re-union with the FRG or would reform at that stage have enabled a genuine, free GDR identity to emerge, with which the people would have identified? After the crushing of the Prague Spring, it seems inconceivable that the USSR would ever have allowed such a policy.

introducing automation into the metal working industries. This led to cuts in consumer goods and in September 1970 the whole policy collapsed.

THE UNITY OF SOCIAL AND ECONOMIC POLICY, 1970–89

Theoretically this new policy, which was introduced by Honecker, was to give the GDR the best of both worlds. Rising economic production was to finance social reform, but the reality was very different:

● Honecker re-introduced the old top-heavy and inefficient centralised bureaucratic system of the 1950s and nationalised the remaining small independent firms;
● The GDR's economy was severely hit by the price rises in oil and other raw materials in 1973. Over the period 1972–75 import prices rose, for example, by 34 per cent, while export prices increased by 17 per cent;
● Spending on welfare was double the rise in the national income between 1971 and 1979.

By the early 1980s the situation had deteriorated to such an extent that the GDR was financially dependent on loans from the FRG. By November 1987 the total value of these had risen to nearly DM 38.5 billion. Honecker's failure to achieve solvency was to be one of the main reasons for the collapse of the GDR in 1989. In 1987 the financial situation was so bleak that the *Stasi* was already reporting that economic problems and shortages were discrediting the regime.

> ## KEY ISSUE
>
> *Why did the economy of the GDR do so much worse than the FRG from 1950 to 1989?*

C *Foreign policy*

The foreign policy of the GDR was essentially determined by the USSR. It was aligned with the Soviet Bloc and had to follow Moscow's lead in foreign and inter-German affairs. Consequently, one of its main priorities became to improve relations with its Eastern European neighbours, particularly Poland, with which it signed the Goerlitz Treaty in 1950, recognising the Oder–Neisse frontier. Officially, the SED leadership supported German unity as long as it would result in a unified Communist Germany, but until 1955 the very existence of the GDR was threatened by various Soviet attempts to halt the Western integration of the FRG in return for creating a neutral Germany. The GDR had little option but to go along with these plans and only when they failed in 1955 did Moscow recognise the independence of the GDR and integrate it into the Warsaw Pact.

In the second half of the 1950s the GDR drew ever closer to the USSR and its allies. There were treaties with China, Mongolia and close cultural contacts with Poland. The GDR tried in vain to break the 'diplomatic blockade' of the Hallstein Doctrine and thus welcomed Khrushchev's ultimatum to the Western powers in 1958, demanding the signing of a peace treaty with the two Germanies and the neutralisation of West Berlin. Over the next two years, as the West

See page 391

See pages 398–9

refused to respond to the ultimatum, Ulbricht began to urge Khrushchev to sign a separate peace treaty with the GDR and recognise its sovereignty over East Berlin. In an effort to put pressure on him he even sent an official delegation to Peking in January 1961 at a time when Soviet relations with China were fast deteriorating. In fact, Khrushchev never did sign a peace treaty with the GDR, but when faced with the imminent collapse of the GDR, he rather reluctantly agreed to the building of the Berlin Wall at the Warsaw Pact meeting in early August 1961.

The SED Party leadership initially viewed the new era of *détente* and *Ostpolitik* that followed the Cuban crisis with considerable suspicion. As early as 1963 Otto Winzer, the GDR's foreign minister, characterised Bonn's developing *Ostpolitik* as 'aggression in felt slippers'. He feared that, through a 'softly, softly' approach, Bonn might gradually undermine the GDR. After the Prague Spring Brezhnev was also aware of its potential dangers to the GDR, even though he remained convinced that the advantages of *détente* were greater than a continuation of the Cold War. Consequently, the GDR had no real option but to go along with *détente* and *Ostpolitik*.

When Brezhnev met Honecker in July 1970 he stressed the solid advantages of *Ostpolitik*: 'its frontiers, its existence will be confirmed for all the world to see', but he also warned him against allowing the 'Social Democratisation' of the GDR: 'it must not come to a process of *rapprochement* [friendly relations] between the FRG and GDR...Concentrate everything on the all-sided strengthening of the GDR, as you call it.'

Once the Basic Treaty was signed the GDR initially acted very defensively towards the FRG and the West. It declared itself a separate socialist nation and in 1975 signed a twenty-five year treaty of friendship with the USSR. Honecker was also a strong supporter of the Brezhnev Doctrine and in 1980–81 urged Brezhnev to crush the Polish *Solidarity* Movement with force. However, there is no doubt that the GDR also gained much from both *détente* and *Ostpolitik*:

See pages 38–9

See pages 178–80

- By 1984 it was recognised by 132 states;
- It joined the UN;
- It participated in the Helsinki Conference of 1975 and signed the Final Act which committed the signatory nations to a mutual recognition of their independence and sovereignty;
- It did, of course, receive large DM loans from the FRG.

See page 39

The contradiction between the GDR's growing financial dependence on Bonn and its loyalty to Moscow only began to emerge with the 'New Cold War' in the early 1980s. By the time the cruise missiles were installed in West Germany in 1983, Honecker, far from seizing the chance to break off links with the FRG, tried hard to insulate inter-German relations from the impact of the growing Soviet–American tension. Even though his visit to West Germany was vetoed by Moscow until September 1987, he did all he could to keep *Ostpolitik* alive.

See pages 414–16

5 ↽ THE REUNIFICATION OF GERMANY

See pages 148–50

In 1953 and 1961 the GDR was on the verge of collapse, but each time it had been saved by decisive Soviet support. By 1989–90 the USSR, virtually bankrupt and weakened by the Afghan War, was no longer able to enforce the Brezhnev Doctrine. Gorbachev wanted to end the Cold War, seek western financial loans and reform the Soviet economy. He was therefore not willing to run the risk of directly intervening in the affairs of the GDR.

A *The collapse of the GDR*

By the early summer of 1989 the GDR was already in serious difficulties and the population was again facing shortages in consumer goods. As we have seen, Honecker reacted to the growing wave of criticism from Christian, environmentalist and human rights groups by reverting to the familiar policy of repression. Within the context of the end of the Cold War this was no longer a realistic policy, as events were to show:

- In May 1989 Hungary began to dismantle the barriers along its frontiers with Austria. In July thousands of East Germans travelled to Hungary in the hope of crossing over to Austria. By 7 August several hundred were camping in the grounds of the West German Embassy in Budapestinin an attempt to force the FRG to intervene on their behalf. On 11 September the Austrians agreed to accept them and 150 000 poured across the border;
- Meanwhile, FRG embassies were similarly besieged by East German 'holidaymakers' in Prague and Warsaw. Unwilling to face an embarrassing showdown just when the GDR was about to celebrate its fortieth anniversary, Honecker bowed to pressure from Kohl to grant the German tourists in Prague exit visas. The GDR–Czech frontier was then closed and the Germans transferred to the West by trains routed through the GDR. At Dresden station riots broke out as crowds tried to storm the trains in an attempt to board them.

TIMELINE

11 Sept 1989	Hungary allowed GDR citizens to cross Austrian frontier
9 Oct	Massive but peaceful demonstration in Leipzig
9 Nov	Berlin Wall opened
18 March 1990	GDR elections
1 July	German Economic and Monetary Union
12 Sept	'Two-plus-four' Treaty
3 Oct	German unification

Honecker's unsure handling of this crisis suddenly made people realise that public protest might at last begin to be effective in bringing about change in the GDR. Leading this movement were such newly formed groups as the New Forum, the Social Democratic Initiative and Democracy Now. They were not concerned with flight to the FRG but with reforming the GDR from within. In Leipzig on 25 September and on three successive Mondays thereafter thousands of demonstrators paraded peacefully through the streets shouting such slogans as 'We are the people' and 'We are staying here', meaning that they wanted to work for reform at home rather than flee to the FRG. Although there were some clashes between the police and the demonstrators, the regime did not forcibly break up the demonstrations as it knew that ultimately Gorbachev would not back a hard-line policy. Neither was it

PICTURE 5
*A souvenir hunter moves in
as the Wall is demolished,
February 1990*

they totally sure of the loyalty of the factory defence groups and the young policemen.

This failure of will played a crucial part in the collapse of the regime and showed that the Party leadership was rapidly losing control of the situation. On 17–18 October Honecker was replaced by Egon Krenz as General Secretary. In a desperate attempt to win support for his government, he opened up the crossing points through the Berlin Wall, but this, far from stabilizing the situation, increased the pressure on the Party. Krenz was sacked by the *Volkskammer* on 13 November and replaced by Hans Modrow, the Dresden Party Secretary, who had a reputation as a reformer. He made further far-reaching concessions:

- He agreed to Church proposals for a 'Round Table' dialogue with the opposition groups on the model of those conducted by *Solidarity* with the Polish Government;
- He also conceded free elections. At first these were to be held in May 1990, but then as a result of growing pressure and unrest – on 13 January, for instance, the *Stasi* headquarters were ransacked – he brought the date forward to 18 March.

See pages 178–9

In these elections the SED, which now called itself the Party of Democratic Socialism (PDS), won only 16.4 per cent of the vote, while the East German CDU and the refounded SPD won over 70 per cent. As one contemporary historian, Konrad Jarausch, has remarked, the 'East Germans had rejected the slow process of constitutional convention and stepped onto the fast track'. A new coalition government was set up, led by the CDU leader, de Maizière.

ANALYSIS

The CDU in East Germany

The CDU in East Germany had been a member of the National Front and was an ally of the SED. Only in December 1989 did it reject Socialism. In February 1990, it formed, together with two new parties, the German Social Union and Democratic Awakening, the Alliance for Germany. The Alliance was subsidised by the West German CDU. In the March elections, the CDU won 40.8 per cent of the vote.

B *Chancellor Kohl seizes the initiative*

At first, like everybody else, Kohl had misjudged the speed with which the GDR was collapsing. In November his ten-point plan had envisaged

MAP 5
Germany after unification

the two Germanies forming a very loose confederation which would only slowly grow into a political union. Events, however, were to convince him that he had to move much more quickly. Just before Christmas he visited Dresden and was given a rapturous reception which left him in little doubt that most East Germans wanted unity as quickly as possible. By February, Kohl had already secured international agreement to German unity. Genscher had been sent to Moscow to square Gorbachev with lavish promises of future West German loans. Then at Ottowa on 12–14 February, he also secured President Bush's agreement to a plan for negotiations on German unity, the Two-plus-Four formula, which would involve the two Germanies plus the four former occupying powers. By the time the East German elections were over, Kohl was ready to seize the initiative and make German unity a reality:

- On 18 May the two Germanies agreed that economic, social and monetary union should start on 1 July;
- On 31 July the Treaty of Unification was signed;
- On 12 September the Two-plus-Four Treaty was signed in Moscow, finally ending the remaining rights of the former occupying powers in Berlin;
- On 3 October Germany was unified.

6 ⌐ CONCLUSION: THE NEW GERMANY

The two Germanies were artificial products of the Cold War. In 1990 Adenauer's belief that a wealthy, prosperous and democratic FRG would act as a magnet for the GDR was proved correct: the population of the bankrupted GDR voted overwhelmingly to join the FRG. By Article 23 of the Basic Law the constitution of the FRG was simply extended to the GDR in 1990. Its former *Länder* were reconstituted and given representation in the *Bundesrat*, while 144 new members representing East Germany joined the *Bundestag*. The triumph of the FRG was total.

In retrospect this seems inevitable, but was it really so? If it had not been for the Korean War and the long post-war boom lasting up to the 1960s, the FRG would have been much weaker economically and politically, and by no means an object of envy for the East German population. In 1952–53 the USSR came very near to pulling out of East Germany. It is possible that only the stubbornness of Adenauer and the fall of Beria in June 1953 prevented a deal being done with the West. At times too – in the late 1950s and the early 1970s – the GDR appeared to come near to achieving a degree of stability that would have enabled it to survive. Yet in the final analysis, its persistent relative economic failure in relation to the FRG and its repressive political system ensured that it did not win the loyalty of the majority of its people.

However, the failure of the GDR did not mean that unification was a painless process. It revealed how far the two Germanies had grown apart. After the initial enthusiasm had died down the East Germans had to come to terms with the economic realities of the union. Their productivity was a mere 30 per cent of the FRG's and their industries, under the impact of the currency union and inflow of West German products, had virtually collapsed. By 1994 13.9 per cent of the workforce in Eastern Germany was unemployed. Throughout the 1990s the former territories of the GDR integrated only very slowly with the Western *Länder*. The East Germans, as Kettenacker put it, had to emerge 'from their sheltered but miserable lives under socialism to a democratic but competitive society'. Inevitably, to some the old GDR began in retrospect to appear, irrationally perhaps, to be a 'paradise lost'. For the majority of East Germans the GDR had been a prison, yet there were some who benefited from its policies. In its early years it offered the children of workers and peasants real opportunites to gain higher education and to move into managerial and technical posts.

In the 1990s the reunification of Germany did not change the essential character of the FRG. It still strongly supported Western integration as its backing for the Maastricht Treaty and the introduction of the European single currency showed. The Bonn–Paris axis continued to dictate the agenda within the EU, and the new Germany, like the FRG, remained shy of playing a world role. Neither was there a sudden break with the traditional pattern of West German politics. Kohl remained Chancellor until 1998. Obviously, in the longer term, re-unification would have a profound impact on the German identity.

7 ↫ BIBLIOGRAPHY

Two informative and well-structured general histories on post-war Germany, which cover both the FRG and the GDR are *Germany since 1945* by L. Kettenacker (Oxford, 1997) and *German Politics 1945–1995* by P. Pulzer (Oxford, 1995). Kettenacker is particularly useful on the social history of the period. There are a large number of books in English on West Germany. *Reinventing Germany. German Political Development since 1945 by* A. Glees (Oxford, 1996) is a clear and accessible introduction to developments in the FRG over this period. Another informative and well-written account is *The Bonn Republic by* A.J. Nichols (London, 1997). A very detailed two-volume 'block buster' which is a useful book of reference is *A History of West Germany*, Vol. 1, *From Shadow to Substance, 1945–63* and Vol. 2, *Democracy and its Discontents, 1963–1991, by* D. Bark and D. Gress; 2nd ed. (Oxford, 1991). The biographies and autobiographies of the major politicians are also important sources for understanding the history of the FRG. The *Memoirs* by Adenauer (London, 1966) and the comprehensive two-volume bigraphy, *A German Politician and Statesman in a Period of War, Revolution and Reconstruction* by Hans-Peter Schwarz (trans.,

Oxford, 1995–97) are important sources for the period 1945–63. A short and concise guide to the economic history of the FRG can be found in a chapter entitled 'The Economy of the Federal Republic since 1949' by R. Overy in *The Federal Republic since 1949* edited by K. Larres and P. Panayi (London, 1996). The fall of the GDR in 1990 inevitably made all the histories of East Germany written before that period out-of-date as historians now have access to the East German archives and are in a position to find out what really happened. *Anatomy of a Dictatorship. Inside the GDR, 1949–89* by M. Fulbrook (Oxford, 1995) is one of the first books in English to use this new material and it has a useful chapter on the fall of the GDR. It will take some time, however, for historians to work their way through the hundreds of thousands of files in the archives and write a new history of the GDR. In the meantime, such older histories as *The GDR since 1945* by M. McCauley (London, 1983) still have considerable value as an overall guide to the history of East Germany. *The GDR: Moscow's German Ally* (London, 1985) by D. Childs remains a useful textbook on political, social and economic aspects of the GDR. There are many detailed studies on the occupation and division of Germany. *Memoirs* by Adenauer (see above) provides an account of politics in the British Zone up to 1945. Good but very detailed studies of American and Soviet policy in Germany are *Retreat from Victory. The American Occupation of Germany* by E. Petersen (Detroit, 1977) and *The Russians in Germany* by N. Naimark (Cambridge, MA, 1995). *Ostpolitik* is well covered in *Willy Brandt: A Political Biography* by B. Marshall (London, 1990) and in *In Europe's Name. Germany and the Divided Continent* by T. Garton Ash (London, 1993), which also traces how *Ostpolitik* develops up to 1990. There are a large number of books on the fall of the GDR. *The Rush to German Unity* by K. Jarausch (Oxford, 1994) is a readable and comprehensive account of events, while *Dissolution. The Crisis of Communism and the End of East Germany* by C. Maier, (Princeton, 1997) is particularly good on the economic collapse of the GDR.

8 ⌐ ESSAY QUESTIONS

1. (a) What was the impact of the Allied occupation on Germany between 1945 and 1948?
    (b) How true would it be to say that the USSR made a far more decisive break with Germany's past in its zone than did the Western powers in the period 1945–48?
2. (a) Outline the key stages in the developments that led to the division of Germany in 1949;
    (b) Who was more responsible for the division of Germany: the Western powers or the USSR?
3. (a) Why did the FRG develop into such a prosperous state under Adenauer?

(b) With what justification has it been claimed that without Soviet support the GDR could not have survived the period 1949–61?

4. (a) What advantages did Adenauer gain for the FRG in the process of Western integration between 1949 and 1963?

    (b) Who gained most from *Ostpolitik*: the GDR or the FRG?

5. (a) Outline the problems which faced the FRG in the period 1963–87. How successfully were they overcome?

    (b) Consider the view that the construction of the Berlin Wall gave the GDR a 'second chance'.

6. (a) Outline the process whereby the two Germanies were unified in 1989–90;

    (b) 'Rather than examining why the GDR collapsed in 1989–90, historians should be asking why the GDR survived for forty years'. Discuss.

9 ᴄ DOCUMENTARY EXERCISE ON THE COLLAPSE OF THE GDR

Study carefully the sources on the GDR and answer the questions which follow:

SOURCE A

Adenauer speaking in the Bundestag on 20 September 1955, after his return from Moscow.

The Government of the so-called 'GDR' was not formed on the basis of truly free elections and therefore has not received any real authorisation by the people. In fact, it is rejected by the overwhelming majority of the population; there is neither legal protection nor freedom in the Soviet occupied zone, and the constitution exists only on paper.

SOURCE B

Extract from a letter from the Government of the FRG to the Government of the GDR on the day the Basic Treaty was signed, 21 December 1972.

In connection with the signing today of the Treaty on the Basis of Relations between the FRG and GDR, the Government of the FRG has the honour to state that this treaty does not conflict with the political aim of the FRG to work for a state of peace in Europe in which the German nation will regain its unity through free self-determination.

SOURCE C

Notes taken on Pastor Tschiche's lecture in East Berlin in 12 November 1985 for the GDR's Ministry of Church Affairs. He saw that those refusing to accept the GDR regime had three options:

– retreat into the inner sphere (niche society);
– infiltration of social institutions in order to alter structures (which has the disadvantage that it might in the process stabilise conditions);
– rejection of current structures, search for lifestyles, freeing oneself from dependence.

The two heads of state agreed to preserve and expand prior achievements, keeping in mind the basic principle that the states respect one another's independence and sovereignty regarding their domestic and foreign affairs. Willingness to negotiate and realism should be the guidelines for constructive, practical cooperation between the two states . . .

SOURCE D
Joint communiqué by Erich Honecker and Chancellor Kohl, 8 September 1987, on the occasion of Honecker's visit to the FRG.

The overwhelming majority of these people has an essentially negative view of problems and failures in the development of [GDR] society, especially in their private lives, personal living standards, and so-called everyday shortcomings; based on this attitude and on comparisons with conditions in the FRG and West Berlin, they assess developments in the GDR negatively.

The advantages of socialism, such as social security and protection, are acknowledged; however, they are no longer seen as decisive factors in comparison with the problems and failures that have emerged. To some extent, they are taken for granted . . .

SOURCE E
Stasi *report on the motives for emigration, 9 September 1989.*

Comrades! We all know the great interest with which the people of the GDR follow our affairs, the radical reorganisation in the Soviet Union. This restructuring is extremely difficult, requiring the greatest exertion of physical, intellectual, and moral strength by the party and the people. But this is an absolutely necessary process for us . . .

SOURCE F
Extract from Gorbachev's speech in East Berlin on the fortieth anniversary of the GDR, 6 October 1989.

Question: Can you see any changes in the status of Germany?
Answer: Yes . . . I don't share the concern that some European countries have about a reunified Germany . . . I don't see Germany, in order to get reunification, going off onto what some are concerned about, and that is a neutralist path that puts them at odds or potentially at odds, with their NATO partners . . .

SOURCE G
President Bush, interviewed by the New York Times, *24 October 1989.*

Q

1. *How reliable is Source A as a guide to the GDR's development from 1949–55? (4 marks)*
2. (a) *Using your own knowledge and Sources B and D, explain why* Ostpolitik *replaced the Hallstein Doctrine as the FRG's main policy towards the GDR. (4 marks)*
(b) *To what extent does Source D contradict Source B? (4 marks)*
3. (a) *Using Source C, explain the three options open to citizens of the GDR as outlined by Pastor Tschiche. (5 marks)*
(b) *Using your own knowledge and Source C, explain why so few citizens of the GDR adopted Option 3 in the period 1961–88? (6 marks)*

Q

4. (a) *Identify the reasons the* Stasi *gave for emigration to the GDR in Source E.* (*3 marks*)

(b) *Why did emigration on this scale again become possible by September 1988?* (*5 marks*)

(c) *In view of the East Germans' experience of unification after 1990, can the comment in Source E by the* Stasi *that 'the advantages of socialism' were taken for granted be justified with hindsight? Using your own knowledge, explain your answer fully.* (*4 marks*)

5. *To what extent do Sources F and G indicate that the two superpowers had decided as early as October 1989 that they would not prevent German unity?* (*5 marks*)

6. *Using your own knowledge and these sources, explain why the GDR was able to survive for forty years only to collapse in 1990.* (*10 marks*)

France: 1944–95

2

INTRODUCTION

The history of France after the Second World War is in many ways a striking success story. The France of the 1990s was a prosperous, modern democracy, dramatically different from the divided and crisis-ridden France of 1944. Despite the successes, however, post-war France remained in some respects a prisoner of the past, still affected by longstanding social and political divisions.

Three periods of crisis and upheaval interrupted the generally successful development of post-war France. The first, in 1944–47, was the difficult transition from the political vacuum at the end of the Vichy years to a restored republican system of government under the Fourth Republic. This phase was marked by economic crisis, fears of Communism, disputes over a new constitution and the shock resignation of de Gaulle in 1946. It lasted until economic recovery began, aided by the Marshall Plan, in 1947.

The second phase, 1958–62, began with a revolt in French Algeria, which led to the return of de Gaulle, the end of the Fourth Republic and the establishment of a new political system under the Fifth Republic. It continued with a succession of violent and divisive events, both in Algeria and mainland France, and was finally ended in 1962 by granting independence to Algeria.

The third phase, 1968–69, was dominated by the 'events' of May 1968, in which student protest combined with more traditional industrial unrest to produce an unexpectedly serious crisis, with the possibility of the army being called in to stop the 'revolution'. The crisis was over quite quickly but led, indirectly, to the resignation of de Gaulle in 1969. It seemed as if 1981 might mark another historic turning point, when the Left gained power and President Mitterand launched an ambitious programme of Socialist reforms. But there was a startling U-turn in 1983 and for the rest of his presidency Mitterand followed a moderate, even right-of-centre line. French politics remained remarkably stable, whether the prime ministers under Mitterand were of the Right or of the Left.

It might be helpful to keep in mind some of the following general factors:

- The importance of the Cold War. Like much of Western Europe, France was heavily influenced by the political, economic and strategic role of the USA;
- The importance of consistent central economic planning, which began in 1945–47 and helped to produce the sustained economic prosperity of France after the war, often known in France as the 'Thirty Glorious Years';

TIMELINE

France 1940–95

1940	Defeat and the end of the Third Republic
1944	Liberation and start of the Fourth Republic
1946	Resignation of de Gaulle
1954	Defeat at Dien Bien Phu
1958	Establishment of the Fifth Republic
1968	The 'events' of May
1969	Retirement of de Gaulle
1981	Election of President Mitterand
1995	Election of Jacques Chirac

See Table 3 on page 64
for a list of the main
political parties of the
Fourth Republic

- The close partnership which existed between France and West Germany after 1950 instead of the historic French–German enmity and which was the basis of France's role in the European Community;
- The nature of French political parties, which were only rarely based on large, stable party organisations. With many smaller, looser parties, often renaming or re-inventing themselves, it is often simpler to focus on general groupings, or 'blocs', of parties of the Left, the Centre, or the Right;
- The frequency with which cabinets and prime ministers changed, especially before 1958. (Against this, it should be noted that there was a long tradition in France of reliable and effective administrators. There was more continuity than the many changes of government would suggest.);
- The way French politics generally drifted towards the Right after 1945. This reflected trends in the rest of Europe, although traditional left-wing attitudes remained stronger in France than elsewhere;
- The legacy of France's colonial past. The process of decolonisation in Indochina and Algeria was painful and divisive and it made France a multicultural society. Social problems concerning immigrant communities were often exploited by right-wing political movements.

Above all, there was the dominant personality of Charles de Gaulle, overshadowing almost the entire history of France since 1940. For Gaullists, the Fifth Republic was the key to French success after 1958. In their view, the Gaullist presidency ended the weak governments and petty party politics of the Fourth Republic and provided long overdue political stability and continuity, even after de Gaulle himself left the stage in 1969. But this rosy view of the last forty years depended upon a one-sided Gaullist interpretation. Many historians would challenge de Gaulle's 'unique greatness' and would defend the achievements of the pre-1958 Republic. There have always been two Frances, two ways of remembering the past.

KEY ISSUE

What was the significance of de Gaulle in French history?

1 ⌁ POLITICAL HISTORY

A *The Fourth Republic*

THE LEGACY OF THE PAST

From the French Revolution in 1789 onwards, there were always two visions of France. One was the revolutionary France which celebrated Bastille Day every 14 July: the France of 1871 and the Paris Commune; of the Popular Front in the 1930s; of the left-wing resisters against Vichy. The other was the France of strong government and national pride: the France of Napoleon I and the First Empire; of Napoleon III and the Second Empire; of the anti-Dreyfusards in the late 1890s and of the right-wing leagues in the 1930s; of the Pétainists who supported the Vichy regime. Between 1875 and 1940, the Third Republic seemed to represent the victory of Republican democracy. The Popular Front government set up in 1936 under Leon Blum was launched on a wave of optimism and passed long-awaited social reforms. But it faced a backlash from the pro-Fascist, anti-Republican elements on the Right. The Popular Front fell in 1937. In 1940 the Third Republic collapsed after defeat in the war against Hitler.

France became the '*État Français*', an authoritarian state, glorifying the cult of Marshal Pétain and dedicated to 'Work, Family, Nation'. The obvious reason for the fall of the Third Republic was a humiliating military defeat; but 1940 was also a political revolution. The Reynaud government was undermined by the defeatists and conservatives set on an armistice and the Pétain regime was installed at Vichy. On 10 July the National Assembly voted, 468–80, to end the constitution of the Third Republic and replace it with the new 'French State'.

Pétain promised to be the 'shield of France', protecting against the worst consequences of defeat and wiping away the hated left-wing and **anti-clerical** traditions symbolised by the Popular Front. From 1940, many attitudes and actions were not only collaborationist but openly in favour of Fascist ideology and social policy. Nor was Pétain only a figurehead. He took an active role in shaping the so-called 'National Revolution'. He was also popular, at least at first. The then little known General de Gaulle represented the will to fight on. His whole career was based on his flight to England and his legendary broadcast on BBC radio on 18 June, 1940. At that time, however, de Gaulle was an unpopular lone voice, and his early military actions as 'leader of the Free French' were seen as unpatriotic. Whatever was claimed afterwards, Pétain's regime started out with mass support.

After 1942, the Germans tightened their grip on so-called 'independent' France. The French forced labour organisation, the STO, conscripted thousands of workers for munitions factories in Nazi Germany. French collaboration led to terrible crimes against French Jews, such as the concentration camp at Drancy and the deportation of the children of Isieu. The SS received eager collaboration from the right-wing French militia, the *Milice*. And, as the war turned against Germany, the French Resistance grew. The '*Guerre–Franco–Française*' (the war between the two Frances) became even more bitter. By 1944, many parts of French society were tainted by active collaboration: from politicians like Pierre Laval, from businessmen, and from many leaders of the Catholic Church. Almost everyone was tainted to some extent by passive collaboration.

Even the Resistance was badly divided, both at national and at local level. There were many feuds between and within right-wing and Communist Resistance groups. It took a long period of political infighting before de Gaulle, from his position outside France, was accepted as leader of a united French Resistance movement. In 1944, France badly needed some patriotic myths to hide some ugly realities.

anti-clericalism
opposition, often from liberals, to the excessive influence of the Church

KEY ISSUE

Which sections of French society supported the Vichy regime and why did they do so?

See *Petain's Crime* by Paul Webster; Papermac, 1992

See 'The Mitterand Affair' on page 86

A famous documentary film, *Le Chagrin et le Pitié (The Sorrow and the Pity)*, was made by Marcel Ophuls in 1971. This film caused a major political storm in France and was not shown on French television until 1981.

This was not only true in 1944–45. Throughout the fifty years after the Liberation, Vichy remained an explosive issue in French life and memory. At almost any time, a film, a book, an incautious remark could re-open old wounds.

The mood of 1944–45 required villains to be punished. Some of the obvious targets were German, such as the SS troops who carried out the notorious massacre at Oradour-sur-Glane near Limoges in 1944. But to help these Germans, there had been French traitors: Pétain; Pierre Laval, the power behind Pétain, who was executed in 1945; Charles Maurras, the leader of the right-wing movement *Action Française*; the leaders of the *Milice*, Joseph Darnand and Paul Touvier. There were also women who had taken German lovers during the occupation, and businessmen who had done profitable deals with the Nazis. There was much talk of *'épuration'* – purifying the nation by purging the collaborators. In reality, many war criminals were not pursued very vigorously and the process of punishment was often uncontrolled and inconsistent. Despite all the bitterness, the number of people killed in revenge during 1944–45 was much smaller than was thought at the time – probably 10 000, not the 100 000 sometimes claimed.

The Liberation myth played an important part in the rebuilding of France after the war. When Paris was liberated, amid unforgettable scenes of wild joy, de Gaulle dominated the scene, not riding on an American tank but walking 'alone', as leader of the Free French, liberating his own people. For months, de Gaulle had fought hard, often infuriating the British and Americans, to ensure that Paris would not be liberated by the Allied armies but by Free French units under General Leclerc – and by himself.

PICTURE 6
A collaborator faces her accusers, 1944

When he made his first speech, de Gaulle said France had been set free by 'the French, with the help of their British and American allies'. Throughout the war, de Gaulle had acted, often rather absurdly, as the embodiment of the French nation. Now in 1944 he claimed to represent, in one man, the unbroken continuity of a legitimate French nation. He refused to proclaim the return of the Republic, on the grounds that the 'real' French nation had remained intact throughout the war. The Vichy years had been wished out of existence. In fact, the Vichy years left lasting marks on France. The economic legacy of Vichy was in many ways beneficial, with the continuation of efficient administrative and organisational methods and national planning. In foreign affairs, however, the legacy of Vichy and the shame of 1940 made the nation, and the army, so desperate to restore national pride that they could not face up to reality over Indochina and Algeria. And the fact that the truth about collaboration was not faced up to meant that what Henry Rousso calls 'the Vichy Syndrome', the inability to cope with the memory of the Vichy years, continued to hang over French life and politics.

KEY ISSUE

What were the effects of the Vichy years on France after the war?

'DICTATOR BY CONSENT' – FRANCE AND DE GAULLE, 1944–46

One of de Gaulle's claims to fame as Head of State in 1944–45 is that he 'saved the nation from Communism'. He did this partly by his own prestige, using to the full the position he had gained as leader of the Free French. One of his great political assets was that he had been out of France since 1940 and had not been involved in the infighting and compromises which had scarred the Resistance within France. The 'Government of National Unanimity' which de Gaulle set up in September 1944 combined all elements of the Resistance, including the Communists. This was not easy. France was in a revolutionary situation in 1944. The Germans were retreating; the Vichy authorities were disintegrating. In many parts of France there was a dangerous political vacuum. The chief source of political power was the FFI (French Forces of the Interior), the combined forces of the Resistance within France, mostly dominated by the Communist Irregulars and Partisans. Two of the three men on the Military Committee of the National Resistance Council were Communists. In many towns and villages, Liberation Committees were set up, in which Communist influence was strong. Even many non-Communists respected the determination of the Communist Resistance which claimed to have lost '75 000 martyrs' in the struggle.

KEY ISSUE

How close did France come to revolution in 1944–45?

There were several reasons why this situation did not lead to a Communist take-over:

● The fact that the ultimate military power in France in 1944–45 was the USA; the Americans simply would not allow it to happen;
● The situation of the French Communist Party. Its leaders, such as Maurice Thorez, badly felt the need to live down the 1939 Nazi–

Soviet Pact. They also followed Stalin's policy that cooperation with the new government would be a better, safer path to power anyway;

● The speed with which de Gaulle moved. He had made plans early in 1944 to enable himself to set up a provisional government as quickly as possible following the Liberation. Well before D-Day, his agents were already active. Once in France, and with the military backing of two American divisions, de Gaulle quickly incorporated the FFI into the Free French Army (27 September) and passed a decree (28 October) dissolving the Communist militias;

● The international situation, which enhanced de Gaulle's prestige. It suited the 'Big Three', including Stalin, to treat France as a great power, taking part in the four-power occupation of Germany.

Politically, de Gaulle cleverly by-passed the National Resistance Council altogether. With his massive public popularity and the political position he had built up steadily since 1940, de Gaulle came to be a 'dictator by consent'. By the summer of 1945, the period of transition was all but over. Central authority had been secured and it was time to devise a new permanent constitution.

For de Gaulle and his supporters, the issue was simple. The old party politics of the Third Republic had failed. France needed a strong presidential system, building on the current sense of national unity and directly in touch with the people. It was a close associate of de Gaulle who said at this time that what France needed was 'a republican monarch'. Many politicians disagreed. The Third Republic might indeed have been a disaster, they argued, but the authoritarian Vichy regime had been worse. There was a deep tradition of democracy in France and a longstanding suspicion of military dictators. It had been agreed in 1944 that there should be a Constituent Assembly to devise and vote on the new constitution. Now, many political parties, both new ones and those from pre-1940 days, were ready to launch into action.

There was an inevitable clash between de Gaulle, who was unanimously elected head of the Provisional Government in November 1945, and the political parties. Ironically, one of de Gaulle's problems was that he did not, then, have a party of his own. Another problem was the difficult economic situation. De Gaulle won the first round. One referendum massively rejected a plan to restore the institutions of the Third Republic, and another referendum backed de Gaulle's view that the Constituent Assembly should only be temporary, until the new system was in place. But when de Gaulle formed his first government, he was forced to accept five Communist ministers in his cabinet. Running the government soon became exactly the kind of party bargaining that de Gaulle hated so much. After two months, stating that he was merely a 'prisoner of the parties', de Gaulle resigned in disgust on 20 January 1946. He had no doubt who was to blame. His farewell statement said:

TABLE 3

The main political parties of France, 1945–47

PCF	Communists (1920)
SFIO	Socialists (1905)
Radicals	Liberals (1901)
MRP	Christian Democrats (1944)
RPF	Gaullists (1947)

See page 87

The dominance of the political parties has returned. I condemn it. But unless I use force to set up a dictatorship, which I do not desire and would doubtless come to a bad end, I have no means of preventing it. So I must retire.

It is clear that he did not expect to be out for long and that he would soon be called back, this time with the strong powers he desired. In the event, for the next twelve years France was to be a parliamentary republic, with de Gaulle out in the political wilderness.

Devising a new constitution was a slow process, even after de Gaulle took himself out of the equation. The constitutional proposals for a **one-chamber system** favoured by the left-wing parties were rejected narrowly in a referendum of May 1946; a second Constituent Assembly was elected and its proposals (for a two-chamber system) were approved by referendum in October 1946. There was a majority of one million, but eight million abstained. The Fourth Republic was to have a political system very like the Third. A President, elected by both houses of parliament, would be in office for seven years and would appoint the Prime Minister. Real power would lie with the National Assembly. The powers of the President were to be limited – which was the chief cause of de Gaulle's disenchantment with the system.

one-chamber or **unicameral system** a parliament with one directly-elected assembly, without an upper house or senate

'TRIPARTISM'

Up to 1947, governments of the Fourth Republic were based on 'tripartism', power-sharing between three main parties. One of the reasons why de Gaulle had resigned, also a widespread popular feeling in France at the time, was the desire to avoid a return to the bad old days of party squabbles. As a result, the political map of the Fourth Republic, at least at first, seemed to be very different. Right-wing parties had been discredited by Vichy. The best-supported single party

De Gaulle's departure from power

Historians differ sharply over the interpretation of de Gaulle's departure from power in 1946. On the one hand, it is clear that de Gaulle had made a massive contribution to the transition to democracy in 1944–46. For Gaullists, and the General himself, 1946 was a wasted opportunity, which meant that France had to suffer twelve more years of weak government before de Gaulle came back to save the nation again in 1958. On the other hand, supporters of the Fourth Republic can make a convincing case that de Gaulle was an authoritarian leader who did not understand the give-and-take of politics; that he was an exceptional man who had handled an exceptional situation well but that now it was time for a return to normality.

ANALYSIS

was the Communist PCF; the second main party-group was the Socialists; the third was a brand new moderate Christian Democrat party calling itself the MRP (Popular Republican Movement) led by Georges Bidault.

Bidault had succeeded Jean Moulin, murdered by the Nazis in 1943, as leader of the National Resistance Council. Bidault and the MRP symbolised one of the most important facts about post-war France – the huge extent to which the experience of resistance moulded French politics. Everyone – de Gaulle himself, the MRP, the Communists – regarded themselves as the defenders of the spirit of resistance and unity. The trouble was that resistance and unity meant only vague ideas, not a practical programme. The three main power blocs all agreed about the need to build a new and better democracy and they all agreed that de Gaulle must be prevented from having too much power, but they agreed about little else. Tripartism, therefore, was always an uneasy compromise and did not last long. It was always up against the following huge difficulties:

See page 87

- The problem of any big, diverse coalition, in which it is hard to agree on detailed policies, especially in France with its rapid turnover of cabinets;
- The difficult economic situation, especially inflation, following the resignation of Pierre Mendès-France in 1945;
- The special problem of the Communists, still treated with suspicion by their Socialist partners and widely regarded as 'unpatriotic' at a time when the Cold War was taking hold;
- Traditional French anti-clericalism. The Christian Democrat MRP were never going to find it easy to cooperate with left-wing allies who were bitterly anti-clerical, especially when it came to key social issues like education.

Worst of all for tripartism was the problem of de Gaulle. The General had opposed the return of a Republican system based on the party politics he had always hated. Now, from his self-imposed political wilderness, he set out to sabotage that system.

De Gaulle had already campaigned against the new constitution in 1946. At Strasbourg in April 1947, he announced the formation of a new political movement, the RPF (Rally of the French People), which he insisted was not a political party but a genuinely national movement. Its only unifying factor, of course, was de Gaulle himself. Though the RPF claimed to be 'the party that was not a party', it acted like a party, campaigning hard in local and national elections; and although its ideal was national unity, its supporters tended to be right-wing and very anti-Communist.

In the process, de Gaulle made life much more difficult for the Socialists and completely undermined the pro-Resistance, pro-de Gaulle MRP. Instead of three party groups combining together, there were now two anti-republican wings, the Gaullist RPF on the Right and the Communist PCF on the Left, with the Socialists, the MRP and the smaller liberal parties caught uneasily in the middle. That same April, a big strike broke out at the Renault car factory, backed by the Communist-dominated union, the CGT.

All this coincided with a tense period in the Cold War. Bidault, the foreign minister, came under pressure from his opposite number in Britain, Ernest Bevin, to prevent Western secrets being transferred straight to Moscow by Communists in the French cabinet. At the same time, there was an urgent French need for Marshall Aid from the USA. The position of Communist ministers in the government, always awkward, became even more so. Early in May 1947, Prime Minister Paul Ramadier dismissed the Communist ministers from the coalition government. It would be 1981 before any Communists became members of the cabinet again.

THE THIRD FORCE

The end of tripartism pushed the politics of the Fourth Republic firmly towards the centre. The Communists were out of the government. The Gaullist RPF (which gathered huge early support and gained 40 per cent of the vote in the municipal elections of October 1947) was a new force on the Right. The moderate parties tried to establish some kind of defensive political alliance, aimed at keeping both the Gaullists and the Communists out of power. This alliance became known as the 'Third Force'.

MAURICE THOREZ (1900–64)

Maurice Thorez was the leader of the French Communist Party in the elections of 1945 and was Vice-Premier in 1946–47. He was a key figure in the shifting fortunes of the French Communists before, during and after the Second World War. The son of a miner and a miner himself, he joined the PCF when it was first founded in 1920, becoming General Secretary of the party in 1930. Thorez had a zig-zag career. In the 1920s, he was frequently in prison. In 1936, he supported Stalin's change of policy, ordering Communists to back the Popular Front. In 1939, Thorez supported the Nazi–Soviet Pact, deserted from the French army and went to Moscow; this resulted in his being regarded as a traitor and sentenced *in absentia* to a long term in prison. In 1944, he was pardoned and returned to France, at a time when Communist influence was very strong, both in the Resistance and in the unions. He played a key role in tripartism until the Communists were dismissed in 1947. Thorez remained a prominent political figure throughout the Fourth Republic but neither he, nor the Communist Party, ever got back the power and influence they had had in 1944–47.

KEY ISSUE

What was the impact of the Cold War on politics in France?

The Third Force was an alliance between the Socialists, the MRP and the Radicals, one of the old liberal parties which had lost ground badly in 1945 but now made a comeback. In one special sense, the governments of the 'Third Force' were very like those of the past. They were based on the support of only about one-third of the electorate and keeping a cabinet together was extremely difficult. Not only was the style of government similar to the past, many of the old politicians were back, too, including Paul Reynaud and Leon Blum. One key politician was Henri Queuille, who had been a member of countless cabinets before 1940 and was now in government continuously from 1948 to 1954, including four spells as Prime Minister. It was Queuille who, in 1951, changed the electoral law to favour coalition groupings more than single parties, such as the RPF or the PCF. It was in the late 1940s that the saying emerged: 'The Fourth Republic has died – it has been replaced by the Third.'

There were tensions within the Third Force. The MRP, with its Catholic Christian Democrat base, could not easily live with the deep-rooted anti-clericalism of the other parties; in 1948, the coalition very nearly split apart over the issue of church schools. Similarly, the Socialists always had difficulty accepting economic policies designed to curb inflation. As with all parties in France, there were particularly heated divisions over the war in Indochina. As far as possible, splits were avoided, and, since governments did not last long, there was a natural tendency to think in the short term and avoid risks. This trend came to be known as 'immobilism' – the politics of no change.

In general, French politics moved towards the Right, partly because of the Cold War, partly also because the Communists were no longer in government. As the RPF did well in the period from 1947 to 1951, there was also a natural tendency for other parties to compete with the RPF for centre-right votes. When a new right-wing party was formed in 1951, the CNIP (National Council of Independents and Peasants), the centrist parties were squeezed even more.

'Immobilism' meant that the Third Force suffered from growing cynicism among the public that nothing was happening and nothing had changed. The 1951 elections produced a crisis. Even though the Gaullist RPF did not do as well as its rivals had feared, the RPF was the largest single party with 120 seats; the Communists had over 100. Then the Socialists refused to cooperate with the MRP any longer, and de Gaulle and the RPF seemed close to gaining power. President Vincent Auriol was determined to avoid this. As he put it at the time:

> ## KEY ISSUE
>
> *How stable was the Fourth Republic by 1950?*

I do not want to call into the government someone whose purpose is to overthrow the constitution of which I am the guardian. He makes a public show of his scorn for the other political parties; his own party is a totalitarian movement, grouped around his personal power. I know de Gaulle is a patriot but I am not going to hand the Republic over to adventure and the unknown.

Auriol managed a skilful balancing act to keep the RPF out, and even persuaded twenty-seven Gaullists into splitting away from the RPF to join the MRP and the Radicals in the government. Gaullism had come very close to power but had been blocked. But the Third Force had fallen apart. The immediate cause was a new row over the 'schools question', the same old problem which had already bitterly divided the Catholic MRP from the anti-clerical Socialists in 1948; but the real reasons were deeper.

From 1952, France was led by a coalition of the MRP and Radicals without Socialist involvement but with support from some RPF Gaullists. French politics had moved a long way from tripartism and the optimism of a new system, united by the resistance experience, of 1945–47. This sense of decline and pessimism was strengthened by a number of factors. In 1952, the new cabinet included many discredited figures from the 1930s, including a number of Vichyites. In 1953, the capable President Auriol was replaced by an unimpressive conservative, René Coty. The bulk of the RPF joined forces with the government in 1953, causing de Gaulle to disgustedly announce his 'real' retirement from political life in order to write his memoirs. 1953 was also the year when an obscure right-wing populist, Pierre Poujade, launched his *Poujadist* movement, yet another right-wing political group discontented with the Fourth Republic and the 'system'. In 1953 and 1954, the Fourth Republic went through a series of dramatic events. There was the 'retirement' of de Gaulle, the rise of Poujade, and the final end of France's long and unsuccessful war in Indochina with the defeat at Dien Bien Phu. These events led to the formation of the most dynamic reforming government of the 1950s, headed by Pierre Mendès-France.

The war in Indochina had caused economic strain and political conflict in France since it began in 1946. By 1953, the war had reached crisis point. One of the reasons why Mendès-France was prevented from becoming Prime Minister in 1953 was the fear that he would pull out from the war, something that right-wingers in France bitterly opposed, even though French public opinion was clearly in favour of getting out of the war. The military situation in Vietnam, however, steadily worsened and in May 1954 the final blow fell when the besieged garrison at Dien Bien Phu surrendered. The result, after an eight-year war and the loss of 21 000 men, was a deep gloom in France and the feeling that the country had been humiliated.

James McMillan claimed that, 'The Fourth Republic died at Dien Bien Phu; though the death certificate was not signed until Algeria four years later', but McMillan's verdict may be unfair to the Fourth Republic. This was a time when the economic policies followed since 1946–47 were beginning to produce solid success. And for seven months the Mendès-France government showed that the political system was still capable of life and energy.

The Mendès-France government lasted less than a year. Many, including some in his own party, regarded him as too likely to give up Algeria. This was one of the key reasons why he was forced out in 1955. (Later, Mendès-France resigned from his post in the Mollet govern-

TABLE 4
Prime Ministers of the Fourth Republic, 1946–51

1946	(Charles de Gaulle)
	Felix Gouin
	Georges Bidault
	Leon Blum
1947	Paul Ramadier
	Robert Schuman
1948	Andre Marie
	Henri Queuille
1949	Georges Bidault
1950	René Pleven
1951	Henri Queuille
	René Pleven

See pages 91–2

See page 87

PROFILE

PIERRE MENDÈS-FRANCE (1907–82)

Mendès-France was one of the key politicians of the Fourth Republic. A brilliant law student, he was elected to the Chamber in 1932 and became a cabinet minister, at the age of twenty-nine, in 1936. He was imprisoned by the Vichy regime but escaped and went to England to join the Free French. He was one of the leading figures in the Provisional Government of 1945 and was admired as a man of principle. He did not believe in fudging issues; one of his favourite sayings was 'to govern is to choose'. He had consistently argued for negotiations to get out of the Indochina War and as soon as he became Prime Minister he quickly achieved a ceasefire and then moved to continue the process of decolonisation in North Africa. He also launched an energetic programme of social and economic modernisation. He persuaded the Assembly to give the government special economic powers in August 1954 and used them to issue more than 120 decrees, giving state backing to schemes in industry, agriculture, housing, education and research.

But Mendès-France was never good at the game of party politics and was not much liked by the politicians or the people, even when he was right, which was often. He lacked the common touch, as was famously shown in 1954 when he launched a very moralist but impractical public campaign to persuade the French to drink more milk and less wine. Also, like Leon Blum in the 1930s, he was often unfairly attacked for being 'left-wing' and Jewish.

KEY ISSUE

What were the achievements of the Fourth Republic?

ment in protest against the use of repression and torture by French troops in Algeria.) Some would argue that the nature of politics in the Fourth Republic, with its short-lived governments, just did not allow enough time for capable leaders like Mendès-France to carry their plans to a finish. When the Fourth Republic ended in 1958, Mendès-France was one of those warning against the perils of dictatorship as de Gaulle returned to power and established the Fifth Republic. After 1959, Mendès-France had no real power base but continued to be an influential lone voice.

THE END OF THE FOURTH REPUBLIC

From 1955 to the end in 1958, the Republic moved uncertainly from one challenge to another, with political difficulties at home intensified by the apparently insoluble problems of France's colonial wars. The politician who made the biggest impact in the mid-1950s was Pierre Poujade and his populist *Poujadist* movement.

The Fourth Republic

The Fourth Republic has frequently been dismissed as a failure. From an early stage, its public image was one of ineffectual, unpopular and short-lived governments. There is nothing unusual about the title of Ronald Matthews' book *The Death of the Fourth Republic* but it is surely worth noting that Matthews wrote it as early as 1953.

Against this, it could be said that the Fourth Republic had many genuine achievements, especially in economic modernisation, avoiding political extremism, and leading the way in European integration. R.E.M. Irving wrote in *The First Indochina War* in 1975 that, 'The Fourth Republic was probably the most successful of all French Republics – except that it failed.' In 1991, Frank Giles, in *The Locust Years* in 1991, claimed that:

> Normality makes for uninteresting reading; good news is no news. This explains why, apart from grumbles and criticism, there is little mention of what life under the Fourth Republic was really like. Political pundits in the capital reported every government crisis with prophecies of doom and disaster. Outside Paris, in the countryside and provincial towns, people went their way largely unconcerned, being content to share in the boom of prosperity which for five years up to 1958 nothing had been able to stop.

ANALYSIS

TABLE 5
Prime Ministers of the Fourth Republic, 1952–58

1952	Edgar Faure
	Antoine Pinay
1953	René Mayer
	Joseph Laniel
1954	Pierre Mendès-France
1955	Edgar Faure
1956	Guy Mollet
1957	Maurice Bourgès-Manoury
	Felix Gaillard
	Pierre Pflimlin
1958	Charles de Gaulle

See pages 92–4

In the 1956 elections, the Poujadists gained 12 per cent of the vote and weakened the other right-wing parties. The Socialist Guy Mollet became Prime Minister, in partnership with Mendès-France, but the government was in a shaky position faced by 146 Communists campaigning for a new Popular Front. This was also a time when foreign issues were very pressing, with the worsening war in Algeria and controversies about French membership of the EEC and the international crises of Suez and the Budapest rising. Mollet tried to appease the army and the Algerian settlers by increased repression in Algeria. This led to a split in the socialist SFIO and to the resignation of Mendès-France. By mid-1957, Mollet's government was brought down by a tactical alliance between the PCF and the parties of the Right. This led to a continuous political crisis during which, as in 1951, five prime ministers were nominated but none could form a government.

As political crisis paralysed politics in Paris, leaving the government, now headed by Pierre Pflimlin, in a weakened state, the settlers and extremist army officers in Algiers moved closer to outright rebellion. And Charles de Gaulle made it more and more obvious that he was 'available' to save France again.

ANALYSIS

See page 85

Poujadism

Poujade was not a mainstream politician. He was an outsider, speaking up especially for the depressed small businesses in regions like the South-West. He attacked the 'system', especially anything to do with taxes. *Poujadism* was a mixed bag of small-town and rural frustrations, sometimes vaguely leftish, often violent, always very nationalist. Some called him a Fascist: his nickname was 'Poujadolf'. One of Poujade's early recruits was the ex-paratrooper J.M. Le Pen, later to become leader of his own party of foreign-hating outsiders, the *Front National* in 1972. From its formation in 1953, Poujade's movement soon gathered momentum, staging a mass rally in Paris, and gaining a lot of support by its hard line on Algeria and by attacks on Mendès-France for 'giving away' Indochina – and for being a Jew. *Poujadism* was never destined to last but it was an important protest movement for a while. It also split the Right, taking many votes away from the RPF.

1958

coup d'état attempt to seize power by force

See page 94

See documentary exercise at the end of the chapter for de Gaulle's role in the Algerian crisis

In May 1958, Algeria was rocked by a revolt by the settlers and army rebels who launched a **coup d'état** code-named 'Operation Resurrection', aiming to prevent what they feared was going to be a surrender of French rule. As the revolt began, France had three distinct centres of potential political power:

- Paris, where the Pflimlin government and President Coty had to defend the Republic;
- Algiers, where General Salan and the rebels were leading the *coup*;
- Colombey les-Deux-Eglises, where de Gaulle was in waiting.

Both in Paris and in Algiers, de Gaulle was seen as the key to the situation. If he joined the revolt, he would virtually guarantee its success; on the other hand, de Gaulle was the one man with the prestige to face down the army and the Right. By now, de Gaulle had become a very skilled political operator. Later, after becoming President on his own terms, he said to a colleague 'I played well.' There is little doubt that he deliberately exploited the crisis as a path to power.

To the militarists and extremists in Algiers, de Gaulle appeared as the strong man who would establish authoritarian rule and save '*Algérie Française*'. Throughout, de Gaulle was careful to avoid direct links with the rebels, although General Salan and the other leaders of the coup expected de Gaulle to back them. For de Gaulle, the revolt was another 1940, requiring once again the 'saviour of the nation'. But, even though there were Gaullist agents, such as Jacques Soustelle and Leon Delbecque, in Algiers and de Gaulle himself may secretly have encouraged the rebels, he preferred to stick to the legal path. He had no wish to become tied down by commitments to the army.

To the parliamentary politicians, de Gaulle's support was a two-edged sword. Yes, he was 'at the disposal' of the Republic – but he would only save the Republic in order to change it. Remembering 1946 and 1951, de Gaulle insisted he would only return if given full powers to revise the constitution and greatly increase the authority of the President. Some politicians, including Mendès-France, opposed this and there was a mass Republican rally in Paris; but the air of crisis caused Pflimlin to resign on 29 May. President Coty invited de Gaulle to form the next government and a panic-stricken parliament voted 329–244 for de Gaulle. He was sworn in as the last Prime Minister of the Fourth Republic on 1 June 1958.

He then moved very swiftly to draw up a new constitution, confirmed by his favourite method of a referendum (79 per cent voted 'oui'). A new Gaullist party, the UNR (Union for a New Republic), was formed to replace the RPF and gained 198 seats in the elections in November. After gaining 78 per cent of the votes in the presidential election, de Gaulle was inaugurated as first President of the Fifth Republic in January 1959.

KEY ISSUE

How far was the fall of the Fourth Republic due to its own weaknesses?

B *The Fifth Republic*

FRANCE AND DE GAULLE

Consolidation 1958–62. The return of de Gaulle was a complex mixture of internal and external politics. The burning issue which brought de Gaulle back to power was the Algerian crisis and how to resolve it without civil war or an army seizure of power. But the priority for de Gaulle was to establish the strong presidential system which he had failed to obtain in 1945–46. By 1958, de Gaulle saw himself as a 'Man of Destiny' whose time had belatedly come.

One of his great political achievements was to avoid being committed either to the army or to politicians in 1958. It is also fair to say that he preserved democracy. French history is littered with soldier-dictators, from Napoleon I to Pétain; de Gaulle did not follow that tradition. He despised the professional politicians (though he was a remarkably clever politician himself) but he aimed for a system in which the people would have a direct link to those who ruled over them. From the start, one of the features of de Gaulle's Fifth Republic was to be the frequent use of the referendum, and of the TV broadcast to the nation, in order to bypass the political parties and reach directly to the people.

In 1958, therefore, de Gaulle took no bold measures over Algeria. His policy was basically 'wait-and-see'. All his efforts went into framing a new constitution. Even though he was the one man who appealed to almost all sections of French politics and society, de Gaulle did not have a completely free hand. Several influential politicians, including Mendès-France and François Mitterand, stubbornly defended the role of parliamentary government against a too-powerful presidency. De Gaulle joked 'Do they think I'm about to start a career as a dictator at the age of sixty-seven?'; but many on the Left opposed him just the same.

Between 1 June 1958, when de Gaulle became Prime Minister with special powers, and the referendum of October 1962, the new Gaullist constitution took shape. The president would continue to be elected for a period of seven years but with much greater powers than before. After the referendum of 1962, the president was to be elected by **universal suffrage**, which strengthened the prestige of the presidency and lessened the influence of parliamentary parties. The president could now appoint the prime minister, dissolve parliament, and declare a state of emergency. Cabinet ministers could no longer keep their seats as members of parliament but had to resign when appointed. A number of other measures reduced the ability of parliament to overthrow governments as in the past.

universal suffrage one-person—one-vote

The presidency now became the focal point of the political system. It must be remembered, too, that politics did not only change in 1958–62 because of the constitution. The personality of de Gaulle himself made the presidency far more powerful than it would have been in the hands of anyone else. Only Charles de Gaulle, for example, could have accompanied the outgoing President Coty to the ceremony at which he, de Gaulle, was sworn in and then left poor Coty standing on the pavement as de Gaulle swept away alone in the presidential limousine.

De Gaulle also had wide all-party support. At the very beginning in 1958, he offered posts in his government to leading figures in all the main political parties except the Communists. He also made effective use of the techniques of government by referendum. It is also remarkable that such a seemingly old-fashioned and pompous man as de Gaulle should be so skilful in his use of the media in general and especially of direct televised broadcasts to the nation.

So de Gaulle moved swiftly to consolidate his position in 1958. He announced his new constitution on 4 September, won the referendum on 28 September, set up the new Gaullist party, the UNR (Union for a New Republic), and won big support in the elections of November. On 21 December, he was elected first President of the Fifth Republic by a massive majority, and was inaugurated on 8 January, 1959. The 1958 elections changed the political map. The UNR gained 198 seats and the centrist parties, the MRP and the Independents, did well, but Communists, Socialists, Radicals and Poujadists all suffered huge losses. De Gaulle appointed Michel Debré as Prime Minister and, although Debré was a faithful Gaullist, frequently bullied him, and the parliamentary majority, in ways which de Gaulle's own constitution did not strictly allow. From 1960, de Gaulle fought a long campaign against persistent opposition to achieve the direct election of the president. This was finally achieved in the referendum of October 1962; but only after a close political struggle during which de Gaulle's Prime Minister, Georges Pompidou was defeated in a vote of censure.

During this period, de Gaulle had one terrific political asset, which he used time and again. France was in a virtual state of emergency while the Algerian problem and the simmering army-settler revolt remained unsolved and de Gaulle was seen as the only man who could rescue France. He was determined to keep up the political pressure while he was still 'indispensable'.

Algeria and France, 1958–62. Among those who showed the greatest enthusiasm for the return of de Gaulle were the rebels who had launched the revolt in Algiers on 13 May, 1958. The revolt was based on an explosive mixture of grievances: from right-wingers in France, elements of the army and, above all, the settlers, the so-called *pieds-noirs*. The *pieds-noirs*, or *'black-feet'*, were the one million people of European descent who lived in Algeria. Though hardly any had ever lived in France, they saw themselves as patriotic French citizens and were totally opposed to any compromise with the **FLN**. A Committee of Public Safety was set up under General Massu, which called openly for the return of de Gaulle. The army men in Algiers, led by General Salan, knew that de Gaulle could never have come to power without the crisis they had caused. They also knew that Gaullist agents had done a lot to help the Algerian crisis along in the weeks leading up to 29 May.

> **FLN** (National Liberation Front) the rebel nationalist movement in Algeria, see page 92

In the event, de Gaulle proved a great disappointment to the rebels. At first, they were optimistic, especially when he visited Algiers on 4 June and told huge crowds of settlers 'I have understood you!'. This typically ambiguous phrase did not, in fact, mean what the crowds hoped it meant. De Gaulle was careful to avoid any open support for the rebels. He then sacked Salan, replaced him with General Challe and set about disbanding the Committee of Public Safety.

At first, de Gaulle had hopes of winning the war militarily and he gave Challe backing to fight the war more aggressively. Always a realist, however, de Gaulle came to the conclusion early in 1959 that the war could not be won. He began edging towards the idea of a negotiated solution and in September 1959 proposed a ceasefire. When Massu opposed this in the newspapers, de Gaulle sacked him. This led to a second revolt in Algiers in January 1960, a mass strike known as the 'Week of the Barricades'. This petered out, largely because the bulk of the French army had no heart to go against de Gaulle.

During 1960, de Gaulle moved further and further in favour of a negotiated settlement, even though his ideas were still far short of outright independence. He won a referendum in January 1961 on proposals for self-determination, within France, for Algeria. The third, most dangerous revolt then broke out in Algiers on 22 April 1961, led by four generals, including Salan and Challe. The situation was so serious that the authorities gave advice on how the citizens of Paris might defend the capital against the paratroopers when they attempted to invade. De Gaulle declared a state of emergency and went on TV dressed in full military uniform to make the most famous of his direct broadcasts to the people.

The crisis was faced down successfully because once again the army rank-and-file would not follow the generals against de Gaulle. By now, however, the conflict had poisoned the politics of mainland France. In Algeria, extremists set up the OAS (Organisation of the Secret Army) and continued a terror campaign, including assassination attempts against de Gaulle.

On 17 October 1961, a mass demonstration in Paris by supporters of Algerian Independence led to vicious police action in which 12 000 were arrested and more than 100 killed, with many bodies dumped in the Seine. The fact that the Paris police chief was Maurice Papon, already criticised for his role as a Vichy official in the deportation of Jews in 1943, made the left-wing political protests within France even more intense. In February 1962, police charged at a left-wing counter-demonstration in Paris, near the Charonne Metro station. There were eight deaths and hundreds injured. This led to another mass demonstration at the funeral of the victims, attended by half a million people.

See page 94

These events culminated in a decisive change of opinion within France. The idea of *'Algérie Française'* was plainly dead; so were de Gaulle's illusions about some kind of home rule for Algeria, but still as part of France. In March 1962 the peace settlement was agreed at Evian. Right-wing opposition remained a danger but an OAS general strike in Algiers on 26 March was quickly put down by the army. A referendum approving independence for Algeria was won with a 90 per cent vote in April.

See page 94

Politically, the ending of the Algerian crisis left scars. There were more assassination attempts, and also the problems of integrating nearly 800 000 Algerian settlers into the life of a mainland France they had never known. The memory of the Algerian War became yet another divisive issue, connected with and making worse other divisive memories from the Vichy past. One of the strands of the appeal of J.M. Le Pen and his FN National Front in the 1980s was a bitter attack on the 'betrayal' of soldiers like Le Pen and on the 'false shame' of having fought in Algeria. But the Algerian nightmare was finally over and de Gaulle was free to turn to his plans for the future of France.

The well-known film *The Day of the Jackal* is based on a real-life attempt to assassinate de Gaulle in 1963

See page 85

France in the 1960s. By 1962, the Fifth Republic was securely established. The new constitution was in place and the colonial nightmare was over. The old political parties had been greatly weakened and new forms of politics began to take shape. On the one hand, the de Gaulle presidency combined many elements of political support, in favour of the new ruling élite. On the other hand, there grew up new kinds of political opposition from left-wing intellectuals and a growing trend towards radicalism in the universities. The mood of French intellectuals in the 1960s was generally left-wing and there were frequent satirical attacks on de Gaulle. The existentialist philosopher, Jean-Paul Sartre, declared that although he was an atheist, if he had to choose between God and de Gaulle, he would choose God because 'God is more modest'.

By the time de Gaulle was due for re-election in 1965, French politics was apparently in a quiet phase. De Gaulle had won most of his political battles and was now chiefly concerned with foreign policy and

TIMELINE

France and Algeria

Nov 1954	Start of the FLN revolt
Dec	20 000 French troops sent to Algeria
13 May 1958	*Group of Seven* attack in Algiers
4 June	De Gaulle's speech in Algiers
Sept 1959	Algeria promised self-determination
Jan 1960	'Week of the Barricades' in Algiers
22 April	OAS assassination attempt against de Gaulle
	Army revolt in Algiers led by General Challe
23 April	National TV broadcast by de Gaulle
25 April	Collapse of the revolt
March 1962	Evian agreements proposed independence
April	Referendum in France (65 per cent to 7)
July	Referendum in Algeria (77 per cent to 0.25)

his plans to restore French '*grandeur*'. Although they sometimes lacked substance, de Gaulle gained credit for a number of striking foreign policy initiatives, both in completing the process of French decolonisation and as a world statesman opening a new relationship with the Soviet Bloc and with the Third World. The new regime could also take the credit for rising levels of prosperity even though, in reality, this owed much to the modernisation of the economy during the Fourth Republic. The media, especially the national television network ORTF, was always ready to publicise Gaullist successes.

See pages 94 and 96

See pages 88–9

When the election came, however, de Gaulle's position was nothing like as invincible as he had expected. Gaullist over-confidence (the great man did not even bother to campaign) turned to anxiety and disappointment when the main challenger, the Socialist candidate François Mitterand, ran surprisingly strongly and forced a second ballot. This was regarded as an insult by de Gaulle who only belatedly campaigned in earnest, being forced to act like a partisan politician when he wished to be seen as being far above petty politics. He won the run-off, with 55 per cent, but his re-election had weakened his position, not strengthened it. It also made a nationally-known politician out of Mitterand, who would eventually win the presidency, at the third attempt, in 1981.

See pages 82–3

By 1967, a lot of de Gaulle's glamour was fading. There was a series of strikes and industrial protests and the elections of March 1967 showed a slippage in Gaullist support. It was also clear that de Gaulle and his Prime Minister, Georges Pompidou, did not always see eye to eye. Pompidou found it difficult to keep the government going, with powerful opposition from Mitterand and the leader of the Independents, Valéry Giscard d'Estaing, not to mention interference from de Gaulle himself. The stage was set for the 'events' of 1968.

See chapters on Germany, Italy, Central Europe and Social and Cultural Trends

May 1968. 1968 was a year of crisis and youth revolution in many countries other than France. French family life was actually rather more stable and traditional than in other countries and French youth culture

PICTURE 7
Paris, May 1968

See page 460

was not thought to be especially rebellious. Even so, the events of May 1968 in France came near to revolution.

The source of the revolution was the universities. It reflected the so-called 'generation gap' and the hostility of radical intellectuals to the rather static and authoritarian Gaullist system, which by 1968 many saw as almost a 'one-party state'. It was also influenced by many outside factors, including protests against the Vietnam War, the influence of Latin American revolutionaries, especially Che Guevara, the civil rights movement in the USA, and the 'Prague Spring' in Czechoslovakia.

The original disturbances began at the overcrowded University of Nanterre in the suburbs of Paris, with demonstrations, arrests and student sit-ins leading to the university being closed down on 2 May. Disturbances then broke out at the Sorbonne. The police were sent in, the Sorbonne was closed and student demonstrators set up barricades in the streets. By the weekend of 10–11 May, the government faced a real crisis of public order. There were disagreements between de Gaulle and Pompidou as to how far force should be used. On 13 May, ten years to the day since the first revolt in Algiers, the left-wing unions declared a one-day strike in support of the students.

The first response of de Gaulle was to go on a scheduled state visit to Romania, an attempt to be 'presidential' which actually made him seem out of touch. On 24 May, de Gaulle made a TV broadcast as he had done so often before; this time it failed to work the usual magic. Pompidou attempted to make a deal with the unions but without success, at least at first. The crisis appeared to be out of control, the split between de Gaulle and Pompidou was increasingly obvious and people reminded themselves that their President was seventy-seven years old. A mass Communist demonstration was announced, to take place on 29 May. Pompidou had tanks brought up to the outskirts of Paris by the army. Then de Gaulle suddenly disappeared and the Fifth Republic seemed to be tottering.

De Gaulle quickly returned and recovered the situation with apparent ease, by means of a radio speech and a mass rally in Paris by half a million Gaullists, but the events of May 1968 had done terminal damage to his prestige and to his prospects of staying in power. This was not obvious at first. Pompidou talked de Gaulle out of the referendum he wished to hold and persuaded him to call elections instead. The Gaullists made huge gains. De Gaulle promptly sacked Pompidou and, against all advice, pushed ahead with his referendum. But in the referendum campaign de Gaulle was opposed not only by the Left but also by his former ally, the Independent leader Giscard d'Estaing. In April 1969, the referendum rejected de Gaulle by 53 per cent. De Gaulle resigned soon afterwards, without fighting back. Despite his authoritarian ways, he had always claimed the voice of the people was all-important. He died quietly at Colombey in 1970.

The importance of May 1968 is difficult to measure. It was undeniably a serious crisis but hardly a real revolution. Much of the student protest, for example, was vague and unrealistic and petered out at the end of term. When it came to the crunch, Pompidou was able to make a perfectly reasonable deal with the unions, in the so-called Grenelle Agreements. What 1968 did show was that de Gaulle and the Fifth Republic had not magically ended all the political problems of modern France. Ten years after de Gaulle had condemned the Fourth Republic for its hopeless failure to deal with the crisis of 1958, he himself had seemed completely at a loss when faced with a less urgent crisis of his own. The Gaullist 'mystique' had been knocked sideways.

See pages 79–80

KEY ISSUE

How impressive were the achievements of Charles de Gaulle? (See the essay-writing exercise for the issue of evaluating the political legacy of de Gaulle.)

ANALYSIS

The mysterious disappearance of de Gaulle, 29 May 1968

One of the great mysteries of May 1968 is the 'disappearance' of President de Gaulle. In the midst of the crisis which had grown out of the demonstrations, with Pompidou calling up tanks to the edges of Paris, and with François Mitterand announcing that he would run for the presidency if the post became vacant – at this moment, de Gaulle seemingly gave up. Early on 29 May, he vanished from Paris by helicopter, leaving Pompidou to deal with the crisis on his own.

Most people assumed on 29 May that de Gaulle had gone back, as so often in his career, to his home at Colombey. In fact, de Gaulle was not even in France. He went to Baden-Baden in West Germany, to meet General Massu, his antagonist in the Algiers revolt of 1958, who was now commander of the French forces in Germany. In Baden, de Gaulle met Massu for a lengthy and apparently impassioned conversation. He then suddenly returned home; the radio news announced that night that the President was back at Colombey. The next day he swept back into Paris and took charge of the government as if he had never been away. Pompidou never really forgave him.

Nobody knew at the time what de Gaulle was up to; nobody really knows now. Maybe not even de Gaulle himself really had a logical explanation. One theory is that he had gone to see Massu to organise military counter-measures against the 'revolution' in Paris. A second theory is that de Gaulle had simply cracked under the pressure. He and Mme de Gaulle took large amounts of luggage as if intending a long stay; Pompidou certainly thought when de Gaulle left that he would not be coming back. Massu also claims that he had to talk de Gaulle out of quitting: Massu's version is that he told de Gaulle,

> My General, it's too bad, what can you do? You're in the shit but you must stay on. Go back to it. You can't do anything else. General de Gaulle is an old fighter and must fight to the end.

According to Pompidou, de Gaulle told him, later, 'For once, my nerve failed. I an not very proud of myself.' According to Mme Massu, de Gaulle told her, 'Providence put your husband my way on May 29.' A lot of convincing evidence suggests de Gaulle intended to give up for good but then changed his mind.

There is, however, room for a third theory. Simply by disappearing, de Gaulle may have planned to shock the nation; he genuinely thought of himself as indispensable. He told his son-in-law, 'I want to plunge them all into doubt and anxiety. That way I will regain control of the situation.' This was very typical of de Gaulle and his masterly way of being ambiguous. If it was a plan, it certainly worked. The politicians were openly relieved when he came back, and half a million people joined the Gaullist march in support. But what de Gaulle said to his son-in-law is contradicted by many other statements.

The mystery may never be solved. In his radio speech to the nation, de Gaulle said, 'For the past twenty-four hours, I have considered every eventuality.'

He probably had.

KEY ISSUE

How far did the events of May 1968 undermine the position of de Gaulle?

GAULLISM WITHOUT DE GAULLE

Georges Pompidou was the logical successor to de Gaulle and in many ways there was a smooth continuation in French politics, even though the events of 1968 had actually driven quite a deep rift between the two men. Robert Gildea claims that:

> Whereas from 1945 to 1968 the French republic had repeatedly been in crisis, after the fall of de Gaulle it enjoyed unprecedented stability.

See *France Since 1945* by R. Gildea (bibliography)

After 1969, Left–Right divisions in French politics lost much of their former edge. Sustained economic growth had established general acceptance of the mixed economy. Gildea describes the France of the 1970s as a 'Republic of the Centre', in which the main parties were closer in outlook than at any time since the earliest days of the Fourth Republic. Traditional politics, in the parties or in the trade unions, lost urgency and appeal. It is probably significant that it was from the 1970s that new and more radical political forces emerged, with the National Front on the Right and the Greens and other fringe parties on the Left.

See pages 89–90

The two leading candidates to succeed Pompidou were Jacques Chaban-Delmas and Valéry Giscard d'Estaing. Chaban-Delmas, first pushed forward by de Gaulle in 1958, was Pompidou's first Prime Minister, with Giscard as Finance Minister. Chaban was an ambitious, progressive politician, who fancied himself as the French John Kennedy, but he soon made himself unpopular with more conservative Gaullists, including Pompidou, partly because of his impatient, rather domineering style, partly because of his supposedly 'left-wing' plans. (It was Chaban who first brought the technocrat Jacques Delors into prominence as one of his key advisers.) Chaban was forced out of power in 1972, partly because of damaging newspaper accusations about irregularities in his personal tax affairs, but there was well-founded speculation at the time that the Gaullist 'barons' had orchestrated the campaign which brought him down.

In 1974, Chaban-Delmas stood in the presidential election but was defeated by a political alliance between Valéry Giscard d'Estaing and the ambitious young Finance Minister, Jacques Chirac. The real challenger to Giscard was François Mitterand, who lost narrowly in the run-off election. Giscard became President, but his own party, the Independent Republicans, was small and it was clear that he would need support from Chirac.

As President, Giscard had two difficult problems. The first was that the OPEC oil-price crisis of 1973–74 undermined the long period of French prosperity. The second was Jacques Chirac. Chirac saw the post of Prime Minister as a political base from which he could make a bid to become President. After numerous clashes with Giscard, Chirac stormily resigned in 1976, founded a new Gaullist party, the RPR (modelled on the old RPF), and got himself elected Mayor of Paris in 1977.

TABLE 6
Presidents of the Fifth Republic, 1958–95

1958	Charles de Gaulle (virtually unopposed)
1965	Charles de Gaulle (vs François Mitterand)
1969	Georges Pompidou (vs Alain Poher)
1974	Valéry Giscard d'Estaing (vs François Mitterand)
1981	François Mitterand (vs Valéry Giscard d'Estaing)
1988	François Mitterand (vs Jacques Chirac)
1995	Jacques Chirac (vs Lionel Jospin)

PROFILE	GEORGES POMPIDOU (1911–74)

Pompidou was a country schoolmaster before the Second World War. He fought with the Resistance and joined de Gaulle in 1944. He became a key assistant to de Gaulle in the 1960s, and was especially important as de Gaulle's chief contact with the Algerian rebels. He entered the Assembly as one of the wave of new Gaullist deputies in 1958, and became Prime Minister in 1962. He served de Gaulle with skill and loyalty until he was sacked in 1968. He won a decisive victory in the presidential election in 1969, having been chosen and supported by the Gaullist 'barons'. As President, Pompidou continued de Gaulle's system, though in a much less autocratic style. Pompidou changed French policy towards Britain and eased the way for British entry into the EEC in 1973. He presided over important aspects of economic modernisation, especially road building and industrial development in the regions. He was also particularly interested in big public projects and urban renewal, especially in Paris. The Pompidou Centre, the most popular museum and public building in France, was not actually opened until after Pompidou was gone, but it rightly links his name with such projects. After a lengthy illness, he died in office in 1974.

With Chirac as such a high-profile rival and the economic situation getting worse, Giscard struggled to live up to his presidential style. His Finance Minister, and then Prime Minister, the economics professor Raymond Barre, was talented but not popular. In the 1978 elections, right-wing parties retained control but lost seats. For the first time since the disastrous defeat in 1969, the Left was making a comeback. This was not as sudden as it seemed. Between 1969 and 1971, a new Socialist party, the PS, had emerged, under the leadership of Mitterand. At the same time, the PS took the big decision to give up on alliances with the centrist parties and to rebuild cooperation with the Communists. The PS committed itself to left-wing policies, especially nationalisation, while the Communist PCF committed itself to democratic politics. Both did well in the 1978 elections, 23 per cent of the votes to the PS and 20 per cent to the PCF. The 'Union of the Left' had become an effective coalition, and the economic crisis was making life difficult for Giscard. The Left was poised for victory in the 1981 elections.

KEY ISSUE

What factors explain the recovery of the Left in France in the 1970s?

THE MITTERAND YEARS

Giscard d'Estaing was unlucky in 1981. The tightening of the economic screws since 1973 had made things very difficult and a new oil price crisis in 1979 came at a bad time. All across Europe, there was a rightward trend in politics: in 1979 Margaret Thatcher came to power

VALÉRY GISCARD D'ESTAING (B. 1926)

Giscard was a contradictory politician. On the one hand, he was a moderniser, who brought the voting age down to eighteen, extended women's rights, and loosened government control of the broadcasting organisation ORTF. On the other hand, he was a vain and autocratic man whose public image was always rather snobbish and élitist. He was not very good at cooperating with the political allies he needed in order to keep his coalition going.

Giscard's father had been in various right-wing groups in the 1930s, including *Action Française* and *Croix de Feu* and later supported Pétain. Valéry, however, was much more on the moderate, centre-right. He was a product of the ENA (*École Nationale d'Administration*) and was part of the 'think-tank' advising the Mendès-France government in 1954–55. He became leader of the Independent Republicans (RI) and then Finance Minister in 1962. He tried hard to keep up a youthful image to match the 'Swinging Sixties', but wearing T-shirts while electioneering was not really his style. Later, as President, he tried to show the common touch by inviting ordinary families to dinner at the presidential residence; but he never escaped his image of belonging to the ruling élite.

in Britain, in 1982 the long period of SPD rule in West Germany ended with the election of Helmut Kohl and the return of the CDU. The stunning victory of Mitterand and the Left in France in 1981 seemed to be out of line with this trend.

This may be an illusion. Despite all the careful rebuilding of the Left in the 1970s, Mitterand's victory was only achieved with the help of damaging splits on the Right. In the first ballot, Mitterand and Giscard both had 26 per cent, with Chirac on 18 per cent and the Communist, Georges Marchais, on 15 per cent. But, whereas Marchais announced full support for Mitterand at the run-off, Chirac made no effort to support Giscard. Many Chirac voters abstained, enough to explain why Mitterand, the 'eternal loser' of 1965 and 1974, triumphed 51 per cent to 48 and became the first non-Gaullist president of the Fifth Republic.

There was wild enthusiasm on election night. Watching it, Mitterand himself said, 'Take a look at this! You'll never see anything like it again.' Perhaps he sensed what was coming. Mitterand did not last long as a left-wing leader. In 1983, there was to be a sudden and total transformation of government policies, with many of the left-wing promises of 1981 abandoned. After the 'U-turn' of 1983, French economic policy moved in the direction of deflation and policies similar to those of other European countries. So the rightward trend affected France after all, but only after an initial flurry of very left-wing policies.

TABLE 7
The main political parties in France since 1969

Greens	(formed 1984)
Communists	(PCF; 1920)
Socialists	(PS; 1971)
Left Radicals	(MRG)
Radicals	(1901)
Democratic Centre	(1969)
Republicans	(RI; 1962)
Gaullists	(UNR; 1958)
	(RPR; 1976)
National Front	(FN; 1972)

See page 90

KEY ISSUE

What were the effects upon France of European and world economic trends?

TABLE 8

Prime Ministers of the Fifth Republic, 1959–95

Jan 1959	Michel Debré
April 1962	Georges Pompidou
July 1968	Maurice Couve de Murville
June 1969	Jacques Chaban-Delmas
July 1972	Pierre Messmer
May 1974	Jacques Chirac
Aug 1976	Raymond Barre
May 1981	Pierre Mauroy
July 1984	Laurent Fabius
March 1986	Jacques Chirac
May 1988	Michel Rocard
May 1991	Edith Cresson
April 1992	Pierre Bérégovoy
March 1995	Edouard Balladur

Once elected President, Mitterand called elections in which the PS (38 per cent) and the PCF (16 per cent) gained control of the National Assembly. There were four Communists in the cabinet, the first since the end of tripartism in 1947. Claiming to be the guardians of the spirit of the Popular Front and the Liberation, the new government launched a programme of nationalisation and other reforms. Thirty-six private banks were nationalised, the death penalty was abolished and new taxes imposed on the 'super-rich'.

In the difficult economic climate of the early 1980s, such measures ran into difficulties, with rising inflation and a balance-of-payments crisis. The Prime Minister, Pierre Mauroy, and Jacques Delors both warned Mitterand that the pressures from the rest of the EEC would be too great to withstand and a deep division grew between these 'Europeans' and the left-wingers who wanted to 'go it alone'. Mitterand waited as long as he dared before making a choice but heavy Socialist losses in the 1983 elections forced his hand. He ordered an end to the 'break with capitalism' and opted for spending cuts and for the market economy. It was one of the most significant moments in the history of France since 1944.

Surprisingly enough, it was not the end, nor even the beginning of the end, for François Mitterand, not even when he had to back down humiliatingly on a plan to reform church schools in 1984. Most of the big plans of 1981 were in tatters but Mitterand survived as strong as ever. The fact that he did so proved how effectively the constitution of de Gaulle's Fifth Republic provided political continuity. Mitterand now chose a moderniser, Laurent Fabius, as Prime Minister, to the fury of left-wing Socialists – but, whatever Mitterand did, the Left was headed for a bad defeat in the 1986 elections.

When Jacques Chirac became Prime Minister, many feared that the combination of a left-wing President and a right-wing Prime Minister would produce a major political crisis like those of the 1950s. This fear was never borne out, partly because of the nature of the de Gaulle presidency, partly because Mitterand himself was such a clever political operator. Edouard Balladur, a key adviser to Chirac, coined the term '*co-habitation*' to describe how opposing President and Prime Minister might work side-by-side, if not together. And, although Chirac inevitably had many clashes with Mitterand, many observers noted the fact that Chirac had got on worse with his 'ally' Giscard, than he now did with his 'enemy' Mitterand.

Co-habitation went remarkably smoothly, in spite of a huge row over privatisation in July 1986. Mitterand was both cunning and realistic. Balladur was a useful go-between. Above all, Chirac was set on becoming President in 1988 and dared not rock the boat too much in a France which plainly preferred *co-habitation* to confrontation. In the 1988 elections, Mitterand played his role skilfully and outmanouvred both Chirac and Raymond Barre to win a decisive victory. In his second term of office, Mitterand remained firmly in control, despite continuing difficulties and disagreements on the Left. Following in the footsteps of Pompidou, Mitterand encouraged a number of impressive public building projects, many of them especially to commemorate the two hundredth anniversary of the French Revolution in 1989.

It was only in 1994, when news came out of his serious illness with cancer, and his revelations of the so-called Mitterand Affair that the 'great survivor' began to lose his grip on power. By then, the French political consensus, the 'republic of the centre', was under great strain. The parties of the Right were increasingly split on the subject of European integration; and they faced a threat from the popularity of the far right *Front National*.

See page 86

The Socialists faced serious problems in finding a candidate for the 1995 elections. The party had never really recovered from the trauma of 1983. One leading figure, Pierre Bérégovoy, had committed suicide in 1993. The man with probably the best hope of winning, Jacques Delors, refused to run. In the end the choice fell on the experienced, but rather uncharismatic Lionel Jospin. Jospin performed better than many had expected and even won the first ballot but the final result was pre-ordained. In May 1995, after almost as long a wait as Mitterand's from 1965, Jacques Chirac became President of the Fifth Republic.

The France of 1995 faced some pressing problems: long-term unemployment, growing doubts both on the Right and on the Left about the move to a single European currency, increased support for far-right politics, social tensions in the new satellite towns. But such problems should not hide the facts of the political and economic recovery of France from the desperate situation at the end of the Second World War. The Years of Division were mostly years of prosperity and stability for France.

J.M. Le Pen and the Front National

ANALYSIS

The National Front, under its leader, the ex-paratrooper J.M. Le Pen, was launched in 1972. Le Pen proved to be an effective leader with the ability to enthuse crowds and a knack for attracting publicity. His message was in some ways similar to *Poujadisme*, attacking the 'establishment', defending the honour of the troops who had fought in Algeria, and often gaining support for anti-immigration, anti-Jewish and anti-European policies. The FN was widely regarded as only a violent fringe movement but, in the circumstances of the 1990s, this began to change. The FN extended the range of its support from the traditional far right to other social groups, playing on fears of unemployment, and doing particularly well in the suburbs of Paris and Marseilles. Le Pen's ambitious younger deputy, Bruno Mégret, led a new breed of outwardly respectable and managerial FN leaders, more willing than Le Pen to cooperate with mainstream parties. As the 1995 elections approached, such cooperation, previously unthinkable, became a serious possibility.

The Mitterand Affair

The 'Mitterand Affair' of 1994 was a sensational episode which re-awakened the ghosts of the Vichy past. Since 1986, these ghosts had already been stirred by the trials of Klaus Barbie and Paul Touvier. In theory, Barbie's case should not have been a problem for the French – Barbie was, after all, an SS war criminal. But Barbie's Communist defence lawyer used the trial to focus uncomfortable attention upon the French collaborators who had willingly aided Barbie. One of these collaborators, Paul Touvier had been allowed to lie low undisturbed for years. In 1989 he was re-arrested and eventually went on trial in 1992 but was, amazingly, acquitted. After a storm of public protest he was retried in 1994 and found guilty. Then René Bousquet, long accused of organising deportations of French Jews in 1942–43, was assassinated at the door of his Paris home in 1993, in the midst of the row over the second Touvier trial. Next, fresh demands were made to re-open the case of yet another Vichy official, Maurice Papon.

Then in 1994 (the fiftieth anniversary of the Liberation) a book was published about the early career of François Mitterand. The book, *A French Youth*, contained sensational revelations: that when Mitterand first came to Paris in 1934 he had joined the youth section of the pro-Fascist *Croix de Feu*, that Mitterand had demonstrated against immigrants in 1935; that he had been a devoted supporter of Pétain and had worked for the Vichy regime, dealing with prisoners of war. Though Mitterand had gone over to the resistance, he did so only in 1943.

It is an important feature of post-war French history that almost all its politicians were 'men of the resistance'. They were all well aware of the fine line between resistance and collaboration. Mitterand's past was not so very bad. But then it was revealed that Mitterand had been a friend of René Bousquet and had helped his career since 1949. In the atmosphere of 1994, even the well-known fact that Mitterand laid a wreath at the grave of Pétain every year, seemed sinister. For many on the Left, it seemed to prove that Mitterand was an opportunist, that his socialism had never been more than skin-deep.

Mitterand's image took a heavy blow. It is hard to explain why such a clever politician would allow himself to be interviewed for the book, called by some his 'political suicide' – perhaps because by then he was dying and knew it; perhaps because he thought he had done nothing wrong; perhaps because the fiftieth anniversary seemed the time to draw a line under the past. The real point is that Mitterand's ambiguous career shows up the difference between the cosy myths of the Resistance and the much more complicated, uncomfortable truth.

2 ⤳ ECONOMIC HISTORY

A *Introduction*

The story of the post-war French economy is one of the most striking aspects of the history of France since 1944. Between the wars, France had been economically stagnant, plagued by low population growth, low productivity and recurrent industrial unrest. But, after the war, France went through a sustained period of economic modernisation and prosperity which has become known as the 'Thirty Glorious Years'. The France of the 1970s was unrecognisable from the France of the 1930s, with higher living standards, healthy rates of population growth, high levels of investment and an urbanised, modern infrastructure.

None of this seemed likely in 1944–47. French industry was backward and demoralised. There were shortages and seemingly chronic inflation. The unions were very strong, often heavily influenced by Communists. There were fears of economic breakdown, made worse by many deep divisions from the 1930s or from the years of occupation, when many French industrialists were accused of profiting from collaboration.

Several reasons can be suggested for the remarkable transformation of the economy from these unpromising beginnings:

* The impact of the Marshall Plan, launched at a vital tine in 1947, which did much to bring economic recovery to France, and elsewhere. The post-war years were a boom period for Western Europe as a whole, not just for France;
* The results of European integration. France, in partnership with Germany, took a leading role in the economic cooperation which culminated in the Coal and Steel Community and the EEC and benefited accordingly;
* The measures previously taken by the Vichy regime. From 1941, technocrats like Jean Bichelonne had begun schemes for centralised national planning, some of them influenced by the central planning of the Nazi war economy under Albert Speer; these schemes were built on after the war. Vichy also had some success with raising the birth rate through generous family allowances.

See pages 336–8

Over and above all these reasons, however, was the Monnet Plan. From 1946, the French economy was directed by a centralised, state-run and consistent form of national economic planning which, almost regardless of political ups and downs, underpinned a continuous process of economic expansion.

B *The Monnet Plan and French economic recovery*

The first attempts to deal with the post-war economic mess were not promising. Pierre Mendès-France became Minister of the National

Economy at the Liberation and put forward bold and comprehensive plans to eliminate inflation, to nationalise key areas of transport, power and banking, and to continue Vichy-style national planning. But Mendès-France ran into powerful opposition from politicians and from business and was not given much backing by de Gaulle. After he resigned in March 1945, the problems of inflation and economic drift worsened. France faced a serious economic crisis in 1946–47, which was a key factor prompting the USA to bring in the Marshall Plan.

In January 1946, Jean Monnet was appointed head of the *Commisariat General du Plan*. Monnet thus became head of a body of about forty economic experts which could virtually ignore parliament and rely on continuity of policy, however often governments came and went. The first economic plan was issued at the beginning of 1947, an ideal time to gain maximum benefit from American aid under the Marshall Plan. Monnet and his colleague Robert Schuman were also the chief architects of the 1951 Schuman Plan, which integrated French and German industry in the Coal and Steel Community and set the model for later European economic cooperation.

The Monnet Plan quickly achieved its targets for post-war reconstruction and soon won over the banks and industrialists who had been so hostile when it was set up. As with West Germany, the Cold War, and from 1950 the Korean War, encouraged the growth of military projects and the economy in general. After Monnet, his successors Etienne Hirsch and Pierre Masse continued the effective and consistent work of the Plan, supported by the so-called *Enarques*, the skilled administrators produced by the ENA (*École Nationale d'Administration*). This central direction of the economy is often called *dirigisme*.

Between 1949 and 1973, investment grew to record levels, while foreign trade and exports, especially to the rest of Europe, increased sharply. Large projects were launched in housing and in transport, especially rail modernisation. In the 1950s and 1960s, French economic growth was sometimes higher than that of West Germany and consistently double that of Britain.

Contrary to popular myths, the economic successes of the Fourth Republic were considerable; though much of the credit for them was claimed by the Fifth. It is true that after 1958 there was growth and sharply rising living standards, but these successes were built on foundations laid earlier. Some key industries were nationalised and steps were taken to ensure government coordination of banking and

TABLE 9

Annual economic growth rates in France, 1949–70

Growth rate (%)	1949–59	1960–70
France	4.5	5.8
West Germany	7.4	4.9
UK	2.4	2.9

TABLE 10

French industrial output, 1929–57

French industrial output	1929	1946	1952	1957
Coal (million tons)	55.0	49.3	57.4	59.1
Steel (million tons)	9.7	4.4	10.9	14.1
Cement (million tons)	6.2	3.4	8.6	12.5
Electricity (billion kilowatts)	15.6	13.0	40.8	57.5

investment. One notable success story was the car industry. Renault came into government ownership and took about one-third of French car production. Other firms such as Peugeot, Citröen and Simca also competed well in the home and European markets.

By 1958, the French economy had achieved modernisation and vastly increased productivity and technical development in key sectors such as steel, railways and electric power. Although marred by a return of inflation in 1957–58, the economy was ready to benefit from the impact of the Common Market; the surge in the economy from 1958 to 1962 owed more to this than to any economic policies of the Fifth Republic. It was ironic that the Gaullists, who had strongly opposed the Common Market, would see France benefit from it perhaps more than any other member state.

During these years, France became an urban country, with far fewer people dependent on the land and a notable shift of population to the cities and the suburbs. French agriculture remained traditional and small-scale but it became much more mechanised and productive, and French farmers did particularly well out of the Common Agricultural Policy after it was set up in 1961. Despite some painful adjustments for farmers, or such outbursts of dissatisfaction as *Poujadisme* in the 1950s, or the industrial problems associated with the protests of 1968, the sustained economic success of the 'thirty glorious years' was genuine. It was symbolised by the cultural confidence of the big public projects begun by Pompidou in the 1970s. But 'the end of the easy times' was coming.

> **KEY ISSUE**
>
> *How extensive was French economic recovery by 1958?*

C *The impact of the 1973 oil crisis*

According to Walter Laqueur, 'the years from 1950 to 1973 were the golden age of the European economy' but, from 1973, there was a prolonged and painful recession, which hit France as it did all the Western economies. The immediate cause was the oil-price crisis of 1973–74. Led by Sheikh Yamani and Saudi Arabia, the Oil Producing and Exporting Countries formed a highly effective cartel to control the production and pricing of oil. The impact of OPEC was to quadruple the price of oil, causing a serious energy crisis, which hit especially hard in France, where 75 per cent of energy was imported. Exports were hit, inflation shot up to 14 per cent and French industry went into recession, producing large-scale unemployment for the first time since the war. A further oil-price crisis in 1979 worsened the recession.

	1970	1975	1980	1985	1990	1993
France	2.5	4.0	6.3	10.2	9.0	11.9
UK	2.2	3.2	5.6	11.5	5.5	10.3
W. Germany	0.6	4.0	3.2	8.0	6.2	8.9
USA	4.8	8.3	7.0	7.1	5.4	6.9
EEC (average)	2.5	4.2	6.2	8.0	8.5	10.7

TABLE 11
French unemployment rates, 1970–93

There were other adverse factors. In 1971, President Nixon changed USA monetary policy and ended the long period of international financial stability which had lasted since the Bretton Woods Conference of 1944. France was hit by a continuous monetary crisis which lasted until the French–German agreement on the EMS (European Monetary System) in 1979. France also suffered from being uncompetitive in world markets, due to the high costs of labour and social security. This was a long-standing problem which had been made worse by the Grenelle agreements by which Pompidou bought off union unrest in 1968, and continued to be a controversial issue in the 1990s. France thus faced deep-rooted problems in energy costs, an adverse balance of payments, monetary instability and rising unemployment.

It was the Giscard d'Estaing presidency that first had to deal with these difficulties. Giscard relied heavily on his favourite economics expert Raymond Barre, who tried a programme of economic stabilisation based on cuts in prices, wages and public expenditure; and on the EMS, introduced in 1979. This policy, in general one of deflation, failed to achieve the rather optimistic targets set by Barre and was also damaged by a new oil-price crisis in 1979. Unemployment levels pushed up above 6 per cent, a factor which had much to do with Giscard's defeat in 1981 and the triumph of Mitterand and the Left.

The new government threw out deflation and gambled on reflation. The aim was to increase spending and boost economic growth in order to pay for reductions in unemployment and for increased social benefits. All these plans depended upon a recovery in world trade which did not happen. France was faced by the twin evils of unemployment and inflation at one and the same time. In 1983 came the great Socialist U-turn. There were tax increases, a freeze on prices and wages, and big cuts in public spending, together with a series of privatisations.

After 1983, the French economy was stabilised in many respects, with inflation and public spending under control but with low growth and continued unemployment. Economic problems were also reflected in social issues such as crime, youth violence and difficult race relations. Against this background, the France of 1995 continued to debate the merits of deflation and economic liberalism (President Chirac) against reflation and job creation (the Socialist Prime Minister Lionel Jospin). In which economic direction France (and Europe as a whole) would move was far from clear.

KEY ISSUE

How did the global economy affect France and other European economies from 1973?

3 ↫ FOREIGN POLICY

Three issues dominated the foreign affairs of France from 1944:

● The problem of decolonisation. The issue poisoned the politics of the Fourth Republic and culminated in disaster in 1954 and 1958;
● The close and lasting partnership with West Germany, often seen as the key to securing French interests in Europe, ensuring peace after

centuries of French–German wars; and providing the basis of France's role in the EC;

● The rebuilding of France as a great power and the development of a distinctive French foreign policy, independent of constraints from the USA (especially important to de Gaulle and the Gaullists).

A *The rebirth of France, 1944–45*

Nothing mattered more to de Gaulle in 1944 than the restoration of national pride. It was a key element in the so-called Liberation Myth that France was set free by the French. Obstinate, touchy, self-important, often absurd, de Gaulle had had difficult relations with 'les Anglo-Saxons' during the war, most of all with Roosevelt and the Americans. It was an open secret in 1942–43 that Roosevelt would have preferred General Giraud, or almost anyone but de Gaulle, as French leader – long after the war, de Gaulle still nursed grievances from the real and imaginary slights he had suffered from his allies. It was significant that de Gaulle even turned against General Spears, Churchill's liaison officer, who had worked so closely with de Gaulle from the beginning in 1940. One cause of this was British–French colonial rivalry over the future of Syria and the Lebanon but the real issue was de Gaulle's determination to have a free hand.

Much was achieved to reclaim French status and prestige in 1944–45. France was one of the four occupying powers of Germany and of Berlin. As the Cold War developed, France became a vital part of the emerging Western alliance. Later, this assisted the economic revival of France through the Marshall Plan. On the other hand, this obsession with wiping away national humiliation meant that post-war France found it almost impossible to handle decolonisation.

B *Loss of empire*

The First World War had already shaken the foundations of European colonialism. The end of the Second World War marked the end of the age of the European powers and the beginning of the age of the superpowers. American ideals of self-determination and Soviet Communism were both hostile to colonialism, and the events of the war itself had bankrupted the European powers and demolished the 'colonial mystique', the myth of the invincible power of the white colonial overlords. Sweeping Japanese victories in Asia in 1942 against the French, the Dutch and the British, removed the basis of French colonial authority. The Vietnamese nationalist movement, the Viet Minh, led by Ho Chi Minh and General Giap, developed into a formidable force fighting against the Japanese. Their aim was independence from the Japanese, not to bring back French rule. After the war, attempts to re-establish French colonial authority in Indochina led inevitably to conflict with the Viet Minh.

It may just have been possible for France to achieve some kind of compromise with the Viet Minh provisional government in 1945–46 and thus keep Indochina loosely within what was now called the French Union rather than the French Empire. Ho Chi Minh came to Paris in 1946, apparently ready to negotiate. Several influential voices in France, including the left-wing parties, politicians such as Mendès-France and even a few realists in the army, were in favour of a deal. But the opportunity was deliberately thrown away. The hard-liners made sure that the new French constitution ruled out independence for the overseas territories. War broke out in December 1946.

French colonial policy was dominated by the so-called 'Saigon clique', a powerful lobby of businessmen, colonial officials and right-wingers, led by the High Commissioner, Thierry d'Argenlieu. As time went on, this lobby talked more and more of anti-Communism as well as of French national pride. The result was a long, 'dirty war' in Indochina, leading to a dreadful waste of lives and a drain on vital resources – and also to divisions in French politics. For a time, the dynamic leadership of General Lattre de Tassigny and considerable amounts of American aid seemed to promise French success. But after the death of Lattre at the end of 1952, the war went steadily in favour of the Viet Minh. This led ultimately to the defeat at Dien Bien Phu.

See page 69

Like the Tet offensive of 1968 which was the beginning of the end for the Americans in Vietnam, Dien Bien Phu was not so much a single decisive battle as a moment of realisation. Even in 1947, less than half of French public opinion had supported the war. In 1954, after Dien Bien Phu, the thought of yet more financial burdens and yet more conscripted French troops being sent to a war thousands of miles away brought a decisive change of mood. Talks began at Geneva in April 1954. In June, Mendès-France became Prime Minister and pulled France out of the war. After the Geneva Agreements were signed, the war itself continued because American support was given to the anti-Communist regime of South Vietnam under the Emperor Bao Dai; but French rule was over.

KEY ISSUE

What was the impact of the defeat in Indochina upon France?

After ending the Indochina war, Mendès-France had some success in disengaging from French North Africa. He granted autonomy to Tunisia and began the talks which led to independence for Morocco in 1956. Algeria, however, presented an insoluble problem. First, the Algerian Muslim nationalists, the FLN, had been inspired by the example of the Viet Minh. The FLN, led by Ben Bella, rapidly developed into a formidable military and political force. Second, many in the French Army, burning to wipe out the double shame of 1940 and 1954, were utterly against any political settlement – or, as they saw it, any 'sell-out' like that of 1954. Worst of all, there were more than a million French settlers in Algeria. They had powerful political influence in mainland France and close links to leading elements of the army. A long and bitter war began which was to last from 1954 to 1962, marked by deepening ideological conflicts, a vicious spiral of atrocities and a poisoning of the politics of mainland France.

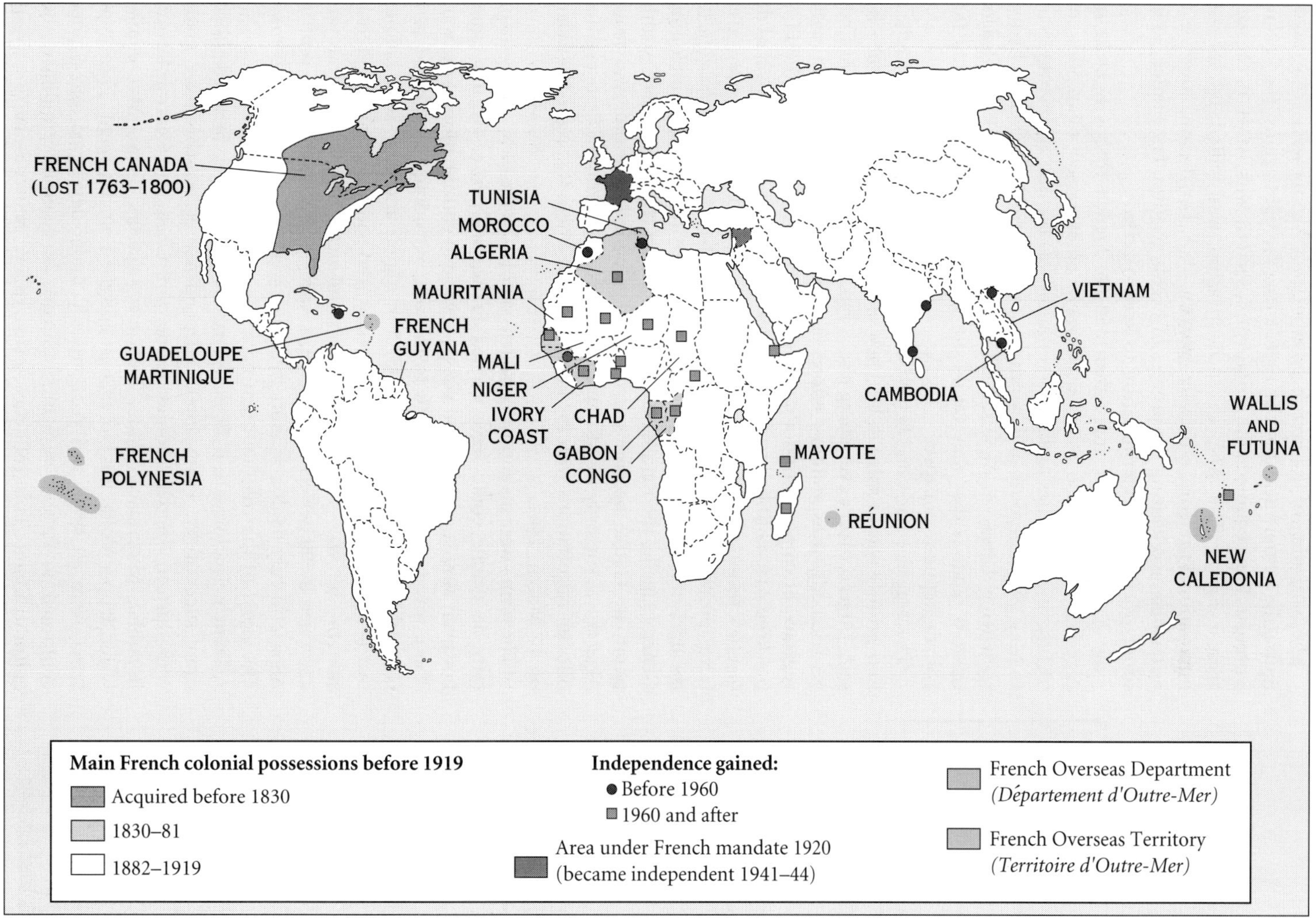
FRENCH CANADA
(LOST 1763–1800)
TUNISIA
MOROCCO
ALGERIA
MAURITANIA
FRENCH
GUYANA
GUADELOUPE
MARTINIQUE
MALI
NIGER
IVORY
COAST
CHAD
GABON
CONGO
FRENCH
POLYNESIA
MAYOTTE
RÉUNION
VIETNAM
CAMBODIA
WALLIS
AND
FUTUNA
NEW
CALEDONIA
Main French colonial possessions before 1919
Acquired before 1830
1830–81
1882–1919
Independence gained:
Before 1960
1960 and after
Area under French mandate 1920
(became independent 1941–44)
French Overseas Department
(Département d'Outre-Mer)
French Overseas Territory
(Territoire d'Outre-Mer)

MAP 6
The French Overseas Empire since 1945

The hardening of the French position over Algeria was accentuated, indirectly, by the Suez Crisis of 1956. Using the fight against the FLN as a pretext, France joined with Britain and, secretly with Israel, in the war against Egypt. The Anglo–French invasion was halted by intense international pressure, especially from the USA. For Britain, Suez was a watershed, accelerating the process of decolonisation. For France, 1956 simply fuelled the determination to keep Algeria.

By 1958, there were more than 350 000 French troops fighting in Algeria. Governments were increasingly embarrassed by reports of torture and atrocities and public opinion was turning against the war. In May 1958, rumours of new peace moves provoked a rebellion by the right-wing 'Ultras' in Algiers. Leading army officers like General Salan, made it obvious that they would not put down the rebellion and the Fourth Republic collapsed.

> The Algerian issue became the central issue in French politics between 1958 and 1962. Its impact is covered on pages 75–6.

The Algerian crisis had helped de Gaulle back to power; de Gaulle's first priority was to solve it. He knew ending the war was essential – he said, 'Algeria blocks everything else' – but he had no clear plan. At first, he tried vigorous military efforts against the FLN, combined with repeated attempts to find a compromise which would satisfy the FLN but keep Algeria linked to France. There was 75 per cent approval of de Gaulle's proposals in a referendum in January 1961; but there were also bitter protests from the settlers and army rebels in Algiers, leading to the uprising in Algiers in April 1961, headed by four generals, including General Challe, the man de Gaulle himself had chosen in 1958. At this point, de Gaulle became convinced that complete withdrawal from Algeria was the only way to save the political situation in France. After difficult negotiations with the FLN, final agreement was signed at Evian on 17 March, 1962.

The terms were an almost complete victory for the FLN; and perhaps only de Gaulle could have carried France with him. By this time, however, almost any solution was preferable to continuation of the war. There was a violent aftermath to the war, including many killed in a General Strike organised by the OAS in Algiers and large-scale killings by the FLN of the *harkis,* those Algerians who had fought on the French side in the war. A referendum on independence for Algeria was approved by 90 per cent in France in April 1962 and by 99 per cent in Algeria in July. Half a million *pieds-noir* were assimilated into France. The worst of the colonial nightmare was over.

French decolonisation in other parts of Africa was handled much more successfully. From 1960, independence agreements were made with thirteen French colonies: Cameroon, Chad, the Central African Republic, Madagascar, Mali, Dahomey, Gabon, Togo, Mauretania, Niger, Upper Volta, the Ivory Coast and the French Congo. These new states were all small and economically under-developed and France continued to have a very big influence in economic, military and cultural affairs. This influence, often called 'neo-colonialism' by its critics, was carefully maintained by successive French governments from the 1960s.

C *France and Europe: the French–German partnership*

French involvement in the European Community was the basis of French policy in Europe after 1950. This was not just for economic reasons; there was also a genuine determination to secure long-term peace in Europe.

See Chapter 8 for the issue of European integration

In the early stages from 1945, French–German relations were not good. French forces were part of the four-power military occupation and there were German grievances against bad behaviour by some French troops. On the French side, there was bitterness following the German occupation of France, and a real fear of a revival of German power. Several French politicians, including de Gaulle, spoke of neutralising Germany by splitting it up into several small states. By 1947–48, under the influence of the Cold War and Marshall Aid, French aims to break up Germany were fading away. It was clear that the Americans wanted a strong, centralised German state and that France had to go along with American policy both for economic reasons and as members of NATO, formed in 1949.

The new French line, of making Germany 'safe' through cooperation, was mostly the work of Robert Schuman, architect of the Coal and Steel Community set up in 1950–51. This arranged for remarkably close and detailed economic links between French and German industry. It gave France direct access to the resources of the Ruhr and the Saar and provided the basis of the economic modernisation of France under the Fourth Republic. At the time, the links with Germany were controversial. Memories of the war were still fresh: the Gaullist RPF vigorously opposed all moves towards the formation of the EEC, which was finally achieved in 1957. During the same period, efforts to set up the EDC (European Defence Community) which would involve a re-armed Germany in European military cooperation, were even more controversial. Political battles over the EDC continued through much of the 1950s.

See pages 336–7

See Chapter 9 for the role of France in the Cold War

When de Gaulle came to power in 1958, his past record suggested he would take a hostile line towards the EEC and towards the Germans. In the event, one of the key features of de Gaulle's policy was to be a close personal alliance with Chancellor Konrad Adenauer, which lasted until Adenauer's retirement in 1963. The French–German partnership stayed strong under de Gaulle. Preserving it was one of the many reasons behind de Gaulle's veto against British membership of the EEC in 1963. Even though de Gaulle often infuriated his European partners by stubborn and unilateral actions (such as his famous 'empty chair' tactics in 1965) there was no question of his deserting the EEC. After 1969, de Gaulle's successors continued to maintain the French–German partnership, though Pompidou opened the way for British membership in 1973. In the 1970s, there was an especially close personal relationship between Giscard d'Estaing and Chancellor Helmut Schmidt, which made French–German ties closer than ever.

Under Mitterand, the French–German partnership remained central, even though the end of the Berlin Wall in 1989 aroused old French fears of an over-powerful Germany. By 1995, there were anxieties in France about the results of German re-unification and about the rush towards a single currency; but the French commitment to European unity and to partnership with Germany stayed strong.

D *President de Gaulle: the politics of 'Grandeur'*

As soon as the Algerian crisis was over, de Gaulle was ready to turn to his cherished ideas of restoring the prestige of France as a great power. This meant standing out against American predominance and finding a truly independent and distinctive French role in the world. Even before 1962, de Gaulle had begun to pull away from the Western alliance, by opposing moves to closer military integration of NATO in 1959 and by pushing for the French independent nuclear deterrent in 1960. He deliberately blocked British entry into the EEC in 1963 and again in 1967, on the grounds that British membership would extend American influence over Europe 'by the back door'.

Thus, Gaullist foreign policy followed two clear lines – to reduce American dominance of the West and to increase French prestige beyond Europe. This led to actions such as withdrawing France from military commitments to NATO late in 1965, making high-profile visits to Moscow in 1966 and to Romania in 1967 and also giving maximum encouragement to the 'non-aligned' countries. There were frequent references to a 'third bloc', balancing the American and Soviet superpowers, to '*détente*' leading to the end of the Cold War, and to de Gaulle's vision of a 'Europe from the Atlantic to the Urals'.

Outside Europe, de Gaulle recognised Communist China in 1964, toured Latin America and, from 1965, began to denounce American policy in Vietnam. The main purpose behind many of these moves may have been to provoke the USA; it was the British and Canadians who were infuriated by de Gaulle's provocative and public support for the French separatists in Quebec during his tour of Canada in 1967. There were also efforts to compensate for the loss of empire by emphasising cultural and economic links with the remaining French colonies.

Few of de Gaulle's high-profile ventures into foreign affairs had any deep or lasting importance. Even French hostility to NATO was mostly an irritant and did not seriously affect the alliance, other than to move its headquarters to Belgium.

The efforts to find a special world role for France carried on after de Gaulle himself was gone. French policy in the Middle East was more pro-Arab than the policy of Britain or the USA and was backed by numerous deals with Arab states to provide French armaments and aircraft. French policy, under both Giscard and Mitterand, was also aimed at maintaining good relations with the Soviet Union. In 1989–90, Mitterand attempted to play a role with Mikhail Gorbachev in negotiating a merger of the two German states until the sudden rush to re-unification overtook them. In

KEY ISSUE

To what extent did the foreign policies of de Gaulle achieve success?

France was also the main supplier of military hardware to Israel until 1969.

the Balkan War from 1991, French policy was often closer to the Russians than the line taken by Western powers.

The most controversial aspects of French foreign policy revolved around the '*force de frappe*' – the independent French nuclear weapons established by de Gaulle and continued by all his successors. This soaked up huge expenditure and also caused large-scale international criticism of France on environmental issues. One notable example of this was the 'Rainbow Warrior Affair' of 1985, when French secret agents were caught in New Zealand after blowing up the Greenpeace

MAP 7
France, 1945–95

ship *Rainbow Warrior*, which had been leading the environmental protest campaign against French nuclear tests in the South Pacific. At the start of his presidency, Jacques Chirac raised an even bigger storm of protest by going ahead with further nuclear tests on Muruoa Atoll.

The post-war era saw some belated success in decolonisation and links with her former colonies. French policy in Europe helped economic modernisation and long-term peace. Strenuous efforts to maintain leadership of the French-speaking world and to defend the role of French as a world language had some success; though the combined effects of international pop music and the Internet threatened to make this a losing struggle in the long term. And the ending of the Cold War meant that there were new challenges to be faced in foreign affairs.

4 ↝ BIBLIOGRAPHY

In the 'Access' series, *France: The Three Republics 1914–69* by P. Neville (Hodder and Stoughton, 1993) includes an up-to-date, well-structured introduction to post-war France and the career of de Gaulle. Two surveys of French history as a whole which have good and accessible sections on France up to the 1990s are *The Cambridge Illustrated History of France* by C. Jones (Cambridge University Press, 1994) and *The Concise History of France* by P. Price (Fontana, 1993). *France Since 1945* by R. Gildea (OPUS, 1996) is an excellent thematic treatment of modern French politics and society. *Twentieth-century France* by J. F. McMillan (Arnold, 1992) is also very useful and follows a more straightforward chronological outline than Gildea. *France Since the Popular Front, 1936–96* by M. Larkin is comprehensive and up-to-date but very detailed. The relevant chapters in *The Collins Illustrated History of the Twentieth Century* by J. A. S. Grenville (Harper Collins, 1994) and *Europe In Our Time* by W. Laqueur (Penguin, 1992) are challenging and interesting. Of the many biographies of de Gaulle, *De Gaulle* by A. Shennan (Longman, 1990) is useful. The definitive work is the massive *De Gaulle: The Ruler, 1944–70* by J. Lacouture (Harper Collins, 1991). Finally, there is a difficult but fascinating book on the history and memory of the Vichy years, *The Vichy Syndrome* by H. Rousso (Harvard University Press, 1991).

5 ↝ ESSAYS

A *Essay questions*

1. (a) What dangers and difficulties faced France after the Liberation?
   (b) How serious were the internal divisions of France in 1944–45?
2. (a) Outline briefly the reasons why France was defeated in Indochina and Algeria;

(b) What impact did these colonial wars have on mainland France?

3. (a) For what reasons and with what justification did de Gaulle withdraw from French politics in 1946?

(b) What was the role and importance of de Gaulle in French politics 1944–58?

4. (a) What factors led to French economic recovery under the Fourth Republic?

(b) Examine the view that 'the achievements of the French Fourth Republic have been greatly underrated'.

5. (a) What social and political divisions characterised the Vichy regime and the Fourth Republic?

(b) How far did the presidency of Charles de Gaulle (1958–69) heal these divisions?

6. (a) How far did the events of 1968 reveal weaknesses and failures on the part of de Gaulle and the Fifth Republic?

(b) In what ways did Georges Pompidou (i) continue de Gaulle's legacy, and (ii) change it?

7. (a) What were the main aims pursued by President Mitterand from 1981 to 1985 and how consistent were they?

(b) Evaluate Mitterand's achievements as President of France.

8. Assess the impact of de Gaulle on the French from 1940 to 1969.

9. 'A great success story'. How justified is this description of the post-war French economy?

10. Discuss the view that the foreign policies of President de Gaulle were 'shallow and provocative'.

B *Answering essay questions*

Question: With what justification has it been claimed that, in the years 1940–1969 'again and again, Charles de Gaulle was the Saviour of France'?

This question has a provocative wording, inviting you to take sides. From the start, your essay should set out a clear point of view: either 'proving' the claim to be true or tackling it head-on. It may be that your view is 'that this statement is true up to a point but...' – even so, you must not sit on the fence! Make a clear, argued case, and even If you strongly disagree with the statement, the 'justification' for the quotation has to be looked at carefully.

Next, it is essential to analyse the key words of the question, to see how they 'fit' your case. 'Saviour' is a loaded word, tending to hero-worship – do you wish to attack it? Even the simple word 'France' needs attention: does this mean the democratic French Republic? Or the Gaullist ideal?

Most of all, the words 'again and again' can be debated. Even critics of de Gaulle would concede de Gaulle saved France at least once, in 1940–44, and might accept a second example, in getting out of the Algerian crisis in 1958–62. But 'again and again' seems to imply an endless list of unique achievements, to see de Gaulle as a great leader who saved France from the permanent party-political weakness which went before him. This question is about de Gaulle but it is also about the history of France since 1940 under Vichy and the Third and Fourth Republics. You need to assess what France needed to be saved from.

Below is a long list of achievements which have been credited to de Gaulle. Use them as a means of drawing up a balance-sheet of your own judgements: those you accept and those you reject. This balance-sheet will decide the overall view you take of de Gaulle, either as the man who saved France from national humiliation and 'eighty years of weak governments', or as an overrated Gaullist myth. It will also provide a framework for evidence and examples:

1940 the decision to fight on alone, de Gaulle's BBC broadcast;
1943 standing up to Churchill and Roosevelt, uniting French resistance;
1944 the Liberation of Paris; 'France liberated by the French';
1945 'dictator by consent', saving France from Communism or civil war;
1946 de Gaulle resigns; France wastes the chance to achieve stability (also proves de Gaulle to be a true democrat, not another Napoleon);
1958 the return of de Gaulle, saving France by a new strong presidency;
1962 de Gaulle as the one man able to free France from the Algerian crisis;
1960s restoring French greatness with '*grandeur*' in foreign policy;
1968 de Gaulle saving France from the 'anarchy' of May 1968;
1969 accepting the will of the people and retiring without protest;
1970 since his death, a legacy of continuity and political stability.

Having chosen which of these claims are (i) true; (ii) false; (iii) exaggerated, you can then apply your judgements to a framework of key events, looking particularly at the crisis points of 1940–46; 1958–62; and 1968–69. You should use these events to *support* your case, not to describe what happened.

C *Comparing the achievements of the Fourth and Fifth Republics*

The evaluation of the successes of the Fourth Republic (and thus, by comparison, of the Fifth Republic) is difficult. Table 12 attempts to sum up the general issues involved and to set out alternatives.

Test the evidence for each of the general claims. Decide, above all, whether claims for the achievements of the Fifth Republic are either exaggerated and insubstantial or actually built on the foundations laid by the Fourth Republic before 1958. This 'balance-sheet' will enable you to marshal the evidence for an overall argument, 'proving' that the Fourth Republic was either a failed system rescued by de Gaulle in 1958 or a deceptively stable and successful system unfairly maligned by its opponents.

TABLE 12

The achievements of the Fourth and Fifth Republics in France

	Successes?	Failures?
FOURTH REPUBLIC		
Political	Restoring democracy 1945	Chronic cabinet instability
	Avoiding Communist take-over	Lack of popular acceptance
	Blocking threats from Gaullism	Short-term politics
	1947–51 and Poujadism in 1950	Destabilised by Gaullists and by 1958
		Algerian crisis
Economic	Social and welfare reforms	
	Recovery from post-war crisis	Chronic inflation and failure to reform
	Monnet Plan: re-structuring of industry	the tax system
	and transport	
Foreign policy	Membership of Western alliance	Failure to win or end wars in Indochina
	Founder-member of EEC	and Algeria
	Geneva talks 1954	Undue dominance from USA
FIFTH REPUBLIC		
Political	Defeat of right-wing revolts	Democratic opposition stifled
	Stable, continuous presidency	Excessive control of media
	Successful succession after de Gaulle	Failure to cope with crisis of 1968
	had gone	
Economic	Rising living standards in 1960s	Industrial unrest, 1967–68
	Prestige transport projects such as	Serious economic problems exposed by
	TGV and Channel Tunnel	'U-turn' in 1983
Foreign policy	French–German alliance	Unnecessary conflict with the USA and
	Independent French deterrent	Britain, 1962–67
	Assertion of French interests against	Lack of substance (and waste of resources)
	USA domination	in pursuit of prestige and *'grandeur'*
	Success in decolonisation	

6 ᗕ DOCUMENTARY EXERCISE ON ALGERIA AND DE GAULLE, 1958

Study Sources A–H and answer *all* the questions which follow.

On 13 April, General Massu declared his aims to cheering thousands in Algiers: 'I, General Massu, have just formed a Committee of Public Safety in Algiers, so that a Government of Public Safety under General de Gaulle can be formed in France!'
Two days later, General Salan harangued another huge crowd. 'Vive l'Algérie Française!' he cried. Just as he was about to move back, the Gaullist Leon Delbecque caught Salan's arm and muttered harshly, 'Shout Vive de Gaulle!'
Salan faced the crowd once more and shouted, 'Vive de Gaulle!'

SOURCE A
'Revolt in Algiers' from De Gaulle: The Ruler, 1944–70 by Jean Lacouture.

The degradation of the state inevitably brings with it disturbance In the armed forces, national dislocation, loss of independence. For

SOURCE B
*General Charles de Gaulle,
public announcement,
14 May.*

twelve years, France, in the grip of problems too severe to be solved by the regime of the parties, has gone through this disastrous process.

Not so long ago, the nation, in its depths, trusted me to lead it to salvation. Today, in the trials that face it once again, let the nation know that I am ready to assume the powers of the Republic.

SOURCE C
*The Gaullist politician,
Gaston Palewski, in a private
conversation, 1984.*

Suppose de Gaulle had disappeared before May 1958, or just done nothing. The uprising in Algiers against the Pflimlin government would not have been contained in Algeria. The government in France would have had no protection against 'Operation Resurrection'. It was a choice between Gaullists on the one hand and Generals Salan and Massu on the other.

SOURCE D
*Speech by Pierre Mendès-
France, 1 June 1958*

A year ago, six months ago, even three weeks ago, I thought de Gaulle might be the salvation of the country. But now a certain event, the sedition in Algiers, has taken place. The General has clearly stood surety for it, whether he intended to or not. I feel torn in two. Whatever my personal feelings, I shall not vote for his investiture as head of government. I cannot accept a vote under the threat of a military uprising. The decision about to be taken is not a free one but has been dictated under the blackmail of civil war.

SOURCE E
*François Mitterand on the
same occasion.*

When the most illustrious of Frenchmen presents himself for our votes, I cannot forget that he is supported, first and foremost, by an undisciplined army. In law, he will receive his authority from the national parliament; in reality he already holds authority by a bid for power. (At this there was loud applause from many on the left). 'You will come round in time', I have been told. Well, if General de Gaulle is indeed the founder of a new form of democracy, the liberator of the African peoples, the restorer of national unity, if he gives France the continuity and authority she needs, then, yes, I shall rally to him.

SOURCE F
 *Memoirs of Hope (1969–
70) by Charles de Gaulle.*

A feeling of immense relief swept over the country. Instantly, the storm clouds vanished from the horizon. Now that the Captain was at the helm of the ship of State, there was a sense that the harsh problems the nation had faced for so long would at last be resolved.

You haven't made a single mistake! That's very good. But you must admit that I, too, have played my cards well!

SOURCE G
Charles de Gaulle, private remark to Leon Delbecque, 3 June 1958.

Before moving into the Prime Minister's residence, de Gaulle went back for the last time to his hotel. The night porter was waiting for him and accompanied him, respectfully, to the lift. The General tapped him on the back and chuckled, 'Albert, I've won!'

SOURCE H
Story told in De Gaulle: The Ruler, 1945–70 *by Jean Lacouture.*

From a study of these sources, consider the following questions:

Q

1. *Explain what Mendès-France meant by the phrase, 'The General clearly stood surety for it' (Source D). (2 marks)*
2. *How useful and reliable is this collection of sources as evidence about the circumstances in which de Gaulle achieved power in 1958? (6 marks)*
3. *In the light of the evidence of these sources, and from your own knowledge, answer the following three questions. In each case give reasons for your choice of 'yes' or 'no':*
(a) *Did the Fourth Republic die of its own accord, de Gaulle doing no more than fill the political vacuum left behind? (4 marks)*
(b) *If military pressure was used to hasten the end of the dying Republic, was de Gaulle aware of it? (4 marks)*
(c) *Did de Gaulle actively help the process by which the Republic was 'killed off'? (4 marks)*
4. *From a study of these sources, assemble a list of reasons why de Gaulle came to power in 1958, arranged in order of importance. (10 marks)*

3   The USSR, 1945–91

INTRODUCTION

Lenin's minority Communist government which seized power in 1917 survived a destructive civil war between 1918 and 1921 whilst trying to lay the foundations of a Socialist state. Following Lenin's death and the rise to power of Stalin by 1929, the Union of Soviet Socialist Republics underwent a massive economic and social transformation. Collectivisation involved the forcible amalgamation of millions of small farms into large collectives, supplying grain to the government; whilst under the five-year plans, a massive, centrally planned and directed programme of industrialisation was intended to turn the country into a modern, industrialised, power. Overseeing the process was Stalin's authoritarian one-party regime, which reinforced its power through a combination of terror and propaganda. Millions of Soviet citizens, mostly innocent of any crime, were killed or imprisoned by the secret police as the regime sought to root out 'spies, wreckers and saboteurs' and other 'enemies of progress'. Despite the disruptions of the 1930s, Stalin's USSR managed to survive a brutal and costly war against Germany between 1941 and 1945.

The themes of this chapter will centre on the politics, economics and foreign policy of the Soviet Union after it emerged from the Second World War as a great European and world power. Although these three strands were closely interwoven, they will be treated separately for most of the chapter. How did Stalin consolidate the USSR's recently acquired superpower status? To what extent did the Stalinist political and economic system survive in the decades after his death? How successfully did Stalin's successors maintain an authoritarian system, cope with economic problems and assert Soviet influence in the world? Were there consistent themes in Soviet foreign policy? How significant were the reforms of the 1980s and why did the USSR finally disintegrate at the beginning of the 1990s?

After 1945 the Soviets sought to consolidate their influence in Eastern and Central Europe. As resulting Cold War tensions with the West increased, so the ideological battle lines hardened, and the Stalinist political and economic systems became even more rigorous. However, the pressure of trying to compete with the USA as a superpower increased the strains on the weaker Soviet economy. These strains prompted pressure for change and eventually led to political and economic reform. But this reforming process, undertaken by Gorbachev in the 1980s, could not be controlled once begun. Along with the added complication of rising nationalist tensions in the constituent republics which made up the USSR, it led to the eventual collapse of the Soviet system and of the federation in 1991.

The history of the USSR after 1945 can only be understood in the context of its experiences during the Second World War. This began for the USSR with the Nazi invasion of June 1941. Although Hitler had planned the attack for some time, it came as a surprise to Stalin. The German attack cut deep into Russia, and the invaders occupied huge tracts of land and killed or imprisoned millions of Red Army soldiers.

What the Germans did not destroy themselves was often destroyed by the Russians as they retreated. Many of the showpiece factories, bridges and dams built during the five-year plans were destroyed. The Germans got to the gates of Moscow and Leningrad late in 1941 before they were held.

The Soviets survived the initial German invasion through a combination of the courage of their soldiers, the difficulties encountered by the Germans in fighting so far from home in difficult conditions and the fact that the Soviets fought a total war from the start. Soviet industrial capacity was not destroyed, and the nature of the Soviet command economy made it relatively easy to transform peacetime industry to a war footing.

Nevertheless, the war inflicted tremendous damage on the USSR. Later the Soviets acknowledged their war dead at about twenty-eight million, probably an underestimate. More than 1710 towns and 70 000 villages were destroyed, along with more than 31 000 industrial enterprises. Therefore, at the end of the war the USSR faced enormous problems. Wartime damage had to be repaired and the economy rebuilt.

There were also other important political issues to be resolved. The Russians had twice been invaded from the West in less than fifty years. Stalin was determined that the area on Russia's western borders should be a secure buffer zone and a Soviet sphere of influence. The opportunity was there because in the process of driving back the German invaders between 1943 and 1945 the Soviets had liberated most of the countries of Eastern and Central Europe and were in a position to help or even enforce the establishment of friendly Communist regimes. However, in so doing, the wartime Alliance dissolved and mutual suspicion developed between the Western democracies and the Communist states. A new threat to security appeared to emerge, particularly as the Americans had a monopoly of nuclear weapons. The USSR struggled to maintain itself as a superpower capable of competing with the USA.

> **KEY ISSUE**
>
> *How significant was the impact of the war on the Soviet economy and attitudes?*

1 ⌐ POLITICAL HISTORY

A *The Soviet system*

Before the war, Stalin's power had rested upon his control of the Communist Party. Although as First Secretary he reported to the Central Committee of the Communist Party, Stalin in reality ruled autocratically. The Party dominated Soviet life, and Stalin's power had been reinforced in two ways: first, by his arbitrary purges of the Party before the war, which had created uncertainty and fear and had made opposition to Stalin both difficult and dangerous; and second, by Stalin's role as a successful wartime leader, which increased his authority inside the USSR and bolstered his prestige outside it.

Many Soviet citizens hoped that after 1945 the wartime alliance would be continued and that the regime would govern less arbitrarily, but these hopes were soon dashed. Stalin was even more concerned to keep foreign influences out of the USSR. Although purges were now less wide-ranging, life was still insecure in a society which demanded conformity in all areas of public and even private life. The internal security apparatus and the propaganda were still all-pervasive.

Soviet political structures and practices underwent no significant changes between 1945 and the period of Gorbachev's reforms in the 1980s. The Soviet Union was a federation of fifteen Union Republics, of which the Russian Federation was the largest. Each Republic had its own legislative body (a Supreme Soviet) and its own government (a Council of Ministers), but the central government in Moscow was responsible for defence, foreign policy, foreign trade, communications and industry.

However, real power lay with the Communist Party: its organisation paralleled that of State bodies. Each Republic had its own Communist Party organisation, but key appointments throughout the Federation were vetted by the central Party organisation.

MAP 8
The USSR, 1945–91

Less than 10 per cent of the Soviet population belonged to the Communist Party, which was the only party, and only a minority of members were full-time Party officials. But membership of the Party was essential for influence in every walk of life. The Soviet Constitution guaranteed the Communist Party a leading role in society.

The Soviet government was elected. Candidates were selected and there was little genuine competition. The population was exhorted to vote for local *soviets* or councils, and for the Soviet of the Union every five years. This body, together with the Soviet of the Nationalities, which represented the different Republics and regions, made up the Supreme Soviet. The Supreme Soviet met rarely, although its function was to approve legislation, and it elected a Council of Ministers to supervise administration.

Many of the deputies to these bodies were also Communist Party members. The Party had its own structural pyramid. Local Party organisations sent delegates to higher committees. Every five years a selection of Party members attended a Party Congress. The Congress approved both Party policy and the list of members proposed for the Central Committee. This was a key body of almost fifty-five members who were responsible for managing the Party in the long gaps between congresses. Technically the Central Committee elected the *Politburo*, which met weekly as a kind of cabinet to direct domestic and foreign policy, and which was supported administratively by the Secretariat.

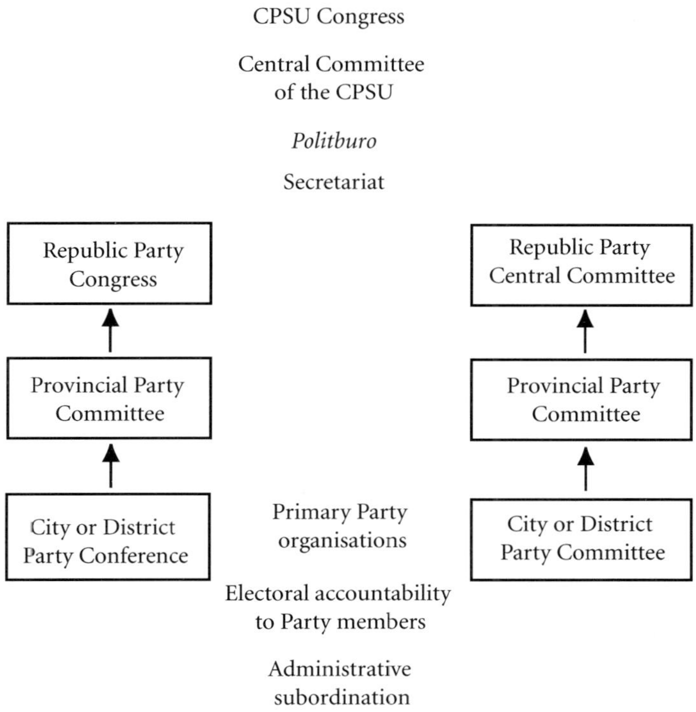

> **KEY ISSUE**
>
> *How did the Communist Party maintain its authority in the USSR?*

CPSU Congress

Central Committee
of the CPSU

Politburo

Secretariat

Republic Party Congress		Republic Party Central Committee
Provincial Party Committee	Primary Party organisations	Provincial Party Committee
City or District Party Conference		City or District Party Committee

Electoral accountability
to Party members

Administrative
subordination

DIAGRAM 1
Organisational structure of the Communist Party

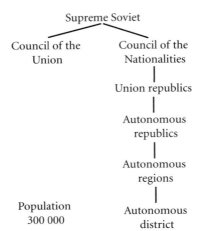

Supreme Soviet

Council of the
Union

Council of the
Nationalities

Union republics

Autonomous
republics

Autonomous
regions

DIAGRAM 2

*Elections to the Supreme
Soviet*

Population
300 000

Autonomous
district

Leadership was either 'collective' as in the period immediately after Stalin's death, or more often it was in the hands of the General Secretary. He – it was always a man – tried to manouevre colleagues in and out of the *Politburo* in order to establish his own dominance. The General Secretary was certainly a more important figure than the President, who was a 'State' representative.

The Party reinforced its dominance by the *Nomenklatura* system: a list of suitable Party members from which important State and Party positions were filled. Everywhere membership of Party and State bodies overlapped, but the Party was in the commanding position. The majority of prominent members in important institutions such as the police, the bureaucracy, industrial enterprises and the army were Party members. The Party's monopoly of power was reinforced by great wealth and by propaganda which constantly emphasised the importance of its role. Only in the period just before the break-up of the USSR did the monopoly of power exercised by the Communist Party come under threat.

Membership of the Party in the middle and higher ranks carried privileges such as access to certain goods and services denied to the rest of the population. Middle-ranking Party bureaucrats often obstructed attempts at reform by more perceptive leaders, notably Khrushchev and Gorbachev: in addition to their ideological commitment to the status quo, many Party bureaucrats had no interest in changing a system under which they had, at least after Stalin, secure positions, status and privileges. It was the middle and lower-ranking bureaucrats who essentially maintained the Soviet system for forty years from 1945, whilst arguments over policy were fought out over their heads in the higher levels of the Party hierarchy.

TIMELINE

The USSR, 1945–64 (Foreign affairs are in italics)

1945	*Yalta Conference*
	Potsdam Conference
1946	Fourth Five-Year Plan
	Purge began in Leningrad
1947	Marshall Aid refused by Stalin
	Cominform established
1948	Leningrad Purge
	Berlin Crisis began
1949	Stalin's 70th birthday
	COMECON established
	Soviet atomic bomb tested
1950	*Korean War (1950–53)*
1951	Fifth Five-Year Plan
1953	'Doctors Plot'
	Soviet hydrogen bomb tested
	Death of Stalin
	Khrushchev elected First Secretary
	Beria executed
1954	Virgin Lands campaign
1955	Malenkov dismissed as Prime Minister
	Warsaw Pact set up
1956	20th Party Congress
	Khrushchev's 'Secret Speech'
	Hungarian Rising crushed
	Sixth Five-Year Plan
1957	Khrushchev's proposals for decentralising the economy
	Cominform abolished
	Plot to depose Khrushchev defeated
	Kaganovich, Malenkov, Molotov, Zhukov demoted
	Launch of *Sputnik I*
1958	Bulganin demoted
	Sixth Five-Year Plan abandoned
	Agricultural and educational reforms introduced
1959	Seven-Year Plan approved
	Khrushchev visited China and USA
1960	Big reductions in Armed Forces
	Khrushchev visited India and France
	US U2 plane shot down
	Aid to China stopped
	Khrushchev walked out of UN
1961	Seventh Five-Year Plan replaced Seven-Year Plan
	Gagarin orbited the earth
	Berlin Wall erected
1962	*Cuban Missile Crisis*
1963	Poor harvest led to food imports
	Test-Ban Treaty
	Border incidents with China
1964	Khrushchev 'retired'
	Brezhnev became First Secretary
	Kosygin became Prime Minister

B *Stalin in power, 1945–53*

Stalin's attitude towards government remained rigid after the Second World War. Although post-war purges were less extensive than in the 1930s, his rule was still arbitrary. In 1949 he purged the Leningrad Party organisation. Despite its heroic defence of the city during the German siege of 1941–44, Stalin had long been suspicious of the loyalty of the Leningrad Party, and its leaders were tried and shot. Stalin's last major purge was against Russian Jews. In 1953 prominent Jewish doctors in Moscow were accused of plotting to murder Stalin and other leading Party figures. Several were arrested, although Stalin suddenly died before a large-scale purge could be implemented.

No one dared to challenge the authority of Stalin or Lavrenti Beria's Secret Police. In 1947 Stalin even began to rule without the Central Committee and the *Politburo*. At the time of Stalin's death in March 1953, millions of Soviet citizens languished in the *Gulag,* the network of labour camps across the USSR. At least one million people died during Stalin's purges between 1945 and 1953. Even so, there was mass mourning at Stalin's funeral: he had been respected as well as feared by most citizens, who had been indoctrinated with his pervasive personality cult, and who had seen in him the strong leader who had led them to victory over Germany.

Although Khrushchev criticised Stalin in a speech to his colleagues in 1956, there was no public criticism of him until 1959. In that year the new edition of the official *History of the All-Union Communist Party*, previously full of praise for Stalin, admitted that many innocent people had been purged, and it condemned his personality cult. However, it also praised his achievements and declared that, overall, Stalin's career had been of benefit to the USSR and to Communism generally.

Several official histories of the Party published after 1975 commented upon the supposed successes of Stalin's policies, but Stalin himself was not mentioned. In other Soviet history books of this period, Stalin's role was generally played down. An exception was Roy Medvedev's *Let History Judge*, published in 1971. Medvedev, a dissident, was critical of Stalin, but also insisted that many others besides Stalin were also responsible for the crimes of the Stalin era.

Western historians were often more critical of Stalin. Leonard Schapiro and Robert Conquest, writing in the 1960s, emphasised Stalin's dictatorial tendencies. Alec Nove and Martin McCauley were prepared to acknowledge Stalin's political skills, but recognised his brutality, whilst also accepting that it was too simplistic to lay all the ills of the Soviet Union at Stalin's door alone.

Assessments of Stalin were particularly painful for Russians, because they had to consider directly the extent to which their own people had assisted Stalin in his policies. The first genuine post-***glasnost*** Soviet biography of Stalin was *Stalin, Triumph and Tragedy* by Dmitri Volkogonov, published in 1988. He emphasised Stalin's 'imperfections', 'negative qualities' and 'mediocrity', which he made up for with cunning and ruthlessness.

KEY ISSUE

Why has Stalin's reputation provoked so much controversy amongst historians?

---

glasnost period of 'openness' in the mid-1980s in the USSR

C *Khrushchev, 1953–64*

KHRUSHCHEV'S RISE TO POWER

There was no obvious heir to Stalin. A collective leadership emerged after his death. Leading contenders were Malenkov, Foreign Minister Molotov, Deputy Prime Minister Bulganin, Kaganovich, Party Secretary Khrushchev, and Beria. The **KGB**'s head, Beria, who was notoriously arbitrary and ruthless, was quickly arrested and executed in December 1953: his Party colleagues agreed that the Secret Police needed to be brought more firmly under Party control, and that it was time to modify the rigid Stalinist method of government.

KGB the Soviet secret police

NIKITA KHRUSHCHEV (1894–1971)

PROFILE

Khrushchev came from a peasant background. He rose to prominence under Stalin, and was put in charge of the Ukraine in 1944. In 1949 Stalin put him in charge of the Moscow Party organisation. Ambitious for power, Khrushchev outmanouvred his colleagues in the uncertainty following Stalin's death, becoming the dominant leader by 1957. His radical attempts to improve the Soviet economy and make the Party less bureaucratic and more adventurous had mixed success. Khrushchev's risky, high-profile foreign policy also caused unrest among his colleagues: particularly the split with China, the disruption caused in the Eastern Bloc by de-Stalinisation and the climbdown over Cuba. Khrushchev's populist, sometimes crude political style also upset conservative colleagues, who secured his removal from the leadership in 1964. They claimed that he had made bad decisions, taken sole credit for Soviet achievements and ignored colleagues.

Opinions about Khrushchev have remained divided. He has been praised for ending Stalin's reign of terror. On the other hand, Khrushchev was brought up within the Stalinist system, and had no intention of releasing the grip of the Party on all aspects of life. Shortly before his death in 1971 he declared, 'My leadership was sometimes more administrative than creative. I was too concerned with restricting or prohibiting.' The British diplomat Sir Frank Roberts, British ambassador to Moscow in the early 1960s, reminisced,

> Khrushchev often reminded me of the driver of an autocar too big and heavy for his skills, too often pressing his foot down on the accelerator around dangerous bends and too often having to apply the brakes jerkily. He lacked Stalin's basic caution, so much closer to Russian traditional policies, and embarked confidently upon adventurous

> courses with attractive options without seeing clearly where they might lead him. When the risks became too great, he had to beat hasty retreats, usually skilfully conducted, but finally too trying for the nerves and patience of his colleagues.

For all the criticism of Khrushchev, some commentators believe that he left the USSR in a better state than he had found it. He himself said, immediately after his dismissal,

> Perhaps the most important thing I did was just this: that they were able to get rid of me by simply voting, whereas Stalin would have had them all arrested.

soviet local council

There was general agreement that Soviet rule should be based more on consensus than terror. Attempts were made to define the rights and duties of citizens more clearly, and to reactivate Party organs, trade unions and local *soviets*. However, this did not mean a significant liberalisation of the Soviet regime. The Party wanted to stimulate economic and social progress without relying mainly on fear. But all Party members assumed that the Communist Party should stay firmly in control. Disagreements were purely about strategies, not principles, and this, together with personal ambition, is what determined the struggle for power among the collective leadership.

Georgi Malenkov, who was Soviet Prime Minister and in charge of the State bureaucracy, wanted to shift the emphasis of economic planning towards agriculture and light industry rather than heavy industry and defence. However, this 'New Course' policy, outlined in 1953, alienated traditional Stalinists and the army. Khrushchev, who had risen by his own abilities from a poor peasant background, was a more dominant personality. He too was willing to reform within certain limits, particularly to achieve higher living standards. But he argued that this should be achieved by expanding agriculture rather than threatening the primacy of the military and heavy industry lobbies, who therefore supported him. Khrushchev was able to promote his policies though Party organs like *Pravda*.

Khrushchev proved the dominant contender by 1955. In May of that year Malenkov was replaced by Bulganin and demoted to a more minor post. Khrushchev then calmly adopted Malenkov's policies of advocating co-existence with the capitalist West and 'goulash Communism', or provision of more consumer goods.

KEY ISSUE

What was the significance of Khrushchev's policy of de-Stalinisation?

THE 'SECRET SPEECH' AND DE-STALINISATION

Khrushchev could not simply override his colleagues, but his dominance was clearly confirmed by his notorious 'Secret Speech' to the Party hierarchy at the Twentieth Congress of February 1956. Khrushchev made the first denunciation of Stalin, attacking his personality cult and responsibility for the purges, as well as other 'mistakes' he had made.

Significantly, the attack was very much a personal one, not an attack on the Party itself or the Stalinist system. Krushchev and his listeners were themselves products of that system and had carried out Stalin's policies. Nevertheless, news of the speech created shock waves: many citizens had their long-held perceptions suddenly challenged. More-over, Khrushchev initiated a policy of 'De-Stalinisation'; this included some relaxation of restrictions on artistic freedom and debate, and a new emphasis on the rule of law. Probably even more significant was the impact on other Communist regimes in Eastern and Central Europe.

Khrushchev was seen by some of his colleagues as a potential new Stalin, and he was still criticised by Malenkov's allies, known as the 'Anti-Party Group'. There were challenges to him, particularly after he began administrative reforms which reduced the authority of central ministries, and thousands of bureaucrats were forced to leave the comforts of Moscow for the provinces. The *Politburo* voted to force his resignation as Party Secretary in 1957. But Khrushchev used his support in the army and the Central Committee to overrule the *Politburo*. Malenkov, Molotov and Kaganovich were forced to resign from the government. Khrushchev then forced the resignation of the leading figure in the army, Marshal Zhukov, fearing that he might become too powerful, and also demoted Bulganin.

Khrushchev became Prime Minister as well as First Secretary, thereby heading the government as well as the Party. Yet although he was largely responsible for shaping Soviet domestic and foreign policy until 1964, he was never all-powerful and remained answerable to colleagues. He upset many by his popularist style – unlike Stalin, Khrushchev loved mixing with the people and was naturally effervescent – and when some of his policies failed, there were colleagues waiting to attack him. Khrushchev never enjoyed total command over the Party or the government machine, and to overcome resistance to reforms, his policies had to be seen to be successful. When they failed, his position eventually became untenable.

> See Chapters 4 and 6

> **KEY ISSUE**
>
> *How different was Khrushchev's method of government from that of Stalin?*

REFORM, CRITICISM AND FALL FROM POWER

Modernisation and reform required a better-educated population. Khrushchev insituted measures in 1958 to open higher education to more students from poor backgrounds. Like several of his reforms, these were largely frustrated by bureaucratic obstructionism. There were legal reforms to enforce the rule of law and reduce the list of capital offences, but no fundamental opposition to the regime was allowed. Khrushchev's attitude towards de-Stalinisation was material rather than intellectual: he had little real interest in intellectual freedom, and there was, for example, a renewal of religious persecution in the USSR, and a reduction in the number of Orthodox churches from 20 000 to 11 500 between 1955 and 1964. There were additional attacks on other churches. For Khrushchev, de-Stalinisation meant more food and consumer goods.

Khrushchev maintained a high profile, despite his criticism of Stalin's cult of personality. Therefore he inevitably attracted criticism himself when policies failed. Several policies were ultimately unsuccessful. Khrushchev's policy of 'Peaceful Co-existence' was unpopular in many quarters, and he alienated the military: although the army hierarchy had supported Khrushchev's rise to power, it disagreed with his attempts to reduce Soviet conventional forces. His climbdown in the Cuban Missiles Crisis after an adventurous challenge to American supremacy, and his failure to repair relations with China, brought about a loss of face. Just as significant was the failure of Khrushchev's economic policy: growth rates fell and food prices had to be raised in 1962, to the accompaniment of riots. His claim in October 1962 that the USSR was well on the way to overtaking the standard of living of any capitalist country seemed absurdly optimistic.

Khrushchev's standing with the Party was a particular problem. Party Secretaries found that their powers were reduced with reorganisation, and many middle-ranking bureaucrats tried to frustrate his reforms. Khrushchev also failed to keep the Central Committee packed with his own supporters.

Whilst Khrushchev was on holiday in October 1964 the *Politburo* decided to remove him. The Central Committee retired him, ostensibly on health grounds. He was allowed to live in obscurity until his death in 1971.

See page 138

KEY ISSUE

Why did Khrushchev fall from power?

D *Brezhnev, 1964–82*

Khrushchev was initially succeeded by another collective leadership: Brezhnev, Kosygin, Podgorny, Shelepin and Suslov. Leonid Brezhnev was to emerge as the front-runner. An early protegé of Khrushchev, he had built up his own power base among the 'Dnieper mafia', members of the military and the bureaucracy from the Dnieper region who supported his move against the former leader.

STYLE AND POWER BASE

In October 1964, Brezhnev was appointed First Secretary, whilst Alexei Kosygin was made Prime Minister. Podgorny became Head of State. The Central Committee decided that no one man should ever again hold both the top posts in the Party and government. Kosygin played an important role in foreign affairs, but did not have Brezhnev's strong base of support in the Party. Podgorny was soon moved into the largely honorary position of President. Brezhnev steadily amassed positions and honours, developed a cult of personality, promoted his supporters, and was widely regarded as being *the* Soviet leader by the end of the 1960s.

Brezhnev was popular with his colleagues because, unlike Khrushchev, he was regarded as predictable, moderate, and a man of consensus

LEONID BREZHNEV (1906–82)

Brezhnev came from a steel town in the Ukraine. During the 1930s he was heavily involved in the collectivisation campaign and the purges. Brezhnev's star rose along with that of his mentor, Khrushchev, but by the time of Khrushchev's fall in 1964, Brezhnev had become one of his critics.

Brezhnev became First Secretary in 1964 and was securely in charge of the USSR by 1969. He was accepted as Khrushchev's successor partly because he was seen by colleagues as cautious and 'safe'. He was adaptable enough in the early 1970s to realise that a policy of *détente* with the West was in Soviet interests. However, the most notable features of Brezhnev's rule were that:

● he presided over a period of economic decline in the 1970s. Brezhnev, in physical decline and dependent upon drugs, was unwilling and incapable of arresting the decline;

● He allowed the power of the Party to remain unchallenged, and even fossilised. Brezhnev had no original ideas and was very susceptible to the flattery which fed his natural vanity.

Brezhnev became the most decorated individual in Soviet history, but was also the butt of many Soviet jokes, for example:

> Brezhnev was rushed to hospital for emergency surgery. 'Is this it? Is he dying?' a frantic doctor asked. 'No,' a colleague replied, 'We just have to widen his ribcage. There's no more room on his chest for his medals.'

Also:

> An embarrassed secretary tells Brezhnev one day, 'Leonid Ilich, one of your shoes is blue and the other is red.' Brezhnev replies, beaming, 'And I have another pair just like these at home!'

TIMELINE

The USSR, 1964–82 (Foreign affairs are in italics)

1965 Arrest of Dissident writers Daniel and Sinyavsky
1966 Eighth Five-Year Plan (1966–70)
1968 *Invasion of Czechoslovakia*
1969 *Border clashes with China*
SALT Talks in Helsinki
1970 *Treaties with Romania, Czechoslovakia and West Germany*
1971 Ninth Five-Year Plan (1971–75)
1972 *Nixon first USA President to visit USSR*
1973 *Brezhnev visited West Germany and USA*
1974 Expulsion of Solzhenitsyn
Presidents Nixon and Ford visited USSR
1975 *Joint USA–Soviet space flight*
Helsinki Agreements signed
1976 Tenth Five-Year Plan (1976–80)
1977 Brezhnev became Head of State
Brezhnev Constitution
1978 Trial of Dissidents Orlov, Scharansky and Ginsburg
1979 *SALT II Treaty signed*
Invasion of Afghanistan
1980 Retirement of Kosygin
1981 Eleventh Five-Year Plan (1981–85)
1982 Death of Brezhnev
Andropov elected First Secretary

who would not rock the boat. But he also secured his own position by promoting trusted colleagues into the *Politburo* and other key positions. For example, Yuri Andropov was made Head of the KGB in 1967 to ensure Party control over it, whilst Marshal Grechko, a Brezhnev supporter, was made Minister of Defence. Rivals were quietly pushed into the background, and the bulk of the Party was content because it was reassured by Brezhnev's conservative approach. Brezhnev was referred to as General Secretary from 1966, and remained securely in control until his death eighteen years later. Only when it was clear that he was dying did former colleagues begin to intrigue over the succession.

Kosygin's reputation suffered from a failed attempt to reform the economy in 1966, and an unpopular move to promote some decentralisation in the bureaucracy. Meanwhile, Brezhnev was strong enough to ignore the earlier constraints imposed by the Central Committee and by becoming President in 1970, once again combined leadership of the Party and State machines. The Party showed signs of stagnation, and whilst the men at the top grew older, the rate at which new recruits joined the Party declined. The Party increasingly became the haven for careerists and those on the make, rather than the home of the ideologically committed. Shortly before Brezhnev's death the entire *Politburo* and Secretariat were re-elected without change, whilst members of his family were promoted to high positions, and in some cases were involved in corruption.

KEY ISSUE

Why was Brezhnev's period in power a 'time of stagnation'?

'DEVELOPED SOCIALISM' AND DECLINE

In 1971 Brezhnev confidently proclaimed 'Developed Socialism', which seemed safer than Khrushchev's rash prediction that the USSR would have become a prosperous, classless, Communist society by 1980. In reality Brezhnev's rule was a time of economic, political and social stagnation. Much-needed reforms were not implemented, and there were even strict limits on what could be discussed. For example, although many experts realised that the system of subsidising prices was expensive and inefficient, no one dared face the social discontent that might follow its abandonment. Statistics were frequently distorted to hide unpleasant truths, particularly about the economy. Since the standard of living of many citizens did gradually rise, it was relatively easy in an authoritarian society to ignore the worrying underlying trend of a drastic decline in growth.

Brezhnev tried to leave his own mark on the USSR by introducing a new constitution in 1977. The country was declared to be a Socialist State, in which the Communist Party was the 'leading and guiding force'. Human rights were guaranteed. In reality, the regime strengthened its hold on the people. Police powers were increased, and any criticism of the Soviet system was regarded at the very best as anti-social, at worst as deviancy or outright treachery. A campaign against dissidents began with the trial of the writers Sinyavsky and Daniel in 1965. The Soviet government endorsed the Helsinki Accord on Human Rights in 1975, but critics of the regime were harshly treated. Many were held in mental institutions. The Nobel prizewinner Andrei Sakharov, the scientist Yuri Orlov and the writer Andrei Ginzberg were harrassed. Many Russian Jews who wished to emigrate to Israel were prevented from leaving. However, most Soviet citizens regarded the activities of dissidents with indifference or contempt, and were much less interested than the outside world in their fate.

Brezhnev's health and dominance began to decline in the late 1970s. Decisions were increasingly delegated to members of the *Politburo*, and Brezhnev's close supporter and confidant Konstantin Chernenko, already an old man himself, was groomed for the succession. But a

PICTURE 8
*Top Soviet military on
parade*

struggle for power was under way before Brezhnev's death in November 1982.

Many jokes about Brezhnev circulated in the USSR during his lifetime, but there was also respect, particularly since the major problems which the country faced were not publicised. However, after his death Brezhnev's memory was strongly attacked: he was the man, who, wishing for stability, had done little to realise the aspirations of the people for more freedoms and material benefits, and who had operated a propaganda machine and a personality cult almost as pervasive as in Stalin's day.

E *Andropov and Chernenko, 1982–85*

ANDROPOV: THE BEGINNINGS OF REFORM

Brezhnev's successors were both old and sick men when they took power, but their brief period of office was important for the future direction of the USSR.

After Brezhnev's death, Yuri Andropov, Head of the KGB, was quickly appointed General Secretary. The process was managed by the *Politburo*, not the Central Committee, and the military and KGB threw their weight behind Andropov. The designated heir, Chernenko, was sidelined for the time being.

Andropov was an austere, relatively unknown figure, who was wrongly thought in the West to have liberal leanings. With access to accurate KGB information about the true state of affairs at home and abroad, he was certainly better informed than most people in the USSR. Unlike Brezhnev therefore, he was prepared to criticise the short-comings of the Soviet bureaucracy and economy. He was realistic enough to want reform, although he was as ruthless as his predecessors in dealing with dissent: Sakharov was exiled to Gorky on his orders.

KEY ISSUE

How important to internal developments in the USSR was the period of power of Andropov and Chernenko?

TIMELINE

The USSR, 1983–91 (Foreign affairs are in italics)

1983 *Korean airliner shot down*
1984 Death of Andropov
Chernenko elected General Secretary
1985 Twelfth Five-Year Plan (1985–90)
Death of Chernenko
Gorbachev elected General Secretary
1986 Gorbachev called for glasnost and perestroika
Explosion of Chernobyl nuclear reactor
1987 Nationalist riots and demonstrations
Supreme Soviet approved economic restructuring
1988 Steps towards a market economy
Withdrawal from Afghanistan began
Serious Nationalist outbreaks
Moscow summit with Reagan
1989 Big cuts in military budget
Serious Nationalist outbreaks
Major changes in Communist states of Eastern Europe
Gorbachev elected Chairman of Supreme Soviet

Andropov moved quickly against Brezhnev's supporters at all levels of the Party and government. He was supported in this by long-serving Foreign Minister Gromyko. Andropov's most important contribution as General Secretary was to promote a number of younger, more vigorous supporters who were to play a key role in Soviet politics: Nikolai Ryzkhov was put in charge of a new economic programme; Grigori Romanov was put in charge of heavy industry; and Mikhail Gorbachev, an expert on agriculture, was soon to become the Number Two.

Andropov's watchwords were discipline and reform. He inveighed against slackness and ill-discipline in the workplace, and the police were sent into the streets to round up absentees from work. More power to make decisions was delegated to factory managers, and wages were linked more closely to production. The realist Andropov declared that the USSR was only just at the beginning of the stage of developed Socialism! He was also unbending in his attitude towards foreign affairs. This was particularly noticeable when in August 1983 a Korean Airlines passenger airliner which had strayed deep into Soviet air space was shot down with large loss of life, provoking vociferous foreign condemnation.

Andropov was too ill to enjoy power for long. He died in February 1984 before much had been changed, and before he had encountered the full weight of opposition which always confronted reformers in the USSR. Yet Andropov had provided two vital services: he had given hope to those people who did want change, and he had promoted younger colleagues who were to be the nucleus of the next generation of reformers.

THE CHERNENKO INTERREGNUM

Some Kremlin officials claimed that Andropov had nominated Gorbachev as his successor. However, the Brezhnev old guard secured the promotion of their candidate, Chernenko. The younger Gorbachev was prepared to wait his turn, and there may have been some sort of agreement that he would eventually succeed the old and ailing Chernenko.

Chernenko was certain to follow the cautious policies of his mentor Brezhnev: he was not known for originality and had no strong power base of his own. He was not an inspiring leader, and Russians joked that 'You can't have a personality cult without a personality.' Chernenko accepted the importance of some reform but also emphasised the need to 'Look before you leap.'

During Chernenko's thirteen months in office there were very few personnel changes at the top. His government was a coalition of Andropov and Brezhnev supporters. The drive against corruption continued, but plans to reform the bureaucracy were shelved. There was no coherent domestic programme, only a declared intention to improve education, and a determination to uphold the Soviet system against dissident criticism. In foreign affairs Chernenko reverted to

Brezhnev's policy of *détente*, which had taken a battering during the Andropov regime.

The leadership issue remained unresolved. There were tensions in the relations between politicians and the army command over military strategy and defence spending. It was also implicitly recognised that Gorbachev was Chernenko's deputy. Gromyko threw his weight behind Gorbachev, and his accession to power was relatively smooth when Chernenko finally died in March 1985. Gorbachev had the support of the Andropov faction, the KGB, and those elements in the administration that did want reform.

F *Gorbachev, 1985–91*

Gorbachev came to power with high hopes of reform, but his tenure of power effectively led to the break-up of the USSR and a collapse of his own reputation within Russia. Gorbachev believed firmly that reform was essential, but also that the Communist Party should remain in control of the process. He wanted the system to work better, not to overthrow it. His period in office saw optimism turn to disillusion.

1990 Serious Nationalist outbreaks
Elections in Soviet Republics
Peace Agreement between NATO and Warsaw Pact
Some Republics declared independence
Gorbachev appointed President of USSR
Agreement on German unification
Yeltsin elected President of Russian Federation
Gorbachev re-elected General Secretary
1991 August *coup*
Establishment of CIS, resignation of Gorbachev
End of the USSR

MIKHAIL GORBACHEV (B. 1931)

PROFILE

Gorbachev came from a peasant family in the Caucasus. He studied law and became a Party expert on agriculture. He was promoted along with his mentor Andropov and was declared General Secretary in 1985 following Chernenko's death. Gorbachev was the first Soviet leader not to have played a role in the Second World War and whose political career was principally in the post-Stalin years, although his apprenticeship had been shaped within the existing system. At fifty-four he was a young leader by Soviet standards. He was the first leader to attempt to reform both the Soviet economy and society through *glasnost* and **perestroika**. Gorbachev also sought a new accomodation with the West and the end of the Cold War. However, the reforms upset conservatives within the Party. More radical reformers like Boris Yeltsin complained that the reforms did not go far enough, particularly in not reducing the monopolistic role of the Communist Party and not moving quickly to a free market economy. Gorbachev still believed that the Party had an important role. He underestimated the destructive effect of ethnic tensions and many of his reforms were too little and too late. It is doubtful anyway whether the system inherited from Stalin could have been reformed from above, and it was incompatible with genuine democracy. Perhaps Gorbachev's

perestroika
restructuring, especially of the economy

own uncertainty was summed up by a Soviet joke current in 1990:

> Gorbachev tells Congress that he wants to change the seating: 'Let all those who want capitalism sit on the right, the rest on the left.' After everyone else has taken their new places, one deputy is still hesitating. Gorbachev asks him what the matter is. 'I believe in socialism but I want to live under capitalism,' the unhappy deputy replies. 'Come and join me on the platform then', responds Gorbachev.

Although Gorbachev survived the *coup* of 1991, the break-up of the Soviet Union signalled his own demise as leader. Ironically, his reputation as a relatively youthful, committed reformer won him a much higher reputation outside his country than within it, where he was widely regarded as weak, and even worse, a failure. When Gorbachev stood for the Russian presidency in June 1996 he received only 0.5 per cent of the votes.

GLASNOST AND PERESTROIKA

KEY ISSUE

What were glasnost *and* perestroika, *and how significant were they?*

What was new about Gorbachev's approach was that he recognised not only the need for economic reform if the decline in the Soviet economy were to be reversed, but he also appreciated that this could not be achieved without a significant change in attitudes. His policies were based on the twin premises of *glasnost* (openness) and *perestroika* (reconstruction). He believed that the USSR could learn from other systems whilst retaining the best of its own.

Like earlier Soviet leaders, Gorbachev had first to consolidate his position as General Secretary by promoting his own supporters and removing his rivals. He was supported by Gromyko, who in nominating Gorbachev as General Secretary referred to his 'brilliant analysis and decision making in both domestic and foreign policy'. Gorbachev promoted three supporters to full *Politburo* membership in April 1985: Yegor Ligachev, put in charge of Ideology, Ryzhkov, and Victor Chebrikov, Head of the KGB. His rivals included Romanov and Victor Grishkin, the Moscow Party boss. Romanov was soon demoted, and Gorbachev was further strengthened by the promotion of Eduard Shevardnadze as foreign minister to succeed the retiring Gromyko. Ryzhkov became Prime Minister in September 1985, and at the end of the year Boris Yeltsin replaced Grishkin.

As Gorbachev strengthened his support at the highest levels, so there was a drastic purge lower down: between 1986 and 1989 all the Republican First Secretaries were replaced, along with more than half of Party officials at district and city level. Over half the Central Committee were new members. Gorbachev seemed relaxed and confident, representative of a new breed of Soviet politicians who were well-educated and comfortable with the media. His reputation blossomed, particularly abroad.

As part of *glasnost*, people were encouraged to voice their opinions about official shortcomings, since Gorbachev felt that reform depended upon an acknowledgement of incompetence and corruption. In contrast, his conservative opponents believed that such openness encouraged social instability. The new attitude took some time to take root: when the Chernobyl nuclear reactor suffered a disastrous meltdown in April 1986, the Soviet media was reluctant to reveal the facts for several days.

Many victims of Stalinist repression were rehabilitated, and censorship was relaxed. The works of banned writers such as Boris Pasternak and Alexander Solzhenitsyn were published in the USSR for the first time. Newspapers and television began to discuss previously taboo subjects such as drugs. However, this was less important to ordinary people than continuing shortages in the shops. Gorbachev himself became less tolerant as criticism of his own policies grew, and in 1990 all media had to be registered with the authorities.

Gorbachev saw *glasnost* as essential to the success of his other major innovation – *perestroika*, or reconstruction. In 1985 and 1986 Gorbachev still hoped to make the existing economic system work better, and believed that one way was to give more initiative to key figures like factory managers. The Soviet economy was ailing, and suffering from long-term deficiences in planning and the attempts to keep up with the United States in military and economic terms. Like Khrushchev before him, Gorbachev faced obstructionism and resistance from those in the lower tiers of the administration whose efforts were necessary for success, and he faced either apathy from ordinary people, or disillusionment when the reforms were seen not to be having an immediate effect.

See pages 130 and 134

Gorbachev faced a dilemma. He would not accept the radical solution of a transition to a market economy. But having told the Central Committee in January 1987 that the economy and society were in 'crisis', he concluded that political reform was essential if any economic reforms were to work. By political reform he meant a degree of democratisation, including genuinely competitive elections at local and Republican level – although he still believed that the Communist Party would remain in control and that Socialism would remain in place.

> ### KEY ISSUE
>
> *What difficulties did Gorbachev encounter in trying to reform the USSR, and why?*

GROWING DIFFICULTIES

In 1987 there were experiments with multi-candidate elections, and elections to a new Congress were held in 1989. By Western liberal standards they were not democratic elections: hundreds of seats were reserved for organisations such as the Communist Party, which was allocated 100, and for districts and nationality areas. 2884 candidates contested 1500 constituencies. 87 per cent of the elected candidates were Communist Party members, more than in the pre-reformed system, whilst the number of female representatives was halved to 17 per cent. It was not an auspicious beginning to political reform. Gorbachev himself was elected to the new post of Chairman of the

Supreme Soviet in May 1989. Ironically, as his hold on the Party strengthened, the Party's influence actually declined: there was a loss of faith in the Party, particularly amongst the young. Power was passing from the Party to other institutions like the Presidency, but these institutions had few roots in a country which had never enjoyed genuine democracy. There was also considerable opposition to *perestroika* from middle-ranking bureaucrats and managers who were being expected to be more accountable. There were fears of unemployment and price rises. The future looked uncertain, particularly when in 1990 Gorbachev was given emergency powers to ban strikes, demonstrations and publications, and could even impose 'temporary presidential rule' over Republics or regions. Severe restrictions placed on the production and sale of alcohol in an attempt to improve health and curb absenteeism brought Gorbachev more unpopularity than any other measure.

Gorbachev later admitted that once having accepted the need for change, he should have committed himself to more radical reform much earlier, but he was faced with tackling powerful institutions like the Party and the bureaucracy firmly as well as changing popular attitudes. He was increasingly caught in the middle between those who wanted him to commit the government to more radical reform, particularly on the economic front, and those who felt that he had gone too far already.

In March 1990 an executive Presidency was established, with the intention of providing strong government to fill the vacuum left by the declining authority of the Party. Gorbachev was elected by the Congress, but in future the President would be chosen by universal suffrage. He held considerable power on paper, including the right to nominate holders of important State positions, the right to head a new Council of the fifteen Republican Presidents, a decision-making body, and the right to head a new Security Council responsible for defence. The first Prime Minister, Valentin Pavlov, was elected in January 1991 and was accountable to the President.

In practice, Gorbachev's power was much less impressive. Both the Congress and the Supreme Soviet called for his resignation, and the Republican governments increasingly ignored federal decrees. But Gorbachev's power, and indeed the future of the entire federation, faced much more serious challenges in the shape of growing nationalist discontent in the Republics.

Nationalist feeling had been brutally suppressed by Stalin, who was even prepared to shift entire national groups around the USSR to lessen the possibility of a serious threat to federal stability. Under his successors one of the tasks of the Communist Party in the various Republics had been to foster a 'Soviet' mentality over local patriotism. As the authority of the Party declined, so outbreaks of ethnic or nationalist discontent became more threatening, a situation scarcely foreseen when Gorbachev came to power. Discontent in the Baltic States led to independence. More violent outbreaks occurred elsewhere. In 1988 Armenians and Azeris killed each other in the disputed area of

Nagorno-Karabakh, ceded to Azerbaidzhan in 1921. Nationalist outbreaks in Georgia were brutally put down in April 1989. There were more killings in Uzbekistan.

Nationalism became a major force in the Russian Republic itself. Some Russians were prepared for the break-up of the Union, but others, such as members of the right-wing organisation *SOYUZ* ('Union') were determined to maintain it. Conflicting political views came to a head in Republican and local elections held in Russia in March 1990. Many new parties were set up, covering all shades of the political spectrum. One of the largest reforming parties was the Bloc of Democratic Russia. The Soviet Communist Party of Bolsheviks claimed to be the successors of the old Communist Party. There were several parties on the Right, the most extreme being the Liberal Democratic Party led by Vladimir Zhirinovsky. Most of the parties had no roots, a fragile organisational base, and political allegiances constantly shifted. Gorbachev himself faced a growing challenge to his authority from Boris Yeltsin. Yeltsin was elected President of the Russian Parliament in May 1990, and the Parliament began to pass laws which conflicted with Union legislation.

Gorbachev's dilemma was this: should he try to preserve the Union by force, or cede sovereignty to the Republics? Yeltsin was more decisive: he realised that he could not dictate policy for the whole Union from the centre, and was prepared to cede sovereignty, although his supporters hoped that the Union would be succeeded by some kind of loose confederation.

A draft Union Treaty was published in November 1990 and was followed in March 1991 by a national referendum, called after the Georgian parliament declared its independence. The question was a loaded one: 'Do you consider it necessary to preserve the Union of Soviet Socialist Republics as a renewed federation of equal sovereign republics, in which the rights and freedoms of an individual of any nationality will be fully guaranteed?'

The result was a resounding success for Gorbachev in some places where the referendum was administered, but the result was incon-clusive in Russia itself, and the Baltic Republics, Georgia, Armenia and Moldavia refused to administer it at all. Gorbachev decided, with Yeltsin's support, to sign the new Union Treaty with the other nine republics. But his idea of a loose confederation with the Republics controlling their own internal security, economic resources and the media, satisfied neither Nationalists seeking independence nor conservatives, who were wedded to the old federal structure.

COUP AND BREAK-UP OF THE UNION

It was the conservatives who moved against Gorbachev. The final straw for them was an apparent move against the Party itself. By 1990 there were competitive elections for some Party offices for the first time, and a reduction in Party posts and personnel. The conservatives had been on the defensive and had no particularly coherent programme, but they were able to play on the fears of ordinary people who were alarmed at

See pages 321–3

KEY ISSUE

What threats to the USSR were posed by the development of nationalism?

KEY ISSUE

*What were the causes
and consequences of the
coup against
Gorbachev?*

the collapse of the *rouble*, price rises and more shortages in the shops. The conservatives also knew that if the Union Treaty were implemented, their own bases of power in the army and the Party would be eroded. They were also threatened by Yeltsin's activities. He banned the formation of Communist cells in all Russian enterprises, and then in the June 1991 Russian presidential election he secured 57.3 per cent of the votes, ahead of rivals who included Ryzhkov and Zhirinovsky. Ironically, the vote was also seen as a protest against Gorbachev's failed reforms and against the conservative Congress of People's Deputies, seen as unrepresentative of the popular mood.

On 18 August 1991 Gorbachev's enemies acted. Whilst he was on holiday in the Crimea, a group which included his Vice-President Gennadi Yanaev put him under house arrest and formed a 'State Emergency Committee' in Moscow. The Committee declared itself to be in power, with the aim of saving Russia from disaster. All the plotters were Gorbachev appointees, and included the Prime Minister, the Ministers of Defence and Internal Affairs, and the Head of the KGB. Armed units surrounded the Russian Parliament building in Moscow.

The *coup* was defeated by the heroism of Yeltsin and ordinary people who refused to be cowed, by the fact that some younger elements in the army and KGB would not support the plotters, and by the indecision and lack of real planning by the plotters themselves. On 20 August some of the wavering plotters defected and fled. Other leaders were arrested. Three days after the *coup* began, Gorbachev was brought back to Moscow as a free man.

Even then Gorbachev acted indecisively and lost his last chance to retain power. Although almost every member of Gorbachev's cabinet had been implicated in the *coup*, Gorbachev continued to declare his faith in the discredited Communist Party. He was publically criticised in the Russian Parliament, and only then did he reluctantly agree that his government should resign. Yeltsin suspended the operations of the Communist Party in the Russian Federation, and the Supreme Soviet did the same for the entire USSR.

Ironically, the plotters had unwittingly hastened the destruction of the Union. Immediately after the *coup*, several Republics declared their independence. The secession of the Ukraine in December 1991 effectively killed off any hopes of retaining a Union of sorts: the Ukraine was the second largest nation in the USSR, and was responsible for half the agricultural products and over one-fifth of the industrial output of the USSR. In the same month Russia, the Ukraine, and Belorussia formed the Commonwealth of Independent States (CIS), soon to be joined by other Republics. Howwever, it was a loose organisation without a parliament or presidency. There were many practical problems to be resolved if the new structure were to be viable.

The redundant Gorbachev resigned the Presidency of the old Union on Christmas Day 1991. The focus of power in Russia had shifted to Yeltsin. Yeltsin's problems were only just beginning. In many of the other Republics, old leaders continued in office, albeit sometimes with renamed parties, and they continued to run authoritarian regimes.

MAP 9

The Russian Federation, following the break-up of the Union in 1991, and its neighbours

Gorbachev had found that once he had embarked upon serious reform, he could not control the process, and expectations turned to disillusionment. The world's first Marxist state had collapsed, and the new era beginning for its constituent parts was fraught with political and economic difficulties.

> **KEY ISSUE**
>
> *Was Gorbachev ultimately a failure?*

Was Gorbachev a failure?

ANALYSIS

Following the break-up of the USSR, historians began to put Gorbachev's career into perspective and to consider his responsibility for events. Whilst most commentators believe that some kind of dramatic transformation of the Soviet Union was almost inevitable, verdicts on Gorbachev's role in the process have generally been unfavourable.

There have been positive comments about Gorbachev. It is generally accepted that he was a reformer, and he did at least prepare the ground for the beginnings of democracy. He took over a declining superpower and tried to manage the difficult transition to a post-Communist society; and for all the problems, the USSR did not suffer the fate of Yugoslavia when it split into its constituent parts. In his foreign policy Gorbachev helped to end the Cold War confrontation and reach an accommodation with the West.

However, negative comments have increasingly outweighed the positive ones. Gorbachev's policies effectively killed off the USSR and lost him his power, neither of which he intended. Gorbachev began positively, leading the movement for *perestroika*. Unfortunately, there were serious flaws in his approach, which reflected the fact that Gorbachev was stronger at short-term tactical manoeuvring than constructing long-term strategic policies. Were there fundamental flaws in *perestroika*? The first reforms centred on the economy, attempting to make management more effective and the workforce more motivated and productive. However, other fundamental problems were not addressed: for example the State remained the dominant force in the economy. The government tried to both increase investment and improve living standards, which were contradictory goals in a declining economy. There was not enough commitment to reform from enough people, particularly in the lower ranks of the Party. The reforms only worsened shortages and increased budget deficits and inflation. Gorbachev hesitated between all-out reform on the one hand, which would have included transition to a market economy and doing away with the leading role of the Party, and moderate tinkering with the economy on the other hand. He succeeded in alienating both radicals and conservatives. By appearing to reduce the monopoly of power for so long enjoyed by the Party, Gorbachev was undermining the one institution that, however inefficiently, had held the system together; and he could offer nothing coherent in its place.

These judgements may seem harsh: the most dangerous time for any authoritarian society is when reforms begin and expectations are raised, and Gorbachev was not responsible for the problems which had arisen in the Soviet economy and society in the decades before 1985. However, Gorbachev began to lose his grip once the initial reforms failed. This was partly due to his own failings: he did not give enough attention to basic administrative details and did not manage his colleagues well. He showed naivety, for example in assuming of the 1991 plotters that because he had appointed them to high posts, they would automatically remain loyal to him. He underestimated the strength of nationalist feeling and failed to anticipate the rise in ethnic tension as control from Moscow weakened. As it became evident that the economic reforms were not working and that resentment was rising, Gorbachev moved to the right from 1989 – shown, for example, in his attempts in 1990 to bully Lithuania into staying in the Union. When the Union began to break up, he had no alternative policies left.

Therefore, the verdicts of historians on Gorbachev have tended to be harsh. John Keep refers to errors such as the undermining of financial stability through overspending, the underestimating of ethnic tensions and the refusal to make the transition to a free market. He asserts, 'All these miscalculations were rooted in a failure to appreciate the true nature of the Soviet political system, which, being totalitarian, was held together ultimately by coercion and mendacious propaganda.' (J. Keep, *Last of the Empires*, OUP, 1995). According to Martin McCauley, 'Gorbachev had difficulty in assessing the consequences of his actions, perhaps his most serious shortcoming.' (M. McCauley, *Gorbachev*, Longman, 1998). According to Robert Service, '*Glasnost* and *perestroika* were undermining the political and economic foundations of the Soviet order. Localism, nationalism, corruption, illegal private profiteering and distrust of official authority: all these phenomena, which had grown unchecked under the rule of Brezhnev, had been reinforced by the dismantlement of central controls undertaken by Gorbachev.' (R. Service, *A History of Twentieth Century Russia*, Allen Lane, 1997).

However, most historians concede that reforming the old USSR was an almost impossible task. McCauley's judgement is that

> Gorbachev's lasting legacy is that he led his people out of the kingdom of certainty into the kingdom of uncertainty. They thereby ceased to be prisoners of an inevitable future. Uncertainty then made them free … Gorbachev gave them something precious, the right to think and manage their lives for themselves.

2 ↬ ECONOMIC HISTORY

A *The Stalinist legacy*

During the 1930s the USSR had been transformed by Stalin into the first centrally planned and directed economy in the modern world. The intention had been to turn a relatively backward agricultural economy into a modern industrial power in the space of a few years, since it was assumed by Marxists that Socialism must be based upon industrialisation.

There were two main prongs to Stalin's approach. One was collectivisation: the replacement of small individually-owned farms by large collective farms, whose prime duty was to supply cheap food to the State. Collectivisation was a brutal process, but the State secured a relatively secure supply of cheap food, which was necessary in order to fulfil the other part of the economic transformation, industrialisation. However, the total quantity of food was never enough to meet all Soviet needs.

Industrialisation was achieved by means of five-year plans, begun in 1928. The State Planning Agency, *GOSPLAN*, determined targets for each industry. Each individual enterprise was given targets, and was allocated resources. The State, not the market, determined priorities: these were investment in capital or production goods such as steel, coal, cement, machine tools and military equipment. Consumer goods were given a low priority. The population was exhorted to make sacrifices and put up with shortages for the sake of a better future. Labour discipline was draconian, and targets were everything.

Industrialisation, like collectivisation, produced enormous economic and social disruption, and not all targets were met. But the economic results were also impressive: huge increases in output in many industries, and the USSR hauled itself into the position of being a leading economic power. In the space of a decade the USSR became strong enough to withstand the strains of a major war between 1941 and 1945.

The post-war years under Stalin were devoted to rebuilding the economy. Collective or State-run farms were re-established in recovered territories, and factories and railways were rebuilt. The population was called upon to make yet more huge sacrifices. Between 1945 and 1950 much of the wartime damage was repaired. However, there were some worrying signs for the Soviet economy: in particular, although some numerical targets were met, there was no significant increase in productivity, and targets relating to agricultural output and the standard of living could not be fulfilled.

The Soviet approach of determining targets, allocating resources and directing labour had initially proved successful in producing a rapid increase in output, because the economy was developing from a primitive economic base. But it was a system based upon quantity, not quality. Managers were concerned only to meet quantitative targets, and if this were to be achieved at the expense of quality, so be it. Managers were disinclined to show initiative or to take risks, since production might be adversely affected. A huge bureaucracy, containing its own internal conflicts over priorities, often made unrealistic demands. As the years of Stalinist terror receded, labour discipline became more difficult to enforce. Workers had few incentives to work hard, except at the end of the month when targets had to be fulfilled. There was officially no unemployment, and many enterprises were over-staffed. On collective farms, peasants put more effort into cultivating their small household plots than into working in the fields, and by Western European standards agricultural yields were low.

The command economy proved inflexible in meeting the needs of a more sophisticated economy in which greater quality was necessary, and in which consumers had increasing expectations. And yet reform was difficult: any suggestion of introducing free market mechanisms was anathema to Communists, who believed that this would mean a return to capitalism and a class-ridden society. And as with political reform, there was a vast bureaucracy of inertia and entrenched opposition to any major change.

> ## KEY ISSUE
>
> *How had Stalin changed the USSR economically?*

> ## KEY ISSUE
>
> *What were the main features of the 'command economy'?*

B *Agriculture*

Soviet farms were of two types. The majority were large collectives. Members of the collective made deliveries to the State at prices determined by the State, and after various other demands had been fulfilled, the remaining proceeds went to the members of the collective. Other farms were directly State-owned and run, and the farm workers were paid a wage by the State.

Agricultural yields remained poor, despite increasing mechanisation. Successive Soviet regimes attempted to improve motivation and output, with limited success. Khrushchev put considerable faith into raising production levels, and promoted the Virgin Lands project between 1953 and 1955. Huge areas of undeveloped land in Kazakhstan and Western Siberia were ploughed up for the first time. State farms were created in these areas, and elsewhere many collective farms, or *Kolkhozes*, were converted into State farms. The number of collective farms was almost halved.

The results of Khrushchev's reforms were mixed. State farms, which were created around large cities, where there was a large market close to hand, did particularly well. Up to 1958 farm incomes rose, and farms began to acquire their own machinery after motor tractor stations, which had previously hired out their services, were abolished. However, in the Virgin Lands the results were frequently unsuccessful: drought and erosion caused poor harvests. The Soviet grain harvest rose from 85 million tons in 1954 to 103 million in 1955 and 125 million in 1956, but fell back to 102 million in 1957. Figures were not much higher by the mid-1960s. Attempts to promote intensive farming by the use of mineral fertilisers and irrigation produced limited benefits. Ambitious targets – such as the trebling of meat production in the Sixth Five-Year Plan – could not be met, although tax incentives were given to peasants, past *Kolkhoz* debts were written off, and more flexibility was given to farm managers. One of the problems for the regime was that rural conditions were generally poorer than those in the overcrowded towns, so that younger men in particular, having completed their military service, preferred to migrate to the cities. Other peasants were denied internal passports and could therefore not move freely within the USSR. Collective farm workers lagged behind urban workers in terms of pensions and other benefits.

Agricultural failure was to be an important factor in Khrushchev's downfall. Special campaigns, such as promoting the cultivation of maize, failed. When the harvest failed badly, as it did in 1963, large amounts of grain had to be bought from the West, making a mockery of Khrushchev's claims that the USSR was becoming a land of plenty.

KEY ISSUE

What was the impact of Khrushchev's agricultural reforms?

	1972	1973	1974	1975	1976	1977	1978	1979
Grain harvest (million tons)	168	222.5	196	140	224	195.5	237	179

TABLE 13
Soviet grain harvest, 1972–79

Brezhnev continued the broad outlines of Khrushchev's policies in agriculture. His 'New Deal' of 1965 raised crop prices and wages in an attempt to give the peasants an incentive to produce more. The policy of amalgamating collective farms and converting many into State farms was continued, and investment in agriculture was increased. The USSR subsidised agriculture more than any other Great Power: the percentage of investment in agriculture increased from 22 per cent of the State's total investment in 1970 to 27 per cent in 1977. Yet agriculture, which in Brezhnev's day employed 22 per cent of the working population, contributed only 17 per cent of National Income. The grain harvest continued to fluctuate wildly, as Table 13 shows.

In 1981 peasants finally acquired the right to internal passports, and the government began to encourage *Kolkhoz* markets at which peasants could sell their own food at free market prices. Collective farmworkers did better in some areas than others. For example, in the Baltic Republics they earned up to double the all-Union average. State farms were even ordered to provide farmers with breeding stock, feed, machinery and credit for use on their private plots. It was a tacit admission that the State sector could not supply Soviet needs without the support of private enterprise and foreign grain imports. But for ideological reasons no one as yet drew the conclusion that collective or State-run farming, the basis of Soviet agricultural practice since the end of the 1930s, was fundamentally inefficient. Measures such as the 1982 'Food Programme' which created large agro-industrial administrations at district and regional levels to coordinate the production, transport, storage and processing of food, simply meant more bureaucracy.

Gorbachev had been given responsibility for agriculture by Brezhnev, and he continued to seek improvements when in power. He created a 'Superministry' to carry out strategic planning in agriculture. The planned increase in agricultural output for 1986–90 was an annual average of 2.7 per cent, but from 1987 onwards this figure was never approached, despite the fact that government investment in agriculture continued at a high level.

Eventually market-style reforms were introduced. Privately-owned businesses and cooperatives were permitted, and farmers were allowed to lease land from the State. However, bureaucratic obstructionism and outright opposition prevented these initiatives from redressing an ailing agricultural sector. There was always a regular supply of food to the State, but never enough in return for the investment put into agriculture, and never enough to make the USSR independent of foreign imports.

> ### KEY ISSUE
>
> *How did Soviet agriculture fare under Brezhnev and Gorbachev?*

C *Industry*

See pages 127–8

The basic characteristics of the Soviet industrial economy outlined earlier continued in their essentials under Stalin's successors: centralised planning and target-setting; central allocation of resources; priority to capital investment and defence spending. The faults generated by this system, such as lack of interministerial coordination, wasteful duplication, low quality goods, low productivity, the hoarding of labour and scarce resources, also continued. The five-year plans, although thoroughly prepared and frequently revised, rarely achieved their targets.

Khrushchev's policies involved some decentralisation in order to provide more incentive for initiative at a lower level of management, but his attempts to rationalise the command economy also led to new layers of bureaucracy. In 1955, *GOSPLAN* was divided into a State Committee for long-term planning (still called *GOSPLAN*) and a State Economic Commission for current planning. Khrushchev also created Regional Economic Councils with general control over enterprises in particular regions.

The Sixth Five-Year Plan was replaced by a Seven-Year Plan (1959–65), with an emphasis on accelerating particular sections of the economy such as cement, and increasing investment in the less developed Eastern regions of the USSR. The degree of success varied. According to Soviet sources, the output of producers' goods almost doubled between 1958 and 1965, whilst the output of consumer goods increased by 60 per cent. Output of steel almost doubled, output of oil and electricity more than doubled. The size of the workforce increased by almost 50 per cent. However, all Soviet statistics have to be treated with caution, since it was admitted in the post-Soviet era that they were subject to doctoring for propaganda purposes or to cover up deficiencies. Also crude statistics give no indication of quality. One historian noted how supply and production requirements often did not mesh:

> Steel sheet was made too heavy because the plan was in tons, and acceptance of orders from customers for thin sheet threatened plan fulfilment. Road transport vehicles made useless journeys to fulfil plans in ton-kilometres. Khrushchev himself quoted the examples of heavy chandeliers (plans in tons), and over-large sofas made by the furniture industry (the easiest way of fulfilling plans in roubles). New designs or new methods were avoided, because the resultant temporary disruption of established practices would threaten the fulfilment of quantitative output targets.
>
> A. Nove, *An Economic History of the USSR* (Penguin, 1972)

KEY ISSUE

How successful were Khrushchev's industrial policies?

Khrushchev's tinkering with the planning system never challenged its fundamentals. Although the Regional Councils, many of which were merged in 1963, determined the use of investment funds, key commodities were still allocated centrally. In 1962 Khrushchev also split the Party into agricultural and industrial wings in an attempt to promote specialisation and efficiency. These administrative changes produced more grumblings from within the Party than positive

	1950	1960	1970
Electricity (milliard kWhs)	91.2	292.3	740
Oil (million tons)	37.9	147.9	353
Steel (million tons)	27.3	65.3	116
Coal (million tons)	261.1	509.6	624
Cement (million tons)	10.2	45.5	95.2
Machine tools (thousands)	70.6	155.9	240
Motor vehicles (thousands)	362.9	523.6	916
Tractors (thousands)	116.7	238.5	459
Television sets (thousands)	11.9	1726	6700
Leather footwear (million pairs)	203	419	676

TABLE 14

Industrial progress in the USSR, 1950–70

(Data from Soviet sources)

progress. In several sectors of the economy, growth rates began to decline.

Inefficiency and failure to modernise were storing up long-term problems for the Soviet economy. However, in the short term the Khrushchev era did see material standards for the urban population rise. Average wages were raised, and there were improvements in social services and secondary education. Nevertheless, standards of living remained low by Western standards. There were also increasing differentials *within* the USSR: for example standards were higher in the Baltic Republics than the Asian Republics. The problem of inadequate urban housing, although being addressed, remained. Certainly, Khrushchev's vision of a Communist utopia remained a long way short of realisation, as did his boast that the USSR would outstrip the West economically within a generation.

Brezhnev's economic policies were cautious, and many problems were swept under the carpet. There were opportunities for industrial development. Oil was struck in Western Siberia in 1964, and vast amounts of mineral and other resources were discovered in this undeveloped region in the 1960s and 1970s. By 1983 357 million tons of oil a year were being extracted from Siberia, representing 60 per cent of Soviet oil production, already the largest in the world. The development of vast reserves of gas and coal was given a high priority in the Tenth and Eleventh Five-Year Plans of 1976–80 and 1981–85. A 3500-mile pipeline was constructed to carry natural gas from Siberia, and the Baikal–Amur Railway (*BAM*) was built between 1974 and 1984 at the cost of 30 billion *roubles*. This railway of over 3000 kilometres was built to the north of the much older Trans-Siberian Railway, but was as much a project to do with prestige as with useful investment.

The government also devoted more attention to the south of the USSR, with investment in the Asian Republics. However, Soviet economic planning took no account of environmental concerns, and huge irrigation schemes such as the diversion of rivers in Kazakhstan had catastrophic ecological consequences over vast areas – the draining of the inland Aral Sea being the prime example.

	1975 (Plan)	1975 (Actual)	1980 (Plan)	1980 (Actual)
Electricity (milliard kWhs)	1065	1039	1380	1290
Oil (million tons)	505	491	640	604
Coal (million tons)	695	701	800	719
Steel (million tons)	146	141	168	155
Cement (million tons)	125	122	145	125
Tractors (million tons)	575	550	590	562
Motor vehicles (million tons)	2100	1964	2296	2199
Leather footwear (million pairs)	830	698		

(Data from Soviet sources)

TABLE 15

Economic performance in the later Brezhnev years

Very little of the investment realised the optimistic hopes of its promoters, partly because of the difficulties of exploiting difficult and inhospitable regions, and partly because the Soviet command economy was inefficiently organised and managed. The rate of industrial growth declined sharply after 1975. Pressure from the agricultural and defence sectors reduced the amount available for investment in heavy industry, whilst labour productivity remained at half the American figure.

The regime knew that there were serious problems. The Tenth Five-Year Plan reduced the emphasis on increasing productive capacity in favour of improving efficiency and quality. There were efforts to form factory workers into 'brigades', with contracts and incentives to improve productivity. But the rate of economic growth was still low.

The Soviet population was either unaware of these facts or accepted them. After all, real wages and social benefits continued to improve gradually, and there was guaranteed employment for all. The five-day working week became the norm from 1967. People were certainly unaware that Brezhnev's government spent far more of its Gross National Product on defence compared to the Western powers. There were still shortages of consumer goods of quality, and the population was paying the price in domestic stagnation of Soviet attempts to match the USA as a world power. It was this awareness amongst younger reformist sections of the Party that finally propelled the USSR into a series of more radical economic reforms in the mid-1980s.

Some of the seeds of Gorbachev's strategy of *perestroika* or restructuring, were sown during Andropov's short-lived regime. However, many of Andropov's efforts concentrated on exhortations for more discipline and increased productivity, rather than radical structural changes. Even so, Andropov was told by the Head of *GOSPLAN*, who had been in post for twenty years, that any economic experiments must proceed 'cautiously'. Andropov began a 'limited industrial experiment' in January 1984, modelled partly upon Hungarian practices. Factory managers were given more influence over decisions concerning production and use of profits, and wages and bonuses were more closely linked to production and sales. But central planning mechanisms remained in place, and managers and workers

KEY ISSUE

Why did the Soviet economy deteriorate during Brezhnev's time in power?

were assured that any 'surplus manpower' resulting from changes would be reabsorbed elsewhere.

From 1985 onwards Gorbachev built upon these earlier efforts. He preferred to talk about 'improving the economic mechanism' rather than reform, and at first thought only in terms of making the existing system work better rather than fundamentally restructuring it. At first Gorbachev blamed the economic slowdown on the reluctance of officials to make necessary improvements – what he called a 'wait and see' mentality. Rather than abolish central planning and introduce a supply and demand economy, Gorbachev hoped to give more initiative to managers at enterprise level and to free central planners to focus upon strategic planning and determining priorities for investment. Gorbachev also wanted an emphasis on quality as well as quantity in order for the USSR to compete with the American, Japanese and Western European economies. This would mean, for example, more investment in high-technology engineering. Several industrial ministries were amalgamated, and three 'superministries' were created for machine building, energy and agriculture.

Gorbachev's plans became increasingly ambitious. The Twelfth Five-Year Plan (1986–90) assumed a doubling of national income by the year 2000, with the bulk of investment going into European Russia rather than Siberia, in a reversal of Brezhnev's policy. However, as Table 16 indicates, the targets were not met.

Under Gorbachev, the annual rate of economic growth was 3.7 per cent, a modest figure comparable with the Brezhnev years. Also, powerful ministries such as the Energy Ministry used their muscle to ensure that they continued to receive the bulk of investment, rather than it going into machine building as Gorbachev had intended.

Gorbachev realised that more radical measures were necessary. In 1987 factory managers were given more say in what to produce and whom to employ. 'Self-financing', by which enterprises paid for operating costs out of their own profits, was introduced between 1987 and 1989. A Quality Inspection Agency was established. A law of January 1987 permitted privately-owned businesses and cooperatives, although bureaucratic restrictions prevented many such activities from being successful.

None of these measures worked. Years of neglect, a reluctance to make changes, bureaucratic obstructionism, all took their toll. The Soviet economy could not achieve higher growth rates and qualitative improvements simultaneously. Private enterprise was discouraged as

KEY ISSUE

What were the main features of Gorbachev's economic reforms?

KEY ISSUE

To what extent were Gorbachev's economic reforms ultimately successful?

TABLE 16

Soviet economic growth, 1986–91 (from official Soviet figures). Figures in percentages.

Average (Plan)	1986–90	1986	1987	1988	1989	1990
National income produced	4.2	2.3	1.6	4.4	2.4	−4.0
Industrial output	4.6	4.4	3.8	3.9	1.7	−1.2
Agricultural output	2.7	5.3	−0.6	1.7	1.3	−2.3

(Data from official Soviet figures)

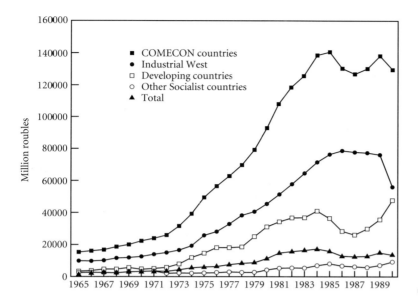

DIAGRAM 3
*The value and direction of
Soviet exports, 1965–90*

encouraging selfish individualism, and therefore privatisation of major industries was rejected as a possible policy by most politicians. Such support as there was for *perestroika* in some quarters began to evaporate as the promised material benefits did not materialise. Gorbachev's industrial reforms were seen as lacking a coherent long-term strategy. In 1990, one of Gorbachev's own advisers, Shatalin, argued for a programme of privatisation reinforced by foreign investment, but this was ruled out as being too radical. Rising inflation

Region	1970	1975	1980	1985	1990
West Europe					
Total trade	16.6	23.4	27.0	21.3	32.4
Exports	15.1	22.4	29.7	23.8	32.6
Imports	18.2	24.4	24.0	18.8	32.2
East Europe					
Total trade	56.9	46.8	46.6	51.5	33.8
Exports	55.3	48.4	46.3	50.6	32.6
Imports	58.7	45.3	47.0	52.5	34.9
North America					
Total trade	1.3	3.9	2.7	2.7	2.6
Exports	0.6	0.6	0.4	0.5	1.0
Imports	2.1	7.1	5.2	4.8	4.0
Asia-Pacific					
Total trade	7.6	7.0	7.2	7.2	9.5
Exports	8.1	5.7	5.3	6.8	10.1
Imports	7.1	8.3	9.2	7.6	8.9
Other					
Total trade	17.6	8.9	16.5	17.4	21.7
Exports	20.9	22.9	18.3	18.4	23.8
Imports	13.9	14.9	14.5	16.4	20.0

TABLE 17
*The distribution of Soviet
foreign trade, 1970–90 (as %
of total trade)*

See graph on page 135

compounded economic difficulties. Exports were switched increasingly towards the western world in a desperate attempt to earn hard currency. Despite this, the Soviet debt to Western banks and governments rose from 10 billion dollars in 1984 to 37 billion by 1989.

Prime Minister Ryzhkov presented a new programme to the Supreme Soviet in May 1990. It provided for a transition to a regulated market economy in three stages by 1995. Eventually the Supreme Soviet adopted a compromise plan in October 1990. In various stages there would be the commercialisation of State enterprises, less central interference in prices, and the *rouble* would become a fully convertible currency on the world market. Gorbachev himself urged caution, but in any case economic reform was being overtaken by events as the 1991 *coup* and its aftermath led to the break-up of the USSR.

Following the break-up, and the establishment of the Commonwealth of Independent States, economic problems continued. Additional difficulties were caused by the disruption of internal trade. Independent Republics, whose economies had been integrated into the USSR with corresponding degrees of enforced specialisation in certain industries, now had to adjust to a life of independence and economic reconstruction of their own. The economic outlook for most of the former Soviet Republics, including Russia itself, looked bleak, and this threatened to compound the difficulties of an already fraught political situation.

3 ↪ FOREIGN POLICY

A *Stalin and the Cold War*

See Chapter 9 for the origins and development of the Cold War; see Chapter 4 for developments in Eastern and Central Europe

Soviet foreign policy before the Second World War was largely dominated by fear of capitalist encirclement. Several foreign powers had intervened in Russia after the 1917 Revolution, and Stalin remained obsessed with the idea that capitalist powers would destroy the USSR if possible. Therefore, Stalin's policy was to strengthen Soviet defences whilst supporting Communist movements elsewhere, provided they followed Moscow's line. The Nazi threat in the 1930s alarmed Stalin, but the failure of the Soviets and the Western democracies to combine against it led Stalin into the Nazi–Soviet Pact of 1939.

Stalin's suspicion of the outside world was reinforced by Hitler's attack in 1941. His insistence on security after the war led to the installing of friendly governments in those countries of Eastern and Central Europe that the Red Army had liberated from German rule. The wartime alliance itself did not survive the strains of mutual suspicion.

Interpretations of the origins of the Cold War have often changed. It is simplistic to assume, as many anti-Soviet commentators once did, that the USSR was simply waiting for an opportunity to invade Western

Legend:
- Western bloc
- Eastern bloc
- Neutral countries

0 200 400 600
Scale (km)

NORWAY · SWEDEN · FINLAND · UNITED KINGDOM · North Sea · Baltic Sea · U.S.S.R. · DENMARK · NETH. · IRELAND · EAST GERMANY · POLAND · WEST GERMANY · BELGIUM · CZECH · HUNGARY · LUX. · AUSTRIA · Atlantic Ocean · FRANCE · SWITZ. · ROMANIA · ITALY · YUGOSLAVIA · BULGARIA · Black Sea · PORTUGAL · SPAIN · CORSICA · ALBANIA · GREECE · SARDINIA · SICILY · MALTA · CYPRUS · Mediterranean Sea · CRETE

MAP 10
*The Soviet defence system:
the Warsaw Pact confronting
NATO*

Europe, and was deterred only by a strong Western response to Soviet provocations, such as the Berlin crisis of 1948–49. The Soviets were certainly prepared to exploit weaknesses in the Western Alliance, but Stalin also had his own legitimate security concerns which explain his policies towards states bordering on the USSR. Also the Soviets did not simply impose Communist regimes in Eastern and Central Europe by force: local Communists had considerable support immediately after the war, although the threat of the Red Army was also in the background to ensure Soviet control.

Stalin's attitude towards the Soviet satellite states hardened from the late 1940s as the Cold War intensifed, rather than being a cause *of* the Cold War. It was from the late 1940s that many features of the Stalinist political and economic system were copied in Eastern and Central Europe. But ultimately Stalin's actions were determined by what he perceived to be Soviet national interests rather than the interests of world Communism, since the two did not always coincide. Stalin was more concerned with economic recovery and in establishing a secure buffer zone than world revolution. Pre-revolutionary Russian foreign policy had been traditionally cautious, and Soviet foreign policy was usually in the same vein. Whatever their policies, it was always likely

KEY ISSUE

*What were Stalin's
ambitions in foreign
policy?*

that the Soviets and Americans would experience difficulties in their relations: before the war both powers had been essentially isolationist in attitude and had little real knowledge of each other. Certainly we should be cautious about assuming that Stalin had a coherent long-term plan beyond his simple determination to enhance Soviet security.

Stalin adhered to many of the agreements he had signed with his Western Allies during the War, although his interpretations of, for example, the Yalta Agreement may sometimes have been different from theirs. He had reduced the size of the Red Army by 1948, and he did not support a Communist revolution in Greece. Disagreements with the West arose partly from attempts to establish precisely where spheres of influence began and ended in the new post-war world.

See pages 389–91

Stalin's distrust of the USA was increased by the Marshall Plan, seen as an attempt to extend American influence in Europe, and by the Truman Doctrine and the formation of NATO. Rivalry with the West became serious during the Berlin Crisis, and the Soviets also fought a war of words with the West in the United Nations. Stalin backed the North Koreans during their war with the South Koreans between 1950 and 1953. Stalin's attitudes towards the outside world had been shaped long before the war, and had been reinforced during it. Soviet foreign policy was not likely to alter course significantly whilst he was alive.

B *Khrushchev and Peaceful Co-existence*

Stalin's successors did not inherit an easy legacy in foreign affairs. The American policy of 'containment' had yielded results in Asia, where the Communist drive into South Korea had been checked; and the USSR was surrounded by defensive alliances. Dulles, the American Secretary of State was preaching 'Brinkmanship' – the art of pushing the other side almost to the point of war – and also 'Massive Retaliation' – the notion that the USA would regard any act of Communist aggression anywhere in the world as emanating from the USSR, which would therefore suffer retaliation when and where the USA chose.

See page 395

KEY ISSUE

Why was 'Peaceful Co-existence' introduced, and with what effects?

Because of these policies the Soviets were anxious to reduce the American lead in military strength, to avoid outright provocation, to break out of containment and possibly create divisions in opposing alliances. Winning support amongst non-aligned nations in the Developing World was another possible strategy.

Khrushchev introduced the new concept of Peaceful Co-existence in 1956. He abandoned the official line that violent conflict between the capitalist and Communist worlds was inevitable as a prelude to world revolution. It was still accepted that the two political and economic systems would compete for supremacy, but it was no longer axiomatic in the nuclear age that this struggle must involve all-out war. Khrushchev was also tacitly admitting that individual nations could determine which political, social and economic system they wished to follow, at least within certain limits.

This was a policy of realism, and not just based on fear. Khrushchev was now speaking from a stronger position. In November 1955 the Soviets successfully tested a hydrogen bomb. They successfully tested an Intercontinental Ballistic Missile in August 1957, and launched the first orbiting satellite, *Sputnik*, in October. In April 1961 Yuri Gagarin became the first man to orbit the world in space. It appeared that the USSR had eroded American superiority, but at the same time, by abandoning a commitment to violent revolution, Khrushchev was able to proceed down the path of better relations with the West. This was also important to him because the Soviets were apprehensive about West German rearmament, which had begun in 1952/53.

The Soviet 'peace offensive' began in earnest in 1955. Although the USSR rejected an American 'Open Skies' proposal, that would have allowed each power to photograph each other's military installations freely from the air, Khrushchev formally ended the state of war with Germany, and signed a treaty ending the joint Allied occupation of Austria. There was optimism before the Geneva Summit Conference of July 1955. In the wake of this conference, Khrushchev proposed a nuclear-free zone in Europe. The Americans could not agree to this because its short-range tactical nuclear missiles, seen as essential to counterbalance the Soviet superiority in numbers of troops, were based in West Germany. In November 1958 Khrushchev proposed that West Berlin should become a free demilitarised zone. Again there was too much mutual suspicion of motives to make acceptance of this proposal likely: were the Soviets hoping to persuade the Western Powers to leave Berlin?

Relations were soon soured again. A planned summit in Paris for May 1960 was called off by Khrushchev, following the shooting down of an American U-2 spy plane over Soviet territory. Soon afterwards, Khrushchev made a provocative speech at the United Nations, proposing major changes in the UN's organisation. Khrushchev's hard line may have been to try to appease his colleagues who were critical of his Peaceful Co-existence policy; and he may also have been trying to impose himself on the new and much younger President John F. Kennedy. At a summit in Vienna in 1961 Khrushchev made threats over the future of Berlin, and the Soviets renewed nuclear testing. Although in 1959 Khrushchev admitted the rights of the occupying powers in Berlin, he was now insisting again that they must leave. The building of the Berlin Wall in August 1961 could have threatened a major crisis, but the situation appeared to stabilise, as both sides came to accept the division of Germany, although the Soviets continued their campaign for the international recognition of East German sovereignty.

Khrushchev's siting of missiles in Cuba was partly prompted by an opportunity to gain a triumph over the USA, and partly by a perceived opportunity to counter American military superiority by stationing Soviet missiles close to American soil. When American determination to force the Soviets to back down and remove their missiles threatened a major confrontation and possibly war between the superpowers, Khrushchev did back down. He lost face with many of his colleagues: he

> ## KEY ISSUE
>
> *To what extent was Khrushchev's foreign policy successful in promoting Soviet interests*

See page 400

See pages 402–5

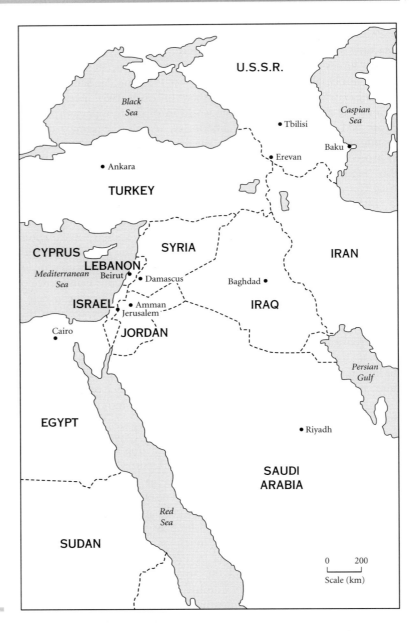

MAP 11
The Middle East

appeared to have embarked upon a policy of dangerous confrontation, and then given way. Had Khrushchev been too desperate for a foreign policy success after earlier failures? Or was he, as some historians later argued, trying to achieve strategic parity with the USA at a stroke and then persuade the Americans into a settlement which would include a resolution of the Berlin issue? Either way, Khrushchev appeared to have miscalculated.

The Soviets continued to seek strategic and tactical advantages elsewhere. In 1956 they provided economic and military aid to

President Nasser of Egypt after the Americans refused to finance the Aswan Dam. Thus began a long period of involvement with the Arab world. When the British and French invaded the Suez Canal Zone during the Arab–Israeli War of 1956, the Soviets threatened nuclear retaliation. The USSR gave aid to a host of countries in North Africa and nearer home: Syria, Afghanistan, Iraq, Tunisia, Algeria, North Yemen, Morocco and Turkey. The Soviets also established contacts with a number of African States, such as Ghana, Mali and Guinea. Khrushchev supported India, giving it aid and support in its struggle with Pakistan. Aid was also given to Burma and Indonesia. However, tangible benefits from these contacts were not great, and the Soviets themselves were often regarded by these states as patronising and arrogant.

One of Khrushchev's failures was his inability to restore unity to the world Communist movement. His biggest failure in this respect was in relations with China. Mao Ze Dong had come to power in 1949 and there had seemed the prospect of an alliance between two huge Communist powers. But the Chinese brand of Communism was very different from the Soviet version, and there was little love lost historically between the two countries. After Stalin's death, the Chinese refused to acknowledge the USSR as the natural leader of the Communist world, and indeed accused the Soviets of betraying the true nature of Marxism. The Chinese also condemned the policy of Peaceful Co-existence with the West. In 1957 the Soviets offered to assist the Chinese in developing their own nuclear weapons, but only in return for control of Chinese foreign policy. Mao preferred to go it alone. In 1962, when China and India were briefly at war, the USSR gave tacit support to India. Fierce quarrelling between Mao and Khrushchev further helped to tarnish Khrushchev's reputation within the USSR.

So Khrushchev's foreign policy ended largely in failure. He had more high-level contacts with foreign leaders than his predecessors, but his objectives were not achieved. He failed to mend relations with China, he was forced to intervene in Hungary in 1956 to suppress the independence movement there, and he failed to get his way over Cuba and Germany. The USSR had certainly become a world power, but it did not appear yet to be very successful on the world stage.

C *Brezhnev's foreign policy*

There were two dominant strands to Brezhnev's foreign policy in the 1960s and 70s. Following the Cuban Missile Crisis and Khrushchev's fall from power, the Soviets sought a worldwide role and the military clout necessary to underpin it. But at the same time, Brezhnev sought an improvement in East–West relations, leading to a period of *détente*. These two strands were not at variance, since the USSR wished to approach *détente* from a position of parity with the USA, not as a weaker supplicant. There were positive achievements on which to build, such as the installation of a 'Hot Line' or direct link between the

See pages 411–13

MAP 12
The Sino–Soviet border

Kremlin and the White House, and the Test Ban Treaty, both signed after the settlement of the Cuban Missile Crisis.

The economic effort involved in developing and maintaining superpower status produced a marked drain on the Soviet economy and contributed significantly to the domestic problems outlined earlier in this chapter.

Brezhnev was also keen to consolidate the Socialist Bloc in Eastern and Central Europe and to reassert the Soviet position as recognised leader of the world Communist movement, which, after Khrushchev, could clearly no longer be taken for granted.

Khrushchev's defence policy had been based upon the principle of minimum nuclear deterrence: that is, the USSR had to maintain sufficient nuclear capability to deter any would-be aggressor and convince it that the Soviets could deliver a devastating nuclear counter-attack even if they were attacked first. Brezhnev modified this doctrine: the USSR must develop a range of conventional and nuclear weapons capable of matching the USA in any sphere: all-out nuclear war, limited nuclear war, or conventional war. It meant, for example, the creation of a Red Navy capable of operating worldwide, to counteract the American naval dominance so clearly demonstrated during the Cuban Missile Crisis. This also represented an important shift in defence thinking: Peaceful Co-existence had been formulated on the premise that any major conflict would inevitably escalate into all-out nuclear war. There was now an assumption, shared with some American strategists, that it might be possible to keep a nuclear war 'limited',

KEY ISSUE

What was the basis of Brezhnev's foreign policy and to what extent was it successful?

either by using only conventional weapons or tactical nuclear ones. However, this flexible view of defence was not shared by most of the Red Army command, which continued to believe that a nuclear war would be 'total' from the start, or very quickly become so.

The possibility of an international crisis degenerating into a mutually destructive nuclear holocaust was an alarming one, and made the search for an improvement in international relations all the more important.

In pursuing their first objective, parity with the USA, the Soviets continued to spend more and more on defence during the 1960s. Work on an anti-ballistic missile (ABM) system around Moscow began in 1966; the Soviet Air Force was modernised; the Soviet Navy appeared in the Indian Ocean for the first time in 1963; and the first Soviet aircraft carrier was launched in 1973. Also military training was extended to men *before* they were conscripted. At the same time, links between the army and the Party were consolidated, partly in order to increase the political reliability of the officer corps. Over 90 per cent of all officers belonged to the Party or the *Komsomol*, its youth wing.

It is difficult to make precise comparisons between the respective forces of the Warsaw Pact and NATO. By the end of the 1960s the USSR probably had more strategic long-range nuclear weapons than the USA. On the other hand, the USA had far more submarine-launched missiles, which were less vulnerable to attack. The Warsaw Pact had larger conventional forces than NATO in Europe, but many of its units were of poorer quality. The two alliances also operated differently. The Warsaw Pact, created in 1955 for the mutual defence of the USSR and its allies in the Eastern Bloc, was more closely controlled by the USSR than was NATO by the Americans. It was certainly implicit in the organisation of the Warsaw Pact that its forces would be under Soviet command in the event of war.

See page 391

Improving Soviet–USA relations in the 1960s was not easy. The USA was heavily involved in the Vietnam War, interpreted in the Communist world as American imperialism. During the Arab–Israeli War of 1967, the Soviets backed the Arab States, whilst the USA traditionally supported Israel. In 1968 the USSR was widely condemned for invading Czechoslovakia to stop reforms there. The American moon landing of June 1969 appeared to have shifted the balance of technological superiority back in favour of the USA; whilst in 1969 President Nixon launched a programme to develop MIRVs (Multiple independently-targetable re-entry vehicles), a new escalation of the nuclear armoury, and also an anti-ballistic missile system, both of which committed the Soviets to more defence spending if they wished to reciprocate.

Nevertheless, *détente* – a relaxation of international tension – was also on the agenda. It was an attractive policy, both from the standpoint of avoiding crises that might escalate to war, and also from that of promising a reduction in military expenditure. There were some successful examples on which to draw. In 1965 the Soviets successfully mediated in a border conflict between India and Pakistan, and the USA

KEY ISSUE

What were the motives for détente, *and how did it affect international relations?*

supported this. The two superpowers signed a treaty in 1967 banning nuclear weapons from outer space, and a Non-Proliferation Treaty in 1968 committed them not to help other powers to attain a nuclear capability that could be converted to military purposes.

Brezhnev had to assure conservatives in the Kremlin that accommodation with the West did not signify a lessening of ideological commitment. Brezhnev insisted that the class struggle of two incompatible political and economic systems would continue, but in an economic, political and ideological context, rather than a military one. However, the difficulty for the USSR lay precisely in trying to compete on these terms. The Soviets could, for example, afford to pump aid into countries on a scale likely to persuade them into a closer political relationship far less than the USA. Brezhnev also argued that *détente* would allow the Soviets to better exploit internal divisions in the capitalist world, but this idea, though superficially seductive, bore few concrete results.

In April 1970 the Strategic Arms Limitation Talks (SALT) marked an important stage in *détente*. The objective of the Talks was arms control – limiting the proliferation of nuclear weapons – rather than the longer-term goal of actual disarmament. In February 1971 the USSR, USA and Britain signed an agreement banning the installation of nuclear devices on the sea bed, and communication links between the Kremlin and the White House were improved. There were further Soviet–USA agreements on economic, technical and cultural links. An ABM Treaty was signed restricting both superpowers to one ABM and one ICBM (inter-continental ballistic missile) site each, to reduce the likelihood of surprise attacks. There were also limitations on the numbers of SLBMs (submarine-launched ballistic missiles).

Brezhnev also sought more friendly relations with Western Europe, and several agreements were signed with individual countries. This was partly because the Soviets were concerned at the possibility of the development of the European Community as a major force in Europe. The Community's longer-term political aim of European union was far more ambitious than the aims of COMECON (the Council of Mutual Economic Assistance), which was designed to encourage and rationalise trade between nations in the Eastern Bloc.

Brezhnev was anxious to secure Western recognition of East Germany as a sovereign State. To this purpose, he cultivated the West German government, and sought a European Security Conference. In the meantime, talks began in Vienna in 1973 on Mutual and Balanced Force Reductions. However, diagreements on what would be 'mutual' and ' balanced' caused the talks to drag on for the rest of the decade, with no agreement.

Brezhnev signed the Helsinki Act of the European Security Conference in August 1973, along with thirty-two other European states, the USA and Canada. There were wide-ranging agreements on political, military, economic, environmental, cultural and human rights issues. However, although this agreement should have brought prestige for the USSR, it also created embarrassments, since monitoring groups were set up all over Europe, and they publicised Soviet violations of human rights.

Brezhnev pressed ahead with a SALT II Treaty, which was finally signed in June 1979 in Vienna. Both superpowers were limited to 2250 strategic missiles and 1320 MIRVed vehicles. However, there were several complications: both sides argued about the status of other weapons which were being developed, such as low-flying Cruise missiles which NATO was installing in Europe. SALT II was not ratified. *Détente* suffered a major blow with the Soviet invasion of Afghanistan in December 1979. In fact, the signs that the Cold War was returning had already been present. For example, President Carter was demanding a big increase in the USA military budget in 1978. Also, several Western-supported regimes were suffering attacks from radical movements, in Vietnam, Angola, Mozambique, Ethiopia, Iran, Nicaragua and South Yemen, and suspicions were fuelled that the Soviets were intent on destabilising tactics. The new American President Reagan was certainly convinced that the Soviets were heavily involved in revolutionary movements in Central America. His response was the Strategic Defence Initiative or 'Star Wars', which by planning for weapons in space, threatened to upset the delicate nuclear balance and therefore alarmed the Soviets.

Brezhnev's regime supported both Socialist and Nationalist regimes in the Developing World. Soviet aid was usually military rather than economic. Between 1965 and 1971 aid was given to the North Vietnamese regime in its struggle against the South and its USA supporters. Brezhnev's help was rewarded when the unified Vietnam which emerged from the war signed a Treaty of Friendship and Cooperation with the Kremlin, which hoped that Vietnam might replace China as its ally in South-East Asia. However, elsewhere the Soviets were often unsuccessful in translating their overseas aid into political influence. This was particularly evident when the Soviets could do little to prevent the overthrow of Allende's Marxist regime in Chile in 1973. The Soviets simply did not possess the economic and political influence of the USA.

The limitations of Soviet strategy were also evident in the Middle East. Having supported and supplied the Arab States, the Soviets then witnessed Arab humiliation in the 1967 war against Israel. After the war, the Soviets re-equipped the Egyptian forces, but then President Sadat ordered the Soviet advisers out. During the Arab–Israeli War of 1973, the American and Soviet navies came dangerously close to confrontation in the Mediterranean. After the 1973 war, despite continued Soviet support for Syria, it was the Americans who clearly had the initiative in the Middle East, as was evident when they hosted the historic Camp David Peace Agreement between Egypt and Israel.

Even in the Indian subcontinent, where the Soviets had maintained friendly relations with India, reinforced by treaties in 1971 and 1976, their influence declined, as relations between India and China markedly improved during the 1970s.

See page 412

KEY ISSUE

Why did détente *run into difficulties in the 1980s?*

See page 415

KEY ISSUE

Why, and with what effect, did the USSR become involved in Afghanistan?

Afghanistan posed even greater problems for Brezhnev. Historically Afghanistan had always been an area of interest to the Russians, since it bordered their territory. A Marxist *coup* took place in Afghanistan in 1978. The new regime was soon under attack from within, and in December 1979 it 'invited' the intervention of the Red Army, which poured 100 000 conscripts into the country within four months. It was not simply a case of Soviet expansionism towards the Indian Ocean. The Kremlin also had genuine concerns about the spread of Islamic fundamentalism from Iran through Afghanistan into its own populous Muslim Republics in Central Asia. According to Brezhnev,

> We had either to bring in troops or let the Afghan revolution be defeated and the country turned into a kind of Shah's Iran...It was not a simple decision to take...There are situations when non-intervention is a disgrace and a betrayal.

The Afghan War proved to be a disaster for the USSR. The Soviets found themselves embroiled in a long and bloody conflict with guerrillas they could not suppress. The Kremlin was unable to hide the extent of the casualties from its own population, and a hostile world condemned Soviet involvement to the extent of some countries boycotting the 1980 Moscow Olympics and the USA putting an

MAP 13
Afghanistan and surrounding countries

embargo on exports of grain and technology to the USSR. It was the first time since 1945 that the Red Army had travelled beyond the borders of Europe to fight, and the experience proved materially and psychologically damaging.

Brezhnev's policy in Eastern Europe proved equally unpopular with the outside world. The liberalisation of Czechoslovakia in 1968 provoked the Warsaw Pact into invading the country in August. The offending regime was replaced.

See page 168

The West was not prepared to intervene in this Soviet sphere of influence, but Soviet actions in Czechoslovakia were widely condemned. In November 1968 the Brezhnev Doctrine was promulgated: the USSR reserved the right to interfere in the internal affairs of any Socialist State should it perceive there to be a threat to Socialism generally. Threats of intervention were actually made in 1980 when the reform movement in Poland took on a strong anti-Communist character.

See page 178

China remained a considerable cause of concern to Brezhnev. In 1969 there were serious armed clashes on the Sino–Soviet border, and throughout the 1970s thousands of Soviet troops were stationed along it. Although tensions lessened in the late 1970s, after Mao's death China did not look likely to return to the Soviet fold.

Brezhnev's foreign policy had therefore not been a marked success. The Soviets had, at great cost to themselves, maintained military parity with NATO, or a situation close to it, but they had few allies, had failed to divide their opponents, and although they had acquired some overseas friends and bases, they lacked the influence of their more powerful rival.

D *Andropov's foreign policy*

Andropov maintained a firm line towards the West on succeeding Brezhnev in 1982. There was considerable continuity with his predecessor's policy, which was not surprising since the long-serving Gromyko was still responsible for foreign affairs. Andropov attacked Reagan's 'Star Wars' policy, declaring that the Soviets were not a 'naive people', but he also expressed the hope of better relations. Continuing Soviet involvement in Afghanistan made this difficult, and the Chinese also showed little interest in improving relations.

Nevertheless, Andropov made new Arms Control proposals in 1983, offering to reduce the number of Soviet SS-20 missiles as part of an agreement which would include British and French weapons in any equation. However, NATO continued to deploy Cruise and Pershing missiles in Europe, so agreement was not reached. Andropov did not improve matters by ill-timed intervention in the West German elections, expressing support for Chancellor Kohl's left-wing opponent.

The most serious blow to East–West relations at this time occurred in August 1983 when Korean Airlines passenger plane KAL 007 was shot down well inside Soviet airspace, with the loss of 269 passengers,

KEY ISSUE

How successful was Andropov's foreign policy?

including several Americans. The official version was that the plane had strayed off course; the Soviets claimed that the plane was on a spying mission over sensitive Soviet territory in the Far East. The Soviets first denied the incident, then defended their actions. The incident, and Soviet handling of it, helped to cause the breakdown of talks in Geneva, which officially foundered on the refusal of the Americans to redeploy their missiles in Europe. The Cold War was still very much alive. Andropov's successor, Chernenko, hoped to restore better relations with the West, and preached Peaceful Co-existence, but President Reagan was intransigent on the issue of 'Star Wars', and Chernenko faced opposition to *détente* from powerful groups within the USSR itself. Just as Chernenko's health was fading, Gromyko announced that agreement had been reached that Arms Control talks would include space weapons, strategic and medium-range missiles.

E *Gorbachev and 'New Thinking'*

Gorbachev inherited an unpromising situation in 1985: a draining war in Afghanistan; the failure to ratify the SALT II Treaty; arguments over 'Star Wars'; the deployment of Cruise missiles by NATO in Western Europe; continuing poor relations with China. To continue traditional Soviet policy would entail the maintenance of massive nuclear and conventional forces whilst pursuing better relations with the West as part of Peaceful Co-existence. But Gorbachev wanted a foreign policy that would take more realistic account of Soviet economic problems. To that extent foreign policy and *perestroika* were closely linked.

In public, Gorbachev took the line that in an increasingly interdependent world, the traditional language of confrontation was both redundant and dangerous. He unveiled his 'New Thinking' at the Twenty-Seventh Party Congress in 1986:

> The changes in the development of the contemporary world are so profound and significant that they require a rethinking and comprehensive analysis of all its factors. The situation of nuclear confrontation calls for new approaches, methods, and forms of relations between different social systems, states and regions.

KEY ISSUE

What was 'New Thinking' and what effects did it have upon Soviet foreign policy?

Gorbachev went on to criticise Brezhnev's policies for failing to keep pace with the needs of the contemporary world. There was certainly far less of the old dogma about differences between incompatible political systems, and far more realism than his audience was used to hearing, although not all liked the message. One of his colleagues, Yegor Ligachev, openly challenged Gorbachev in August 1988, insisting that Soviet foreign policy should still be based upon the 'class character of international relations'.

Gorbachev committed the USSR to a more active role in the United Nations, and also claimed that 'New Thinking' meant a greater awareness of the interdependence of the modern world, not just in a political or economic sense. He showed an interest in environmental issues and called for freer trade. The USSR began to attend meetings of GATT (The General Agreement on Trade and Tariffs) and applied to join the International Monetary Fund. Gorbachev also promised an increased commitment to human rights.

Another change in emphasis was Gorbachev's promise that the USSR would no longer support revolutionary movements in other countries: a considerable change, since the export of Communism had always been on the Soviet agenda, even though the degree of commitment had varied from time to time.

Even more important in the short term was Gorbachev's rejection of the Brezhnev Doctrine. The USSR would no longer claim the right to intervene in the internal affairs of other Socialist states. This was of crucial importance in the late 1980s: Gorbachev positively encouraged reform in the Eastern Bloc and clearly stated in talks with Communist leaders that the USSR would not support hard-line regimes resisting change. Without Gorbachev's attitude, the changes in Eastern and Central Europe would almost certainly have been more painful and possibly violent than they were. Without the promise of Soviet backing, always present in the past, other Communist regimes lacked the confidence to resist increasing demands for reform.

Gorbachev had to tackle the long-standing issue of arms control negotiations. In November 1985 he met Reagan in a 'fireside chat' and offered to make reductions in numbers of Soviet missiles and balance them against NATO weapons. But the talks were unsuccessful, because Reagan was not prepared to abandon his 'Star Wars' initiative. Nevertheless, Gorbachev did announce a reduction in the Soviet strategic missile armoury in January 1986, and in September a preparatory treaty on conventional disarmament was signed between NATO and the Warsaw Pact. The sense of growing optimism seemed misplaced when there was further stalemate in arms control negotiations at a summit meeting in Reykjavik between Gorbachev and Reagan.

The third Reagan–Gorbachev summit at Washington in December 1987 produced a major breakthrough. For the first time there was an agreement on disarmament, without a reference to 'Star Wars'. The first dismantling of short-range missiles in Europe began.

Following the final Reagan–Gorbachev summit in Moscow in the summer of 1988, troop reductions were agreed. Progress was continued under Reagan's successor, President Bush, who met Gorbachev off Malta in December 1989. When they met again in Moscow in July 1991 they agreed to reduce their stocks of weapons by 30 per cent.

It is scarcely surprising that given the long years of haggling and disappointment, the success of arms control and disarmament negotiations in the late 1980s gave Gorbachev a reputation as an international statesman far higher than his reputation at home with the Soviet people.

> ### KEY ISSUE
>
> *Why was it so difficult to achieve real progress in arms control and disarmament negotiations?*

Gorbachev also showed statesmanship in the Middle East. He attempted to improve relationships with Israel whilst continuing traditional ties of friendship with the less radical Arab States. He faced a delicate situation during the Gulf War, which began with Iraq's invasion of Kuwait in August 1990. The Soviets had ties with Iraq, and were not prepared to intervene militarily against them, although Gorbachev supported UN resolutions to liberate Kuwait. He overrode criticism within the USSR that he was relinquishing the Soviet role as a world power and thereby harming Soviet prestige.

Gorbachev also grasped the nettle of ending the unpopular and unsuccessful intervention in Afghanistan. Soviet troops were withdrawn between 1986 and 1989, although inevitably the Soviet-backed regime which remained after the withdrawal was very fragile and survived only because its own enemies were divided.

Another issue seemed to have been resolved when trade and diplomatic agreements were signed with China in 1985 and 1986. Diplomatic relations were also improved with Japan, an old enemy of the USSR, and other Asian countries such as Thailand, Malaysia, Indonesia and Singapore.

Gorbachev's foreign policy was not just based on ideological considerations. A major incentive for improving relationships was Gorbachev's open recognition that the USSR must reduce its defence expenditure if his domestic economic reforms were to have a realistic chance of success. It seemed that the Cold War had come to an end, and possibly the world was a safer place. However, it was pointed out by one Western historian, Stephen White, that this was the 'diplomacy of decline', in that the Soviets were relinquishing hard-won spheres of influence that had symbolised their superpower status. This was not lost on Gorbachev's own domestic opponents, who regarded Gorbachev as unable to maintain Soviet interests abroad. Ironically, for all Gorbachev's successes and his high reputation abroad, the Soviet Union itself was coming to the end of its existence, and internal Nationalist problems were claiming more attention than Russia's world or even European role as Gorbachev came to the end of his period in office.

> **KEY ISSUE**
>
> *What was the 'diplomacy of decline' and is it a valid description of Gorbachev's foreign policy?*

4 ↪ BIBLIOGRAPHY

There are several useful books on the Stalin and Khrushchev periods of Soviet history, far fewer on the Brezhnev and Gorbachev periods. There are a few books which cover the whole period from 1945 to 1991. One is *The USSR 1945–1990* (Hodder and Stoughton 'History at Source', 1991) by J. Laver. It is written for the 16–19 age group and contains brief introductions to several topics on domestic events and foreign policy, along with collections of documentary and visual sources, source-based exercises, essay titles and plans, and advice on how to tackle sources and essays. *Last of Empires* (OUP, 1996) by J. Keep is a useful history of the period 1945–1991. *Stalin and Khrushchev: The USSR 1924–64* (Hodder and Stoughton 'Access To History', 1990) by M. Lynch is written for the 16–19 age group. In addition to a mixture of narrative and analysis, it contains some source-based questions, advice on note-taking skills, and essays. A similar approach is followed in *Stagnation and Reform: The USSR 1964–1991* (Hodder and Stoughton 'Access To History', 1996) by J. Laver, which deals exclusively with the period from Brezhnev to Gorbachev and the break-up of the USSR.

A useful combination of sources, critical narrative and analysis on the Khrushchev period can be found in *The Khrushchev Era 1953–1964* (Longman Seminar Studies, 1995) by M. McCauley. *Khruschchev: A Biography* (Sphere, 1968) by E. Crankshaw is an interesting interpretation.

There are no concise studies of Brezhnev. However, a useful, if detailed study of the Gorbachev period and its immediate aftermath is *After Gorbachev* (Cambridge University Press, 1993) by S. White. *Gorbachev and his Reforms* (Philip Allan, 1990) by R. Sakwa, *Soviet Society under Perestroika* (Unwin Hyman, 1990) by D. Lane and *Gorbachev* (Longman, 1998) by M. McCauley are also useful.

General histories of the post-1945 period in Soviet history rarely deal satisfactorily with the later years of Brezhnev, or the period after 1982. However, the revised edition of *A History of the Soviet Union* (Fontana, 1990) by G. Hosking is very readable; and *The Soviet Superpower: The Soviet Union 1945–80* (Heinemann, 1982) by P. Mooney is still useful, both on domestic and foreign policy.

There are also some worthwhile videos on this period of Soviet history, including the *Red Empire* series.

5 ↜ ESSAY QUESTIONS

1. (a) In what ways was the USSR affected by the Second World War?
   (b) To what extent had the USSR recovered from the effects of the war by the time of Stalin's death in 1953?
2. (a) What were Khrushchev's motives for de-Stalinisation?
   (b) How successful was this policy?
3. 'A failed reformer'. How valid is this assessment of Khrushchev?
4. (a) What were the main political and economic changes made by Brezhnev during his period in office?
   (b) 'Political stability at the expense of economic stagnation'. To what extent is this an accurate description of the USSR during Brezhnev's dominance in the late 1960s and 1970s?
5. Compare the achievements of Khrushchev and Brezhnev in managing the Soviet economy.
6. (a) What prompted Gorbachev's policies of *glasnost* and *perestroika*?
   (b) How successful were they in transforming the USSR?

7. (a) What immediate events led to the conservative *coup* against Gorbachev and the break-up of the Soviet Union in 1991?
   (b) To what extent was Gorbachev responsible for the break-up?
8. (a) What were the main features of Khrushchev's foreign policy?
   (b) To what extent did Khrushchev's foreign policy differ from that of Stalin?
9. '*Détente* was the only success of Soviet foreign policy in the period between the death of Stalin and the accession to power of Gorbachev (1953–85).' How valid is this assessment?
10. (a) What was Gorbachev's 'New Thinking' in Soviet foreign policy?
    (b) How different was it from previous Soviet foreign policy?
11. How accurate is it to describe the period from 1953 to the break-up of the USSR in 1991 as one of 'stagnation and missed opportunities'?
12. (a) What were the main political and economic features of Stalinism?
    (b) To what extent was the USSR still Stalinist by the time of its break-up in 1991?

6 ↜ DOCUMENTARY EXERCISE ON THE USSR BETWEEN THE 1960S AND 1980S

The following are all Soviet sources about problems and progress in the USSR between the 1960s and the 1980s. Study all of them carefully and answer the qustions which follow:

The Soviet Union is a socialist state. The Soviet people have built socialism in accordance with Lenin's instructions under the leadership of the Communist Party. The Soviet Union has become a powerful and advanced world power. It has achieved this because the people who run the country are the working people who make the machines, build the houses and grow the grain. The factories, the railways, the land and all its riches belong to the people. In this socialist country there is nobody who can do nothing and live off the labour of others...All are equal, men and women and people of all nationalities. Soviet citizens elect their representatives to the Soviets of Working People's Deputies who possess all the power in the country...

The Soviet people are building communism. Under communism work will be the most important and necessary thing in a person's life. Everyone will be well educated and a conscious citizen of society. Thanks to the effort of all, there will be such a large variety of food and other things that everyone will have everything he needs to live, work and relax. A person will work according to his ability and receive according to his needs...Work will become more and more interesting. Life and work in the country will be almost the same as in the towns...

Soviet people help each other unselfishly in every way. Many live as the Communist Party teaches them, according to the principle: 'Man is friend, comrade and brother to man...'

At its Twenty-second Congress in 1961 the Communist Party of the Soviet Union adopted its programme for the building of communism in the USSR which the Soviet people are now successfully carrying out...

'The fact that the USSR was the first to build a socialist society and was the first to demonstrate in practice the real meaning of equal fraternal relations between peoples, will undoubtedly be remembered and valued by all peoples for all times to come,' said Leonid Brezhnev, General Secretary of the CPSU Central Committee.

In February 1976, the Twentieth Congress of the Communist Party of the Soviet Union met to review, among other things, the results of the successful ninth five-year plan, and define targets for the country's economic development in the tenth five-year period (1976–1980) ...

By fulfilling the tenth five-year plan targets the country will make another big stride towards communism.

The land of victorious socialism is confidently marching ahead.

SOURCE A
From A Child's Textbook,
1976.

In the autumn of 1965, the Soviet Union began to carry out economic reform. Its prime objective was to raise the efficiency of social production, to secure a steady growth of labour productivity, to improve national economic management through striking a happy balance between centralised planned management and the encouragement of economic initiative and autonomy of enterprises, to provide more attractive financial inducements to groups of workers and individual workers in the results of their work...Soviet industry was placed on the basis of economic accounting...

The measures carried out by the Communist Party and the Soviet Government resulted in a fresh upsurge in the national economy. By the mid-1970s the USSR's economic potential had doubled compared with what it was in the mid-1960s...

The rapid economic progress made in the USSR convincingly attested to socialism's great advantages. In fifty years of Soviet power the USSR maintained an average annual growth rate of 9.9 per cent in industrial output versus 3.7 per cent in the USA...In some sectors Soviet industry has outstripped US industry. Soviet agricultural output had nearly trebled over these fifty years...

The USSR has long eliminated unemployment, the inequality of women, and social ills...

The collective efforts of the USSR's peoples have guaranteed the rapid improvement of living standards in all the republics. A new historical community of people has emerged in the USSR – the Soviet people, an amalgam of freely developing nations and nationalities and ethnic groups fused together by the Marxist–Leninist ideology and by a singleness of aims of building a communist society. By now the salient features of the Soviet man have taken shape: commitment to communist ideals, Soviet patriotism and internationalism, the desire and ability to work well and be highly active in social and political life, an intolerable and uncompromising attitude to oppression in any form whatsoever, to national and racial prejudice. Generations of internationalists have grown up...

Of late, reactionary circles in the West have mounted a hysterical propaganda campaign to protest 'violations of human rights' allegedly committed in the USSR... The Soviet Union has made a marked contribution to the elaboration of the Universal Declaration of Human Rights and later to the International Covenant on Economic, Social and Cultural Rights, and the Final Act of the Helsinki Conference on Security and Co-operation in Europe... In capitalist society, rent as it is by unresolved and unresolvable contradictions, elementary human rights are being grossly violated. Millions of unemployed, oppressed ethnic minorities are condemned to a life of poverty and misery which insults human dignity. The hullabaloo raised by the ideologists of capitalism about the alleged violations of human rights in socialist countries is solely designed to deceive world public opinion. This dirty smear campaign is, of course, doomed. The Soviet reality refutes the false assertions of Western propagandists.

SOURCE B
From History of the USSR: An Outline of Socialist Construction, *by Y. Kukushkin, 1981.*

Every readjustment of the economic mechanism begins with a readjustment of thinking, with a rejection of old stereotypes of thought and actions, with a clear understanding of the new tasks. This refers primarily to the activity of our economic personnel, to the functionaries of the central links of administration. Most of them have a clear idea of the Party's initiatives and seek and find the best ways of carrying them out... It is hard however, to understand those who follow a 'wait and see' policy, or those who do not actually do anything or change anything. There will be no reconciliation with the stance taken by functionaries of that kind. We will simply have to part ways with them. All the more so do we have to part ways with those who hope that everything will settle down and return to the old lines. That will not happen, comrades!

SOURCE C
From Gorbachev's Report to the Twenty-Seventh Congress of the Party, *February 1986.*

We have got to be self-critical: we must see clearly that despite all the positive effects, the state of affairs in the economy is changing too slowly... In substance, the increase we have achieved in food output has largely been used to cover the demand connected with the growth of the population...And those who are holding up the process, who are creating hindrances, have to be put out of the way. Difficulties arose largely due to the tenacity of managerial stereotypes, to a striving to conserve familiar command methods of economic management, to the resistance of a part of the managerial cadre...And what is most intolerable is that enterprises are being compelled by means of State orders to manufacture goods that are not in demand, compelled for the simple reason that they want to attain the notorious 'gross output' targets...Enterprises that have been given the right to reward their more efficient workers and cut down on the incomes of those that are lazy, wasteful or idle, are using it much too timidly in fear of offending anyone. To put it plainly, the reform will not work, will not yield the results we expect, if it does not affect the personal interests of literally every person.

SOURCE D
From Gorbachev's Address to the Special Nineteenth Party Conference, *June 1988.*

	Produced national income	Gross industrial production	Gross agricultural production	Labour productivity	Real incomes per head
1951–55	11.4	13.0	4.2	–	–
1956–60	9.1	10.4	6.0	–	–
1961–65	6.5	8.6	2.3	6.1	3.6
1966–70	7.8	8.5	3.9	6.8	5.9
1971–75	5.7	7.4	2.5	4.5	4.4
1976–80	4.3	4.4	1.7	3.3	3.4
1981–85	3.6	3.7	1.1	3.1	2.1
1986	4.1	4.9	5.1	3.8	2.3
1987	2.3	3.8	0.2	2.4	2.0

TABLE 18
(Source E) Average annual rate of Soviet economic growth (in %), 1951–87, compiled from Soviet sources.

The Secretariat and *Politburo* of the central committee of the Communist party of the Soviet Union did not come out against the coup d'etat.

The central committee did not manage to take a firm position of condemnation and opposition and did not call on communists to fight the trampling of constitutional law. Among the conspirators were members of the party leadership. A number of party committees and the mass media supported the actions of the state criminals.

This put millions of communists in a false position. Many members of the party refused to collaborate with the conspirators, condemned the *coup*, and joined the fight against it.

No one has the right to blame wholesale all communists, and I as President consider it my duty to defend them as citizens from unfounded accusations. In this situation, the central committee of the CPSU must make the difficult but honest decision to disband itself.

The fate of republican Communist Parties and local party

SOURCE F
Gorbachev's statement of resignation as General Secretary after the coup *of August 1991.*

organisations should be decided by themselves. I consider it no longer possible to continue to carry out my duties as general secretary of the central committee of the Communist Party of the Soviet Union and I relinquish corresponding authority.

I believe that democratically minded communists, who remained faithful to constitutional law and to the course of the renewal of society, will speak up for the creation of a new basis of a party capable, together with all progressive forces, of actively joining in the continuation of fundamental democratic reforms.

1. *Compare the content and tone of the propaganda in Sources A and B. (6 marks)*
2. *Using the sources and your own knowledge, explain in what ways, and why, the message of Sources C and D is different from that of Sources A and B. (7 marks)*
3. *Using Source E and your own knowledge, explain which of Sources A, B, C or D presents a truer picture of Soviet economic perormance. (7 marks)*
4. *What reasons were given by Gorbachev in Source F for resigning and suggesting the dissolution of the Communist Party? (4 marks)*
5. *Are Sources C, D and F from the post-*glasnost *era more useful to the historian of the USSR than Sources A and B, from the pre-*glasnost *era? Explain your answer. (6 marks)*
6. *Study the following cartoons from Soviet magazines of the 1980s, and answer the questions which follow:*

PICTURE 9
(Source A) 'You substitute a false label "fresh" for "sour" and you can send them to Murmansk!' from Krokodil, *1984.*

PICTURE 10

(Source B) 'Pass it through these wonderful cast-iron railings!' from Krokodil, *1984.*

PICTURE 11

(Source C) 'Work without quality is not work, but self-seeking' (The apple bears the motto 'Bonus') from Krokodil, *1984.*

PICTURE 12

(Source D) 'Now Sidorov, don't return without spare parts! The State farm will take care of your family until you return' from Krokodil, 1986.

PICTURE 13

(Source E) 'Excuse me, but he has a more weighty argument for admittance' from Krokodil, 1986.

(Source F) 'I am reporting: the region's telephone system is completely working!' from Krokodil, 1986.

(Source G) The documents read 'Orders, Instructions, Appendices, Decrees' from Krokodil, 1986.

PICTURE 16

(Source H) 'We are keeping in step with the times – we are developing glasnost!' The posters read 'Our Miscalculations, Our Shortages, Slackers, Defects' from Krokodil, 1987.

Q

1. *All these cartoons suggest problems with the Soviet economy or society in the 1980s. Identify what seems to be the message of each source. (24 marks)*
2. *What more general points do these sources suggest about the USSR at the time of Gorbachev's accession to power in 1985? (6 marks)*
3. *Why did the regime allow this sort of material to be published, even before 1985? (4 marks)*
4. *Using your own knowledge, explain the extent to which Gorbachev's reforms successfully resolved any of the problems you have identified. (6 marks)*

Central Europe, 1945–92

4

INTRODUCTION

Czechoslovakia, Poland, Hungary and Austria occupied a key position in Europe, not just because they are geographically central, but because they were sandwiched between the Western European members of NATO and the Soviet Union. As such they were involved in the Cold War politics which dominated much of the post-1945 period.

Austria, like Germany, was a defeated country in 1945 and experienced a joint occupation. However, from 1955 it reverted to its sovereign status, on the condition that it remained neutral. Austria faced the problem of coming to terms with its Nazi past. It also had a distinctive diplomatic status, comparable only with Switzerland and the Scandinavian States in Europe – that of being outside the Communist Bloc but not part of the Western anti-Communist alliance.

Czechoslovakia, Poland and Hungary were very much part of the Eastern Communist Bloc. They had a common political system – they were effectively one-party authoritarian states with similarities to Stalin's USSR – and they were also members of a supranational economic organisation (COMECON) and of a military alliance (the Warsaw Pact). All three countries experienced a Communist takeover in the aftermath of the Second World War, and the Communist regimes in each of them were overturned at the end of the 1980s. However, there were also differences between their experiences. Both Hungary and Czechoslovakia experienced Soviet-led invasions when reformers attempted radical political changes. Poland did not, although it was subject to Soviet pressure. There were also significant differences in the ways in which the three economies were managed and differences in the ways in which the Communist regimes came to an end, and in the methods by which post-Communist regimes tackled the residual political, economic and social problems.

These themes and events will be developed in this chapter. However, it will differ from the format of some of the other chapters in this respect: Czechoslovakia, Poland and Hungary, as part of the Soviet-controlled Eastern Bloc, and Austria as a neutral power, scarcely had independent foreign policies in the way that most modern sovereign states had. Therefore although political and economic developments will be covered in some detail, foreign relations will be included in the relevant 'political' sections, rather than being considered independently.

1 ⤳ CZECHOSLOVAKIA

A *Introduction: Czechoslovakia to 1945*

The state of Czechoslovakia was carved out of the Austro–Hungarian Empire at the end of the First World War. It was an artificial creation, comprising mostly Czechs and Slovaks, plus a large German minority. Czechoslovakia was unique in Central Europe in that it was a democracy, and a relatively developed and prosperous one. However, in 1938 and 1939 it was carved up by Germany, Poland and Hungary. The Czechoslovak lands were spared massive material damage in the Second World War, but they did suffer the rigours of a brutal Nazi occupation.

MAP 14
Eastern Europe in 1945

MAP 15
*Central and Eastern Europe
in 1994*

Resistance to the Germans after 1941 was dominated by Communists in both the Czech lands and the Slovak Protectorate. In London, a Czech government-in-exile was headed by former President Beneš. Stalin recognised this government in 1943, although some of the Czechoslovak Communist leaders like Klement Gottwald were in Moscow, and he agreed to respect Czechoslovakia's pre-war borders. The Red Army helped the partisans to drive out the German occupiers by May 1945. Stalin's intentions for post-war Czechoslovakia were not clear. However, he confirmed his 1943 decision after further negotiations in March 1945.

B *Political history*

FROM LIBERATION TO *COUP*

The Czechoslovak government agreed on by the Allies in 1945 contained several political parties. However, the Communists controlled the police and armed forces. The considerable pre-war popular support for the Communists was continued, and indeed strengthened by their record of wartime resistance after 1941.

Gottwald, back in Czechoslovakia, emphasised peaceful cooperation with other organisations and parties, including the Socialists. The restored President Beneš was wary of Soviet influence, and hoped that Czechoslovakia could act as a bridge between East and West, without becoming committed to either. Soviet forces were withdrawn from Czechoslovakia at the end of 1945 and elections were held in May 1946. The National Front of Communists and Socialists won an overall majority of votes, its support coming from both rural and urban areas. Gottwald became Prime Minister of a coalition government which included representatives of both the London government-in-exile and the Communist leadership back from exile in Moscow. Gottwald's policy of a gradual approach to Socialism appeared to be paying off. However, he faced a situation in which there was an undercurrent of Slovak resentment against more prosperous Czech neighbours, and this was reflected in the Slovak Communist Party, as well as in the nation at large.

Gottwald encountered problems in his relations with the Soviets. In July 1947 the Czechoslovak government declared its willingness to accept Marshall Aid. The Soviets forced Gottwald to reverse this decision. He also faced a challenge to his authority from Rudolf Slánsky, who controlled the security forces and wanted to reduce the domination of the National Front by Party bureaucrats.

The lead-up to the election of May 1948 was critical. Non-Communists were concerned at the gradual but steady growth of Soviet influence, although there was no clear evidence of an organised Communist plot to seize total power. Several non-Communist ministers resigned from the Government, hoping to force a showdown and prompt Beneš into calling an election and taking more decisive action against the Communists.

In the West these events were often interpreted as an attempted Communist *coup* against Beneš and the State, but it was the non-Communists who provoked a crisis. If the intention was somehow to push Beneš into adopting an anti-Communist stance, the move backfired. Beneš accepted a Communist-dominated government, and it was the Communists' opponents who had placed themselves in the political wilderness. The Communists achieved power without having to take up Stalin's offer of direct Soviet intervention.

FROM THE COMMUNIST TAKEOVER TO THE PRAGUE SPRING

From February 1948 Communists held the key government posts and effectively chose who held the others. The most prominent non-

See pages 387–8

KEY ISSUE

How and why did the 'coup' of 1948 come about?

Communist was Jan Masaryk, Minister of Foreign Affairs and son of Czechoslovakia's founder. In March he died in suspicious circumstances: although officially the death was suicide, there was evidence of Soviet complicity. The Communists moved quickly to consolidate their authority. New elections were held, this time not contested. Gottwald replaced Beneš as President, and Antonín Zápotocký became Prime Minister.

As was common in Communist states, purges were implemented to reinforce the authority of the regime and remove possible rivals to the leadership. Over 500 000 ordinary Party members, bureaucrats and military personnel were sacked or imprisoned. Slánsky was tried and executed in 1952. Soviet pressure was behind the purging of Slánsky, a victim of anti-semitic persecution, and he was also accused of contacts with Israel and Yugoslavia, both outside the Eastern Bloc.

> ### KEY ISSUE
>
> *What was Gottwald's contribution to the establishment of Socialism in Czechoslovakia?*

TIMELINE

Events in Czechoslovakia

April 1945	National Front government formed
May 1946	Czech Communists did well in elections
	Gottwald became Prime Minister and Communists got government posts
Feb 1948	Communist-dominated government set up
May	Single list of National Front candidates put forward for election
June	Gottwald replaced Beneš as President
Sept 1949	Purges of leading Communists began
Jan 1968	Dubček replaced Novotný as First Secretary
March	Beginning of 'Prague Spring'
Aug	Czechoslovakia invaded by Warsaw Pact
April 1969	Husák became First Secretary
Oct 1969	Czechoslovakia formally agreed to stationing of Soviet troops
Jan 1977	Dissident civil rights group 'Charter 77' formed
Dec 1987	Husák resigned Party leadership
	Replaced by Jakeš
Nov 1989	Opposition groups formed
	Communist leadership resigned
Dec	Čalfa formed a mainly non-Communist government
	Václav Havel elected President
June 1990	Civic Forum and Public Against Violence won elections
June 1991	Beginning of large-scale privatisation
	Withdrawal of Soviet troops completed
June 1992	Klaus and Mečiar became Prime Ministers of the Czech Republic and Slovakia respectively
July	Havel resigned Federal Presidency
Jan 1993	Formal separation of Czech and Slovak Republics
	Havel elected President of Czech Republic
Feb	Kovač elected Slovak President
Oct 1994	Mečiar's coalition government in Slovak Republic slowed down economic reform
	Instituted restrictions on the media
June 1996	Right-wing government formed in Czech Republic
July 1997	Czech Republic invited to join NATO

PROFILE

ALEXANDER DUBČEK
(1921–92)

PICTURE 17
Dubček, President Novotný and GDR leader, Walther Ulbricht, celebrate the anniversary of the 1948 Communist takeover of Czechoslovakia, Prague, February 1968

Dubček had spent his youth in the Soviet Union. He later recalled seeing starving peasants and victims of purges, but he never blamed the Communist system itself, only the people who operated it. He was a committed supporter of the Soviet system and was an active and orthodox member of the Slovak Communist Party from 1939. Dubček later faced strong opposition from Novotný and his supporters, who unfairly branded him a 'Slovak nationalist'. Dubček had Soviet backing when appointed leader in January 1968, and Brezhnev doubtless expected him to be a compliant ally.

Dubček encouraged reform but naively assumed that the Communist Party could be geninely popular and retain control of events. The reality was that Dubček was swept along by the tide of events. He was bullied into accepting Soviet intervention, and told by Brezhnev that 'You have let us all down.'

After the Soviet invasion, Dubček was made President of the new Federal Assembly (August 1968–September 1969) and was ambassador to Turkey (December 1969–June 1970). He was then expelled from the Party and relegated to a minor administrative post in Slovakia.

In December 1989, Dubček re-emerged from obscurity to be elected speaker of the post-Communist Czech Parliament. He was killed in a car crash in 1992.

Some of Dubček's reforming ideas were taken up almost twenty years later by the Soviet leader Gorbachev. When visiting Prague in 1989, Gorbachev was asked what the difference was between himself and Dubček. 'Nineteen years', was his reply.

Most historians accept that Dubček was naive and not capable of standing up to Brezhnev's USSR. He has been described, along with the Hungarian reformer Imre Nagy, as 'well-meaning but lightweight reformers who were soon out of their political depth and destined to become figureheads and later martyrs for their cause' and 'indisputably losers'. (R. Pearson, *The Rise and Fall of the Soviet Empire*, Macmillan, 1998).

Meanwhile, Communist control was also reinforced by the creation of Soviet-style Party structures and practices. These survived the de-Stalinisation which went on in Khrushchev's USSR. Czechoslovakia acquired the reputation of being a hardline Communist state.

Gottwald died in 1953. His successor as Party leader was Antonín Novotný. Novotný ousted some of the leading pro-Stalinists in the Party in 1963, but he was renowned for his own hardline approach, especially towards Slovakia, traditionally the junior and neglected partner in the hybrid state of Czechoslovakia. Novotný's constitution of 1960 asserted that Czechoslovakia had attained socialism, but it also did away with many Slovak institutions on the grounds that separate representation was not necessary to protect the interests of workers.

Novotný resisted Soviet pressure to rehabilitate victims of earlier purges, and even carried out more. He set his face against reform. When Novotný faced criticism from within the Party, he organised a coup against his opponents, but was blocked by his own security forces. The Soviet leader Brezhnev would not back him and he was forced to resign the Party leadership in January 1968, although he retained the presidency.

Novotný's successor was the First Secretary of the Slovak Communist Party, Alexander Dubček. Soon after his appointment events took a radical turn. Reformers within the Czech and Slovak Communist Parties argued for major political and economic reforms. Novotný was replaced as President by a retired general, Ludvík Svoboda. New freedoms were granted to the media. Dubček gave the impression of being swept along by events. He was not a great innovator: his declaration that the Party must have genuinely popular participation to justify its right to rule was largely borrowed from the Hungarian reformers of 1956. Dubček allowed intellectuals, journalists and reformers to make their voices heard, whilst somewhat naively believing that in a genuinely democratic system the Communists would manage by popular consent to retain their leading role in society. However, Dubček could not stem the tide of popular protest and expectations which marked this growing period of freedom, the so-called 'Prague Spring' of 1968.

THE INVASION OF CZECHOSLOVAKIA

The Soviet leaders decided that Dubček could no longer be trusted, although he frequently and genuinely protested his loyalty to the USSR and to Socialism. He also insisted that he did not intend to take Czechoslovakia out of the Warsaw Pact. However, Brezhnev could not tolerate the Czechoslovak version of 'Socialism with a human face': economic experimentation was one thing, but radical reforms were something else, and might affect other Eastern Bloc countries.

The Warsaw Pact had already issued warnings to Dubček to reassert firm control over the media and organisations. The Czechoslovak and Soviet leaders met at Cierna nad Tisou in Slovakia between 29 July and 1 August 1968. Although the Czechoslovaks renewed pledges of loyalty, the Warsaw Pact decided to intervene. On the night of 20–21 August 1968 200 000 troops from the USSR, East Germany, Poland, Hungary and Bulgaria invaded Czechoslovakia. The Warsaw Pact constitution did not allow for intervention in the internal affairs of member states, but it was claimed that counter-revolution threatened. Although there was some resistance in Prague, the invasion could not be stopped. The West protested, but was not prepared to intervene in what was accepted as a Soviet sphere of influence.

The Soviets could not produce a collaborationist government with sufficient authority. Therefore they arrested Dubček, Svoboda and other Czechoslovak leaders and bullied them into signing the Moscow Agreements, by which they agreed to reverse the changes made during the Prague Spring.

HUSÁK'S CZECHOSLOVAKIA

The process of reversing reforms, purging reformers and reconstituting the leadership was called 'Normalisation'. One of the few protests was the suicide, by burning, of the student Jan Palach. It took place in Prague's Wenceslas Square in January 1969. Dubček now carried little credibility, and following public celebrations of a victory by the Czechoslovak ice hockey team over the Soviets, he was forced by the Soviets to resign seven months after the initial invasion.

Dubček's successor as First Secretary was Gustav Husák, who had left the reformist wing of the Slovakian Communist Party just before the invasion. Husák had survived a turbulent political career, which included imprisonment for 'Slovak bourgeois nationalism', a spell as a construction worker, and rehabilitation into the Party. By the 1970s he was steering a middle course between Left and Right, becoming Head of State in 1975. He suppressed outward shows of dissent, as was expected by Moscow, and was popularly despised as the 'Russian

---

KEY ISSUE

What were the main features of the 'Prague Spring' and why did it come about?

KEY ISSUE

Why did the USSR invade Czechoslovakia?

goose'. When an organisation called Charter 77 called for human rights, several members were arrested. There was little more overt dissent – most people settled for quiet conformity, and even the Communist Party was beset by apathy. Husák was seen as increasingly hard line, and he listened with distaste to Gorbachev's pronouncements on reform in the 1980s USSR. Only token efforts of reform were attempted in Czechoslovakia. Husák was forced to resign in December 1987 and was eventually expelled from the Party in 1990.

Miloš Jakeš succeeded Husák. He was an old Stalinist, and could not dam the growing pressure for reform, despite the arrests of notable dissidents such as the playwright Václav Havel.

THE VELVET REVOLUTION

The Czechoslovak regime held out against real reform for as long as it could. However, the breaching of the Berlin Wall in November 1989 acted as a flashpoint. Demonstrations in favour of reform broke out in several cities: their relatively restrained nature led to the term 'Velvet Revolution'. Two political groups set themselves up in opposition to the regime. In Prague there was the Civic Forum, which included Havel. In Slovakia there was Public Against Violence. Very late in the day, the Communist leadership took heed of the warning signs and desperately tried to make the Party reformist. The leadership resigned *en bloc* and a new government was set up under Ladislav Adamec in December 1989. It contained some non-Communists, but the opposition would not recognise it, and the government resigned in the same month.

The opposition finally won the day. A Government of National Understanding was set up by Civic Forum and other non-Communist groups, under the former Communist Marián Čalfa. Husák resigned the presidency, and the Czech lands and Slovakia were granted separate republican governments to function alongside the new federal government. Havel was elected President of the National Assembly, and Dubček emerged from obscurity to be its chairman.

Twenty-three parties fought the general election of June 1990. Civic Forum and Public against Violence won convincingly, and both were strongly represented in Čalfa's new government. However, there were complex arguments about the pace of economic reform, whilst a resurgence of nationalism, especially in Slovakia, threatened long-term stability.

THE VELVET DIVORCE

Although economic and social reforms continued apace, the national question occupied most attention. The separation of the Czech and Slovak Republics was announced in 1992. However, both Civic Forum and Public Against Violence had already split into factions in 1991. Civic Forum split in February into the Civic Democratic Party and the Civic Movement, the latter led by Václav Klaus, who favoured moderate economic reform. The Slovaks argued more about federal issues than economics: the Slovak Prime Minister Vladimir Měciar

> ### KEY ISSUE
>
> *How and why was Communism overthrown in Czechoslovakia?*

formed the Movement for a Democratic Slovakia. However, he was accused of pro-Soviet intrigue and was replaced by the Christian Democrat leader Ján Carnogurský, who was supported by what remained of Public Against Violence. This atmosphere of faction and bickering enabled the Communists to retain a respectable level of support in both Republics.

Federal President Havel failed to persuade the Federal Assembly to agree on the format for a referendum in 1991 to resolve the national issue. It was eventually resolved by elections in June 1992. Klaus and Měciar, who had the greatest political support, could not form a federal government, so agreed that the old state should divide. Havel resigned as Federal President in July 1992.

Party	Votes (%) 1992	Votes (%) 1996	Seats (no.) 1996
Civic Democratic Party and Christian Democrats	29.7	29.7	68
Communist Party	14.1	10.3	22
Social Democratic Party	6.5	28.4	61
Liberal Social Union	6.5	–	–
Christian Democratic Union/ People's Party	6.3	8.1	18
Republican Party	6.0	8.0	18
Civic Democratic Alliance	5.9	6.4	13

TABLE 19
Czech general election results, 1992 and 1996

(N.B. The 1992 results were for the Czech National Council, which became the Czech Parliament in January 1993.)

Party	Votes (%) 1992	Votes (%) 1994	Seats (no.) 1994
Movement for a Democratic Slovakia	37.3	35.0	61
Party of the Democratic Left	14.7	–	–
Christian Democratic Movement	8.9	10.1	17
Slovak National Party	7.9	5.4	9
Hungarian Alliance	7.4	10.2	17
Social Democratic Party	4.1	–	–
Civic Democratic Union	4.0	–	–
Democratic Party	3.3	–	–
Others	12.4	13.1	0

TABLE 20
*Slovak general election
results, 1992 and 1994*

A new coalition was formed to carry through the peaceful 'velvet divorce'. On 1 January 1993 the Federation was dissolved. Havel was elected the new Czech President, and Michal Kovač was elected Slovak President. The Czech Constitution of January 1993 created a parliament comprising a 400-member House of Representatives and a Senate of eighty-one members. Klaus, leader of the Civic Democratic Party, continued with economic reform, and the Czech Republic proved to be one of the most stable of the post-Communist states, at least until Klaus's coalition lost its majority in June 1996.

Slovakia's Parliament was a National Council, and the first coalition government comprised the Movement for a Democratic Slovakia and the Slovak National Party, with MDS leader Mečiar as Prime Minister. Slovakia faced many problems, such as a relatively undeveloped economy and the issue of how to deal with over half a million ethnic Hungarians who lived in a country of under five million inhabitants. Opinion polls in Slovakia during 1990–93 suggested that four-fifths of its inhabitants would have preferred to live in a common state with the Czechs. Governments lacked stability, and Mečiar was ousted in March 1994, only to return in October. His government then began to slow down economic reform and to pass laws making criticism of itself more difficult.

C *Economic history*

SOCIALIST CZECHOSLOVAKIA

The pre-1939 Czech lands had been one of the most economically developed regions of Central and Eastern Europe, with a substantial industrial base. Slovakia was more rural and undeveloped. The Stalinist command economy model, imposed on Czechoslovakia after 1945, did not benefit a relatively sophisticated society. It was a model which could produce rapid growth results in an undeveloped economy, but not improve a more complex one in which quality was as important as quantity. A crude industrialisation drive based on central planning and direction of resources took little account of consumer need and

Stalinist economics did little to help the long-term growth prospects of the Czechoslovak economy.

Nationalisation was extended to all enterprises of over 150 workers in October 1945. 80 per cent of industries and services were nationalised by 1948, and the process was completed during the next four years. Many peasants were gratified to receive land taken from the one million Sudeten Germans driven out of the borderlands in 1945 and 1946.

The Czechoslovak economy emerged from the war relatively unscathed compared to its neighbours, and this made the failure to secure Marshall Aid easier to bear. However, planning took little account of consumer demand, real wages fell, and there were protests by workers in 1953.

Following Khrushchev's economic reforms in the USSR, there was half-hearted tinkering with the Czechoslovak economic structure in the 1950s. In 1958 the number of industrial enterprises was reduced from over 1400 to less than 400. Managers were given more say in investment decisions, but there was little impact on the low growth rates, and the reforms were reversed in the early 1960s. Czechoslovakia found it difficult to export its traditional product – machinery – outside COMECON markets. An economic crisis in 1962–63 led to a major rethink: levels of investment were targeted on specific areas, and the over-ambitious Third Five-Year Plan (1960–65) was suspended. The drive towards collectivisation of agriculture was halted. The rate of growth in National Income declined from 11 per cent in 1959 to zero by 1963, when Czechoslovakia became the first European Communist country to record an absolute decline in National Income.

Clearly, decisive action was needed. The 'New Economic Model' was implemented in 1967. It allowed for some decentralisation of planning and freedom for individual enterprises. However, the model was never fully implemented because of apathy and opposition from entrenched conservative bureaucrats. The essentials of the centrally planned economy remained, and the regime would not accept that political reform was also necessary for economic reform to succeed. Novotný resisted calls for further economic reform and the liberalising hopes of economic reformers in the 'Prague Spring' of 1968 were dashed by the Warsaw Pact invasion. In the 'normalisation' which followed, full economic controls with centrally planned targets and allocation of resources were re-imposed.

The discrediting of reform simply compounded Czechoslovakia's economic problems. Growth rates continued to decline and the once prosperous state slipped behind some of its neighbours. Further tinkering with the economy in the later 1970s did not help. Defence spending was cut, and the USSR subsidised oil supplies to Czechoslovakia. However, a continued decline in internal investment damaged the economy. The protest movement which eventually overthrew Husák was fuelled by economic pressures on ordinary Czechoslovaks, particularly when he refused to follow Gorbachev's reforming example in the USSR.

KEY ISSUE

How did the Czechoslovak economy fare under the Communist regime?

FROM SOCIALISM TO CAPITALISM

Even after Husák's removal, most reformers were reluctant to institute radical measures, because of the dislocation which would inevitably occur in the short term. Both Federal and Republican Governments did agree to introduce a reform programme in 1991, to include some measure of privatisation and a liberal pricing policy, phasing out subsidies. In June 1990 fifty of the largest state enterprises were put on the market for foreign investors, whilst enterprises were allowed to submit their own privatisation plans for official approval. If market reforms were to be effective, there had to be some popular participation. So in February 1991 laws were passed returning expropriated property to its previous owners, and in October privatisation vouchers were put on sale to the public.

The benefits of these policies were not immediately obvious. Economic progress was hindered by political uncertainties. Industrial production continued to fall during 1991, unemployment rose (at twice the rate in Slovakia as in the Czech lands) and the collapse of markets in the COMECON Bloc hit the economy hard. Popular capitalism proved difficult to take root. Early in 1992 citizens who bought investment vouchers were allowed to exchange them for shares in state-owned companies. However, most shares were bought by investment trusts, and therefore although the bulk of capital was no longer state-owned, it was still concentrated in relatively few hands.

The final stage of privatisation in the Czech Republic took place towards the end of 1993, involving 770 enterprises, with the vouchers on sale to all citizens. In Slovakia, privatisation involved a mixture of vouchers and direct sale. Because the Slovak economy was less developed than its Czech counterpart, the Slovaks sought close economic relations with their neighbours: in December 1992 the Czech, Polish and Hungarian governments reached agreement to reduce tariffs on trade between their countries.

The experience of forty years of State Socialism had, on balance, not been beneficial for the Czechoslovak economy and its people. It is true that the living conditions of the various social groups showed fewer marked differences than in some other Eastern Bloc countries. Also, the population benefited from guaranteed employment and a basic level of social services. However, Czechoslovakia also experienced some of the social problems common in Eastern Bloc states: for example, urban overcrowding and a housing shortage, despite a fall in the birth rate, accentuated by a move of the agricultural population to the towns. As in all Communist states, the lot of women was hard: in spite of legal equality, they worked full time but also bore the brunt of shortages and the burden of running homes.

The dismantling of Communism and the difficult transition to capitalism did not bring immediate improvements. However, after the creation of the Czech and Slovak Republics, some of the political uncertainties were eased, confidence began to grow and the economy showed some improvement. The long-term prospect of economic integration with Western Europe offered further hope.

> **KEY ISSUE**
>
> *How did the overthrow of the Communist regime affect the Czechoslovak economy?*

2 ᔧ POLAND

A *Introduction: Poland to 1945*

The once-powerful State of Poland had been partitioned by powerful neighbours in the eighteenth century. A national State was only resurrected after the First World War. Tragedy repeated itself in 1939 when Poland was carved up by Germany and the USSR at the beginning of the Second World War. The occupation of Poland resulted in proportionately more casualties and damage (over six million dead) than any other combatant country and the experience of the war simply reinforced Polish fear and hatred of German and Soviet neighbours.

Politics in wartime Poland were complex. Like the Czechs, the Poles had a government-in-exile in London. It commanded a resistance force, the Polish Home Army. The Polish Communist Party, whose leadership had been purged by Stalin before the war, was encouraged to ally with other left-wing parties and form a Popular Front. At the same time Stalin, always suspicious of the Poles, developed a parallel Polish Communist leadership in Moscow should he need to intervene more directly in Poland. Wladyslaw Gomulka, the Communist leader in Poland, followed Stalin's orders and negotiated both with the government-in-exile and the Socialists in the hope of forming a Popular Front. However, Stalin sent another prominent Polish Communist, Boleslaw Bierut, to work alongside Gomulka. The two were rivals, and Bierut opposed negotiations with the Socialists.

Stalin eventually backed Bierut and sent the Red Army into German-occupied Poland early in 1944. Bierut was made President of the Polish Committee for National Liberation, based in Lublin, and consisting of Communists once based in Moscow. Although the Socialists agreed to ally with the Communists, the situation was complicated by a civil war between the Communists and the Polish Home Army. After the Germans were driven out of Poland, the Committee became the provisional government of Poland, with Bierut as President. Thousands of anti-Communists were rounded up and killed in the following months.

> **KEY ISSUE**
>
> *How and why were the Communists able to come to power in Poland?*

B *Political history*

THE CONSOLIDATION OF COMMUNIST RULE

The Western Allies only recognised the provisional government in June 1945 after it agreed to appoint some non-Communists. The government contained members of the Communist, Socialist, Peasant and Catholic Labour Parties. The Prime Minister was the Socialist Edward Osóbka. His government implemented the Potsdam Agreement: the frontiers of Poland were shifted westwards into former German territory to compensate for the loss of Polish land in the East to the USSR.

> See map on page 385

MAP 16
Poland after the Second World War

The unity of the government was short-lived. First, the Communists (called the Polish United Workers' Party or PUWP) and Socialists instituted radical economic and social reforms. Second, the Communists were closely controlled from Moscow, which regarded Poland as integral to Soviet defence and therefore interfered in Polish affairs whenever it saw fit. A referendum on issues including land reform was held in June 1946, and the new Polish Peasant Party did well. It was admitted in 1990 that the referendum had been manipulated, accounting for the majority in favour of Communist proposals.

See page 183

Not all was plain sailing for the Communists. Gomulka disagreed with some of his own colleagues on several issues, and he was also at odds with Stalin: Gomulka did not want to join the new **COMINFORM**, regarding it as an instrument of Soviet control; and he did not want rapid collectivisation of agriculture. Gomulka paid the price for his 'nationalist deviation', as Moscow saw it. He was replaced as Party leader by Bierut in September 1948. Bierut followed the Moscow line. Soviet officials were in the Polish security forces, and the Minister of Defence was Konstantin Rokosowski, a Soviet marshal. Poland was seen as a key area in the developing Cold War confrontation between East and West, and Stalin was taking no chances on its loyalty. In 1948 the Socialist Party was merged with the Communists.

COMINFORM or Communist Information Bureau: an organisation of communist states formed after the Second World War

THE RETURN OF GOMULKA

Under Soviet control, political stability seemed assured until the uncertainties created by Khrushchev's attack on Stalin's memory in 1956 and the resulting policy of de-Stalinisation. Bierut died in March 1956 and his successor, Edward Ochab, rehabilitated the disgraced

TIMELINE

Events in Poland

Feb 1945	Allies recognised provisional government in Poland
Aug	New Polish–German border agreed
Jan 1947	Communists and Allies won general election
Sept 1948	Gomulka resigns Polish leadership
Dec	Communists and Socialists merged
June 1956	Workers' riots in Poznań
	Gomulka appointed First Secretary
Dec 1970	Food riots
	Gierek replaced Gomulka as leader
June 1976	Strikes and disturbances suppressed
July– Sept 1980	Strikes at Gdańsk and elsewhere
	Gierek replaced as leader by Kania
	Recognition of *Solidarity*
Feb 1981	General Jaruzelski became Prime Minister
Dec	Martial law declared and *Solidarity* banned
Nov 1985	Jaruzelski became President
Feb 1989	Polish government held talks with *Solidarity*
March	*Solidarity* legalised
June	*Solidarity* won first free parliamentary elections
July	Jaruzelski elected President
	Tadeuz Mazowiecki appointed first non-Communist Prime Minister
Dec 1990	Lech Wałęsa elected President
Jan 1991	Bielecki's 'Government of Experts' formed
Dec	Centre-right Catholic coalition under J. Olszewski
July 1992	Suchocha government appointed
Oct 1993	Pawlak coalition government formed
Nov 1995	Wałęsa lost presidential election to former Communist A. Kwasniewski
July 1997	Poland invited to join NATO

Gomulka. Censorship was relaxed and some political prisoners were released.

However, workers in Poznań, unhappy with their working conditions, rioted. The army had to restore order and there were several deaths. It was the first major public challenge to Communist policies in the Eastern Bloc. There were arguments in the PUWP about responsibility for the disturbances, but those advocating moderate reform won the day. In October 1956 Gomulka, who had considerable popular support, was appointed First Secretary by the *Politburo*.

Gomulka's appointment was opposed by Moscow-backed hardliners, named the Natolin Group after a village near Warsaw. Fears increased when Khrushchev arrived in Moscow to attend a special PUWP Party Congress, and warned the Polish Communists of the possibility of Soviet intervention. However, the Party called the Soviet bluff, and made some changes of personnel. The Soviets did not intervene, possibly because they were still smarting from international condemnation of their intervention in Hungary, but most likely because they feared mass resistance from Polish workers.

See page 188

Gomulka followed up his success by sending Marshal Rokosowski and thousands of Soviet officers back to Moscow and winning an assurance from the Soviets that they would respect Polish sovereignty. The Kremlin also accepted that the bulk of Polish agriculture would remain uncollectivised, one of the ways in which Poland was unique in the Eastern Bloc.

Gomulka did not retain his reputation for adaptability and political skill. Initially his regime seemed very radical: in 1957 Poland had the first contested elections in the Eastern Bloc, when 750 candidates contested 459 parliamentary seats. But by the 1960s, it was the reformers who were dissatisfied, as party discipline was tightened up and dissidents were persecuted. There was harassment of Jews, who had traditionally been persecuted in Poland, after the Arab–Israeli War of 1967. Expressions of sympathy for the Czechoslovak reformers of 1968 were muzzled. However, Gomulka's orthodoxy and his increasingly hardline approach won him the continued support of the USSR. He was eventually undermined by economic failure, although he contributed to his downfall by expending more energy on trying to outflank his rivals and factional groups in the Party than on tackling Poland's social and economic ills.

KEY ISSUE

How successful was Gomulka's regime in establishing stability in Poland and maintaining a stable relationship with the USSR?

GIEREK'S POLAND

Gomulka's fall was sparked off by escalating strikes and demonstrations following a 30 per cent increase in the price of food in December 1970. The Central Committee, alarmed, removed Gomulka and installed Edward Gierek as new Party leader. Gierek had a reputation as an effective administrator. He adopted the short-term solution of making concessions to the workers and reversing the price increases in February 1971. He then planned a more substantial package of economic reforms and attempted to involve more ordinary citizens in the Party's activities.

Gierek also sought compromise with the Catholic Church. The Church in Poland occupied a unique position in the Eastern Bloc. Despite the prevailing anti-religious Marxist orthodoxy, the Church was supported by the majority of the Polish population, including many Party members. Earlier attempts to curb the power of the Church, including its separation from the State, nationalisation of its lands and the imprisonment of the influential Cardinal Wyszynski, had simply boosted its popular support. Gierek recognised the value of the Church's support, and he allowed religion to be taught in Polish schools. The reconciliation was aided by the appointment of the Pole Karol Wojtyla as Pope John Paul II in 1978.

Gierek did not forget where his base of support lay. His 1976 Constitution, which announced that Poland had become a Socialist state, also emphasised the leading role of the Party. Relations with the USSR and fellow Eastern Bloc states were strengthened. However, Gierek suffered the same fate as Gomulka. Economic problems demanded action. In June 1976 the announcement of a 60 per cent rise in prices was predictably met by mass demonstrations and strikes.

KEY ISSUE

To what extent did Gierek's regime succeed in achieving stability and popularity within Poland?

PROFILE

LECH WAŁĘSA (B. 1943)

Wałęsa was the son of a village carpenter who had spent some time in a Nazi concentration camp. He became a shipyard electrician and fellow workers elected him to the strike committee in the Lenin shipyard at Gdańsk in 1970. There, Wałęsa learned not to take on the police in the streets but to passively resist and occupy the workplace until the authorities negotiated:

> A wall cannot be demolished with butts of the head. We must move slowly, step by step, otherwise the wall remains untouched and we break our heads.

Wałęsa was frequently in trouble with the authorities for his trade union activities. He came to national prominence as the leader of the Gdańsk strike in the late 1970s, his leadership of *Solidarity* and his strong opposition to government policies.

Wałęsa proved adept both at appealing to a mass audience and negotiating coolly with the authorities. He also knew when to compromise. However, he was imprisoned under martial law in December 1981, then released eleven months later. Wałęsa was awarded the Nobel Peace Prize in 1983. Although he continued to guide *Solidarity*, Wałęsa refused office when it joined Poland's non-Communist government in September 1989. He was elected to the presidency in 1990, but was defeated in the 1995 presidential elections by a former Communist.

Wałęsa's politics were a mixture of realism and romanticism. Although he became a national symbol abroad as well as at home, he was not a lover of western-style capitalism. At the time of *Solidarity* Wałęsa declared,

> We don't want to go back to capitalism or copy Western models. We live in Poland and must find Polish solutions. Socialism isn't a bad system. Let it remain – as long as it is controlled.

Wałęsa was deeply Catholic and patriotic but not an intellectual. His achievement was to turn a shipyard protest into a nationwide movement.

Although militants were arrested, an organised opposition began to emerge. Students, workers and intellectuals formed the Committee for the Defence of Workers (KOR). The Church supported the opposition and underground organisations distributed protest literature.

THE ERA OF *SOLIDARITY*

There was a similar pattern of unrest in 1980. More price rises were met with strikes. The focus for discontent was the Lenin shipyard in

Gdańsk. The demonstrations of 1970 had begun here. The strikers' leader was Lech Wałęsa.

Attempts to divide the strikers failed and strike committees produced demands for independent unions. The government was divided about how it should respond. Eventually Gierek offered reforms and negotiated with the new organisation *Solidarity*, the first independent, self-governing union in the Communist world. The Party agreed to sign an agreement because the combined threat of a general strike and massive social unrest was too horrendous to contemplate. The USSR allowed the agreement to be signed, probably because the Polish Party persuaded the Kremlin that it was still in control – although the Warsaw Pact did conduct menacing manoeuvres on Poland's borders in 1980 and 1981.

The strain was too much for Gierek. After a heart attack he was replaced by Stanislaw Kania. Kania's background was in security and his appointment was approved by the Kremlin. *Solidarity* itself was only formally recognised in November 1980 after another threat of a general strike. There were more confrontations before moderates won the day. In February 1981, the army chief General Wojcieck Jaruzelski was appointed Prime Minister. At an Extraordinary PUWP Congress in July most of the Central Committee and many other important Party functionaries were replaced. Both Kania and Jaruzelski declared their commitment to reform, despite opposition from some Party hardliners.

Solidarity's victory created problems for itself. It set up branches across Poland and held a Congress in September and October 1981. However, the movement was difficult to control: there were disagreements amongst its members about how far they should engage in traditional union activities, and how far they should become a political organisation and put pressure for change on the Party.

In October 1981 Kania was replaced as PUWP leader by Jaruzelski, already Prime Minister and Minister of Defence. Jaruzelski tried to reduce *Solidarity*'s influence by proposing to include it as just one of several parties and public organisations in a 'Front for National Cooperation', whilst the Communists remained very much in control. *Solidarity* refused. Jaruzelski, under pressure from the Kremlin and his own hardliners to take decisive action, declared martial law on 12 December 1981. He created a Military Council of National Salvation and arrested *Solidarity*'s leaders. Trade union activity was suspended. There were also promises of economic reform, but the measures taken were very limited.

Solidarity was formally abolished in the autumn of 1982. However, many of its several million members continued to operate underground. In contrast, Communist Party membership declined and there was considerable apathy amongst members. Although martial law was lifted in July 1983, other repressive laws remained. In retaliation, *Solidarity* urged Poles to boycott local elections. Jaruzelski was appointed President in November 1985.

KEY ISSUE

How significant was the rise of Solidarity *in Poland and the rest of the Eastern Bloc?*

THE TRIUMPH OF *SOLIDARITY* AND THE END OF COMMUNIST RULE

Once again, economic problems provoked major change. Economic problems were mounting, without much prospect of improvement. The PUWP's Tenth Congress in June 1986 was attended by Soviet leader Gorbachev, who had begun his own reform programme in the USSR. Jaruzelski announced that all political prisoners would be released. A referendum on political and economic reform in November 1987 aroused little enthusiasm, and new price increases in 1988 fomented more discontent and strikes. Eventually, the government attempted a compromise with its opponents. In January 1989 the PUWP decided to legalise *Solidarity* and recognise other political parties. This major step led to 'Round Table' negotiations between the government, Church and *Solidarity*, and had a considerable impact on promoting change elsewhere in the Eastern Bloc.

It was agreed that 35 per cent of parliamentary seats could be contested by opposition candidates in the forthcoming elections. Elections to the new Senate (Upper House) would be completely free and open. In the first round of elections in June 1989 the Communists did poorly, whereas *Solidarity* won most of the parliamentary and Senate seats open to it. There was a similar result in the second round of elections. Wałęsa declared, 'This is the beginning of democracy and a free Poland.'

Jaruzelski was narrowly elected by Parliament to the new post of Executive President in July 1989. However, the recent election results led Jaruzelski to invite *Solidarity* to join a coalition government. He also resigned the PUWP leadership in favour of the previous Prime Minister, Mieczyslaw Rákowski. *Solidarity*, wary of a coalition with the Communists, refused to cooperate. Jaruzelski effectively admitted defeat on 20 August 1989 by inviting Tadeusz Mazowiecki, editor of the *Solidarity* newspaper, to form a new government. The Communists still controlled the army and internal security, but nevertheless it was the first government in the Eastern Bloc since the late 1940s not controlled by Communists. In addition to two Communists, there were eleven *Solidarity* members and representatives of other parties in the government. Equally significant was the fact that the USSR allowed it to happen. A clear message had been sent to the rest of the Eastern Bloc that the USSR would not intervene to prop up Communist regimes. It was perhaps no coincidence that the breaching of the Berlin Wall and other radical developments occurred shortly after these events in Poland.

POST-COMMUNIST POLAND

Mazowiecki's government took immediate measures to dismantle the Communist apparatus. Poland became a simple 'Republic' and Party control over the police and army was removed. The PUWP dissolved itself and was reborn as the Social Democrat Party, in January 1990.

Focus now shifted to a presidential election. Lech Wałęsa was a candidate since, although re-elected Chairman of the *Solidarity* trade

> **KEY ISSUE**
>
> *How and why was Communism overthrown in Poland?*

Party	Votes (%) 1991	Votes (%) 1991	Seats (no.) 1993
Democratic Union	12.3	10.6	74
Democratic Left Alliance	12.0	20.4	171
Polish Peasants' Party	8.7	15.4	132
Centre Alliance	8.7	4.4	–
Catholic Electoral Committee	8.7	–	–
Confederation for an Independent Poland	7.5	5.8	22
Liberal Democratic Congress	7.5	4.0	–
Polish Peasants' Party (Peasant Alliance)	5.5	2.3	–
German Ethnic Minority	1.2	0.7	4

TABLE 21
Polish general election results, 1991 and 1993

union in April 1990, he also wanted a political base. However, now that it was operating openly and successfully, *Solidarity* was divided: a Centre Alliance supported Wałęsa's campaign, whilst ROAD (the Democratic Action Civic Movement) supported Mazowiecki. Jaruzelski resigned the presidency in September 1990.

The result of the first round of the elections in November 1990 was a surprise. Wałęsa won 40 per cent of the vote but no overall majority. The largely unknown Stanislaw Tyminski, a Polish-born Canadian Peruvian businessman, got 23 per cent of the vote. Mazowiecki, a poor third, promptly resigned as Prime Minister. Wałęsa won a clear majority in the second round, with 74 per cent, and was sworn in as President. The new Prime Minister was the businessman Krzysztof Bielecki.

Clearly reform was expected, but the situation was difficult. There was still a majority of old Communists in Parliament, and the new parties often lacked coherence and stability. The first fully free and open parliamentary elections did not take place until October 1991, long after several other former Communist states had passed through the process. On a low turn-out, probably reflecting a mixture of confusion and apathy in the electorate, no party secured more than 12 per cent of the vote. It was therefore difficult to form a new government. Eventually Jan Olszewski was appointed Prime Minister, but in July 1992 he was dismissed in favour of Waldemar Pawlak, leader of the Peasant Party. He, in turn, was soon replaced by a member of the Democratic Union, Hanna Suchocha, who headed a seven-party coalition. To a large extent these frequent changes reflected arguments about the nature and pace of economic reform.

Unemployment, strikes, political disputes – all augured ill for the new democracy. Suchocha's government received a vote of no confidence in May 1993. In new elections the Union of the Democratic Left and the Polish Peasant Party, both successor parties to the Communists, combined to win a clear majority. *Solidarity* parties received little support because of their internal divisions. Pawlak became Prime Minister. Supporters of democracy were concerned by the increase in support for Nationalist parties, disillusionment with the new democracy, and nostalgia in many quarters for the 'security' which many people remembered under the old authoritarian Communist

KEY ISSUE

To what extent did the post-Communist regimes in Poland succeed in restoring stability?

regime. Political stability was not helped by a power struggle between President Wałęsa and the government, with Wałęsa attacking a slowing down of the reform process. Wałęsa himself was defeated in the November 1995 presidential election by Alexander Kwasniewski, an ex-Communist. Poland's prospects would depend largely on the future of the economy and how ordinary people felt about their living and working conditions.

C *Economic history*

The economy was crucial to events in Poland. It was unrest sparked off by price rises which triggered major political crises in 1970 and 1980, and lay behind the rise of *Solidarity*. It was the inability of post-Communist governments in the years immediately after 1989 to reform the economy, which prompted fears that the new democracy would not survive. And yet, ironically, the price rises were part of what more enlightened Poles accepted as inevitable if real economic problems were to be addressed.

Poland emerged from the Second World War devastated, with an estimated billion dollars' worth of damage, in addition to the loss of tens of thousands of its most able and youngest citizens. However, the Communists expected to transform the economy regardless of the cost: even before the end of the war social and economic reform had begun. Committees were established in factories with worker representatives on management boards. Following a law of January 1946, large factories were nationalised and the State soon controlled all industry. The Soviet model of the five-year plan was adopted, with due emphasis upon rapid industrialisation and collectivisation of agriculture. The targets were not fulfilled, partly because Poland simply could not afford the necessary investment. There were shortages and rationing, and inflation ran at 80 per cent in the early 1950s. Social problems, in particular urban overcrowding and a high birth rate, compounded economic problems. The urban population increased by one-third between 1950 and 1970.

The Polish economy differed from the orthodox Eastern Bloc model in one important respect: 75 per cent of farmland remained uncollectivised, and Poland remained a country of relatively small farmers. Many farms, already collectivised, were broken up in 1956. Small independent farmers were harder for the Party to control. But even Stalin accepted the situation, declaring that 'Communism fits Poland like a saddle fits a cow'. The 1956 riots showed the dangers of instituting policies which were resented by large sections of the population, and the Soviets seemed prepared to accept economic 'deviations' provided that the Polish Communists remained in control. Poland also showed its independence in other ways, for example by continuing extensive trade with the West, and accepting American aid to buy grain from abroad.

See page 176

KEY ISSUE

To what extent was the organisation of the Polish economy typical of economies in the Eastern Bloc?

However, Gomulka faced similar economic problems to some of his Eastern Bloc counterparts. Poland's growth rate was one of the lowest in Central and Eastern Europe. It was difficult to satisfy the material expectations of the population. A joint Party–Government Economic Council set up in 1956 proposed a limited relaxation of economic controls. The number of economic targets was reduced, workers' councils were given more say in the running of enterprises and there were more direct links made between profits and workers' bonuses. This was too radical for some in the PUWP, and the councils were put under trade union (and therefore Party) control in May 1957. The Economic Council was wound up in 1962, before its proposals for less central planning could be implemented. Further calls for more reforms of the pricing and incentive structures were mostly discredited by the serious workers' riots of 1970 and later. Pricing remained one of the biggest problems for the regime. Peasants needed the stimulus of higher prices to encourage them to produce more. The government could subsidise prices, an inefficient strategy, or try to pass higher prices on to the consumer. Whenever it adopted the latter approach, strikes and demonstrations followed, and sometimes also a political crisis.

In the 1970s Gierek sought a way out of this impasse by trying to benefit from the trade, technology and credit facilities of the West. A Committee for Modernising the Economic System and the State was set up in 1971, and its plan was implemented in 1973. Larger enterprises were given rights to engage in foreign trade. However, the essentials of the planned economy were still in place. More concessions were made to independent farmers, who no longer had to suffer compulsory purchases of their produce, and from 1977 they received the same social benefits as industrial workers. Modernisation brought a rise in living standards in the early 1970s, but problems soon re-emerged. As demand outstripped domestic food production, so food imports and Poland's foreign debts soared. Food imports quadrupled during the 1970s. Relatively little investment went into private farms, although they supplied 80 per cent of the nation's food. The neglect of agriculture was reflected in the exodus of farmers to the cities, adding to the social problems there. By 1976 food subsidies made up 12 per cent of Poland's gross domestic product. So it was not surprising that in 1976 and 1980 the government reverted again to raising prices, although they were defeated by the predictable social discontent that followed. Economic problems increasingly fed political demands.

See page 177

KEY ISSUE

How successfully did the Polish Communist regimes deal with economic problems?

The prospects for reform under the Jaruzelski regime looked grim. In the early 1980s, the government talked about decentralisation and greater autonomy for enterprises, but central controls actually increased. Poland looked abroad for help. A decline in the provision of Western credit was balanced by more Soviet aid: a Polish–Soviet trade agreement was signed in May 1984, and Poland became more involved in COMECON. However, growth rates remained low and inflation grew. More successful was the development of the 'Polonia' sector. This comprised companies (700 by the mid-1980s) that were run as private enterprises by returning Polish emigrés. There were also several thousand privately-owned workshops and service enterprises. But the Jaruzelski regime, like others in the Eastern Bloc, was eventually brought down by economic failure. The hard currency foreign debt was massive by 1988, and inflation was running at 2000 per cent by 1989. A referendum in 1987 produced only a small majority in favour of an austerity package. More price increases sparked off discontent again and increased support for *Solidarity*.

The post-Communist Mazowiecki government made economic reform a priority. A plan drawn up in January 1990 was designed to resolve the problems of inflation and shortages, and then speed up the transition to a market economy. Wage controls were retained but prices and imports were deregulated. The currency was made convertible and most subsidies were abolished. Inefficient enterprises faced closure. It was a traumatic period for many Poles, but probably one that was necessary. Inflation did fall, but so did wages, and unemployment rose. In April 1991 the International Monetary Fund offered new loans to Poland, despite Polish inability to pay off previous ones.

In July 1990 a law on privatisation was passed. Shares in some pilot enterprises were put on offer, then in June 1991 400 major enterprises (25 per cent of the total) were sold off under a scheme by which 30 per cent of an enterprise remained state-owned, 10 per cent was owned by the employees, and 60 per cent belonged to a 'National Wealth Fund', which comprised shares owned by individuals.

Problems persisted: inflation remained high, and unemployment continued to grow, reaching 2 000 000, or 12 per cent of the workforce, in 1992. Discontent showed itself in 6000 strikes in 1992 alone.

Persistent economic problems did not bode well for political reconstruction and democracy. It was extraordinarily difficult to reconcile the short-term expectations of ordinary people with the painful belt-tightening measures necessary to put the economy on a sound long-term footing. There were signs of increasing support for nationalist parties and nostalgia for the predictabilities of the Communist past. As the political situation stabilised from 1992, so the economy improved. The experience of transition to a market economy, typical in many respects of all the countries of the former Eastern Bloc, was fraught with difficulty.

> **KEY ISSUE**
>
> *How healthy was the Polish economy under post-Communist regimes?*

3 ↝ HUNGARY

A *Introduction: Hungary to 1945*

At the end of the First World War, Hungary had to concede territory to its neighbours. Many ethnic Hungarians inhabited Transylvania, which was given to Romania. In all, 30 per cent of Hungarians lived outside Hungary. Between the World Wars Hungary fell under a right-wing dictatorship. Hitler allowed Hungary to gain territory from the break-up of Czechoslovakia in March 1939 and during the Second World War

MAP 17
*Hungary after the Second
World War*

Hungary became Hitler's ally, although it tried to stay neutral towards the USSR.

Hungary was occupied by Germany in 1944 as the Red Army moved into Central Europe. Left-wing parties, including the small illegal Communist Party, were suppressed. However, the Communists profited from the Soviet invasion of Hungary in September 1944: a National Independence Front was set up, comprising several political groups but heavily influenced by the Communists. On Stalin's orders, the Hungarian Communists, led by Mátyás Rákosi, supported the idea of a coalition government. Stalin trod cautiously, since as a defeated Axis power, Hungary was subject to an Allied Control Commission. A peace treaty was not signed until 1947, when the Red Army left Hungary.

B *Political history*

THE ESTABLISHMENT OF COMMUNIST RULE

Rákosi's policy of coalition meant that the Communists made no overt bid for power, and they were not the most popular party. In the November 1945 elections the Smallholders won considerably more votes than the Communists and Socialists combined. However, although the Allied Control Commission had insisted on a coalition government, the Communists steadily increased their influence. They controlled the Ministry of the Interior, they increased their influence in the trade unions, and they further split an already-divided opposition by forging alliances with other groups such as the Social Democrats.

In 1946 a Republic replaced the monarchy. A left-wing alliance dominated the governing coalition, which was involved in considerable political infighting and manoeuvring. In the spring of 1947 the Smallholders' leader, Bela Kovács, was arrested on charges of conspiracy against the new Republic and offences against the Red Army. The Prime Minister, Ferenc Nagy, also a Smallholder, was forced

TIMELINE

Events in Hungary

Nov 1945	Broad coalition government formed
1946	Communists manoeuvred control of the government
June 1948	Social Democrats forced to merge with Communists
	One-party rule under Rákosi
May 1949	Communists took power in Popular Front, replacing
	Communist-dominated coalition
1950–51	Collectivisation and nationalisation
July 1953	Nagy became Prime Minister
1955	Rákosi instituted hard-line regime
Oct–Nov	Hungarian rising crushed
1956	Kádár appointed First Secretary
Jan 1968	Kádár's regime began New Economic Mechanism
May 1988	Karoly Grősz became Prime Minister, replacing Kádár
Jan 1989	New constitution and new political parties allowed
March	Round-Table opposition formed
Sept	Hungary opened its border with Austria
March 1990	Democratic Forum won elections
	Coalition government formed
May	J. Ántáll formed centre-right coalition
May 1994	Hungarian Socialist Party (former Communists) won power
June 1995	A. Gőncz re-elected President
July 1997	Hungary invited to join NATO

KEY ISSUE

How and why did the Communists succeed in coming to power in Hungary?

---

to resign. The Communists and Socialists benefited from these events, winning 45 per cent of the votes in rigged elections in August 1947. Several parties, including the Communists, were given posts in the new government.

Stalin had been broadly content with events in Hungary thus far, but now had cause for concern. Some Socialists were arguing for a break with the Communists; Stalin was also worried by long-standing links between Hungarian Communists and Tito's Yugoslavia, which had recently fallen out with Moscow. Therefore the Hungarian Communists now adopted a more forward policy. In 1949 some prominent Communists were purged. The Roman Catholic Primate Cardinal Mindszenty was sentenced to life imprisonment and there was a campaign against the Catholic and Protestant churches.

Members of other left-wing parties were pressurised into amalgamating with the Communists, who had become the Hungarian Workers' party (MDP) in June 1948. In 1950 several prominent Socialists were put on trial. When Rákosi became Prime Minister in 1952, the Communists further increased their influence in the State apparatus, and Hungary had become a one-party authoritarian state. Rákosi was renowned for his hardline Stalinist approach, and in the early 1950s over 200 000 Party members were dismissed or imprisoned.

IMRE NAGY AND THE 'NEW COURSE'

Rákosi was forced to resign the Party leadership in 1953 following criticism of Hungary's poor economic performance. His successor,

IMRE NAGY (1896–1958)

From a poor background, Imre Nagy had been taken prisoner in Russia during the First World War whilst fighting in the Austro–Hungarian army. In 1918 he joined the Hungarian section of the Russian Communist Party. On his return to Hungary in 1921 he joined the Socialist Workers' Party, because the Communists were banned. After some time in prison he returned to the USSR, where he became a collective farm director in 1937 and an agricultural expert. He was also a friend of Georgy Malenkov, a Soviet exponent of 'goulash Communism'. This was a policy of putting more emphasis in planning on the production of consumer goods for the benefit of ordinary people.

Nagy was expelled from the *Politburo* in 1949, after being attacked by Rákosi. However, he was foisted on the Hungarian government by the Soviets in 1953. He opposed a policy of rapid collectivisation of agriculture. His ideas on 'democratising' the Communist Party also caused great concern amongst orthodox Communists, who believed in the concept of an élite Party or who were concerned with their own power and privileges. Nagy echoed Djilas's concerns in Yugoslavia about the unrepresentative nature of a one-party bureaucratic state. However, like Gorbachev in the USSR many years later, Nagy naively believed that the Communists would maintain popular support and power in a genuinely democratic system.

Nagy was expelled from the government and the Party in 1955, his cause not helped by Malenkov's demotion in the USSR. He continued to hope for rehabilitation, writing that the Soviet model of Socialism was defective and that nations should develop their own paths to Socialism by

> ...systematically decreasing the use of force and utilising democratic methods in the interest of close cooperation on the widest possible scale with the masses of working people.

Executed and discredited after the rising had failed, Nagy's reputation was rehabilitated after the fall of Communism in Hungary over thirty years later. Most historians doubt whether Nagy's reformist ideas were workable: his views on the possible democratisation of the Party were naive and 'He had not clearly linked economic problems to shortcomings in the socio-economic infrastructure.' (G. and N. Swain, *Eastern Europe Since 1945*, Macmillan, 1993)

KEY ISSUE

What was Imre Nagy's 'New Course'?

Ernst Gerö, was another Stalinist. However, the more moderate Communist Imre Nagy was appointed Prime Minister. With Soviet support, Nagy implemented a 'New Course', telling his colleagues that 'we failed to realise the basic law of socialism – the constant raising of the standard of living of the population'.

Nagy aroused concern amongst more orthodox Marxists by proclaiming a desire to go much further than material betterment. He also wanted to increase genuine popular participation in the Hungarian Workers' Party, and make it more than a rubber stamp for leadership decisions. He proposed a new Patriotic People's Front, a democratic organisation to involve Communists and non-Communists. Nagy assumed that the Communists would still exercise leadership, but nevertheless his views were radically different from the Leninist conception of the élite, disciplined Party as the vanguard of the proletariat.

Nagy was strongly attacked by Rákosi and others for his views and actions in relaxing police controls. In 1955 Nagy was expelled from the *Politburo*, the Central Committee and the Party. Rákosi reinstated a hardline regime. Nagy continued to expound his views, and was supported by a group known as the Petofi Circle, which by 1956 had developed into a nationwide opposition movement. The USSR became concerned by the divisions and dissatisfaction evident in Hungary. The Soviets were concerned about the future of the Soviet Bloc. They were afraid of a repeat of the 1948 Yugoslav break with Moscow and a 'domino' effect, with other nationalist movements developing within their sphere of influence. Khrushchev engineered Nagy's rehabilitation in the Party in an attempt to stabilise the situation. However, on 23 October 1956, the Petofi Circle called for a mass demonstration against the presence of Soviet troops in Hungary, and in support of the return of Nagy as Head of the government. The demonstration went ahead, despite a government ban and Nagy's own reluctance to commit himself firmly to one side or the other.

THE 1956 HUNGARIAN RISING

Popular protests were the start of the Hungarian Rising. The government was unsure of how to respond, and persuaded Nagy to appeal for calm. Gerő returned from a visit to Belgrade and denounced the demonstrators on the radio. The demonstrators responded by converging on the Budapest radio station and capturing it on 24 October, after violent clashes with the authorities. Gerő requested Soviet support and on the same day Soviet tanks entered Budapest to begin four days of bitter fighting. Meanwhile, Nagy was still waiting on the sidelines for all the necessary official procedures for forming a government to be completed. He was in an impossible position, without the support of either the Hungarian Communist establishment or many of the reformers.

On 25 October the Soviets agreed that János Kádár should replace Gerő as Party leader, with Nagy as Prime Minister. Nagy broadcast appeals for a ceasefire and the withdrawal of Soviet troops. On 30

October he formed a multi-party government, against Soviet wishes. Nagy did not denounce a declaration by the newly-formed Revolutionary Committee of Defence that Hungary should leave the Warsaw Pact, and on 4 November, having obtained the consent of its allies, the USSR invaded Hungary. The excuse was that Hungary faced the threat of counter-revolution. The Soviets backed Kádár to form a new government and the centres of Hungarian resistance were mopped up. Nagy was captured by Soviet troops and later executed. During the entire Rising about 3000 Hungarians were killed and 13 000 wounded. A further 2000 were later executed, and 200 000 Hungarians fled to the West.

There were strong complaints in the West against Soviet intervention in Hungary, but no action. The Western powers were involved in the Suez Crisis, and in any case, it was tacitly accepted that Hungary was within the Soviet sphere of influence – as was the case with Czechoslovakia in 1968.

KÁDÁR'S HUNGARY

Kádár had been put in place by the Soviets, not by popular support. There followed a major purge inside and outside the Party. However, once the Rising had been crushed and the opposition quelled, he did implement policies designed to win over the Hungarian people. The USSR assisted with unprecedented amounts of financial aid in an attempt to reconcile the population to Communist rule – a policy that was in part, successful. Kádár carried out some of Nagy's more moderate reforms, and expelled Rákosi and his supporters from the Party in 1961. In January 1962 Kádár felt secure enough to declare, 'Whereas the Rákosites used to say that those who are not with us are against us, we say, those who are not against us are with us.' The implication was that the regime would not look for much more than outward conformity, and would not indulge in the fervent political indoctrination typical of Stalin's period. There was a rehabilitation of victims of earlier purges and an **amnesty** for those involved in the 1956 Rising. Censorship was relaxed, and foreign influences allowed into Hungary to a greater extent than in most Eastern Bloc countries. There was also reconciliation with the Catholic Church.

Kádár achieved this without unduly alarming the USSR about Hungary's loyalty to the Eastern Bloc. Indeed, some of his economic reforms influenced future Soviet leaders Andropov and Gorbachev. The fact that Kádár appeared to have reduced direct Soviet influence in Hungary won him some popular support which led to an increase in Party membership and contributed to his lengthy period of office.

Even political reform was undertaken. In 1966 candidates were linked to specific constituencies, and some elections were contested. The 1972 Constitution, whilst declaring that Hungary was a Socialist state, explicitly recognised the break with Stalinism. However, the experience of Czechoslovakia in 1968 was a brake on radical changes, and earlier economic successes were threatened by recession in the 1970s.

KEY ISSUE

Why was Hungary invaded in 1956?

See pages 192–3 for Kádár's attempts to liberalise the economy

amnesty a one-off release of prisoners

KEY ISSUE

Why did Kádár's regime survive for so long in Hungary?

See page 168

The pace of reform picked up again in the 1980s. Multi-candidate elections became compulsory in 1983. In the 1985 elections, in what was a first in the Eastern Bloc, some independent deputies were elected, and some prominent Communists were defeated. There remained limits to reform: strong criticism of the regime could still mean censorship or arrest. As the mood for reform strengthened in Eastern and Central Europe, reformers regarded Kádár as too rigid, despite his earlier success in appeasing the Soviets and heading a relatively moderate regime. Kádár's problem, like that of several Eastern Bloc leaders, was that the threat of Soviet intervention was steadily evaporating as Gorbachev unfolded his own reform programme in the USSR, and as anti-Communist reformers were increasingly bold in their expectations and demands. Above all, it was the failure to sustain economic growth, admitted by Kádár at the Party Congress in 1985, which fed the opposition.

THE OVERTHROW OF COMMUNISM

An important breakthrough for the opposition came in 1987, with the formation of the Hungarian Democratic Forum (HDF) followed by the Alliance of Young Democrats (FIDESZ) and the Alliance of Free Initiatives. Former parties such as the Smallholders and Social Democrats were also resurrected. Reformers among the Communists saw the threat and summoned a special MDP Conference in May 1988. Kádár, who ultimately sided with the conservatives, was one of the Conference's first victims: he was sacked, along with several colleagues, having been in power for over thirty years.

The pace of change then quickened. Early in 1989 the Communists committed themselves to multi-party politics and announced that they would join a coalition government. The reform-minded Communists also agreed to hold 'Round Table' talks with opposition groups. During the talks the Hungarian government opened its border with Austria, thereby allowing thousands of East Germans supposedly holidaying in Hungary to escape to the West. The Round Table talks reached an impasse in September 1989: despite the commitment to a multi-party democracy; FIDESZ and the other groups wanted parliamentary elections to take place prior to presidential elections before they would sign an agreement.

KEY ISSUE

How was Communism overturned in Hungary?

In October 1989, the MDP held an Extraordinary Congress at which the reformers changed the Party's name to the Hungarian Socialist Party (HSP), leaving a small Communist rump behind. The Party gave up its 'leading role' in the new 'Republic of Hungary'.

There was no unanimous agreement on the way ahead, and therefore a referendum was planned for November 1989, to determine issues such as the date of the presidential elections. The Democratic Forum advised its supporters to abstain, and the opposition was clearly divided. Nevertheless, the HSP did badly. The first completely free parliamentary elections in the Eastern Bloc were held in Hungary in March and April 1990. There was no decisive result, but the Democratic Forum led by Jozsef Ántáll formed a coalition government

Party	Votes (%) March 1990	Votes (%) May 1994	Seats (no.) 1994
Democratic Forum	24.7	11.7	37
Alliance of Free Democrats	21.4	19.4	70
Independent Smallholders	11.7	8.9	26
Hungarian Socialist Party	10.9	33.0	209
FIDESZ (Alliance of Young Democrats)	8.9	7.0	20
Christian Democratic People's Party	6.5	7.1	22
Hungarian Socialist Workers' Party	3.7	3.3	–
Agrarian Federation	3.1	2.3	1

TABLE 22
Hungarian general election results, 1990 and 1994

with the Smallholders and Christian Democrats. This was Hungary's first post-war non-Communist government, and the HSP had secured a low percentage of the votes in the election. FIDESZ was one of the opposition groups, but the democratic parties were very divided amongst themselves.

Árpád Göncz, a Free Democrat, was appointed President in August 1990. It was a difficult situation for the new democracy, since he disagreed with Parliament on constitutional reforms, and the coalition government faced conflicting demands from its supporters about how to prioritise reforms. Late in 1990 the government introduced an austerity package, which included a 65 per cent rise in the price of petrol. This sparked immediate strikes and demonstrations by lorry and taxi drivers. Although the government withdrew the price rises, its popularity fell, despite other attempts to boost its position: notably a compensation law of June 1991 allowing individuals and organisations like the Church, which had had property expropriated by the State since 1948, to seek its return, and a visit to Hungary by the Pope in August 1991 to mark improved relations with the Catholic Church. The government's problem was that economic reform, involving the transition to a market economy, produced dislocation such as unemployment and dashed expectations, at least in the short term. Ántáll favoured moderate reform, and justified his policy by the fact that Hungary had avoided major social disruption or violence. However, his approach to reform was too cautious for some, and he was frequently at odds with the President.

Political disillusionment amongst Hungarians was reflected in the falling membership of parties and the cancellation of some by-election results because of a very low turn-out. Remnants of the old authoritarianism were still in place: political influence in the media was still such that the heads of Hungarian radio and television were sacked in January 1992. The HSP began to do well in local elections and by-elections.

In January 1993 Ántáll was re-elected Chairman of the Democratic Forum, and his centrist stance in politics appeared to pay dividends. The most promising sign for future progress was the granting of associated European Union status to Hungary in December 1991. Closer integration with Western Europe probably offered Hungary the

See Table 22 above

KEY ISSUE

How successfully did post-Communist regimes restore stability in Hungary?

best hope of reinforcing democracy and stimulating economic development, rather than just relying on its own efforts or alliance with its neighbours in the former Eastern Bloc. However, the former Communists made a comeback when the HSP won a majority in the May 1994 general election. The Democratic Forum vote collapsed. The Socialists formed an uneasy coalition with the Alliance of Free Democrats, but did manage to restore confidence with an economic austerity package.

C *Economic history*

THE NEW ECONOMIC MECHANISM

Hungarian economic development after 1948 exhibited some features unique in the Communist world, and was a stimulus for some of the economic reforms attempted elsewhere, particularly in the USSR in the 1980s. However, in the initial stages of Communist control, economic development followed an orthodox Stalinist model. Pre-war Hungary had been a semi-feudal society, with land and economic power concentrated in the hands of a relatively small élite. Much of that land was nationalised, and the Soviet model of a planned economy with centrally-determined targets and a central allocation of resources was adopted. It was difficult to meet the early targets, and a rapid rise in the urban population produced strains, so that the targets of the Five-Year Plan of 1950–54 were not met. Awareness of the strains imposed by rapid economic change led Nagy to oppose rapid collectivisation of land in the early 1950s, and to take more account of the everyday needs of consumers.

Kádár's appointment in the wake of the 1956 Hungarian Rising was a crucial factor in economic development. Although a Marxist, Kádár was also a pragmatist, and he realised that economic growth and a rise in the standard of living were essential if popular support or acquiescence for the regime were to be achieved. The process was gradual. In 1959, a three-year process of reimposing collectivisation was recommended, and in 1962 the Party agreed on the need for further industrial concentration. However, in the early 1960s some important decisions on reform were taken. Detailed deliberations culminated in the implementation of the New Economic Mechanism (NEM) in January 1968.

Ironically, this reform was implemented in the same year that Hungary participated in the suppression of the Czechoslovakian reform movement. But the Hungarians were careful to emphasise that the NEM did not involve political reform, although it was radical. The premise of NEM was that it was possible to run a 'socialist market economy' – an economy in which market forces would play an important role within the framework of an authoritarian one-party state. Central planning and the central allocation of resources were abandoned, although they had been key elements of the Soviet Stalinist model. Experts would have more say in decision making. Individual

KEY ISSUE

What was the significance of the New Economic Mechanism?

enterprises were expected to make profits, and not just to meet quantitative targets. Supply and demand, not the State, would determine how resources were allocated – although the State offered some protection against international competition and fluctuations in world prices. Small-scale enterprises were legalised and encouraged.

A principal aim was to do away with central control over heavy industry, but to retain some control over the production of consumer goods for the benefit of the ordinary citizen. Therefore, whilst producer goods were sold through wholesale enterprises at prices agreed by buyer and seller, consumer goods and services were still regulated by the government. The principle was straightforward, but the system was complex: for example, some prices were entirely free, some were closely regulated, and some were allowed to fluctuate between limits set by the State.

Agriculture also experienced changes. Small-scale private plots were encouraged as elsewhere in most of the Eastern Bloc; and collective farms were given the responsibility of managing their own production and marketing.

The early results of NEM were promising. Output in agriculture and consumer goods increased significantly, and real wages doubled. There were more goods in the shops than could be found in most parts of Central and Eastern Europe. Not surprisingly, reform-minded Communists and economists throughout the region showed interest in the Hungarian economic experiment.

ECONOMIC PROBLEMS

However, economic progress stuttered during the 1970s. Performance levels were not always sustained, and the foreign trade deficit grew. COMECON did not prove a great benefit to Hungary. Hungary was adversely affected by the world oil crisis. There were arguments within the Hungarian leadership between those who wanted the trend towards decentralisation reversed, and those who believed that NEM must be extended and market forces given even more scope. In 1973, the conservatives won a victory: some large enterprises accounting for over half of national production were given protection against market forces, and several prominent reformers were sacked. A new State Planning Committee was established. However, some conservatives were sacked following the Eleventh Party Congress of March 1975.

At one stage Hungary almost achieved self-sufficiency in agriculture. However, low prices proved a disincentive to peasants to maintain large herds, and there were soon shortages again. Labour productivity fell, and living standards were only maintained with Soviet aid and by reducing military spending. The position of the State in the economy was actually strengthened, and one of the faults of NEM was that although market forces were encouraged, there was little attention paid to structural changes in the economy, so technology lagged behind developments in the West. From the late 1970s, the government adopted an austerity programme to reduce domestic consumption. However, failure to sustain a rise in living standards, which

> **KEY ISSUE**
>
> *Why did Hungary experience increasing economic problems?*

Communists had always promised would be achieved under Socialism, reduced the credibility of the regime. In order to acquire foreign aid, Hungary joined the International Monetary Fund and the World Bank in 1982. There was also further economic restructuring: all industry was put under the control of a single ministry, although some large industries were broken down into smaller units. The depth of Hungary's problems was summed up by one commentator as follows: at the end of the 1970s Hungary had

> ... massive, unmanageable hard currency debts, inefficient and outdated production structures, budget deficits, and an inflationary excess of purchasing power in the hands of the population.

(J. Batt, *East Central Europe from Reform to Transformation,* Royal Institute of International Affairs, 1991)

REFORM

More radical measures followed. In 1982–83 enterprises were permitted to issue bonds, and in 1985 the government ceded virtual autonomy to firms, which could choose to be managed by an enterprise council or an elected leadership. In 1986 joint-stock companies were permitted for the first time, and in 1987 competing banks were opened up. The State sector of the economy, which accounted for 73 per cent in 1975, was reduced to 65 per cent in 1985. In that year, there were 600 small cooperatives in existence and some 20 000 Enterprise Economic Work partnerships. The latter were groups of workers who were allowed to use their workplaces to work for themselves on a profit-making basis, outside of normal working hours. Depending on one's point of view, this was either an ingenious method of increasing worker motivation, or a tacit admission that 'moonlighting', a key feature of all Eastern Bloc economies, with workers putting more effort into their own activities than their official jobs, was happening anyway and should be acknowledged.

None of these measures solved Hungary's problems. State subsidies were increased, the private sector continued to expand, but Hungary's external debt doubled between 1985 and 1987 alone. Even reformers within the MDP recognised the need for change. Karoly Grősz, Kádár's successor as Party leader, had already presented a reform package to Parliament in September 1987, and radical reformers had already reached the conclusion that more economic reform was impractical without accompanying political reform.

The new opposition parties at the end of the 1980s had radical economic plans. The Smallholders were most concerned for the return of state-owned farmland to private hands. All the parties were committed to a market economy, although there were disagreements about the pace of change. Prime Minister Ántáll favoured moderate reform rather than the 'shock therapy' advocated by some: he seemed vindicated when there was a drastic response to the price rises of 1990.

See pages 190–2

However, unemployment continued to rise, and so the process of privatisation was speeded up. In 1990 it was announced that twenty major companies were to be privatised. In September 1991 'self-privatisation' was introduced for smaller companies. Citizens were to receive credit vouchers enabling them to purchase State property, repaying the cost over fifteen years.

The success of these measures was limited. Trade with the West increased, and more foreign firms were established in Hungary than in other Eastern Bloc countries. However, overall trade levels declined. A tough austerity programme had to be introduced in 1995 in order to balance the budget, and this hit groups such as pensioners. Future membership of the European Union was seen as Hungary's best hope of sustained growth. The New Economic Mechanism had been a bold economic experiment, and one that proved that State Socialism, even when it provided social security and a basic standard of living, could not attain the levels of economic success of the more dynamic Western economies. However, Hungarians found that a transition to capitalism carried with it a new set of difficulties.

> **KEY ISSUE**
>
> *How successfully were Hungary's economic problems resolved by the overthrow of Communism?*

4 ⌐ THE COMMUNIST STATES OF EASTERN AND CENTRAL EUROPE — A COMPARATIVE ANALYSIS

The states of Czechoslovakia, Poland, Hungary, Romania and Bulgaria had many common characteristics during the period covered by this book. This was also true of Yugoslavia and Albania to a lesser extent.

> See Chapter 6

A *How they became Communist*

During and immediately after the Second World War Communist Parties dominated **popular front** organisations and were included in coalitions. Gradually the Communists came to dominate the coalitions, recruited mass memberships, established one-party rule (sometimes through rigged elections), merged with Socialist parties and then established Stalinist-style regimes. The Communists succeeded because of Soviet support, the weakness and mistakes of democratic parties, and the failure of the West to resist the process.

> **Popular Fronts**
> coalitions of left-wing parties

B *How they remained Communist*

These states exhibited several features which characterised Stalinist rule in the USSR, among them:

- One-party rule, based on an all-embracing ideology (Marxism–Leninism);
- The use of repression and propaganda to maintain one-party rule;
- State control of the economy;

See Tables 23 and 24 for comparative statistics on standards of living

TABLE 23

Estimated annual income per head in Central Europe, 1985 (in US$)

Albania	860
Bulgaria	3200
Czechoslovakia	6000
GDR	5400
Hungary	1722
Poland	1900
Romania	2687
Yugoslavia	1850
USSR	4200
UK	7156

Source: *The World in Figures* (Economist Publications, London, 1987)

- Party control over all State and bureaucratic institutions.

There were differences – for example, in Hungary some private enterprise was tolerated, in Poland agriculture was not collectivised, Poland remained overtly Catholic, and levels of economic and social development varied considerably – but these were less obvious than the similarities.

C *Why the regimes were overturned in 1989*

Several factors were at work. The USSR, for so long the arbiter of the Eastern Bloc's destinies, was itself undergoing major changes under Gorbachev and was not prepared to support threatened regimes. By 1989 the regimes had lost any semblance of real popular support – they had proved incapable of producing a Socialist utopia, and worse than that, were in economic decline, or even facing bankruptcy. In an age of global mass communication, these facts could no longer be hidden from ordinary people. The example of the West added to the pressures.

D *The nature of the post-Communist regimes*

The post-1989 regimes developed some of the features of the older liberal democracies of the West, but only to a certain degree, which was hardly surprising, given their prevous historical development. Parliamentary elections giving the electors genuine choice were introduced, although they were sometimes manipulated. Personal freedoms were enshrined in constitutions. However, political parties were often poorly organised and did not represent the aspirations of ordinary citizens adequately. The States were still quite centralised and there was not a strong concept of the separation of powers between government, parliament and the judiciary, as was held dear in some Western democracies. Old habits died hard: for example, corruption remained a strong feature of post-Communist societies at all levels, and in several cases governments were reluctant to give up control of the media.

Economic problems were also common, characterised especially by a growing gap in wealth between different sections of society and

TABLE 24

Possession of luxury items, 1987 (per 1000 of the population)

	Radios	TVs	Cars
Albania	167	83	1.6
Bulgaria	221	189	115
Czechoslovakia	256	285	171
GDR	663	754	199
Hungary	586	402	135
Poland	289	263	98
Romania	288	173	11
Yugoslavia	235	209	125
USSR	685	310	40
UK	1145	434	292

Source: *The World in Figures* (Economist Publications, London, 1987)

unemployment as inefficient economies were exposed to the blast of competition.

The growth of Nationalist tensions also threatened the stability of new States or the security of minority groups such as Hungarians in Romania.

E *Political developments*

Large numbers of parties sprang up, often based around anti-Communist alliances but lacking discipline and strong organisation. In some cases, for example Romania and Bulgaria, Communists stayed in power under another guise. The first post-1989 governments suffered a backlash of unpopularity once it became evident that they could not solve all the problems overnight. In Poland, Hungary and Bulgaria in particular, this led to the return to power of former Communists. The parties generally suffered from lack of close identification by voters and a tendency to fragment easily. The new parliaments tended to be subservient to the governing party or president, as in Romania for example, or chaotic because of the lack of party discipline, as in Poland. Presidents were either directly elected or elected by parliaments.

F *Economic and social developments*

Several post-Communist societies wanted to adopt a 'Third Way' between capitalism and Communism, for example combining a market

See Table 25 for the difficulties experienced during the period of transition

	Economic growth (%)			Inflation (%)		
	1988	1989	1990	1988	1989	1990
USSR	6	3	−4	7	9	10
Poland	5	0	−12	60	241	800
Yugoslavia	0	1	−10	194	1256	550
Romania	0	−11	−12	1	2	20
Czechoslovakia	2	1	−3	0	1	14
Hungary	2	1	−5	16	17	29
Bulgaria	1	0	−11	1	9	50

Source: *Rebuilding Eastern Europe* (Frankfurt, Deutsche Bank Economics Department, 1991)

TABLE 25
The difficulties of economic transition

	Jan 1988	June 1989	June 1991
Albania	28.8	28.8	3.6
Bulgaria	21.0	21.0	8.5
Czechoslovakia	29.5	29.5	8.7
GDR	32.2	32.2	20.4
Hungary	20.9	20.9	7.0
Poland	20.2	13.5	13.5
Romania	34.4	34.4	3.6
USSR	31.1	15.3	15.3

TABLE 26
Percentages of women holding seats in Parliament, 1988–91

economy with an extensive welfare state. This proved impractical and other models were followed: shock therapy, where reforms or austerity packages were implemented wholesale; or a gradualist approach, as in the Czech Republic. Economic reform proved difficult for several reasons: few people had the capital to buy into businesses; people lacked purchasing power; exchange rates were unstable; inefficient firms continued to be subsidised; unemployment and corruption grew; there were growing disparities of wealth between individuals and regions. Social progress was sometimes slow: for example, the number of women in the new parliaments actually went down.

See Table 26

5 ⌐ AUSTRIA

A *Introduction: Austria to 1945*

Until 1918 Austria was at the hub of the Hapsburg Empire, dominating the Danube Basin and much of Central Europe. As the Empire broke up at the end of the First World War, Austria was left as a small state, banned from uniting with its ally Germany, and suffering losses and restrictions as a defeated combatant. Social and political divisions made it more vulnerable, and it succumbed without resistance to Nazi occupation in 1938. Austria, absorbed into Hitler's *Reich*, was part of the Axis alliance during the Second World War, although there was some anti-Nazi resistance, particularly from Communists, after 1941.

The Allies were uncertain whether to treat Austria as a separate state 'conquered' by Germany, or as an enemy power. Like all combatant states, Austria had suffered. There was damage from air raids after 1943, and only 5000 of Austria's pre-war 220 000 Jews survived the war. Almost 250 000 Austrian soldiers had died, and 750 000 were in captivity. Austria was fortunate to be treated ultimately as a victim of Nazi aggression rather than as Hitler's ally. This was reflected in the Moscow Declaration of November 1943, by which the USSR, Britain and the USA declared that Austria should be a 'free and independent state'. Stalin agreed to this, because as the war went in his favour, he probably expected that Austria, like other Central and Eastern European states, would emerge with a pro-Communist regime. The Allies actually doubted Austria's continued viability as a small independent state, and Churchill advocated combining Catholic Bavaria and Austria. Some Western statesmen favoured a Danubian federation. However, Stalin opposed this.

In the spring of 1945 Vienna fell to the Red Army, dashing British hopes of getting there first. Austria's situation was complicated by the existence of the Hapsburg heir Otto. Some of Austria's former political leaders had already met in December 1944 and agreed on a provisional National Committee. At the end of the war they formed a city administration in Vienna under the Social Democrat Theodor Korner.

In July 1945 Austria was divided into four occupation zones, as agreed in 1943. The USA occupied Salzburg and part of Upper Austria;

KEY ISSUE

How and why was Austria divided at the end of the Second World War?

the USSR occupied Burgenland, Lower Austria and part of Upper Austria; Britain occupied Carinthia, East Tyrol and Styria; and France occupied the Tyrol and Vorarlberg. Vienna itself was partitioned. An Allied Council coordinated the administration of the zones, with each of the four powers having the power of veto over decisions. The Western powers set up provisional governments in their zones. As World War gave way to Cold War, Vienna, like Berlin, became a focal point of mistrust between East and West, although tension between the former allies in Austria was never as great as it was to be in Germany.

In the following sections, Austrian foreign policy will not be dealt with separately, but as part of political events: as Austria was occupied until 1955, and followed a neutral foreign policy after independence, foreign affairs did not play a prominent part in Austria's post-war history.

B *Political history*

In 1945 the pre-war Social Democrats and Revolutionary Socialists combined to form the relatively moderate Austrian Socialist Party (SPO). Its leader was Adolf Scharf, whilst the veteran Karl Renner was on the Right of the Party. The pre-war Christian Socialists reorganised as the Austrian People's Party (OVP), supported mainly by a mixture of farmers, white-collar workers and businessmen. Its leaders included the rising political star Leopold Figl, who had suffered for several years in Nazi concentration camps. The Communist Party was boosted by the Soviet presence in Austria.

The first post-war provisional government was led by Karl Renner. Although he had supported the union with Germany in 1938 he was acceptable to Stalin as a possible leader of a left-wing Popular Front. Renner reassured Stalin in April 1945 by urging him to take Austria 'under his mighty protection' and pledged that Social Democrats would 'work fraternally with the Communist Party to refound the Republic step by step together' – a move scarcely calculated to reassure the West of Austria's long-term independence. Stalin ensured that two Moscow-based Communists were included in Renner's government: Ernst Fischer for Popular Enlightenment, Education and Culture, and Franz Honner for the Interior. Many of the other ministers were moderate Socialists.

Britain and the USA refused to recognise what they regarded as a stooge regime imposed by Moscow, and they argued with the Soviets at the Potsdam Conference (July–August 1945). It was agreed that Austria, as a victim of German aggression, need not pay reparations. The West only recognised Renner's government in late October 1945, when he agreed to change its composition and hold a general election. Decisions of the government had to be approved by the Allied Council.

The Council agreed at its first meeting to make its immediate priority the elimination of Nazi influence from Austrian life – an aim never completely fulfilled.

Austria's first free election since 1930, held in November 1945, reassured the West by resulting in a conservative majority. The People's Party won almost 50 per cent of the votes; the Socialists won 44.6 per cent; and the Communists trailed badly with 5 per cent.

Figl replaced Renner, who became Federal President in December. Figl's government was approved by the Allied Council. It was a coalition of the People's Party, Socialists, Communists and non-party representatives. This coalition system lasted until 1966, although the Communists withdrew in 1947.

Figl was a forthright, popular leader who worked well with the Allied Council. He began the process of recovery from the war, working within the limits imposed by the Allied occupation which lasted ten years. Economic recovery was the first priority. As in other war-torn areas, the Black Market ruled. Rations were very low. At Christmas 1945, Figl could offer his people little but patriotism: 'For your Christmas tree, even if you have one, I can give you no candles, no crust of bread, no coal for heating and no glass for your windows. We have nothing. I can only beg of you one thing: believe in this Austria of ours.' Recovery came slowly.

Figl faced formidable problems. He was expected to root out the strong Nazi legacy. He had to tread a delicate balance between not antagonising the wartime Allies, whose Council he had to work with, and carrying out the important task of trying to establish a real Austrian – as opposed to German – identity. All public posts in the bureaucracy, higher education, industry and the media were shared out between political parties. Therefore most influential postholders in Austria regarded their first allegiance as being towards their party, rather than to the State. Policy was determined by party leaders and then approved by Parliament. It did not always make for democratic government, but did lead to firm government, which was important if Austrian politicians were to maintain any influence with the occupying powers, and in particular if they were to stand up to Soviet harassment.

Figl secured an important measure of autonomy in June 1946 when the Soviets agreed that in future any law proposed by the Austrian government would automatically become law unless the four members of the Council unanimously objected to it, replacing the possibility of the single veto.

In 1945, the West feared that Austria might become a Communist state. By the end of the 1940s any extremist threat appeared to be coming from the Right. The right-wing Union of Independents (VDU) was founded in 1949. It soon became the third largest party, with some influence in coalition politics. Several ex-Nazis joined the Party.

There was a swing to the Right in the 1949 election. The People's Party won 44 per cent of the vote, the Socialists 38 per cent, the Union of Independents 11 per cent. The coalition of the People's Party and the Socialists continued. Support for the Communists declined, partly because of ill-feeling towards the USSR for its policy towards Austria and also because the economy began to recover. The Austrian Communists sought to cooperate with other parties; however, when the former Revolutionary Socialist Erwin Scharf supported closer ties with the Communists, he was expelled from the Socialist Party in 1949.

The USSR demanded that Figl and his apparently pro-Western government should be replaced. Between 1948 and 1950 the Soviets provoked industrial unrest inside Austria in an attempt to pressurise the government into changes or possibly even to bring it down. The attempt failed, and Figl sacked some known Communists from the police. It was the last significant show of strength by the Left. Thereafter, Soviet hostility became less intense, particularly after Stalin's death in 1953.

The Soviets correctly interpreted Austrian policy as pro-Western, despite the officially 'neutral' status of the country. During Figl's premiership the Austrian army cooperated with Western forces and drew up joint contingency plans for the possibility of a Soviet invasion or Berlin-style blockade.

In May 1951 Korner was elected President. In April 1953 Julius Raab succeeded Figl as Chancellor and head of his Party. In the 1953 election the Socialists won 42 per cent of the vote, the People's Party 41 per cent, the Union of Independents and their allies 11 per cent, and the Communists 5 per cent. By 1959 the Communists had lost their representation in Parliament.

Austria's international status had been complicated by developments in neighbouring countries and Cold War politics. After 1947, Yugoslavia demanded reparations from Austria and campaigned to acquire Carinthia. Once the USSR had secured Western approval for its peace treaties with Romania, Hungary and Bulgaria, it supported the Yugoslav claims. However, the claims were dropped after the split between Yugoslavia and the USSR, the Yugoslavs settling instead for an Austrian guarantee of Croat and Slovenian minority rights.

On the Northern border, Germany was very much the focal point of the Cold War. While the two superpowers confronted each other in Germany, there seemed little prospect of either side giving up its occupation of Austria and ceding an advantage to the other side. Although the four occupying powers held extensive discussions between 1947 and 1953 on the status of Austria, the USSR vetoed most proposals for change. Soviet concerns were understandable, given the fact that several prominent Austrian politicians openly advocated that an independent Austria should apply to join NATO.

The prospects of progress improved with Raab's accession to power, and the Socialist leader Bruno Kreisky becoming Foreign Minister. However, the change of leadership in Moscow was even more important. Khrushchev was far more prepared to be flexible on Austria than his predecessor Stalin had been, partly because Tito was insisting that Soviet troops must leave Austria before he would respond to Khrushchev's efforts to heal the breach between Yugoslavia and the USSR.

The Soviets showed a willingness to compromise and all the occupying powers began to reduce the size of their occupying forces. In 1955 Molotov dropped the Soviet insistence that the Austrian

KEY ISSUE

How was Austria affected by involvement in Cold War politics?

occupation could not end until a peace treaty had been agreed for Germany.

The Soviet change of heart was prompted partly by the declining value of Austria as an asset. Attempts to win the population over to Communism had failed miserably, as was confirmed by the poor showing of Austrian Communists in elections. Moreover, the Soviets having stripped their zone of many of its valuable assets, Austria was now actually becoming a drain on Soviet resources. Strategic calculations were also crucial. The creation of the Warsaw Pact in 1955 gave the Red Army rights to station troops in neighbouring Hungary and Romania, further reducing the value of an Austrian base to the USSR. Also, an independent Austria might benefit the USSR more than the West, given that the West would lose a direct and continuous link between its zones in Germany and a fellow NATO state in Italy.

When in April 1955 the Soviets suggested a permanently neutral status for Austria, Raab readily agreed. A treaty in May provided for occupying forces to be withdrawn within ninety days. The agreement was therefore one made between the Austrian government and the Kremlin, although Britain, France and the USA gave their assent. The treaty included a declaration preventing union between Austria and Germany, safeguards for Croatian and Slovenian minorities, and a ban on a Hapsburg restoration. The occupation forces had all departed by 25 October 1956. Austria's neutral status prevented it from making any military pacts or from allowing any foreign military bases on its territory. However, Austria did join the United Nations in December 1955. Austria's main concern was to keep out of Cold War conflicts, and therefore it did not play a prominent part in wider European affairs.

Under the Austrian Constitution, the President was elected by universal suffrage every six years, and his duties were mostly ceremonial. Of the two parliamentary houses, the most important was the *Nationalrat*, elected by a system of proportional representation every four years. The other house was the *Bundesrat*, or Federal Assembly, elected indirectly by the nine provincial legislatures.

The main feature of Austrian politics for many years was cooperation. Even the Socialists moved towards the centre ground in their anxiety to distance themselves from the Communists, and their 1958 programme was designed to win support from middle-class and Catholic voters. The People's Party drew its main strength from the provinces. It retained the support of many Catholics because of its emphasis on conservative family values, although it lost some influence as the relative importance of farming to the Austrian economy declined. The right-wing Union of Independents was reorganised in 1956 as the Freedom Party (FPO), firstly under the ex-Nazi Anton Reinteller and from 1958 under the ex-SS officer Friedrich Peter, who led the Party for twenty years. The FPO declared that Austria was a German state, but also supported the concept of a united Europe.

The newly independent Austria soon gave the Soviets cause for concern. During the 1956 Hungarian Rising, Austria gave asylum to

150 000 Hungarian refugees. But thereafter Austria adopted a low international profile, the government turning its attention to domestic affairs. There was a consensus on most issues for eleven years after 1955, aided by economic prosperity. Under an arrangement called *Proporz*, government offices were shared out by coalition partners after an election in proportion to the votes gained. The People's Party usually gained the Ministries of Education, Finance, Trade, Agriculture and Defence. The Socialists received the Ministries of Justice, Social Affairs, Transport and the Interior. Each minister would have an undersecretary from the other party. All decisions in the coalition cabinet had to be unanimous. The President and Chancellor were usually from different parties.

KEY ISSUE

Why were politics in Austria so stable?

The system made for stability, but was not particularly conducive to democracy: there was no effective parliamentary opposition and decisions were mostly made behind closed doors. No law could be introduced into the *Nationalrat* unless it had previously been approved by a political or parliamentary committee or some official body, and therefore disagreements had usually been ironed out before discussion in the *Nationalrat* itself. Civil servants often stood for office themselves. It was a system which allowed for corruption.

The balance of support for the main parties changed little in the *Nationalrat* elections before 1966. In the 1956 election the OVP won eighty-two seats, the Socialists seventy-four, the Freedom Party six and the Communists three.

In the 1959 election the Socialists won a majority of the votes cast, but did not secure a majority of seats, getting seventy-eight compared to seventy-nine for the OVP. The Freedom Party won eight seats, and the Communists none, possibly a reaction to the Soviet suppression of the Hungarian Rising of 1956. In May 1961 Raab, who had gained considerable prestige for his part in negotiating the Austrian State Treaty, resigned, and was replaced by Alphons Gorbach. In the 1962 election the OVP won eighty-one seats, the Socialists seventy-six and the Freedom Party eight.

Meanwhile, in the 1957 presidential election, as Korner had died, the Socialist Scharf won a narrow victory. Bruno Pittermann replaced Scharf as Head of the Party and as Vice-Chancellor. In the 1963 presidential election, Scharf was re-elected with 55 per cent of the vote. Raab, backed by Gorbach, lost, partly because of increasing criticism of his leadership by reformers within his party. The new Party Chairman was Josef Klaus, who was less willing to compromise with the Socialists. The Socialists themselves were increasingly split by internal divisions, and in September 1975 a splinter group called the Democratic Progressive Party was formed under Franz Olah.

The 1966 election was a landmark. The years of post-war coalitions were over. Olah had split the Socialists, and the fact that the Communists advised their supporters to vote for the Socialists possibly frightened off some voters. The People's Party under Josef Klaus won an absolute majority, pushing the Socialists into opposition. The People's Party won eighty-five seats, the Socialists seventy-four, and the

Freedom Party six. Negotiations to continue the coalition, as desired by the Socialists, broke down, and so Klaus organised the first one-party government in post-war Austria. Plans for the reorganisation of industry were put forward. However, Klaus's plans were not popular in many quarters.

The Socialist comeback was mainly due to Bruno Kreisky, who achieved considerable respect at home and abroad. Born in 1911 into a middle-class Jewish background, he suffered imprisonment in the 1930s for membership of the illegal Socialist Party. After a diplomatic career after the war, he became Foreign Minister in Raab's government in 1959. He became the Socialist leader in 1967, ending divisions in the Party through his popularity with ordinary people and his pragmatism. In contrast, Josef Taus, the new OVP leader from 1975, was seen as uninspiring, and the policies of his party were difficult to distinguish from those of the Socialists.

Kreisky's policy was to hold the central ground, to retain some working-class support whilst also reassuring middle-class voters. He promised reform but not revolution, and denounced Communism. In 1970 his Party won eighty-one seats, the OVP seventy-nine, and the FPO five. It was therefore a minority government. Another election in October 1971 was more decisive: the Socialists won ninety-three out of 183 seats. When Franz Jonas defeated Kurt Waldheim in the April 1971 presidential election, the Socialists also controlled the presidency. In 1974 Jonas died. His successor was Rudolf Kirchschlager, a non-party man but supported by the Socialists. He won the 1974 presidential election, and was unopposed in May 1980.

The Socialists' modest measures of social reform were unopposed in the *Nationalrat*. Workers received more benefits, the length of military service was reduced, the forty-hour week was introduced in 1975, and there were some educational reforms. In contrast, a law passed in 1973 to make abortion easier to obtain aroused strong opposition, not just from the Catholic Church but also from the OVP and FPO.

The 1975 election confirmed the Socialists in power. They received ninety-three seats, the OVP gained eighty, and the FPO ten. Kreisky continued to distance his Party from Marxism, and promised moderate policies which would appeal to both Catholics and non-Catholics. The Socialists included a commitment to 'Christian values' in their 1978 programme. Unsurprisingly, the Socialists cashed in on Kreisky's popularity by running in the 1979 election on the slogan 'Austria needs Kreisky'. He won an impressive victory, the Socialists winning ninety-five seats, the OVP seventy-seven and the FPO eleven.

Economic growth assisted stability. Domestic issues arose mainly from Austria's past. In the 1960s there were terrorist outrages in the South Tyrol, which became the dominant controversy. The region had been given to Italy after the First World War, although it contained 250 000 German speakers, some of whom complained at attempts to 'Italianise' this former region of the Hapsburg Empire. Western governments supported Italian claims. At first the Austrian government supported the Tiroleans in their desire to escape Italian jurisdiction.

KEY ISSUE

Why was Kreisky successful in Austria's politics for so long?

Austria went to the United Nations in 1960, and the UN tried to get Italy and Austria to negotiate. Nationalist groups began a bombing campaign to draw international attention to their cause. In 1967, continued stalemate led Italy to veto Austria's attempt at closer association with the European Common Market. Eventually agreement was reached in 1969 for the Tirolean province of Bozen to be given more autonomous rights. Although both the Austrian and Italian governments approved the agreement, the Austrians still resented the fact that they were not allowed to intervene in Tirolean affairs.

There was also controversy over the Burgenland. The 25 000 Croats and up to 50 000 Slovenes living there were guaranteed minority rights in the 1955 State Treaty. However, a 1972 law promising dual language signs wherever there was a minority of at least 20 per cent caused violent protest from some German inhabitants. Yugoslavia protested. The Ethnic Groups Act of 1977 allowed for the signs wherever over 25 per cent of the population was not German-speaking, and the Austrian government also agreed to subsidise Slovenian newspapers and radio broadcasts.

An issue even closer to home was the legacy of Austria's imperial past, the main issue of public controversy between 1955 and 1966. A 1919 law banned members of the imperial family from entering the new Republic unless they swore allegiance to its constitution. The imperial heir, Otto Hapsburg, was granted Austrian citizenship in 1956 and renounced his dynastic claims two years later. However, he was not prepared to promise to desist from political activities. Anti-monarchists still feared a possible imperial comeback. In 1963, a court ruled in support of Otto's return, but Parliament declared against it. The Socialists and the Freedom Party were both against Otto's return. He was allowed to visit Vienna in 1966.

Austria's complicity in Nazi activity between 1938 and 1945 and the way in which the process of denazification had been handled also became a focus of international attention in the 1980s. The responsibility for denazification was given by the Allies to the Austrian government in February 1946. During the following ten years over 13 000 Austrian Nazis were found guilty of various offences: there were fines and imprisonments, and ten death sentences were passed. Over 500 000 Austrians out of a population of less than 7 000 000 were affected in some way by denazification. However, the process was often arbitrary, being conducted by various means such as questionnaires. Some prominent Austrian Nazis, notably Adolf Eichmann, escaped justice. Many ex-Nazis continued in important posts, including the civil service. Some amnesties were issued in 1948 and several ex-Nazis got back on to voting lists. Generally, the official tone was to play down the widespread complicity in Nazism of the war years, and this accorded with the popular mood. A poll of Austrians in 1947 suggested that more Austrians thought that Nazism was a good idea that had simply been badly implemented, rather than having been a bad idea in the first place. Simon Wiesenthal, prominent campaigner for justice for the victims of Nazism, published a memorandum in 1966 emphasising

KEY ISSUE

Why was denazification a major issue in Austria?

that the Austrians had been far less thorough than the Germans in investigating their Nazi past. As a result, many war crimes had not been properly investigated or resolved, and many prominent ex-Nazis remained at large.

The issue of Austria's Nazi past intensified in the 1980s due to the activities of Kurt Waldheim. He was Austrian Foreign Minister between 1968 and 1970, and United Nations Secretary-General between 1972 and 1982. In 1986 Waldheim campaigned to be elected Austrian President, standing for the right-wing People's Party. During the campaign foreign sources published his wartime record. He was accused of complicity in reprisal actions against partisans whilst serving with the German army in the Balkans, without having actually taken part in reprisals himself. Waldheim had not been a Nazi, but his apparent forgetfulness of his wartime exploits created a poor impression in some quarters. Although he won the presidential election in June 1986, the international controversy continued. Waldheim asked for an international commission of military historians to look into his case. Its report, published in February 1988, cleared Waldheim of personal involvement in atrocities, although it did accuse him of 'proximity to legally incriminating acts and orders'. The strength of feeling evoked by the whole issue was the major reason that Waldheim did not run for the presidency again in 1992.

There was also growing concern in Austria over environmental issues. Austria committed itself to developing nuclear power in the 1960s, concerned by its dependence on oil from the Middle East, natural gas from the USSR and coal from the Soviet-controlled Eastern Bloc. A nuclear plant was planned in the late 1960s, and Kreisky planned to build three more by 1990. A plant built at Zwentendorf, only forty miles from Vienna and near a geological fault, was planned to provide 12 per cent of Austria's energy needs. However, public concern caused the main parties to agree on a referendum, Austria's first ever, in November 1978. Kreisky decided to treat the referendum as a vote of confidence in himself. Although 50.47 per cent of the vote was against the plant, Kreisky did not resign. However, a parliamentary bill to close the plant was passed in December 1978.

There was also controversy when the government planned a hydroelectric plant at Hainburg, thirty miles from Vienna. Environmentalists protested at the prospect of the destruction of natural marshland, and the building plans were postponed in 1985.

Austrian governments had generally kept a low profile in foreign affairs because of their neutrality, although they had denounced Soviet intervention in Hungary in 1956. Austria took in many Hungarian refugees, and also gave temporary refuge to 90 000 Czech refugees in 1968. However, Austria also kept links with the Eastern Bloc and joined the Soviet-dominated Danube Commission in 1960. Kreisky followed the *Ostpolitik* policy of his friend Willy Brandt in Germany, although relations with Eastern Bloc states varied. Relations with Hungary were better than with Czechoslovakia.

See pages 38–9

Kreisky enjoyed his international reputation and wanted Austria to have a role in the world. He built the Vienna International Centre as a base for some UN agencies, and in 1970 Austria became a nonpermanent member of the Security Council. Austrian troops joined UN peacekeeping forces in the Middle East, although Kreisky was criticised by Israel for being too friendly to Arab states. Vienna was also the headquarters of OPEC and the centre for superpower talks on arms control and other issues.

In the 1980s, the long-established Socialist regime was accused of complacency and corruption. In the 1983 election the Socialists finally lost their overall majority. Although the largest party with ninety seats, the People's Party won eighty-one and the FPO twelve. Kreisky resigned, and his influence came to an end. In May 1983 a coalition was established under Fred Sinowatz as Chancellor and Norbert Steger of the FPO as Vice-Chancellor. The People's Party under Alois Mock was in opposition.

In the 1986 election the SPO won eighty seats, the OVP seventy-seven, the FPO eighteen and the Greens eight. In January 1987 a coalition was agreed with Franz Vranitsky as Chancellor and Mock as Vice-Chancellor and Foreign Minister. The two main parties agreed on a four-year programme to restore Austria's deteriorating financial situation, and the government continued well into the 1990s. Thomas Klestil of the People's Party was elected President in 1992.

As Austria entered the 1990s, its prospects for prosperity and stability seemed good, despite some concerns about the power vacuum developing along its Southern border with the break-up of Yugoslavia. Austria was becoming more involved in the wider European and world community. In 1991 Austria became a temporary member of the UN Security Council and therefore participated in the decision to take military action against Iraq. There was also a vigorous debate about the pros and cons of joining the European Union. Over 80 per cent of eligible voters turned out in a referendum in June 1994, and a big majority voted in favour of joining. Austria's accession to the European Union was bound to have far-reaching consequences, particularly since it might call into question Austria's cherished neutrality. Whatever the future, Austria's Second Republic had achieved much to its credit. Despite limited resources it had modernised the economy, and as politics moved towards the Centre, most Austrians felt a strong degree of social harmony and common interest.

See page 351

C *Economic history*

Austria's first economic priority in 1945 was recovery from the war. Direct assistance came from the United Nations and private organisations. Only with the help of Marshall Aid, which provided $280 000 000 in 1948, did life really begin to improve. By 1949 flour and bread rationing was ended, and production was rising. But inflation rose, and disgruntled workers went on strike, dissatisfied with the leadership provided by the Socialist-dominated Austrian Federation of Trade Unions. However, the currency was gradually stabilised, despite the fact that many factories and other resources were taken from their zone by the Soviets, who continued to press for reparations. They dismantled factories and confiscated assets in their zone. In contrast, the Western Allies renounced any claims on their zones. Between 1945 and 1955 Austria received $1 585 000 000 in foreign aid from the West, mostly from the USA. Between 1950 and 1960 Austria's GNP increased by an average of 6 per cent a year. Between 1960 and 1970 the average growth rate was 4.7 per cent, and between 1970 and 1979 it was 4.3 per cent. Unemployment was low at less than 2 per cent by the 1970s, and over 200 000 Turkish and Yugoslav workers emigrated to Austria in 1973 alone.

In July 1946 the government nationalised much of the economy in an attempt to prevent assets being stripped, a move supported by the West but opposed by the Communists. The degree of public ownership of resources in Austria was higher than in any other non-Communist European state. Two-thirds of industry was controlled or influenced by the State, and by 1972 almost 30 per cent of the workforce was employed in the public sector, contributing 20 per cent to Gross National Product. In 1991 50 per cent of production still came from the State-owned or State-protected sector.

As Austria recovered, a model of cooperation was established between employers and workers. In 1957 the Parity Commission for Wages and Prices was set up to produce a 'Social Charter' governing worker–employer relationships, and was renewed regularly. The Commission brought together representatives of the employers, trade unions and government. The Commission not only determined wages and prices but set out Austria's general economic policy. Generally, the government managed to implement policies with little opposition.

The economy improved, despite the fact that Austria's historic focus of economic activity, the Danube Basin, had largely been closed to it by the Iron Curtain, behind which Communist states formed their own trading block. Tourism was an important bonus, aiding Austria's 'economic miracle', which also reaped the benefits of a build-up of heavy industry begun before the war, and the fact that during the war there had been an emphasis on producing capital goods rather than consumer goods.

The collapse of Communism in the late 1980s opened up new possibilities for Austria. It was close to Hungary, the Czech Republic, Slovakia and the entire Danube region. Tax concessions and the prospect of Austria becoming a focus for trade between East and West persuaded many foreign firms to set up in Vienna. By 1993 Austrian firms had concluded 7500 joint-venture agreements with enterprises in Eastern Europe. The Austrians conducted a big marketing operation in the old Soviet Bloc, although they were overtaken by the Germans.

Another great opportunity was promised by the European Union, particularly since Italy and Germany were Austria's most valuable trading partners. Germany made massive investments in Austria. In the

> ## KEY ISSUE
>
> *How successful was the post-war Austrian economy?*

1970s over 40 per cent of Austria's imports were from Germany, and three quarters of tourists to Austria were from Germany. Austria had been represented on the Council of the OEEC, formed in 1948, and had been one of the founder members of EFTA. However, Austrian farmers were against the EEC, and some Austrian firms feared being swamped by foreign competition. Others, particularly Socialists, feared that Austria's extensive social system might be threatened by Community membership. Nevertheless, the majority of the population was in favour of membership. Austria sought associate membership of the EEC in 1961, despite Soviet protests that this represented a violation of Austria's neutral status. In July 1972 Austria received tariff privileges from the EEC, along with other EFTA members. At the same time Austria traded with the COMECON states and joined the Soviet-dominated Danube Commission in 1960.

6 ↪ BIBLIOGRAPHY

The history of Czechoslovakia, Hungary and Poland during this period is covered in more detail in *The Eastern and Central European States 1945–1992* by J. Laver (Hodder and Stoughton, 1999), a book which also gives advice to students on note making and essay writing. There are other useful books which cover the history of the region. The *Columbia History of Eastern Europe in the Twentieth Century*, edited by J. Held (Columbia University Press, 1992) not only traces the history of individual countries from the early twentieth century to about 1990, but helps to explain the background of events. *Eastern Europe Since 1945* by G. and N. Swain (Macmillan, 1993) is useful. *Central Europe Since 1945* by P Lewis (Longman, 1994) does not follow a country-by-country approach, but draws out general themes. *Revolution in East–Central Europe* by D. Mason (Westview Press, 1992) is good on the dramatic events of 1989 to 1992. *We The People – The Revolution of 1990* by T. Ash (Penguin, 1990) is one of several vivid journalists' accounts of the collapse of Communist rule in Poland, Czechoslovakia and Hungary. There is not a lot of material on Austria, but *Austria Between East and West 1945–1955* by W. Bader (Stanford University Press, 1966), *Austria Since 1945* by W. Wright (University of Minnesota, 1982) and *Modern Austria* by B. Jelavich (Cambridge University Press, 1987) can all be recommended.

7 ↪ ESSAY QUESTIONS

1. (a) Why did the Czechoslovak Communists not come to power until 1948?
   (b) Why did the Communist regime stay in power for so long?
2. (a) What reforms were undertaken by Dubček's regime in Czechoslovakia in the 1960s?

(b) Why was the regime overthrown by Czechoslovakia's allies?

3. (a) Why was Czechoslovakia's Communist regime overthrown in the 1980s?

(b) What were the consequences for Czechoslovak political and economic life?

4. How and why did the Polish Communists come to power after the Second World War?

5. (a) Outline Poland's relations with the USSR between 1945 and 1989;

(b) To what extent did the USSR intervene in Polish affairs?

6. How successfully did Poland's Communist regime manage the Polish economy in the four decades after coming to power?

7. (a) Why was *Solidarity* formed in Poland?

(b) What influence did *Solidarity* have on subsequent Polish affairs?

8. (a) What political and economic reforms were undertaken by Poland's post-1989 governments?

(b) How successful were they in solving Poland's problems?

9. Account for the rise and fall of Imre Nagy in Hungary.

10. (a) What caused the Hungarian Rising of 1956?

(b) Why did it fail?

11. (a) What were the main features of Hungary's New Economic Mechanism?

(b) How successful was it in meeting Hungary's economic needs?

12. How significant were the achievements of any *two* of the following: Novotný; Husák; Kádár; Jaruzelski?

13. Why, and with what consequences, was Austria divided in 1945?

14. 'Peace and consensus.' To what extent did Austrian governments achieve these aims after 1955?

15. Compare and contrast any *two* of the following regimes in their approach to politics and economics in the period between the late 1940s and the late 1980s: Poland; Czechoslovakia; Hungary.

16. Compare the reasons for, and the consequences of, Soviet intervention in Hungary in 1956 and Czechoslovakia in 1968.

8 ⌒ INTERPRETING PHOTOGRAPHS AND A PHOTOGRAPHIC EXERCISE ON THE HUNGARIAN RISING OF 1956

Photographs are just one of many sources of evidence available to the student of modern history. They can be excellent sources of primary evidence. At one level they can show details of everyday events, people, fashions and so on, and possibly be used in a comparison of the past and present. On another level, photographs can record significant events, or at least record a moment of time during a significant event. Photographs can help to recreate atmosphere and capture a moment of emotion or tension not evident in moving film or other sources, bringing us as close as possible to an event which we did not directly experience ourselves.

Nevertheless, like any form of evidence, photographs have to be treated with care by historians. Some famous photographs have been faked or staged: examples include the raising of the Stars and Stripes by American soldiers on the recaptured island of Iwo Jima in World War Two, and the many doctored photographs of Stalin's USSR which 'removed' the disgraced Trotsky from Lenin's side in an attempt to obliterate him from history altogether. Popular newspapers still sometimes fake photographs or manipulate images to produce a desired effect.

Therefore, as with any form of evidence, the student using photographs as historical evidence should ask questions not just about the content of a photograph but also the following:

- What, if any, were the motives of the photographer, and to what use might the photograph have been put?
- To what extent do these and other factors affect a photograph's value as evidence?

The following are other questions you might well ask of a photograph (as indeed of some other kinds of evidence):

1. *What does the photograph actually show?*
2. *Do we know whether the photograph is authentic? Is there a caption or other form of attribution? If we do not know anything about the photograph, what is the probability of it being authentic?*
3. *Is it likely that the photograph was taken for a particular purpose? If so, what was it? Was it produced for purposes of information or propaganda?*
4. *Is the photograph reliable as evidence? If so, reliable for what?*
5. *How might the photograph or series of photographs affect our interpretation of events? Can we learn anything of significance from this evidence?*
6. *What are the uses and limitations of the photograph as evidence?*

As always, when discussing evidence, you should relate your analysis to the context of the particular photograph, and avoid making generalised comments about the value of *any* photograph.

Bearing these points in mind, study the following collection of photographs A–G taken during the Hungarian Rising of 1956, and apply the questions above to them. Finally, answer this additional question: to what extent do these photographs assist our understanding of the Rising?

PICTURE 19
(Source A) Stalin's bust being pulled off its pedestal, Budapest

PICTURE 20
(Source B) Stalin's statue being moved by tractor from Stalin Square to the Hungarian National Theatre, Budapest

PICTURE 21
(Source C) Russian tanks in Budapest

PICTURE 22
(Source D) One of the Hungarian leaders of the uprising addresses a crowd in Budapest

PICTURE 23
(Source E) Civilians and soldiers fire from behind a barricade, Budapest

PICTURE 24
(Source F) A victim of the street fighting in Budapest, 1956

PICTURE 25
(Source G) Hungarian refugees flee across a broken bridge over the Einsen Canal into Austria

5

Southern Europe, 1945–95: Italy, Spain and Portugal

See page 66

INTRODUCTION

Though each is a separate country with its own distinctive character and history, important common themes link together the post-war experience of Italy, Spain and Portugal. All three share the social and cultural features of Southern Mediterranean Europe, in particular the lasting influence of traditional Catholicism. All three are societies deeply influenced by the rule and legacy of three dictators, Mussolini, Franco and Salazar. All three went through a subsequent transition to democracy and to membership of the European Community. All are countries affected to a significant degree by regional differences, particularly Spain and Italy. The difference is that both Spain and Portugal maintained a position of neutrality throughout the Second World War, while the history of Italy was decisively affected by Mussolini's decision to enter the war as Hitler's ally in 1940.

1 ⌐ ITALY, 1943–94

A *Introduction*

For fifty years after the Second World War, the history of Italy followed a pattern that was set in the 1940s and did not substantially change until the early 1990s, when it experienced something close to a political revolution. Several key factors shaped the history of post-war Italy, some of them special to that country, others similar to those elsewhere in Western Europe. They included:

● The legacy of Fascism. After 1945, all three main parties in Italy, and the Constitution of the Republic, were avowedly anti-Fascist. As in the French Fourth Republic there was no mainstream right-wing party;

● Political instability. Governments in Italy were invariably coalitions, which, on average, lasted less than a year. Party politics were based on patronage and personalities;

● The impact of the Cold War. The USA played a particularly important role in the domestic affairs of Italy, both economically and politically, pouring support into 'the defence against Communism';

- The dominance of the Christian Democratic Party. The DC emerged after the war as a new centre-right party and held power for most of the next fifty years, with a system of patronage that was open to influence-peddling and corruption. Italy showed some of the features of a 'one-party state;

- The influence of the Catholic Church. The special place of Catholicism in Italy was reinforced by anti-Communism after 1945, and by direct Catholic influence on the leaders of the Christian Democrats;

- The post-war economic recovery of Western Europe. Italy was a founder member of the EEC and shared in the general prosperity of the 1960s;

- The 'European social revolution'. Italy experienced deep social and cultural change in the 1960s and 1970s, including a period of student radicalism and urban terrorism.

MAP 18
Italy, 1943–95

B *Political history*

THE LEGACY OF THE PAST

Italy was an old civilisation but a relatively new state. Unification had been accompanied by high hopes in the 1860s but Liberal Italy struggled to cope with deep divisions between Church and State and between North and South. Entry into the First World War in 1915 led to military failure and economic strain. In 1919, Italy was left with a sense of national humiliation following the post-war peace settlement. There was widespread industrial and political unrest. In 1922, Italian democracy collapsed and Mussolini came to power.

From 1922 to 1940, Fascist Italy, at least on the surface, seemed to achieve considerable political and economic success at home and significant prestige abroad. Mussolini was the first Fascist dictator, the first pioneer of new techniques of mass propaganda. He was credited with bringing about national unity and pride, with reconciling the Catholic Church to the Italian State in 1929, and with making Italy into a great power and himself into a world statesman. Many of these achievements were shallow ones, exaggerated by Mussolini's flair for propaganda presentation.

From 1935, Mussolini moved into a dangerous alliance with Hitler's Germany. Even so, he was enough of a realist to avoid involvement in the Second World War in 1939. He tried hard to persuade Hitler not to launch a war, saying that Italy would not be ready for war until 1942. It was still possible that Italy might stay neutral, perhaps even join in on the winning side, as in 1915. In the event, Mussolini made a fatal miscalculation. In June 1940, believing the outcome of the war to be decided beyond any doubt, he joined forces with Hitler and invaded France – late enough to be safe from a serious conflict but soon enough to share in the glory of victory. Mussolini had gone to war hoping not to have to fight a war. But the war did not end, as he hoped, after the defeat of France. The European war became a world war in 1941, with disastrous consequences for Italy and for Mussolini.

In 1940, Italy had a second-rate navy (without a single aircraft carrier) and a third-rate army and air force. Although Mussolini had boasted about 'eight million bayonets', he knew that it was empty propaganda. The Italian war effort went hopelessly wrong. Both in North Africa and in the Balkans, Italian forces failed so badly that Hitler was compelled into large-scale intervention by German armies to rescue the situation. The Italian fleet was virtually destroyed by the Royal Navy at Taranto and Cape Matapan. Italy became totally subordinated to German interests. It was a symbol of the way that Italy had become so tied to Germany that units of the Italian army were destroyed in 1942–43, fighting for their German allies at Stalingrad in the USSR. In May 1943, the last Axis forces pulled out of North Africa. In July, the Allies invaded Sicily.

Fascist rule crumbled with remarkable speed as even Mussolini's own hand-picked Fascist Grand Council turned against him. The almost-forgotten King of Italy was brought back into action to dismiss

Mussolini on 25 July 1943. Hardly a single Fascist tried to fight back. Mussolini was imprisoned and a new government was set up under the army chief-of-staff, Marshal Badoglio. At first, Badoglio and the King attempted to keep their options open and see how the invasion of Italy turned out before committing themselves, but events ran away with them. Badoglio and the King fled from Rome and surrendered to the Allies. On 10 October, they were forced to sign a declaration of war making Italy a 'co-belligerent' against Germany. Mussolini's Fascist regime had ruled for twenty-one years and allied itself to Nazi Germany. It collapsed, and became allied to Germany's enemies, in the space of only forty-five days.

But the war, and Fascist influence, did not end as neatly as had been hoped. The German armies fought tenaciously and it took over a year of bitter fighting before German armies were driven out of northern Italy. The whole history of post-war Italy was decisively influenced by the events of the nineteen months between the fall of Mussolini and the end of the Second World War.

'THE TURNING POINT OF MODERN ITALIAN HISTORY':
ITALY, 1943–45

The men who had got rid of Mussolini (the King, Badoglio, and dissident Fascists) hoped to keep power in the hands of the old political establishment, to negotiate with the Allies, to get German troops out of Italy – and to do all this quickly and painlessly. They were wildly over-optimistic, for several reasons:

- The German forces did not leave Italy quickly and quietly. They remained in control of northern Italy throughout most of 1944;
- With the protection of the German presence, Fascist sympathisers made a comeback and set up the so-called Italian Social Republic, usually known as the 'Salo Republic' because its 'capital' was the lakeside resort of Salo;
- The end of Mussolini brought out into the open all kinds of democratic political groups who had been suppressed during the 1920s and 30s. Within a short time, six anti-Fascist parties had been formed;
- The Communists took a leading role in building up an Italian Resistance through well-armed bands of partisans. As in France after the collapse of Vichy, the Communists, led by Palmiro Togliatti, wanted to be seen as the patriotic backbone of the anti-Fascist Resistance, earning a legitimate place in the new government of Italy after the war.

The old-style manipulative political fixers around the 'Royal Government' of the King and Badoglio could not control these pent-up factions. The result was a nasty and divisive Civil War, with the German armies in the north, the slowly advancing allied armies in the south, and millions of Italian civilians caught up in between. Numerous resistance groups emerged, involving peasants, workers and middle-class intellectuals. All were supposedly joined together in a National Liberation Committee, but actually had almost no agreed aims except to fight the Germans.

Opposing the Resistance, alongside the Germans, was the 'Salo Republic' and its collection of Fascists and right-wingers. In the anarchy of the Civil War, there were many violent revenges. Many Fascists were shot without trial. German forces and Italian collaborators carried out a number of atrocities, including the massacre of 300 left-wing prisoners in the Ardentine Caves, near Rome, in 1944. Eventually, the German forces pulled out and the Salo Republic collapsed. In April 1945, Mussolini was captured by Communist partisans and shot. His body, together with that of his mistress Clara Petacci, was exhibited in the square in Milan.

In 1945, the Italian political scene was in ruins. The Allies regarded Italy with contempt, following the slogans KID ('Keep Italy Down') and MIP ('Make Italy Pay'). The economy had been badly damaged by the war and was almost completely in the hands of the black market. The King and the old-style political establishment were discredited, as were those people associated with Fascist rule. Many were suspicious of Togliatti and the Communists, fearing excessive Soviet influence in Italy. In addition, Italy was plagued by age-old problems: the economic division between the poor, backward South and the advanced, industrial North, and the position of the Catholic Church. The Church was discredited by its collaboration with Fascism but was bound to play a key role in any efforts to block the Communists after the war.

The troubled nature of Italian society at this time is strikingly portrayed in the work of two famous Italian film directors, Roberto Rossellini (*Rome: Open City*) and Vittorio de Sica (*Bicycle Thieves and Umberto D*). See page **427**.

KEY ISSUE

In what ways was Italy affected by Mussolini's legacy after 1943?

THE CONSOLIDATION OF THE ITALIAN REPUBLIC, 1945–49

Italy was under military occupation when the war ended. Italian politics had to begin again almost from scratch. The first stage was local rule by partisan committees, during which time many Fascist collaborators were executed out of hand. The second stage was a temporary government based on the National Liberation Committee and led by Ferruccio Parri, a moderate socialist. Parri was soon undermined, however, by conservative opposition and replaced by the Christian Democrat leader, Alcide de Gasperi, in December 1945. The third stage was a referendum to decide whether Italy should remain a monarchy or become a republic. The voting, in May 1946, went in favour of a republic, but only by 54 per cent to 46. The fourth stage was a Constituent Assembly to devise a new and permanent political system.

Of the many political groupings active in 1943–45, three main mass parties emerged from the elections for the Constituent Assembly:

- The Communists, led by Palmiro Togliatti, and the only party able to keep nationwide party unity, avoiding any north–south split – 19 per cent;
- The Italian Socialist Party, now led by Pietro Nenni – 20 per cent;
- The Christian Democrats, a new right-of-centre party, led by Alcide de Gasperi, partly based on the old '*Popolari*' party founded by Don

Sturzo in 1919 and strongly supported by the Catholic Church – 35 per cent.

In addition, there were numerous small parties, who, in total, got just over 20 per cent. It became clear that the Christian Democrats would be the basis of the new government but would have to share power with other parties in a coalition. This set the pattern for years to come. De Gasperi stayed in power until 1953 and the Christian Democrats dominated Italian politics until 1992.

The political divisions of the Republic were intensified by continuing bitter enmities arising from the war, by urgent economic difficulties and by external factors. Just as in 1919, many Italians resented the post-war settlement, which took away Italy's colonies and transferred territory to Yugoslavia. American influence pushed Italy in a firmly anti-Communist direction. These external factors became mixed with the internal situation. There was serious industrial unrest in 1946–47,

See pages 229–30

PALMIRO TOGLIATTI (1893–1964)

PROFILE

Palmiro Togliatti was leader of the Italian Communists (PCI) from the formation of the party in the 1920s until his death in 1964. Born into a middle-class family in Genoa, he was wounded in the First World War, and started his career as a Socialist journalist in 1919. He led a breakaway group which split from the PSI in 1921 to form the Communist Party. Exiled by Mussolini, he was based in Moscow from 1926 to 1944. He also took a leading role in the Spanish Civil War, in charge of the Comintern agents on the Republican side. Like the French Communist leader Maurice Thorez, Togliatti became a key figure in 1944–45, as the Fascist regime collapsed and there was a surge of support for left-wing, anti-Fascist resisters. He was Deputy Prime Minister in 1945 and later Justice Minister but the pressures of the Cold War led to de Gasperi expelling the Communists from the government in 1947. Togliatti narrowly survived an assassination attempt in 1948.

Although the Communists got 135 seats in the 1948 elections, the Italian Left remained split and never broke through to achieve power. Togliatti was always handicapped by his associations with Stalin and the USSR but he was not a dogmatic ideologist. After Stalin's death, and especially after 1956, he took a very flexible approach to Communist theory. He accepted that Italy was a Catholic country and believed in an 'Italian road to socialism'. His ideas of Eurocommunism were taken up elsewhere in Western Europe and by the PCI leadership, especially Enrico Berlinguer in the 1970s.

See page 222

and such a serious food supply crisis that thousands took part in a 'hunger march' in Naples in 1947. USA policy-makers became increasingly concerned about the rise in support for left-wing parties. It was these worries about the situation in Italy, and in France, that led to the Marshall Plan.

The political developments in Italy, therefore, resembled those in France at the same time. The Communists seemed in a very strong position but were hampered by taking part in a coalition government. Politics drifted to the Right and the PCI was expelled from the government in 1947. The Marshall Plan accelerated this process. By April 1948, the economic crisis had been stabilised. In the first elections under the new permanent Constitution, de Gasperi and the Christian Democrats fought a well-financed campaign, with massive backing from the Catholic Church, and won a decisive victory. The vote for the Left also held up well – Italian politics were becoming polarised.

The Christian Democrats were able to rely on support from the northern industrialists, from the great landowners of the south, and from the USA. Italy was a founder member of NATO in 1949, more for political reasons than for military ones. Anti-Communism became a basic prop of Christian Democrat rule. So did manipulation of the police and local government, although Italy was very definitely a democracy, not an authoritarian system like that of Franco or Salazar. The pattern of post-war Italian politics was set.

See pages 387–9

KEY ISSUE

What factors prevented the Italian Left from achieving more lasting political success after the fall of Mussolini?

ANALYSIS

American influence in Italy, 1946–48

The Cold War had a huge influence upon post-war Western Europe, perhaps more so in Italy than anywhere. In the economic and political chaos of 1946, American policy was deeply concerned about Italy 'going Communist'. Long before the Marshall Plan was thought of, murky actions were being taken to head off the threat of Communism in Italy. One was the role of CIA agents in assisting the escape of Nazi war criminals who might be useful in the fight against Communism. The main 'ratline', or escape route to South America, for German, Austrian and Croatian ex-Nazis was through Italy, often with direct help from the Catholic Church and from CIA agents. At one point, the same building in Rome was being shared by the American agents trying to arrest these ex-Nazis, and by other American agents helping them to escape.

Another American step, which had dire consequences, was the re-introduction of the *Mafia* into Italy. One of Mussolini's few genuine achievements was to clip the wings of the *Mafia*. Now in 1946, agents of the OSS (the wartime American secret service and forerunner of the CIA) brought the notorious gangster, 'Lucky'

Luciano, to Italy to help ensure that Communist influence in the Italian south was minimised. At the same time, the USA funded a secret 'stay-behind' network, known as *Gladio*, which was to monitor the Communist Party and take action if ever it attempted to seize power. Together with more open examples of American influence, such as Marshall Aid and the lavish funding of the DC election campaign, it is hardly surprising that some left-wingers in Italy regarded Alcide de Gasperi as an 'American agent'.

'STABLE INSTABILITY': ITALY, 1948–68

The Christian Democrats were Italy's dominant party for four decades. From 1948 to 1987 their share of the vote never dropped below 34 per cent. The DC provided every Prime Minister of Italy from December 1945 to 1981, and several after that. DC local councillors controlled most major cities. Men appointed by the DC managed much of industry and public finance.

The DC could rely on massive support from the Catholic Church. It also got long-term support from the USA. It was the natural choice for anyone who feared the rise of the Italian Left. And, once in power, the DC established a system of mass patronage that ensured that huge numbers of jobs depended upon political support for the Christian Democrats. The DC drew its support from various elements of Italian society (women voters, the elderly, small landowners), but the key factors holding it together were always the same:

- Catholic religious loyalties;
- Cold War anti-Communism;
- Patronage and the resulting links with business and public sector jobs.

Martin Clark called this 'the triumph of Low Politics':

It practised the politics of compromise and patronage, of temporary deals and temporary governments, of granting favours and buying support, and of political interference in the administration. Many Italians regarded it as inherently corrupt.

Modern Italy by M. Clark (see bibliography)

Although the long dominance of the DC provided continuity, there was a polarisation of politics in Italy. Despite splits between the PSI, the PCI and the Social Democrats, support for left-wing parties remained strong. The system also depended upon coalition governments, with the DC in partnership with other parties. Sometimes, governments were 'centre-right', allied to the Social Democrat PSDI, sometimes 'centre-left', including the Socialists, and sometimes 'national unity', with the Communists.

Main parties	1948 % D	1953 % D	1958 % D	1963 % D	1968 % D
PCI (Communists)	(31%)	23% 143	23% 140	25% 166	27% 177
PSI (Socialists)	(183)	13% 75	14% 84	14% 87	(15%)
PSDI (Social Democrats)	7% 33	5% 19	5% 23	6% 33	(91)
PRI (Republicans)	3% 9	2% 5	1% 6	1% 6	2% 9
DC (Christian Democrats)	48% 304	40% 263	42% 273	38% 260	39% 266
PLI (Liberals)	4% 19	3% 13	4% 14	7% 39	6% 31
PNM (Monarchists)	3% 14	7% 40	5% 25	2% 8	1% 6
MSI (Neo-Fascists)	2% 6	6% 29	5% 25	5% 27	5% 23

% D: share of the vote and number of deputies elected.

TABLE 27

Political parties and election results in Italy, 1948–68

See pages 338–9

Italy Since 1800 by Roger Absalom (see bibliography)

Alcide de Gasperi lost control of his party in 1953 and was forced to resign. He was succeeded by Amintore Fanfani. By then, however, the position of the DC in Italian politics was already established and de Gasperi had committed Italy to membership of the European Community. It was in Italy, at Messina in 1955 and in Rome in 1957, that the EEC took shape. Italy began to share in the general economic recovery and full employment of Western Europe in the 1950s and 60s. Italian politics remained in a set pattern – which Roger Absalom has described as 'stable instability'.

In one sense, there was serious instability. Divisions between Left and Right ran deep. There were two different 'sub-cultures' in Italy: one Catholic, the other Socialist. These sub-cultures, with their own newspapers and social organisations, were so self-contained and so different that they amounted to two different ways of life. Governments were also short-lived, with shaky coalitions based on shifting alliances between groups and individuals. Between 1945 and 1970, Italy had twenty-eight governments and twelve prime ministers. But this 'stable instability' reflected a basic situation of relative economic prosperity and continued Christian Democrat dominance.

There was a political crisis in 1960, when the Christian Democrat Prime Minister, Fernando Tambroni, made an alliance with the neo-Fascist MSI. This led to mass demonstrations and violent clashes with police in Genoa. The Tambroni 'experiment' was abandoned after four months; the DC never again went so far to the Right. Then there was an economic and political crisis in 1962–63, with serious industrial unrest and a decline of support for the DC in the 1963 elections, but this rearranged the political system more than altered the basic pattern. From December 1963, the DC held power through a four-party coalition, in partnership with the PSI, the PSDI and the Republicans, with Aldo Moro as Prime Minister. Moro's coalition was similar in some ways to the 1966 'Grand Coalition' in West Germany. It was not until 1968 that new social and political forces challenged the system.

KEY ISSUE

Why was the Christian Democratic Party so successful for so long?

ITALY, 1968–80

By 1968, post-war prosperity had brought substantial social changes to Italy, as it had throughout Western Europe. The long dominance of the

DC meant that new forms of political protest emerged. The 'cultural revolution' of 1968 affected Italy more deeply, and for much longer, than the more famous 'events of May' affected France. In Italy, 1968 led to the 'hot autumn' of 1969 and a decade of political violence.

See pages 458–63

There were several strands in the upheavals of 1968–69: student radicalism, discontented factory workers, pressures for change in the lives and status of women, the liberalisation of the Catholic Church, urban terrorism and the revival of Fascism. There were serious clashes between police and students in 1968 and a wave of unrest and violence in 1969. Urban terrorism came both from the Left and from the Right. The most famous of many left-wing radical groups were the so-called 'Red Brigades', founded in Milan in 1970. The Red Brigades began with political kidnappings and bank robberies but this escalated into bombings and killings in 1974. In 1978, they kidnapped the former Prime Minister, Aldo Moro. When their demands for the release of terrorists from prison were refused, they murdered Aldo Moro and dumped his body in a Renault 5. Later, scraps of paper with Moro's handwritten notes were discovered in the villa where he had been kept prisoner.

Right-wing violence began as a backlash against the student protests of 1968–69. Neo-Fascists were responsible for the first and the last big terrorist outrages of the decade. In December 1969, they killed sixteen people by a bomb in a public square in Milan. In 1974, sixteen were killed when the Rome–Munich express was derailed. In August 1980, they blew up the restaurant in Bologna railway station, killing eighty-five and injuring more than 200. The murder of Aldo Moro and the Bologna station bomb actually marked the end of the decade of urban terrorism. Previously, terrorism had been regarded as commonplace, even acceptable. Now there was a revulsion against it.

From 1973, the new PCI leader, Enrico Berlinguer, pushed forward the ideas of Eurocommunism and proposed a 'historic compromise' between the Communists and the Republic. Efforts were made to include the PCI in the government coalition. These efforts failed but the more moderate image of the PCI became accepted. Control of the government remained with the DC under its leader, Giulio Andreotti. 'Stable instability' continued as usual.

ITALY, 1980–92

Outwardly, Italian politics continued in its familiar groove throughout the 1980s. In reality, the system was facing long-term problems. The great upheavals of 1992–94 were not as sudden as they seemed. In 1981, for example, Italy briefly had a non-Christian Democrat Prime Minister for the first time since 1945. In the 1983 elections, the DC share of the vote dropped sharply, from 38 per cent to 33. The Socialist leader, Bettino Craxi, became Prime Minister and stayed in power for most of the period until 1987. In 1984, Umberto Bossi began stirring up northern discontent with his Lombard League. In 1989–91, when the Cold War ended, the structures of Italian politics were fundamentally altered. Perhaps most of all, there was a growing public reaction against

The fight against organised crime

In 1981, a major scandal erupted when documents were discovered showing hundreds of judges, journalists, politicians and public officials to be members of the influential, secretive Masonic Lodge *P2*. It was alleged that *P2* was closely connected to the DC, to the Catholic Church and to the *Mafia*. In 1982, Roberto Calvi, a financier with the *Banco Ambrosiana*, and an adviser to the Vatican, was found dead in London, hanging from Blackfriars Bridge in highly suspicious circumstances. His death drew attention to the murky role of *P2*. To many people, it also looked very like a *Mafia* execution.

The *Mafia* was almost part of the political scenery in Italy. It had been reintroduced, with American help, in 1943–46 and had wide-ranging influence in numerous sectors of the economy. (Strictly speaking, the *Mafia* was in Sicily. In Calabria, organised crime was called the *'ndrangheta'*; in Naples it was the *Camorra*.) The police did not try very hard to make arrests. If arrests were made, there were many *Mafia*-friendly judges to quash the sentences. Many believed that Giulio Andreotti, the DC leader, had *Mafia* associations. Now, in 1982, the authorities really took on the fight against organised crime and appointed a special anti-*Mafia* unit under General Carlo Alberto Dalla Chiesa, who had established a good name fighting the urban terrorists in the late 1970s.

Within a short time, Dalla Chiesa and his wife were murdered but, unlike previous occasions, the murder did not deflect the crusade against organised crime. Dalla Chiesa's colleagues, Giovanni Falcone and Paolo Borsellino, continued to gain vital information from *Mafia* 'supergrasses' such as Tommaso Buscetta and rounded up 456 *mafiosi* for a mass trial in Palermo in 1987. All were imprisoned, including some top bosses like Toto Rina.

The *mafiosi* were not bothered – they felt certain that their friends in the legal system would let them out on appeal. But the tainted judges were removed and the appeals were turned down. The *Mafia* took immediate revenge and killed Silvio Lima, their contact man with the politicians in Rome. Then, in two huge, separate bomb attacks in 1992, they murdered Falcone and Borsellino. The result was a wave of revulsion against the *Mafia* and against their political friends. Organised crime was in fact badly weakened in 1992 and the murders helped to cause a 'legal revolution' in Italy.

PICTURE 26
*Some of the 456 Mafia
leaders awaiting trial in
Palermo, 1987*

the corruption of public life in Italy. In the 1980s, a series of high-
profile events brought the issues of corruption and crime into the
limelight and provided the backdrop for the 'legal revolution' to come.

ITALY, 1992–95: THE COLLAPSE OF THE FIRST REPUBLIC

The Italian Republic was the republic of the Cold War, built on the
twin pillars of anti-Fascism and anti-Communism. The end of the Cold
War, therefore, had a massive impact on Italy. The fall of Communism
weakened the PCI and deprived the DC of one of the key reasons for its
very existence. The 1992 elections showed how far people had lost faith
in the system. Only 47 per cent bothered to vote at all, regarding
national politics as a corrupt national joke. For the first time ever, the
DC vote dipped below 30 per cent. The PCI slumped to 17 per cent.
The PSI might have expected to make gains but remained stuck at 13
per cent. All this left a huge hole in Italian politics, which Martin Clark
has called a 'Legitimacy Crisis'.

This hole was filled by new forms of politics:

- In 1990–92, there was a surge of support for the *Northern League*,
  led by Umberto Bossi. The *Lega* was an amalgamation of several
  leagues that had grown up in the 1980s, especially Bossi's 'Lombard
  League'. Bossi was an effective propagandist, winning support by
  populist attacks against 'southern' corruption, and also stressing

> ### KEY ISSUE
>
> *In what ways and to
> what extent had Italian
> society and politics
> 'fundamentally
> changed' between 1968
> and the mid-1980s?*

See pages 284–5

TIMELINE

Italy, 1943–94

1943 The fall of Mussolini
1944 The Salo Republic and
–45 Civil War
1945 The Constitution of
–46 the Republic
de Gaspari Prime
Minister
1947 The Marshall Plan
–48 PCI excluded from
government
1953 De Gaspari replaced
by Fanfani
1955 Messina Conference
1957 Treaty of Rome
1960 Riots against DC–MSI
alliance
1968 Prolonged clashes
–69 between police and
radical protesters
1978 Murder of Aldo Moro
1980 Bologna station bomb
1982 Murder of General
Dalla Chiesa
1983 Elections showed
decline of DC
1987 456 *Mafiosi* on trial
in Palermo
1992 Murders of Falcone
and Borsellino
1993 Corruption charges
against Craxi and
Andreotti
1994 'Revolution' in election
results
Berlusconi Prime
Minister

how the advanced, prosperous north was subsidising the rest of the country. Bossi also argued for big cuts in public spending and reducing the power of the State. The *Lega* seemed to threaten the break-up of the unified Italian State, as actually happened with the breakaway of Slovenia from Yugoslavia;

● Another new 'anti-party' was the populist political movement *Forza Italia (Go Italy!)* led, and financed, by the media tycoon Silvio Berlusconi. *Forza Italia* was based on a mixture of soccer-style supporters clubs, massive advertising and brilliant television presentation. Berlusconi was originally a crooner on cruise ships. By the 1980s, he possessed a huge media empire. Italians watched television on Berlusconi's three TV channels, where the adverts provided by Berlusconi's massive advertising agency *Publitalia* extolled the goods sold in Berlusconi's supermarket chains. If they did not watch TV, they read Berlusconi's numerous newspapers and magazines. Most of all, he owned the giant football club *AC Milan,* which gave him almost unlimited media opportunities. He had previously depended upon close links with politicians, especially Bettino Craxi. Now he struck out on his own. *Forza Italia* rocketed from nowhere to gain 20 per cent of the vote in the 1994 elections;

● Alongside *Forza Italia*, the right-wing National Alliance also made big gains. The Alliance was headed by the neo-Fascist MSI and its leader, Gianfranco Fini. The MSI had been a fringe party for years and had never come near to power apart from the brief Tambroni episode in 1960. Now, with Fini as a capable and energetic leader, support for the far Right surged. The MSI was also enlivened by the contributions of Mussolini's granddaughter. Alessandra Mussolini was youthful, blonde and glamorous, though at times it was difficult to tell if she wanted to succeed in politics or just to make it as a show-business celebrity. In the mood of 1993–94, anyone so different from the old-style politicians was an asset.

The way for these new political movements was opened by rejection of the mainstream parties and also by changes in the system. The President of the Republic, Francesco Cossiga, launched a big attack on political corruption in 1991. A maverick DC politician, Mario Segni, promoted the idea of 'taking politics out of the hands of the politicians'. The result was a new voting system based on proportional representation, and a rush of new laws passed by referendum. In 1992, these changes loosened the grip of the old parties.

In 1993, support for the new movements mushroomed as there were more and more revelations about the extent of political corruption and links with organised crime. In Milan, a magistrate, Antonio de Pietro, opened a legal investigation called *Operation Clean Hands*, exposing massive bribery of politicians and public officials. Bettino Craxi was indicted on corruption charges and ran away to Tunisia. Nearly 400 members of parliament were under investigation. In the south, the murder of Judge Falcone in 1992 was a turning point in the fight against the *Mafia* and exposed the extent to which leading politicians had allowed organised crime to flourish. In 1993, Giulio Andreotti, the man who had been Prime Minister seven times, who served in twenty-three different cabinets, who had been close to four popes, the man who symbolised the whole DC era, was charged with extensive collusion with the crime bosses. Italy became obsessed with the past, re-opening forgotten controversies about Fascist atrocities in 1944, or the 'dirty tricks' against the Communists in 1945–47.

The indictment of Andreotti really did mark the collapse of the old ways. The mood of the time was 'Old is bad. New is good'. The whole political culture was on trial. In the 1994 elections, the overriding purpose of the voters was to 'get rid of the corrupt old gang'. All three main parties were big losers. Berlusconi and *Forza Italia* got 20 per cent. Gianfranco Fini, leader of so-called National Alliance (the neo-Fascist MSI and parties on the Right) got 23 per cent. Bossi's *Northern League* got over 20 per cent of voters in the North.

Silvio Berlusconi became Prime Minister. Most of his cabinet came from outside the previous political élite. The new coalition was not stable as most of the force behind it came from negative voting. Berlusconi's policies were running into trouble even before sensational charges of corruption were made against his brother. Soon, Silvio Berlusconi himself was charged with illegal business dealings. Italy already had three recent Prime Ministers, Craxi, Giovanni de Mita and 'Don Giulio' Andreotti, in imminent danger of going to jail. Now Berlusconi, the recently-elected 'Mr Clean', joined the list.

In 1995, Italy was in a political no-man's land. The Cold War era was over and the old Christian Democrat system was discredited but no new permanent replacement had established itself. A stop-gap Prime Minister, Lamberto Dini, and a stop-gap President, Romano Prodi, kept the government going, but the long-term outcome of the 'legal revolution' of 1992–94 remained unknown.

> **KEY ISSUE**
>
> *In what respects and to what extent did Italy experience a 'political revolution' between 1992 and 1994?*

C *Economic history*

In 1945–46, the Italian economy was in a terrible state. Agricultural production was one-third of the 1938 level. Industrial production was even less. Real wages were barely half of pre-war levels for workers, about two-thirds for public servants. War damage was severe. The finance minister, Luigi Einardi, announced:

> Two million dwellings destroyed. Five million damaged. Railways lacking 50 per cent of rolling stock. 10 per cent left of pre-war merchant shipping. At least three billion *lire* needed for essential reconstruction.

Einardi proposed a policy of free-market capitalism. The proposals by Togliatti's Communists and Nenni's Socialists for wholesale nationalisation did not gain enough support. There was also a strong reaction against the Fascist 'corporate state'. Italy missed the chance of a major restructuring of the economic system. There was a rapid return to economic normality, but in Italy normality meant deep-rooted structural problems: the North–South divide, outdated technology, high unemployment and a huge bureaucracy. Italy had no real equivalent to the French Monnet Plan.

The first key to Italian economic recovery was the Marshall Plan. From 1947, Italian industrial production rose steadily and reached 140 per cent of pre-war levels by mid-1952. Recovery was also boosted by the discovery of big natural gas deposits in the Po valley; for the first time ever, Italy had its own cheap energy supply. But unemployment persisted in the north and rural poverty was still endemic in the south. In the 1950s, Italy began to benefit from the general economic boom in Europe. Under de Gasperi, the DC committed Italy to membership of the EEC. Combined with other favourable factors (low inflation, an artificially low exchange rate for the *lira*) this enabled a surge of economic activity. There was a human flood of unskilled workers from the south into the key 'triangle' of industrial development between Milan, Turin and Genoa. The EEC also provided job opportunities for thousands of Italian migrant workers elsewhere in Western Europe.

Efforts were made to build up the economy of the *Mezzogiorno* through regional investment schemes but these had little success and were often open to corruption. The North–South divide remained. Overall, however, Italy shared in the European 'economic miracle' of the late 1950s. Ownership of cars and televisions shot up. Italian firms such as Fiat, Olivetti, Pirelli and Montecatini became international giants. Italy was in the forefront of fashion and design. There was a massive expansion of higher education. By 1980, Italy ranked seventh in the table of industrial economies.

Along with the 'economic miracle', Italy shared in the European 'social revolution'. Despite vigorous opposition from Catholic conservatives, Italy legalised divorce in 1974 and abortion in 1976. Affluence, feminism, youth culture, tourism and the deregulation of the media affected Italy in the same ways as elsewhere. Economic prosperity was not uninterrupted. There was a sharp downturn in 1962–63, leading to a wave of strikes. Italy was badly affected by the impact of the oil-price crisis after 1973. The chemical industry was caught up in a terrible disaster in 1976 when there was an escape of deadly dioxins from the Seveso plant. The burden of state spending remained very heavy. Overall, however, the economy of the Italian

---

KEY ISSUE

How successfully and for what reasons did the Italian economy recover from its problems after the Second World War?

See Chapter 10

TABLE 28

Economic growth and unemployment in Italy, 1951–70

	1951–58	1959–63	1964–65	1966–70
Growth of GDP	5.0%	6.3%	3.2%	6.0%
Unemployment	7.0%	5.0%	3.0%	5.6%

GDP: Gross domestic product

Republic was a remarkable success story, bringing Italy closer to the levels of the rest of Western Europe than at any time in the history of united Italy.

D *Foreign policy*

The foreign policy of post-war Italy closely controlled by external factors. The peace settlement of 1947 was imposed on Italy, not negotiated. An independent foreign policy was impossible. More than in any other European country except West Germany, governments in Italy were totally identified with the Cold War policies of the USA. Membership of the European Community also placed Italian policies within a multinational framework. The key patterns of Italian foreign policy, therefore, were established at a very early stage, with the Marshall Plan of 1947 and the determination of Alcide de Gasperi to lead Italy into NATO and the EEC.

Some particular Italian issues had to be dealt with. There was a long-running dispute with Austria over the German-speaking South Tyrol, still part of Italy after 1945. This was settled in 1960 by granting cultural rights. A more serious dispute concerned the borders with Yugoslavia, especially Trieste. In 1953, Tito attempted to take over Trieste, bringing Italy and Yugoslavia close to war. The crisis was defused by the Western Allies and Trieste was formally handed to Italy in 1954 – as in 1947, this was an imposed decision, not one negotiated by Italian diplomats. Most Italians were happy to ignore foreign policy. A survey in 1958 showed that 50 per cent of Italians had no idea what NATO was. There was no Italian equivalent to de Gaulle's dreams of great power standing. The EEC, and the Americans, could take care of everything.

This changed somewhat in the 1980s, when the Foreign Minister, Gianni de Michaelis, tried to establish a distinctive Italian approach to Eastern Europe. After the fall of Communism, Italian governments became particularly concerned with the break-up of Yugoslavia and with the problems of refugees from the Balkan War and from Albania. The biggest change concerned relations with the USA. The end of the Cold War took away the basis of USA–Italian relations. Italy mattered less to the USA. Italy also gave offence by offering only lukewarm support at the time of the Gulf War in 1991. In 1992, the USA showed no particular desire to prop up Christian Democrat rule as it had so often done in the past. For the most part, foreign policy issues were still completely overshadowed by domestic affairs.

2 ∽ SPAIN, 1945–95

A *Introduction*

In the years before 1945, Spain experienced political upheavals that scarred the nation. In the 1920s, Spain experienced a form of

TIMELINE

Spain, 1931–95

1931	Foundation of the Spanish Republic
1936	Outbreak of Spanish Civil War
1939	Final Nationalist victory
1940	Franco's meeting with Hitler
1945	The survival of Franco's regime
1953	Pact of Madrid
1969	Nomination of Juan Carlos as Franco's successor
1975	Death of Franco
1981	Failure of right-wing *coup d'etat*
1982	Election of Socialist government
1986	Spanish membership of EU
1992	Olympic Games in Barcelona
1995	Javier Solana appointed Secretary General of NATO

dictatorship under the leadership of Primo de Rivera. In 1931, the monarchy became a democratic republic. Between 1936 and 1939, the Republic was overthrown in a bitter civil war. Spain became an isolated 'outlaw' state, economically ruined, ruled by a dictatorship and torn by deep political and religious hatreds. The history of Spain for the next thirty-six years was to be completely identified with the personality and rule of one man – General Francisco Franco.

This section considers a number of key issues concerning modern Spain. How did Franco maintain his power for so long? How much of a break with the past was Franco's death in 1975? How far did Spain follow, or diverge from, the European mainstream? Most of all, how completely did Spain overcome the dreadful legacy of the Spanish Civil War?

PROFILE

FRANCISCO FRANCO (1893–1975)

Francisco Franco Bahamonde was born in the seaport of El Ferrol, in the north-western region of Galicia. Several members of his family had been naval officers but Franco entered the Toledo Military Academy in 1910 and soon became a rising star in the Spanish army. He made his name in colonial wars in North Africa, leading the fight against the Moroccan guerrilla leader Abd al-Krim. In 1927, aged only thirty-four, he was appointed Principal of the Military Academy at Saragossa. Although Franco's career suffered a setback in 1931 (because a keen monarchist like him was out of place in the new Republic), he continued his rise through the army élite and became Chief of the General Staff in 1935 and then Governor of the Canary Islands in 1936.

When elements of the army prepared to revolt against the Republic in 1936, Franco at first hesitated to join the rebels but then committed himself to a leading role. In June, he led troops from Morocco into Spain and set up a rebel Nationalist government at Burgos. Franco was not only the military leader of the Nationalist armies. He was also immensely skilful as a political leader, keeping together the diverse anti-Republican forces. In 1937, after the death of its leader, Jose Antonio Primo de Rivera, Franco took over the Spanish Fascist movement, the *Falange*. He also accepted considerable assistance from Nazi Germany and Fascist Italy and thus became closely associated with Hitler and Mussolini. In reality, Franco was not an ideologist. He used Fascism but Fascism never captured him. Franco was much more a Francoist than a Fascist.

Victory in the Spanish Civil War made Franco the master of Spain in 1939. It also gave Franco a deserved reputation for ruthlessness and brutality. Vicious reprisals followed the end of the war in 1939. Until his death in 1975 at the age of eighty-two, Franco continued to show the same ruthlessness and skill in preserving his own power by repression, manipulation and the tactics of 'divide and rule'. He did all this without overworking. Franco was a man who knew how to keep power while leaving the detail to loyal subordinates. He enjoyed hunting, golf, fishing trips on his yacht *Azor,* and never missed *Match of the Day* on TV. 'I do not', he boasted later in his career, 'find Spain difficult to govern.'

Against all expectations, Franco survived the downfall of Fascism in 1945 and outlasted Hitler and Mussolini by thirty years. In the process, for good or bad, he moulded the history of modern Spain.

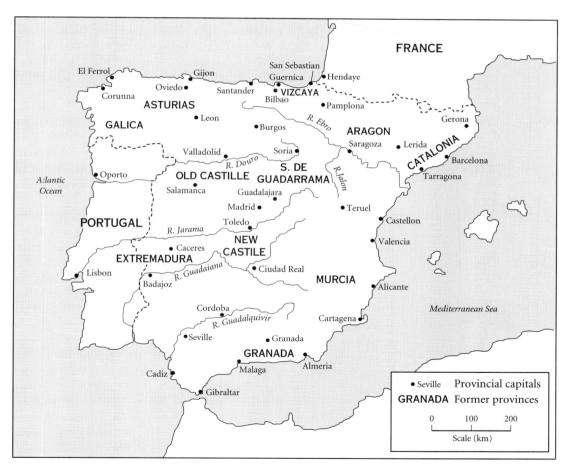

MAP 19
Spain and Portugal, 1945–95

B *Political history*

THE LEGACY OF THE PAST: THE SPANISH CIVIL WAR
The Spanish Civil War was not one war but three parallel wars:

- The international conflict involving support for the Nationalists from Germany and Italy, while the Republicans received limited help from the Soviet Union and from the volunteers of the International Brigade;
- The struggle between the central government and the separatist forces seeking self-rule for Catalonia and the Basque country;
- The main conflict between Left and Right – the diverse forces supporting the Republic and the equally variegated elements of the Nationalists.

Each of these conflicts left an important legacy. In the Western democracies, especially Britain and France, Franco was a hate-figure for all liberals and left-wingers. As long as Franco ruled, Spain would always be outside the mainstream of Western Europe. Separatism was defeated in 1939 but not removed. Catalonia, and its capital, Barcelona, remained sharply different from the rest of Spain and Basque nationalism remained a thorny issue, especially when the Basque terrorist organisation *ETA* began a campaign of bombings in the 1970s. Above all, the bitter legacy of 1939 left Spain itself torn by continuing political conflicts. Countless thousands were killed or purged under the policy of *Limpieza,* the reprisals and punishments handed out by the Nationalists after the war. Hundreds of thousands were in exile, many of them leading figures in Spanish culture. The first part of Franco's career did much to intensify these conflicts; from 1939 the rest of his career was spent perpetuating them and coping with the consequences.

SPAIN AND THE SECOND WORLD WAR
Some of the most important events in history are the events that do not happen. The basis of Franco's long career after 1939 was that, unlike Mussolini, he avoided involvement in the Second World War.

This was not easily done. In 1940, Hitler looked unstoppable and Franco was tempted to join the Axis for imperialist reasons. The defeat of Britain would mean that Spain could win back Gibraltar. Franco had made his name fighting in North Africa and was eager to make territorial gains there. He came under pressure from right-wing elements in his own regime, especially in the *Falange*, who were strongly in favour of Spain joining a 'Fascist crusade'. In the end, Franco resisted these pressures but it was a close-run thing.

In October 1940, it seemed very likely that Spain would indeed side with Hitler. Franco's very pro-Axis brother-in-law, Ramon Serrano Suner, became Foreign Minister. Heinrich Himmler was given a lavish welcome when he made an official visit to Spain. But when Franco went to meet Hitler on 23 October, at Hendaye on the French border, the meeting did not go well. Franco was disappointed that Hitler did not promise big rewards. Hitler was simply disappointed with Franco and is

KEY ISSUE

In what respects and how deeply was Spain affected by the Civil War?

said to have muttered afterwards, 'There is nothing to be done with this man.' Later, Hitler privately described his long meeting with Franco as 'worse than going to the dentist' and referred to Franco as 'conceited, arrogant and stupid. A clown!'

There are differing interpretations as to why Franco avoided entering the war. Franco's admirers like to stress how cleverly he defended Spain's interests at Hendaye, 'holding back Hitler, where the French had failed'. The Francoist version stresses the strong, far-sighted policy by which the *Caudillo* kept Spain out of Hitler's clutches. According to Paul Preston, it was more luck than cleverness. Preston argues that the Franco of 1940 was 'a greedy imperialist' and that, if Hitler had offered more, Franco would have gone for it.

> *Franco* by Paul Preston (see bibliography)

But Franco was prudent as well as lucky. Unlike Mussolini, he waited long enough to see whether Hitler really was going to win. In the meantime, he had many dangers to avoid. Franco had to worry about the possibility of Hitler invading Spain, as Goering told Hitler to do in 1940. He had to worry about Britain choking off Spain's food and fuel supplies if he entered the war. Franco also had to worry about his own political position. Spain's economic situation was desperately bad in 1941 and there were tensions within his regime, especially between the army and the Falangists.

In December 1941, with the German armies held up in Russia and American entry into the war, it became clear to Franco that Hitler had got into serious difficulties. Franco still hoped for an Axis victory but began to seek better relations with the USA. These efforts weakened the position of Ramon Serrano Suner. Franco became less obsessed with gaining an overseas empire and more concerned to protect his power at home. In February 1942, Franco met the Portuguese dictator, Salazar, in Seville and agreed a joint policy of neutrality. Later in 1942, in a decisive shift of policy, Franco sacked Serrano Suner. Luck, fear of Allied retaliation and cautious political calculation ensured the neutrality that safeguarded the continuation of Franco's rule in Spain more than any other factor.

From 1942, Franco worked hard to keep good relations with both sides, often by dishonest methods. The fall of Mussolini in 1943 tipped Spain closer towards the Western allies. Franco began stressing that the real threat to the world was now the Soviet Union and that he, Franco, would be a valuable ally in the fight against Communism. Even as late as 1944, 70 per cent of Spain's exports were to Germany or to Nazi-occupied countries and German radar stations were allowed to continue operating in Spain right to the end of the war. What efforts Franco did make to ingratiate himself with the Allies had little success. His main plan appeared to be to do nothing and hope that the Allies had too many other problems to be bothered with Spain.

Ultimately, this plan worked. In May 1944, the oil sanctions that had so damaged the Spanish economy were lifted. Although both Britain and the USA wanted Franco removed, it was clear by 1945 that they would not use force to do so. And when Stalin, Truman and Churchill met for the peace negotiations at Potsdam in July 1945, Stalin got no

---

KEY ISSUE

By what methods and with what results for Spain was Franco able to avoid involvement in the Second World War?

See pages 383–5

support for immediate action against Franco's regime. Even the election of a Labour government did not change British policy as expected. Franco had already managed to protect his grip on Spain by avoiding the Second World War. Now he was going to protect it further by 'playing the Cold War card'.

SPAIN AND THE COLD WAR, 1945–53

The condition of Spain at the end of the war in 1945 was disastrous. 700 000 people had been killed in the Spanish Civil War. Another 15 000 were killed in the period of revenge from 1939. Nearly 200 000 Spaniards were in exile. Economic measures against Spain during the World War had squeezed a vulnerable economy to the limit. Trade with Germany was finished. The French Fourth Republic closed the border with Spain in 1946. Spain had no chance of joining the United Nations, nor of gaining economic help from the Western democracies. Franco's Spain was isolated, unpopular and broke.

Franco's internal position did not seem much better. Elements of the army wanted to get rid of him and restore the monarchy. The *Falange* was not easy to control. To make matters worse, the Republican opponents of the regime were now in a position to fight back. In 1945 Republican forces began a guerrilla war in Northern Spain, which was a serious threat until 1947 and not finally called off until 1951. And, as always, there were serious internal differences between the many factions within the Nationalists.

Several key factors saved Franco from the ruinous position he faced in 1945:

- The first, immediate rescue was an injection of food supplies from his fellow dictator, Juan Peron of Argentina, in 1946;
- The second was Franco's skill as a politician and manipulator. Paul Preston emphasises 'the world of experience separating the cautious and cunning Franco of 1945 from the eager imperialist of 1940';
- The third was repression. In and after 1945, the regime continued the same brutal methods of censorship, arrests and executions that had been in place ever since 1939;
- The key to the long-term survival of his regime was the USA. Spain's geography, Franco's anti-Communism and his tactics during the latter part of the Second World War made it possible for Spain to gain economic salvation by being on the right side in the Cold War.

This process took time. In 1946–47, Spain was still in international disgrace and the economic crisis was severe. In May 1947, a wave of violent strikes hit Catalonia, the Basque country, Galicia and Madrid. The effect of this industrial unrest was actually to benefit Franco. At the very time the Marshall Plan was being devised, there seemed an urgent need to shore up Spain and keep out the menace of Communism. Spain was excluded from the countries receiving aid under the Marshall Plan at first but Cold War attitudes were hardening rapidly in the USA. In 1947, Franco made constitutional changes, making his regime seem less Fascist and more traditional through the Law of Succession, 'camouflaging the regime with the trappings of acceptability'. In 1948, Franco's man in the USA, Jose Felix Lequerica, spent $250 000 in bribes as part of a diplomatic offensive to maximise conservative and Catholic support in the USA. These efforts were ultimately successful. Spain received a loan of $25 million early in 1949.

The course of the Cold War did the rest. In June 1950, the start of the Korean War convinced even the Franco-hating Harry Truman that his military advisers were right and Spain should be brought out of diplomatic isolation. European hostility to Franco was still strong enough to prevent Spain being admitted to NATO but what really mattered to Franco was a two-way relationship with the USA. In November, Spain was promised that an American ambassador would be posted to Madrid; and received a secret loan of $62 million. This opened the way for Spain to come out of the diplomatic cold: in 1952, Spain was admitted to UNESCO, in 1953, Spain signed a Concordat with the Vatican, and in 1955 it was admitted to the United Nations.

Most important of all, in September 1953, Franco agreed the Pacts of Madrid with the USA, now led by President Eisenhower. In return for four key Spanish bases, the airfields at Torrejon, Moron and Zaragoza, and the naval base at Rota, the USA committed $241 million to Spain. (Between 1951 and 1957, USA aid to Spain totalled $625 million.) After the Pacts of Madrid, Franco's political position was completely secure.

THE FRANCO REGIME, 1953–69

By 1953, the Francoist regime was safely established. Franco had gained complete mastery over the key 'families' upon which his regime depended, the Falangists, the Army, the Church and the Monarchists. He knew how to 'divide and rule'. He knew how to delegate authority to trusted subordinates without letting them get too powerful. He could rely on a ruthless and efficient system of repression and on an effective propaganda machine. Franco's regime had been developing for fifteen years and would now continue unchallenged until the 1970s.

The first basis of the regime was the FET (*Falange Espanola Tradicionalsta*) formed by Franco and Serrano Suner in 1937. The Falangists, however, never gained the dominant role they expected. Many Fascist, 'syndicalist' social policies were adopted but Francoism was always a flexible system, balancing a variety of traditionalist and more modern elements. The title FET was gradually used less and replaced by 'National Movement', or 'New State':

- The apex of the regime was the *Caudillo* himself. He was the '*Jefe Nacional*', the '*Generalissimo*' who won the Civil War. In the 1947 Law of Succession, he had cemented his position as Head of State. Any opposition to his rule was weak and fragmented, held down by an efficient system of repression. The 1939 Law of Political Responsibilities gave huge powers to the police. At any one time 40 000 people were in prison. Close to Franco were a few reliable

> **KEY ISSUE**
>
> *Why was Franco able to continue in power for so long?*

subordinates, such as Serano Suner, Jose Felix Lequerica and, most trusted of all, Admiral Luis Carrero Blanco;

- Falangists were very influential in the regime even after 1945, especially through organisations like the Youth Front, the Women's Section and the propaganda machine. But radical Falangists were marginalised by 1942 and the Falangists who did remain in the cabinet were more moderate, and also carefully balanced against other groups;

- The army was an essential pillar of the regime. It was where Franco had his original power base and the army was also an important part of internal repression. During the guerrilla war in 1945–48, Spain was under martial law, with each region of Spain controlled by an army Captain-General who was backed by the paramilitary police, the *Garda Civil*, and a network of army-run concentration camps. All soldiers were automatically party members and were often given government posts;

- The Catholic Church was another pillar of the regime. Francoism called itself a 'moral crusade' and the Church was a natural ally against anti-republicanism and anti-Communism. In 1953, Franco signed a Concordat with the Vatican. Catholics were prominent in the regime at all levels but Catholic influence in areas like education had to be balanced against the Falangists and organisations like 'Catholic Action' had to compete with equivalent Falangist organisations;

- From the 1950s, traditional Catholicism also had to compete with *Opus Dei*, the powerful, élitist lay Catholic organisation. *Opus Dei* was socially very conservative but modern, managerial and 'technocratic' in its approach. Franco relied on *Opus Dei* technocrats such as Laureano Lopez Rodo, his Technical Secretary from 1956, to oversee the process of modernisation. It also suited him to play rival wings of Catholicism off against each other;

- The final pillar of the regime was provided by the Monarchists, though they overlapped with many other groups such as Church and army. Here, too, Franco cleverly used the tactics of 'divide and rule'. The issue of the monarchy never interfered with Franco's position as Head of State and Franco kept the monarchists guessing until 1969.

PROFILE

LUIS CARRERO BLANCO (1903–73)

Perhaps the most important individual in the regime apart from Franco himself, Luis Carrero Blanco, started out on a naval career, specialising in submarines. He joined Franco's government in 1941 and soon became a trusted confidential adviser, 'the invisible man who was always present, always making himself useful'. It was Carrero Blanco who supervised the ruthless purge of Republican opposition after the Civil War, as head of the 'Tribunal for the Repression of Freemasonry and Communism'. From this point, he remained a key figure of the regime for thirty years: cabinet minister in 1951, Rear-Admiral in 1957, Admiral in 1966, Deputy Head of Government in 1967, and finally Head of Government in 1973. He might well have played a big role in the succession to Franco but for the fact that he was assassinated in December 1973 by an ETA car bomb. Not long after his death, Edouard de Blaye summed up Carrero Blanco's role in Francoism:

> Anti-Communist, anti-Semite, anti-Freemason, he was one of the 'ultras' of the regime. No one was closer to Franco than this professional sailor who had more experience of sailing the troubled waters of politics than voyaging across the deep blue sea. For thirty-three years, he had talks with the *Caudillo* almost every day. Keeping in the background, he secretly pulled the strings, insinuating, advising, suggesting. While in the end it was the *Caudillo* alone who decided, the governing idea behind his decisions often bore the signature of Carrero Blanco or of Laureano Lopez Rodo.

Franco and the Politics of Spain, by Eduoard de Blaye (Penguin, 1974)

Carrero Blanco's special relationship with Laureano Lopez Rodo was almost as vital to the regime as his relationship with Franco. In 1955, Lopez Rodo, a young law professor and militant member of *Opus Dei*, was asked to help save Carrero Blanco's marriage, which was on the point of breaking up. His advice was a brilliantly successful: he not only reconciled husband and wife but also so impressed Carrero Blanco that the two men established a lasting partnership in politics. It was Carrero Blanco who brought Lopez Rodo into the government in December 1956 and, from 1957, it was the Carrero Blanco–Lopez Rodo team that was behind the drive to bring the technocrats into prominent roles in industry and finance. It was also the Carrero Blanco–Lopez Rodo team that carried out 'Operation Juan Carlos' in 1969, pushing the ageing Franco into nominating Juan Carlos as his successor.

The Franco regime was authoritarian but flexible enough to allow for a degree of change. In 1957, a big reorganisation of the civil service and the government gave a leading role to the modernisers of *Opus Dei*, backed by the close alliance between Luis Carrero Blanco, and the leading *Opus Dei* technocrat, Laureano Lopez Rodo. In 1959, a Stabilisation Plan was set up to modernise the economy. In 1966, Manuel Fraga introduced the 'Organic Law of the State'. This gave the Spanish Parliament, the *Cortes*, some vaguely democratic window-dressing and paved the way for solving the problem of the succession by making separate the posts of President and Head of State. The essential nature of the regime, and Franco's control over it, did not change much. But in the 1960s, Spain went through a 'social revolution'.

See page 246

See the section on economic history, pages 245–8

The future king of Spain?

In theory, the Spanish Civil War should have led to the restoration of the monarchy in Spain. Franco, however, had no intention of bringing back the monarchy while he was still alive. He had the Falangists to think about and he wanted to be his own Head of State. There were rival claimants to the throne, the 'Carlists' and the Bourbons. Franco preferred the Bourbons but at different times encouraged the hopes of all the various candidates. The 'Carlists' did not finally lose hope until Prince Carlos Hugo was expelled from Spain in 1968. The 'official' Bourbon claimant to the throne was Don Juan, the son of Alfonso XIII (who had been King until 1931 and who died in exile in 1941) but in 1948, Franco arranged for Don Juan's young son, Juan Carlos, to be brought up and educated in Spain. This was typical of the way Franco cleverly exploited the divisions between the various monarchist factions, but he could always rely on the monarchists supporting his regime. They always depended on Franco more than he depended on them.

For the next thirty years, Franco kept the monarchists dangling. Don Juan refused to give up his claims and kept pushing forward the idea of a liberal, democratic monarchy, while Francoist conservatives hoped that Juan Carlos would be in favour of maintaining an authoritarian regime. Juan Carlos himself was careful to say nothing. Many had the impression that he was Franco's stooge. In 1958, Franco again promised the return of the monarchy 'one day' but it seemed that that day was a long way off. In an interview with a British newspaper in 1965, one of Franco's ministers let it be known that Juan Carlos would be chosen, but not until Carrero Blanco and Lopez Rodo pushed him hard in 1969 did Franco formally nominate Juan Carlos as his heir.

Franco's Spain managed to combine social transformation without fundamental change in the political system. Managing this contradictory situation was one of Franco's more striking achievements but, by 1969, it was already clear that political change would be inevitable once Franco had gone.

THE LAST YEARS OF FRANCO AND THE TRANSITION TO DEMOCRACY, 1969–81

Between 1969 and 1981, Spain went through a period of fundamental change. The key event in this process was the death of Franco, but even before 1975 there was an important period of political uncertainty, 'the crisis of the late years of Francoism'; and after 1975 there was a time of suspense until it became clear that there would be no successful anti-democratic backlash against the fragile new constitutional monarchy. In the event, Spain managed a remarkably smooth transition from dictatorship to democracy; but this was not something which could have been confidently predicted in 1975.

1969 was a turning point in the history of Spain. The Basque separatist movement, ETA, emerged as a dangerous opponent of the regime. Franco at last nominated Juan Carlos as his successor. He also delegated a considerable degree of power to Luis Carrero Blanco. The new 'homogenous' government reflected the influence of the modernisers and showed Franco, now seventy-six, to be moving to the sidelines as he set out to 'get his affairs in order'.

There were many pressures for change building up between 1966 and 1975, both from external factors and from within the crumbling regime itself:

- the impact of mass tourism and of Spaniards working temporarily abroad;
- the realisation that Franco could not go on forever, that change was inevitable;
- the fact that integration with Western Europe required democracy in Spain;
- the side effects of the 1974 revolution in Portugal. This alarmed the USA and led to American pressure on Spain to carry out political reforms;
- Spain's own economic progress, encouraging the growth of an articulate middle class, demanding higher living standards and more freedoms;
- the revival of an effective opposition against the regime from Socialists, Communists, progressive businessmen and liberal Catholic reformers;
- the 'generation gap' and the restlessness of youth, especially university students.

KEY ISSUE

In what ways and why did the Franco regime change after 1969?

Franco hoped to ensure that most of the elements of his authoritarian regime would keep going after he was dead. He aimed to satisfy the army and the old conservatives by bringing back the monarchy; and to please moderates by making some seemingly democratic political reforms, while real power would actually stay with Franco loyalists like Carrero Blanco. Franco believed he had the situation under control (he is said to have claimed that 'it's all tied up') but it is unlikely that his plan would have worked out as he hoped, even if Carrero Blanco had not been killed by ETA terrorists, who blew up his car in December 1973. The murder of Carrero Blanco sparked off a series of repressive measures, cancelling many of the cautious reforms made since 1966.

After the death of Carrero Blanco, the regime began to disintegrate. Much of the stability of Franco's rule had depended upon the feeling that the old man would be there forever. Now even Francoists knew that some kind of change was inevitable and, for the first time since the 1940s, the hopes of the opposition were stirred up by the prospect of change. The previously divided opposition groups at last began to work together in the so-called *Junta Democratica*. The pressure for change was also increased by the economic impact of the 1973 oil-price crisis. The new head of the government, Carlos Arias Navarro, found that the supporters of the regime were badly split between hard-liners (known as the 'Bunker') and the liberalisers. What Paul Preston calls the 'internal contradictions of Francoism' were coming to the surface.

Arias talked about liberalisation but dared not actually implement it because he was afraid of the army. In 1975, the Arias government was reinforced by an *Opus Dei* moderniser and adviser to Juan Carlos, Fernando Herrero Tejedor, but within a few months Herrero was killed in a road accident. Then Franco caused a storm of protest by ordering the executions of five revolutionaries, despite appeals from the Pope and Juan Carlos. The Franco regime was rotting from within while Spain waited for Franco to die.

Franco died in November 1975, aged eighty-two. Juan Carlos was made King two days later. The government was rejigged, to include several reform-minded Francoists, but it could not control the situation. Rising prices led to a wave of strikes and demonstrations and violent clashes with the police. In July 1976, Juan Carlos persuaded Arias to resign and instead appointed an almost unknown Francoist reformer, Adolfo Suarez.

Suarez knew the Franco system inside out. He knew exactly how and where to graft real democratic structures onto the manipulated 'pretend-democracy' already there. The Francoist *Cortes* voted itself out of existence. A Political Reform Act was passed, with democratic elections to be held at the end of 1976. The Act was approved by a huge majority in a referendum. Next, Suarez legalised political parties, including the Communists. In June 1977, Suarez won Spain's first democratic elections since 1936.

What followed was a period of consensus, disillusion and then consolidation. The consensus was a desire not to rock the boat. Most Francoists knew their day was over and had little enthusiasm to fight back. Most of the opposition was so relieved to have democracy and reform that they did not want to push too hard. Memories of the Civil War were so sharp that there was a general fear of it happening again. The disillusionment was inevitable. Fixing a new constitution was difficult. Nobody had experience of running a democratic government and the parties of the Left and the Centre still had many divisions.

Despite this, the consolidation was achieved with relative ease. In the *Moncloa Pacts* of 1977, the government compromised with the opposition both on economic measures and on negotiations about a new constitution. The left-wing parties abandoned the ideas of *ruptura*, a complete break with the past, and agreed a policy of wage restraint to avoid inflation. The Suarez government bought time for its gradualist policies to work.

A new Constitution was set up in 1978 but the new democracy was not yet safe. Economic problems and disappointment with the lack of fundamental reforms caused a low turnout at the 1979 elections. There were fears of a backlash from the army, especially when ETA bomb attacks led to new demands for strict law and order policies. In February 1981, an attempt at a *coup d'etat* was launched by the *Garda Civil* led by Lieutenant-Colonel Antonio Tejero Molina. The Parliament was stormed and many MPs were held hostage for thirty-six hours. Other army units revolted in the regions.

But this was not 1936. Ever since 1976, people had been afraid that a *coup* might show how weak and unstable the new system was. The Tejero *coup* actually showed how strong it was. The bulk of the army stayed loyal and the revolt collapsed. Above all, there was a massive public reaction in favour of democracy and a wave of demonstrations in which everyone from Francoists to Communists joined. In 1983 Spain went to the polls again and, in an atmosphere of normality and calm, elected to power a Socialist government, headed by Felipe Gonzalez. Franco was truly dead and democracy was here to stay.

MODERN SPAIN

The political parties of the new Spain took shape in the elections of 1977. On the Left were the Socialists and the Communists. On the Right was the 'Popular Alliance' led by an old Francoist, Manuel Fraga. The most powerful group was a loose centrist coalition of liberals and Christian Democrats, the UCD (Democratic Centre Union), led by Adolfo Suarez. The 1979 elections produced similar results, with the UCD still in power and the Socialist vote up to 31 per cent. In 1980, however, the UCD did badly in the regional elections and Suarez resigned. Soon after this, the Tejero Molina *coup* was launched.

Suarez' successor as Prime Minister, Leopoldo Calva Sotelo, proved unable to keep the UCD together and it broke up into a number of smaller parties. In new elections in 1982, the UCD vote collapsed to 7 per cent. The Socialists, led by Felipe Gonzalez, won decisively with 46 per cent. The conservative Popular Alliance, now seen as a reassuringly respectable party, became the main opposition. The UCD never recovered. Spain virtually became a two-party system. Politically, Felipe Gonzalez was in a strong position, but the economic situation in the early 1980s made life difficult for him. He was forced into devaluation and spending cuts and had to accept high levels of unemployment, all of which went against the hopes of his supporters.

Party							
PCE (Communists)	9%	10%	4%				
	19	23	4				
U (United Left)				5%	9%	10%	11%
				7	17	18	21
PSOE (Socialists)	29%	31%	48%	45%	40%	39%	38%
	110	121	202	184	175	159	141
UCD (Democratic Centre Union)	36%	35%	7%				
	166	168	11				
SDS (Social Democratic Centre)				3%	9%	8%	2%
				2	19	14	0
PP (People's Party; Popular Alliance)	16	9	107	105	107	141	156

TABLE 29
National elections in Spain, 1977–96

Despite these problems, the speed with which Spain was integrated with the rest of Europe was remarkable. Spain joined NATO in 1982 and, after seven years of negotiations, joined the EC in 1986. The Socialists had originally opposed Spanish membership of NATO and demanded a referendum on the issue, but Felipe Gonzalez changed tack and campaigned in favour when the referendum was held in 1986. He then used the referendum 'yes' vote as a springboard for success in the 1986 elections.

Gonzalez and the PSOE, therefore, were the dominant force in national politics through most of the post-Franco period. The end of the Franco regime also meant big changes for the regions. The Franco era had been ruthlessly centralist and the new democracy moved quickly to allow devolution. In 1979–80, the 'historic nationalities' – Catalonia, the Basque country and Galicia – were all granted statutes allowing a considerable degree of self-rule. There was then a great controversy over which other regions might qualify for autonomy. A 'pact with the regions' was agreed in 1981. By 1983, Spain was divided into seventeen autonomous regions. In 1992, a second 'pact with the regions' took devolution further. Devolution was successful in many respects but it failed to end the problems of Basque separatism. The ETA bombing campaigns continued.

Felipe Gonzalez' government ran into difficulties in 1987–89, with a wave of strikes and ETA terrorist attacks. There was also an internal split as the interests of the PSOE and the traditional trade union leaders diverged. Even so, the Socialists were able to win 40 per cent of the votes in the 1989 elections and narrowly retained power again in 1993. By then, the People's Alliance Party had been revamped with a new name, the People's Party, and a new leader, José Maria Aznar. At first, Aznar found it difficult to compete with Felipe Gonzalez in terms of popular appeal but he was an effective party organiser. After narrow defeat in 1993, Aznar led the PP to an election victory in 1996.

By 1995, twenty years after the death of the *Caudillo*, the political, economic and social transformation of Spain was complete. The monarchy had achieved acceptance to an astonishing degree – any Civil War veteran who saw Juan Carlos and Sofia being spontaneously applauded on the streets of Barcelona at the time of the 1992 Olympics would have rubbed his eyes in disbelief. The two main political parties represented the moderate Socialist Left and the respectable Conservative Right. Apart from the continuing ETA bombing campaign, regional issues had been dealt with successfully. Spain's modernity and prosperity were symbolised by the high-tech fast train, the *AVE*, whisking its passengers in silent comfort from Seville to Madrid in three hours. The social and cultural life of Madrid and other Spanish cities was vibrant, youthful and optimistic. How much all of this occurred because of the legacy of Franco's long rule, or in spite of it, remains a very good question.

KEY ISSUE

In what ways and to what extent did the legacy of Franco assist or hinder the development of Spain between 1975 and 1995?

C *Economic history*

FROM CIVIL WAR TO COLD WAR

The economic situation of Spain in 1939 was appalling and the Second World War made it worse. The Civil War had caused massive damage, huge loss of life and had dislocated the economy. It also ruined Spain's foreign trade and left Spain badly isolated throughout the Second World War. There was large-scale trade with Nazi Germany during the war, amounting to 40 per cent of Spain's total exports, with another 30 per cent going to Nazi-occupied countries. The defeat of Germany brought this trade to an end with painful results. Spain had also suffered severely throughout the war from having oil supplies strictly rationed by the Allies.

By 1944–45, living standards in Spain were below the levels of 1914. Rural poverty was acute. After the war, towns and cities became choked with the rural unemployed. Spain was totally without friends in Europe and the French Fourth Republic closed the border with Spain in 1946. Only substantial food supplies sent by President Juan Peron from Argentina late in 1946 saved many Spaniards from starvation. Peron's aid was vital but could only be a short-term measure. The long-term economic salvation of Spain depended upon outside factors. The economic crisis facing France and Italy in 1946–47 was solved first by the Marshall Plan and then by the integration of the European economy through the Schuman Plan and, later, the EEC. The hostility to Franco in 1947 made it impossible for Spain to be granted help under the Marshall Plan at first; Spain was not able to join the European Community until 1986, long after Franco was dead.

See pages 350–1

See the section on political history, pages 236–7

It was only the Cold War that offered the Franco regime a way out. Despite fierce opposition from President Truman, who loathed Franco, American banks loaned Spain $25 million early in 1949. Later in 1949, negotiations began to work out a deal based on massive USA economic assistance in exchange for Spanish bases. Between 1950 and 1953, a new economic relationship was formed and culminated in the Pacts of Madrid, bringing into Spain aid totalling nearly $220 million. The ending of Spain's isolation guaranteed its economic survival.

Franco and his admirers claimed that this showed the success of his patient and determined policies. Franco's critics suggest that a democratic Spain could have had all this and more years before, and that Franco's foreign policy was all about strengthening Franco, not the Spanish economy. They also point out that Franco chose incompetent ministers in economic matters and damaged the economy by nationalistic insistence on an unrealistically high valuation of the *peseta*. Even so, after 1953, the way was open for a degree of economic recovery.

ECONOMIC MODERNISATION AND 'SOCIAL REVOLUTION': SPAIN, 1953–75

The original aim of Francoist economic policy was *autarky*, or self-sufficiency. During and after the Civil War, the economic policies of the regime were based on an ideological crusade to wipe out the Socialist evils of the Republic. The regime did everything possible to preserve private property in the hands of supporters of the Nationalists. There was also a huge amount of State intervention, both to smash union opposition and to let loose the corporatist ideas of the Falangists. State control of industry was set up through the INI (*Instituto Nacional de Industria*) and trade union organisations were tightly controlled by the *Falange*. These policies were generally maintained throughout the period from the Civil War to 1953 but by the mid-1950s the regime realised that autarky was failing. There was a serious balance of payments problem and government subsidies could not carry on at their existing levels. The regime reorganised in a major cabinet reshuffle. The future of the economy lay in the hands of the technocrats of *Opus Dei*.

The key individuals were Alberto Ullastres and Navarro Rubio, placed in charge of commerce and finance at the beginning of 1957, and Laureano Lopez Rodo, who was already Franco's Technical Secretary. These were the men behind the 1959 Plan for Stabilisation and Liberalisation, intended to slash public spending, reduce inflation and open Spain up to foreign trade and investment. The Plan had some resemblance to the French Monnet Plan of 1946 and the technocrats had real power within the regime. It was a big change in the direction of the economy and one that Franco was not enthusiastic about but felt forced to accept.

The Stabilisation Plan was well timed. It coincided with the general economic boom in Western Europe which enabled large-scale foreign investment into Spain. The boom also fuelled the rapid expansion of mass tourism, which was the biggest single factor in economic growth in Spain in the 1960s, and enabled one million Spaniards working abroad to send home significant amounts of money. From 1960 to 1973, Spain experienced an 'economic miracle', with annual average growth in the GDP above 7 per cent, second in the world after Japan. Spain also benefited from a special trade arrangement with the EEC, even though Spanish membership was out of the question. As the Spanish economy changed, so did Spanish society. Spain became an urbanised country, with barely 20 per cent of the population in agriculture. Industries like steel, shipbuilding and car manufacture expanded. There was also a huge expansion of service industries, especially in banking and tourism, and of higher education. A large urban, professional middle class emerged.

Such extensive social and economic change inevitably created problems. Growth was uneven and some regions did badly by comparison with others. INI could not cope and became a bloated bureaucratic monster, prone to corruption. In 1969, there was a massive scandal, the Matesa affair, which led to serious divisions within the regime. In the early 1970s, a number of economic problems faced a regime which did not seem able to deal with them. Above all, the problem was the nature of the regime itself. Francoism was repressive and socially extremely conservative. This was a society in which girls were chaperoned, and there was widespread censorship. Not only divorce but also adultery was illegal. Rapid economic and social change such as Spain experienced in the 1960s implied that the regime must adapt or break. Outwardly, the Franco regime kept the lid on. Spain had no equivalent to the student radicalism or sexual revolution so visible in France and Italy, and the machinery of repression stayed in place. But for how much longer?

Social revolution in Spain

The question of how far Spain experienced a 'social revolution' during the Franco era is an important one for historians assessing the legacy of the Franco regime. It can be argued that Franco's Spain was a repressive society, holding back the economic modernisation and social advance happening elsewhere in Western Europe. Alternatively, it can be argued that Franco was a cunning, flexible realist who allowed gradual change within the framework of political stability.

According to Grugel and Rees:

> Economically, Spain was a very different country in the 1970s compared to the 1940s. The Franco regime presided over the most important economic transformation in Spanish history, turning Spain into a fully industrialised and urban society. Yet Franco's regime first delayed this process through its reactionary policies, then managed change badly, and finally made itself redundant.

Franco's Spain, by J. Grugel and T. Rees (see bibliography)

Note the words 'presided over'. This verdict is hardly a lavish compliment to Franco. Franco himself was not in favour of change and one of his key long-term advisers, Luis Carrero Blanco, was of the opinion that 'to offer change to a Spaniard was like giving drink to an alcoholic'. In the early 1970s, many committed Francoists were so hostile to change that they were known as the 'Bunker'. Franco himself was particularly opposed to any liberalisation of culture or the media. On the other hand, 'presided over' suggests what Franco was prepared to tolerate within his regime in order to keep a balance and to adjust to necessity. He did allow the technocrats to take over from 1957, even if he had little sympathy with what they were doing.

According to Raymond Carr:

> Spain became the playground of Europe, with its beaches and sunny days a valuable asset exploited to saturation point by package-tour agencies. Spain was the service area of northern Europe, supplying workers to the factories of France and Germany. Between 1960 and 1970, the number of cars per thousand of population rose from 9 to 70. For televisions, the figures rose from 1 per cent to 90 per cent.

Modern Spain, 1875–1980 by Raymond Carr (see bibliography)

KEY ISSUE

What was the social, economic and cultural legacy of the Franco era?

See page 242

In structural terms, Spain changed more rapidly between 1957 and 1978 than in the previous century.

Against this, social attitudes in Spain continued to reflect the intensely traditional outlook of the Catholic Church, which virtually controlled education and social policy. The cultural atmosphere of Spain before 1975 was still extremely conservative and anti-feminist. It was under the Second Republic after 1975 that there was a sense of release and rapid change, leading to a 'generation gap' that remained noticeable for the next twenty years.

The simple explanation may be that the economic changes hit Spain in the 1960s and the social and cultural effects followed in the 1970s. It remains a matter for debate whether Francoism 'managed change badly', or 'allowed change to happen slowly and without pain'.

THE SPANISH ECONOMY AFTER FRANCO

The compromise between all the political parties in the *Moncloa Pacts* of 1977 allowed for wage and price controls, and a wide range of social reforms, such as legalising abortion and decriminalising adultery. The new democratic Spain had a broad national consensus on economic and social issues. This was just as well because the economic situation after 1977 was very difficult. Unemployment went up to 12 per cent by 1980. Spain relied heavily on oil imports and suffered badly from the after-effects of the oil-price crises of 1973 and 1979. In the 1980s, like other governments in Western Europe, Spain was forced into policies of devaluation, spending cuts and a wage freeze. The SEAT car firm was privatised and the Spanish shipbuilding industry was slimmed to a fraction of its former size.

The restructuring of the Spanish economy was painful but effective, and was helped by entry into the EC in 1986. Spain achieved annual growth rates of above 5 per cent in the late 1980s, outstripping European neighbours to the point where some analysts talked of a 'second economic miracle'. Foreign investment flooded into Spain. Then this brief boom was knocked sideways by the impact of world recession and the government was forced into sharply deflationary measures. The economy also came under pressure from the need to meet the 'convergence criteria' laid down in the Maastricht Treaty. The value of

TABLE 30

The Spanish economy and its European competitors, 1992

	Population (millions)	Gross domestic product ($ bn)	Personal income ($ per capita)
Spain	34.1	574	14 731
Italy	57.8	1224	21 176
Portugal	9.8	84	8521
Germany	80.6	1775	22 032
UK	57.8	1041	17 987

the *peseta* fell. Despite these problems, the Spanish economy in the mid-1990s was healthy and it was considered probable that Spain would qualify for entry to the Single European Currency in time for 1999.

D *Foreign policy*

As has been made clear, Spanish foreign policy was very much subordinated to the needs of domestic politics. When the National Movement began, foreign policy was highly ideological – anti-Communist, pro-Fascist and dreaming of imperial grandeur. Of all this, only the anti-Communism survived. The defeat of the Axis drove Franco into international isolation. In 1947, Franco was pathetically grateful to the Peron regime in Argentina, first for granting vital food supplies and then for sending the glamorous Eva Peron on a state visit to Spain, Italy and France. This allowed Franco to make a splash of Evita's tour of Spain and to pretend that his isolation was not complete. It was not Francoist foreign policy aims but the needs of economic and political survival that pushed Franco into the arms of the USA. From 1953, it could be argued, Franco did not really have his own foreign policy at all, being totally dependent upon an unequal relationship with the USA. $1.5 billion received from the USA mattered more than the Cold War.

There were a few remnants of his foreign dreams that Franco could still pursue. From time to time, Spain raised the issue of Gibraltar, demanding its return from Britain. In 1964, Britain was so angered by Spanish pressure over Gibraltar that a big order for ships to be built in Spain was cancelled. The Gibraltar issue was useful as a way of stirring up national feeling but not much else. Franco periodically involved himself in disputes over Spanish Morocco and the Western Sahara but made little headway. From 1962, Spain made repeated efforts to gain membership of the EEC but these had no chance of success while Franco was in power. One surprising shift of policy was towards the USSR and Eastern Europe. The old anti-Communist warrior Franco began opening links to the Soviet Bloc in the 1960s and a number of trade agreements were signed. Overall, the international position of Spain was so constrained that foreign affairs had relatively little significance.

After the death of Franco, the new democratic Spain had infinitely better relations with the outside world but foreign policy was still largely in the hands of others. Domestic political considerations came first and most important international issues were seen by Spain as European questions, rather than Spanish ones.

3 ↫ PORTUGAL

A *Introduction*

The history of Portugal in many ways paralleled that of Spain. A declining monarchy gave way to the First Republic in 1910. The

KEY ISSUE

Why was Salazar able to maintain his regime for so long?

republic failed to establish itself and, in 1926, was overthrown by a right-wing military revolt. In 1932, the military handed over power to an obscure professor of economics, Dr Antonio de Oliviera Salazar, who then proceeded to set up a Catholic authoritarian regime which controlled Portugal for more than forty years.

Similarities between Spain and Portugal went further than the fact that each had a dominating leader who mixed a National movement with Fascism and stayed in power from the 1930s to the 1970s. Like Franco's Spain, Salazar's Portugal stayed neutral in the Second World War. Similar geographical and political considerations meant that Portugal remained isolated from the mainstream of Western Europe after 1945 but became an integral part of the Western military alliance. Like Spain, Portugal benefited hugely from the boom in mass tourism. Like Spain after Franco, Portugal after Salazar moved relatively easily towards democracy and membership of the European Community. This 'era of democracy' became particularly associated with Mario Soares, who was the first Prime Minister of post-Salazar Portugal.

This section considers three key aspects of the history of Portugal: the long rule of Salazar; the successful evolution of a democratic system after the Revolution of 1974–76; and the long, painful process of decolonisation.

B *Political history*

PORTUGAL, 1945–74

Like Franco's Spain, Portugal was isolated both geographically and diplomatically in 1945. By then, the Salazar regime was already long established. After the defeat of the Axis, Salazar came under pressure to democratise his very authoritarian system. There was also serious industrial unrest. In 1947, a military *coup d'etat* was attempted but was put down by Salazar loyalists with relative ease. The Salazar regime was not a true Fascist dictatorship but it was extremely efficient at the business of internal repression. Another of the many similarities with Franco's Spain was the way Salazar profited from the Cold War. Portugal was a founder member of NATO in 1949 and was able to develop excellent long-term relations with the USA, including substantial economic aid in return for bases. Portugal remained economically backward but politically stable.

There was little effective opposition to the regime. In 1958, General Humbero Delgado ran against Salazar's hand-picked candidate in the presidential elections but the voting system was so easily manipulated by the regime that he had little chance of success. Along with other opposition figures, including the Bishop of Oporto, Humberto Delgado was sent into exile and was later murdered. Another attempted military rising was crushed in 1959.

The Salazar regime seemed immovable but economic pressures were building up, intensified by the huge costs of colonial wars, and Portugal could not be insulated completely from the social changes affecting the

ANTONIO DE OLIVIERA SALAZAR (1889–1970)

Salazar was the son of an innkeeper. He originally trained to be a priest but became an academic instead. In 1919, at the age of thirty, he was appointed Professor of Economics. He went into politics and rose swiftly until he was given the post of Finance Minister in the military government in 1928. He proved to be immensely successful in this post and the military leaders selected him as Prime Minister when they handed over power to a civilian government in 1932. A seemingly colourless man, who never married and never travelled outside Portugal, except for the odd trip to Spain to see Franco, Salazar was anything but a glamorous, charismatic leader. He was, however, an extraordinarily capable and controlled politician. He became a virtual dictator and utterly dominated all aspects of politics in Portugal until he suffered a stroke in 1968 and handed over power to Marcello Caetano.

Like Franco, Salazar mixed his own personal rule with traditional Catholic conservatism but also with Fascist-style social policies. In 1933, he set up a new constitution, proclaiming Portugal as an *Estado Novo* (New State) and outlawing all political parties except his own Portuguese National Union. *Estado Novo* was a neo-Fascist one-party state, heavily influenced by the example of Mussolini's Italy. Salazar was a man who hated almost everything about the twentieth century, although he did push through a number of social and economic reforms, in spite of fierce opposition from the old-fashioned conservatives on the other wing of the National Union.

Salazar had no interest in democracy. He once said, 'all government is saving the people from themselves'. He kept power under his own close control. For a long period, he was Minister of War and Foreign Minister, as well as Head of Government and State. He kept Portugal neutral throughout the Spanish Civil War and the Second World War. The blind spot of this skilful political realist was colonialism. He stubbornly refused to accept that Portugal's overseas colonies could no longer be maintained after 1945. Where other countries reluctantly gave in to decolonisation, Salazar fought to the bitter end, causing heavy costs and alienating the army generals. By the time Salazar died in 1970, Portugal was heading for a revolution.

rest of Europe in the 1960s. In 1968, Salazar suffered a stroke and, after almost forty years of virtual one-man rule, handed over power to Marcello Caetano. Even before Salazar died in 1970, major political change was inevitable. The Socialist Party was reformed under the able leadership of Mario Soares in 1973. There were outbreaks of urban terrorism not unlike those in Italy at the same time. When the revolution happened in 1974, however, it was not started by the political opponents of the regime but by army rebellion.

THE PORTUGUESE REVOLUTION, 1974–76

See page 255

See pages 60–73

See Timeline on page 253

The problems associated with the loss of empire dominated Portugal after the Second World War. In many ways, the situation of Portugal was similar to that of the French Fourth Republic with an explosive mixture of national pride, economic burdens and a divided, resentful army – but Portugal had no de Gaulle and no quick exit. There was a particular problem with the low morale of army conscripts serving far from home in an unpopular war. Between 1968 and 1973, a liberal general, Antonio de Spinola, tried to bring in reforms and raise morale but Caetano sacked him early in 1974. This sparked off the Revolution.

The events of 1974–76 were turbulent and confusing. Many observers, including policy makers in the USA, were seriously concerned about the dangers of a Communist take-over. In the 'hot summer' of 1975, Portugal was virtually out of control. Domestic politics became interwoven with the issues of African independence. The army split into several, heavily politicised factions. There were some consistent general themes that may give some coherence to the complex ebb and flow of the Revolution:

- The MFA (Armed Forces Movement), led at first by Major Otelo de Carvalho, represented the younger generation of army officers and had distinct left-wing tendencies which led it to side with the Communists. There was a close alliance between one of the left-wing MFA leaders, Colonel Vasco Goncalves, and the Communist leader Alvaro Cunhal. The 'Revolutionary Council' (and the army security organisation COPCON, set up by Carvalho in 1975) was very left-wing. Its three-man leadership, Costa Gomes, Goncalves and Carvalho, was also badly split;
- Other elements of the army were moderates or traditional Catholic conservatives, anxious to restore discipline and order. It was these elements who put out the 'Document of the Nine', demanding moderation, and who later seized power in November 1975;
- The influence of events in Africa was significant. Many of the Marxist attitudes in parts of the Portuguese army had been picked up from their opponents in the wars of liberation. Disagreements over which African independence movements should be handed power helped to bring down Spinola in 1974;
- Popular support for the Communists was never as strong as was originally feared. All elections in 1975–76 showed consistently greater support for the Socialists, with the liberal-centrist Popular Democrats in second place. The personal qualities of Mario Soares were a vital aspect of this. There had been no political alternatives in Salazar's time and the speed with which Soares gained a national image and united the moderate Socialist Left played a big part in stabilising Portugal in 1976.

KEY ISSUE

What were the causes of the Portuguese Revolution of 1974?

TIMELINE

The Portuguese Revolution

April 1974	Overthrow of Caetano
	Military *Junta* established by Otelo de Carvalho
	Spinola made President and elections promised
May	Large-scale demonstrations in Lisbon
	Civilian government set up, with Mario Soares as Foreign Minister
July	Spinola's reforms blocked by alliance of MFA and Communists
Sept	Resignation of Spinola after row over Angolan independence
	Presidency taken over by General Costa Gomes
Jan 1975	New arrangements for Angolan independence under MPLA rule
March	Failure of attempted *coup* by pro-Spinola army officers
	Spinola exiled
	Government controlled by 'Revolutionary Council'
April	Victory for Socialists in elections for the Constituency Assembly
May	Demonstrations against Costa Gomes, Goncalves and Carvalho
Aug	*Document of the Nine* issued by army officers
Nov	Parliament attacked by strking workers
	Government 'on strike'
	Seizure of power by moderate army officers
April 1976	New constitution established
	Elections won by Socialists
June	General Eanes elected President
	Mario Soares made Prime Minister

After the chaotic events of 1974–76, Portuguese politics settled down surprisingly quickly. The elections of 1976 showed mass support for democracy. After some early successes, Mario Soares found it difficult to cope with the political and economic difficulties facing him. Inflation was high and the tourist industry had collapsed. After the events of 1974–76, there was no chance of cooperation with the Communists and Soares was always leading a minority government. He resigned in 1978 and, after a period during which no stable government could be formed, the combined liberal–conservative 'Democratic Alliance' came to power.

MODERN PORTUGAL

The Democratic Alliance government linked together various elements from liberals to conservative monarchists. Its leader, Sa Carneiro, aimed to take Portugal away from nationalisation and high public spending towards privatisation and a competitive free-market economy. He was also determined to get Portugal into the European Community. His policies were frequently hindered by President Eanes, who was influenced by the still-powerful Revolutionary Council. Then Sa Carneiro was killed in a car crash. The government failed to cope with inflation and lost power in 1983.

Mario Soares returned to lead a new government coalition but lost power, for the last time, in 1985. He was elected President in 1986 and re-elected in 1991, a symbol of democratic stability. From 1985, the government was led by the Social Democrats, who 'went it alone' without their conservative allies, making big gains in the elections of 1985 and again in 1987. Entry to the EC was granted in 1986 and the Portuguese economy improved steadily, though it remained the poorest in Western Europe. By the early 1990s Portugal was, like Spain, an established two-party democracy, in the European mainstream.

See pages 350–1

C *Economic history*

Portugal was not a developed country in 1945. North of Lisbon there was a traditional smallholders' peasant economy. In the south – the Alentejo region – huge traditional landed estates were farmed by a peasantry which was desperately poor and often illiterate. (The south often provided mass support for the Communist party; the small farmers of the north were politically and socially conservative.) The Salazar regime did develop a managerial class but there was little industrial development and Portugal remained extremely backward compared to the rest of Western Europe.

To an even greater extent than Spain, many Portuguese found work as migrant workers elsewhere in Europe, Brazil or North America. In the 1960s, one of the chief sources of income for thousands of families was money remitted home from people working abroad. Another source of wealth in the 1960s was the development of mass tourism, particularly in the Algarve. This did not grow as fast or as big as tourism in Spain but it was a major aspect of the economy until it was temporarily interrupted by the 1974 Revolution.

Portugal's colonies provided some economic advantages – exports to the colonial market, imports of cheap labour and mineral resources, including iron ore and diamonds – but the economy was put under heavy strain by the huge costs of fighting colonial wars in Angola and Mozambique. By 1973, 2 per cent of the entire population was in the army and military spending was soaking up half of the national income. The immediate spark for the Revolution in 1974 was a military rebellion, but economic discontent was a key underlying factor.

The events of 1974–76 made the economic problems worse. The little trade and industry Portugal had was dislocated by repeated strikes, and the violent disturbances temporarily destroyed the tourist industry. The measures taken by various left-wing governments in 1975 involved heavy public spending and caused dangerous levels of inflation which persisted well after the Revolution was over. One of the problems that brought down the Soares government in 1978 was the economic legacy of the Revolution. Another problem was that the rigid Salazar regime had closed off all alternatives. After 1976, economic management in Portugal almost had to start from scratch, and was often in the hands of people who had been out of the country for years. Economic recovery involved painful cost-cutting measures, high interest rates and dependence on foreign loans.

After 1980, the Carneiro government tried to move in the direction of privatisation and 'monetarist' policies. These policies had no magic effect. Portugal in the early 1980s was still plagued by low living standards, high inflation and extensive illiteracy. But membership of the EC from 1986 brought distinct economic benefits, including regional grants and improvements to the infrastructure. The tourist industry also expanded rapidly. Portugal was also affected by the general 'social revolution' that occurred throughout Western Europe from the 1960s. The Salazar regime had held back these trends but not avoided them completely. After 1976, Portuguese society opened up considerably, with the expansion of higher education and many social reforms. By the early 1990s, admittedly from a low base, Portugal's growth rate was above the EC average, unemployment was down and public spending was more or less under control. The long sleep of the Salazar years and the upheavals of 1974–76 had been overcome.

> **KEY ISSUE**
>
> *What factors enabled the economic modernisation of Portugal from the 1970s?*

D *Foreign policy*

ISOLATION, COLD WAR AND THE EUROPEAN COMMUNITY

Portugal under Salazar was content to be isolated from the world outside. The country maintained neutrality throughout the Second World War, partly because Salazar's natural sympathy with Fascist regimes had to be balanced against Portugal's long-standing and valued alliance with Britain. During and after the war, Salazar found himself naturally allied to Franco's Spain and, like Franco, was regarded as an old-fashioned right-wing dictator, past his sell-by date. Portugal was important to the Western alliance, however, and became a founder member of NATO, gaining considerable financial and diplomatic support from the USA. This was a lasting relationship. In the superpower confrontation during the Arab–Israeli War of 1973, when Henry Kissinger found his requests for support rejected even by Britain, Portugal was the only European ally to offer the use of its bases to the Americans.

After the 1974–76 Revolution, and with Salazar gone from the scene, the way was open for Portugal to join the European Community. This took several years to accomplish, not least because of the economic gulf separating Portugal from the rest of the EC, but Portugal was formally admitted in 1986.

See pages 350–1

LOSS OF EMPIRE

By far the most important issue in foreign policy was the Portuguese Empire overseas. No European country, not even Britain or France, found the process of decolonisation as difficult and as painful as the end of Portugal's historic overseas Empire. The long, losing struggle to defend this Empire against the forces of nationalism did more than any other single factor to bring Portugal to chaos and revolution by 1975.

Portugal had the oldest of European empires overseas. It was the thing that defined the nation's history, through the colonial pioneers such as Prince Henry the Navigator, who sent seamen to explore Africa and the Atlantic islands from the 1420s, or Vasco da Gama and Alfonso d'Albuquerque, the founders of the maritime Empire in India between 1498 and 1515. The most famous work of Portuguese literature was *The Lusiads* by Camoens, celebrating the sea pioneers of discovery and empire. In 1945, Portugal still possessed colonies as far-flung as Goa in India, Macao in China and the huge territories of Portuguese East Africa (Mozambique), Portuguese West Africa (Angola) and Portuguese Guinea. There was also a large white settler population in Angola which had grown to over 300 000 by 1970. These settlers were, like the *pied noirs* in French Algeria, a strong influence on the government at home. Maintenance of this Empire was a burning desire on the part of conservatives, much of the army and of Salazar himself.

The tide of history was running in the opposite direction. Already loosened by the impact of the First World War, European colonial dominance was under fierce pressure after the Second World War. The old colonial powers, Britain and France, were weaker. The new superpowers were both, in theory, hostile to colonialism. Many nationalist movements had taken shape, or grown stronger, during the war. At first, the irresistible pressures working against colonialism and in favour of movements of national liberation affected Africa much less than Asia but by the late 1950s, the British were beginning to accept that the 'wind of change' meant giving independence to their African colonies. Portugal could not be insulated from the process.

In 1961, Portugal lost Goa, seized by India when negotiations were refused. In the same year, Holden Roberto founded the FNLA movement, fighting for the liberation of Angola. Within a few years, this movement split into three warring factions: Roberto Holden and the FNLA; Agostinho Neto and the Marxist MPLA; and Jonas Savimbi's UNITA. In 1964, a similar guerrilla campaign was launched by FRELIMO in Mozambique. In Portuguese Guinea, the PAIGC movement led by Amilcar Cabral had gained control of most of the colony by 1967. Leading generals informed Salazar that these colonial wars could not be won, but the regime refused to countenance withdrawal or even compromise. Even after 1968, Marcello Caetano stuck to the hard line. The 1974 Revolution really began with General Spinola publishing a book, *Portugal and the Future*, which virtually demanded that the African wars were given up.

At the same time, and with tragic long-term consequences, the colonial struggle was overtaken by the Cold War. In Angola, Neto and the MPLA had been supported extensively by the USSR from the start. Later, they were helped by troops from Cuba when it looked like they might lose to Savimbi. UNITA was supported directly from Zaire and indirectly from South Africa and the USA. From 1974, FNLA was backed by Communist China. In Mozambique, FRELIMO became a

KEY ISSUE

Why was the loss of empire so long and painful a process for Portugal?

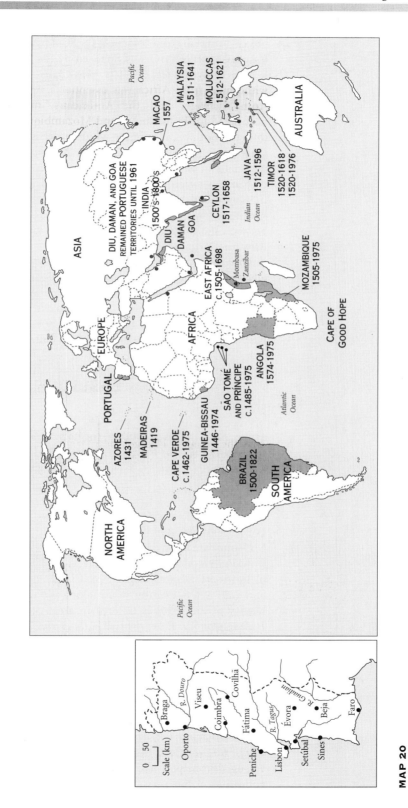

MAP 20
Portugal's Overseas Empire, 1960–75

proxy army for one side of the Cold War, while the right-wing movement RENAMO was financed by the other.

The army revolt of 1974 was based on the assumption that withdrawal from Africa was essential. Despite pressure not to do so from Kissinger and the Americans, independence was quickly negotiated for both Guinea and Mozambique. Angola was much more difficult, both because of the white settler issue and because there were three rival liberation movements. Attempts were made in 1975 to negotiate an end to the war in Angola, but they were hampered by the divisions between the African leaders and within Portugal. Eventually, in November 1975, a complex deal for Angolan independence was hammered out in Lisbon. This *Alvor Agreement* set up a coalition between the three liberation movements and set February 1976 as the date for Portuguese troops to be pulled out. The Portuguese Empire did not end well. Decolonisation was delayed too long and it had a very adverse effect upon Portugal. After independence, superpower interference ensured that the wars in Angola and Mozambique continued well into the 1980s, doing lasting damage to the new states. But, for Portugal, the end of its empire made it possible to start overcoming the past and to forge new relationships in Europe.

4 ↪ BIBLIOGRAPHY

GENERAL

There are useful short outlines of Italy, Spain and Portugal during this period in *Cold War Europe, 1945–1991* by J. Young (Arnold, 1991) and *Europe In Our Time* by W. Laqueur (Penguin, 1992).

ITALY

A lively introductory survey is *Italy: The Unfinished Revolution* by M. Frei (Mandarin, 1996). The key events of 1940–46 and the legacy of Mussolini are covered well in *Liberal and Fascist Italy 1870–1946* by M. Robson (Hodder and Stoughton 'Access', 1993). Two expert outline histories are *Modern Italy* by M. Clark, 2nd edition (Longman, 1996) and *Italy 1801–1995* by R. Absalom (Longman, 1995). The complex history of the 1990s is covered in great depth and detail in *The New Italian Republic: From the Fall of the Berlin Wall to Berlusconi,* edited by S. Gundle and S. Parker (Routledge, 1996).

SPAIN

A good overview of the period is in *Modern Spain:1875–1980* by R. Carr (OPUS, 1980). An up-to-date analysis, aimed at undergraduates, is *Franco's Spain* by J. Grugel and T. Rees (Arnold Contemporary History, 1997). *Contemporary Spain: A Handbook* edited by C. J. Ross (Arnold, 1997) has a great deal of accessible and up-to-date information arranged in helpful brief chapters. The best biography of Franco is the authoritative but very lengthy *Franco* by P. Preston; the same author has contributed a number of excellent brief articles, well-suited to A-level students, to *Modern History Review*. A reliable shorter alternative to Preston's biography is *Franco* by Shelagh Ellwood (1994). There is a comprehensive analysis of the key period 1969–81 in *The Triumph of Democracy in Spain* by P. Preston (Routledge, 1987).

PORTUGAL

An interesting survey of modern Portugal and its geographical and historical background is *The Portuguese* by M. Kaplan (Penguin, 1992). An excellent in-depth account of the Salazar regime and its aftermath is *The Making of Portuguese Democracy* by K. Maxwell (CUP, 1995).

5 ↫ ESSAY QUESTIONS

A *General questions*

1. (a) Outline the ways in which Italy was damaged by the legacy of Mussolini and the Second World War;
   (b) How completely did Italy overcome these problems between 1945 and 1953?
2. (a) Explain the methods by which the Italian Christian Democratic Party maintained itself in power after 1945;
   (b) Why were left-wing parties in Italy unable to achieve more than they did between 1944 and 1964?
3. (a) Outline the ways in which Italy experienced a 'social revolution' in the 1960s and 70s;
   (b) Compare the events of 1968–69 in Italy with those taking place in France at the same time.
4. (a) Outline the reasons for the sudden rise to prominence in the 1990s of Silvio Berlusconi;
   (b) Explain why the established political parties suffered such a complete collapse in 1992–94.
5. (a) Outline the various elements of the Franco regime and 'Francoism';
   (b) Analyse the reasons why Franco was able to maintain himself in power in 1945 and for so long afterwards.
6. Consider the view that 'by 1980, most Spaniards had cause to be grateful to Francisco Franco'.
7. (a) Outline the ways in which the history of post-war Spain was similar to that of Portugal;
   (b) Explain the reasons for these similarities.
8. (a) Why did Portugal find the process of decolonisation so difficult?
   (b) Compare and contrast the experience of 'loss of empire' after 1945 by Portugal and France.
9. Discuss the significance for his country of the career of any *one* of the following:

Palmiro Togliatti; Giulio Andreotti; Silvio Berlusconi; Felipe Gonzalez; Antonio De Oliviera Salazar; Mario Soares.

10. With reference to the history of Italy, Spain and Portugal, examine the influence of any *one* of the following:

- the legacy of Fascism;
- the Cold War policies of the USA;
- the problems of one-party rule;
- membership of the European Community;
- social and cultural changes after 1960.

B *Answering essay questions on Franco and Spain*

History essay questions are almost always either 'Give a list of reasons why' or 'How far do you agree that...?'. Franco's rule in Spain is ideally suited to each type. One keynote question might be '*Why did Franco remain in power for so long?*' Another might be '*With what justification has it been claimed that "by 1980, most Spaniards had cause to be grateful for Franco's legacy"?*'

The answer to any 'how far?' question is usually 'up to a point but ...'. This does not mean that you should always look for a half-way house. Many excellent history essays take a bold, assertive view. The following planning advice suggests ways of assessing Franco's legacy in order to have the best of both worlds – an awareness of the alternatives, but also a decisive opinion.

The first step is the decisive interpretation. You might broadly agree with the quotation – arguing that Spaniards were indeed grateful by 1980 because:

- Franco saved Spain from Communism, chaos and disintegration in 1936;
- unlike Mussolini, Franco kept his country out of the Second World War;
- like de Gaulle in France in 1944–46, Franco provided stability in the dangerous crisis after the war and, again, 'saved Spain from Communism';
- Franco guided Spain into a secure place in the NATO alliance;
- he provided Spain with stability and continuity, avoiding frequent changes of government;
- the Spanish economy prospered in the 1960s;
- Spain's social transformation was gradual, avoiding the widespread upheavals of 1968;
- Franco prepared for the succession by nominating Juan Carlos;
- there was a smooth transition to democracy after Franco was dead.

Well, yes, this can seem a pretty impressive list. Some reasons appeal mostly to Francoist supporters but several are plainly true and convincing. On the other hand, you might be tempted to argue very strongly in the opposite direction, asking exactly which Spaniards were grateful:

- Those killed by the Nationalists in the Civil War?
- Those murdered, imprisoned or exiled in 1939 or in the thirty-six years afterwards?
- The writers, artists and intellectuals driven out of Spain?
- The rural migrants who nearly starved in the late 1940s, when Frenchmen and Italians received aid that Spaniards could not receive because the rest of the world hated Franco?
- The Spaniards who worked abroad and knew how much poorer Spain was than the EEC – and who knew what a free press and free media could be like?
- The Falangists who felt betrayed when Franco gave up on Fascism?
- The monarchists and Catholic conservatives he used and lied to for so long?

Further arguments might be that many of the advantages of modern Spain would have happened anyway – that Franco made no difference, or made them happen less, or later.

A good essay would need to 'prove' one of these arguments convincingly, but also to deal with the alternative case. If you attack Franco as a nasty, murderous, deceitful dictator, make sure you explain away the apparently beneficial aspects of his legacy. If you assess Franco's legacy more positively, it is absolutely essential to show awareness (and specific examples) of the ugly side of the regime.

6

South-Eastern Europe

See map on page 419
for geographical
positions of these
countries

INTRODUCTION

By the time of the First World War, the emergent nations of South-Eastern Europe or the Balkans, notably Greece, Romania and Bulgaria, had succeeded in freeing themselves from the rule of the weakening Turkish Empire. Albania was created just before 1914, and Yugoslavia soon after the war. Turkey itself underwent a superficial westernisation.

After 1918, much of South-Eastern Europe remained undeveloped and at risk from the imperialist aspirations of Germany, Italy and the USSR. Most of the region was involved in the Second World War. After 1945, the paths of the various states diverged considerably. Romania and Bulgaria became Communist states. Yugoslavia developed a distinctive brand of Socialism and remained outside the Eastern Bloc. An artificial state, bottling up many ethnic and nationalist tensions, by the 1990s Yugoslavia had degenerated into a destructive civil war that threatened the peace of the entire region. For most of this period, Albania was a hardline Stalinist state, isolated from the rest of Europe. Greece experienced both developing democracy and rule by a military dictatorship. Turkey, although principally an Asian power geographically and historically, was increasingly drawn into the European and Western orbit. It also experienced periods of military intervention.

Because there were disparate political and economic developments in the region, this chapter will examine the separate histories of each country after 1945, keeping where possible to the division of political history, economic history and foreign affairs, although these divisions are inevitably often artificial.

1 ⇨ ROMANIA

A *Introduction: Romania to 1945*

Romania acquired territory from Hungary and the Russian Empire after the First World War. An economically undeveloped country, despite large oil resources, Romania was ruled by a pro-German right-wing authoritarian regime. The USSR annexed Bessarabia and Bukovina from Romania in 1940. Romania joined Germany in invading the USSR in 1941, and suffered as the Soviets won back the initiative from 1942 onwards.

The internal political situation of Romania was complex. The Communist leader from 1944 was Gheorghe Gheorghiu-Dej, imposed on the Party by Stalin with instructions to negotiate an alliance with other parties. Young King Michael overthrew the pro-Nazi dictator Antonescu in August 1944, and Romania switched to the Allied side. The Communists and Socialists formed a National Democratic Front, which was included in a coalition government in November 1944. In February 1945, with the USSR about to intervene directly, a *coup* in Bucharest resulted in a Communist-dominated government.

B *Political history*

'NATIONAL COMMUNISM' UNDER GHEORGHIU-DEJ AND CEAUŞESCU

The Socialists and Communists merged in March 1946, and the resulting 'Popular Front' did well in elections. At first Gheorghiu-Dej dutifully followed Soviet policies whilst ruthlessly purging those who disagreed with him. However, he soon began to follow an independent line, in 1956 requesting that Soviet troops leave Romania. Gheorgiu-Dej objected to COMECON proposals that Romania concentrate its economic efforts on agriculture. Romania wished to industrialise and not to be dependent on more powerful neighbours. Romania also refused to participate in Warsaw Pact exercises. This independent stance was continued by Nicolae Ceauşescu, who came to power when Gheorghiu-Dej died in 1965. The Soviets tolerated this independent attitude, in contrast to events in Hungary in 1956 and Czechoslovakia in 1968, because Romania was too small to threaten Soviet hegemony in Eastern Europe and internally it showed no signs of relaxing strict Party control of all aspects of life.

> ### KEY ISSUE
>
> *What were the main features of Romania's 'independent' Communism?*

Nicolae Ceauşescu established one of the most autocratic dictatorships in the Eastern Bloc. In 1974 multi-candidate elections to Parliament were introduced. But the impression of popular participation was a smokescreen behind which the Party's hold over the population was steadily increased. In the 1980s Ceauşescu pumped money into prestige projects and implemented brutal social policies. To reverse a decline in the birth rate, abortion was forbidden. Under the 'Systemisation Policy', first introduced in 1974, whole villages were destroyed and their populations shifted to new industrial complexes. There were renewed attacks on religious practices.

Romania's large minority population of ethnic Hungarians, absorbed after the First World War, also suffered. A policy of 'Romanianisation' meant attacks on the Hungarian language and culture, and the region experienced the lowest level of economic development in Romania.

THE ROMANIAN REVOLUTION

Romania was one of the last of the Eastern Bloc countries to experience change in the late 1980s, and when it came, the Romanian Revolution was the most violent. There had already been unrest amongst miners in

<table>
<tr>
<td>

PROFILE

</td>
<td>

NICOLAE CEAUŞESCU (1918–89)

Ceauşescu was born into a peasant family and joined the Communist Party in 1936. He endured several spells in prison, then rose rapidly in the Party after the war, becoming Party leader in 1965 and Head of State in 1967, the youngest Eastern Bloc leader of that time. He developed a pronounced personality cult and promoted his ruthless wife Elena, and several members of his family, to important positions. Large areas of Bucharest were bulldozed to make way for sumptuous palaces for the Ceauşescu family, whilst the ordinary people were amongst the poorest in Europe. Ceauşescu was Party leader, President and holder of several other important posts. His regime was buttressed by extensive propaganda and a large and feared secret police force, the *Securitate*. He was feted and given state visits to Britain and other Western countries, which sought to exploit his disagreements with the USSR. Ceauşescu's power was never seriously threatened before 1989. Then, in the last of the Eastern Bloc revolutions, he and his wife escaped by helicoptor from the roof of their palace, only to be later captured, given a mock trial and summarily executed on Christmas Day.

</td>
</tr>
</table>

the 1970s and 80s, and in 1987 there were demonstrations in the industrial town of Brasov, all violently suppressed. Ceauşescu ruled out reform, although living and working conditions progressively deteriorated.

The spark for the 1989 Revolution was the attempt by the authorities to deport a popular Hungarian priest from the town of Timisoara. In the resulting demonstrations, the *Securitate* (secret police) killed seventy-one demonstrators. As outrage grew, Ceauşescu called two rallies in Bucharest. Instead of support, he was met with jeers and then demonstrations. The army sided with the people against the *Securitate*. The Ceauşescus escaped from Bucharest but were soon captured and shot. Many members of the *Securitate* were hunted down and killed.

ROMANIA AFTER CEAUŞESCU

At the time of Ceauşescu's flight from Bucharest a National Salvation Front (NSF) was set up. It was led by Ion Iliescu, and included many Communists. Other new parties were formed, but suspicion remained that the Old Guard was still in charge. In the May 1990 elections the NSF won a majority, and Iliescu was elected President. Effectively, the old Communist élite was still in power and ensuing demonstrations were violently suppressed.

Some economic reforms were attempted, but price increases provoked strikes and demonstrations, culminating in a march by

TIMELINE

Events in Romania

March 1945	Formation of Communist-dominated National Democratic Front government
July 1946	Peace treaty with USSR
Nov	NDF Government won two-thirds of votes in disputed general election
Dec 1947	King Michael abdicated and Republic declared
1948	Social Democrats and Communists merged to form Romanian Worker's Party
June 1952	Gheorghiu-Dej became Prime Minister
July 1958	Soviet troops withdrew from Romania
March 1965	Ceauşescu became Party leader
Nov 1987	Riots in Brasov brutally suppressed
Dec 1989	Revolution deposed Ceauşescu
May 1990	Election victory of National Salvation Front Ion Iliescu became President
Dec 1991	New constitution approved, with wide presidential powers
March 1992	Split of NSF
Sept	Iliescu re-elected President
Oct 1993	Romania joined Council of Europe
Dec 1996	General election won by reform candidate

TABLE 31
Romanian election results, May 1990, number of seats

National Salvation Front	263
Hungarian Democratic Union	29
National Liberal Party	29
Christian Democratic National Peasants' Party	12
Ecological Movement	12
Romanian Unity Alliance	9
Agrarian Democratic Party	9
Romanian Ecological Party	9
Socialist Democratic Party	5

miners on Bucharest in September 1991. There was parliamentary reform: a powerful presidency was created, along with a two-house parliament modelled on the French example. The NSF split in March 1992. Some members formed the Democratic National Salvation Front (FDSN) to support President Iliescu, and the new party won the election of September 1992. The party changed its name to the Party of Social Democracy of Romania in 1993. Successive government coalitions lacked stability, and the transition to post-Communism in Romania was proving far from smooth. The real process of political and economic reform had scarcely begun before 1995.

C *Economic history*

In the late 1940s Gheorghiu-Dej implemented Soviet-style policies, creating a centralised command economy and collectivising agriculture. The economy remained under central control, although occasionally the Party paid lip-service to the principle of worker participation in decision making.

As in politics and foreign affairs, the regime was determined to follow an independent line in economic policy. It rejected Khrushchev's conception of 'Socialist division of labour', with its implication that Romania would provide food for other states in the Eastern Bloc. The Romanians deemed a strong industrial base integral to power and independence.

However, Romania's ambitious economic targets could not be realised. In 1978 the 'New Economic and Financial Mechanism'

KEY ISSUE

What were the main features of Communist economic policy in Romania and how successful was it?

prescribed that enterprises should be more cost-efficient and self-reliant, but the regime was not prepared to relax centralised control. During the late 1970s, annual growth rates seriously declined. Little incentive was allowed: even collective farm workers found their freedom to work on private plots of land circumscribed.

Romania's determination to avoid over-dependence on COMECON markets led it to expand trading ties with the developing world, although it classified itself as a 'developing nation' in order to get preferential trade terms from the European Community. The non-Communist world, eager to exploit an apparent chink in Socialist solidarity, obliged: Romania was allowed to join the General Agreement on Trade and Tariffs in 1971 and the International Monetary Fund in 1972. However, in order to pay off large debts to the West, the regime instituted a rigorous and unpopular austerity package in the 1980s. This included bread rationing and the banning of the use of household appliances in order to save on electricity. The peasants also suffered because the price for their produce was determined by the State. Economic and social discontent undoubtedly fuelled the dissatisfaction which suddenly exploded on to the streets in 1989.

Reforms followed the overthrow of the Ceauşescu regime. In 1990 some land was returned to private ownership and foreign ownership of Romanian property was permitted. A National Privatisation Agency was set up. However, the ending of subsidies caused prices to rise, provoking strikes and demonstrations. Prices were then frozen. But Romania's economic problems were immense as it entered the post-Communist era.

D *Foreign policy*

Initially the Romanians were loyal to their Soviet mentors. They dutifully denounced the Yugoslavs following Tito's split with Stalin. As a result, the COMINFORM headquarters were removed to Bucharest. However, Gheorghiu-Dej later developed ties with Tito, and during the Hungarian Rising he declared the 'inadvisability of foreign intervention in the affairs of other countries'.

Romania was clearly determined to develop an independent foreign policy. This stance continued under Ceauşescu, who went on to establish close ties with China, Albania and Yugoslavia, all at loggerheads with Moscow. In 1958 the Romanian and Soviet governments reached agreement on the departure of Soviet troops from Romania. Later Romania refused to participate in Warsaw Pact exercises, although Romania remained in the Alliance.

The Romanian stance, although irritating to the Soviets, was tolerated. Romania showed no interest in dismantling Socialism, and provided an extra indirect channel of communication to Western powers, which cultivated Romania. Romania was also the only Eastern Bloc state to maintain diplomatic relations with Israel. In 1968 Romania criticised the Warsaw Pact for intervening in Czechoslovakia, and in 1979 Ceauşescu refused to support the Soviet invasion of Afghanistan.

Despite later condemnation of Ceauşescu, he was vigorously courted by Western Powers for many years: they hoped to use his desire for independence to cause dissension in the Eastern Bloc.

2 ⇌ BULGARIA

A *Introduction: Bulgaria to 1945*

As a defeated power in 1918, Bulgaria was forced to surrender parts of Northern Macedonia to Yugoslavia, Dobrudja to Romania, and Western Thrace to Greece. Like Romania, Bulgaria became an ally of Hitler's Germany, although it did not declare war on the USSR in 1941. During the Second World War, Bulgarian Communists fought as **partisans** against their own government. The West was reluctant to support them, fearing a Communist revolution, so the Communists looked to Moscow instead for help. The veteran Dimitrov, former head of the Communist International, argued for a popular insurrection, with Stalin's blessing.

partisans guerilla fighters, often politically motivated, fighting against governments or occupying powers

Bulgaria was never occupied by Germany, but was invaded by the Red Army in September 1944. On the day after the invasion, the Communists carried out a *coup* in Sofia and set up a Fatherland Front government. This was a coalition of several groups, but was dominated by the Communists. At the end of the war Bulgaria was supervised by an Allied Control Commission, which insisted that all parties be free to participate in elections. An election in October 1946 secured the Fatherland Front 75 per cent of the vote. The Allies declared themselves satisfied, despite many complaints of electoral abuses, and signed a peace treaty with the Bulgarian government in February 1947.

The Bulgarian Communists were now free to consolidate their power. For the next forty years they were to prove the USSR's most consistent and loyal ally. However, despite Bulgaria's stability and some economic progress, it succumbed, as did its Communist neighbours, to pressures for change in the late 1980s.

B *Political history*

COMMUNIST CONSOLIDATION

The Communist takeover in Bulgaria was a bloody affair. Even before the peace treaty, the Communists exacted revenge on their opponents. Over 30 000 representatives of the previous regime were shot, including 100 prominent politicians on one night alone in February 1945. Several priests were also tried, and by early 1947 all opposition parties had been outlawed. Nevertheless, the Communists had considerable support on account of their record of resistance to a widely hated regime during the war. Dimitrov died in 1949. The Party leader from 1950 was Vulko Chervenkov, and he was loyal to Moscow.

Bulgaria was not greatly affected by the events of 1956 in Hungary, but afterwards Chervenkov resigned the party leadership to Todor Zhivkov.

ZHIVKOV'S BULGARIA

KEY ISSUE

What were the main features of Zhivkov's domestic policies in Bulgaria?

Zhivkov's loyalty to the USSR was demonstrated by Bulgaria's participation in the invasion of Czechoslovakia in 1968, and he followed Brezhnev's policy on *détente*. At home, Zhivkov did not pursue radical policies and his regime encountered no serious internal opposition until the late 1980s. He also secured the support of the Orthodox Church. The Communists were firmly in control, and the 1971 Constitution declared the party to be the 'leading force' in what was described as an 'advanced socialist state'.

The one major source of internal friction was Bulgaria's large Turkish minority. Relations had been reasonably friendly, but in 1984 the government launched a campaign to assimilate the Turks into a 'Bulgarian national culture'.

PROFILE

TODOR ZHIVKOV (1911–98)

Zhivkov was born into a poor peasant family. Between the wars he joined the Communist Party and had a good record of resistance against the Nazis. By 1950 he was Secretary of the Central Committee and became First Secretary following Khrushchev's 'secret speech' in the USSR. With Khrushchev's support he defeated his rivals and established himself as an astute leader. He became the longest-serving leader in the Eastern Bloc, surviving an army plot against him in 1965 and remaining a loyal ally of the Soviet leadership. Although sometimes criticised from within Bulgaria for what was seen as subservience to Moscow, Zhivkov's survival depended partly upon his recognition of the advantages of Soviet support, his eradication of internal opposition, his firm control of domestic and foreign policy, and the fact that many of his economic policies were relatively successful. Zhivkov was trusted by both East and West and sometimes acted as spokesman for the whole Eastern Bloc. The Kremlin found him useful as a channel for communications with the West at times when the Cold War was tense.

Following his fall from power, Zhivkov was arrested on charges of embezzlement in 1992. He was released from house arrest in 1997 and died the following year.

REVOLUTION AND BEYOND

As Bulgaria's economy ran into difficulties in the 1980s, Zhivkov's position became much less secure. Gorbachev's reform programme in the USSR undermined much of what had been orthodox practice to the Bulgarian regime. Although Zhivkov had shown himself adaptable in the past, he only paid lip-service to the new concept of *perestroika*, or restructuring. Opposition to his regime grew as reforms occurred elsewhere in the Eastern Bloc. Reform societies were set up in Bulgaria in 1989, despite some arrests.

The day after the Berlin Wall was breached in November 1989 a reluctant Zhivkov was forced to resign. Colleagues jumped on the reform bandwagon in order to save themselves. Zhivkov's successor was Peter Mladenov, who recognised opposition groups, legitimised dissident activity, and ended the programme of Turkish assimilation. This last concession was very necessary: before his fall, Zhivkov had briefly opened the border with Turkey, and over 300 000 ethnic Turks had immediately left Bulgaria. This figure embarrassed a government which had claimed that the Turks were well treated. Mladenov invited the Turks to return, and hoped to keep Communist control through a 'revolution from above', purging the hard-liners.

Despite Mladenov's concessions, the opposition continued, and a new grouping appeared – the Union of Democratic Forces (UDF). Mladenov held a 'Congress of Renewal' early in 1990, then negotiated a political agreement with the UDF and the Agrarian Union. The Communists became the Bulgarian Socialist Party (BSP), and Mladenov became first President of a new Republic. The following general election proved inconclusive, the BSP gaining a small parliamentary majority. Although the result showed the strength of the Communist legacy, it also reflected the growing power of the opposition, which by now included the Party of Rights and Freedoms. This party represented ethnic Turks.

Stalemate followed. The government was reluctant to embark on a reform programme without the support of the opposition, but the UDF refused to cooperate. Mladenov resigned in favour of Zheliu Zhelev, the UDF leader, in August 1990. However, there was a general strike and continued confusion. A temporary government led by Dimitur Popov adopted a new constitution and implemented reforms. In the election of October 1991 the BSP won 33 per cent of the vote. The UDF, although split into factions, won 36 per cent and formed Bulgaria's first post-war non-Communist government. Zhelev narrowly won the presidential election from the Communist candidate in January 1992.

The revolution had finally been achieved. By now, the mood for change was very strong, although there was continued instability, leading to fears that a dictatorial figure might emerge to take control. In December 1994 the former Communists won an outright majority in Parliament, with 43 per cent of the votes. The BSP's leader, Zhan Videnov, announced a slowing down of the economic reform process. His government blamed the UDF government of 1991–92 for economic problems and instituted new controls over the media. Popular

TIMELINE

Events in Bulgaria

1944	Communist-dominated Fatherland Front *coup*
Oct 1946	Fatherland Front won rigged election Dimitrov formed government
Dec 1947	Soviet troops withdrawn from Bulgaria
Dec 1949	Beginning of large purge of Communist Party
Aug 1948	Social Democrats merged with Communists
March 1954	Zhivkov appointed First Secretary
April 1965	Unsuccessful *coup* against Zhivkov
1971	Zhivkov became President
1984	First assimilation campaign against Turks
May–Aug 1989	300 000 ethnic Turks expelled to Turkey
Nov	Resignation of Zhivkov
May 1990	Bulgarian Socialist Party won election
Aug	Zhelev elected President in place of Mladenov
July 1991	New constitution approved
Nov	First wholly non-Communist government
April 1992	Privatisation Law
Dec 1994	Former Communists (BSP) won electoral victory

TABLE 32

The Bulgarian general election, December 1994

Party	Seats
BSP	125
UDF	69
National Union	18
Movement for Rights and Freedoms	15
Bulgarian Business Bloc	13

KEY ISSUE

How successful was Bulgaria's economic development during and after Zhivkov's time in power?

dissatisfaction led to President Zhelev's defeat by the UDF candidate in preliminary presidential elections in June 1996.

C *Economic history*

From 1945 the Communists began to transform the Bulgarian economy. All land over twenty-five hectares, and land belonging to collaborators, was seized and collectivised. Factories were nationalised. There was talk of economic reform in the 1950s and 1960s, but little action.

The Bulgarian economy had a weak industrial base: almost half the working population was still employed in agriculture and forestry. Even so, wheat had to be imported in 1962 to compensate for domestic shortfalls. From 1964 there were experiments allowing local initiative in determining wages and prices, in both agriculture and industry, but these were abandoned early in 1968.

The need for economic reform became more evident in the 1970s when the growth in national income slowed rapidly. However, the trend was for more centralisation. In 1973 three new industrial ministries were created, removing power from lower-level associations. Several enterprises were amalgamated. In rural areas, collective farms were replaced by large agro-industrial complexes.

Zhivkov's aim was to expand Bulgaria's industrial and technological base. He achieved this without some of the more drastic social consequences experienced by neighbouring Romania. In 1979, Bulgaria's own 'New Economic Mechanism' attempted to encourage more enterprise autonomy. Small semi-autonomous units were set up within larger enterprises. Banking facilities were extended and a Bulgarian Industrial Association was formed to offer advice to businesses. However, the rate of growth declined again in the 1980s, and foreign debts mounted. This decline, at a time of reform in the USSR, created more pressures inside Bulgaria. However, the Communist regime still believed in a planned Socialist economy.

Even after the fall of Zhivkov it was difficult for Bulgarians to agree on a radical programme of economic reform, because of near-stalemate between the Bulgarian Socialist Party (the former Communists) and the new opposition. Popov's government, formed in 1991, abolished price subsidies, causing prices to rise by over 1000 per cent. Unemployment also rose. Although privatisation went ahead, progress was hampered by an obsolete industrial structure and conservative traditions. Limited progress had been made by the mid-1990s.

D *Foreign policy*

During the late 1940s there were signs that the new Bulgarian Communist regime would follow an independent line. In January 1948 Dimitrov proposed a large Balkan and Danubian federation to offer mutual support to the smaller powers in the region. Stalin vetoed the proposal.

Thereafter Bulgaria loyally followed Soviet foreign policy, in contrast to Romania. Bulgaria was a loyal member of the Warsaw Pact. Given Bulgaria's limited resources, Zhivkov managed Bulgaria's international standing skilfully and won international respect He cultivated good relations with West Germany, which could provide some of the economic and technological expertise that Bulgaria required. Zhivkov also pursued the Soviet objective of *détente*.

The few international ripples caused by Bulgaria were in relation to Turkey and Yugoslavia. In 1969, the Bulgarians resurrected an historic claim to Macedonia, insisting that two thirds of Yugoslavia's Macedonian population were ethnically Bulgarian. Tension over Macedonia increased when Yugoslavia began to break up at the end of the 1980s. Tension was raised by the policy of assimilating ethnic Turks and Bulgaria's reputation was also tarnished by the government's involvement against dissidents abroad. However, Bulgaria was generally thought of as a stable member of the Soviet alliance.

KEY ISSUE

What were the main features of Bulgaria's foreign policy?

See pages 283–4

3 ⤳ YUGOSLAVIA

A *Introduction: Yugoslavia to 1945*

Yugoslavia was created mainly out of the defeated Austro–Hungarian Empire at the end of the First World War. It comprised seven principal nationalities, one of which, the Albanians, was non-Slav. In most areas the different ethnic groups intermingled. The Serbs and Croats were the largest groups, followed by the Slovenes. There were also Macedonians, Albanians (in Kosovo), Hungarians (in Vojvodina), Romanians (in the East), Italians (on the Adriatic coast), Muslim Slavs and Croats in Bosnia, and Macedonians (ethnically Serbian). It was a hotchpotch of peoples and religions, principally Roman Catholicism, Orthodox Christianity and Islam.

The Croats wanted a federal rather than a unitary state, and won an agreement in 1939 for autonomy within Yugoslavia. However, the political situation remained volatile. The Communist Party could not take advantage of instability because it was itself divided and suspect in its loyalty to Stalin. The Party was suspended by the USSR in 1938–39, and during that time Josip Broz, later known as Tito, became caretaker leader.

In the Spring of 1941 Hitler invaded Yugoslavia, which was carved up between Germany, Italy and Bulgaria. Tito quickly organised resistance against the occupiers. However, there were bitter internal divisions. The Germans allowed the Croat *Ustasha* regime to set up an independent state of Croatia (including Bosnia-Herzegovina). This regime was dedicated to eliminating Croatian Serbs. Resistance movements were at odds with each other as well as fighting the occupiers and their puppet regimes. The Serbian leader and royalist Draza Mihailović fought against Tito's Communist partisans, and

MAP 21

Yugoslavia, 1945–91: Republics and autonomous regions

MAP 22

National and ethnic distribution in Yugoslavia

JOSIP TITO (1892–1980)

Josip Tito was born in Croatia in 1892, one of fifteen children born to a Croatian father and Slovenian mother. He had been a corporal in the Austro–Hungarian army in the First World War and a prisoner of the Russians, witnessing the Revolution in Moscow. As a Communist and metalworker, he returned to Yugoslavia in 1920. He served five years in prison from 1929 for organising illegal activities. In 1937 he became First Secretary of Yugoslavia's Communist Party of about 12 000 members. He was loyal to Moscow and brought the Party back into line, whilst continuing opposition to the Yugoslav regime until 1941.

He led Yugoslav partisan forces against Germany following the Nazi invasion. Although Tito wrote that almost half his forces were Serbian, he was willing to recruit from all the peoples of Yugoslavia.

Although initially loyal to the USSR, Tito was not prepared to be Stalin's lackey after 1945. He believed that his version of Socialism would triumph. He did achieve a higher standard of living for his people than the Czechoslovak or Hungarian regimes, which ruled over countries both more developed than Yugoslavia had been in 1939. Tito held Yugoslavia together – but no individual had the ability, character or experience to fill the void left by his death.

PICTURE 27
Josip Tito

wanted an ethnically pure Greater Serbia. The bitter internal rivalries were to come to the fore again in the 1980s and 90s. Tito's disciplined partisans waged all-out war against the Axis occupiers, and Tito's call for 'Brotherhood and Unity' appealed to many Yugoslavs more than Mihailović's Serbian nationalism or the Croatian nationalism of the *Ustasha*.

When it was clear that Mihailović's forces were collaborating with the Axis against the partisans, the Western Allies gave Tito their firm support, despite his revolutionary objectives. However, Stalin pressurised Tito to adopt a 'united front' policy of cooperation with non-Communists. Even before the end of the war, Tito's concern was to secure Yugoslavia's independence: he got an assurance from Stalin in September 1944 that the Red Army would leave Yugoslavia as soon as Belgrade was liberated, a feat achieved in the following month. So Yugoslavia escaped the fate of the countries of Central and Eastern Europe, which fell directly under Soviet influence at the end of the war.

Tito was not interested in reconciliation. At the end of the war he insisted that those non-Communist Yugoslavian partisans on Allied territory should be returned home. Many were handed over, and up to 250 000 were immediately slaughtered on their return.

KEY ISSUE

How did Tito succeed in getting to power in Yugoslavia?

TIMELINE

Events in Yugoslavia

Nov 1945	People's Front won election
1946	Tito became President under new constitution
June 1948	Yugoslavia expelled from Cominform and subject to Soviet economic blockade
June 1950	Workers' councils established in industry
June 1956	Relations with USSR restored
1968	Major protests in Croatia and revolt in Kosovo
1971	Collective presidency established
Feb 1974	New constitution gave more power to Republics
May 1980	Death of Tito
May 1987	Milosović won control of Serbian Communist Party
Jan 1989	Markoví appointed Federal Prime Minister
May	Milosović elected Serbian Prime Minister
1990	Republican elections showed anti-Communist sentiment in Slovenia and Croatia, but Communist strength in Serbia and Montenegro
March 1991	First inter-ethnic fighting between Croats and Serbs
June	Croatia and Slovenia declared independence from Yugoslavia
July	War between Serbia and Slovenia
Sept	Macedonia declared independence
Oct	Bosnia declared sovereignty
Nov	EC sanctions against Yugoslavia
Jan 1992	West recognised Croatia and Slovenia
Feb	Bosnia-Herzegovina declared independence
	Bosnian Serbs declared an independent state
April	EU and USA recognised Bosnia
Sept	Yugoslavia expelled from UN
Oct	Vance-Owen Peace Plan
April 1993	Serbs rejected UN peace plan
Aug	NATO agreed to air strikes
1994	NATO attacks on Serb forces
Oct 1995	Bosnian ceasefire
Dec	Dayton Peace Agreement
	First UN troops arrived to enforce the peace

B *Political history*

TITO'S YUGOSLAVIA

In March 1945 Tito joined a coalition government of the 'Democratic Federative Yugoslavia'. However, he wanted power. He ignored Stalin's instructions to act cautiously and appease the Allies. One of Tito's first priorities was to eliminate domestic opposition. A civil war continued against Mihailović's forces. Mihailović was finally captured in March 1946, and executed. Politicians and some Catholic priests were tried for alleged war crimes and other offences. Islam was also persecuted: many Muslim schools and mosques were closed. Several thousand Yugoslavs were imprisoned or executed in 1945 and 1946. The press was muzzled and there was no legal opposition. Tito's authority was reinforced by the Yugoslav People's Army, whose commanders were almost always Party members.

The new Federal Republic comprised six Republics and two autonomous regions. One of the latter was Kosovo, given autonomy *within* Serbia in 1945 with the intention of protecting the Serbian minority which lived amidst a predominantly Albanian population. Kosovo was economically the most undeveloped region of Yugoslavia. Nationalist unrest there in 1981 was to emerge as a major threat to the stability of the Federal Republic.

Tito organised the Communist Party on Stalinist lines and there was a programme of rapid industrialisation. Under the 1946 Constitution there were six central ministries. Six Republican ministries also meant six separate regional bureaucracies – a cumbersome system. The Communists emphasised the national identity of 'Yugoslavia'. However, Republican loyalties were often stronger than national ones, especially after Tito's death. The 'right' of the Republics to secede was bogus, because the Constitution asserted that the Yugoslav people had declared a wish to live together forever.

From 1946 the Popular Front was a Communist-dominated coalition which brooked no opposition. Communist authority was reinforced by the State Security Administration, with unrestricted powers to arrest and even summarily execute political opponents.

Tito's break with Stalin was to be a momentous event in Yugoslavia's history. A struggle for influence rather than ideology was at the root of the dispute. Stalin stuck to the terms of his wartime agreements with the Allies and would not support Tito's claim to Trieste or back his support for the Greek Communists and a Balkan Federation. Tito in turn opposed the Cominform. Stalin wanted influence over the Yugoslav Communist Party (KPJ). Tito attempted a compromise, but Yugoslavia was expelled from the Cominform in June 1948.

The Yugoslav Party claimed that Stalin had abandoned Marxist–Leninist principles, and Tito declared in 1951,

> ...we cannot quite say that the Soviet Union is in general not a Socialist country, that is, that all the achievements of the Revolution have been destroyed; rather that the leaders and responsible figures are not socialists.

The break with the USSR lasted several years and had both domestic and international consequences. However, Tito continued Soviet-style policies. Forcible collectivisation of agriculture was implemented in 1949, and industrial development continued. As the KPJ grew, so the purges intensified. In 1948 and 1949 27 000 Party members were expelled for suspected Soviet sympathies. Officially there were 16 000 arrests, in reality many more. Four-fifths of the victims received no trial, but were sent to notorious concentration camps. Tito's excuse for creating a centralised dictatorship was that it was necessary to counter a perceived Soviet threat.

The main initial impact of the breach with Stalin was to point Yugoslavia more towards the West. The West was eager to exploit the

KEY ISSUE

What were the main features of Tito's Yugoslavia and what were the similarities and differences with other Communist states in Europe?

KEY ISSUE

Why did Yugoslavia and the USSR split, and what were the consequences?

crack in Socialist unity. The USA provided military and economic aid from 1950, enabling Tito to maintain his independence of the Soviet Bloc.

As the split with Moscow intensified, so the ideological differences widened. The political system was overhauled in 1950. The number of official Party and State jobs was halved as responsibilities were increasingly shifted from the Federal to the Republican or local levels, in contrast to the Stalinist model of rigid centralisation. In June 1950 a law authorised workers' councils in industry and the Central Planning Commission was abolished. Local committees were given extensive governing powers. In 1952 the KPJ was renamed the League of Communists of Yugoslavia (LCY). Separate Party organisations were set up in the Republics.

Under the 1953 Constitution the Chamber of Nationalities was replaced by a Federal Chamber of Party members or representatives approved by the Party. The Republics lost the rights of sovereignty and secession granted in 1946. Tito was named as President, governing with the aid of a Federal Executive Council (SIV), which replaced the Council of Ministers. The result was a dual authority between Federal and Republican structures, a system which survived until Tito's death but then shifted in the Republics' favour, eventually with disastrous results for the Federation. There was an increasing preponderance of Serbs in political and military structures.

Tito now talked of the Party distancing itself from the direct control of central government. However, these changes did not satisfy an increasingly vociferous critic, the leading Communist Milovan Djilas. In 1953 Djilas argued in the Party newspaper for genuinely contested elections in which non-Communist candidates could stand and a new Socialist organisation would be formed separate from the Party. He thought that the Party should 'wither away' and declared that 'the Leninist form of the Party and state has become obsolete'. The Party 'would merge with the Socialist Alliance, and the Communists would merge with ordinary citizens'.

This was too much for Tito, who told the Central Committee in January 1954,

> I was the first to speak of the withering away of the Party, the withering away of the League. However, I did not say that it ought to happen within six months or a year or two, but that it would be a long process. Until the last class enemy has been rendered incapable of action, until socialist consciousness has penetrated all layers of our citizenry, there can be no question of the withering away of the League of Communists or of its liquidation.

Djilas was expelled from the Central Committee in January 1954 and imprisoned in 1956. The Communists were still very much in control, dominating local committees and workers' councils. Tito himself was firmly at the helm as President and Commander-in-Chief of the Army.

His international reputation grew as he seemed to have secured Yugoslavia's independence, and he avoided the disturbances which affected much of the Soviet Bloc in 1956. Tito felt secure enough by the 1960s to relax some ideological controls. Compared to the Soviet Bloc, Yugoslavia experienced intellectual and cultural diversity. A 1954 law reversed previous religious persecution, guaranteeing freedom of religious practice, although churches were put under State control. In 1958 promises were made to relax one-party rule and central planning, with the Party having only a 'guiding', not a 'leading' role in Yugoslav life. The Communist Programme declared that

> Nothing in our established practice may ever be considered so sacred that we dare not move on and replace it with practices that are more progressive, freer, more humane.

But there was no substantial loss of Communist power.

There were some social and educational advances and the different ethnic groups co-existed reasonably amicably. In 1971 ethnic Muslims were granted full national status.

The restoration of friendly relations between Yugoslavia and the USSR also helped to maintain stability. Khrushchev visited Belgrade in May 1955 and publically regretted the earlier Soviet attacks on Tito. A joint declaration in June 1955 referred to 'mutual respect and non-interference in one another's internal affairs'. In June 1956 Tito returned the visit to Moscow and there was a declaration restoring relations between the Yugoslav and Soviet Communist Parties.

Meanwhile, continued American aid to Yugoslavia helped to gloss over economic deficiencies and a growing disparity in the prosperity of the various Republics. However, politicians and economists began to debate the pros and cons of centralised government and more devolution of power to the Republics.

The 1963 Constitution increased the independence of the Republics at the expense of the Federal government for the first time. Four separate Chambers were created to deal with economic questions, education and culture, welfare and health, and organisational policy. Deputies in the Chambers were nominated by enterprises and institutions and were elected by 400 communal assemblies. The deputies persuaded Tito to restore the Republics' right to secession on the condition that all agreed. Republican Communist Parties began to organise their separate conferences, although they also formed the Confederation of the League of Communists of Yugoslavia. Tito maintained his supremacy over Republican leaders, and the Constitution allowed only him to hold high office in both State and Party, but the dangers of this system for the homogeneity of the Yugoslav State were to become evident following his death.

In several ways the 1960s and 70s were a watershed for Yugoslavia. The 1960s saw more contact with the West and more cultural freedoms. Some religious publications were permitted in 1966 and new churches

KEY ISSUE

How significant were the political changes made during Tito's time in power?

were built in Serbia. In 1966 an agreement was signed with the Vatican to exchange diplomatic representatives. However, social progress was uneven: it was less evident in the countryside, where in the early 1960s one-third of all children over five still did not attend school. In Kosovo 41 per cent of the population was illiterate.

From the late 1960s Yugoslavia's economic problems mounted and there were ethnically-generated disagreements. First, in 1967 some Croatian intellectuals demanded more status for their language and traditions. More serious were separatist-inspired outbursts. Although a complex electoral framework ensured that the Communists maintained a monopoly of power at local, Republican and Federal levels, the challenges were growing. In June 1968 students at Belgrade University went on strike in protest at police heavy-handedness in response to earlier disturbances. Several protesters also objected to market-orientated economic reforms.

Serious disturbances broke out in Kosovo, which suffered from high unemployment, low levels of income, and an administration which comprised 50 per cent Serbs and Montenigrins. Even Kosovan Communists felt disadvantaged and wanted full Republican status. In November 1968 battles with the police led to several deaths. Thereafter, Kosovo was effectively under military occupation. Several Party members in Kosovo were expelled although some concessions were made, such as the appointment of more Albanian officials.

In 1969 Slovenia witnessed its first overt protests against Federal authority, when the Federal government passed restrictive laws on commercial road transport, hampering Slovenian attempts to widen access to markets in Western Europe.

Further constitutional amendments did not resolve disputes between Federal and Republican authorities. In 1967 the Chamber of Nationalities, representing Republican interests, had already been given broader powers. In 1968, a new Federal Chamber had to approve all legislation. In April 1969 direct elections were introduced for all Republican and provincial Chambers.

There were prolonged complaints in Croatia between 1967 and 1973 against perceived inequalities such as unfair taxation. Tito responded by purging prominent liberals in Croatia and other Republics.

Reformers faced a classic dilemma: many wanted less central control, associated with dictatorship, but a weakening of central control meant weakening the Party; and without its unifying role, dangerous nationalist and ethnic tensions might be unleashed.

Serbian nationalism posed the greatest threat to unity. Serbia was in a powerful position: Yugoslavia was governed from Belgrade, the Serb capital, and Serbs occupied key positions in the Party and the army. Much clearly depended upon the ageing Tito and there was concern for the future stability of Yugoslavia. In 1971 a collective presidency was established. Tito became President of the Yugoslav Federation for life *and* President of the collective presidency, which comprised two members from each Republic and one from each autonomous province, making a total of fourteen. The arrangement was designed

KEY ISSUE

Why did nationalist and separatist unrest grow in Yugoslavia?

to achieve an ethnic balance. The Federal Executive Council (SIV) was the only coherent organisation for directing central government policy, but it contained five inter-Republican committees responsible for determining common policies. It proved a clumsy instrument, incapable of resolving issues such as the Croatian crisis, and it demonstrated the growing weakness of federal power.

The 1974 Constitution sought a compromise between central control and Republican autonomy. It kept a key role for the Party. Tito retained overall command of the army. The two autonomous provinces became Republics in all respects other than that they lacked rights of citizenship and secession. This inflamed those Serbs in Kosovo who thought that Tito was prejudiced against them.

The Constitution set up complex structures. The Federal Chambers were reduced from five to two: the smaller Chamber of Republics and Autonomous Regions was the more powerful, handling legislation affecting the Republics. It comprised deputies from all the Republics and autonomous provinces. The deputies voted in groups, as directed by their own assemblies. To become law, Republican bills had to be agreed by all eight groups. In effect, the Constitution gave the Republics a veto on issues affecting themselves, leaving the Belgrade federal leadership with little power.

The larger Federal Chamber comprised 220 deputies from the Republics and autonomous provinces. The deputies were elected indirectly and could make majority decisions on some relatively minor issues.

The requirement for unanimity in the Federal Chamber and among the collective presidency, was to prove the major drawback of the 1974 Constitution. Tito tried to achieve greater balance in the top ranks of the Party, by recruiting more younger workers and old partisan officers, and altering the ethnic balance of the Central Committee, of which over 40 per cent were Serbs or Montenigrins. However, he had limited success. Tito's declining years were marked by growing economic difficulties, which in turn fed Republican discontent.

Tito's death in May 1980 was widely grieved. His pragmatic rule had seen a form of 'democratic socialism'. However, progress had not been uniform throughout the country, and political change had lagged behind economic change. Tito had done little to prevent growing political fragmentation.

> ### KEY ISSUE
>
> *What were the main achievements and limitations of Tito's regime in Yugoslavia?*

YUGOSLAVIA AFTER TITO

After Tito's death there were power struggles between his old partisan colleagues and a new generation of political leaders who owed their loyalty to the Republics first, and Yugoslavia second. They were unwilling to risk their positions by seriously reforming the Party. The political heads of the various Republics increasingly used nationalism to reinforce their own power, but disagreed amongst themselves about the structure of the State: the Serbs wanted a strong federal government; the other leaders wanted a weak confederation, power staying with the Republics.

Kosovo was soon a focus of discontent again, particularly from those wanting its accession to Albania. In 1981 there were serious disturbances, encouraged by Albania. Serbian nationalists eventually used this to destroy Kosovo's autonomy, despite the protests of the other Republics.

The members of the nine-person presidency that succeeded Tito were virtual nonentities until the emergence of Milka Planinc, a veteran Croat partisan. She was elected by the National Assembly in May 1982 to be Chair of the Federal Executive Council and was the first senior political figure for years to force reluctant Republican leaderships and assembly delegates to face up to Yugoslavia's mounting foreign debts. She persuaded a group of foreign bankers and the IMF to provide new loans.

The Bosnian Croat Branko Mikulić succeeded Planinc in May 1986. Although Mikulić succeeded in forming a new Council, he faced immediate difficulties in attempting to implement reform. He secured a $1.3 billion foreign loan, but he and his Cabinet faced increasing criticism from assertive Republican leaderships. Mikulić was further weakened by revelations of financial scandals in Bosnia and by spiralling inflation. He failed to implement any serious structural measures to tackle economic problems and was forced to resign in December 1988.

Mikulić's resignation marked a further major decline in the power of the federal government. The outbreak of serious ethnic disturbances and political squabblings soon marked a rapid descent into civil war. The Party was unable to hold the country together and maintain a monopoly of power. Eastern Bloc regimes broke free of Soviet power and Communist one-party rule in the same period, with relatively little bloodshed. However, the additional and disastrous factor in Yugoslavia's case was the stirring up of ethnic rivalries in a way not seen in Central and Eastern Europe. In Soviet Bloc countries economic dissatisfaction was channelled into demands for political reform and an end to Communist rule; in Yugoslavia it was channelled not into demands for democracy but into heightened ethnic rivalries. By 1989 the League of Yugoslav Communists was effectively defunct, leaving only the Yugoslav People's Army (JNA) as a federal organisation capable, at least in theory, of holding the federal state together.

Mikulić's successor, and the last federal Prime Minister, was Ante Marković. He was unable to secure political agreement or reform, since Republican leaders saw him as a threat to their own nationalist ambitions. His failed attempt to introduce a new union effectively marked the end of Yugoslavia as a coherent entity. The Serb leader Slobodan Milosević undermined Marcović and his Yugoslav Reform Party, which stood for an undivided Yugoslavia, a market economy and democratic rights.

The Republican leaders who filled the vacuum left by Tito's death were already very powerful and skilled at playing the ethnic card. Two prominent leaders had emerged in 1986: Milan Kucan in Slovenia and Milosević in Serbia. Milosević secured eight votes in the collective

---

KEY ISSUE

Why did Yugoslavia descend into civil war in the years after Tito's death?

presidency by 1989 for his proposal to restructure Yugoslavia on lines favouring Serbia. His power grew steadily in the 1980s, chiefly through exploiting Serbian discontent with the economic situation. A former Belgrade Party chief, Milosević consolidated his own power by championing Serbian nationalism and presenting the Serbs as victims in Yugoslavia's ethnic struggles. In 1988 the Serbian Communists refused to recognise the authority of the Yugoslav League of Communists. Nationalism proved stronger than Party loyalty. Milosević was overwhelmingly elected Serbian President in May 1989. He had no detailed reform programme, but promised strong leadership to the Serbs at a time of uncertainty and he ran a Stalinist-type authoritarian party.

Having silenced opposition within Serbia, Milosević turned his attentions outside, attacking the leaderships of Vojvodina, Kosovo and the federal leadership. Milosević's motto was 'Serbia will be united or it will not exist.' The Party leaderships in Vojvodina and Montenegro were replaced with Milosević's appointees, who then carried out purges. Milosević secured Serbian dominance in the Federal Central Committee, preventing any internal challenge to himself.

Milosević's championing of Serbian nationalism caused concern, particularly in Slovenia. Slovenia was the most prosperous of the Republics, and sought closer links with Italy, Austria and Hungary, but experienced its own economic difficulties in the 1980s. It was increasingly resentful of having to contribute a quarter of the federal budget although it contained only 8 per cent of Yugoslavia's population. Slovenia quietly began to dismantle Communist rule from the mid-1980s, and new political groups began to form.

In 1989 the Slovenian Communists renamed themselves the Party of Democratic Reform, and championed Slovenian causes. A coalition of anti-Communist parties called DEMOS also supported Slovenian sovereignty. The former Communist leader Milan Kucan supported a campaign by student leaders against compulsory service in the Yugoslav army. Slovenia's parties were committed to national sovereignty and democratisation. Already by 1989, hostility between Slovenia, seeming to represent a more liberal trend in Yugoslavia, and Serbia, seeming to represent intolerance and oppressive nationalism, embroiled the other Republics. Serbia instituted an economic boycott against Slovenia when the latter rejected Serbian attempts to restructure the Federation in Serbia's interests. Slovenia retaliated by reducing its contribution to the federal budget by 15 per cent. Kosovo, Vojvodina and Montenegro were part of Serbia from March 1989. Against Serbia were ranged Slovenia, Croatia, Bosnia-Herzegovina and Macedonia.

During 1989 and 1990 Federal Prime Minister Marković and President Drnovsek tried to effect radical economic reforms to control inflation, but they were increasingly operating in a power vacuum. Events took an extreme turn in Croatia at the end of 1989. The Croatian League of Communists elected a new leader, Ivica Racan. However, the Croatian Democratic Union (HDZ) had already been illegally formed by Franjo Tudjman, a former partisan and historian.

Extremists in the HDZ began to attack Serbs, and in response Croatian Serbs, who made up 11 per cent of the population and were prompted by Milosević, began to demand autonomy for themselves within Croatia.

The last Federal Party Congress was held in January 1990. Influenced by events in Eastern Europe, the leading role of the Communists was removed from the Constitution. The Slovenians walked out, followed by the Croatians. Although the Federal Republic lasted for another one-and-a-half years, while Marković introduced market reforms, it was increasingly impotent. Marković's new nationwide party, the 'Movement for Yugoslavia', had a small following and was virtually irrelevant from the start. Marković's government resigned in December 1991. Milosević took over most of the remaining federal institutions, purged them, and set up a new federal government under Milan Panić. When Panić opposed Milosević's policies, the Panić government resigned in October 1992, and Milosević won the subsequent election in December.

The battleground shifted to multi-party elections in individual Republics, although they were boycotted by the Kosovo Albanians in protest at having lost their Assembly. The situation was complicated by the army, which formed a new party – the League of Communists – in December 1990. The army was trying to stake its own claim as an arbiter in Yugoslavia's precarious future, although its sympathies were clearly with Serbia.

Communist parties were defeated in four of the six Republican elections of 1990, although former Communists won the presidential elections in every Republic except Bosnia-Herzegovina.

The first elections were in Slovenia in April 1990. The reconstituted Communist party (ZKS–SPD) won fourteen of the seventy-three seats. A coalition of six other parties won forty-seven seats. However, Kucan won the presidency. A referendum in December 1990 saw a 95 per cent vote in favour of independence.

Elections were held in Croatia in April and May 1990. The reformed Communists (SKH–SPD) and Liberal Centrists won 57 per cent of the vote. But the Croatian Democratic Alliance (HDZ) won 42 per cent. In May Franjo Tudjman was elected President. He had been a partisan in the Second World War and then the youngest general in Tito's army until being imprisoned for Croat nationalism. After the elections, many Croatian Serbs were forced out of administrative and other important positions. The Croatian Communists quickly disintegrated as an effective force. Tudjman increased his own political power whilst mounting a fierce nationalist campaign. He also formed a Croatian army of over 100 000 men, armed with weapons bought from Germany. A coalition government was formed under the Communist Stipe Mesić. However, a referendum on independence was not held until May 1991.

In Serbia, Milosević was the only old Republican leader to win with his own party in control. The Serbian League of Communists became the Socialist Party of Serbia (SPS) in July 1990. As well as playing the nationalist card, Milosević also created a personality cult around himself. In the parliamentary election of December 1990 the SPS did not secure an overall majority of votes, but won 194 of the 240 seats. Milosević won 65 per cent of the votes in the presidential election. He claimed to be speaking for *all* Serbs in Yugoslavia, not just in Serbia, and his policy seemed to be to manipulate or redefine the federal structure in Serbia's interests, or destroy it altogether.

The six largest parties which fought the Macedonian elections of November 1990 wished to preserve a reformed federal state. Marković's Alliance won nineteen of the 120 seats; the restructured Communists won thirty; a nationalist coalition, the Internal Macedonian Revolutionary Organisation (UMRO) won thirty-seven. The new parliament elected Kiro Gligorev, a reform Communist, as President and Head of Government. However, the Macedonian successor regime, unlike the others in former Yugoslavia, was not recognised by the international community. This put Macedonia in a vulnerable position: with a quarter of its population of Albanian, Bulgarian or Turkish origin, Macedonia feared its borders might be breached by stronger neighbours. So in the 1980s Macedonia supported federalism, and then a strong Serbia. After declaring independence in November 1991, the Macedonian government, with a precarious economy and threats to its border, faced an uneasy future.

KEY ISSUE

What was the significance of the 1990 republican elections?

The Montenegrin elections were held in December 1990, amidst widespread evidence of electoral irregularities. A young reform Communist, Momir Bulatović, won the presidency, whilst the reconstituted Communist Party won two-thirds of the parliamentary seats. Like Gligorov in Macedonia, Bulatović supported Marković's reforms and attempts to preserve a Yugoslav Federation.

Elections in Bosnia-Herzegovina were held in December 1990. Before 1987 the Bosnian Party leadership had been conservative, supporting the status quo in the belief that Bosnia was safest in the Federation. The Bosnian leaders had even supported Milosević against the Slovenian reformers until they came to fear his Serb nationalism as the greater evil. In the election Marković's Alliance won only thirteen out of 240 seats in the first round and none in the second. The reconstituted Communists won eighteen seats. Most seats were won by ethnically-based parties. The Muslim Party of Democratic Action (SDA), led by the dissident Alija Izetbegović, won eighty seats in the second round. He wanted to keep Bosnia-Herzegovina together as one entity, afraid of partition between Serbia and Croatia otherwise. Tudjman's HDZ Party won forty-four of the forty-nine seats secured by Croat candidates. Radovan Karadzić, a former Sarajevo psychiatrist and leader of the nationalistic Serbian Democratic Party (SDS), won seventy-two of the eighty-five seats won by Serbs. His platform was to defend Serb rights. Izetbegović formed a coalition of the three main parties. In those areas where one particular ethnic group was in a majority, tensions grew.

As Republican differences hardened, Milosević seemed to be in a very powerful position. The secession of Slovenia and Croatia from the Yugoslav Federation effectively left him in control of Serbia, Kosovo, Vojvodina and Montenegro. Izetbegović's government could not tolerate Milosević's strident nationalism, so on 3 March 1992 Bosnia declared its independence. This in turn ensured that Bosnian Serbs would seek to separate their territory from the rest of Bosnia. This was a crucial point in the break-up of Yugoslavia: on 6 April, Europe and the USA recognised Bosnia-Herzegovina as an independent state. War began two days later when Serbian troops clashed with Muslims and Bosnian Croats.

WAR AND BREAK-UP

Milosević's desire to turn Yugoslavia into a Greater Serbia was a major factor in causing war. Serbia's refusal to compromise and to allow the Croatian representative to take his turn as Yugoslav President led Slovenia and Croatia to hold referenda and to declare independence. The federal army attacked Slovenia but withdrew after a two-week war. A ceasefire was signed on 28 June after the threat of European Union sanctions against Serbia. Also Serbia did not have a border with Slovenia, and Milosević probably decided that Slovenia was outside his ambitions. Although the Slovenians agreed to suspend their independence for three months, they had effectively broken away. Yugoslavia now existed in name only.

The war in Croatia was to be more drawn out and bloody. In February 1991 the Croatian Serbs declared their own autonomous region and secession, and the Croatian government responded by forming its own army. The Serb-dominated Yugoslav army deployed against Croatia. Tudjman refused to attend meetings of the collective state presidency, and broke off relations with Serbia on 4 August. Serbian forces occupied one-third of Croatia, claiming that they were defending Serbs against a 'fascist regime'. Croatia survived and got international recognition. But EU attempts to get a ceasefire in the autumn failed. The United Nations did succeed in establishing a ceasefire in December 1991, but by then Serbia was well on its way to creating a Greater Serbia, eliminating non-Serbs. In December 1991 the EU, under German persuasion, agreed to recognise Slovenia and Croatia. Attention then shifted to Bosnia.

The Serbian assault on Bosnia-Herzegovina was more devastating. The Serbs were one of three recognised national groups in Bosnia and were represented in the Assembly and the government. But before the attack, the Serbs in Bosnia set up their own National Assembly and National Council, and created six 'Serb Autonomous Regions'. The Serbian army then established 'corridors' between the regions, 'cleansing' them of non-Serbs. The Serbs resisted attempts by other groups to allow Bosnia-Herzegovina to remain an independent state. In October 1991 the Bosnian Assembly declared that its borders were inviolable and supported the concept of a Yugoslavia consisting of sovereign states. But the Serb Democratic Party (SDS), which controlled seventy-two of the 240 seats in the Bosnian Assembly and was led by Radovan Karadzić, walked out of the Assembly and declared the separate sovereign 'Serb Republic of Bosnia-Herzegovina'. The Croatian Democratic Union established two 'Croat Communities' to protect Croats living in the Republic. Although Croatia did not initiate

	1961	1971	1981	1991
Bosnia-Herzegovina	100	100	100	100
Serbs	42.8	37.3	32.3	31.4
Muslims	25.6	39.6	39.5	43.7
Croats	21.7	20.6	18.4	17.3
Yugoslavs	8.4	1.2	7.9	5.5
Others	1.5	1.3	2	2.1
Croatia	100	100	100	100
Croats	80.2	79.4	75.1	78.1
Serbs	15	14.2	11.6	12.2
Yugoslavs	0.4	1.9	8.2	2.2
Others	4.4	4.5	5.1	7.5
Kosovo	100	100	100	100
Albanians	67	73.7	77.5	90
Serbs	23.5	18.4	13.3	10
Montenegrins	3.9	2.5	1.7	
Others	5.6	5.4	7.5	

TABLE 33
The ethnic populations of Bosnia-Herzegovina, Croatia and Kosovo, 1961–91 (as percentages)

war in Bosnia, and denied having territorial ambitions, to many people outside Bosnia it seemed that the Croats were acting in a similarly destructive way to the Serbs.

Following the EU recognition of Croatia and Slovenia in January 1992, it then offered to supervise a referendum in Bosnia in March 1992 on the question 'Are you in favour of a sovereign and independent Bosnia-Herzegovina, a state of equal citizens and nations of Muslims, Serbs, Croats and others who live in it?' Two-thirds, mostly Muslims and Croats, voted in favour. EU recognition of Bosnian independence was followed by a Bosnian Muslim attack on Serbs in Sarajevo and Serbian retaliation. The Serbians then intensified their programme of 'ethnic cleansing', a euphamism for expelling Muslims in order to create a 'corridor of Serbs' between Western Bosnia and Serbia. By the autumn of 1992 Bosnian Serbs, supported by the Yugoslav army, had captured two-thirds of Bosnia-Herzegovina.

Events took place in Yugoslavia without decisive intervention by the rest of Europe. European powers were preoccupied with the Gulf War and the break-up of Communist power in Eastern Europe. The British and French were reluctant to act without American help. Many politicians misjudged the situation, believing that the war would end following the cessation of hostilities between Croatia and Serbia. There were also rumours that the European powers did a behind-closed-doors deal in Maastricht in December 1991 to adopt a joint policy towards Yugoslavia, but that Germany then broke ranks by unilaterally recognising Croatian independence in January 1992, thereby prompting other European countries and the USA to follow suit.

A federal state was reconstituted in April 1992, but it was a rump consisting of Serbia, Montenegro, Kosovo and Vojvodina. It was now clear that the USA and EU had abandoned support for 'Yugoslavia' and were supporting the successor states instead. In September 1992 the Federal State of Yugoslavia was excluded from the United Nations.

KEY ISSUE

*What was the outcome
of the Civil War in
Yugoslavia?*

Milesović retained his support in Serbia, winning the presidential
election in December.

In October 1992 the American and European-sponsored Vance-
Owen Peace Plan attempted to transform Bosnia into ten self-
governing districts or 'cantons' to appease Serbs, Croats and Muslims.
There were to be three identified for each of the three main ethnic
groups, with a mixed prefecture in Sarajevo. This was rejected by the
Bosnian-Serb Assembly in April 1993. There followed the equally
unpopular Owen-Stollenberg initiative to divide Bosnia-Herzegovina
into three quasi-Republics linked in a loose federation.

Bosnia was in a very weak position to resist attack. It was
unprepared, weapons had been confiscated by the army, and foreign
powers put an arms embargo on Bosnia but did not help to defend it.
The West condemned Serbian behaviour, agreed to initiate a war
crimes tribunal and imposed economic sanctions against Serbia, but
did not stop the aggression. The West did not insist that those
Republics seeking international recognition should give a firm
guarantee to protect minority rights. Although a tenuous peace was

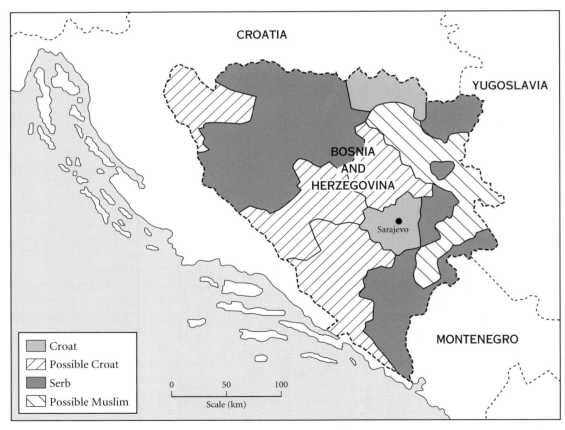

MAP 23

The planned division of Bosnia-Herzegovina under the Vance–Owen Peace Plan

PICTURE 28
Muslim refugees

proclaimed between Bosnia and Croatia, arms continued to flow into both territories and many Croatians still hoped to annex part of Bosnia. A long-term settlement still seemed a long way off. There were thirty-six ceasefires between 1991 and 1995. The Serbs continued their attacks on Sarajevo and elsewhere. Eventually NATO intervened to attack Serbian positions from the air, in mid-1995. Serbia remained defiant, so in July 1995 the UN indicted Karadzić for crimes against humanity. Following a new ceasefire in October, a peace agreement was signed in Dayton, Ohio, in December 1995. Bosnia was divided into two areas, 51 per cent Muslim/Croat and 49 per cent Serb. The UN's economic sanctions against Serbia, imposed in 1992, were lifted. An uneasy peace prevailed, and opposition to the Government within Serbia itself made significant progress for the first time.

PICTURE 29
Sarajevans run from snipers

Several issues remained unresolved, notably the situation of the Albanians in Kosovo: they suffered violent suppression from the Serbians again in 1998. Western policy from the start had been anti-Serb, based on a perception that the Serbs had initiated war, although all sides committed atrocities. The West failed to recognise the Serbs and Bosnian Serbs as two distinct groups. It also recognised the breakaway states too early in 1991–92; and then threatened military intervention for too long before taking decisive action. In the end, large-scale military action ended more through the mutual exhaustion of combatants rather than as the result of Western intervention.

C *Economic policy*

Yugoslavia had been economically devastated by the Second World War. Tito's government had some success in promoting economic recovery. However, existing economic imbalances between the Yugoslav Republics widened. From the late 1940s the Yugoslavs pursued their own Socialist experiment, but in the long run it failed.

Five years of war had left over 1 700 000 Yugoslavs dead, 11 per cent of the pre-war population. 15 per cent of housing, 40 per cent of industry, 50 per cent of railways and over 50 per cent of livestock and agricultural machinery were destroyed or damaged. Initially, Tito's regime secured a rapid economic recovery, partly due to reconstruction work carried out by Communist youth brigades, prisoners and forced labour. But it was also due to massive foreign aid. The United Nations Rehabilitation Agency donated $415 000 000, more than to any other European country. The Yugoslavs also signed bilateral trade agreements with the USSR and other Communist regimes, and after the breach with the USSR, they received massive amounts of American aid.

In April 1945 an Agrarian Reform Law limited the size of landholdings, expropriated land from wartime collaborators, and allocated four-fifths of the land to war veterans and landless labourers. However, initial attempts to impose a Soviet-style command economy proved relatively fruitless. The First Five-year Plan of 1947–51 was a

PICTURE 30

Checking a mass grave at Srska – victims of ethnic cleansing

	Marshall Plan, 1949–52	Mutual Security Act, 1953–61	Foreign Assistance Act, 1962–67
Grants	186.8	617	91.9
Loans	422	444.5	
Military assistance	310	412	1.8

TABLE 34
US aid to Yugoslavia, 1949–67 (US$ million)

disaster. The targets were wildly ambitious. Peasants were expected to provide food surpluses to feed the army and industrial workers and to earn export revenue. There was widespread resistance from peasants to making grain deliveries to the State and to joining cooperatives. Many were arrested but had to be released in 1946 and 1947 to prevent the uncollected harvest from rotting in the fields. Even so, in 1949 the regime decided to collectivise agriculture forcibly. Continued peasant resistance led to falls in output.

Industrial development also posed problems. Following Yugoslavia's expulsion from the Soviet Bloc, the regime attempted a policy of autarky or self-sufficiency. Foreign trade declined. Defence was a growing economic burden, absorbing over 16 per cent of national income in 1950. Tito realised that a Soviet-style economy was not working, and from 1949 the regime began to consider alternatives to a central command economy. It developed a policy of decentralisation. In 1950 management of most federal economic enterprises was transferred to Republican or local control. In June 1950 workers' councils were authorised. The Central Planning Commission was abolished: in its place, local committees had to bargain for a share of investment funds, and received a guaranteed share of profits from enterprises in their region. Local committees became powerful because they controlled local government and access to Republican and federal authorities. This 'bottom up' model seemed to be in stark contrast to the Soviet model of centralised decision making and control from above. However, the State still controlled banking and most investment. Only 25 per cent of total investment was financed by enterprises themselves. American aid enabled Tito to continue investing in industry and defence without diverting resources into agriculture.

Although Yugoslav investment was concentrated on heavy industry, consumers were able to buy food and Western imports. The population was also allowed to travel relatively freely. It seemed more relaxed than Soviet Socialism, although the Party dominated workers' councils and other local committees, so local democracy was stronger on paper than in reality.

The Yugoslav regime was the first Communist one largely to divorce itself from running the economy. At the Sixth Congress of 1952, the Party declared that 'the Yugoslav League of Communists is not and cannot be the direct operative manager and commander in economic, state or social life'. However, it was difficult to reconcile coherent nationwide planning with local democracy, and in 1953 Tito was already adopting a more orthodox approach and calling for a

KEY ISSUE

How successful was Socialist economic policy in Yugoslavia?

See page 276

reassertion of the Party's leading role 'to counteract disruptive forces'. It was this change of tack which prompted Djilas's protests. Workers' management did not bring the benefits expected. Poorer educated workers tended to rubber stamp management proposals, and managers still had most influence.

Yugoslav enterprises had to become more efficient to compete with trading partners. For this reason, the government introduced radical market-style reforms in the mid-1960s. The reconciliation with Khrushchev brought recognition of the Yugoslav right to pursue their own path to Socialism, although Yugoslavia began to increase its trade with COMECON countries, while Soviet exports of oil and gas, plus massive military aid from 1957, were invaluable to Yugoslavia and reduced its economic dependence on the USA. Nevertheless, American agricultural and military deliveries continued, whilst American and United Nations' loans to finance investment continued until well into the 1980s. Trade with Western Europe was also important: Italy was Yugoslavia's biggest trading partner from 1954.

The growth of the Yugoslav economy in the 1950s was as rapid as any country in Communist Eastern Europe. This was reflected in the successful Second Five-Year Plan. Industrial production and exports of manufactures rose by 11–12 per cent a year. This was achieved not just by foreign aid but by massive capital investment and the employment of more workers rather than by increasing individual productivity, which was the hallmark of more sophisticated economies. Many enterprises remained inefficient, managed by people appointed because of Party connections rather than for their expertise. Likewise, many foreign loans were spent subsidising consumer spending or grandiose projects, rather than being used to increase productivity or to improve the country's basic infrastructure. There was a growing imbalance in the relative prosperity of various Republics. Hence the debate over market-style reforms in the 1960s.

Inflation and a rise in the cost of living became persistent problems from the early 1960s. A wage freeze was introduced in 1962 and more radical reforms were shelved. Even so, there was a decline in industrial production. The arguments over reform continued. Tito changed tack again. In 1963 he declared himself against further reform, and a campaign against private enterprise led to the closing of many small shops and workshops. But in the mid-1960s Tito permitted more

TABLE 35

Yugoslavian socio-economic indicators, 1950–70

	1950	1960	1970
Gross domestic product per head (1966 prices)	216	333	520
Automobiles (per 1000 persons)	0.4	2.9	35
Radio receivers (per 1000 persons)	21	78	166
Infant mortality (per 1000 live births)	118.6	87.7	55.2
Population per doctor	3360	1474	1010
Population % urban	21	28	39
% non-urban	79	72	61
% rural	64	50	38

	Western Europe and the USA (% of total)		USSR (% of total)		Other E. Europe (% of total)	
	Exports	Imports	Exports	Imports	Exports	Imports
1954	76.8	81.1	0.5	0.3	2.8	0.7
1956	65	68	23	22		
1958–59	58	70.7	29.6	26.2		
1960–62	51.9	29.7	8	6.8	20.6	18.7
1963–64	65.7	56	11.9	7.2	24.6	18.6
1965	42.2	66.9	17.2	8.4	24.8	21.4
1966–68	48.5	57.6	16.6	9.8	18.6	18.1
1969–71	50.3	69.3	14.4	7.7	18	14.7
1972–80	34.7	45.4	20.7	12.3	20.1	14

TABLE 36
Yugoslavia's balance of foreign trade, 1954–80

decentralisation, in line with the 'self-managed society' promised in the 1963 Constitution. Regional banks replaced smaller communal banks and by 1971 there was a Federal National Bank and eight separate national banks. The tax system was reformed. Workers' councils had their powers increased: they could determine wage rates and appoint managers from lists of approved names submitted to them. However, although enterprises were given increasing autonomy, they did not actually own their own assets. In the countryside, peasants were given loans to buy equipment. The currency was devalued. However, levels of investment scarcely rose, although unemployment and inflation did. From around 1968 the economy was in serious trouble, and the situation was worsened by the oil crisis of the 1970s. By 1979 inflation was running at over 100 per cent a year.

Yugoslavia's economic difficulties contributed to, and were themselves exacerbated by, regional and ethnic tensions. There were debates on how to assist the less developed, poorer regions: for example, by 1960 Slovenia's per capita income was five times that of Kosovo's, and the disparities were increasing. Investment was pumped into the less developed areas. However, this had a depressing effect on overall growth rates and led to grumblings from richer regions which contributed most to the federal budget. Montenegro received over 200 per cent more than the average amount of capital investment in Yugoslavia, yet remained poor, particularly since political motives sometimes overrode economic common sense. For example, in order to favour an area in Montenegro which had supported partisans during the war, a fridge-making factory was built on top of a mountain accessible only by an unpaved road impassable for much of the year. Following the 1974 Constitution, energy and transport were organised along Republican lines. By the 1980s there was considerable duplication of industry and services and only one-third of goods and services produced within Yugoslavia actually crossed Republican or provincial borders.

There were also social disparities. In the early 1960s a third of Yugoslavia's rural population did not attend school. The rate of illiteracy in Kosovo was 41 per cent. Unemployment, inflation and economic recession all fed ethnic unrest. However, reform was not always welcome. In the late 1960s there were student riots in Belgrade and elsewhere in favour of 'Socialism', rather than market reforms.

Tito's death made serious economic reform even less likely. Individual Republics borrowed without federal government permission and ran up big debts. The national infrastructure declined as economic planning was left to individual Republics from the 1970s. The Sixth and Seventh Five-Year Plans of 1976–80 and 1981–85 met none of their targets. An austerity programme introduced in 1982 and involving currency controls, devaluation, import restrictions and petrol rationing, actually increased unemployment.

Economic grievances were taken up by feuding politicians, but the real problems were papered over. Some foreign firms, particularly American ones, were encouraged to set up in the 1980s. But in the 1970s and 80s the Yugoslav economy was run mainly on foreign borrowing. Yugoslavia owed $2 billion in 1968, and $20 billion by 1982. By 1984 one quarter of all families were below the poverty line. Foreign debts rose by 20 per cent a year. However, even modest reforms were opposed, and Mikulić's attempts to restructure the economy foundered as Yugoslavia began to break up. One of Yugoslavia's previous success stories, foreign tourism, was also seriously damaged by the ensuing conflict. Ante Marković had a temporary success in 1990 in halting inflation by revaluing the currency and liberalising trade and employment laws. However, inflation resumed in the second half of 1990. The ending of state subsidies hit enterprises, whilst the Serbian government robbed federal funds to pay wages and pensions. Then came civil war, which ruined the economy, just as the German invasion had over forty years before.

D *Foreign policy*

Yugoslavia occupied a sensitive geographical and political position in post-1945 Europe, in the forefront of the Cold War and occupying a region which had historically been a source of international tensions. Interest in Yugoslavia extended beyond the Balkans.

Tito made a conscious effort to extend Yugoslavia's influence well beyond its borders. During the war, the Communists proposed a Balkan Federation, to balance superpower influence. Preliminary treaties were signed with Bulgaria and Albania, but after Yugoslavia's isolation from the the Soviet Bloc in 1948 the idea of a federation died.

Yugoslavia's expulsion from the Cominform in 1948 and its split with Moscow made Tito the focus of American and Soviet attention. This presented both dangers and opportunities for Tito. The danger was of Soviet intervention, either economic blockade or invasion, in order to bring Yugoslavia back within the orthodox Communist fold. The opportunity was for Tito to exploit the ideological differences between East and West, which he did skilfully, mainly by inducing the

PICTURE 31
*'No, Comrade Stalin!
Everyone is out of step except
Marshal Tito.' The* Daily
Express *comments on Tito's
position in relation to the
USSR and the Eastern Bloc.*

Americans to provide massive aid to shore up Yugoslavia's economy and defence. The implied promise in return was that Tito would not allow Yugoslavia to become a Soviet puppet state. Although Yugoslavia became reconciled with the USSR, and the Soviets retained a keen interest in Yugoslav affairs, Tito managed to maintain an independent stance in foreign affairs.

Tito sometimes strayed into sensitive areas. In 1950 he supported the UN decision to defend South Korea from Communist attack. In 1956 he initially supported Imre Nagy in Hungary but switched sides and supported Soviet intervention, arguing that it was necessary to preserve Socialism in Hungary. In 1957 Yugoslavia officially recognised the East German State, and began to receive large quantities of Soviet military aid, although in the same year Tito refused to acknowledge the supremacy of the Soviets in the world Communist movement.

Yugoslavia actively participated in the UN's Economic and Social Council, although its most significant contribution to international relations was its prominent role in the non-aligned movement. This attracted countries in the developing world which wanted to avoid ideological commitment in the Cold War. Tito's commitment to non-involvement grew partly out of the good relations he developed with Ethiopia, India and Egypt in 1955, and led him to deplore the concept of two hostile power blocs.

Tito enjoyed his influence. At the Non-Aligned Conference in Belgrade in 1961, Tito was proclaimed 'Father of Non-Alignment'. Even after the restoration of relations with the USSR in the 1950s, Tito maintained his involvement.

Tito lost some goodwill for his backing of Egypt in the 1967 Arab–Israeli war, but won admiration in the West for his stand against the Warsaw Pact invasion of Czechoslovakia in 1968. Tito's international influence reached its peak in the next decade, but declined from 1976: Yugoslavia became more dependent on the West for economic help again, and the Soviet invasion of Afghanistan in 1979 reawakened fears of outside intervention in its own affairs. Yugoslavia's influence in the Non-Aligned Movement was usurped by Cuba, which pushed the

KEY ISSUE

*How successful was
Tito's foreign policy?*

movement more towards the Soviet camp, despite opposition from Tito.

None of Tito's successors had anything like his prestige outside of Yugoslavia. As the problems of the 1980s degenerated into civil war and the break-up of Yugoslavia as a federal state, it is meaningless to talk about a Yugoslav foreign policy. The various Republics became battlegrounds of competing factions. Even when the fighting stopped and rehabilitation had begun, the influence of individual Republics was inevitably limited. Even Slovenia, the most developed of the former constituent parts of Yugoslavia, was not considered ready for European Union membership in 1997.

4 ∽ GREECE

A *Introduction: Greece to 1945*

In 1940 Greece was invaded by Italy and then by Germany. Communists were prominent in the Resistance. However, in 1944 Stalin promised his Western Allies that he would not support the Greek Communists in their attempt to seize power. Thus Greece did not become part of the Soviet-controlled Eastern Bloc. There was a gradual move from authoritarian government towards democracy, punctuated by a period of military dictatorship, and a conscious move by Greece to associate itself more closely with the liberal democracies of Western Europe.

B *Political history*

ESTABLISHING STABILITY

In 1945 the Greek government was headed by Georgios Papandreou. It took a civil war which lasted until 1949 before Greek Communists were defeated and democracy was established. In the meantime, in 1947, Britain handed over its protector's role in Greece to the Americans, who provided massive aid to Greece and also interfered in the running of the country.

Greek Rally won 82 per cent of the seats in the 1952 election, ushering in twenty years of right-wing rule. There were stringent laws against left-wing activity. Economic progress brought some stability.

KARAMANLIS AND PAPANDREOU

Konstantinos Karamanlis was dominant in Greek politics for thirty-five years from 1955. He transformed Greek Rally into the National Radical Union. From 1958 the United Democratic Left became the principal opposition party. There was an increasing polarisation in politics between Left and Right until 1961 when Papandreou re-emerged to join the centre parties into the Centre Union, which then became the chief opposition to Karamanlis.

TIMELINE

Events in Greece

1945 –49	Civil War
1952	Greece joined NATO
1955	Karamanlis in power
1961	Georgios Papandreou formed Centre Union
1964	Centre Union in power
1967	Military *coup*
1974	Return to civilian rule under Karamanlis Partition of Cyprus
1981	Greece joined European Community PASOK government under Andreas Papandreou

Karamanlis narrowly lost to Papandreou in the 1963 election. He left Greece to live in France for eleven years before making a dramatic return to Greek politics. Papandreou's Centre Union had a big parliamentary majority from 1964. He made his son, Andreas, Economics Minister and implemented reforms. However, he struggled to control the army, and argued with young King Constantine II. Eventually, Papandreou resigned and a group of junior army officers, opposed to the Centre Union, seized power in a *coup*.

KEY ISSUE

How significant were the contributions of Karamanlis and Georgios Papandreou to Greek political life?

GREECE UNDER THE COLONELS

The surprise *coup* met no resistance. The King agreed to a civilian government, a facade behind which a military *Junta* of 'Three Colonels' ruled. The **Junta** arrested thousands of left-wing politicians, including the Papandreous.

King Constantine fled after his own poorly-planned *coup* against the Colonels failed in December 1967. Colonel Georgios Papadopoulos now ruled directly. His regime was tacitly accepted by Greece's Western allies because of its anti-Communism. But economic problems undermined the *Junta*. In 1973, Papadopoulos deposed the exiled King and proclaimed himself as President. However, following further demonstrations, his own hardline colleagues, led by Brigadier Dimitrios Joannidis, deposed him. Then Joaniddis's commanders refused to contemplate war over Cyprus. They demanded a return to civilian rule and invited the experienced Karamanlis to return to Greece as Prime Minister again in July 1974.

Junta a ruling group of army officers

KEY ISSUE

What were the causes and consequences of the military coup?

See page 297

CIVILIAN GOVERNMENT AGAIN: NEW DEMOCRACY AND PASOK

Karamanlis skilfully guided Greece through the transition to civilian rule at a time of uncertainty and tension over Cyprus. He headed the new Democracy Party, successor to the National Radical Union. A new party, the Panhellenic Socialist Movement (PASOK), led by Andreas Papandreou, gained support. PASOK's programme was 'National Independence, Popular Sovereignty, Social Liberation and Democratic Structures'. The Centre of Greek politics was being squeezed as the parties of the Left and Right now showed a more cautious approach to most issues.

Karamanlis's 1975 Constitution created a strong presidency. Karamanlis, President himself from 1980, became increasingly preoccupied with foreign affairs and Greece's application to join the European Community. In 1977 PASOK became the main opposition party to New Democracy.

In 1981 PASOK formed a government. Papandreou introduced reforms, such as the introduction of a National Health Service. Economic reforms were less successful. In 1985 Papandreou introduced an austerity package. He was criticised for his private life and several PASOK ministers were implicated in corruption, although Papandreou himself survived attacks in Parliament.

KEY ISSUE

What key developments in Greek politics took place between 1974 and the 1990s?

KEY ISSUE

What developments took place in the Greek economy between 1945 and the 1990s?

There was stalemate after two general elections in 1989. New Democracy narrowly failed to achieve an absolute majority, whilst support for the new 'Alliance of the Left and of Progress' fell considerably. PASOK recovered ground. From 1990 New Democracy had a narrow majority, whilst Karamanlis was re-elected President.

As Greek politics moved into the 1990s, the prospects for continued stability seemed mixed. Greece was now a member of the European Community, and both Left and Right appeared to be committed to democracy. However, it proved difficult to form majority governments, there was still a taint of corruption in political life, the economic outlook was worsening, and developments in Cyprus, Yugoslavia and Albania all threatened serious complications for Greece. It was too early to take a stable and secure democracy in Greece for granted.

C *Economic history*

Economic recovery in Greece after the Second World War was slow. Growth was stimulated mainly by means of a building programme, the massive merchant fleet, and tourism. Between 1945 and 1975 12 per cent of the Greek population emigrated.

Like many European economies, Greece was hit hard by the oil crisis of the early 1970s. Inflation also remained a problem. Social reform was hampered by economic and financial constraints. Large foreign loans contributed to a balance of payments deficit.

Post-war Greek governments nationalised many firms and banks. Probably two-fifths of the Greek economy was 'unofficial', with Greeks working entirely for themselves and not paying taxes. Membership of the European Community did not resolve all the problems. Greece entered the 1990s facing economic as well as political uncertainties.

See page 350

D *Foreign policy*

Greece had a high international profile in the Cold War: it was embroiled in civil war soon after the Second World War, the Eastern Mediterranean and Aegean regions were important strategically, and Greece's neighbours quickly established Communist regimes or had Communism foisted upon them. Therefore, the future of Greece was particularly important to the West. The Greek government was aware of the country's vulnerability should Stalin break his wartime agreement not to interfere in Greece. So the Greeks joined Turkey in NATO in 1952. However, tension between Greece and Turkey was always on or just below the surface.

The British base of Cyprus became the flashpoint for a new conflict. Its population was 80 per cent Greek and 20 per cent Turkish. Greek Cypriots had long demanded *enosis* ('union') with Greece. When Britain refused to cede sovereignty of Cyprus to Greece, a campaign of civil disobedience and violence began on the island in April 1955. It was organised by General Georgios Grivas, a Cypriot-born Greek army officer. His National Organisation of Cypriot Fighters (EOKA) was supported by Makarios III, Archbishop of Cyprus. The Turks demanded *taksim* ('partition') of Cyprus.

In 1959 Greece and Turkey reached agreement for Cyprus to become an independent Republic within the British Commonwealth. Britain would retain sovereignty over two bases and guarantee the settlement. Turkish and Greek Cypriot leaders were not consulted about the agreement and signed it unwillingly. In 1960 Makarios became President of the new independent Republic of Cyprus. Grivas never accepted the agreement. In November 1963 Makarios demanded fewer powers for the Turkish minority and when the Turkish government refused, fighting broke out between the two communities on Cyprus. The USA pressurised the Turkish government not to intervene. A UN peacekeeping force was sent to Cyprus and most of the Turkish population was transferred into enclaves from which the Greeks were excluded. The UN force was still there thirty years later.

When Greece flexed its muscles over Cyprus again in 1967, it had to back down. Turkey had much stronger forces. Makarios's relations with the Greek government deteriorated, and the Greek military *Junta* carried out a *coup* to briefly depose him. Turkey reacted by invading Northern Cyprus on 20 July 1974. 200 000 Greek Cypriots fled to the South of Cyprus, and the weak Greek response humiliated the *Junta*. Many Greeks demonstrated against the USA for supposedly favouring Turkey. Cyprus was partitioned between two communities.

There were further disputes between Greece and Turkey in the 1970s and 80s. Turkey protested at Greek fortification of islands in the Aegean, and there were serious arguments about the extent of coastal waters and air traffic space, and also border clashes. In 1984 the Greeks declared that the main threat to their security came from Turkey, their NATO ally.

> **KEY ISSUE**
>
> *Why was Cyprus a flashpoint in international relations?*

> **KEY ISSUE**
>
> *Why were relations between Greece and Turkey frequently strained?*

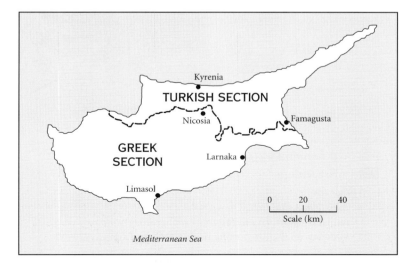

MAP 24
The partition of Cyprus, 1974

In January 1988 Greece and Turkey signed the Davos 'no war agreement'. Steps were taken to improve relations. However, the issue of Cyprus remained potentially explosive. Greece sought additional security outside NATO by joining the European Union. The European Community agreed that Greece should have full membership from 1981. Although originally hostile to membership, PASOK accepted it once in power. However, Papandreou refused to cooperate with NATO.

The ending of the Cold War at the end of the 1980s did not resolve all areas of concern. Instability in Albania, Yugoslavia and Macedonia threatened possible insecurities for Greece.

Greece was proud to have established its independence in the modern world. It was not a great power, but as Greece entered the 1990s it could hope to play a greater part in Europe through its membership of the European Union – and acceptance of Greece as a full European power had been the main aim of all progressive Greek politicians in the twentieth century.

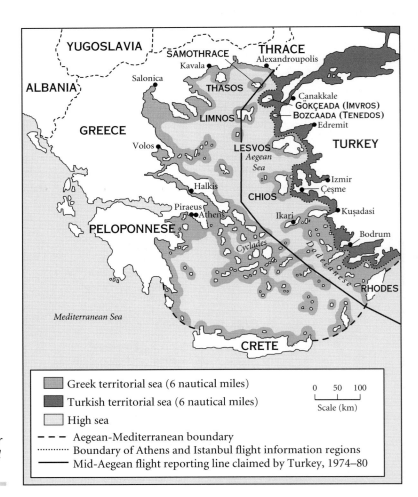

MAP 25

The Aegean: the area under dispute between Greece and Turkey

5 ↷ ALBANIA

A *Political history*

HOXHA'S ALBANIA

Albania was occupied by Italy and Germany during the Second World War. Enver Hoxha succeeded in establishing a Communist government in 1944 without direct Soviet help.

A committed Stalinist, Hoxha resented the Soviet leadership's attack on Stalin's reputation in 1956. In 1961, Albania ended formal relations with the USSR and turned to China instead. More radical policies were introduced. The Church was abolished in 1967, priests were persecuted and Albania became the first atheist state. Propaganda and purges kept the army, the Party and the population generally in line and Hoxha faced no significant challenges to his authority.

Albania became the most isolated state in Europe, resisting change. When Hoxha finally died in April 1985 his protegé Ramiz Alia was smoothly and unanimously elected First Secretary of the Party.

Hoxha had survived as leader for an impressive period of over forty years. He succeeded in his goal of preserving the independence of his small and undeveloped country. He could claim to have destroyed the

TIMELINE

Events in Albania

1944	Enver Hoxha established Communist power
1961	Break with USSR
1968	Albania left the Warsaw Pact
1978	Break with China
1985	Death of Hoxha Appointment of Ramiz Alia as First Secretary
1991	First free post-Communist elections Ramiz Alia elected President

KEY ISSUE

What were the distinctive features of Hoxha's Albania?

MAP 26
Albania

old regional loyalties which had plagued Albania's previous history, and he had at least begun a period of social and economic development.

However, all this had been achieved at the cost of rigid ideological conformity and a cult of personality.

THE POST-HOXHA ERA

KEY ISSUE

How significant were the political changes made after Hoxha?

See page 301

Albania's reputation as an isolated, repressive, backward Stalinist state seemed increasingly unattractive. Ramiz Alia's first tentative steps towards reform were a milder version of Gorbachev's *perestroika* in the USSR, and they were based on the same assumption that the Party would retain control of the process. However, the collapse of Communist power in Eastern Europe in 1989 pushed the regime into further changes such as the 'New Economic Mechanism', which partly decentralised the economy.

Political reforms were very limited. The reformers appeared to be winning when a multiparty political system was approved. The Democratic Party (DP) became the first legal opposition party in Albania since the Communist takeover. There was a guarantee of human rights, a reform of the penal code and a lifting of the ban on religion. Albania's notorious self-imposed isolation was beginning to break down.

The first free elections for seventy years were held in March 1991. The Communists continued to do well. The main opposition party, the DP, won 39 per cent of the vote. In violence following the election, several DP Party workers were killed.

Ramiz Alia was elected President in May 1991. The new 'Republic of Albania' had finally entered the mainstream of European politics after fifty years of isolation, but it proved difficult to shake off the legacy of an authoritarian past. Lack of democratic traditions and economic difficulties rendered the future uncertain. The problem of Kosovo and relations with Yugoslavia remained. The fragility of the regime was emphasised in the mid-1990s when thousands of optimistic Albanians who had put their savings into worthless pyramid investment schemes were left bankrupt, without government support. There was looting and violence, old regional divisions re-emerged, and more Albanians tried to flee the country. As in some other previously Communist countries, the transition to new political and economic structures proved fraught with difficulty, and was compounded by Albania's continuing reputation as the poorest country in Europe.

B *Economic history*

As a committed Stalinist, Enver Hoxha followed the Soviet model of centralised planning of industry and collectivisation of agriculture. Albania had valuable chrome resources to exploit. It also had oil, copper, iron and nickel, and could develop hydroelectric power. Therefore, as in most undeveloped economies which adopted an industrialisation drive, the initial results were impressive. In the 1950s there was a growth rate of 20 per cent a year.

The Soviets designated Albania as a source of food and raw materials for Eastern Europe, and therefore Khrushchev urged Hoxha to reduce industrial investment. Hoxha refused and this was a key factor in Albania's diplomatic break with the USSR in 1961, and the ending of Soviet aid.

China replaced the USSR as Albania's sponsor. The Chinese assisted an industrialisation drive involving the building of oil refineries, ore-processing plants, chemical food processing and machine-tool factories, hydroelectric plants and a steel mill. Communications were also improved: much of the railway system was built by volunteer Young Communists. The road system remained primitive.

China's aid programme stopped in 1978. Albania was completely alone and industrial and agricultural growth suffered. By 1967 all land was collectivised. But self-sufficiency was never achieved and food was still imported in the 1980s because the increase in agricultural output scarcely kept pace with the rise in population.

In recognition of this fact Ramiz Alia's 'New Economic Mechanism' of 1989–90 was more radical. Farmers were allowed to double the size of private plots, sell on the open market, and repossess 'collectivised' herds of cattle. Subsidies and price controls for inefficient industries were to be stopped. Foreign investment in Albania was encouraged, including joint Albanian/foreign business ventures. Some economists wanted to go further and implement a full market economy.

Reforms were slow to take effect. Unemployment, strikes and absenteeism actually rose. Albania entered the 1990s with a declining National Income and a rising trade deficit.

C *Foreign policy*

Until 1948 Hoxha's regime was dependent on its most powerful neighbour, Yugoslavia. The Yugoslavs had been influential in helping Albania to fight its Axis occupiers during the war. The Albanians were forced to accept the Yugoslav acquisition of the Albanian-populated province of Kosovo in 1946. In the same year the Yugoslavs and Albanians signed an agreement to integrate their economies. However, relations were broken off in 1948. Hoxha moved Albania firmly into the Soviet camp.

Britain and the USA made several secret attempts to destabilise and overthrow Hoxha's regime after 1949. But Albania's relations with the Eastern Bloc strengthened. It joined COMECON in 1949 and the Warsaw Pact in 1955. However, relations between Albania and the USSR were seriously affected by the death of Stalin in 1953. Hoxha did not have the same respect for his successors. After ending relations with the Kremlin in 1961, Albania ceased to participate in COMECON and following the Soviet invasion of Czechoslovakia in 1968, Albania left the Warsaw Pact.

KEY ISSUE

What were the main features of Albania's economy and economic policy during and after the Communist regime?

KEY ISSUE

What were the causes and consequences of Albania's isolationism?

In 1961 Hoxha pronounced his 'Dual Adversary' theory. This postulated that true Marxist–Leninist states (that is, Albania and China) had to fight the twin adversaries of 'imperialism' and 'Soviet-led modern revisionism', both of which threatened true Communism. Having moved out of the Yugoslav and then the Soviet orbit, Hoxha's friendship with China lasted from 1961 to 1978. However, after Mao's death, China attempted to improve relations with Yugoslavia and other European nations, and it reduced its aid to Albania. Chinese military and economic aid to Albania was halted in 1978, leaving Albania effectively alone. Albania's economy was seriously damaged by its isolation, so in the early 1980s new ties were established with nearby countries – Greece, Turkey, Austria and Italy.

Albania gradually opened up after Hoxha's death. After 1987 diplomatic relations were re-established with West Germany, Canada, the USSR and the USA. Albania's integration into the international community was almost complete.

6 ⌁ TURKEY

A *Introduction: Turkey to 1945*

Although geographically situated between Europe and the Middle East, modern Turkey has regarded itself as part of Europe. After 1945 Turkey became closely tied to the rest of Europe through military alliances and a system of parliamentary democracy unique in the Middle East.

B *Political history*

Until 1945 Turkey's governments were authoritarian and dominated by the Republican People's Party (RPP). In May 1945 moves towards democracy were announced, although parties representing the extreme Right or Left, and religious political groups, were not permitted. In 1945 the National Development Party was founded, followed by the moderate right-wing Democratic Party (DP). The latter formed a genuine opposition, winning sixty-two parliamentary seats in 1946.

The RPP was in a dilemma as to whether to carry out reforms or to suppress the opposition. President Inönü determined on moderation and ensured that Turkey became a multi-party state, although new Communist and Socialist parties were suppressed.

The DP faced problems when a Muslim faction broke away to form the Nation Party in July 1948. Nevertheless, the DP won Turkey's first genuinely free election in May 1950. The Army offered Inönü a military *coup* to nullify the election, but he declined and resigned the presidency. The new Assembly elected Celal Bayar as President and Adnan Menderes as Prime Minister.

Menderes was a charismatic, strong individual who dominated Turkish politics for ten years after 1950. The DP won a landslide

MAP 27
Turkey

election victory in 1954, but its fortunes then declined. The economy ran into difficulties and DP reforms aroused controversy. A relaxation of punitive laws against Islam had already begun. However, this liberalisation was accompanied by a revival in Islam and the formation of Muslim political groups, although they were illegal. There were fears that the secular state would be undermined. In 1955 some liberals defected from the DP to form the Freedom Party, which then merged with the RPP.

Menderes launched the Fatherland Front to try to mobilise popular support for the DP. But tensions, fuelled by economic failures, led to a military *coup* in May 1960, led by General Cemal Gursel. President Bayer, Menderes and all DP ministers were arrested. Gursel headed a National Unity Committee (NUC). Menderes and another leading Democrat were hanged. Several other Democrat politicians were imprisoned and there was a purge of the army and other institutions.

Conflict soon broke out within the army between those who wanted to stay in power and push through reforms, and those anxious to return to constitutional government. The constitutionalists won: in November 1960 the NUC was purged, and an Armed Forces Union of senior officers ran the country. A Senate was created to balance the powerful National Assembly.

In 1961 the ban on political activity was lifted. In the October 1961 election the RPP failed to win an overall majority, to the disappointment of the army. Close behind the RPP was the new Justice Party (JP), effectively the successor to the DP. Although some officers wanted to annul the election, democracy prevailed. The NUC disbanded itself.

> ## KEY ISSUE
>
> *What were the main features of Turkey's political development between 1945 and the 1990s?*

Gursel was elected President, and a coalition government of the RPP and JP was formed

RPP leader Ismet Inönü persuaded extremist forces to adopt democratic ways. There were no radical reforms, but DP leaders were released in 1964, and their political rights restored in 1969. In 1965 the JP won a majority.

The JP leader and new Prime Minister of the single-party government was Süleyman Demirel, an engineer aged forty-one, who was to be a dominant force in Turkish politics. He promised the army that the State would not interfere in its internal affairs. Demirel's concern was economic progress and political liberalisation. The government encouraged foreign investment, with impressive results, as industry began to overtake agriculture as Turkey's prime source of wealth.

Although the JP won a majority again in 1969, Demirel could never feel secure. His own Party represented diverse interests. Radical forces were developing in 1960s Turkey, particularly amongst students and intellectuals. Some activists turned to violence. Workers were also active: trade unions secured the right to strike in 1963, after which they grew rapidly. The Turkish Workers Party (TWP), supported by workers and Kurds, was founded in 1961.

The Right was also active, although two attempted *coups* failed. The Republican Peasants National Party (RPNP) was led by Colonel Alpaslan Turkes, a former member of the NUC. It was militantly nationalist, pan-Turkish and anti-Communist. Turkes also tried to appeal to Muslims and his Party became the Nationalist Action Party in 1969, with a paramilitary youth wing called the Grey Wolves.

The JP finally split in 1970. Demirel, left in charge of a weak minority government, could not cope with a rising tide of violence, particularly in universities and Kurdistan. Another right-wing party, the National Order Party (NOP) was formed by Nesmettin Erbakan in January 1970.

Violence from the Left and Right led General Memduk Tagmac to force Demirel's resignation in March 1971. A conservative government was installed and martial law declared. Some civil freedoms were suspended. The new government was led by RPP member Nikat Erim, and then Ferit Melen of the Reliance Party, while Ecevit replaced Inönü as RPP leader.

The army was in a dilemma: its leaders did not wish to take power themselves, but disorder forced them to intervene frequently in politics. In 1973 a coalition government of Ecevit's RPP and Erbakan's NOP was formed. Ecevit's strident stance in the Cyprus crisis brought him popularity, and he resigned, intending another election to increase his vote. But the other parties negotiated and Demirel formed a new coalition of the JP, NOP, NAP and defectors from the RPP.

There were further short-lived governments under Ecevit and Demirel. Clearly parliamentary government was not working effectively. Failure to achieve stable majority governments allowed a disproportionate influence to small extremist parties, and prevented effective social and economic reform. Violence from both Left and

KEY ISSUE

Why did the army frequently intervene in Turkish politics?

See page 307

Right and from Kurdish separatists was growing. In the final seven months of 1980 alone, there were 1250 political deaths.

The growth of a religious Islamic party, encouraged by the Iranian Revolution of 1979, also posed a threat to the secular State. A reluctant army had had enough of the paralysis, and army leader General Kenan Evran intervened on 12 September 1980. Leading politicians were arrested and parties banned. A five-man National Security Council took control, dissolved Parliament, and issued martial law throughout Turkey. Thousands on the Right and Left were arrested, imprisoned and tortured. General Evran, who was declared Head of State, saw his task as preserving the Constitution from incompetent or corrupt politicians. Experienced politicians were banned from political activity.

A civilian government was appointed, as the army always intended, although a new Constitution provided for a strong President who appointed the Prime Minister and could dismiss Parliament. Evran became President. The press and trade unions were closely controlled.

In the November 1983 election only three parties were approved by the army. Turgut Özal's Motherland Party (MP) won. Özal was popular and able. He was determined to restore the pre-eminence of civil politics. He secured more victories in 1985 and 1987. However, the MP faced difficult circumstances. Violence continued, and the government's tough response attracted some liberal criticism outside Turkey. In the economy, the gap between rich and poor widened. In 1987, Turkey's application to join the European Union was turned down on the grounds that it had not adapted enough to the standards of existing members. Arguments over Turkey's prospective membership continued well into the 1990s.

In 1987 the ban on old politicians was lifted. They resumed their careers, but their parties had new names. The old RPP was resurrected as the Social Democratic Populist Party (SDPP) under Erdal Inönü. The old JP appeared as the True Path Party (TPP) led by Demirel. Together they provided the main opposition group in the Assembly. The Welfare Party, led by Erbakan, aimed for an Islamic state. Communism was illegal, but Radical and Green parties began to emerge.

The MP suffered from this competition, and Özal was criticised for nepotism and increasing authoritarianism. In October 1989 he succeeded Evren as President. A new Populist Social Democratic Party (SHP) emerged to challenge for the central ground. As various political parties took root the prospects for democracy seemed good. In October 1991 the True Path Party and the Social Democrats formed a coalition government, and Demirel became President after Özal's death. In 1993 Tansu Çilla became Turkey's first female Prime Minister.

The Kurdish issue was still unresolved. The Kurds, who resisted modernisation and had retained their tribal organisation, lived in Turkey, Iran, Iraq and Syria. In Turkey they were subject to deportations, military administration and a ban on their own language until 1991. The Kurds fought back. During the 1960s the Kurdistan Labour Party (PKK) aimed for an independent Kurdish state, and set up enclaves in Turkey and Iraq. When Saddam Hussein tried to

TIMELINE

Events in Turkey

1950 Celal Bayer became President and Adnan Menderes Prime Minister

1952 Turkey joined NATO

1960 Military *coup*

1965 Süleyman Demirel appointed Prime Minister

1974 Bulent Ecevit appointed Prime Minister

1975 Right-wing coalition under Demirel

1978 Ecevit appointed Prime Minister

1979 Demirel appointed Prime Minister

1980 Military *coup* by General Kenan Evren

1983 Turgut Özal appointed Prime Minister

1987 Turkey's application to join the European Community

1989 Özal elected President European Community rejected Turkey's application

1991 Demirel appointed Prime Minister

1993 Demirel elected President
Tansu Çilla appointed Prime Minister
Re-establishment of Republican People's Party

1995 SDPP and Republican People's Party reunited under Hikmet Cetin
Resignation of Çilla

exterminate the Kurds in Iraq, they rebelled in March 1991. 1 500 000 Kurds fled to Turkey and Iran. The Turkish army attacked the PKK's guerrilla bases in South East Turkey and Northern Iraq. The Turkish government was also concerned by the growth of support for a militant Islamic state.

An austerity programme in 1994 in turn sparked off discontent. The pro-Islamic Welfare Party did well in local elections but the pro-Kurdish Democracy Party was closed down. In March 1995 the SDPP and Republican People's Party reunited under Hikmet Cetin. In September Çilla resigned after divisions in the governing coalition. Turkey's progress towards a Western-style democracy was still uneven.

C *Economic history*

Turkey was assisted after 1945 by Marshall Aid from the USA. It remained primarily an agricultural country; as late as 1989 only 20.5 per cent of the population worked in industry. The majority of peasants were smallholders, and in 1973 only 20 per cent of farming families were living above survival level.

There was some rapid economic growth as Turkey recovered from the war, but the boom was over by the mid-1950s. Turkish investment was frequently uncoordinated, although there was a planning office which produced five-year plans for the State sector from 1960. Foreign investment was allowed from 1955, but not in oil. State-owned companies were financed by banks and there were close links between political parties and industry. In 1963 there were 238 state plants, employing 25 per cent of the working population.

The government's protectionist policies were not very successful. Imports exceeded exports, which grew slowly. The oil crisis of 1973–74 hit the economy. Governments in the 1970s tried to deal with the crisis by borrowing, printing money and imposing more import restrictions. The result was higher inflation and negotiations with the IMF, the World Bank and OECD. Demirel had to carry out substantial reforms in order to get credit: the measures included abolishing import and export controls, cutting subsidies, raising prices and reducing government expenditure. These measures were very unpopular.

During the 1980s Özal attempted fundamental economic changes, extending a free market economy and reducing inflation. There was some success: growth rates and exports grew. However, inflation also rose and real wages fell considerably. After 1985 there were cyclical movements of growth and recession. More foreign investment and tourism were encouraged. The 'South East Anatolia Project' was a huge complex of dams on the Euphrates and Tigris rivers to provide irrigation.

A rapid rise in population from 13 000 000 in 1923 to 50 000 000 by the 1980s added to economic and social strains. By 1980 there were 2 500 000 emigrant Turkish workers in Western Europe, including 800 000 in Germany. About half of Turkey's population had no social security and a third of all Turks were still illiterate in 1989.

KEY ISSUE

How successful was the Turkish economy after 1945?

Clearly, remedies were necessary if Turkey were to join the European Union, which it had decided upon in 1963. The Sixth Five-Year Plan of 1990–94 set unrealistically high growth targets at a time of high inflation, low growth, growing unemployment and increasing differentials between rich and poor, with resulting unrest. The Turkish economy entered the 1990s still with major problems.

D *Foreign policy*

Turkey's geographical position gave it a strategic importance and an important role in Cold War politics. Although Turkey emerged from the Second World War on the Allied side, it was under pressure from the USSR even before the war's end. Moscow demanded a change in the status of the **Straits** and a revision of its frontier with Turkey. The Soviets wanted free access through the Straits confined to those states such as the USSR which had borders on the Black Sea. Stalin refused to accept a situation in which, he declared, 'Turkey had a hand on Russia's throat'. In June 1945 the USSR laid claim to Kars and Ardakan, and much of Turkey's Black Sea Coast. The Soviets, under Western pressure, dropped their demands in October 1946, but continued to subvert Turkey.

Turkish concern over Soviet behaviour led it to join NATO in 1952. Nevertheless, the Turks sometimes acted independently, as when they adopted a pro-Arab stance after the 1967 Arab–Israeli War. Relations with the USSR improved, partly due to Turkish disillusionment with a lack of American support in its dispute with Greece over Cyprus. Turkey invaded Cyprus and occupied parts of it in 1974. Nevertheless, Turkey stayed relatively close to the USA, which saw Turkey as a valuable ally in the Middle East. In 1990 Turkey sent troops to the Gulf, and also signed the 'Charter for a New Europe' in Paris, pledging its commitment to democracy and the rule of law. In 1992 Turkey signed an agreement with other states bordering on the Black Sea. Clearly Turkey, with its ambition of joining the European Union, was keen to demonstrate its responsibility and commitment to the new Europe.

> **Straits** the narrow stretch of water separating the Black Sea from the Meditranean sea

> ### KEY ISSUE
> *What were the main features of Turkey's foreign policy?*

> See page 304

7 ⌐ BIBLIOGRAPHY

Events in Romania and Bulgaria are covered in *The Eastern and Central European States 1945–92* by J. Laver (Hodder and Stoughton, 1999) and in several books on the Eastern Bloc generally, including *Eastern Europe Since 1945* by G. and N. Swain (Macmillan, 1993) and *Revolution in East-Central Europe* by D. Mason (Boulder, 1992). Romanian history receives detailed treatment in *Romania: Politics, Economics and Society* by M. Shafir (Pinter, 1985) and *Romania In Turmoil* by M. Rady (Tauris, 1992). Bulgaria's history receives detailed treatment in *Bulgaria: Politics, Economics and Society* by R. McIntyre (Pinter, 1988). Yugoslavia before its break-up is covered in *Yugoslavia: Politics, Economics and Society* by B. McFarlane (Pinter, 1988). *The Fall of Yugoslavia* by M. Glenny (Penguin,

1992) is a useful account. Also useful are *The Changing Face of The Balkans* by F. Carter and H. Norris (UCL Press, 1996), *Tito, Yugoslavia's Great Dictator: A Reassessment* by S. Pavlowitch (Ohio State University Press, 1992), *Broken Bonds: Yugoslavia's Disintegration and Balkan Politics in Transition* by L. Cohen (Westview, 1995), *The Destruction of Yugoslavia: Tracking the Break-up, 1980–92* by B. Magas (Verso, 1993), and *The Death of Yugoslavia* by L. Silber and A. Little (Penguin, 1995). Greek history is dealt with in *A Concise History of Greece* by R. Clogg (CUP, 1992) and *Parties and Elections in Greece: The Search For Legitimacy*, also by R. Clogg (C Hurst, 1987). Albanian history is dealt with in *Albania* by N. Panov (1989).

8 ↝ ESSAY QUESTIONS

1. Compare and contrast the impact of Communist rule on Romania and Bulgaria between the late 1940s and the overthrow of their Communist regimes in the late 1980s.
2. (a) Outline the steps by which Communist rule was established in *either* Romania *or* Bulgaria;
   (b) How successful were the economic and social policies of the Communist regime chosen in part (a)?
3. (a) What were the principal changes made by Tito to Yugoslavia's political and economic system between 1945 and his death in 1980?
   (b) 'Tito made post-1945 Yugoslavia. He alone kept the country in one piece.' To what extent is this a valid assessment of Tito's significance in Yugoslavia's history?
4. (a) What were the principal features of Yugoslavia's political and economic systems under Tito?
   (b) Why were Tito's successors unable to repeat his achievements?
5. (a) Outline the steps by which the Yugoslav Federation degenerated into civil war after the death of Tito;
   (b) Assess the consequences of the break-up for any *two* of the following: Slovenia; Croatia; Serbia; Bosnia.
6. (a) What were the main achievements of Georgios Papandreou and Konstantinos Karamanlis in Greece?
   (b) Why, and with what consequences, was there a military *coup* in Greece in 1967?
7. (a) Outline Enver Hoxha's political and economic policies in Albania;
   (b) What were the causes and consequences for Albania of its isolation in foreign affairs?
8. How successfully was a democratic political system established in Turkey in the four decades after the Second World War?
9. (a) Compare the role of the military in Greek and Turkish politics between the 1960s and 1990s;
   (b) Why were relations between Greece and Turkey often strained during this period?

Northern Europe

7

INTRODUCTION

Scandinavia comprised Denmark, Norway, Sweden, Finland, Iceland, the Faroes (which became self-governing in 1968) and Greenland (granted home rule by Denmark in 1979). Together with the Baltic States of Estonia, Latvia and Lithuania, Scandinavia has not only been on the geographical periphery of Europe but also often out of the political mainstream. However, in recent history the Scandinavian States became more involved in European issues, particularly economic ones. In the same period, the three Baltic Republics graduated to a somewhat uncertain independence from the former USSR.

The main themes of this chapter will be:

● In what ways, and why, did the Scandinavian States develop politically and economically in the way they did?
● To what extent did they become more outward looking in their relationship with the rest of Europe?
● How, and with what consequences, were the three Baltic Republics able to achieve their independence from the Soviet Empire?

1 ⌐ SCANDINAVIA

Introduction: Denmark, Norway, Sweden and Finland to 1945

The history of the Scandinavian states has always been closely interrelated. In 1397 Denmark, Norway and Sweden had been united under the Danish Crown. In 1523 Sweden had separated from Denmark. Finland went its own way, being absorbed into the Russian Empire in the early nineteenth century. Norway secured its independence from Denmark in 1905, and Finland achieved its independence in 1917, after the Russian Revolution. The Scandinavian states were neutral in the First World War, and were widely regarded as peripheral to European affairs, because of their geographical location, their limited natural resources and small populations. It was also a self-imposed isolation. The democratic and populist tradition which emerged from struggles to overturn the autocratic monarchies of Sweden and Denmark fed a desire to avoid the entanglements of great power politics.

The Scandinavian states asserted their neutrality in 1939. However, it could not be sustained. Finland, always vulnerable because of Soviet ambitions to control the Baltic region, was forced into the 'Winter War' in 1939 after refusing to cede to the USSR territory near Leningrad. In retaliation, the Finns joined the Germans in attacking the USSR in 1941, only to suffer eventual defeat by the Soviets again.

Denmark and Norway were overrrun by Germany in the spring of 1940. Only Sweden managed to maintain its independence and neutrality, whilst continuing to trade with Germany. After the war the Scandinavian states quickly reaffirmed their neutrality, although armed forces were maintained to deter would-be aggressors.

There were many similarities between the political systems of Denmark, Norway and Sweden. They had parliaments and electoral systems which often produced coalitions. For three decades after the war Social Democratic parties dominated Scandinavian politics, until Conservative parties made a comeback in the 1980s. Norway, Sweden and Denmark had constitutional monarchies which kept a relatively low profile. Their populations had a high standard of living and generous welfare provision for much of this period. Later, these countries faced more economic pressures and were forced to redefine their attitude towards the European Community.

> **KEY ISSUE**
>
> *Why was Social Democracy such a strong force in several Scandinavian states?*

2 ⤳ DENMARK

A *Political history*

Denmark was occupied by Germany for most of the Second World War, but suffered relatively little material damage. It made a smooth transition to the post-war world. King Christian X and his government had remained in Denmark during the war, whilst avoiding any taint of collaboration. Political life was resumed almost from the position of 1940, although some Resistance leaders were drafted into the government, which also contained some Communists. The Social Democrats remained the largest party, as they had been before the war.

There was an extensive purge of wartime collaborators of the Nazis. Many Danes were banned from professional life. Otherwise, political life proceeded smoothly. From 1972, Denmark's constitutional monarch was Queen Margrethe II. The 135 MPs in Parliament were elected by proportional representation for a maximum of four years.

The Social Democrats generally won about 40 per cent of the vote in general elections, and were either the governing party or were part of governing coalitions for several decades, apart from a time in opposition between 1950 and 1953 when the Liberal Peasant Party (the *Venstre*) was in power. There was also a Socialist People's Party, founded by Aksel Larsen in 1958. He was the former Danish Communist leader, but having been disowned by Moscow he formed his own party, splitting the Communist vote and gaining some votes from the Social Democrats. The Socialists had radical social policies and supported a policy of neutrality in foreign affairs, but were weakened by internal disagreements. However, in 1966 Larsen gained

11 per cent of the electoral vote, and his support became necessary for the Social Democratic government to gain a working majority.

In 1968, following a period of economic difficulties and the devaluation of the *kronar*, the Social Democratic government was replaced by a coalition of the Centre. It was led by Hilmar Baunsgaard, head of a breakaway group from the *Venstre*. Then, in 1973, again at a time of economic recession, the Progressive Party gained 10 per cent of the vote. It demanded big tax cuts. However, the Social Democrats were soon back in power.

The period of Social Democratic dominance ended in 1982 when the Conservatives, led by Poul Schlüter, won power. His government included Conservatives, Liberals and Radical Liberals, but no Socialists, and had only a small majority. The Conservatives were in power for most of the 1980s, but had not only the problems of economic recession to handle, but also the issue of the future development of the European Community. Danish opinion was strongly divided on moves towards closer union. Until the ending of the Cold War there was also a division within the governing coalition about membership of NATO. Denmark felt particularly vulnerable because of its close proximity to large Warsaw Pact forces in East Germany. In order to avoid any accusations of provocation, Danish governments, despite their NATO commitments, refused, along with Norway, to have NATO bases on their territory or NATO ships or nuclear weapons in their waters.

See page 350

KEY ISSUE

What was Denmark's attitude towards involvement in NATO and the European Community?

After the ending of the Cold War, the Social Democrats experienced a revival. In 1990 they were the largest parliamentary party, with 37 per cent of the votes. A coalition government of Conservatives and Liberals was established under Poul Schlüter. It was replaced in 1993 by a coalition of Social Democrats, Radicals, Centre Democrats and the Christian People's Party, with Social Democrat Poul Rasmussen as Prime Minister. Political controversy centred on the European Union. A referendum in 1992 produced a narrow majority against ratification of the Maastricht Treaty, a decision narrowly reversed in another referendum in May 1993.

See page 360

B *Economic history*

All the Scandinavian countries experienced an industrial revolution in the second half of the nineteenth century, although Finland's was a generation behind the others. After 1945, governments were forced to reconsider policies and look further outside their own region to develop trade. All the Scandinavian states experienced a decline in both their primary and industrial sectors, alongside a big increase in the service sector, which accounted for over 60 per cent of the workforce across the region by the 1990s.

Agriculture remained important to the Danish economy. In 1945 over 60 per cent of Danish land was cultivated. Before 1939 much of the farming had been on a cooperative basis. After 1945 many farms were consolidated, so that by Western European standards the average

Danish holding was second in size only to a British farm. Agricultural produce made up one-quarter of all Danish exports. Britain was a big market, and to preserve this trade Denmark joined the EEC in 1973, at the same time as Britain.

Denmark's industrial and service sectors expanded rapidly. Between 1960 and 1970 investment in manufacturing more than doubled, accompanied by a rate of urbanisation that was double the European average. The government was so concerned by an exodus of the rural population that a Regional Development Act was passed in 1958 to stimulate rural employment: industries received grants and cheap loans to set up in rural areas. There were also efforts to encourage economic activity on Denmark's sixty-five small islands.

Denmark's fishing industry prospered. Fishing catches tripled in size in the 1960s, and entry into the EEC also gave Danish fleets access to other waters. In 1988 the Danish fishing catch outweighed Norway's. The service sector also expanded: it employed over 75 per cent of Denmark's work force by 1990. In contrast, the shipbuilding and textile industries were devastated by competition from Pacific states.

Mainly due to a boom economy in the late 1950s and early 1960s, Denmark's population of approximately five million had one of the world's highest standards of living. It also had a generous welfare state, governments spending over 10 per cent of Gross National Product on social services during the 1960s. However, there were also strains. Parts of the economy stagnated in the 1970s and 80s, with a growth rate falling below 1.5 per cent by the end of the 1980s, and then below zero at a time when some neighbouring economies were prospering. Inflation was also a periodic problem, at times running at over 10 per cent, and attempts to curb it had variable success. Economic concerns fuelled the major debate over further progress towards economic and monetary union within Europe at the time of the Maastricht Treaty negotiations in the 1990s.

KEY ISSUE
How and why did the Danish economy run into difficulties from the 1970s?

3 ↪ NORWAY

A *Political history*

The Germans still occupied Norway in May 1945. Although outright collaboration had not been extensive, after the war there were 18 000 arrests for Nazi activities, and many Norwegians were banned from the professions and lost their civil rights.

King Haakon VII and his government-in-exile returned from London in 1945. Norway was a constitutional monarchy: a 165-member parliament, the *Storting*, had sovereign power. Post-war politics were dominated by the Social Democrats, led by Einar Gerhardsen. The Communists had increased their support during the war, but it declined afterwards. Eventually the Social Democrats were weakened by the defection of a left wing, which became the pacifist Socialist People's Party. In 1965 the Social Democrats were finally defeated and a coalition government of four Centre parties succeeded them. From 1973 the Conservatives almost doubled their electoral support, at the expense of the Centre. However, for most of the period between 1963 and 1981, and again between 1986 and 1989, the Social Democrats were in power. A new phenomenon in the 1980s was the advent of the radical Progress Party, which gained 13 per cent of the vote in 1989. It complained particularly about high taxes and immigration. It was the Centre which lost support.

Norway had the most westward orientation of the Scandinavian states. It joined NATO, and its long coastline and natural harbours made it strategically important to the Alliance. However, like Denmark, Norway was anxious to avoid provocation and refused access to NATO ships, nuclear warheads or bases. NATO had to rely instead on bases in Greenland and Iceland to guard the Northern approaches to the Atlantic.

Norway applied to join the EEC at the same time as Denmark and Britain, but withdrew its application after a negative vote in a referendum. This result was repeated when Norway renewed its application in November 1992. A coalition government was formed after the 1989 election, in which Labour emerged as the largest party with sixty-three seats, followed by the Communists with thirty-seven. The government resigned in October 1989 over the issue of Community membership. It was succeeded by a minority Labour government under Gro Harlem Brundtland, and this government survived for several years.

> **KEY ISSUE**
>
> *Why did Norway reject membership of the European Community?*

See pages 349 and 351

B *Economic history*

The development of Norway's industry had been heavily influenced by the application of cheap hydroelectric power in the late nineteenth century. This in turn encouraged the development of high-energy industries like aluminium smelting. A second industrial revolution occurred in the late 1960s with the discovery of off-shore oil. By the 1990s oil and gas made up 49 per cent of Norway's exports. The income earned helped to pay for major improvements to Norway's communications network and Norway developed from the poorest into the richest Scandinavian state.

Then Norway's economy, like that of most European states, suffered a recession in the 1970s, partly due to the oil crisis. There was another economic boom in the 1980s, based on North Sea oil. However, there were also worrying signs. One was foreign competition: this particularly affected Norway's shipbuilding industry. There were disputes with Russia over rights to natural gas below the sea level in the Barents Sea. Even more worrying was the gradual exhaustion of the oilfields and a fall in oil prices from 1986. Two of Norway's staples, agriculture and fishing, also faced an uncertain future.

Norway's farms were small, family-run and uncompetitive, even when subsidised by the State. Farmers were therefore very unenthu-

> **KEY ISSUE**
>
> *Why, and with what results, did the Norwegian economy boom and decline in this period?*

siastic about the European Community. Nevertheless farming declined, and there was rural depopulation in the South and West as towns expanded. Agriculture, forestry and fishing made up only 5.8 per cent of Norway's workforce by 1990. Yet Norway's merchant and fishing fleets had been vitally important to the economy, the fishing fleet in particular having expanded from 4 000 000 to 14 000 000 tons between 1948 and 1987.

The slowdown of growth in the late 1980s, accompanied by inflation and unemployment, provoked strikes and a debate over Norway's future. Governments tried to encourage the development of engineering and other industries to provide a secure long-term base for growth. Inevitably, possible membership of the European Union was a major issue.

4 ⌐ SWEDEN

A *Political history*

Neutral Sweden traded with Germany during the Second World War, but was also nervous of a German invasion. Sweden's neutrality provoked a strong debate after 1945, for example about whether the country should have done more to accept refugees. There was also controversy in the 1990s when it was publically revealed that Swedish governments had made extensive preparations to accommodate the Nazis and implement racist policies should Swedish independence be seriously threatened.

In 1945 there was unanimity that Sweden's neutrality should continue, and that there should be no commitments to either side in the Cold War. Political life was relatively uneventful. The monarch, as Head of State, did not participate in government. A one-chamber Parliament of 349 members was elected for a three-year period (four years from 1994). However, Sweden was a decentralised State, with local authorities having considerable powers.

As in Denmark and Norway, the Social Democrats were a strong force, and under Prime Minister Erlander they dominated post-war politics, governing Sweden between 1933 and 1976 and from 1982. They consistently gained 45 per cent of the electorate's vote, and their dominance was built upon material prosperity: Sweden was one of the wealthiest countries in Europe and for two generations was a model of equality, social welfare and stability. After a decline in the 1960s, the Social Democrats rallied and beat off the Centre in 1968. Other parties succeeded in forming a coalition government between 1976 and 1982, and after that date the Social Democrats relied upon the support of the relatively small Communist and Ecology Parties for a majority. Otherwise, the relatively moderate Swedish Communists exerted little influence. The Liberals were the strongest of the Centre parties. The Greens had twenty members of parliament by 1988. The relative decline of Social Democrat fortunes in the later 1980s reflected growing concerns that Sweden could no longer afford what was probably the most extensive welfare state in the world.

There was a political crisis in 1986 when Prime Minister Olaf Palme was assassinated in mysterious circumstances. Palme's successor, Ingvar Carlsson, was forced to impose a freeze on wages and prices and a ban on strikes in 1990. This was evidence that Sweden's much-vaunted model welfare state could no longer be financed by an economy running into serious problems, although Sweden remained wealthy by European standards.

The Social Democrats were finally defeated in the September 1991 election. They secured 37.6 per cent of the vote. However, a 21-member coalition government was set up comprising Moderates, Liberals, the Centre Party and Christian Democrats, and the Moderate Carl Bildt became Prime Minister. There was an unprecedented period of political and social disagreement, ending the clear political consensus which had held that for much of the post-war period, Sweden's welfare democracy had been the best system for everybody.

B *Economic history*

Until the 1980s the Swedish economy was the most successful of all the Scandinavian economies. Like Norway, Sweden had undergone an industrial revolution in the late nineteenth century, based upon hydroelectric power, an important factor given Sweden's relative lack of alternative power sources. Nevertheless, by the 1970s Sweden had to import 75 per cent of its energy needs, despite the high cost of oil. Inevitably, the Swedes looked for alternatives: by the 1990s almost 20 per cent of energy needs were met by nuclear power, although this policy was controversial, and the Swedish Parliament planned to close all nuclear plants by 2010.

The economy was relatively unaffected by the Second World War. After 1945 growth rates were high, and industrial output doubled in the ten years after 1954. Exports doubled between 1955 and 1965. However, in addition to the growing energy problem, by the 1980s Sweden's traditional industries of steel and shipbuilding were collapsing. Expensive and high-quality Swedish exports became uncompetitive, a serious problem for a country which exported half of its industrial output. The economy grew by less than 2 per cent a year in the 1980s, and the currency was devalued by 16 per cent in 1986.

Newer industries did better than traditional ones. The motor industry was crucial, exporting 75 per cent of its output. Electrical goods, chemicals, plastics and engineering products were also important to the export market. Swedish farming was relatively large-scale but not dependent on the export market. More and more people worked in the service sector, which employed 75 per cent of the work force by 1990.

Many people at home and abroad regarded Sweden as a social experiment. There was a generous welfare system, paid for mainly by

> **KEY ISSUE**
>
> *How important were the Social Democrats in Sweden, and what was the significance of Sweden's welfare state?*

> **KEY ISSUE**
>
> *How significant were political changes in Sweden in the 1980s and early 1990s?*

> **KEY ISSUE**
>
> *What developments took place in the Swedish economy during this period, and with what results?*

the State. For a long time unemployment was virtually non-existent, and there was a high proportion of women in the labour force. Wages, and indirect taxes, continued to rise. However, there were growing problems. Swedes saved little and spent a lot on consumable goods. There were social strains, reflected in a high divorce rate. The recession in the 1980s meant shortages of services and housing, and strikes by dissatisfied workers. World recession, foreign competition and an expensive welfare state meant that even a model social democracy like Sweden could not live beyond its means forever. Swedes entered the 1990s less confident about their future than for several decades. Applying to join the European Community in July 1991 was seen as a possible way of easing economic and social concerns.

See page 351

5 ⤳ FINLAND

A *Political history*

Finland occupied a unique political position among the Scandinavian States after 1945. Following their victory over Finland in the Second World War, the Soviets continued to regard it as part of their sphere of influence. Although Finland was not part of the Soviet Bloc, the Kremlin interfered openly in Finnish politics, making for uncertainty. The USSR also made use of a Soviet–Finnish Defence Treaty, which provided for joint military consultations, to send its troops into Finland.

Unlike its Scandinavian neighbours, Finland was a republic. There was one parliamentary chamber of 200 members, elected by proportional representation for a four-year period. The President was elected for six years by direct popular vote. The Social Democrats did not have the same hold in Finland as in other Scandinavian states, mainly because until 1966 the USSR insisted that they be kept out of government. Instead, the Soviets approved the election of Juko Paasikivi as President until 1956, followed by Urho Kekkonen. Both men were leaders of the Agrarian Party, and the Kremlin worked openly to secure Kekkonen's election.

The Finnish Communist Party was much stronger than its counterparts in other Scandinavian states. It made a failed attempt at a *coup* in 1948. Thereafter it competed in parliamentary elections, and frequently gained up to 20 per cent of the vote.

Soviet interference, and the refusal of political parties other than the Agrarians and the Simonites, a breakaway group from the Social Democrats, to work with the Communists, made it difficult to achieve stable government. Elections were fought by several parties, and there were eight major parties in Parliament. In the twenty years after 1945 there were twenty-five different governments.

Finnish governments were sometimes criticised abroad for 'Finlandisation', or allowing the USSR to dominate a supposedly independent country. But the Finns could not risk upsetting such a powerful

KEY ISSUE

Why was Finland so closely tied to the USSR, and with what consequences?

neighbour which had been a recent enemy, and were understandably reluctant to do anything, particularly in foreign policy, which might annoy the Kremlin. Therefore the Finns adopted a policy of neutrality. After Kekkonen's death in 1981, the USSR became preoccupied with its own problems and Soviet influence declined. Nevertheless, in 1982 the Kremlin still conspired with the Centre Party to prevent the election of the Social Democratic Mauno Koivisto as President. The attempt failed, and Koivisto was also re-elected in 1986. The Social Democratic Martii Ahtisaari was elected President in 1994.

The failure of the Left was reflected in the fortunes of the Finnish Communist Party, whose support declined to about 10 per cent of the popular vote from the 1970s onwards. The Communists were also split between hardline supporters of the Moscow line and 'EuroCommunists', who followed a more independent stance. In 1987 Gorbachev's USSR accepted a Conservative, Harri Holkeri, as Prime Minister for the first time, and 1980s Finnish governments were coalitions of Social Democrats and Conservatives. In the March 1991 elections the largest parties were the Centre Party with fifty-five seats (24 per cent of the vote) and the Social Democrats with forty-eight seats (22 per cent). A coalition government of the Centre Party and the Conservative National Coalition Party was set up with the Centre Party's Esko Aho as Prime Minister. Finland had finally escaped from the shadow of its once-powerful neighbour.

> **KEY ISSUE**
>
> *How and why did Soviet influence in Finland decline?*

B *Economic history*

Historically the Finnish economy had lagged behind that of its Scandinavian neighbours. It remained relatively undeveloped after 1945: almost 50 per cent of Finns lived from farming or forestry. The economic situation was hampered by Finland having to give manufactured goods to the USSR as reparations for the war.

However, the Finnish economy underwent a dramatic transformation from the late 1950s. There was industrial development, particularly in engineering and metal goods. Many of these products were exported to the USSR and Finland's EFTA partners. Other exports included electronic goods, shipping, chemicals and processed food, whilst forestry products made up 36 per cent. However, Finland became heavily dependent on imports of raw materials. Because oil was expensive, Finland developed a nuclear energy programme in the 1950s: it accounted for 15 per cent of energy needs by the 1990s.

By the 1980s the Finnish economy had been transformed. In 1992 only 8.6 per cent of the workforce was in agriculture, compared to 22.7 per cent in industry and 63.7 per cent in the service sector. Finns had a higher standard of living even than their Swedish and Danish neighbours. The growth rate of the economy was consistently above the European average, whilst inflation and unemployment were low. Foreign investment in Finland increased. However, in the late 1980s these trends were reversed. Industry became less competitive, imports

> **KEY ISSUE**
>
> *In what ways, and with what consequences, did the Finnish economy undergo changes in this period?*

increased faster than exports, and Finland fell behind Sweden and Denmark economically. It was hoped that membership of the European Community would benefit the economy, and Finland applied for membership in March 1992.

6 ⤳ THE BALTIC STATES

A *Introduction: The Baltic States to 1945*

The peoples of Estonia, Latvia and Lithuania were descended from settlers on the shores of the Baltic; and occupied lands much fought over by neighbours to both East and West. By the late eighteenth century the region was part of the Russian Empire, and later subject to a policy of 'Russification', which included the imposition of Russian as the official language. However, the Baltic peoples retained their national and cultural characteristics, expressed particularly through religion. Most Lithuanians were Roman Catholic, whilst Latvia and Estonia were predominantly Lutheran.

After the First World War the new Soviet army was expelled from what were by now three independent Republics. The interwar period saw attempts to establish fragile democracies in States without democratic roots. Parliamentary government proved weak and indecisive, and authoritarian regimes were set up in all three States. There was discrimination, particularly against Jews and Poles in Lithuania.

The three states were well aware of their strategic vulnerability. In a desperate search for security the Republics signed non-aggression pacts with the USSR, whilst at the same time hoping to keep Stalin at arm's length. Although the Western powers acknowledged the independence of the Republics, in reality they accepted, like Stalin, that the Baltic lay within the Soviet sphere of influence. Stalin saw the Republics as a defensive barrier against Germany.

The Baltic States were doomed from the moment that the Germans agreed to Soviet annexation in a supplementary protocol to the Nazi–Soviet Non-Aggression Pact of 23 August 1939. The Soviets forced the three Republics to accept Communist-dominated Popular Front governments which 'requested' accession to the Soviet Union in August 1940.

The Baltic States suffered terribly in the Second World War. Under Soviet occupation thousands, including the intellectual élite, were deported and killed. Consequently, many inhabitants welcomed the invading Germans as liberators in June 1941. However, Nazi policies were equally brutal. The Baltic Germans were resettled in German-occupied Poland whilst the three Republics, along with Byelorussia, were formed into the German province of *Reichskommissariat Ostland*. Baltic Jews were massacred wholesale, often with the assistance of the local populations. Some inhabitants volunteered, or were pressed into German military service. The rest of the population lived miserably: for

> **KEY ISSUE**
>
> *Why were the Baltic States insecure in the interwar period?*

example, Estonia's population declined by one-quarter under Nazi occupation. There was so much long-term damage that by 1950 Latvia was the only European state whose population had declined in absolute terms since 1900. The Western Allies largely ignored the fate of the Baltic peoples for several reasons: they were inaccessible, the West did not wish to antagonise its Soviet ally by championing their cause, and there was considerable ignorance about the region, summed up by a comment by the British Minister Lord Halifax in 1941 that 'he did not think that the Baltic peoples were peoples who deserved very much respect or consideration'.

In 1944 the Red Army re-entered the Baltic States. Partisans resisted these new invaders into the 1950s. Reincorporation into the USSR was accepted by the West as a *fait accompli*. Latvia, Lithuania and Estonia were the only pre-war members of the League of Nations not to be restored as independent states in 1945.

Since, for most of the period of this book, the Baltic Republics were part of the Soviet Union, their political and economic history will be dealt with in the following pages, but they had no independent foreign policy to consider.

> **KEY ISSUE**
>
> *What impact did the Second World War have on the Baltic States?*

B *Political history from 1945*

Soviet policy in the Baltic region was brutal. Stalin formed 'Left Fronts' led by non-Communists, but dominated by the leaders of small Communist parties (there were only 700 members in Estonia). There were mass executions and deportations in an attempt to enforce compliance from the inhabitants. Deportation was also part of the enforced collectivisation of agriculture, largely complete by the end of the 1940s. By 1952 about 250 000 Lithuanians, 136 000 Latvians and 124 000 Estonians had been deported; the survivors were allowed by Khrushchev to return after 1956. In addition, Estonia had to cede 5 per cent of its territory to Russia, and Latvia 2 per cent.

As political entities Estonia, Latvia and Lithuania virtually disappeared until the late 1980s, becoming part of the Soviet political structure. Because of the region's proximity to NATO countries, the Soviets were sensitive about security and packed it with military hardware. They also flooded the area with Russian immigrants, upsetting the demographic balance of a region which already suffered from a low birth rate and ageing population. By 1970 Estonians made up 60 per cent of Estonia's population, compared to 88 per cent in 1939; whilst the percentage of Latvians in Latvia fell from 75 to 57 per cent. 80 per cent of Lithuania's population in the 1980s was still indigenous, partly because other than Jews and Poles, it had suffered fewer deportations and depletions during the war.

The Soviet authorities suppressed any shows of dissent. Religious practice was also periodically persecuted. Occasionally, shows of dissatisfaction broke out. In 1972 a group of Estonians appealed to the United Nations against oppression, Soviet troops had to suppress

> **KEY ISSUE**
>
> *How did Soviet occupation affect the political and economic life of the Baltic region?*

MAP 28
The Baltic States

How effectively did the Soviet government enforce conformity in its Baltic territories?

riots in Lithuania and seventeen Latvian Communists described Soviet policies as 'non-Marxist'. However, individualism was expressed mostly through cultural activities, particularly the great annual folk-song festivals.

The USSR also used the Republican Communist parties to enforce conformity, rather than relying on direct control from Moscow. After 1945 many Party members of Baltic descent, but who had been born or educated in Russia, were put in key posts in the three Republics. For example, there were 100 000 of these *Latovicki* in Latvia. They were generally despised by the local populations. Moscow became concerned at the development of 'national Communism', which meant local Communists identifying more with their local power bases than with the political dictates of the Kremlin. Estonia presented a prime example. The Estonian Communist Party was purged in 1950 and Johannes Kabin was appointed First Secretary. As a Russian-educated and Moscow-trained activist, the Kremlin expected him to be its mouthpiece. However, during his lengthy period in office to 1978 he gradually became more sympathetic to his fellow Estonians, and disregarded Soviet orders. Consequently, he was succeeded by a Siberian, Karl Vaino.

'National Communism' also emerged in Lithuania. Antonas Snieckus was First Secretary of the Lithuanian Party until his death in 1974. He promoted several native Lithuanians and tried to avoid the intrigues of Kremlin politics.

The Latvian Communist Party was the most vociferous in challenging Moscow's authority. In 1958 a faction led by Deputy Prime Minister Eduards Berklavs took control of the Party and tried to resist Russification and central control from Moscow. He also tried to end the much-resented immigration of outsiders into Latvia. Khrushchev purged Berklavs and many colleagues on the grounds that 'out of false fear that the Latvian Republic could lose her national character, some comrades tried to artificially hinder the objectively determined process of population resettlement'. The new First Secretary, Arvids Pelse, was Kremlin-trained, and carried out his own purges. In 1966, Pelse became the first native Baltic Communist to be appointed a full member of the Soviet *Politburo*.

KEY ISSUE

What was the significance of 'National Communism'?

Despite outbreaks of 'National Communism' and a fierce determination to preserve their cultural distinctiveness, there was never any question of the Baltic peoples achieving political autonomy before the 1980s. Tensions increased between the indigenous populations and immigrant Russians, the latter often manual workers attracted by the higher standard of living in the three Republics. Only Gorbachev's campaign for reform in the mid-1980s encouraged Baltic reformers and nationalists to believe that autonomy or independence were possibilities.

In the mid-1980s there were demonstrations in support of human rights and commemoration of the signing of the Nazi–Soviet Pact and the 1941 deportations. Reforming Communists increasingly replaced Conservatives at the forefront of Republican parties. The situation was complicated by the emergence of Popular Fronts in all three Republics. These were not political parties but coalitions of reformers, both Communist and non-Communist. Gorbachev, meanwhile, was determined to retain the Republics as integral parts of the Soviet economic and defence structures.

Demands for change soon escalated. The Latvian People's Front, organised in October 1988, was probably the first modern organised political opposition in the USSR. It demanded independence *within* a Socialist federation. In the same month the Popular Front *Sajudis* was founded in Lithuania. It soon announced its 'moral independence' from the USSR. A 'Popular Front for the Support of *Perestroika*' was promoted in Estonia under a former planning official, Edgar Savisaar. A declaration of 'no confidence' in the Soviet government followed. The popular movement for change was also reflected in the great

KEY ISSUE

What was the significance of the Popular Front movement in the Baltic Republics?

'singing revolution' in the autumn of 1988: millions of Baltic citizens 'sang for freedom' in great festivals.

The situation was complicated by the attitude of Russian immigrants. Some of these welcomed the prospect of reform as much as the indigenous populations. Others were anxious to preserve a federal structure which they saw as their best protection. Some Russians, supported by Moscow, formed 'Interfront' movements in late 1988 in Latvia and Estonia, and the pro-Moscow *Yedinstvo* or 'Unity' movement in Lithuania in May 1989. These all aimed to protect Russian interests and opposed new laws which removed voting rights from Russians and removed the status of Russian as the official language. The Interfronts organised strikes.

Prospects for change would largely depend on the relationship between the Republican Communist Parties and the Popular Fronts. In Estonia, where Vaino Valjas was Party leader, the relationship was fruitful. However, there were also more radical voices which, far from seeking an accommodation with the USSR or a new federation, wanted nothing to do with the Soviets. They based their stand on the illegal annexation of the Baltic States in 1940.

The Supreme Soviets of the Baltic Republics made declarations in 1989 and 1990 that they would only recognise federal laws in which they had had a say in formulating. There was an opportunity for ordinary citizens to have their say when elections to the Supreme Soviet of the USSR were held in March 1989. Previously such elections had been a rubber stamp for Soviet policies. This time there was an opportunity for individual candidates to oppose the official Communist Party nominees. Some Party members stood as individuals because of the unpopularity of the official parties, and if they were approved by the Popular Fronts, they were frequently unopposed. Most seats were won by candidates backed by the Popular Fronts, whilst Interfront candidates generally did badly. Nationalist affiliations proved more important than political allegiance.

The election was followed in May 1989 by a joint inaugural assembly of the three Popular Fronts in Tallinn. It passed a resolution 'to coordinate joint policies of the biggest popular movements of the Soviet Baltic countries and to make the general public of the Soviet Union and the world at large aware of the democratic aspirations pursued by the Baltic popular movements'.

Of more dramatic and immediate effect was the 'Baltic Way' of 23 August 1989, the anniversary of the Nazi–Soviet Pact: a human chain of one million Estonians, Latvians and Lithuanians linked hands across the Republics. This event prompted Gorbachev's first openly hostile public statement about developments in the region: he warned against 'nationalist excesses'. Gorbachev was anxious to avert the possibility of Baltic Communist Parties identifying with the Republics and breaking away from Moscow. However, by insisting in effect that they choose between breaking with the Popular Fronts and sticking with Moscow, or distancing themselves from Moscow, he unintentionally pushed them into the latter course. In December 1989 the Lithuanian

KEY ISSUE

How and why did the break with the USSR come about?

Communist Party voted for independence from the USSR and the creation of an independent Socialist Lithuania. Gorbachev visited Lithuania in January 1990 and promised a new law of secession, therefore appearing to accept the *fait accompli.*

C *Independence*

Events were moving quickly towards independence. Elections to the Lithuanian Supreme Soviet were held in February 1990. *Sajudis* candidates were victorious and set up a parliament, the *Seim.* It voted for independence in March. The *Sajudis* leader Vytautas Landsbergis became President of the new Republic.

The Popular Fronts in Latvia and Estonia also came out in favour of independence before the end of 1990, prompted partly by the emergence of more radical 'citizens' congresses' in the Republics, which were demanding a break with Moscow. The Estonian Supreme Soviet declared its independence in March 1990, followed by Latvia in May. The three Republics drafted laws preventing conscription of their citizens into the Red Army. Also in May they formed a Baltic *Entente* and established a joint Council, hoping to enlist international support.

Gorbachev reacted strongly. An economic blockade was imposed against Lithuania. Gorbachev proposed a cumbersome method of secession designed to make its realisation difficult, and ultimately dependent upon the approval of the full Soviet Parliament. However, Gorbachev's own difficulties closer to home opened the way for full independence without an all-out confrontation. Boris Yeltsin, now in power in the Russian Republic, declared his support for Baltic independence. In June 1990 Gorbachev offered the Republics 'special status' in a new federation: something which the Baltic Republican governments had requested in 1988, but which they now considered far too inadequate.

Effectively there was a stalemate, broken only by the dramatic Moscow *coup* of 19 August 1991. The coup threatened to produce a hardline Soviet regime opposed to any concessions. Equally, a weakened Yeltsin regime would be less able to resist audacious moves towards independence by the Republics. On the day after the *coup* the Estonian Parliament declared its full sovereignty. It was recognised by Yeltsin on 24 August and then by the European Community. In September Estonia became a member of the United Nations. A referendum in June 1991, in which Estonia's 475 000 Russian inhabitants were not allowed to vote, approved a new Constitution. The subsequent parliamentary elections were won by the National-Conservative Party, with Mart Laar as President.

See page 123

Events also moved quickly in Latvia. Following Latvia's declaration of independence in May 1990, Moscow had moved troops into Latvia, and in January 1991 these had occupied the press building in Riga, causing several fatalities. In a referendum in March 1991, 73.7 per cent of Latvian voters chose independence. On the day of the Moscow *coup*, the Red Army Commander in the Baltic declared a state of emergency, and on 20 August the Latvian Parliament voted for immediate independence. Yeltsin gave his recognition, and some Russian troops were withdrawn in September. The first full and free Latvian elections were not held until June 1993.

Meanwhile Lithuania was suffering from the Soviet economic blockade, which caused disruption, particularly to oil supplies. A compromise in June 1990 led to a suspension of the declaration of independence whilst trade sanctions were lifted. But there was criticism and rumours of plots. In the uncertainty following Prime Minister Kasimiera's resignation in January 1991, Soviet paratroopers stormed the press building and television tower in Vilnius, and occupied the Ministry of Internal Affairs. Thirteen civilians were killed. The Lithuanian government responded with a referendum in February. This produced a vote of almost 80 per cent in favour of independence. There were border incidents, and on 19 August Soviet forces again stormed the Vilnius radio and television stations. As elsewhere, the Moscow *coup* was decisive: on 22 August 1991 the Lithuanian Supreme Soviet banned the Communist Party and confiscated its assets. There were similar measures in Estonia and Latvia. Russian troops were soon withdrawn from Lithuania, and there was Soviet recognition of its independence in September. An agreement to withdraw Soviet troops permanently from Latvia was signed in March 1994. The Red Army was prepared to leave the Baltic States because it faced its own problems of finance and morale at home, there was the threat of pressure from the West, and because the apparent ending of the Cold War made the Baltic region less strategically significant.

The Baltic States were determined to go their own way. Unlike other former Soviet Republics they refused to join the Commonwealth of Independent States, and they reduced their trade dependence on Russia, creating more links with the West instead.

Lithuania's politics remained volatile after independence. There were four Prime Ministers during 1992, and *Sajudis* was well beaten in parliamentary elections by LDAP, the Democratic Workers' Party of Lithuania, which contained many ex-Communists. The presidential election of February 1993 was comfortably won by the ex-Communist Algirdas Brazauskas, ahead of Landsbirgis. Under Brazauskas's leadership, Lithuania applied to join NATO and established diplomatic relations with Poland.

In Estonia the government of Mart Laar faced difficulties from people who objected to its tough economic policies designed to prepare the way for a market economy, and also from a Parliament dominated by the right wing. In local government elections in October 1993 the opposition made big gains, with Russians often supporting former Communist candidates. President Lennart Meri was sometimes at loggerheads with Parliament and nationalist groups increased their support, especially the Popular Front of Edgar Savisaar and 'Secure Home', led by Tiit Väki. Estonia's Democratic Labour Party was led by

KEY ISSUE

How significant were the political developments that took place in the Baltic States after independence?

the virulently nationalist Juris Bojärs, who attacked free market reforms.

The situation was most difficult in Latvia. It had the largest Russian population of the three Republics, and over one-fifth of the electorate was not Latvian in origin, and voted for candidates who were often former Communists or represented the interests of Russian speakers. The government elected in June 1993 was a coalition of the centrist 'Latvia's Way' (containing former Communists and nationalist members of the Popular Front) and the Farmers' Union, with some support from the Democratic Centre and Christian Democrats. Radical nationalists provided the main opposition.

Therefore the three Baltic Republics entered the second half of the 1990s still with uncertainties ahead. The future was particularly uncertain for those Russians who had settled there during Soviet rule. They were excluded from automatic citizenship of the new states. Tensions did not erupt into violence, but Russians were apprehensive of naturalisation laws passed in 1993, and which restricted alien working and language rights. The Latvian law was so strict with its quotas and ten-year residence qualification that it evoked protests from the Council of Europe. Perhaps more alarming was the opposition to the new regimes from virulent nationalists inside Russia, particularly Vladimir Zhirinovsky, who threatened a new military crusade.

D *Economic history*

The three Baltic Republics were amongst the most productive regions of the USSR, although integration into the Soviet economic system after the Second World War caused considerable disruption as the Baltic economies were subjected to the rigours of the Stalinist command economy. Integration was successful to the extent that within forty years of the 1940 annexations, 90 per cent of Baltic industries were run solely or jointly by All-Union authorities.

After 1945 the Soviets instituted a large-scale industrialisation programme, regardless of environmental consequences. The programme necessitated the large-scale immigration of Russian industrial workers, which created social and political problems. Immigration particularly affected the more industrialised Estonia and Latvia.

There was heavy Soviet investment in the Baltic Republics, particularly large capital projects. The principal emphasis was on manufacturing, and also the oil shale industry in Estonia, used to provide energy for Leningrad. There was extensive urbanisation: by 1970 65 per cent of Estonians lived in cities, where the main industries were oil shale, cement, chemicals and textiles. 62.5 per cent of Latvia's population was urban by 1970, and Russians were concentrated in Latvia's cities. Less than 40 per cent of Riga's population was ethnically Latvian. The principal Latvian industries were steel, agricultural machinery and motor vehicles. 50 per cent of Lithuania's population was urban by 1970. A notable feature of the Lithuanian economy was

> **KEY ISSUE**
>
> *What were the effects of Soviet economic policy in the Baltic Republics?*

the large power plants which served other Soviet Republics besides Lithuania.

Agriculture in the Baltic Republics was less developed. It was disrupted by forced collectivisation after 1945. Estonian agriculture was amongst the most productive in the USSR, but it only regained pre-war levels by the 1960s, and much of the farm produce came from the small household plots allowed to peasants.

The future direction of the Baltic economies became a major issue of controversy during the struggle for autonomy and then independence in the later 1980s. The Soviets were anxious to maintain economic ties, which they claimed to be of mutual benefit to themselves and the Baltic Republics. In May 1989 the Baltic Popular Fronts called for economic independence by 1990, but throughout 1989 Moscow continued to assert its control of crucial areas like heavy industry, fuel and raw materials. Because of the close integration of the Russian and Baltic economies, even had there been a genuine desire for separation on the Soviet side, the practical difficulties would have been immense. As it was, the problems were compounded by the Soviet reaction to Lithuania's breakaway, involving a blockade on oil and gas supplies.

During 1990 the three Baltic Republics sought further economic cooperation between themselves. Economic agreements signed in April 1990 were intended as a first move towards a 'Baltic Common Market' and market economies. When a breakaway was inevitable, Russia embarked on a series of trade agreements with the three states. Russia was concerned not just with its own well-being, but that of its citizens still living in the Baltic Republics.

Independence meant an uncertain future. The experience of Estonia provided a good example of optimism and harsh reality side by side. Small private businesses were quickly established: 20 000 (including 5000 private farms) were set up within one year. Moscow recognised Estonia's economic autonomy in November 1989. In 1990 Estonia's State and private businesses were put on an equal tax footing. However, the real problems began as Estonia tried to disentangle its economy from the Russian one. The Estonian and Soviet budgets were separated in 1991, and Estonia began to introduce decontrol of prices. The result was rampant inflation, rationing and severe food shortages, and a political crisis. Estonia introduced its own currency in 1992, and the economic situation gradually improved, but life remained difficult. This was hardly surprising given that 90 per cent of Estonia's trade had been with its old Soviet neighbours, Russia and the Ukraine.

Latvia and Lithuania experienced similar problems of economic readjustment. The price of political independence proved high. However, economic conditions gradually improved. Currencies were stabilised and austerity programmes were introduced to meet IMF rules on lending. Although austerity measures were unpopular with many of the population, particularly those who found it difficult to seize the advantages possible in a free market economy, they did encourage foreign investment in the region. Estonia in particular developed into one of the fastest growing economies in Europe.

KEY ISSUE

How successfully did the Baltic economies cope with independence?

7 ↬ BIBLIOGRAPHY

The history of Northern Europe is a comparatively neglected area of study outside of the region itself, and this is reflected in the relatively small number of accessible books available. A general background history of Scandinavia is *A History of Scandinavia* by T. Derry (London, 1979). A useful book on Denmark is *The Danish Economy in the Twentieth Century* by H. Johansen (London, 1987). Some relatively recent Norwegian history is covered in *A History of Modern Norway 1814–1972* by T. Derry (OUP, 1973). Two useful books on modern Sweden are *Swedish Politics During the Twentieth Century* by S. Hadenius (Stockholm, 1988) and *Sweden: The Nation's History* (University of Minnesota Press, 1983). Studies of Finland include *Finland in the Twentieth Century* by D. Kirby (2nd edition, London, 1984), *A Brief History of Finland* by M. Klinge (Helsinki, 1987) and *Finland at Peace and War 1918–1993* by H. Tillotson (London, 1993).

There is little available on the Baltic States. However, *The Baltic Revolution: Estonia, Latvia, Lithuania and the Path to Independence* by A. Lieven (Yale University Press, 1993) is useful, as is *The Baltic States: Years of Dependence 1940–1991* by R-J. Misiunas and R. Taagepera (2nd edition, Farnborough, 1993).

8 ↬ ESSAY QUESTIONS

1. (a) Outline the main political developments in any *two* of Denmark, Norway, Sweden or Finland in the forty years after the end of the Second World War;
   (b) 'Moderate government and model social democracies'. How accurate is this description of the political and social life of the two countries you have chosen?
2. (a) Why was the European Economic Community an important issue for the Scandinavian states?
   (b) Compare and contrast the policies of any *two* Scandinavian states towards the European Economic Community between the 1940s and the 1990s.
3. How accurate is the judgement that 'It was inevitable, but with much reluctance, that the Scandinavian states abandoned their traditional isolationism in favour of integration into the mainstream of European affairs in the second half of the twentieth century?'
4. How successfully did the Scandinavian states adapt to new economic circumstances in the second half of the twentieth century?
5. (a) Outline the stages by which Estonia, Latvia and Lithuania achieved their independence from the USSR;
   (b) Why did it take them more than forty years after the Second World War to achieve it?
6. What were the political and economic consequences of achieving independence for the Baltic States?

9 ∽ INTERPRETING CARTOONS: A SOURCES EXERCISE

Many of the points that need to be considered when analysing cartoons as a form of historical evidence are similar to those involved in evaluating photographs. However, it is also important to consider the specific implications of analysing cartoons.

See page 211

Cartoons are often used to illustrate an event or topic in a satirical way. They usually have a humorous element but also employ a range of techniques – often sarcasm, irony or outright ridicule – in order to make a particular point. Some historical cartoons have achieved a fame which survives long after the event itself has faded in the memory: a classic example is the *Punch* cartoon of the German Kaiser Wilhelm II 'dropping the pilot', his Chancellor Bismarck, in 1890.

Usually the cartoonist is trying to make a particular point, and in order to do so, exaggeration may be more important to the cartoonist than the literal truth. Cartoons **can** be a valuable source of historical evidence if interpreted with care. When faced with a cartoon to analyse, start with the 'simple' questions:

- What event or topic is being represented? Can any individuals be identified?
- There is usually a caption or attribution. What information does it give?
- There are often symbols in cartoons. If so, what do they represent and how are they used?

Having worked out the message of the cartoon, consider these points:

- What point is the cartoonist trying to make? Is it a serious or satirical point? Has the cartoonist got a particular point of view?
- Is the cartoon a reliable source of evidence about the topic? Is it just the point of view of the cartoonist? Why was it produced? What was the likely intended audience?
- Does the message represent a widely-held view at the time?
- What are the uses and limitations of the source as evidence? Does it give any historical insights?

As with historical photographs, you must make your analysis of cartoons specific to the particular example, and not make generalised comments about cartoons without any particular context.

Bearing these points in mind, study the following collection of Danish cartoons, which have been translated into English, concerning the debate over Denmark's entry into the European Community. For each cartoon answer the questions above as well as you can, and consider the extent to which the cartoons add to our understanding of the issues involved.

PICTURE 32
'Party leaders in the Socialist People's Party are at a loss over EU policy.'

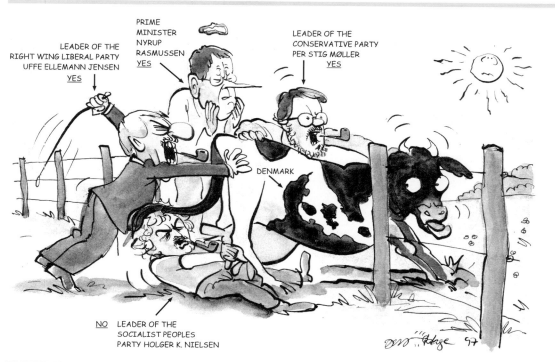

PICTURE 33
'The debate about the Amsterdam Treaty is still at a rather low level.'

PICTURE 34

'It looks as if we are going to have another vote on the EU.'

PICTURE 35

'Danish Prime Minister Paul Nyrup Rasmussen tries to sell the Amsterdam Treaty to the Danes.'

PICTURE 36

'Danish politicans try to talk a voter into saying "yes" to the Amsterdam Treaty.'

8 Integration and Cooperation in Europe

INTRODUCTION

The idea of a united Europe is not new. At the beginning of the nineteenth century Napoleon had tried to unite Europe by force. Later there were attempts at integration which were confined to economic objectives: notably the *Zollverein*, or economic association of German states which preceded the creation of the German Empire in 1871.

After 1918, some groups advocated integration as a means of avoiding the national rivalries regarded as the root cause of the catastrophic First World War. In 1920s European interest in federalist ideas was shown by statesmen such as Briand in France and Beneš in Czechoslovakia. In 1930, Briand advocated a European union to operate within the framework of the League of Nations. However, during the 1930s Western European leaders were preoccupied with Hitler's expansionism and mostly lost interest in such schemes.

The Second World War renewed interest in some form of integration. There were idealists who felt, as in 1918, that integration was the only long-term alternative to national conflict. But there was also short-term reasoning based on a realisation that Europe's once pre-eminent position in the world had been damaged, probably beyond repair. In 1913 Western Europe had accounted for almost half the world's industrial production, a figure down to one-quarter by 1945. Much of Western Europe was devastated or bankrupt. Therefore, there were sound practical reasons for mutual help between nations. This chapter traces the development of the European Union from its beginnings after the Second World War to the expansion and closer integration of the early 1990s, by which time it was one of the largest economic blocs in the world, and examines some of the issues that both united and divided the Union along the way.

1 ⌐ 1945–57: THE ORIGINS OF THE COMMON MARKET

A *Introduction*

In 1944, even before their countries had been liberated from German occupation, the exiled leaders of Belgium, the Netherlands and Luxembourg agreed that after the war their economies should be linked. The resulting Benelux Customs Union came into being on 1 January 1948. Its eventual goal was full economic union.

The victorious British were also concerned about the future, carrying a huge external debt of £4.7 billion. Like other Western European countries Britain was aware of the expansion of Soviet influence in Eastern Europe. Western leaders were concerned that 'going it alone' would make their countries vulnerable to Communist expansion. The USA also favoured European cooperation for this reason. There was also the dilemma of Germany: Western leaders wanted Germany to recover, as a bulwark against Communism, but there was also an understandable fear of a strong Germany. Containing Germany within some form of European organisation might be a solution to the dilemma, as recognised by the Resistance leaders in 1944 when they had declared, 'Only a Federal Union will allow the German people to participate in the life of Europe without being a danger for the rest.'

The French were particularly conscious of the disadvantages of both a weak Germany, susceptible to Communist influence, and a strong Germany which at the very least might compete with France in industrial power. Such fears led to the Brussels Treaty of March 1948, a defensive pact between Britain, France and the Benelux countries. This agreement created the Western European Union (WEU) 'for collaboration in economic, social and cultural matters and for collective self-defence'. The WEU remained in being after 1949 even though the formation of NATO appeared to supersede it.

> **KEY ISSUE**
>
> *What were the attractions of a common market to Western European countries after 1945?*

B *The OEEC*

Jean Monnet, usually regarded as the chief apostle of European unity, saw the advantages of linking Germany so closely with its Western neighbours that cooperation rather than competition would prevail. The Americans were also committed to rebuilding Western Europe through Marshall Aid, and an intergovernmental organisation was required to administer it. Hence the establishment in April 1948 of the Organisation for European Economic Cooperation (OEEC). It represented sixteen states, and although the distribution of Marshall Aid lasted only three years, the OEEC remained as a useful instrument for promoting economic recovery. Its terms of reference were later extended to include all the advanced industrial economies in the non-Communist world, and in 1961 its name was changed to the Organisation for Economic Cooperation and Development (OECD).

See pages 335–6

TIMELINE
Some important dates in European integration

Oct 1947	Formation of BENELUX: customs union of Belgium, The Netherlands and Luxembourg
1948	OEEC set up to administer Marshall Aid
Jan 1949	Formation of COMECON
May 1950	Schuman Plan
April 1951	Setting up of European Coal and Steel Community (ECSC)
March 1957	Treaty of Rome setting up the Common Market
Jan 1958	EEC came into effect
May 1961	European Free Trade Association (EFTA) set up
1961	Britain, Ireland and Denmark applied for membership of EEC
Jan 1962	Agreement to introduce Common Agricultural Policy in 1964
Jan 1963	Negotiations with Britain broken off after de Gaulle veto
July 1967	EEC, ECSC and EURATOM merged into European Community (EC)
	Britain, Ireland , Denmark and Norway re-applied to EEC
July 1968	EC abolished internal tariffs
	Common external tariff established
Dec 1969	Agreement at The Hague to enlarge the EC
Sept 1972	Norway rejected EC membership
Jan 1973	Britain, Ireland and Denmak joined the EC
June 1975	British referendum in favour of continuing membership
March 1979	European Monetary System (EMS) introduced
June 1979	First direct elections to the European Parliament
Jan 1981	Greece joined EC
Dec 1985	Agreement on Single European Market by 1992
Jan 1986	Spain and Portugal joined EC
Dec 1989	Negotiations between EC and EFTA to form European Economic Area (EFA)
July 1990	Beginning of first stage of European Monetary Union (EMU)
Sept 1991	Dissolution of COMECON
Dec 1991	Maastricht Treaty implemented
	European Community becomes the European Union (EU)
Jan 1955	Austria, Finland and Sweden joined EU
July	Under Schengen Agreement, several member states removed all border controls
Dec 1996	Plans to introduce single 'Euro' currency confirmed
	Agreement for Poland, Hungary, the Czech Republic, Slovenia, Estonia and Cyprus to negotiate membership

In May 1949 the Council of Europe was formed. Its objective was to promote European unity in several areas and to protect human rights. At first it had little effective power, despite its declared aim that countries should 'merge certain of their sovereign rights'. Its ineffectiveness was partly due to the opposition of the British, who also objected to proposals for promoting monetary cooperation made by the European Payments Union, created in July 1950.

C *Attitudes towards cooperation*

Britain's attitude towards post-war continental commitments remained ambivalent. Winston Churchill, Britain's wartime leader but now no longer in power, made a speech in Zurich in September 1946 combining vision and realism: he called for cooperation between France and Germany as the basis for a new Europe. He contemplated European unity from the perspective of avoiding future conflict rather than from enthusiasm for potential economic gains. Significantly, he did not mention Britain as a leader of Europe. Like many in Britain he believed that the British were in a unique position in Europe: Britain was Head of the Commonwealth and also had a 'special relationship' with the USA. Therefore, it was felt, Britain could not commit itself wholeheartedly to European union. This belief that Britain was somehow 'different' held it back from full participation in European developments for many years. Britain was also less convinced than its European allies by arguments for European integration because its experience of the war had been different: not having been occupied, and having stood at one stage alone against the enemy, Britain felt a moral superiority, more confident in its isolation and less willing to cede sovereignty to a supranational institution. In contrast, other countries in Western Europe saw distinct advantages in close cooperation. West Germany saw the opportunity of political rehabilitation and economic recovery, although it had stronger economic ties with states in Central Europe. France saw the opportunity to increase its agricultural exports and its industrial growth, whilst tying Germany into a relationship that would prevent future conflict. Italy, Belgium, the Netherlands and Luxembourg saw the possibilities of large export markets for their relatively smaller industries.

Other countries were debarred from membership of a potentially close-knit organisation. The post-war settlement required Austria and Finland to be neutral. Switzerland and Sweden had long-standing traditions of neutrality which might be compromised by membership of a larger union. Spain and Portugal had authoritarian governments and would be uneasy partners. Therefore when the European Economic Community was founded, it actually *increased* the fragmentation of Europe by highlighting the differences between one group of states and others.

See page 370

KEY ISSUE

What was the British attitude towards involvement in Europe?

D *Monnet, the Schuman Plan and the ECSC*

After the war Jean Monnet made significant moves towards integration. Monnet had been Deputy Secretary-General of the League of Nations. During the war he had helped to coordinate allied economic warfare. After the war he became head of the French planning organisation. Although often regarded as an idealist, Monnet also possessed a strong dose of realism. In 1945 he declared,

> The nations of Europe are too circumscribed to give their people the prosperity made possible, and hence necessary, by modern conditions. They will need larger markets ... Prosperity and vital social progress will remain elusive until the nations of Europe form

KEY ISSUE

What part did Monnet and Schuman play in European integration?

a federation or a 'European entity' which will force them into a single economic unit.

Monnet was particularly concerned about Germany and the prospect of its renewed economic dominance after recovery. He persuaded the French foreign minister, Robert Schuman, to adopt the Schuman Plan of May 1950. It was actually drafted by Monnet, but Schuman persuaded the French cabinet to accept it. The Plan pooled the coal and steel resources of Western Europe, to be administered by a joint High Authority. Schuman declared that 'the solidarity between the two countries established by joint production will show that a war between France and Germany becomes not only unthinkable but materially impossible'. The Schuman Plan resulted in the European Coal and Steel Community (ECSC), agreed by the Treaty of Paris in April 1951 and implemented in August 1952. The signatories were France, Germany, Italy and the Benelux countries.

The West Germans and Americans were given advance notice of the Schuman Plan. German Chancellor Konrad Adenauer readily agreed, since the Plan appeared to restore Germany to equality with other states. Britain was not given advance notice, because it was known that Britain would object, and countries had to agree to the principle of **supranationality** before being allowed to take part in negotiations. The British Labour and Conservative parties were united in opposition to ceding any sovereignty. Churchill told his doctor in January 1952, 'I love France and Belgium, but we must not allow ourselves to be pulled down to that level.'

supranationality giving up national sovereignty to an international body

The ECSC's overt objective was to create a common market for coal and steel, with no trade barriers, but rather a common tariff against non-members. However, the motivation behind the organisation was as much political as economic. The Treaty declared that 'the pooling of coal and steel production should...provide for...a first step in the federation of Europe'. The USA backed the ECSC, despite the potential competition it offered to its own economy.

Even more significant in the long run was the fact that the ECSC was to be an important model for the European Community, establishing a structure for integration. Monnet insisted upon this. The High Authority represented the 'general interest of the community': it was supranational, with both a political and administrative role. It could make policy in some areas, for example deciding on a levy on coal and steel firms in order to finance the ECSC. There were also a Council which had the right to approve some decisions; an Advisory Assembly, the precursor of a European Parliament; and a European Court of Justice. For the first time national governments had voluntarily surrendered some of their sovereign powers.

KEY ISSUE

What was the significance of the ECSC in the development of European integration?

The ECSC survived until 1967. It helped to promote economic progress towards a common market in coal and steel, but not without problems. In 1959, when there was overproduction of coal, the Council overruled the High Authority, because national governments refused to cede powers to make decisions on cutbacks. The ECSC was a model for other institutions, but did not directly promote political integration.

E *Defence*

At first little progress was made towards closer European integration in transport, agriculture, health and communications. The first significant step towards cooperation after the creation of the ECSC was the European Defence Community (EDC), set up in May 1952. The idea of a European defence force was supported by Monnet, and arose partly out of fears of West German rearmament, something backed by the USA in its anxiety to increase Western military capability in Europe. The proposals for a European defence organisation were outlined in the Pleven Plan. This gave the strongest say to a Council of Ministers in order to allay fears, particularly British ones, that national armies would be subject to external control. The Plan also specified that the German government would not have control over its own forces: instead these would be under the control of a European army, which would direct only part of member states' forces.

The ECSC Assembly recommended the creation of a European Political Community (EPC), which would have placed the ECSC and EDC under the same umbrella. This was too ambitious a proposal for most politicians. However, the failure to get the EDC off the ground was primarily due to French opposition, despite the fact that the concept had originated in France. The French Assembly rejected the EDC Treaty in August 1954. Although the Treaty attempted to control German rearmament, many people in France did not want any German rearmament at all. There was also strong opposition, particularly in Gaullist quarters, to the idea of having any French forces subject to external control. In any case, the motivation for a European force seemed less urgent after the thaw in the Cold War which followed the ending of the Korean War and the death of Stalin in 1953.

The failure of the EDC led to an extension of the 1948 Brussels Treaty on mutual defence, originally signed by Britain, France and the Benelux countries, to include Germany and Italy. The result was the Western European Union (WEU). It was strictly intergovernmental, with no provision for national forces to be put under external controls and had little real impact. NATO came into existence in 1949 as a defence organisation that was to be the fulcrum of Western European defence policy.

The WEU was revived in 1984 when its Council of Ministers agreed to meet twice a year, with the presidency rotating annually between member states. A Permanent Council met weekly and there was a WEU Assembly in Paris. In 1994 Belgium, France, Germany, Greece, Italy, Luxembourg, the Netherlands, Portugal, Spain and Britain were all members, with Denmark and Ireland as observers, and Norway and Turkey as associate members. The St Petersburg Declaration of January 1992 stated that the WEU should have a military capability enabling it to take part in peacekeeping and humanitarian operations at the request of other international organisations.

F *The creation of the EEC*

KEY ISSUE

What was the motivation for signing the Treaty of Rome?

See page 95

Meanwhile, following the failure of the EDC, attempts at integration shifted to other directions. Monnet concentrated his efforts on economic union. In February 1955 he left his post of President of the High Authority to form a pressure group, the Action Committee for the United States of Europe (ACUSE). For other politicians, the pressure for European cooperation derived from an awareness of post-war realities. The 1956 Suez crisis demonstrated the inability of Britain and France to exert their muscle beyond Europe without the cooperation or consent of the superpowers. Western European countries had to stand by as the USSR crushed the Hungarian Rising in the same year. The movement for independence from European colonial rule amongst emerging nations in Africa and Asia was further evidence of the declining power of individual European powers to influence events significantly.

Nevertheless, political integration or the erosion of national sovereignty was still a radical concept. Charles de Gaulle, rapidly rising to prominence in France, adopted a strongly anti-federalist stance. The focus was still on economic and social issues. As trade recovered from the dislocation of the war years, at the same time as there was increasing competition in global markets, the benefits of closer economic cooperation seemed more evident.

The Foreign Ministers of the six ECSC states had already met in Messina in June 1955 to propose 'a new phase on the path of constructing Europe'. They agreed to seek integration in the areas of atomic energy, transport and social policies, and to establish an investment bank and a customs union. A committee was formed under Belgian Foreign Minister Paul-Henri Spaak to investigate the possibility of a common market. The British representative on the committee was withdrawn after fears that it was pursuing too radical a policy. However, the Spaak Report was approved by the ECSC foreign ministers in May 1956. The committee became a conference, and drafted two treaties, both signed in Rome in March 1957. One treaty established the European Atomic Energy Community (EURATOM). The other was the Treaty of Rome, signed on 25 March, which established the European Economic Community (EEC). Both treaties were ratified by the six parliaments and took effect from 1 January 1958.

2 ⟿ THE ORGANISATION AND WORKINGS OF THE EUROPEAN COMMON MARKET

A *The Treaty of Rome*

The Treaty of Rome had 248 articles, divided into two main categories. There were provisions to do with setting up a common market: the removal of tariffs between member states, then the imposition of a common tariff against imports from outside the EEC. There was also to be an eventual customs union, and steps towards the free movement of people, capital and goods between member states, all necessary if there were to be a genuinely free, competitive internal market.

The second category of articles dealt with other important measures which went beyond the strict notion of a market, but were designed to develop common policies: on agriculture and transport, the creation of a European investment bank to provide loans for economic expansion and the creation of a European Social Fund to support vocational training and full employment policies. Reference was made to long-term objectives such as economic integration, the coordination of national economic and monetary policies, and raising the standard of living of member populations.

The six founding members did not intend the EEC to be exclusive. Article 237 allowed any European state to join, provided it met certain conditions. There would also be opportunities for non-members to have 'associate status'.

The EEC was created in a spirit of optimism, but there were potential difficulties or contradictions from the start. The Treaty was liberal in its emphasis on removing barriers between states – echoing the old nineteenth-century belief in free trade as a means of promoting the creation of wealth and mutual support and understanding. However, by implication some of the articles were interventionist, because member states would have to conform to an overall policy in certain areas, at least in the long term. For this reason the Treaty allowed for member states to opt out of certain provisions if in economic difficulties or if they had concerns over national security. The Treaty was also vague in not stating how particular provisions would be implemented.

B *Economic progress*

Conditions for success seemed good in 1958. After 1945 economic recovery in Western Europe had been slow. But with Marshall Aid, the recovery of Germany, monetary reform and more liberal trade policies, economic prospects had improved. Reconstruction, a stable international exchange system, a boom in the demand for consumer goods, technological advances and high investment rates stimulated growth in the 1950s. The economies of Western Europe were growing at a rate of 4.4 per cent a year, well above the world average, although since several non-EEC economies were also prospering, it is not certain to what extent early high growth rates in the Community were due to the existence of the EEC, or to other factors. Growth continued into the 1960s although threatening signs appeared: large American trade deficits meant that the USA was less able to underpin international growth, although its economic presence in Europe continued to expand. Higher labour costs reduced profits and investments in several member states. These problems became far more serious in the 1970s when the world economy went into recession.

Meanwhile the process of integration continued. The ECSC, EEC and EURATOM were amalgamated in the European Community (EC) on 1 July 1967, and the planned customs union was achieved ahead of schedule in 1968. EURATOM played a relatively minor role in the process of integration, as governments showed little interest in cooperative projects which might lessen national control over such a sensitive issue as nuclear power.

See page 344

KEY ISSUE

How successful was the Common Market in its early years?

See Diagram 4 on page 342

C *EEC institutions and individuals*

The EEC had four major institutions to conduct its business: the European Commission; the Council Assembly; the Parliamentary Assembly; and the Court of Justice. There were also other important institutions. The European Investment Bank provided loans to member states for expansion. The Economic and Social Committee (ECOSOC) was an advisory body of employers, trade unions and 'general interest' groups. The Court of Auditors ensured that the budget was properly managed. The Committee of Permanent Representation comprised delegates of ambassadors and civil servants of member states, and it prepared the work of the Council of Ministers.

ANALYSIS

How the European Community worked

The European Commission was based in Brussels. It comprised two members each from Germany, France and Italy, and one each from the Benelux countries. The Commission's function was to ensure the implementation of the Treaty of Rome, and to both initiate and administer Community policy. It provided the bureaucracy. The Commission and its President were appointed by the Council of Ministers for a period of four years. Commissioners were each given areas of responsibility, and the Commission itself usually met weekly.

The Council of Ministers, also based in Brussels, was the main decision-making body. Often its decisions were based upon proposals made by the Commission. Its members were usually the Foreign Ministers of the member states, and most decisions had to be unanimous. The presidency of the Council rotated every six months. The Council met between eighty and ninety times each year, and voted on legislative measures. There was a 'qualified voting system', votes depending on the size of the country: after the Community's enlargement in the 1970s, Germany and Britain each had ten votes, Denmark and Eire had three votes each. The Council was really *the* key institution, since its consent was necessary to initiate action on most issues.

The Parliamentary Assembly, which was eventually to become the European Parliament, contained 142 members nominated by their governments. Although in theory it could dismiss the Commission, its role was mainly to advise both the Commission and the Council and to monitor their activities. The Assembly had to approve the Community budget, and refused to accept it on three occasions. Much of the Assembly's work was done in committees, and it met in Strasbourg.

Party of European Socialists	198
European People's Party (Christian Democrats)	162
Liberal, Democratic and Reformist Group	44
Greens	28
European Democratic Alliance	20
Rainbow Group	16
Technical Group of the European Right	14
Left Unity Group	13
Non-affiliated	23

TABLE 37
Political groupings in the 1989–94 European Parliament

From 1979 elections to the European Parliament were direct. By 1984 there were 434 members: eighty-one each from France, Germany, Italy and Britain; twenty-five from the Netherlands; twenty-four from Belgium and Greece; sixteen from Denmark; fifteen from Ireland; and six from Luxembourg. Later there were to be sixty Spanish and twenty-four Portuguese Euro-MPS. Euro-MPS were elected for five-year terms by different systems in member states, but all except Britain operated some system of proportional representation. Once in Parliament, Euro-MPS sat not in national groups but in groups determined by their political convictions. In the 1989–94 Parliament there were eight groups (plus twenty-three 'independent' MPs).

Under the Single European Act of 1986 the Parliament was granted increased powers to delay Community legislation, and a unanimous vote in the Council was required to overturn a parliamentary decision. The Maastricht Treaty of 1991 further extended Parliament's powers.

The fourth major Community institution, situated in Luxembourg, was the *Court of Justice*. Its function was to interpret Community treaties and settle disputes which arose over Community law. By 1993 it had dealt with 8293 cases.

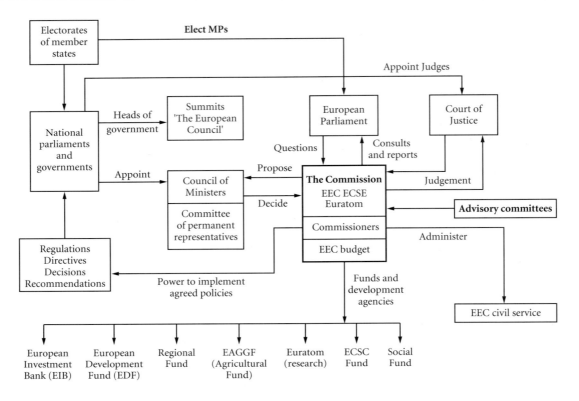

DIAGRAM 4
How the European Community works

Progress within the Community was affected by the personalities and interaction of individuals. The early enthusiasts of the Community were both idealists and realists. The pragmatic de Gaulle usually got on well with Adenauer of Germany. Until they lost power at the beginning of the 1980s, Giscard d'Estaing of France and Helmut Schmidt of Germany also worked well together. Their successors, Mitterand and Kohl, got on less well and so progress in the Community was slower. Mrs Thatcher, British Prime Minister in the 1980s, was regarded as intransigent by colleagues for her strident championing of British interests.

Individual commissioners also played an important role. The Luxembourger Gaston Thorn was much less influential than his predecessor, the British ex-minister Roy Jenkins. In the early 1990s Jacques Delors, despite frequent fallings out with the British government and media, restored drive to the Community in its progress towards a single market.

D *Progress and controversy*

Economic progress helped the reputation of the Community in the 1960s. However, the question of national sovereignty halted progress in other directions, as governments began to look beyond trade and economics. Was the EEC to be an organisation which worked on an intergovernmental basis, with member states retaining their national sovereignty and exerting a power of veto on Community decisions of which their governments disapproved? Or was the EEC to become a genuinely supranational institution, with the highest authority centred in Strasbourg or Brussels?

During the 1960s several states tried to join the Community, by then seen as an economic success. Meanwhile President de Gaulle in France tried to divert the Community away from an integrationist model. He wanted a *Europe des Patries*: that is, a community of sovereign nation states. He also wanted to extend French influence. De Gaulle's close collaboration with Chancellor Adenauer led to a Franco–German Treaty in January 1963, to coordinate the two countries' foreign, defence, information and cultural policies. France and Germany became the two pivotal powers of the EEC .

However, France created problems for its partners in Europe. In 1965 it effectively halted the work of the European Commission. De Gaulle produced the Fouchet Plan, named after a French ambassador. It had five main elements: a commitment to regular meetings of the Heads of State or Foreign Ministers of member states; a commitment to unanimous decision making; the creation of a permanent EEC secretariat in Paris; the creation of permanent intergovernmental committees for foreign, defence, commercial and cultural affairs; and a European Assembly appointed by member governments, which would have deliberative but no decision-making powers. Britain was excluded from the negotiations.

The Plan was clearly designed to preserve national sovereignty and to scotch ideas of supranationalism. However, it was unwelcome to other states. The Fouchet Plan did not sit easily with the Treaty of Rome and existing organisations like the ECSC, and involvement in foreign policy decisions might conflict with the role of NATO. A crisis developed in relations between France and its fellow members, and Community work was disrupted as France boycotted the Council of Ministers for seven months. The first President of the EEC Commission, the German Walther Hallstein, was a believer in a supranational Europe, and he clashed with de Gaulle. De Gaulle also objected to the idea of majority voting, due to be implemented in 1966, and to Commission proposals to increase its own powers and those of the European Parliament. There were also arguments over proposals to switch the financing of the Community from direct national contributions to revenue from tariffs, which had hitherto 'belonged' to the Community as a whole.

De Gaulle faced pressure to compromise not just from the other member states but also from within France, whose farmers wanted the protection promised by the EEC. Therefore he accepted the

> ## KEY ISSUE
>
> *Why did France cause strains in the Community in the 1960s?*

'Luxembourg Compromise' of January 1966. This allowed member states a national veto on EEC proposals which they felt threatened 'very important interests', although these were not defined. Unanimity in the Council was preserved, and moves towards supranationality were blocked, so that the compromise was, if anything, a French victory. Hallstein resigned over this issue, and later Commission Presidents had less power.

E *The European Community (EC) and recession*

Following the Luxembourg Compromise the European bandwagon started to roll again. The Hague Summit was held in December 1969. It was the idea of George Pompidou, de Gaulle's successor as French President. The Summit considered issues relating to the enlarging of membership of the Community, economic and monetary union, progress in cooperation on technological and social policies, and also provided for more regular discussions between Foreign Ministers. Whilst it was difficult to reach agreement, at least the EC was making some progress on cooperation.

However, progress was seriously hampered by the onset of a world economic recession. The 1973 Arab–Israeli War led to an Arab embargo on oil supplies and a four-fold increase in oil prices. This had a devastating effect on oil-dependent economies. Disagreements and paralysis as governments sought a way out of the crisis shattered optimism. Ironically, in 1972 on the eve of the first crisis, a summit was held of the six EC states and the prospective members (Britain, Denmark and Ireland), which committed the Community to complete the internal market with common tariffs, a common currency and a central bank, all by the end of the decade. This was very optimistic and the EC failed to present a coordinated policy to the outside world. Instead, member states sought a way out of recession by unilateral action. For example, France negotiated separate deals with Saudi Arabia, and Britain with Iran. Cooperation was minimal. However, it is possible that without the existence of the Community, the effects of the recession on the economies of individual member states might have been even worse.

The second oil crisis of 1979–80 followed the outbreak of war between Iran and Iraq. There were also other problems: particularly a reluctance to reverse the rises in real wages that had occurred in the 1960s and which led to businesses putting up prices and reducing investment instead. The high-wage, high-cost economies of Western Europe were increasingly challenged by Japan, the newly-industrialising countries of Asia and Latin America, and even parts of Eastern Europe. The Community was slow to respond to the challenge.

The trade policies of the EC contributed to economic difficulties by allowing the build-up of trade surpluses. The American economy suffered and the world monetary system was severely dislocated, disrupting trade and investment. The 1970s slowdown turned into the

---

KEY ISSUE

What were the causes and impact of the economic crises of the 1970s?

1980s recession. The EC suffered more than the USA and Japan from reduced growth, inflation and rising unemployment. For most of the 1980s the annual growth rate of the EC economies was 2.2 per cent, compared to an average of 3.7 per cent for Japan and 3.6 per cent for the USA. Between 1973 and 1985 the Community's share of world trade in manufactured goods fell from 45 per cent to 36 per cent. Car exports from the EC fell by over one-fifth.

Several EC countries adopted protectionist policies. Some politicians adopted a more nationalist stance in response to the crisis, some pressed for more reforms, some sought more integration and quicker progress towards a single market as a way out of recession.

The picture was not all black. Throughout the period between 1958 and 1980 trade *between* member states increased by a factor of 23, whilst EC trade with the rest of the world increased by a factor of 11. The major industrial economies of the EC conducted over half their trade with each other.

Some member states' economies performed better than others. West Germany was the greatest success story. During the 1960s and 70s its economy continued to expand both in absolute terms and in relation to other member states, and it accounted for a quarter of all imports and exports between EC countries. Next was France, which accounted for 18 per cent of imports and 16.3 per cent of exports. Germany had a relatively low rate of inflation and a healthy balance of payments; it was the world's largest exporter of industrial goods, and managed to increase its exports to other EC members even when the EC's total share of world trade was decreasing. In contrast, the French economy suffered, and unemployment rose in several other member states.

The EC found it difficult to coordinate industrial policies to meet adverse economic circumstances. Germany and Britain opposed attempts to rationalise and restructure industry in a way which conflicted with national policies. The ECSC did succeed in implementing a steel policy in 1980, setting national production quotas and reducing government subsidies to steel industries. However, the more usual response to economic difficulties was to resort to protectionism.

	Exports (million ECU)	Imports (million ECU)	Exports as % of GDP
Belgium–Luxembourg	71 068	70 401	58.7
Denmark	22 126	23 639	26.3
France	121 377	130 551	16.5
Greece	5950	11 550	14.2
Ireland	13 621	11 821	51.4
Italy	99 401	101 947	16.2
The Netherlands	85 851	81 279	48.0
Portugal	7319	9608	25.3
Spain	26 982	33 299	11.6
UK	131 621	127 524	19.4
West Germany	247 517	194 368	27.2

TABLE 38
Trading performance of Community members in the mid-1980s

Despite these difficulties, the EC attracted large amounts of foreign investment, particularly from the USA, Japan, Sweden and Switzerland. Britain received the largest share of this investment, followed by Germany, France and the Netherlands. By the mid-1980s the twelve nations of the EC comprised a substantial economic bloc, standing comparison with the two superpowers, as Table 39 shows.

Within the EC itself there were considerable variations, particularly in industrial output, as shown in Table 40.

F *Farming*

Agriculture was a contentious issue for the European Community. In 1958 it was still a major employer, accounting for 25 per cent of the French and 35 per cent of the Italian workforces. The Treaty of Rome assumed a growth in agricultural productivity and stable food supplies, and expected farmers' incomes would increase at the same time as food was supplied to consumers at 'reasonable prices'. These were contradictory objectives. The French, Germans and Italians were very keen to protect their small farmers, even inefficient ones. The Dutch were more interested in modernising their farms and exporting produce.

The controversial Common Agricultural Policy (CAP) was launched in 1962. Prices of farm products were agreed and set at a level above world prices. If agreed targets were not met, the EC would buy up the

TABLE 39

Comparative economic resources of the EC, USA and the USSR in 1985

	EC	USA	USSR
Population (millions)	322	239	279
Gross Domestic Product (1000 m ECU)	3231	5172	Not available
Exports (million ECU)	849 923	279 319	116 154
Steel production (million tonnes)	136	81	154
Grain production (million tonnes)	162	320	179
Motor car production (millions)	10.9	8.2	1.3
Coal production (million tonnes)	227	464	360
Merchant shipping (million tonnes gross)	88.2	19.5	24.7

TABLE 40

Distribution of industrial output within the EC in the 1980s

	% share of EC population, 1985	% share in EC industrial output, 1985	Change, 1985–90 (1985 = 100)
West Germany	18.8	24.3	118
Italy	17.7	17.1	118
UK	17.6	18.9	109
France	17.2	18.6	113
Spain	12.0	8.2	116
The Netherlands	4.5	4.7	109
Belgium/Lux	3.2	2.7	115
Portugal	3.2	1.5	135
Greece	3.1	1.2	103
Denmark	1.6	1.2	107
Ireland	1.1	0.9	144

surplus. This was an expensive policy: huge surplus stocks became embarrassments such as the 'butter mountain' and 'wine lake'; surpluses were wasted or sold off cheaply outside the Community. Controversy was compounded by a French refusal to accept the principle of majority voting on CAP issues.

CAP did succeed in protecting farmers and ensuring Europe's self-sufficiency in food supplies. Agricultural self-sufficiency amongst the six Community members in 1958 was 91 per cent. This figure rose to 108 per cent amongst ten member states by the early 1980s. Agricultural exports from the EC tripled. However, consumers paid high food prices, whilst the cost to the EC's budget was enormous. In the mid-1960s CAP accounted for about 17 per cent of the total EC budget. By 1972 this proportion had risen to a staggering 75 per cent, reducing the amount that the Community could allocate to other projects. In 1991 CAP was still taking up 57 per cent of the budget. As a result, 'set aside' policies were implemented, with farmers paid to take some fertile land out of cultivation. The intention was to reduce spending on agriculture to 46 per cent of the total budget by 1999. Export subsidies on food were to be reduced, allowing prices to fall more into line with world levels. There was to be less emphasis on price support and more on directly supplementing farmers' incomes. Diagram 5 shows how the proportion of the rapidly growing Community budget spent on agriculture and fisheries between 1973 and 1994 did decrease considerably.

A further difficulty was created because agricultural products from the Mediterranean regions of newer member states were either excluded from EC support or received a smaller subsidy than the products of the 'Northern' states. There were accusations of unequal treatment.

By 1997 CAP was costing £30 billion a year. As the prospect of the poorer counties of Eastern Europe joining the Community increased, so it seemed that taxation would have to rise if the levels of farm support were not changed. Therefore the European Commission proposed major cuts to production subsidies and cutting guaranteed prices for crops, meat and milk. However, many farmers felt threatened by the suggested changes: they would need to become more competitive to survive without existing high levels of farm support.

KEY ISSUE

What difficulties did farming cause the Community, and how successfully did it deal with them?

3 ⌐ ENLARGING THE COMMUNITY

A *The 1970s: Britain, Denmark and Ireland*

Enlarging the Community was on the agenda in the 1960s. The original EEC Charter committed the Community to making membership available to all 'suitable' European states. The initial economic successes of the EEC and the changed circumstances of several countries encouraged applications.

MAP 29
The enlargement of the European Community, 1957–95

Legend (on map):
- 1957 (founding members)
- 1973
- 1986
- 1990 (E. Germany)
- 1995

The British government's desire to join the Community was fuelled by the impressive growth rates of member states, combined with a more realistic perception of Britain's post-war role in the world power stakes. During the 1960s more and more investment within Europe was being channelled into Germany rather than Britain. The economic advantages of joining a larger grouping seemed obvious.

However, many British people continued to have reservations. There were concerns over national sovereignty. There were also pressing economic issues, particularly agricultural ones. Farming comprised a relatively smaller sector of the British economy compared to existing member states, and much of Britain's food was imported from outside the Community. Yet agriculture played a key role in Community economic policy.

Britain applied for full membership of the EEC in July 1961, followed by Denmark, Ireland and Norway. Britain's application was rejected by de Gaulle in January 1963, partly because of Britain's 'special

KEY ISSUE

Why did Britain apply to join the Community in the 1960s, and why was its application rejected?

relationship' with the USA, which, it was claimed, made Britain less committed to Europe; and partly because the French President feared that British membership would challenge Franco–German domination of the still relatively small Community. Negotiations also stalled over CAP, with the British wanting a long transition to full participation in the Community and concessions for the Commonwealth, whose trade was threatened by the common external tariff of the Community.

Denmark, Norway and Ireland withdrew their applications after the rejection of Britain's bid. Other member states disapproved of France's rather high-handed rejection of Britain.

The four countries re-applied in 1967, the British Labour government reversing its previous opposition to joining the Community. Despite the support of the Commission for British membership, it was vetoed again by de Gaulle in November 1967. The reason cited was the weakness of the British economy, which had recently undergone a sterling crisis and devaluation.

De Gaulle having resigned the French presidency in 1969, agreement to enlarge the Community was finally reached in June 1971, to take effect from 1 January 1973. It was the first enlargement the Community had undergone. Many in France were still unenthusiastic about Britain's application, but others saw Britain as a possible counterweight to an increasingly successful and confident West Germany.

It was agreed that the new members would undergo a five-year transition period. Because the Common Agricultural Policy would mean higher food prices, Britain's participation in it would be gradual. Britain was to contribute 8.64 per cent of the EC budget in 1973, rising to 18.92 per cent by 1977. There was no agreement on a permanent arrangement after that date. Britain was expected to make a large budgetary contribution because of the relatively small size of its agricultural sector and high levies on food imports.

Various arrangements were also made to ease the difficulties of the Commonwealth, which exported food to Britain and would now be subject to a Community tariff. The new members were also granted special fisheries arrangements, necessary because a fisheries policy initiated at the same time gave all Community members equal and free access to each others' waters. The new members all had extensive fishing fleets and would therefore suffer most from competition.

Norway did not join. A Norwegian referendum voted 53 per cent against joining, mainly due to concerns over Norway's fishing industry and its relationship with its Scandinavian neighbours. A Danish referendum voted 63 per cent in favour of membership. It was expected that Danish agriculture would benefit from the Common Agricultural Policy, and Denmark's chief export markets were Britain and Germany. An Irish referendum produced a positive result of 83 per cent, a logical outcome given that 70 per cent of Irish exports went to Britain.

The expansion of the Community from six to nine members was expected to give it a new boost. Unfortunately, the enlargement took place just as the Community became embroiled in problems and

See page 314

See page 311

KEY ISSUE

What were the consequences of the enlargement of the Community in 1973?

economic recession. British Prime Minister Edward Heath later declared,

> After the oil crisis of 1973–74, the Community lost its momentum and, what was worse, lost the philosophy of Jean Monnet: that the Community exists to find common solutions to common problems.

Britain held a retrospective referendum on its membership of the Community in June 1975. The political and economic establishments broadly supported continued membership and the vote in favour was 67 per cent. However, British governments continued to argue over their high budgetary contributions in Council of Ministers' meetings until well into the 1980s. Eventually it was agreed in 1984 that the British contribution should be reduced from 3000 million ECUs to 1600 million, whilst France, Germany and Italy agreed to larger increases.

B *1986: Greece, Spain and Portugal*

Greece had associate membership of the Community from 1962. Spain and Portugal had special trade relationships from 1970 and 1972 respectively. Once all three countries overturned their dictatorships in 1975 and 1976, their governments applied for full membership. Some Greeks opposed membership, rightly predicting that the relatively undeveloped Greek economy would suffer from open competition. After joining, Greece's trade balance was to deteriorate, and inflation rose. Greece tried to renegotiate its terms of membership immediately after entry, and was to earn a reputation along with Britain and Denmark for being 'difficult' when it came to policy negotiations.

See page 296

Spain, Portugal and Greece, as poorer members of the Community, were all likely to draw heavily on the Community's Social and Regional Funds. France and Italy were concerned about competition from cheap Spanish farm produce. The Common Fisheries Policy opened up the prospect of intense competition from the Spanish fishing fleet, which was almost as large as the other members' fleets combined. There was also concern over competition from the low-wage Spanish and Portuguese economies, and their large steel and textile industries, areas in which there was already overcapacity in the Community. However, there were also hopes among other member states that the accession of Spain, Portugal and Greece would be the best security against a relapse into dictatorship. After lengthy negotiations, all three countries were admitted in January 1986. The twelve member states of the Community now contained 345 million out of a European population (excluding the USSR) of 500 million. The twelve accounted for almost 20 per cent of the world's Gross National Product, just behind the American share but double that of Japan.

C *Enlargement in the 1990s*

Community membership was still an attractive prospect for many countries. Turkey applied for membership in 1987. A decision was deferred in 1990, because of concerns as to whether Turkey met the relevant political and economic criteria for membership. Malta and Cyprus applied for membership in 1990. Austria had long been debarred from membership by its neutral status, but applied in July 1989, principally because two-thirds of its trade was with Community members. Norway reapplied for membership in 1992, but another referendum voted against joining. Sweden had rejected membership in 1958 because of its traditional neutral status, because it had reservations about the Common Agricultural Policy, and because its taxation and welfare systems were not in harmony with those of many Western European states. However, it applied for membership in 1991, followed by Finland.

> **KEY ISSUE**
>
> *What were the implications of the enlargement of the Community in the 1980s and 90s?*

4 ↪ ECONOMIC AND MONETARY UNION

A *Problems of EMU*

Despite the addition of new members to the Community in the early 1970s, efforts to 'deepen' the organisation by economic and monetary union were unsuccessful for a long time. Union would depend upon fixed exchange rates between currencies. These already existed between individual states, but further progress was difficult. The Hague summit in 1969 agreed to aim for Economic and Monetary Union (EMU) by 1980, to be achieved in stages, but there were disagreements about the best route. 'Monetarists' believed that EMU would be best achieved by fixing exchange rates as quickly as possible. 'Economists', particularly in Germany and The Netherlands, believed that monetary union would fail unless there were genuine movement towards economic union first.

The first stage of EMU involved the narrowing of permitted fluctuations in the exchange rates between member states, and the promise of financial assistance to those states with weaker currencies to enable them to stay in the system. Fluctuation in rates between currencies was limited to a band of 1.2 per cent of the central parities, the so-called 'Snake', which would operate within a wider band of 1.5 per cent (the 'Tunnel') against the American dollar. Eventually wider bands of fluctuation were allowed, and the Snake was finally launched in April 1972, with a band allowing for fluctuations of up to 2.25 per cent. But the pound sterling was soon under pressure and Britain had to leave the system after only eight weeks. Denmark, Italy and Ireland also left the system temporarily. In March 1973 the system of fixed exchange rates collapsed completely and the Tunnel was abandoned. The Snake continued. Germany revalued its currency.

After one year the Snake was readjusted and no longer included all the major currencies. France left the Snake in January 1974, rejoined

KEY ISSUE

How successful was the move towards economic and monetary union before the 1990s?

the following year, and left again in 1976. Adjustments to the central rate became common, and soon the Snake was confined to Germany and those smaller countries which linked their currencies to the *Deutschmark*.

Attempts at monetary cooperation, let alone integration, were thus proving difficult. This was partly due to adverse economic circumstances – the effects of the oil crises and the collapse of the general international system of fixed exchange rates. But there was also a lack of real political will. Business might see the advantages for trade of an integrated and stable monetary system, but any move towards monetary integration raised the same concerns about loss of sovereignty as moves towards integration in other areas.

B *EMS and ERM*

Paradoxically, some politicians and economists argued that the adverse economic circumstances which helped kill off EMU made cooperation in the form of fixed exchange rates even more essential. Therefore the Snake was eventually replaced by the less ambitious European Monetary System (EMS), agreed at the Bremen and Brussels Summits in 1978. The French and Germans were prime movers in supporting this. Britain was not part of the negotiations, despite strong support from Roy Jenkins, President of the European Commission between 1977 and 1981.

KEY ISSUE

How successful was the European Monetary System?

The EMS took effect from March 1979. The European Currency Unit (ECU) was introduced as a means for monetary authorities in the Community to settle transactions between themselves. The Exchange Rate Mechanism (ERM) was also introduced: it allowed currencies to fluctuate up to 2.25 per cent either side of a central rate, before dropping out of the system. The *Deutschmark* was selected as the central currency of the ERM, reflecting Germany's economic dominance. There were seven realignments between currencies in the first four years of ERM. However, it did have some positive effect in reducing some of the discrepancies in national inflation rates and the wide variations in exchange rates which disadvantaged trade.

Britain joined the EMS but not the ERM, because the Conservative government was not prepared to agree to what was regarded as a loss of sovereignty.

Other measures followed the establishment of the EMS. Credit facilities were provided for countries experiencing problems with stabilising their currencies. Cheap loans were provided for less prosperous economies. A European Monetary Fund was planned, but not set up.

5 ⌐ RELATIONSHIPS OUTSIDE THE COMMUNITY

A *Relationships with EFTA*

The European Free Trade Area (EFTA) could never really compete with the EC economically, because only Britain of EFTA's members was on an industrial par with the major EC powers among the original six. However, there were close links between the two organisations even before the accession of some EFTA members to the EC. As the latter expanded, much of the rationale for the existence of EFTA began to disappear. Nevertheless, negotiations between the EC and EFTA began in June 1990. They resulted in the establishment of the European Economic Area, which came into being in January 1994: it covered eighteen countries and accounted for 43 per cent of the world's international trade. Switzerland rejected membership after a referendum.

See pages 364–5 for the history of EFTA

B *Relationships with the developing world*

The European Community established relations with several other organisations and countries for their mutual benefit. This was also done to counter accusations that the Community was too inward-looking and was in effect a 'fortress' designed to protect the interests of a small group of rich nations.

See Picture 37

Trade agreements had been signed with all the Mediterranean states except Albania and Libya by the 1970s. The countries concerned received assistance from the European Investment Bank and got free access to the EC for most of their industrial products. Bilateral trade agreements were signed with several developing countries outside Europe in the 1970s and 80s.

The Lomé Conventions in the 1970s, 80s and 90s eventually provided aid and trade assistance packages to over seventy African, Caribbean and Pacific states. Between 1985 and 1990 8 500 000 000 ECUs of aid were provided. Industrial products from these countries were allowed into the EC without being subject to tariffs or quotas. However, since the beneficiaries did not produce many industrial goods for export, competition with Community markets was not intense, and the majority of aid to the developing world still came from individual governments rather than from the EC as an institution. Commonwealth countries were compensated from the Stabilisation Fund for anticipated loss of export earnings from trade with Britain.

C *Relationships with COMECON*

Central and Eastern European states had less developed economies than the West. Largely unsuccessful talks between the EC and COMECON were held between 1977 and 1980. However, as Communist control in the Eastern Bloc was challenged after 1986, agreements were made

See pages 366–8 for the history of COMECON

PICTURE 37
'The fortress of the rich' (The Guardian, 14 February 1994)

between the EC and individual COMECON states in Europe and with China. In 1989 the European Commission coordinated Community aid to the Eastern Bloc countries, in addition to signing trade and cooperation agreements with both them and the USSR. Further long-term agreements were signed in December 1991. From that date, the emerging democracies of Central and Eastern Europe were hopeful of changing these agreements into full membership of the Community once they met the necessary political and economic conditions.

D *Foreign relations*

Sometimes the Community managed to speak with a common voice on events outside Europe, under what was known as the European Political Cooperation (EPC) procedure. After 1975 there was a common policy on applying sanctions against Rhodesia, which had declared independence from Britain; and against the USSR over Poland in 1981. The Community spoke with one voice at the 1975 Helsinki

Conference on Security and Cooperation. It sometimes acted as one in the United Nations.

However, the Community could not agree on sanctions against Israel over its involvement in the Lebanon; or against Argentina over its occupation of the Falklands. Nor could the Community agree on a policy towards the Turkish invasion of Cyprus in 1974; and it made an unconvincing response to the Soviet invasion of Afghanistan in 1980 and the Soviet shooting down of a Korean airliner in 1983.

Some critics argued that these failures demonstrated that the Community was only prepared to act together when members' material interests were directly at stake. On the other hand, some supporters of limited integration argued that the ability of the Community to speak with a common voice on at least some issues proved the possibility of effective cooperation without individual governments having to surrender sovereignty.

KEY ISSUE

How successful was the European Community in its dealings with the outside world?

6 ⌐ MORE PROGRESS AND CHALLENGES: THE 1980S AND 1990S

A *Introduction*

The Community made progress but also ran into difficulties as it moved into the late 1980s and the 1990s. One proposal not adopted was a draft treaty of European Union. The draft was approved by the European Parliament in February 1984, and would have increased the powers of the Commission and the Parliament, thereby reducing those of the Council. The aim was to promote supranationalism over intergovernmentalism. It was rejected for this reason: national governments preferred to maintain their sovereignty. The acceptable alternative was a series of formal summit meetings of the leaders of member states, known as the European Council. Regular summits were held two or three times a year. The summits set the agenda for future development of the Community and even took on some of the responsibilities of the Commission. Sometimes the European Council was used as a forum to settle major disagreements, as over the British budgetary contribution. Governments preferred this approach to the idea of majority voting. The latter tactic was used in 1982 when farm prices were raised in the face of a British veto, but it was rarely invoked.

B *The social and regional dimension*

There were other positive developments. The European Social Fund and the European Regional Development Fund actively supported projects during the 1980s. Social issues addressed included the free mobility of labour within the Community, equal pay for equal work, and protecting the interests of migrants and the dispossessed. In 1990 forty-four million EC citizens were still identified as living in relative

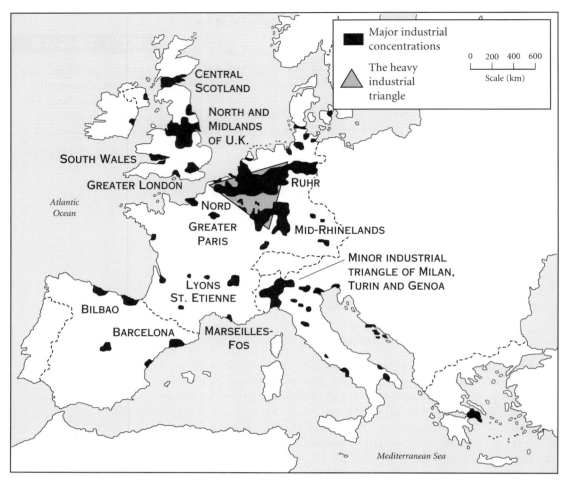

MAP 30

Major concentrations of industry in the European Community

poverty. Sometimes firm action was taken: in 1986 Britain was obliged to introduce a Sex Discrimination Act because of discrimination against women in employment. In 1989 the EC Commission issued a draft Social Charter, which included guarantees of free movement between member states. All member states except Britain signed the Social Charter in 1990.

The Regional Development Fund was set up in January 1975 with the aim of reducing regional inequalities. It supplemented regional policies of national governments, rather than replacing them. In the early days of the Community regional concerns had tended to focus on unemployment and the problems of old declining staple industries like coal and steel, but by the 1990s they were shifting to other issues, such as urban regeneration. A policy on the environment had first been drawn up in 1973. It was followed by a series of resolutions about environmental concerns such as pollution and the quality of drinking water. The 'First Framework Programme' (1984–87) was the first real Community industrial policy, attempting to integrate research and development activities.

The Common Fisheries Policy (CFP) was renegotiated in 1983, after years of disputes about fishing rights and free access. Member states all had fishing limits of up to 200 miles. The new agreement retained the principle of free access, but committed the Community to policies of conservation and assistance to those regions heavily dependent on fishing. The agreement did not assuage national and regional concerns, and there were periodic outbreaks of dissent, particularly in those countries with large fishing fleets, dissatisfied with their quotas.

C *Financing the EU*

In the 1980s there was also a change in the system of financing Community activities. Until 1980 the Community relied upon direct contributions from member states, which had caused controversies. From 1980 there was a move towards 'own resource' financing. Under the new system, criticised by Britain, more of the Community's income would come from the common external tariff, levies on agricultural imports, and up to 1 per cent of VAT receipts. Even this system did not seem equitable. For example, The Netherlands was a small state, but paid a high budgetary contribution in relation to its size because of its large international ports – it was at these ports, entry points into the Community as a whole, that duties were levied. Richer states received preferential treatment because VAT made up a smaller proportion of their total revenue. Britain paid high import levies because it imported a lot of food. Yet since Britain produced a relatively small amount of food itself, it received proportionately smaller handouts of CAP payments. In 1985 Britain contributed almost 20 per cent of the EC budget, but accounted for only 12.6 per cent of EC expenditure. Germany contributed 28.2 per cent of the budget and received 17 per cent back.

The budget remained a source of controversy. Two-thirds of revenue was spent on supporting agricultural prices, which were set well above world levels. The Council and Parliament disputed control of the budget and their respective powers. Britain frequently pressed for reform of both the budget and CAP, and at the Dublin Summit of 1979 Prime Minister Margaret Thatcher demanded a £1 billion rebate. Britain eventually received a two-thirds rebate in 1984.

Funding was a persistent problem because the Community's range of activities was constantly increasing. The total EC budget grew from 35 million ECU in 1958 to 59 billion ECU in 1991. The growth of trade between member states and reductions in tariffs actually reduced Community revenue. Therefore a summit meeting at Fontainebleau in June 1984 agreed not just to readjust the British contribution but to take other measures. These included raising the ceiling on VAT

> **KEY ISSUE**
>
> *Why did funding remain a major issue for the Community?*

See page 350

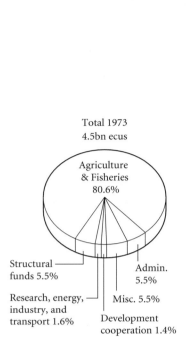
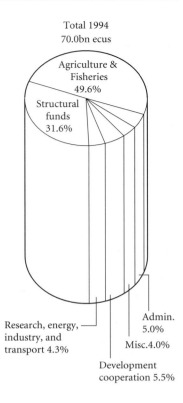

Total 1994
70.0bn ecus

Agriculture &
Fisheries
49.6%

Structural
funds
31.6%

Total 1973
4.5bn ecus

Agriculture
& Fisheries
80.6%

Structural
funds 5.5%

Admin.
5.5%

Research, energy,
industry, and
transport 1.6%

Misc. 5.5%

Development
cooperation 1.4%

Research, energy,
industry, and
transport 4.3%

Admin.
5.0%

Misc.4.0%

Development
cooperation 5.5%

DIAGRAM 5

*The Community budget,
1973 and 1994*

contributions and reducing expenditure on CAP. For the first time a limit was put on the level of guaranteed agricultural prices. This was a turning point in agricultural policy, and revenue and expenditure were brought more closely into line in the second half of the 1980s, although there were still budgetary deficits in 1985 and 1986.

In 1988 a committee was set up under Jacques Delors to make progress on monetary union. At Brussels in February 1988 the Delors 1 package was agreed. The British rebate was to continue. Spending on CAP was to be limited to 74 per cent of the overall growth rate of the Community's GNP. Although Britain and Germany continued to pay proportionately larger contributions, there was some redistribution within the budget to benefit poorer Community members such as Portugal and Greece.

At the subsequent Edinburgh Summit the Delors 11 package was agreed for the 1990s. Spending on agriculture was to be further controlled and there was to be less reliance on VAT for revenue.

D *The Single Market and Treaty of Maastricht*

Despite the concerns, there was also renewed optimism about the future of the Community in the late 1980s. The experience of recession had sometimes encouraged selfishness by individual governments, but also taught the possible benefits of cooperation and reform. The ending of the Cold War appeared to offer new opportunities for progress. There was talk again of integration. It was agreed in 1985 that a single market should be achieved by January 1993. Both Denmark and Ireland held referenda before agreeing to the Single European Act. This increased Parliament's powers by requiring its approval by an absolute majority to the accession of new member states; and the use of qualified majority voting was extended to areas other than taxation.

Three hundred measures were identified as being necessary to complete the single market. The Single Market Programme (SMP) included freedom of movement of people, goods, services and capital throughout the Community, and it was emphasised that governments should take account of the needs of ordinary people, for example by following non-inflationary policies. The SMP prepared the way for the Treaty of European Union signed at Maastricht. However, it proved easier to relax restrictions on capital movements than to relax frontier controls on people and goods and to harmonise national taxation policies, all measures which appeared to have more direct implications for national sovereignty.

> ## KEY ISSUE
> *What was the significance of the single market and the Maastricht Treaty?*

The Council of Ministers implemented 60 per cent of the three hundred measures by 1990. Most measures concerning energy, transport and telecommunications were still outstanding. Protective subsidies by governments also remained a sticking point, as when the British government subsidised the sale of the Rover Car Company to British Aerospace, bringing accusations of unfair favouritism.

The break-up of Communist regimes in the late 1990s, leading to the reunification of Germany and the break-up of the USSR, created new challenges for the Community. There was also the Gulf War, which required a united political response. Conferences at Strasbourg in December 1989 and Dublin in June 1990 revealed diverging views about the future of the Community. Despite these differences, Community members signed the Treaty of European Union (TEU) at Maastricht in December 1991. The Treaty had several provisions, some quite radical. It was stated that the new Community would build on existing treaties and that the ultimate objective was economic and monetary union. Foreign policy, defence, justice and home affairs would remain the preserve of member states. British reservations won the British government an 'opt out' clause, enabling it to determine when it would join the third stage of economic and monetary union.

Britain also refused to sign the Social Protocol, by which eleven Community members committed themselves to promoting employment and better living and working conditions. Britain's reservations were partly due to concern for competitiveness at a time of economic recession, if for example, wages were raised.

Maastricht also led to institutional reforms. Qualified majority voting in the Council and Parliament's powers were extended. Parliament was empowered to set up committees of enquiry. A Regional Committee was set up, enabling regional representatives to participate in decision making. A Cohesion Fund was to progress environmental and transport projects in less developed areas. The concept of common citizenship was emphasised.

Finally, the principle of *subsidiarity* was adopted: this meant that policy decisions should be taken at the appropriate level. Britain interpreted this as offering a means by which the powers of the European Commission could be restricted.

The Maastricht Treaty turned the Economic Community into the European Union (EU). However, the Treaty did not come into effect until November 1993, eleven months late, because several states had difficulty in ratifying it. Referenda were held in three member states. Ireland voted in favour of the Treaty. France voted narrowly in favour (51.05 per cent to 48.95 per cent against). The Danes voted against ratification (50 per cent to 49.3 per cent against) in June 1992. They voted in favour in a second referendum in May 1993 (56.7 per cent to 43.3 per cent against) after Denmark was offered an opt out from the third stage of EMU. It was clear that in some member states at least, public opinion was dubious about closer European integration. It was also unclear how the Treaty would affect practice, since some member states such as Britain were reluctant to commit themselves to EMU or were doubtful whether they could meet the criteria necessary to be accepted as part of the first wave of implementation. There was increasing talk of a 'multi-speed Europe' in which some member states would progress towards integration at a much faster rate than others.

Monetary Union was still very much on the agenda. It had been agreed in 1989 that all Community members should join the ERM in July 1990, subject to certain conditions. The second stage began in January 1994 with the creation of the European Monetary Institute in Frankfurt. Stage Three, involving the transfer of full economic and monetary authority to the EU and the irrevocable fixing of exchange rates, was to begin in January 1997 for those states meeting the convergence criteria. However, this was delayed. Spain (in 1989), Britain (in 1990) and Portugal (in 1992) joined the ERM, leaving only Greece outside. But economic recession, high German interest rates and a stagnant American economy caused the virtual collapse of the ERM in 1992. Italy and Britain left the ERM, accusing Germany of supporting the franc at the expense of the pound. Several other member states had to devalue their currencies. Even Germany, hit by the high cost of reunification, doubted whether it would be prepared for monetary union by 1997, and indeed it did not come about.

The role of the European Parliament also changed as the Community matured. Early limitations on Parliament's powers reflected the fact that federalism had few prominent supporters. Most member states wanted cooperation to stay at the level of intergovernmental agreement and no further. In December 1990 there were intergovernmental conferences to consider political as well as economic and monetary union. But there were strong disagreements about the allocation of power between Parliament, the Council of Ministers and the Commission. At one extreme the Italian Government supported federalism, at the other Britain wanted to retain virtually full national sovereignty. In all member states there were large numbers of opponents as well as supporters of the idea of further integration of both institutions and policies.

E *Further enlargement of the EU*

The late 1980s saw several applications for membership of the Community as the Soviet-dominated Eastern Bloc collapsed. As the Community was enlarged, non-members were increasingly concerned about the consequences of being left out in the cold. The Community had to handle applications for membership at the same time as working out its own programme for the increasing integration of existing members. Different terms were offered to a range of applicants.

On the principle that it was best to be part of the decision-making process, Austria, Sweden and Finland all joined the Community in 1995. Norway did not join after another negative referendum vote. Apart from Iceland and Switzerland, which had bilateral agreements with the Community, Norway was the only Western European country still outside the European Union.

The Central and Eastern European states keen on membership of the EU faced a different challenge. Their economic development lagged behind that of existing member states, so their economies would have been too vulnerable for immediate exposure to the full blast of Western European competition. Poland, the Czech and Slovak Republics, Hungary, Romania and Bulgaria were granted ten-year 'Europe Agreements' which allowed them free trade with the Community in industrial goods, but only limited concessions in the case of agricultural and other goods. However, full membership was still the goal of these states. Poland and Hungary formally applied to join the European Union in 1994. East Germany was reunified with the West in 1990, and survived integration into the European Union only because the strong West German economy bore most of the costs. Problems appeared to reinforce the warnings of those like Martens, the Belgian Prime Minister, who had warned in March 1990 that the Community must not pursue the goal of integration with Eastern Europe to the exclusion of other ideals. He further warned against the Community 'melting away under the warm glow of pan-Europeanism'.

In July 1997, it was agreed that Poland, Hungary, the Czech Republic, Slovenia, Estonia and Cyprus had achieved the necessary economic and political reforms to allow negotiations to join the Union to begin in 1998 and it was expected that the fifteen members would become twenty-one by 2004. Latvia, Lithuania, Romania, Bulgaria and Slovakia were ruled out of membership on the grounds that they still had significant political or economic problems. There were already considerable disparities between the economies of existing member states, and so the Community was cautious about taking on new members.

KEY ISSUE

What were the implications of further enlargement of the Community in the 1990s?

Elsewhere, Turkey's long-standing application for membership had to be addressed. Turkey's dispute with Greece over Cyprus, an existing member of the Union, was a problem. There was also the prospect of non-aligned countries like Malta and Cyprus joining the Union: how could the Union then follow a common foreign policy? Would a larger membership mean more bureaucracy and greater difficulty in reaching decisions? The admission of more members would complicate budgetary issues. Existing practices such as the high level of agricultural support required a radical overhaul, although that in turn would cause problems with French farmers, traditionally a strong voice in the EU. A larger and more diverse membership made a 'multi-speed Europe' more likely, although that would have been against the spirit of the original Treaty of Rome.

F *Challenges to the developing Union*

At the same time as agreeing to the new admissions, the European Commission announced radical reforms to the Common Agricultural Policy, involving big cuts in production subsidies and guaranteed prices to farmers. These measures were deemed necessary since the World Trade Organisation was insisting upon free trade, and because the accession of new and poorer members to the Community would put an enormous strain on Community finances.

Not surprisingly, changing circumstances and priorities altered perceptions of the European Union's structure and functions. Certain ideals remained central to the EU from its foundation: notably the ideals of cooperation and avoiding internal conflict. However, there were also changes of emphasis in the decades after 1957, due to circumstances and the fact that there were always contradictions within the European Community. The enlargements of the Community from the 1970s presented new challenges and opportunities. Also, from the early 1980s there was a shift in the balance of world power. The European Community grew up in a world dominated by the superpower rivalry of the USA and USSR. Europe was part of the Cold War battleground, and many Western European politicians saw the need for Europe to speak with one voice if it were to have a significant say in its future. Europe did achieve this to some extent, despite the negative impact of world recession in the 1970s. However, in the 1980s the USSR faded as a competitor on the world stage, and so conditions changed. New competition to the Community appeared in the 1980s in the shape of Japan and countries of the developing world.

In addition to dealing with these challenges, the EU continued to suffer tensions caused by conflicting goals and competing institutions. There were disagreements between institutions and governments of member states. The Union contained visionaries who believed in an eventual federal or united Europe, whilst others saw it merely as a vehicle for cooperation or harmonisation of economic and perhaps other policies. Governments were sovereign; that is, they owed

KEY ISSUE

How successful had the movement for European unity been in the fifty years since the Second World War?

allegiance to no higher authority, but this conflicted with federalism. In practice, in the first forty years of its existence the Community operated as an intergovernmental institution, with tensions strongest when individual governments tried to override Community directives of which they disapproved. There were occasional outbursts against what were perceived as attempts to squash individual differences, as in Mrs Thatcher's accusation against the Commission in September 1988 that it was trying to create an 'identikit European personality'.

Other contradictions were not resolved or were largely ignored. The Treaty of Rome referred to the aim of reducing gross inequalities between peoples and between member states. However, its other objective of stimulating growth and competition inevitably widened differences, and the Social Fund could not ameliorate the effects of this. The Treaty of Rome emphasised the importance of competition in business, but the Community also encouraged the development of large supranational companies, capable of competing with giant American companies and scarcely designed to promote competition *among* member states. In order to compete with the American and Japanese economies, the Community put increasing emphasis on larger markets and increased productivity and competitiveness. Regional differences also widened, despite the efforts of the European Regional Development Fund to reduce them. Pursuing economic goals frequently clashed with environmental issues, which were increasingly highlighted in the 1980s and 90s.

Political contradictions persisted within Community structures. Power was divided between the European Commission, the Council of Ministers and the European Parliament. From an early stage, although the Commission could initiate policies and challenge the actions of member states, even as far as taking them to the European Court, its actions and finances ultimately had to be approved by the Council of Ministers.

At different times in the Community's history political and economic concerns came to the fore. By the end of the 1980s the European Union was still principally an economic organisation. Many uncertainties remained in the 1990s. How would the world economy develop? How would the revised political order in Eastern Europe affect developments?

As the 1990s progressed, the EU could point to many economic initiatives and at least qualified success as an economic market. It was in the area of political initiatives that the limitations of the Community were still most evident. A common foreign and security policy, to which the Community was committed under the 1991 Maastricht Treaty, still seemed a long way off. The limitations were particularly evident in the Community's failure to resolve the conflict in the former Yugoslavia. It was a new departure for the Community to try to play a mediating role beyond its own frontiers, sending its foreign ministers to arrange a cease-fire and arranging a peace conference in the Hague. However, the European Union achieved little and eventually handed the problem over to the United Nations.

A United States of Europe was still a long way beyond the horizon, and was not on the agenda of many Europeans, who preferred to keep cooperation at an intergovernmental level. Few politicians could agree on the exact parameters of power in the European Union, although most agreed that they would rather be in the Community than outside it.

7 ↝ EFTA

Britain originally proposed an industrial free trade area, through the OEEC, as an alternative to the EEC. The European Free Trade Association (EFTA), was established by the Stockholm Convention of 1960. Its founder members were Britain, Austria, Denmark, Norway, Portugal, Sweden and Switzerland. It was designed as a zone of free trade, without the EEC's ideals of political integration. EFTA inspired no fear of a loss of national sovereignty among non-federalists. It was intergovernmental, and represented the 'outer Seven' of Europe against the 'inner Six'. EFTA's Charter referred to 'the abolition of all tariffs on industrial goods between the seven member states'. It was not a customs union and there were no external tariffs. Britain saw EFTA as a halfway house between isolation in Europe and full membership of the EEC, for which it was waiting in the 1960s.

Since European Community and EFTA members already had mutual trade links and links with the outside world, the division between the two organisations was somewhat artificial. Attempts were made to establish a more formal relationship. Britain was usually the prime mover in these efforts, since economically it had more in common with the EEC countries. The combined population and market of the other six EFTA members was little bigger than Britain itself, and EFTA certainly had difficulty competing with the Community.

There was a feeling in some quarters in Europe that EFTA gave Britain an unfair advantage by getting access to Europe for British products, whilst Britain continued to benefit from free trade with the Commonwealth. However, Britain came to realise that the weakness of sterling, balance of payments crises and lower growth rates, combined with declining influence over the Commonwealth and a falling off in the 'special relationship' with the USA, were not compensated for by membership of EFTA. Britain somewhat reluctantly saw its future in the wider Community, although it continued to resist federalism. Denmark and Britain left EFTA when they joined the EC, although the remaining EFTA members continued in partnership.

Since 75 per cent of the Community's external trade was with the EFTA states, from the early 1980s EFTA and the EC states moved steadily towards a multilateral arrangement known as the European Economic Area (EEA). This allowed EFTA states to participate in a single market whilst remaining outside the European Community. It satisfied governments that wanted an economic relationship without taking on board the implications of political or social integration.

KEY ISSUE

How successful was EFTA in fulfilling its objectives?

% of total EFTA exports to European Community = 57.9
% of total EFTA imports from European Community = 60.8
% of total European Community exports to EFTA = 10.3
% of total European Community imports from EFTA = 9.6
% of exports to other EEA countries in 1992:

Austria	68.8
Finland	68.9
Iceland	73.4
Norway	80
Sweden	70.9

TABLE 41
Trade between EFTA and the
European Community, 1990

However, from 1995 the four non-EU members of the EEA from 1993 had to obey rules made by fifteen EU members without having any say in their formulation.

8 ↝ OTHER EUROPEAN ORGANISATIONS

There were other major organisations which complemented the European Union.

The *Council of Europe* was set up in 1949 to promote economic and social progress. Defence was excluded from its remit. The founder members included most of the later EU members, joined by Hungary in 1990, Czechoslovakia and Poland in 1991, Bulgaria in 1992, Estonia, Lithuania, Romania and Slovenia in 1993. An intergovernmental Committee of (Foreign) Ministers could make recommendations to governments and a Parliamentary Assembly. Assistance came from a secretariat and committees of experts. The Parliamentary Assembly had 224 members appointed or elected by national parliaments. As such it became the widest parliamentary forum in Western Europe, operating mainly by making recommendations on issues such as human rights and the environment. By 1994 the Council had signed 148 conventions on matters as diverse as wild life conservation, the transport of animals and archeological heritage. However, the Council had no legislative powers and therefore its overall impact was limited compared to EU institutions.

The Conference on Security and Cooperation in Europe (CSCE) held its first summit in Helsinki in July–August 1975. It laid down ten principles on human rights, self-determination and intergovernmental relations. Further conferences were held in Belgrade in 1977–78, Madrid 1980–83, Stockholm 1984–86, and Vienna 1986–89. The original charter was signed by the USA, Canada and all European states except Albania. There were fifty-three members by 1983. The charter committed signatories to observe human rights, democracy and the rule of law. The Conference met annually. As a result of its activities, at a Paris summit in November 1990 NATO and the Warsaw Pact signed a Treaty on the Reduction of Conventional Forces in Europe. In July 1992 the Conference agreed in principle to the setting up of an armed peacekeeping force, although this did not materialise.

The European Bank for Reconstruction and Development (EBRD) was inaugurated in April 1991. There were fifty-nine members by 1994, including all the former Soviet Republics. The EBRD's objective was to lend funds at market rates to Eastern European companies and countries committed to multi-party politics and market economies. As such it was an important part of European attempts to assist the transition of countries with former authoritarian regimes to a new era of liberal democracy. There was a widespread recognition that the political credibility and survival of post-Communist regimes might well depend on their ability to achieve economic stability and growth in difficult circumstances.

9 ⌐ COOPERATION IN CENTRAL AND EASTERN EUROPE: COMECON

A *Introduction*

Following Communist takeovers in many Central and Eastern European countries in the aftermath of the Second World War, there was a movement by Moscow and the new regimes to establish a trading bloc covering the new Socialist economies. COMECON (or SMEA) – the Commission for Mutual Economic Aid – was set up in Moscow in January 1949 by the USSR, Poland, Czechoslovakia, Romania, Hungary and Bulgaria. Albania joined later in the year, although its membership effectively ceased from 1961. The East German regime joined in 1950. Later Cuba, Mongolia and Vietnam also joined.

Western governments claimed that COMECON was the Soviet answer to the Marshall Plan of 1947, which had been designed to assist countries to recover from the ravages of war, whilst at the same time increasing American influence in Europe. The Soviets denied this claim, although the communiqué establishing COMECON referred to the planning of 'broader economic cooperation between the peoples of the people's democracies and the Soviet Union', because 'these countries do not consider it possible to subordinate themselves to the dictates of the Marshall Plan, as this plan infringes on the sovereignty of countries and the interests of their national economies'.

B *Aims and organisation*

The stated economic aim of COMECON was 'to exchange economic experience', extend technical aid and encourage mutual trade between members. There was also a declared political aim: 'to strengthen the unity and solidarity of members' and to encourage cooperation 'in the interest of the building of socialism and communism'.

COMECON did seem at first to be little more than a propaganda exercise, since it remained largely inactive until 1954 when a Secretariat was created. COMECON's governing Council met twice in 1949 and

---

KEY ISSUE

Why was COMECON set up?

See pages 387–8

then only once more before 1954. After 1955 the Council usually met twice a year. Only in December 1959 was COMECON's Charter of Organisation signed in Sofia. After that, the essentials of the organisation remained unchanged, and it played a more active role: in particular, under Khrushchev's influence from 1956 it attempted to coordinate national five-year plans. It also encouraged member states to specialise in certain areas and cooperate on a trading basis, particularly in chemicals and engineering, so as to eliminate costly competition and encourage efficiency. This frequently clashed with the policies of individual regimes, which were reluctant to trust each other and wanted to promote self-sufficiency. The Romanians in particular objected to attempts to make them specialise in agriculture in order to feed the rest of the Soviet Bloc.

See page 266

In reality much of the trade between COMECON members continued to be on a bilateral basis, and the organisation was clearly not one of equal members: the Soviets maintained a controlling hand, with their personnel in most key positions, and the Secretariat was eventually concentrated in Moscow.

COMECON's Executive Committee contained six high-ranking permanent delegates from member countries, and they were responsible for implementing policy. There were twenty-one Standing Commissions by 1988, comprised of experts who assisted in the formulation of policy.

C *Achievements and decline*

Was COMECON successful? It did fulfil one of its aims, since trade between COMECON members was greater than between member states and non-member states, as Table 41 shows:

The USSR bought about half the exports of machinery and manufactured goods produced by other COMECON members. Member states were guaranteed energy supplies from the USSR. However, different rates of development between member states, mutual suspicion, and lack of good credit and other market facilities restricted trade.

There were attempts to increase cooperation following the Czechoslovakian crisis of 1968. However, concerns about declining growth rates tended to make the Communist regimes look to internal reforms rather than to greater regional cooperation, and various schemes to expand COMECON's activities were mostly quietly

	Between member states (%)	Developed market economies (%)	Rest of world (%)
1948	44	40	16
1958	61	19	20
1968	64	21	15
1977	55	29	16

TABLE 42
COMECON's trading patterns, 1948–77

TABLE 43

Average annual rates of growth (in %) of COMECON's European members (including the USSR)

	1951–55	1955–60	1961–65	1966–70	1971–75	1976–80	1981–85	1986–88
Bulgaria	12.2	9.7	6.7	8.8	7.8	6.1	3.7	5.6
Czechoslovakia	8.2	7.0	1.9	7.0	5.5	3.7	1.7	2.4
GDR	13.1	7.1	3.5	5.2	5.4	4.1	4.5	3.5
Hungary	5.7	5.9	4.1	6.8	6.3	2.8	1.3	1.7
Poland	8.6	6.6	6.2	6.0	9.8	1.2	0.8	3.9
Romania	14.1	6.6	9.1	7.7	11.4	7.0	4.4	5.1
COMECON as a whole	10.8	8.5	6.0	7.4	6.4	4.1	3.0	3.0

KEY ISSUE

How successful was COMECON in meeting its objectives?

forgotten from the 1970s onwards. When Gorbachev began his reform programme in the USSR in the mid-1980s, he did resurrect the idea of reform of COMECON, but also tried to strengthen Soviet control over it. His efforts met with considerable opposition from other member states, especially when the idea of a common market on Western European lines was mooted.

The rapid break-up of the Soviet Bloc at the end of the 1980s made the likelihood of regional cooperation even less. As the European Union expanded, so its Eastern counterpart steadily declined. It came as no great surprise when the dissolution of the COMECON Executive Committee was announced in February 1991, and the Organisation formally dissolved itself in the following September.

10 ⮌ BIBLIOGRAPHY

There are many specialist books on different aspects of European organisations, particularly the European Union. However, there are not many general books suitable for this level which also cover all the principal areas. A useful introduction to the history of European integration after 1945 is *The Community of Europe* by D. Urwin (London, 1991). Also useful is the *Reconstruction of Western Europe* by A. Milward (London, 1984). The institutions and workings of the European Community are described in *The Government and Politics of the European Community* by N. Nugent (London, 1989). The growth of the Community is covered in *From the Six to the Twelve* by F. Nicholson and R. East (London, 1987). *European Community: the Building of a Union* by J. Pindar (Oxford, 1991) considers the development of the Community from a federalist standpoint. Britain's relations with Europe are dealt with in *An Awkward Partner* by S. George (Oxford, 1990). A personal viewpoint of the ideals of the community can be found in *Memoirs* by Jean Monnet (Collins, 1978). Developments in Eastern Europe feature in *Economic Integration in Eastern Europe* by J. van Brabant (New York, 1989).

11 ⟿ ESSAY QUESTIONS

1. (a) Why was the EEC formed in the 1950s?
    (b) Why was the original membership of six not enlarged until the 1970s?

2. (a) Outline the main terms of the Treaty of Rome (March 1957) and the Maastricht Treaty (1991);
    (b) 'An economic success but a political failure'. To what extent is this a valid judgement on the history of the European Community between these two treaties?

3. To what extent did the European Community fulfil its objectives, in the thirty-five years following the Treaty of Rome (1957), in any *two* of the following: industrial and regional policy; agricultural policy; social policy; economic and monetary union; defence; foreign policy.

4. (a) Outline the main features of the organisation of any *two* of the following: the European Union; EFTA; COMECON;
    (b) What were the main strengths and weaknesses of your two choices during any twenty-year period between their formation and 1991?

5. Why did it prove difficult to achieve full political and economic union in Western Europe in the fifty years after the ending of the Second World War?

6. (a) Outline the policies of any *two* of the following towards European unity in *either* the period 1945–69 *or* 1969–92: France; Britain; Germany; Italy; Denmark; Norway;
    (b) To what extent did the two countries influence the direction of European unity during the period you have chosen?

7. (a) Outline the objectives of *either* COMECON *or* EFTA: France; Britain; Germany; Italy; Denmark; Norway;
    (b) To what extent did the organisation you have chosen fulfil those objectives in the period down to the early 1990s?

12 ⟿ DOCUMENTARY EXERCISE ON EUROPEAN INTEGRATION

Study carefully the sources on European integration below and answer the questions which follow.

> We must build a kind of United States of Europe. In this way only will hundreds of millions of toilers be able to regain the simple joys and hopes which make life worth living. The process is simple. All that is needed is the resolve of hundreds of millions of men and women to do right instead of wrong and gain as their reward blessing instead of cursing...

SOURCE A
Winston Churchill speaking at Zurich, 19 September 1946.

We British have our own Commonwealth of Nations... And why should there not be a European group which could give a sense of enlarged patriotism and common citizenship to the distracted peoples of this turbulent and mighty continent...

I am now going to say something that will astonish you. The first step in the re-creation of the European family must be a partnership between France and Germany. In this way only can France recover the usual leadership of Europe. There can be no revival of Europe without a spiritually great France and a spiritually great Germany. The structure of the United States of Europe, if well and truly built, will be such as to make the material strength of a single state less important... Great Britain, the British Commonwealth of Nations, mighty America, and I trust Soviet Russia... must be the friends and sponsors of the new Europe and must champion its right to live and shine.

SOURCE B
Schuman's Declaration *of 9 May 1950, which led to negotiations to set up the European Coal and Steel Community.*

The contribution which an organised and living Europe can bring to civilisation is indispensable to the maintenance of peaceful relations... Europe will not be made all at once or according to a single plan. It will be built through concrete achievements which first create a *de facto* solidarity. The coming together of the nations of Europe requires the elimination of the age-old opposition of France and Germany. Any action which must be taken in the first place must concern these two countries. With this aim in view, the French Government proposes that action be taken immediately on one limited but decisive point. It proposes that Franco–German production of coal and steel as a whole be placed under a common High Authority, within the framework of an organisation open to the participation of the other countries of Europe...

The solidarity in production thus established will make it plain that any war between France and Germany becomes not merely unthinkable, but materially impossible. The setting up of this powerful productive unit, open to all countries willing to take part... will lay a true foundation for their economic unification.

Under cover of the 'unification' of Europe, the imperialist promoters of integration have divided Europe into economic, political and military groups opposed to one another; they have created an aggressive military bloc of Western European powers aimed against the Soviet Union and the popular democracies... the agreements on the Common Market, Euratom and Eurafrica represent in reality an alliance of the most powerful monopolies, cartels, and trusts of the industry and banks in these six countries...

Behind the project for a Common Market and the other

measures already taken by the monopolists of the Six lies the desire to unite the forces of imperialism with a view...to doing battle against socialism and against the movements of national liberation of the colonised peoples and in the lands under their thumb...

The Treaties establishing the EEC and Euratom provide for the setting up of various controlling organs...The transference to these institutions of certain important competencies in the economic, political and military fields will result in the curtailment of the sovereignty of the weaker states; it will inevitably limit the rights of the Parliaments of these countries to make important social and national decisions.

SOURCE C
A Soviet view of the Common Market, from the Seventeen Theses on the Common Market, *issued by the Institute of the World Economics and International Relations, Moscow, 1957.*

Although the Treaty of Rome is concerned with economic matters, it has an important political objective, namely, to promote unity and stability in Europe which is so essential a factor in the struggle for freedom and progress throughout the world. In this modern world the tendency towards larger groups of nations acting together in the common interest leads to greater unity and thus adds to our strength.

I believe that it is both our duty and our interest to contribute towards that strength by securing the closest possible unity within Europe...I do not think that Britain's contribution to the Commonwealth will be reduced if Europe unites.

SOURCE D
The British Prime Minister, Harold Macmillan, declares Britain's intention to apply to join the Community, Parliament, 31 July 1961.

It makes good sense for our jobs and prosperity . . . it makes good sense for world peace. It makes good sense for the Commonwealth. It makes good sense for our children's future...

Our friends want us to stay in. If we left we would not go back to the world as it was when we joined, still less to the old world of Britain's imperial heyday. The world has been changing fast...Outside, we should be alone in a harsh, cold world, with none of our friends offering to revive old partnerships...

Why can't we go it alone? To some this sounds attractive. Mind our own business. Make our own decisions. Pull up the drawbridge. In the modern world it is just not practicable...

Our traditions are safe. We can work together and still stay British. The Community does not mean dull uniformity. It hasn't made the French eat German food or the Dutch drink Italian beer. Nor will it damage our British traditions and way of life...

English Common Law is not affected . . .

Staying in protects our jobs . . .

Secure food at fair prices.

SOURCE E
Arguments for Britain to stay in the European Community, from the Britain in Europe *campaign leaflet, May 1975.*

Re-negotiation. The present Government, though it tried, has on its own admission failed to achieve the 'fundamental re-negotiation' it promised at the last two General Elections...

What did the pro-Marketeers say? Before we joined the Common Market the Government forecast that we should enjoy – A rapid rise in our living standards; A trade surplus with the Common Market; Better productivity; Higher investment; More employment; Faster industrial growth.

In every case the opposite is now happening...

Our legal right to come out... there is nothing in the Treaty of Rome which says a country cannot come out.

The right to rule ourselves. The fundamental question is whether or not we remain free to rule ourselves in our own way. For the British people, membership of the Common Market has already been a bad bargain...

Your food, your jobs, our trade. We cannot afford to remain in the Common Market because: it must mean still higher food prices...

Your jobs at risk. If we stay in the Common Market, a British Government can no longer prevent the drift of industry south-wards and increasingly to the Continent...

Taxes to keep prices up. The Common Market's dear food policy is designed to prop up inefficient farmers on the Continent by keeping food prices high...

Commonwealth links. Our Commonwealth links are bound to be weakened much further if we stay in the Common Market...

Britain a mere province of the Common Market? The real aim of the Market is, of course, to become one single country in which Britain would be reduced to a mere province.

SOURCE F
Arguments for Britain to leave the European Community, from Why You Should Vote No, *a National Referendum Campaign leaflet, May 1975.*

Q

1. *Using your own knowledge, explain why Britain did not join the Community until several years after its creation.* (6 marks)
2. *Compare Sources A and B in their arguments for European cooperation or integration.* (6 marks)
3. *Using Source C.*
(i) *Identify the elements of propaganda in Source C.* (4 marks)
(ii) *Explain the Soviet objections to the Common Market.* (5 marks)
4. *How reliable is Source D as evidence of the British government's attitude towards membership of the Community in the 1960s.* (4 marks)
5. (i) *What is the message of the cartoons in Source G?* (6 marks)
(ii) *What are the uses and limitations of the cartoons in Source G as evidence of attitudes in Britain towards the European Union?* (7 marks)
6. *Using Sources E and F and your own knowledge, discuss the advantages and disadvantages for Britain of membership of the European Community since 1973.* (12 marks)

"*MY PERSONAL VIEW IS THAT IT'S ALL THE FAULT OF THE EU*"

An election candidate blames a water shortage in Britain on the EU, 16 April 1997

"WE SHALL DEFEND OUR ISLAND, WHATEVER THE COST MAY BE, WE SHALL NEGOTIATE ON THE BEACHES, WE SHALL NEGOTIATE ON THE LANDING GROUNDS, WE SHALL NEGOTIATE IN THE FIELDS AND IN THE STREETS, WE SHALL NEGOTIATE IN THE HILLS; WE SHALL NEVER DECIDE."

Conservative leader John Major and Labour leader Tony Blair and a parody of a wartime speech by Winston Churchill, 23 April 1997

PICTURE 40

A Conservative election poster showing German Chancellor Helmut Kohl as a ventriloquist's dummy on Prime Minister Tony Blair's knee, 8 June 1997

The Cold War, 1943–91

9

INTRODUCTION

The Cold War was the dominant factor in the history of modern Europe from 1945 to the collapse of the Soviet Union. It was the key to the division of Europe between East and West, it was the main legacy of the Second World War, and it marked the end of the age of the European powers and the beginning of the age of the American and Soviet 'superpowers'.

The Cold War began in Europe, above all in Germany. And it was in Germany, with the opening of the Berlin Wall, that it ended. In between times, the Cold War spread to China and Korea, to Cuba and Vietnam, to Africa and the Middle East. In the process, it shaped the society, economy and politics of the superpowers and of the countries they dominated.

In this chapter, the emphasis is on the division of Europe – but one of the key issues of the Cold War was the way in which Europe itself became less in control of its own destiny and more affected by global economic and military factors. The following general points may be helpful:

- The Cold War was a substitute for the general peace settlement which failed to materialise in 1945. It established 'unwritten rules' for the post-war world, not negotiated or official, but permanent ones just the same;
- The Cold War was deceptively stable. Despite dangerous flash-points such as Cuba or Berlin, and despite the emotive fear of nuclear weapons, it provided continuity and security in a state of 'hot peace';
- The Cold War did not only divide Europe along military and strategic lines. There were also important economic and ideological factors. The Cold War was possibly the biggest single factor in explaining the sustained economic prosperity of Western Europe (and Japan) from the late 1940s;
- The Cold War was a worldwide confrontation between the USA and the Soviet Union but it was Europe which provided the main battleground. It was the defeat of Nazi Germany which 'made' the new superpowers and brought them into the heart of Europe;
- The Cold War was intertwined with the issue of decolonisation. Just as the power vacuum in Europe in 1945 led to the involvement of the superpowers, so the decline of the European empires led to superpower rivalries in numerous post-colonial conflicts;

See pages 136–50 for an account of Soviet foreign policy.

- The Cold War was a war of propaganda and indoctrination. Even though the Cold War became history in 1991 and the Soviet archives are now available, it remains difficult to establish a balanced and objective view. (It is advisable to avoid automatic acceptance of Western interpretations and to understand how differently the causes and nature of the Cold War were perceived on the other side of the Iron Curtain.)

1 ⤳ THE ORIGINS OF THE COLD WAR, 1939–49

A *The legacy of the past*

The Cold War that took shape between 1945 and 1949 was not as new, nor as surprising as it seemed at the time. In the first flush of victory, there were high hopes that the wartime Grand Alliance would lead to a better post-war world. It was hoped that the United Nations would succeed where the League had failed and that the cooperation during the war would carry on through the rebuilding of Europe afterwards. At the time, it appeared that a great opportunity to secure a lasting peace was being wasted. In reality, most of the factors leading to the division of the continent were already in place.

The origins of the Cold War went back well before 1945, perhaps as far as the Bolshevik Revolution of 1917. From the outset, 'Bolshevism' was a frightening menace to the capitalist West. The formation of the 'Comintern', the Third Communist International, in 1919, dedicated to promoting Communist world revolution, intensified Western fears of Communist subversion. The Treaty of Brest–Litovsk in 1918, by which the new Bolshevik regime made peace with Germany, was regarded in

ANALYSIS

Torgau-on-the-Elbe, 1945

In April 1945, American forces advancing eastwards through Germany reached the river Elbe, near the small town of Torgau. Here they met up with units of the Red Army. Despite the doubts of their commanders, especially on the American side, Soviet and American troops fraternised cheerfully, celebrating victory over the common Nazi enemy and trying to cross the language barrier with smiles, drinks, cigarettes, chocolate bars and family photographs. They were eagerly encouraged by news reporters and cameramen, who turned the join-up at Torgau into such a media event that it was re-enacted for the cameras a few days afterwards.

The friendships and optimism of Torgau were misleading. Two men, one from the Ukraine and one from the American Midwest, met on that day, became friends and promised to meet again soon, when the war was over. They next met in 1985, at another media event on the occasion of the fortieth anniversary of the end of the war. By then, both men were familiar with decades of indoctrination; each had seen members of their families go off to fight in Vietnam or Afghanistan. The friendships of Torgau had been overruled by the realities of the Cold War.

the West as a betrayal. There were grievances on the Soviet side, too. The Allied Intervention in Russia in 1918–20 was seen as an attempt to kill the Soviet State at birth. Russia was ignored at the post-war peace conferences. By the death of Lenin in 1924, there was already a gulf of fear and ideological dislike between Soviet Russia and the West. Neither side understood much about the other. Each side vastly exaggerated the extent to which the other was a threat.

Between 1929 and 1935, Stalin was content to seal the USSR off from the outside world. The Western powers, especially with the USA following a policy of isolationism, were content to leave Soviet Russia

> **KEY ISSUE**
>
> *How important were long-term factors after 1917 in causing the division of Europe after 1945?*

alone. The Comintern remained in existence but was held on a tight leash by Stalin. European Communist parties followed the Moscow line that they should have nothing to do with non-Communist Socialist parties until this changed fundamentally with the rise of Hitler. In 1935, Stalin reversed his policy and called for Fascism to be opposed by the formation of Popular Fronts in which all left-wing parties would combine forces. A French–Soviet pact was signed to guarantee the joint defence of Czechoslovakia. From 1935, the possibility existed of an anti-Hitler alliance to restrain German aggression by the threat of a two-front war.

This alliance was never formed. In 1936–37, Stalin's intervention on the Republican side in the Spanish Civil War did not cement Soviet–Western relations but made them worse. In September 1938, the Munich Conference 'solved' the crisis over Czechoslovakia without involving the USSR, or the Czechs. With some justification, Stalin decided that cooperation with the West was not going to provide the security he desired. Although he continued to play along with the idea of an alliance, and a British–French military mission was in Moscow for talks in the summer of 1939, he went ahead with the previously-unthinkable Nazi–Soviet Pact, announced on 23 August.

There are many interpretations of the Nazi–Soviet Pact: that it proved Stalin was devious and unreliable; or that the problem of Poland was insoluble; or that the Western powers were following a cynical anti-Communist policy and that Stalin was entirely justified in protecting his own best interests. Whichever interpretation is chosen, there are two all-important issues:

● The pact led to intense anti-Soviet attitudes in the West. Stalin was seen as making a cynical deal with his most bitter ideological enemy, leaving Britain and France to face Germany on their own and apparently proving right all those who regarded him as evil and untrustworthy. Hostility and suspicion against Stalin in 1939 was very like the hostility and suspicion after 1945;

● The pact not only gave Stalin security, for the time being, against a German invasion. The USSR also made significant territorial gains in Eastern Poland, the Baltic States and in the Balkans. The 'Soviet Empire' now extended as far as the empire of the Tsars; and the gains made by Stalin by avoiding war in 1939 were remarkably similar to the gains he made by winning the war in 1945.

KEY ISSUE

How similar were Stalin's aims, and gains, in 1939 and 1945?

B *The Grand Alliance*

When the pact with Hitler was made in 1939, Stalin seemed to have the best of the bargain. He expected a long war, similar to 1914–18, in which all his enemies would be exhausted and weakened. But Stalin had placed too much faith in the French army. The rapid collapse of France in 1940 left Hitler in charge of the continent, with the Soviet Union hopelessly vulnerable.

Then, in June 1941, Hitler's invasion of the USSR meant that Britain and the Soviet Union, so hostile in 1939, were now allies. In December, the Japanese attack at Pearl Harbour brought the USA into the war. The so-called Grand Alliance was formed, led by the 'Big Three', Stalin, Roosevelt and Churchill. If not full-hearted allies, the Big Three were fighting against some of the same enemies for some of the same reasons. The crucial link between Stalin and the Western Allies was fear of Hitler. Neither the USA nor the USSR had entered the war voluntarily. In each case, they had been utterly determined to avoid war. In 1941, each was attacked without warning and literally bombed into the war. Ironically, this war they had tried so hard to avoid turned each of them into an military and industrial world power by 1945.

So, in 1941–42, the objective of the Grand Alliance was survival. But by the summer of 1943 the tide of war was turning. The Red Army won its decisive victories at Stalingrad and Kursk. The Battle of the Atlantic was effectively won in May–June 1943. Italy changed sides. The Japanese were on the defensive in the Pacific, leaving the Americans to pour more and more men and resources into the war in Europe. The emphasis began to shift from fear of Hitler to what would happen after the war; and in this the allies had very different aims. The Cold War began to take shape, at the latest, in 1943.

From 1943 to 1945, many long-term factors, especially deep disagreements about the fate of Poland and Germany, began to fray the outward unity of the Grand Alliance. These tensions ultimately undermined the prospects of a post-war peace agreement. The emergence of the Cold War from 1945 was possibly a disappointing failure but it should not have been a surprise.

One of many causes of friction within the Grand Alliance was the issue of a Second Front. To Stalin, it was obvious that the Red Army had borne the brunt of the war since 1941 and that his allies should relieve the pressure by opening a second front in Europe. Stalin was not satisfied by landings in North Africa and Italy and he was not convinced by Western claims that the technical difficulties of invading France from the sea made it impossible to do so in 1943. As the emphasis shifted from fighting the war to preparing for the results of victory, a series of summit conferences brought the Big Three together, at Tehran in 1943 and at Yalta and Potsdam in 1945. Several other important meetings took place, for example between Churchill and Roosevelt at Casablanca in 1943 and between Churchill and Stalin in 1944. These wartime conferences became all the more important because there was no final peace settlement after the war.

C *Tehran, November–December 1943*

By the time the Big Three met at Tehran, the Grand Alliance was already under strain. At Casablanca in January 1943, Churchill and Roosevelt had agreed that the main invasion of France would have to wait until 1944, even though this was bound to get a hostile response

TIMELINE
The origins of the Cold War

1917 Bolshevik Revolution
1918 Brest–Litovsk Treaty
1918 Allied intervention
  –20
1919 Comintern formed
1933 Hitler in power
1935 Stalin's call for Popular Fronts
1938 USSR excluded at Munich
1939 Anglo–French mission to Moscow
  Nazi–Soviet Pact
1941 German invasion of the USSR
  American entry into the war
1943 Casablanca Conference
  Katyn Forest massacre revealed
  Tehran Conference
1944 Warsaw rising crushed
1945 Yalta Conference
  End of war in Europe
  Potsdam Conference

from Stalin. It was also agreed at Casablanca to demand unconditional surrender from Germany, partly to reassure Stalin that the West would never make a separate peace.

There was also tension over Poland. In March 1943, the German news service announced the discovery of the mass graves of 7000 Polish army officers in the Katyn Forest, near Smolensk. The facts about the Katyn massacre are clear. These were Polish officers killed by Stalin's NKVD in 1940 and not, as Stalin insisted, by the Nazis. (The Soviet Union never admitted responsibility for Katyn. It was only in 1993, after the collapse of Communism, that the Russian Federation opened its archives and confirmed what serious historians had known all along.) Katyn seriously damaged Stalin's relations with the West, both in 1943 and for decades afterwards. It was one of many issues leading to a split between the Polish government-in-exile in London and the pro-Soviet Polish leadership in Moscow. Suspicions of Stalin's motives were intensified by the rapid advances by the Red Army after the great victory at Kursk, which ensured that Stalin's armies would liberate Poland and most of East Central Europe.

At Tehran, therefore, Stalin was in a strong position. Tehran was also the last occasion when Churchill could act as an equal in the Big Three. During 1944, it was more and more obvious that the USA was the dominant partner in the Western alliance; Stalin was quick to see American–British differences and to exploit them. At Tehran, Stalin got assurances about the invasion of France in 1944 and he set out his claims for a return to the pre-1921 Polish–Russian frontiers. Stalin and Churchill also discussed how post-war Germany might be weakened by moving the German–Polish border west to the river Oder.

D *From Tehran to Yalta*

Between Tehran at the end of 1943 and the next summit at Yalta early in 1945, several important developments influenced relationships within the Grand Alliance. One was the military situation. After the Normandy landings, there was no instant collapse of the German armies in the West. By the time of Yalta, American and British forces had only just crossed the Rhine; the Red Army had already pushed deep into Germany. Soviet forces, and Stalin's hand-picked political agents, had already liberated Poland, Hungary, Romania and Bulgaria and were poised to enter Prague, Vienna and Berlin. As the invasion of Japan was likely to be difficult, the USA wanted Soviet help against Japan once Germany had been defeated.

A second factor was disagreement among the Western Allies as to how Stalin should be handled. For Churchill and a number of American diplomats, Stalin was a ruthless, single-minded leader who needed tough negotiation, even confrontation. For Roosevelt, Stalin was just a normal politician with whom deals were perfectly possible. After Tehran, Roosevelt said:

> I got along fine with Marshal Stalin. He combines relentless determination with stalwart good humour. He represents the heart and soul of Russia. We're going to get along very well with him and with the Russian people – very well indeed.

A third central issue was Poland. As soon as Soviet forces entered Eastern Poland early in 1944, Stalin set up a Communist-dominated Committee of Polish Liberation in the town of Lublin (hence the name 'Lublin Poles'), rivalling the authority of the nationalist Polish government-in-exile which had been based in London (and thus known as the 'London Poles') since 1939. The question of Poland, therefore, was already bound to cause tension. This tension was maximised by the Warsaw Rising.

See page 174

Not long after the Warsaw Rising, in October 1944, Churchill flew to Moscow to meet Stalin. Before leaving London, Churchill told one of his advisers:

> Make no mistake, all the Balkans apart from Greece are going to be Bolshevised and there's nothing I can do to prevent it. There's nothing I can do for Poland, either.

Churchill discussed with Stalin how separate spheres of influence might be agreed. He scribbled figures on a scrap of paper and handed it to Stalin:

Romania:	90% Soviet	Greece:	90% British
Yugoslavia:	50% each	Hungary:	50% each
Bulgaria:	70% Soviet		

According to Churchill:

> Stalin took his blue pencil, made a large tick on it and passed it back. I suggested to Marshal Stalin that we should burn the paper because it might seem cynical that we had decided such fateful issues in such an off-hand manner. Stalin replied, 'No. You keep it.'

The Warsaw Rising

ANALYSIS

With the Red Army nearing Warsaw in July 1944, the main Polish Resistance forces, the AK, or Polish Home Army, launched a mass rising against the German occupiers. The AK assumed that, with the Soviet armies so close just across the Vistula river, the rising would enable the Poles to take part in liberating their own capital city. The outcome was a tragic event which, together with the Katyn massacre, ruined Soviet–Polish relations for years to come. The Red Army halted its advance. Soviet forces did not enter the city until nearly five months later. Stalin claimed this was because his forces had to rest and re-group. This was possibly true – but Stalin also refused repeated British requests to use Soviet airfields to fly in supplies for the AK. In a telegram to Churchill, Stalin described the AK as 'a bunch of criminals'.

Meanwhile, the SS forces in Warsaw crushed the rising and destroyed the city block by block. In sixty-three days of fighting, 200 000 Poles were killed; afterwards another 150 000 were sent to Soviet labour camps.

It is possible to make a defence of Stalin's role in the Warsaw Rising. Stalin regarded the nationalist AK (and the London Poles) as fundamentally anti-Soviet, which was at least partly true. For Stalin, the liberation of Poland was an 'internal matter'. He would not interfere with the Western powers in the liberation of France, so why could they not leave him alone in Poland, which was such a vital concern for Russian security? But many saw Stalin's actions as proof that he had no intention of cooperating with the West and was ruthlessly using force to take control of Poland and most of Central Europe.

E *Yalta, February 1945*

Yalta was the last summit before the end of the war. Stalin's bargaining position was strong. Churchill had virtually given up on the Balkans and Poland. Franklin Roosevelt was already a dying man. Yalta was never intended as a 'final' negotiation, only as one more step to an eventual peace settlement, but no final treaty was ever signed. The imprecise Yalta agreements became the basis of the post-war map of Europe.

ANALYSIS

Interpretations of the Yalta Conference

Yalta remains controversial. Many historians and right-wing politicians still speak of Yalta as a betrayal of the 'Little Democracies', especially Poland. Norman Davies writes that 'Poland was handed to Stalin on a plate'. According to this view, Stalin played on the 'gullibility' of the West and exploited the divisions between Churchill and Roosevelt. Roosevelt's defenders saw it differently. For them, Yalta was the basis of a good settlement; the problems came later, after Roosevelt was dead, when the Yalta agreements were not respected by either side.

The American historian Daniel Yergin calls the liberal, Rooseveltian line the 'Yalta Axioms' – belief in cooperation and in understanding legitimate Soviet interests. It can indeed be argued that Stalin made the Yalta agreements in good faith and did not break them afterwards; that, for example, he genuinely believed that 'free elections' meant something different from Western interpretations. Yergin calls the alternative view the 'Riga Axioms' – the view that Stalin did not understand cooperation, only force, and that Stalin saw confidence-building measures merely as weaknesses to be exploited. (American diplomatic experts such as George Kennan and Charles Bohlen had used Riga as a base from which to observe Stalin's Russia in the 1930s.)

After the war, these 'Riga Axioms' gradually dominated the thinking of the Truman administration and became the basis of the policy known as 'containment'.

At Yalta, it was agreed that Soviet forces would share as soon as possible in the war against Japan. Zones for the occupation of Germany were tentatively on the map. Much time was spent on Poland and on the plan to move the Soviet–Polish border westwards, with Poland to be compensated by territory taken from Germany. Thus Polish cities like Lvov became part of the USSR, while historic German cities like Breslau became Polish. This was accompanied by the mass migration of millions of refugees.

The new Polish government set up at Lublin was to be the basis of post-war Poland; but Stalin agreed that there would be a share in the government for the London Poles and he accepted the need for 'free and unfettered elections'. Publicly at least, the Western leaders regarded Yalta as a success at the time. Later, Cold War hostility took over. How much this was due to the devious long-term plans of Stalin, or how much it was due to the fact that Roosevelt died and his successors set out to 'implement Yalta by changing it', is still a question for debate.

> *Shattered Peace* by Daniel Yorgin (see bibliography)

See map on page 385

> **KEY ISSUE**
>
> *Why was there no agreed peace settlement in 1945?*

F *Potsdam, July–August, 1945*

When the victorious powers met at Potsdam in July 1945, the situation was very different from Yalta. The war in Europe was over. Potsdam itself was in the heart of ruined Berlin. The advancing Allied armies had stopped, on the orders of General Eisenhower, leaving most of the capital cities of Central and Eastern Europe, including Berlin, under Soviet control. At San Francisco in April, the conference on the new United Nations Organisation had shown many of the tensions emerging between Soviet Russia and the West.

Perhaps above all, Roosevelt's successor as American President, Harry Truman, came to Potsdam with a very different attitude to dealing with the Soviet Union. Convinced that the USA held the whip hand in military and economic power, Truman assumed that Stalin would give in to pressure. In Washington in April 1945, eleven days after becoming President, Truman took an aggressive, almost bullying line in a personal meeting with the Soviet Foreign Minister Molotov, laying down the law about elections in Poland. Molotov protested that 'he had never been spoken to like that in his life'. The next day, Stalin wrote to Truman:

> Poland borders on the Soviet Union. I do not know whether a genuinely democratic government has been established in Greece or Belgium; the Soviet Union does not claim the right to interfere in those matters, because it recognises how important Greece and Belgium are to the interests of Great Britain. You evidently do not agree that the Soviet Union is entitled to seek a government in Poland which would be friendly to it. The Soviet Union cannot agree to the existence of a government in Poland which is hostile to it.

This had little effect on Truman and the new Secretary of State, James Byrnes. Truman was convinced that a firm line was the right line. What happened at Potsdam deepened a divide which was already there.

At Potsdam, the main issues concerning the occupation of Germany and the four-power control of Berlin were clarified. The German border with Poland was finalised, if not really agreed. At Yalta, the line along the river Oder and the river Neisse had been discussed; now, at Potsdam, Stalin set the border on the western branch of the Neisse, 100 miles further into Germany. The 'Oder–Neisse line' became a keen German grievance after the war.

The war in the Pacific was ended without the need for Soviet military help, because the atomic bomb had been successfully tested and was now to be used at Hiroshima and Nagasaki. Some historians claim that the decision to drop the bomb was made not so much to accelerate the defeat of Japan as to 'impress the Russians'. In any case, the mere fact that the USA possessed such a weapon was bound to make Soviet–American relations worse.

See documentary exercise on pages 423–5

TIMELINE
The wartime conferences

Jan 1943	Casablanca	Churchill, Roosevelt
May 1943	Washington	Churchill, Roosevelt
Aug 1943	Quebec	Churchill, Roosevelt
Nov 1943	Cairo	Churchill, Roosevelt, Chiang Kai-shek
Nov 1943	Tehran	Churchill, Roosevelt, Stalin
Dec 1943	Cairo	Churchill, Roosevelt
Sept 1944	Quebec	Churchill, Roosevelt
Oct 1944	Moscow	Churchill, Stalin
Jan 1945	Malta	Churchill, Roosevelt
Feb 1945	Yalta	Churchill, Roosevelt, Stalin
July 1945	Potsdam	Churchill (Attlee), Truman, Stalin

In mid-conference, Churchill left the stage because of his defeat in the British general election and was replaced by Clement Attlee. It was already plain well before Potsdam that the Big Three had become the Big Two. Stalin raised the question of how to remove Franco from power in Spain but got little encouragement. Truman was keen to internationalise key European waterways. Stalin kept pushing Soviet demands for reparations. Little of this was resolved; mostly, positions were staked out. Although in theory Potsdam was just one more step towards a final post-war peace settlement, it was clear, when the conference broke up on 2 August, that no such settlement would ever take place. The Cold War happened instead.

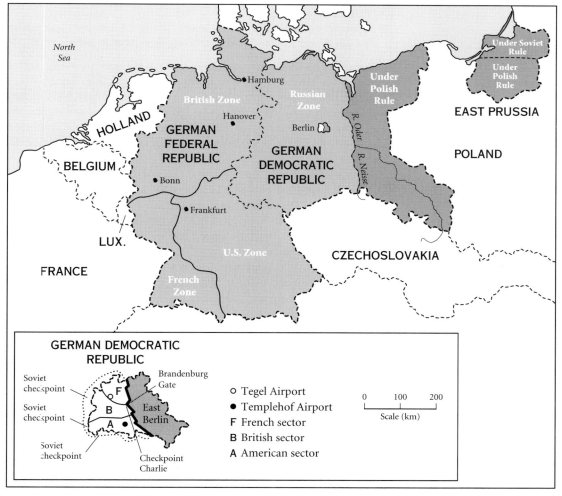

MAP 31
Europe after Potsdam

G *The division of Europe*

After Potsdam, the issues separating the new 'superpowers' made a long list. At the top of the list were the linked questions of Germany and Poland. Poland had already dominated relations up to Potsdam; Berlin would be the central issue from 1945 to 1949. But there were many other factors:

- Ideological – fear of Communism (or, in the other direction, of capitalism) went back to 1917;
- Military – the Soviet Union was alarmed by the American monopoly of the atomic bomb; the West was worried about the massive presence of the Red Army deep into Central Europe;
- Economic – the Americans feared a new great depression and wanted to keep Europe open to American trade; the Soviet Union had suffered enormous losses in the war and feared American economic domination;
- Specific regional issues – in Greece, where a bitter civil war was in progress and in Iran, where interests clashed over oil.

Daniel Yergin is convinced that there were also powerful vested interests. He writes of 'the rise of the National Security State', which combined diplomats, the intelligence services, the military, big industry and key politicians. These groups had gained massive power during the war; now they needed the 'Red Menace' to justify their continued expansion. A similar 'military-industrial complex' developed inside the USSR.

Even after Potsdam, not everyone saw the Cold War as inevitable. Many still hoped for peace and cooperation with 'our gallant wartime ally, Stalin'. In December 1945, the Moscow Conference of Foreign Ministers seemed to hold out real hopes of mutual concessions. Molotov and James Byrnes mapped out the basis of an agreement on Bulgaria and Romania, and on a UN atomic commission. But Byrnes was overruled by Truman, who took a stern anti-Soviet line in a letter to Byrnes in January 1946. In the same month, the virtual economic division of Germany was signalled when the British and American zones of occupation merged into a single economic unit that came to be known as 'Bizonia'. In response, Stalin linked the economies of the Soviet Bloc together in the economic organisation COMECON.

These growing differences, and the continuing uncertainties in American policy, explain why Winston Churchill's famous 'Iron Curtain' speech at Fulton in March 1946 was important. By now, Churchill was only a private citizen. But he still had huge prestige and influence. The Fulton speech was what Truman and many of his advisers wanted to hear. It gave a stark warning about the spreading Soviet sphere of influence and the need for urgent action to stop it expanding further. Churchill could no longer control British policy but he could influence American policy in what he thought was the right direction. It is possible, however, that Churchill was overstating the case and that, like Truman's letter of January 1946, the speech

See page 424

accentuated Soviet fears and pushed Stalin into a defensive and hostile stance.

It was also in 1946 that George Kennan's 'Long Telegram' was circulated in Washington and the policy of 'containment' began to take shape. Kennan was a well-informed observer. He knew that there was no real prospect of Stalin's Russia using armed force to invade the West; but this was not how everyone perceived it in 1946. There were genuine fears of Communist influence infiltrating Iran, Turkey, Greece and Italy, and exaggerated fears that Stalin was set on achieving 'world conquest'.

See page 425

H *The 'Truman Doctrine' and the Marshall Plan*

In 1946–47, the fears of Soviet expansion were intensified by the worsening economic situation in Western Europe. Britain was close to bankruptcy and informed the Americans in February 1947 that British support for Greece and Turkey would end in six weeks. (This was a significant stage in British acceptance of a reduced world role and of dependence on the USA. In the same year, Britain took the decision to pull out from India and Palestine.)

The British withdrawal from Greece was a key factor in Truman's decision to announce the Truman Doctrine in his speech to Congress on 12 March 1947, committing the USA to the policy of 'containing' Communism. Later in 1947, the democratic parties in Hungary made way for a Communist one-party state; in February 1948, the Czech Communists under Klement Gottwald took power in a bloodless *coup* in Prague. These Communist gains seemed to prove that containment was necessary.

See page 164

The main issue was still the economic situation in Western Europe, especially in France and Italy, where there was inflation, serious industrial unrest and strong support for the Communist parties. The situation in the Western zones of Germany was also acute. The economic crisis led to a fundamental alteration in American policy. The Truman Doctrine had to be accompanied by the Marshall Plan.

General George Marshall was an immensely respected figure who had very nearly been chosen as Allied Supreme Commander in preference to Eisenhower. He was called into action by Truman in February 1947 and announced his Marshall Plan in a speech at Harvard University in June. Discussions began immediately with the British and French foreign ministers, Ernest Bevin and Georges Bidault, who were in Paris for the latest conference of foreign ministers.

There is no doubt about the importance of the Marshall Plan for the economic recovery of Western Europe. The Plan was the first essential step in the generation-long prosperity which lasted until the 1970s. It is difficult to imagine the history of the Cold War, or of European integration, without it. There are two key questions, however, concerning American intentions:

PICTURE 42

*Faces of a divided Europe,
1946*

- Was the plan altruistic (Churchill called it 'the most unselfish act by any great power in history')? Or was it designed to protect American interests and to enable the American economic domination of Europe?
- Was the Plan designed to aid Europe as a whole, or was there a deliberate aim to exclude the Soviet Bloc and to consolidate the American economic sphere of influence in the West?

Initially, Molotov showed enthusiasm for the Plan. After all, the Soviet Union was in dire need of economic help. But Molotov was pressurised by Stalin into taking a hard line. The Paris Conference broke up. In the next few months, Soviet policy ruthlessly ensured that the states East of the Iron Curtain would refuse Marshall Aid, even though the Czechs had already indicated that they wanted to accept. The Czech Government was summoned to Moscow and bullied into changing its decision. (The Czech Foreign Minister, Jan Masaryk, later claimed this was 'the moment when Czechoslovakia ceased to be an independent country'.)

The West claimed that Stalin and Molotov had rejected a fair offer. The Soviet Union claimed that the offer had deliberately been framed in order to ensure refusal. Either way, the impact of the Marshall Plan was enormous. Between 1947 and 1952, more than $13 billion was pumped into sixteen countries. The result was an economic division of Europe as clear-cut as the Iron Curtain itself.

This economic division had political effects. In France, the Communists were pushed out of the ruling coalition. Nearly $3 billion of USA aid did much to stabilise the economy, and the politics, of the Fourth Republic.

In Italy, apart from economic help under the Marshall Plan, massive funds were spent by the CIA to ensure that the Christian Democrats defeated the Communists in the 1947 elections. By 1952, even the 'outlaw' regime of General Franco in Spain was able to gain large-scale American aid in return for providing bases for USA bombers.

See pages 236–7

In September 1947, Stalin launched the new Communist Information Bureau, 'Cominform', as a direct response to the Marshall Plan. This involved the Communist parties of Poland, Hungary, Czechoslovakia, Yugoslavia, Romania, Bulgaria, France and Italy in a body which was a replacement for the old 1919 Comintern, which Stalin had dissolved in 1943 as a reassuring gesture to his allies. One of the Cominform's first actions was to give backing to the big strikes which rocked France and Italy in 1947–48. The existence of the Cominform led to even more money and power for Cold War organisations in the USA, such as the National Security Council and the CIA.

KEY ISSUE

What was the role of economic factors in causing the Cold War?

I *The Berlin Blockade*

By 1948, the Cold War in Europe was firmly in place. It only remained to settle the last and biggest problem, which was Germany. Germany had proved a great disappointment to Stalin since 1945 when, at the cost of 100 000 lives, his forces reached Berlin first and controlled the city for ten weeks without any Western interference. The 'Ulbricht Group' had secured political control in key positions and forced through a merger of the SPD (Social Democrats) with the Communist Party in 1946 which produced the Communist-dominated SED (Socialist Unity Party). At that time, Western Europe appeared weak and vulnerable. There seemed good reason to hope that the Americans might disarm and go home, as they had done in 1919–20.

See pages 9–10

None of this happened. The Western powers asserted themselves through the Allied Control Commission and ensured that four-power rule of Berlin was observed. Soviet demands for reparations were blocked. (Many Western analysts remembered the disasters resulting from the issue of reparations after 1919 and wished to avoid repeating the same mistakes.) From Stalin's point of view, it seemed like a wilful refusal to acknowledge the terrible Soviet losses in the Great Patriotic War.

In 1947–48, the situation in Germany was apparently drifting out of Stalin's control. The Western powers were running their occupation zones in such a way as to rebuild the industrial base of Germany. Stalin feared the rebirth of Germany as a pro-Western military power; he also feared the power of the dollar. When the Western powers unilaterally introduced a single currency into 'Bizonia', Stalin launched the Berlin Blockade.

See Chapter 1

It is probable that Stalin's main aim was defensive, that he was simply trying to recover the control of the city he had held in 1945 and then lost. To achieve this, Stalin believed he had the perfect bluff. Even in the uncertain situation of 1948, there was almost no possibility that the West would start World War Three over access to Berlin. Late in June 1948, the Soviet authorities cut off all access to Berlin by road, railway and canal. This was blackmail, to force the Western allies to renegotiate the arrangements for Berlin and for Germany as a whole.

The Western response was the Berlin Airlift. The Second World War had revolutionised air power to an extent Stalin had not realised. The logistical skills and the massive resources behind the airlift enabled the long-term supply of the basic needs of a major city, for eleven months and throughout a bad winter. It also completed the psychological change of the Cold War. Former Soviet allies were now the Communist enemy; former Nazi enemies were now the gallant defenders of freedom in Berlin. The concept of West Berlin as a separate city was born before there was a West German state.

Now it was the West that had the perfect bluff. The only way to defeat the airlift was to shoot down the aircraft. The planners of the

TIMELINE
From Potsdam to Berlin, 1945–49

Feb 1945	Yalta Conference
May	End of the war in Europe
	San Francisco UN Conference
July/Aug	Potsdam Conference
	USA atomic bomb
	End of war with Japan
Sept	Failure of the London Conference of Foreign Ministers
Nov	Crisis over Soviet pressure on Turkey and Iran
Dec	Outline agreement between Byrnes and Molotov in Moscow
Jan 1946	Turman's hostile letter to Stalin
Feb	Stalin's 'Cold War' speech in Moscow
	Kennan's Long Telegram
March	Churchill's Iron Curtain speech
	Disputes in Berlin over reparations
April	Deadlock of Foreign Ministers' Conference in Paris
May	Re-opening of civil war in Greece
Jan 1947	Western zones merged into 'Bizonia'
	Formation of COMECON
March	Truman's speech to Congress setting out the 'Truman Doctrine'
June	Marshall Plan launched
	Foreign Ministers' Conference in Paris
July	Soviet rejection of the Marshall Plan
Sept	Formation of 'Cominform'
Feb 1948	Communist takeover in Czechoslovakia
April	First discussions about an Atlantic security system
June	Yugoslavia's break with Moscow
	Start of the Berlin Blockade
April 1949	NATO Treaty signed in Washington
May	Lifting of the Berlin Blockade
Aug	Konrad Adenauer elected Chancellor of the West German Federal Republic
Sept	Successful test of first Soviet atomic bomb
Oct	New People's Republic of China proclaimed by Chinese Communists

defence of West Berlin, General Lucius Clay and Robert Murphy, were sure that Stalin would never go that far. When Stalin called off the blockade in May 1949, the last pieces of the Cold War jigsaw puzzle fell into place. Later in 1949, the NATO treaty was signed and the separate states of East and West Germany came into existence.

See Chapter 1

On the surface, the Berlin Blockade was a dangerous flash-point in the Cold War but, in reality, it confirmed the 'diplomatic revolution' which had been happening since 1945. NATO now added a military dimension to political and economic divisions which already existed. According to Philip Windsor:

> Before the Berlin Blockade, there was a lot of uncertainty and casting around. Afterwards, everyone knew the rules and everything began to settle down.

From *World Powers in the Twentieth Century*, BBC radio broadcast

The deceptive stability of the long Cold War had begun.

J *NATO and the Warsaw Pact*

KEY ISSUE

In what ways did the Berlin Blockade influence the course of the Cold War?

Although it did not take place immediately, the inevitable Soviet response to the formation of NATO was a matching military alliance. Just as the Marshall Plan led to the formation of COMECON in 1947, so, in 1955, West German membership of NATO led to the formation of the Warsaw Pact.

The emergence of NATO (North Atlantic Treaty Organisation) began with the Brussels Pact of March 1948, in which Holland, Belgium and Luxembourg established cooperation with Britain and France. At that time, Germany was still perceived as the possible enemy; but worries about the USSR were already growing. In July 1948, talks about an 'Atlantic Pact' involving the Brussels Pact countries, the USA and Canada, began in Washington. The Berlin Blockade made the issue an urgent one: on 4 April 1949, the NATO Treaty was signed. As well as the original negotiating powers, the Pact was joined by Italy, Portugal, Norway, Denmark and Iceland. Greece and Turkey joined in 1952, at a time when the Korean War was causing serious tension. (From 1952, NATO was headed by a Secretary-General, always a European, to match the Supreme Allied Commander Europe (SACEUR) who was always American.)

The most controversial issue was the problem of West Germany. From 1952, efforts to establish a European Defence Community (EDC) caused a long debate about West German re-armament which was finally blocked by France in 1954. The outcome was West German membership of NATO in 1955, a step which seriously alarmed the Soviet Union and led directly to the formation of the Warsaw Pact. From 1955 until the end of the Cold War, NATO remained the key to Western defence, though it was disrupted by the policies of de Gaulle after 1958 and moved its headquarters from Paris to Brussels in 1967.

The Warsaw Pact was signed in May 1955, only a week after West German membership of NATO. The USSR, Poland, Czechoslovakia, Hungary, Bulgaria, Romania and Albania agreed to a joint military command under a Soviet Supreme Commander. The Pact incorporated all the various agreements made before 1955. It was originally a twenty-year treaty and was renewed in 1975 and again in 1985. The Pact established the principle of 'fraternal mutual aid' but did not provide for the use of force, nor interference in the internal affairs of member states. The military intervention in Hungary in 1956 was actually conducted outside the terms of the Warsaw Pact. In 1968, the new 'Brezhnev Doctrine' was intended to justify armed intervention in Czechoslovakia that would otherwise have been prohibited under the Warsaw Pact Treaty.

Like NATO, the Warsaw Pact remained a permanent feature of the Cold War – though Yugoslavia was never a member, Romania got Warsaw Pact troops withdrawn in 1958, and Albania left the Pact altogether in 1968. The following table shows the development of the two military alliances, illustrating the nature of the military division of Europe set in train in 1949.

See page 147

KEY ISSUE

What were the aims and achievements of the Warsaw Pact?

	NATO	Warsaw Pact
Sept 1947		Formation of 'Cominform'
March 1948	Brussels Pact	
July 1948	Talks between USA, Canada and Brussels Pact countries	Yugoslavia expelled from 'Cominform'
April 1949	NATO treaty signed in Washington	
Dec 1950	Eisenhower appointed SACEUR (Supreme Allied Commander in Europe)	
1952	Entry of Greece and Turkey First Secretary-General appointed	
Aug 1954	EDC blocked by France 'Balkan Pact' signed by Greece, Turkey and Yugoslavia	
May 1955	West German membership	Warsaw Pact Treaty signed in Poland
Nov 1956		Inclusion of East Germany Soviet intervention in Hungary
1958		Warsaw Pact troops out of Romania
1959	French fleet withdrawn from NATO	
1966	French troops withdrawn	
1967	SHAPE command moved to Brussels	
1968		Warsaw Pact invasion of Czechoslovakia
1982	Spain admitted to membership	
1990	German re-unification	Warsaw Pact disbanded

TABLE 44
Development of the military alliances of NATO and the Warsaw Pact

2 ↩ THE COLD WAR IN EUROPE AND ASIA, 1949–61

A *The widening of the Cold War*

From 1949, the Cold War in Europe became 'institutionalised' and permanent. On each side of the Iron Curtain, political, military and economic patterns had been established. Once these patterns were fixed, they became very difficult to escape from. Ideas and attitudes hardened. On both sides, what was in newspapers, textbooks and feature films followed an orthodox line that was a mirror of what was put out by the other side. The Cold War was always one of propaganda.

Within the Soviet Union, there was a renewed clamp-down on all forms of internal dissent. In Eastern Europe, Stalin imposed tight control on the Communist parties of the satellite states, with 'show trials' in Hungary in 1949 and in Czechoslovakia in 1951. Above all, the Cold War spread outside Europe. From 1945 to 1949, the main focus of superpower rivalry had been on Germany and Poland. Then came the Communist Revolution in China and the Korean War. From 1949, the Cold War was no longer 'just' about Europe and the Iron Curtain. The bipolar relationship between Washington and Moscow became a Cold War triangle involving Beijing and the 'Bamboo Curtain'.

See pages 164 and 186

The victory of Mao Zedong and the Communists in China did not have much to do with Stalin. It was the outcome of a civil war against Chiang Kai-shek and the Chinese Nationalists which had been going on since 1927. During the Second World War, while China and the Western powers had been allies fighting against the Japanese, the civil war had been overshadowed, but from as early as 1944 China specialists in the USA State Department had warned that the Communists had mass support in north China and that Chiang's regime could not last. From 1946, the USA poured aid into supporting Chiang and the Nationalist Kuomintang but, in April 1949, Chinese Communist forces captured Nanking and in October Mao proclaimed the new People's Republic of China. Chiang controlled only the island of Formosa (Taiwan).

This Chinese Revolution brought the Cold War to Asia. The Americans had been deeply involved in Asia already, as the occupying power in Japan. Now, just like the other former enemy, West Germany, Japan came to be seen as a vital outpost in the defence against Communism. At the same time, American attitudes towards the old colonial empires in Asia changed. It was now seen as vital to help the French in the struggle against the Nationalists (now 'Communists'), in Vietnam and, if necessary, the British against the Communist insurgency in Malaya. American commentators became obsessed with the question 'Who lost China?', even though all the experts agreed that Chiang had lost by himself. When the news broke in September 1949 that Soviet scientists had exploded an atomic bomb, it seemed as if all

See pages 91–2

the certainties of victory in 1945 had been taken away. Someone had to be to blame.

American policy was now dominated by the idea of a monolithic Communist world conspiracy, headed by the USSR and China and threatening freedom and democracy everywhere in the world. Within the USA, this led to the vast expansion of the armed forces and of the 'National Security State'. In April 1950, a key report, NSC-68, proposed a military budget of $59 billion, more than four times larger than before. NSC-68 marked American acceptance of the role of military superpower, deeply involved in Europe and Asia. The scene was now set for American involvement in the Korean War.

B *The Korean War*

In June 1950, North Korea, led by the Communist Kim Il Sung, invaded South Korea, ruled by the pro-Western regime of Syngman Rhee. It was assumed by most USA commentators that the invasion had been ordered by Stalin. A civil war in Asia became a Cold War battleground and the Truman Doctrine now applied to Asia as well as to Europe.

The American reaction to the invasion by North Korea was to organise military intervention by the United Nations and to place the hero of the war against Japan, General Douglas McArthur, in command of the defence of the South. Britain sent forces to fight in Korea but the military effort (and some would say the UN itself at this time) was plainly under American control.

By late September, the armies of the North had been driven back to the border but American policy now changed from the original stated aim of 'limited defence'. McArthur led UN forces in an invasion of the North which reached as far as the North Korean–China border on the Yalu river. McArthur made no secret of his desire to smash the North and, if necessary, invade China. Truman blocked this. This began a long series of disagreements that ended, in April 1951, with Truman sacking McArthur for insubordination.

The war ceased to be a civil war and became a 'proxy war' between the Chinese and American-led UN forces. In October 1950, Mao put Chinese troops into the North, almost certainly for defensive reasons. He pressed the Soviet Union for help. Stalin sent 150 modern MIG 15 fighters, disguised in Chinese insignia. In Korea, the Cold War was showing some of its long-term features. Conflicts occurred; but within limits. American intelligence officers knew about the Russian MIGs but did not broadcast the fact because they did not want the war to escalate. Stalin gave only as much, or as little, support as was necessary. Mao joined the war cautiously, only after giving two warnings. Truman sacked McArthur. But the Cold War divide widened just the same. It also suited both sides to have a powerful enemy whose existence justified Cold War attitudes and huge military spending. In the words of the American historian Stephen Cohen, 'it took partners to create the Cold War'.

From *Stalin: The Generalissimo*, Thames Television

There were two more years of fighting, during which UN forces were under pressure from Chinese attacks. Eventually, after heavy losses on both sides, a truce was agreed at Panmunjom in 1953, setting the North–South border almost exactly where it would have been if peace had been agreed in October 1950.

Korea was left badly scarred by the physical and economic legacy of the war but the wider effects of the Korean War were significant:

- the almost complete American domination of the UN;
- the completion of the militarisation of the USA, based on huge arms spending and a commitment to the role of 'world's policeman';
- the long-term isolation of China;
- the formation of SEATO (South East Asia Treaty Organisation) in 1954;

ANALYSIS

McCarthyism

During the Korean War, American politics was overrun by the anti-Communist hysteria known as 'McCarthyism'. Senator Joseph McCarthy used the House UN American Activities Committee (HUAC), supported by the FBI, to carry out a witch-hunt aimed at searching out supposed Communist sympathisers. Many hundreds of people were 'black-listed', including diplomats, academics, and prominent figures in the film industry. Notable victims included the atomic scientist Robert Oppenheimer, the diplomat and China expert Alger Hiss, and Julius and Ethel Rosenberg, who were convicted of spying in 1951 and controversially executed in 1953. McCarthy eventually overreached himself and was discredited in 1954 but the effects of his campaign were long-lasting. Two future American presidents, Richard Nixon and Ronald Reagan, both made their names in the HUAC hearings.

McCarthyism was mostly about domestic American politics, especially a Republican attack on Truman and the Democrats, but it did have a significant influence in Britain and Europe through the press, radio and television. The sensational case of Burgess and MacLean, two British diplomats who were revealed as Soviet spies when they defected to Moscow in 1952, intensified anti-Communist attitudes and also damaged British–American relations. Although McCarthyism in its extreme form died down after 1954, the ideas behind it continued to dominate policies throughout the western alliance.

See Chapter 1

KEY ISSUE

What was the impact of the Korean War upon the Cold War in Europe?

- a boost to the economic recovery of West Germany and, even more so, of Japan, because the USA needed everything that Japanese and West German industry could produce;
- a hardening of attitudes in the USA, both in foreign policy and in domestic political and public opinion.

Both Truman and his successor as President, Dwight Eisenhower, took a fairly moderate line in dealing with the Soviet Union. But Eisenhower's choice as Secretary of State, John Foster Dulles, was a committed anti-Communist. Dulles personified the policy of 'brinkmanship', the policy of diplomatic confrontation to the brink of war. Dulles strongly influenced the policies of the Western alliance until his death in 1959. It was under Dulles and Eisenhower that the so-called Domino Theory developed, basing American policy on the principle that if one 'domino' fell to Communism, all the others would fall in turn. It was also under Dulles and Eisenhower that the focus of the Cold War shifted from Korea to Vietnam.

See pages 91–2

In 1954, the long French struggle in Indochina ended with the decisive defeat at Dien Bien Phu. Originally, American policy had been anti-colonial, firmly opposed to French ambitions to hang on to Indochina. As the Cold War developed, American policy-makers saw Ho Chi Minh less and less as a nationalist and more and more as a Communist leader. By 1953, the Americans were desperately trying to keep the French military effort going. As a last resort, Dulles even briefly considered the use of nuclear weapons. When the French pulled out and peace talks began at Geneva, Vietnam was partitioned. The Americans now inherited the policy of propping up South Vietnam against the Communist North. Ten years later, in the Gulf of Tonkin Resolution, the USA would be drawn into another Asian civil war even more difficult and dangerous than Korea.

C *Europe and the Cold War after Stalin*

By the time the Korean War ended, the two superpowers were under new leadership. After the 1952 election, Truman handed over the USA presidency to Eisenhower. In March 1953 Stalin died, leaving power to a collective leadership in which the dominant personality proved to be Nikita Khrushchev. Stalin's death also paved the way for peace talks at Geneva in 1954, set up to finalise the situation in Korea and to seek a settlement in Vietnam.

The next issue to be negotiated was the integration of Western Europe. Economically, this proceeded successfully, though without British participation, through the Coal and Steel Community of 1950 to the formation of the EEC in 1955–57. Militarily, the issue was much more difficult. American policy, backed by Britain and by the West German Chancellor Konrad Adenauer, was in favour of forming a European Defence Community, with full West German participation. But in France both the government and the Gaullist opposition were

See Chapter 8

hostile to the idea of re-arming Germany. Lengthy negotiations led nowhere and the EDC project was eventually dropped.

See page 337

The outcome was a compromise agreement in London in 1954. As a result, West Germany became a full member of NATO in 1955, but with a pledge never to acquire nuclear weapons. To reassure France, Britain made a commitment to continue stationing substantial armed forces in Germany. The issues involved in 1954–55 explain the popular saying that:

> The purpose of NATO was to keep the Russians out, the Americans in, and the Germans down.

West German membership of NATO was perceived in the Soviet Bloc as a threat. In May 1955, the Warsaw Pact was formed to counter this threat. Even so, the prospects for 'peaceful co-existence' at this time were good. Europe had been stabilised and prosperity was on the way. Stalin was dead and Khrushchev was eager to begin the internal reform of the USSR through 'de-Stalinisation'. He also aimed to bring about a 'thaw' in the Cold War.

In May 1955, the same month that the Warsaw Pact was signed, Khrushchev met the French, British and Americans in Vienna and negotiated the end of four-power occupation. Austria became neutral, providing a model for future agreement on Berlin and Germany. A summit was held at Geneva in July, followed by a visit to Moscow by Adenauer. Khrushchev also moved to dismantle Stalin's legacy of repression. Thousands were released from the camps; in 1956, Khrushchev stunned the Soviet Communist Party with his so-called Secret Speech to the Twentieth Party Congress.

See page 202

See page 112

It seemed possible to achieve a fundamental change in East–West relations; but these hopes were not fulfilled, partly because of entrenched Cold War attitudes and the effects of confrontations since 1945, but mostly because of the combined impact of key events in 1956, in Poland, Hungary and Egypt.

See pages 176 and 188

The Budapest Rising followed serious disturbances in Poland. The Hungarian Party leader, Imre Nagy, was unable to control demands for reform and the Communist government in Hungary virtually collapsed. Soviet military forces were attacked by a homemade army of students and workers and Khrushchev pulled Soviet troops out of Budapest. This seemed like a great victory at the time and led to a few days of intense optimism in Hungary, encouraged by anti-Communist broadcasts from the CIA-funded Radio Free Europe. But at this precise moment, British and French forces, in collusion with Israel, began the invasion of Suez. The Suez invasion went badly wrong. President Eisenhower made it plain that there would be no American backing and virtually forced the British into pulling out. (Some historians argue that John Foster Dulles, unofficially, wanted the invasion to continue in spite of public American protests.)

KEY ISSUE

How was the Cold War in Europe affected by the events of 1955–56?

Nuclear balance 1955-80

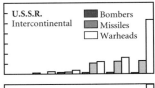

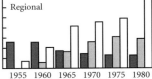

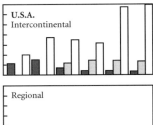

1955 1960 1965 1970 1975 1980

TABLE 45
Development of nuclear missiles by the USA and the USSR, 1955–80

See page 139

Suez had important consequences. Firstly, it drove a wedge between British and American policy. It ended British illusions of being a world power and within a few years led to rapid British decolonisation in the rest of Africa. Suez also pushed the Egyptian leader, Gamel Abdel Nasser, into closer alignment with the Soviet Union. The Middle East became yet another setting for Cold War conflict. Finally, the Suez crisis was the distraction Khrushchev needed to do what he wanted to do anyway, which was to send the Red Army back into Budapest and smash the rising. The Cold War froze solid again.

Budapest and Suez showed the permanent factors at work in the Cold War. There was a point beyond which peaceful cooperation would not go; equally, there was a point at which confrontation would always stop short of all-out war. The crushing of the Budapest rising caused an out-pouring of anti-Soviet feeling in the West but, whatever was said at the UN or on Radio Free Europe, there was never any realistic chance that the West would intervene. These dual tendencies continued between 1956 and 1961, with frequent clashes interspersed with periods of calm and cooperation.

One surprising cause of tension was *Sputnik*, the first space satellite, launched in 1957. This was a shattering blow to the USA, seemingly showing the Soviet Union far ahead in technology. In 1961, the first manned space flight by Yuri Gagarin had a similar effect. American politicians demanded massive new resources for nuclear defence shelters, weapons research and the expansion of higher education to help catch up the 'missile gap'. The late 1950s were an especially tense period in the 'arms race', with the development of the ICBM (intercontinental ballistic missile) and of advanced weapons systems such as the American 'Polaris' submarine.

Despite these problems, Nikita Khrushchev seemed to hold out genuine possibilities for cooperation. Khrushchev was impulsive and a gambler, keen on travel and summit meetings. He made a favourable impression on his visit to the USA in 1959 and then arranged a successful visit to Moscow by the British Prime Minister, Harold Macmillan. A summit meeting was arranged for 1960, in Paris, and it was hoped that Eisenhower might end his presidency on a high note. (One of the reasons for optimism was that John Foster Dulles was no longer an influence. He died in 1959.) But Khrushchev, with his sudden and eruptive style, was always as likely to be involved in confrontation as in moves towards peace. The Paris summit was overtaken by a major international crisis in 1960–61.

D *The Berlin Crisis, 1958–61*

Khrushchev first made an issue of Berlin in 1958. The Soviet Union was deeply concerned about the unexpected and unwelcome success of the West German State. Its 'economic miracle' was leaving East Germany far behind and causing a serious drain of youth and skills to the West. The integration of West Germany into the EEC was leading in a direction that Soviet leaders had never anticipated. And the increasing involvement of West Germany in NATO stirred up old Soviet fears about the rebirth of German militarism.

Accordingly, in January 1958, Khrushchev took the radical step of offering Soviet acceptance of the re-unification of Germany as long as Germany was made neutral, as Austria had been in 1955. This led to some strange reactions. On the Western side, many politicians were suspicious and were reluctant even to discuss the Khrushchev offer. In the Soviet Bloc, there were many, especially the Chinese, who thought Khrushchev had gone too far. Mao Zedong strongly urged Khrushchev to take a tougher line.

This difference in policy between Khrushchev and Mao was part of the build-up to the so-called 'Sino–Soviet Split' which came into the open later. It was also in 1958 that China chose to bombard the islands of Quemoy and Matsu, off Taiwan, raising fears of a new war against Chiang Kai-shek. The USA gave strong, very public, support to Chiang, while Khrushchev more or less told Mao to back off. The crisis over Quemoy and Matsu ended quietly but it stoked up the general air of tension in 1958.

Seeing no response to his original concessions over Berlin, Khrushchev decided to try pressure. If there were talks within six months, Khrushchev announced, 'he would not take action'. The clear threat was that without any talks he would. Why Khrushchev would make a crisis over Berlin when he had just defused one over Quemoy and Matsu is not clear. He may have simply hoped to push the West into negotiations. He was without doubt very worried about West German re-armament, and about the rising numbers of East Germans crossing into the West. Once again, Berlin was the centre of the Cold War.

Tensions eased in 1959, with Khrushchev's successful visit to the USA. There was genuine optimism in 1960 that the Paris summit might resolve many issues, especially Berlin. In the event, the summit never took place. It was aborted as a result of Khrushchev's reaction to the U-2 incident.

Spies in the sky: the U-2 affair

ANALYSIS

In May 1960, just as the Paris summit was about to begin, Khrushchev made a public announcement that an American spy-plane, the U-2, had been shot down in Soviet air space. The official American response was that the aircraft was not spying but was a civilian flight off-course. Khrushchev was able to expose this cover story by producing the captured U-2 pilot, Gary Powers, and numerous cameras and other pieces of espionage equipment. President Eisenhower was challenged to say he had no knowledge of the U-2 flights. In fact, he knew all about them and they had been going on since 1957.

The U-2 flew a one-way route at 70 000 feet, originally well above the height Soviet fighters or missiles could reach. Its pilots were given special drugs to cope with the altitude problems and were also issued with suicide capsules. The cameras had amazing definition. Eisenhower had been given a photograph of himself playing golf at Camp David, taken from 70 000 feet, in which he could easily identify himself and his golf ball.

Eisenhower accepted responsibility for the spy flights and publicly announced that they had been stopped. (In fact, the flights had nearly been stopped earlier; the Powers mission took place because the CIA pleaded for one last flight to search for missile bases in the Ural mountains.) For Khrushchev, simply ending the U-2 flights was not enough. He put pressure on Eisenhower for a full apology and rejected efforts at mediation by Macmillan and de Gaulle. The Paris summit collapsed. It appeared that one spy flight had derailed one of the best chances to end the Cold War, but the U-2 incident may not have been the only cause of the collapse of the 1960 summit and the crisis which followed. A month after the Paris fiasco, Soviet delegates walked out of the Geneva disarmament talks. Both Eisenhower and Macmillan found it difficult to understand why even the impulsive Khrushchev would swing so violently back to confrontation. The real reason may have been pressure on him from within the Soviet Bloc; the U-2 may have given Khrushchev a way out from a summit he actually wanted to avoid.

KEY ISSUE

Why did the Paris summit fail?

Pressures on Khrushchev came from hard-liners in the Party and especially from the military, who were worried about Khrushchev giving away too much in Paris and who were hostile to the deep cuts he was making in the Soviet armed forces. Even more important was the Sino–Soviet Split. Soviet–Chinese relations had been deteriorating for some time. Mao had been against the 1956 Secret Speech; there had been the row over Quemoy and Matsu in 1958; Mao had never much trusted the Soviet Union since Stalin's time anyway. In 1959, a personal visit to Beijing by Khrushchev was full of friction. Now, in the summer of 1960, Khrushchev made the split public with a detailed attack on the Chinese while he was visiting Bucharest. It suited him to be tough over the U-2. From early 1961, Khrushchev was also tempted into an aggressive line by the arrival of a new American President, John F. Kennedy. Khrushchev reckoned that Kennedy was young and inexperienced and might get rattled if challenged. This impression was quickly reinforced by the disastrous American-backed invasion of Cuba at the Bay of Pigs.

See page 403

Kennedy started his presidency with a wave of ambitious policy statements, which he summed up as his 'Freedom Doctrine'. Kennedy spoke as if the West were losing the Cold War and something had to be done about it. When Kennedy met Khrushchev in Vienna, the meeting went very badly, with particular disagreements about the Third World, and ended with a fresh row over Berlin. Khrushchev demanded progress on the issues he had raised in 1958. He threatened to close off Western access to Berlin unless there were a settlement of the status of Berlin and East Germany. Both leaders talked loosely about a possible nuclear war. Khrushchev was also under pressure from the East German leader, Walter Ulbricht, who was desperate to do something about the flood of East Germans fleeing to the West. On one day in August, a record 2000 refugees crossed the border.

See page 44

On the night of 12 August 1961, the Berlin Wall went up. To rub in the message, Khrushchev authorised a series of nuclear test explosions. Briefly, American and Soviet tanks confronted each other at close range near the Berlin border crossing, 'Checkpoint Charlie'. The division of Germany, shaped in Berlin in 1949 by the Berlin Blockade, was now completed in Berlin by the ultimate concrete symbol of division; the Berlin crisis, which had been brewing since 1958, boiled over.

PICTURE 43
Soviet and American tanks near 'Checkpoint Charlie', 1961

In 1961, Berlin was part of the propaganda war. The East suffered from the obvious image problem that the Wall had been built to make prisoners of its own people. At first, West Berliners were angry that nothing was done about the Wall – but Kennedy sent his vice-president, Lyndon Johnson, and the hero of the Berlin Airlift, Lucius Clay, on a very successful mission to show support. The West could boast of its success in 'standing up to Communism'; and of the showy wealth of West Berlin as proof of capitalist economic superiority. Both Kennedy (who came to Berlin in 1963 to make his famous 'Ich bin ein Berliner' speech) and Willy Brandt, the mayor of West Berlin, gained a lot of prestige out of the crisis.

In reality, the 1961 Berlin crisis showed once again the deceptive stability of the Cold War. The tanks which faced each other 'nose to nose' figured in dramatic photographs but not in a shooting war. The Wall, and the divided States of East and West Germany, stayed in place for another twenty-eight years. Meanwhile, the active dangers of the Cold War were transferred outside Europe and attitudes towards the Cold War, both in the USA and in Western Europe, became much more complicated.

3 ⤺ EUROPE AND THE GLOBAL COLD WAR, 1962–73

A *Introduction*

As the Cold War in Europe became surprisingly permanent and stable by 1961, so the focus shifted. Cold War tensions spread dangerously to a number of regional conflicts: in Cuba, in South East Asia, in the Middle East, in Africa, and finally in Afghanistan. In every case, special, local issues were involved but, as in Korea, the influence and interests of the superpowers distorted these regional conflicts into sub-plots of the Cold War. The most dramatic of these sub-plots was in Cuba.

As the Cold War rippled outwards from Europe in the 1960s, a number of new general factors became important and should be taken into account from the European perspective:

- Different attitudes and policies within the Western alliance. In the 1950s, there was basically one, American-led agenda but, by 1961–62, there were divergences, both between the USA and Europe and within Europe, especially after de Gaulle came to power in 1958. While Britain maintained the 'special relationship', de Gaulle accentuated the French alliance with West Germany and the need to avoid American dominance;
- The Sino–Soviet split and the growing impact of China as a separate force;
- The process of decolonisation. In theory, both the superpowers were fundamentally anti-colonial, but the USA was already very 'colonialist' in its approach to Latin America and was repeatedly

drawn into post-colonial conflicts in the Cold War period, above all in Vietnam. The USSR sided with independence movements all over the world but ruled over one of the last and greatest of colonial empires in Eastern Europe;

● The movement in the 1960s to develop the consciousness of the non-aligned, or Third World countries. This was encouraged particularly by Yugoslavia, the one Soviet satellite to escape, and by de Gaulle, who saw the Third World as a counterbalance to the superpowers, and who hoped that he might be the mediator to bring an end to the Cold War.

In the Cuban crisis of 1962, not all these factors applied. There was massive, almost unquestioning support for the USA from public and political opinion in Europe, not least from de Gaulle himself. But this unity was misleading. From 1962 to 1973, European and USA policies moved in very different directions.

B *The Cuban Missile Crisis, October 1962*

In 1959, the Nationalist leader Fidel Castro overthrew the Cuban dictator Fulgencio Batista. Cuba was only ninety miles from Florida and the rise of Castro alarmed American political and business interests. Relations between Cuba and the USA broke down badly. Castro then nationalised key economic concerns and turned to the Soviet Bloc for economic support. In 1961, President Kennedy inherited from the Eisenhower–Nixon administration a planned counter-revolution by Cuban exiles, backed by the CIA. Kennedy unwisely put this plan into operation. The result was the humiliating failure of the Bay of Pigs. The invasion of Cuba, by American-backed Cuban exiles, was a fiasco and American guilt was obvious. The Kennedy presidency had begun with an incompetent and immoral failure. Castro was strengthened. Khrushchev was encouraged to keep Kennedy on the run.

Khrushchev took the typically bold gamble of placing Soviet missiles in Cuba. He saw a chance to correct the Cold War balance: Soviet missiles so close to the USA would equate to NATO missiles based in Turkey. (Soviet medium-range missiles were numerous and technically advanced. But in long-range ICBMs, the USSR was far behind the Americans.) In July, the CIA reported sixty-five Soviet ships on the way to Cuba. On 14 October, U-2 flights over Cuba identified SS-4 missile sites being installed. According to Martin Walker, 'the next thirteen days were the most dangerous period of the whole Cold War'.

From *The Cold War* by Martin Walker (see bibliography)

Both Kennedy and Khrushchev handled the crisis better than their more war-mongering advisers. Kennedy could claim to have 'shown strength in standing up to nuclear blackmail'. He gained almost unanimous support from the press, public and politicians throughout Europe. He also impressed Khrushchev, who decided he had underrated Kennedy in 1961.

ANALYSIS

Thirteen days

14 October: Presence of missile launching-sites was confirmed

16-20 October: Lengthy discussions took place in Washington about USA action. The initiative in the Cuban crisis was Khrushchev's but the key decision – how to respond to the missiles – was American. There were five options:

- to do nothing (which was not even discussed);
- to bomb the SS-4 sites without warning (thought too risky and too 'warlike');
- to act through diplomacy and the UN (rejected as too slow and too 'weak');
- to launch a full-scale invasion of Cuba (planned, but only as a last resort);
- to blockade Cuba by establishing a naval exclusion zone round the island.

22 October: The fifth option was the one adopted. Kennedy announced the presence of the missiles, and the naval 'quarantine' round Cuba, in a national TV broadcast. To gain international support, the U-2 photographic evidence was published at a general session of the UN.

Kennedy's stand in public was firm and reasonable. Recent transcripts of the private White House discussions also show the President to be seeking the most moderate solution possible, supported by his brother, the Attorney-General, Robert Kennedy. But an alarming number of Kennedy's advisers demanded extreme action, not only well-known 'hawks' like General Tommy Powers and the air-force General Curtis Le May, but experienced diplomats like Dean Acheson and Paul Nitze. After the crisis was over, Khrushchev told Kennedy:

> It was easier for me. I wasn't surrounded by people who wanted a war.

24 October: USA forces were placed on DEFCON-2 alert (the highest stage of readiness short of war) while Soviet ships carrying warheads for the SS-4 missiles were steaming towards Cuba.

26 October: A moderate letter from Khrushchev arrived in Washington, suggesting that, if the USA gave assurances not to invade Cuba, 'then the necessity for Soviet military specialists in Cuba would disappear'.

27 October: A second, much more aggressive, Khrushchev message was broadcast on Moscow radio, demanding withdrawal of American missiles from Turkey. The same day, a U-2 was shot down over Cuba.

The solution decided upon in Washington (apparently by a narrow margin) was to publicly accept the first, conciliatory

Khrushchev message and ignore the second, threatening one. This defused the crisis: the Soviet ships turned back. (In private, Kennedy accepted Khrushchev's second message, too. Soviet diplomats were quietly informed that the USA missiles in Turkey would be dismantled.) The dangerous Thirteen Days were over.

However, Kennedy did not impress his right-wing generals. Curtis LeMay told him:

This is the biggest defeat in our history. We should invade today.

For his part, Khrushchev could claim to have protected Cuba and to have won his point over Turkey. In his memoirs, he boasted:

The Caribbean crisis was a triumph of Soviet foreign policy and a personal triumph in my own career. We achieved, I would say, a spectacular success without having to fire a single shot!

On the other hand, the Cuban crisis badly weakened Khrushchev at home. The accusation that he had been first unnecessarily provocative and then 'weak' was a big factor in his removal from power in 1964. As for Castro, he was now a permanent enemy of the USA but was assured of long-term Soviet military and economic backing.

The outcome of the Cuban crisis was ironic. Having come so close to war, the result was the further stabilisation of the Cold War. Relations between Kennedy and Khrushchev were much better than before. A 'hot-line' telephone link was established between Moscow and Washington to reduce the danger of future accidents. In 1963, Kennedy and Macmillan met Khrushchev in Moscow to sign the nuclear test-ban treaty. However, the unity of the Western alliance which had been so marked during the Cuban crisis was misleading. By 1963, there were serious policy disagreements both between Europe and the USA and within Europe itself.

KEY ISSUE

How did the Cuban Crisis affect the Cold War in Europe?

Regional conflicts and the Cold War

ANALYSIS

Cuba was only one of many regional conflicts in which the superpowers pursued Cold War rivalries outside Europe. Between 1962 and 1980, these regional conflicts brought serious confrontations between the superpowers and also provoked grave divisions in the Western alliance. They included:

South East Asia

(1954)   American involvement in the defence of South Vietnam following French withdrawal

1963   Escalation of USA 'advisers' in South Vietnam to 15 000

1964   American ships attacked by North Vietnam in the Gulf of Tonkin

The 'Gulf of Tonkin resolution' pushed through Congress to enable full-scale USA engagement in the war

1966   Total of 380 000 US troops in Vietnam

1968   USA forces besieged at Khe Sanh

Large-scale 'Tet Offensive' launched by Viet Cong

Growing anti-war protests in the USA and Europe

Resignation of President Johnson

1970   USA bombing campaign widened to include Cambodia and Laos

1972   Nixon–Kissinger policy of 'Vietnamisation'

The withdrawal of US combat troops

1975   Victory for North Vietnam

Final American evacuation ordered by President Ford.

The Middle East

1967   Israel's victory over Egypt and Syria in the Six-Day War

1970   Jordan in conflict against the PLO (Palestine Liberation Organisation) and Syria

1973   'Yom Kippur' War between Israel, Egypt and Syria

Major superpower confrontation

Serious divisions between the USA and Western Europe

1976   Breakdown of relations between Egypt and USSR

1979   Revolution in Iran and the seizing of American hostages

1980   Start of Iran–Iraq War

China

1969   Clashes between Chinese and Soviet troops on Amur–Ussuri border

1979   Renewed fighting on the Ussuri border

Start of war between China and Vietnam

Africa

1974   Portuguese rule replaced by Marxist governments in Mozambique and Angola

1975   Cuban forces air-lifted to Angola by the USSR

1977   The 'Ogaden War' – Soviet backing for Ethiopia, USA backing for Somalia

Afghanistan

1979   Soviet invasion of Afghanistan

1980   85 000 Soviet troops tied down in unsuccessful war against the 'Mujehaddin'

C *The loosening of the Western Alliance, 1963–68*

After the Cuban crisis, Kennedy was a popular hero in most of the Western world. Western unity was, however, misleading. Despite Kennedy's good personal relationships with Macmillan, Adenauer and de Gaulle, attitudes towards the Cold War were already diverging, even before Cuba. Between 1963 and 1968 the full extent of these differences came into the open.

Several key factors were involved:

● Reduced European dependence on the USA. Fears of economic collapse had disappeared; the danger of a war in Europe was small;
● Disagreements over nuclear weapons. Britain was determined to keep its nuclear deterrent; de Gaulle's France was determined to acquire one. There was also a vocal anti-nuclear campaign in Britain and Germany;
● The question of European integration. This complicated the triangular relationship between Britain, France and the USA;
● The divisive impact of the Vietnam War;
● The influence of personalities. In 1963, both Adenauer and Macmillan retired and Kennedy was assassinated. The new President, Lyndon Johnson, had poor relationships with European leaders, especially with de Gaulle and Harold Wilson, who became Prime Minister in 1964. The only major Western leader still in power was de Gaulle – and in 1963 de Gaulle had already committed France to a much more independent policy.

FRANCE AND THE COLD WAR

From the moment he came to power in 1958, it was always likely that de Gaulle would alter French policy from the very pro-American line followed by the governments of the Fourth Republic. De Gaulle had clear, fixed aims:

● He was set on a special alliance with Adenauer and West Germany, which the Americans regarded as undermining their own position;
● He wished to alter France's role in NATO and to limit American dominance;
● He was set on France developing her own nuclear weapons;
● He was opposed to British membership of the EEC, almost entirely on the grounds that Britain would be a 'Trojan horse' for American influence in Europe (and also interfere in his partnership with West Germany);
● He was also opposed to American policy in Indochina. As early as 1961, de Gaulle had sent an envoy to President Kennedy:

> Tell him not to get caught up in the Vietnam affair. The United States could lose not only her armed forces but also her soul.

See page 348

In 1963, the latent tensions between France and the USA blew up into a crisis. First came a formal French–German treaty, strongly opposed by the USA because it was made completely outside NATO. Then came the French veto on British membership of the EEC, which was seen by many as motivated by anti-Americanism. Next, de Gaulle rejected American proposals for a multilateral force (MLF) and insisted that there must be an independent French deterrent. Later in 1963, de Gaulle refused to join with the other nuclear powers in the Moscow test-ban treaty. He then withdrew the French Mediterranean fleet from NATO command. When Johnson succeeded Kennedy in November 1963 a strained relationship became even worse.

Between 1963 and 1968, French policy continued to challenge the American view of the Cold War. Since de Gaulle's main aim was to get away from the domination of the two superpowers, he made every effort to open up *détente* – the more the Cold War thawed, the more room there would be for European, especially French, independence. De Gaulle wrote in his memoirs:

> My aim was not to disengage France from the western alliance but to avoid the complete integration of NATO under American command. I aimed to establish relations with the states of the Eastern Bloc, first and foremost with Russia, bringing about understanding and cooperation; to do likewise, when the time was right, with China; and finally to provide France with a nuclear capability. But I was anxious to proceed gradually, keeping up France's traditional friendships.

In March 1966, France pulled her military forces out of NATO. (NATO moved its headquarters from Paris to Brussels in 1967.) In June 1966, de Gaulle made a high-profile visit to Moscow, the most important of numerous attempts he made to break up the 'bipolar' Cold War, and to promote his cherished idea of 'Europe from the Atlantic to the Urals'. In 1967, de Gaulle openly attacked Israel's role in the Six-Day War, and the territorial gains made from it. This attack was almost certainly motivated by purely French concerns but the USA regarded it as undermining the Cold War defences against Communist-backed regimes in Egypt and Syria. And by 1967–68, French policy and French public opinion were totally opposed to Lyndon Johnson's handling of the war in Vietnam.

BRITAIN AND THE COLD WAR

British policy was never as independent as de Gaulle's, nor as openly critical of the Americans. British governments, both Conservative and Labour, were eager to preserve the so-called 'special relationship'. This relationship had been strained in 1956, over Suez, and again in 1962, when the Americans suddenly cancelled work on *Skybolt*, the missile which was to have been the basis of the British independent deterrent. But the *Skybolt* row ended highly satisfactorily from Macmillan's point

of view, when Britain was given the superior *Polaris* missile instead. In 1962 and 1963, British and American policies were closely united over the Cuban crisis and the test-ban treaty, and cemented by the personal friendship between Macmillan and Kennedy.

This unity did not continue under Johnson and Wilson. Part of this was political: American policy-makers were suspicious of a Labour government, especially one with a vocal left wing in sympathy with the Campaign for Nuclear Disarmament. Part of it was personal: the two men simply did not like each other. But the main reason was Vietnam.

Wilson made several attempts to mediate over Vietnam and to prevent escalation of the war. What Johnson wanted was not mediation but British military and political support in the war. Great American pressure was applied, especially in 1966, to persuade Wilson to send even a small token force to Vietnam. American policy towards Britain's role east of Suez changed, now encouraging the maintaining of British bases in Singapore and the Persian Gulf. But, to Johnson's frustration, Britain stayed out of the war.

In 1967, Wilson discussed possible ways of ending the war during a visit to Britain by the Soviet premier Alexei Kosygin. These discussions ended badly, amid British recriminations that President Johnson had sabotaged agreement by imposing an unreasonable deadline. For the Americans, matters were made worse by the financial crisis which hit Britain in 1967 and led the Wilson government to announce that Britain would withdraw from all bases east of Suez except Hong Kong, by 1971. Wilson was furiously condemned in the USA for not doing enough to support the Americans in the Cold War, and by left-wing opinion in Britain for doing far too much.

D *The crisis of American leadership*

See page 78

In 1968, political and public opinion in Europe turned decisively against the war in Vietnam. In Grosvenor Square in London, there were violent demonstrations outside the American Embassy. Protest against the war was an important element in the unrest of May 1968 in Paris. The American defence expert, Paul Nitze, expressed shock at attitudes in Europe:

> Vietnam has become a disastrous side-show, to the point where we are in danger of losing our European allies.

Another leading American diplomat said:

> Yellow men in Asia, black men at home, that ridiculous de Gaulle in Europe, Nasser threatening our oil supplies – Americans aren't used to this.

Then came the 'Tet Offensive' against the American forces in Vietnam. Militarily, this was a disaster for the Viet Cong, who suffered horrendous losses from which they never really recovered. Psychologically, however, it was a stunning victory. It seemed to prove that the war was 'unwinnable' and gave strong impetus to the already growing opposition against the war, both in Europe and within the USA. Soon afterwards, Johnson announced that he would not run for the presidency again.

See pages 147 and 168

1968 was a momentous year in the Cold War. In much the same way as the USA, the Soviet Empire was subjected to severe pressures – from the widening rift with China, and from the ferment in Eastern Europe which culminated in the intervention in Czechoslovakia by Warsaw Pact forces and the assertion of the 'Brezhnev Doctrine'.

KEY ISSUE

What was the impact of the events of 1968 on the relationships between the superpowers and the European States?

Between 1968 and 1973, the USA had to adjust to new realities of power. After vain attempts to continue the war in Indochina, President Nixon and his foreign policy expert, Henry Kissinger, turned back to the peace talks Nixon had deliberately undermined in 1968. American troops began to withdraw in 1972 and were finally evacuated in 1975. Relations with Europe continued to be difficult, partly because of economic pressures on the USA and the growing feeling that it was time for prosperous Western Europe to pay more for its own defence.

In Washington, Senator Mike Mansfield began a vocal campaign to reduce the American commitment in Europe. He demanded to know:

> Why is it that, after twenty years, 250 million west Europeans are unable to organise effective defence against 200 million Russians (who are contending at the same time with 800 million Chinese) but must continue to rely on 200 million Americans for their defence?

The divide between Europe and the USA was at its widest in October 1973, during the Yom Kippur War. Israel was caught unprepared by the initial attack from the Soviet-equipped armies of Egypt and Syria and seemed to be under serious threat of defeat. The USA organised a round-the-clock air-lift of supplies and approached its European allies for the use of NATO airfields. Most European leaders, including the British Prime Minister Edward Heath, were very reluctant to act and highly critical of American policy. Only Salazar's Portugal and The Netherlands offered their bases willingly.

A few days later, when the war had moved decisively in favour of Israel, Moscow threatened direct military intervention to save Egypt from total military defeat. Henry Kissinger, who was in almost total control of USA policy while Nixon was pre-occupied with the Watergate Affair, placed all American bases in Europe on DEFCON 3, the highest nuclear alert, without consulting his European allies. The bluff worked and the Soviet Union backed down – but the strained relations between the USA and Western Europe were a far cry from the united front over Cuba in 1962.

Nixon and Kissinger had more success with their moves to open links with China. By this time, Soviet–Chinese relations had reached an all-time low – they came to the edge of open war in 1969–70. Kissinger made a secret visit to Beijing in 1971. Nixon followed this with an official visit in 1972 and was well received by Chou-en-Lai. This was one more part of the process by which the original simple demarcation lines of the Cold War became blurred.

4 ↜ THE BREZHNEV ERA, 1968–85

A *Détente*

The conflicts and confrontations of the Cold War were always interspersed with attempts at peaceful co-existence. The Brezhnev era included many flash-points and many boasts that the USSR was 'winning the Cold War'; but there was also a long series of arms-limitation talks, an 'era of negotiations' which came to be known as *détente*.

See page 147

See page 148

See pages 38–9

See pages 48–9

See page 144

The events of 1968 had shown the dangerous internal pressures developing in Eastern Europe and led to the 'Brezhnev Doctrine', justifying military intervention by the Warsaw Pact to prevent divergent policies within the satellite states. For the USA, the shocks of the late 1960s and early 1970s and the massive economic burden because of the war in Vietnam made cuts in arms spending look attractive. Another factor was that, for Nixon and Kissinger, *détente* did not only mean negotiating with the USSR. They intended to balance Soviet power by opening up American links with China.

(In 1969–70, China and the USSR were close to war. Huge Soviet forces were concentrated on the Chinese frontier and the Soviet leadership seriously considered a nuclear strike against China's test sites.)

American weakness meant that European leaders began to look for policies less dependent on the USA. There had already been the independent policy of de Gaulle, and European economic growth was such that Europe's share of world trade had overtaken that of the USA. The EEC expanded to take in new members, including Britain, in 1973. In 1969, the new West German chancellor, Willy Brandt, pushed forward his policy of *Ostpolitik*. This was intended to normalise relations between West Germany and the Soviet satellites and to avoid domination by Washington and Moscow. *Ostpolitik* had some successes, such as a treaty with Poland in 1970 and arrangements for family visits between West and East Germany. This led to the signing of the Basic Treaty in 1972. In the end, *Ostpolitik* achieved less than Brandt hoped, partly because Brandt himself lost power in 1974, and partly because the 'unwritten rules' of the Cold War prevented it.

Brezhnev wanted *détente* because he was convinced that the USA would be weakened, at least in the medium-term, by Vietnam and that the USSR had caught up both militarily and economically. He was content to stabilise the existing situation in Europe, which would mean legitimising his Soviet Empire, while pushing ahead forcefully with the Cold War in other promising areas, especially the developing world. Thus, for both superpowers, *détente* was not only, or even mostly, about peaceful co-existence. By 1979, the era of *détente* had done more to intensify the Cold War than to end it. Nevertheless, there were several developments which encouraged optimism at the time, especially negotiations on arms control. ('Arms limitation' was not disarmament. The aim was to freeze or slow down the arms race, in order to cut spending and secure a balance of force.)

In 1970, the SALT (Strategic Arms Limitation Talks) began, leading to the first ABM (Anti-Ballistic Missile) Treaty of 1972, which established a balance of nuclear warheads between the superpowers. The SALT talks continued the attempt to find a basis for agreed arms reductions until 1979, when the SALT II treaty was signed. In 1975, the Helsinki Treaties agreed to recognise the existing borders of Europe (a clear gain for Brezhnev) and also to monitor human rights issues (which was to do much to undermine the Soviet position in the satellite states, especially through the organisation called *Charter 77*). But *détente* had limits and could go only so far.

One of the limits to *détente* was that the arms race was so difficult to stop, even though it was regarded by many as incredibly dangerous, and expensive, and there was always a substantial anti-nuclear protest movement, especially strong in Britain and West Germany. (Key scientists behind the first atomic bombs, the American Robert Oppenheimer and the Russian Andrei Sakharov, both turned against the weapon they had created and became peace campaigners.)

But there were many who regarded the arms race as a guarantee of safety as long as both sides cancelled each other out in the 'balance of terror'. And, on both sides of the Iron Curtain, there were powerful military and industrial vested interests which wanted to keep arms spending high for ideological and business reasons. *Détente* was up against powerful, entrenched opposition.

The secret Cold War

ANALYSIS

It is no surprise that the Cold War inspired innumerable spy thrillers. From beginning to end, the Cold War was all about secrets, in spying and electronic information-gathering and in keeping secret the latest developments in new weapons. By the early 1960s, Berlin probably had the biggest concentration of spies, both human and electronic, in history. Countless intelligence organisations were active: not only American and Soviet but also from the two Germanies and from all over Europe. There were other listening-posts in places like Beirut and Hong Kong.

Most espionage and electronic surveillance was focussed on the secrets of the arms race. The first sensational spy case was the passing of atomic secrets to the Russians from 1945 by the British scientists Klaus Fuchs and Alan Nunn May. Others included the defection to Moscow by the British diplomats Burgess and MacLean in 1952, followed by the 'third man' Kim Philby in 1960. In 1974, the revelation that his aide Gunter Guillaume was a long-standing East German spy was a key reason for the resignation of Willy Brandt as West German Chancellor. Throughout the Cold War, countless diplomats, journalists and businessmen were involved in spying, were captured and were exchanged. One of the most famous symbols of the Cold War was the Glienicke Bridge in Berlin, where many spies were traded back.

Real life was as bizarre as any fiction. In the 1950s, an elaborate plan to undermine the Soviet satellites through spying and subversion was code-named *Operation Splinter Factor*. It failed and scores of agents lost their lives. Soviet-backed agents did kill the Bulgarian dissident Georgi Markov in London with a poison-tipped umbrella. Soviet Bloc agents were implicated in the plot to kill Pope John Paul II in 1980.

The electronic war was almost as mind-boggling. In the ferocious climate of Alaska, more than forty American radar stations made up the Dew Line, watching for a sudden Soviet attack. A few miles away, Soviet 'weather experts' were carrying out a similar watch. American and Soviet nuclear submarines shadowed each other deep under the sea; U-2 planes high in the sky and satellites in space photographed military installations in fine detail. All over the world, listening stations intercepted and decoded radio traffic.

The secret war was also fought in films and popular novels. James Bond was only one of many fictional heroes thwarting the vicious Communist menace. In the 1960s, John Le Carré's *The Spy Who Came In From The Cold* showed a complex world with villains on both sides. In the Watergate–Vietnam 1970s, most thrillers revealed paranoid CIA conspiracies. In the Gorbachev 1980s, books like Frederick Forsyth's *The Fourth Protocol* showed Soviet and Western intelligence working together against rogue elements. When the Cold War ended, thriller writers, like the military men, found a world without the secret war very difficult to come to terms with.

B *The end of* Détente *and the 'New Cold War',* *1980–85*

For most of the 1970s, it appeared as if the USSR was 'winning the Cold War'. The USA was struggling with the legacy of the Vietnam War, with the impact of the Watergate Affair, and with the economic problems following the OPEC oil price crisis of 1973. The Soviet economy was apparently forging ahead with the exploitation of huge new oil and gas finds in Siberia. Soviet SS-20 missiles were numerous and formidable. The Soviet navy was massively expanded under Admiral Gorchkov.

In fact, Soviet successes were overrated. The economy produced more but was lagging far behind the West in key areas such as computing. The Soviet system was riddled with corruption and propaganda lies. Above all, it was hopelessly over-stretched. The huge weight of arms spending, domestic output and support for regimes abroad was too much to carry. (In the early 1970s, American analysts estimated Soviet defence spending to be between 12 and 16 per cent of GDP (Gross Domestic Product). After 1992, Russian officials admitted that it had actually been 25 per cent.)

Even so, Soviet claims were widely believed in the West. Anxiety about Soviet military power caused a shift away from *détente* back to re-armament. The Democrat President Jimmy Carter, the Labour

Prime Minister James Callaghan, and the SPD Chancellor Helmut Schmidt, all became convinced of the need to build up Western forces to counter the Soviet threat. Spending was increased and the decision was taken to deploy large numbers of American *Cruise* and *Pershing* missiles in Europe.

In 1979–80, with the revolution in Iran and the Soviet invasion of Afghanistan, *détente* ended and the 'New Cold War' began. A key factor intensifying this was the emergence of five firmly anti-Communist new leaders in the West:

● Ronald Reagan, who won the 1980 presidential election partly by his promises of an aggressive foreign policy against the 'evil empire';
● Margaret Thatcher, who came to power in 1979 and soon earned the nickname 'Iron Lady';
● Pope John Paul II (Karel Wojtola), the former Archbishop of Cracow, whose resolute anti-Communism alarmed the Kremlin, especially when he drew staggering crowds on his visit to Poland in 1980;
● Helmut Kohl, who continued West German policies almost unchanged after he replaced Helmut Schmidt in 1982;
● François Mitterand, who became the first Socialist President of France in 1981 but, surprisingly, turned out to be the most loyal supporter of the Western alliance to lead France since 1958.

The so-called New Cold War was based on re-armament of the West and rolling back Soviet influence. The crushing of *Solidarity* in Poland in 1981 added to the process. In 1979, *Solidarity*, the independent Polish trade-union and political movement, had won big concessions. John Paul II's visit further boosted national feeling. When the Polish leader, General Jaruzelski, sent in tanks to impose martial law in 1981, the result was an intense anti-Soviet backlash in the West, similar to 1956 and 1968.

See page 180

The New Cold War was divisive in Europe. Vocal opposition was raised against the deployment of *Cruise* and *Pershing* missiles. There was a revival of CND in Britain, including the long-running protest of the 'Greenham Women' at the main USA base in Berkshire, and vigorous activity by the Greens and anti-nuclear protesters in West Germany. In 1983, Willy Brandt split the SPD by pushing for separate European disarmament.

Reagan and Thatcher ignored all this and took a straightforward and confrontational approach. Reagan drove through an enormous expansion of the arms budget and proposed going even further, out-spending the Soviet Bloc to the point where it simply could not compete. *Cruise* and *Pershing* were deployed despite the protests. American missiles were made available to the *Mujehaddin*, the anti-Soviet guerrillas fighting in Afghanistan. Reagan set out on his 'Star Wars' project, the Strategic Defence Initiative, which aimed to place in space an unbreakable shield against any missile attack.

The tone of the early 1980s was set by hostile language and by confrontations reminiscent of the 1950s. In 1983, Soviet air defences

ANALYSIS

Crisis and Co-existence

In the Cold War, there was always a balance between confrontation and cooperation. The following chronology illustrates the counterpoint between crisis and co-existence in the long years after the death of Stalin:

	Crisis and Confrontation	Cooperation
1954		Peace talks in Geneva on Korea and Indochina
1955	Warsaw Pact formed	Austrian neutrality agreed in Vienna
1956	Budapest and Suez	
1958	Start of Berlin crisis	Crisis over Quemoy and Matsu resolved quietly
1959		Successful visit to the USA by Khrushchev
1960	U-2 incident	Planned summit in Paris
1961	Berlin Wall crisis	
1962	Cuban missile crisis	Moscow–Washington 'Hot Line' agreed
1963		Moscow test ban treaty
1964	American escalation in Vietnam	
1965		Meeting between Brezhnev and Johnson in USA
1967	Six-Day War	
1968	'Prague Spring' crushed	Nuclear Non-proliferation Treaty signed
1969		Start of *Ostpolitik*
1972		ABM Treaty (SALT II) signed
1973	Crisis during Yom Kippur War	
1975	Cuban troops placed in Angola	Helsinki Accords on human rights
1979	Soviet invasion of Afghanistan	SALT II Treaty signed (but not ratified)
1980	Boycott of Moscow Olympics	
1983	KAL-007; 'Able Archer' war scare	
1986		Gorbachev–Reagan summit at Reykjavik
1989	Tiananmen Square massacre	Peaceful end of the Berlin Wall

shot down a Korean airliner, KAL 007, killing all on board, when it strayed into Soviet air space. The incident caused an international storm similar to the U-2 in 1960. A few months later, a huge NATO 'war game', code-named *Able Archer 83*, caused such panic in the Soviet high command that all Soviet forces were placed on full nuclear alert.

5 ⌐ THE END OF THE COLD WAR, 1985–91

When Brezhnev died in 1982, it was not obvious how soon the Cold War would be over. The New Cold War was in full swing. In reality the world was already changing. The revival of Western policy under Reagan and Thatcher and the growing strains within the Soviet satellite states presented a huge challenge to the crumbling Soviet system. Brezhnev's successor, Yuri Andropov, planned fundamental changes. He promoted several reformers to prominent positions, including the then little-known Mikhail Gorbachev.

Andropov died prematurely in 1983 and was replaced briefly by the last of the Brezhnevite old guard, Konstantin Chernenko; but the death of Chernenko in 1985 paved the way for Gorbachev to come to power.

See Chapter 3

Gorbachev was so set on internal reform in the USSR that he was willing to give away the 'outer Soviet Empire' in order to achieve it. Gorbachev was certain that the 'Brezhnev era' could not carry on. He was determined to end the Cold War in order to save the Soviet Union. In doing this, he was aided by the fact that he was the first leader of the USSR who did not have a Stalinist past. He was also popular in the West. Gorbachev's first dramatic move was at the Reykjavik summit in 1986, where he offered Reagan massive cuts in Soviet armaments, leading to the 'Zero Solution' – a complete elimination of nuclear weapons within ten years. An immediate and stunning agreement was prevented by Reagan's reluctance to let go of his pet 'Star Wars' programme, and Reykjavik did not finish what it began. But it led to another summit in Washington in 1987 which was a huge media success and sparked off the phenomenon of 'Gorbymania'. The New Cold War was over.

Gorbachev was back in 1988 to address the United Nations in New York. This speech virtually spelled out the end of the whole Cold War. Gorbachev renounced ideology, claiming that the Bolshevik Revolution was 'in the past'. He renounced the Brezhnev Doctrine, and stated that force should not be used to overrule freedom of choice, thus opening the way for the satellite states to go their own way. Finally, he announced that the USSR would withdraw from the arms race, by cuts in nuclear weapons, reducing the Red Army by half a million men and pulling thousands of tanks and troops out of East Central Europe. Work had already begun on dismantling SS-20 missiles and with-drawing Soviet forces from Afghanistan. Negotiations were in hand to get Cuban troops out of Angola.

The speed of all this was unsettling. The new American President, George Bush, was warned by some of his advisers that Gorbachev's 'peace offensive' was only a ploy to get the West off balance. There were many nervous and violent moments in 1989. In Poland, the reformers who negotiated free elections to be held in June were afraid of another 1981. In June 1989, the massacre of political protesters in Tiananmen Square in Beijing by the Chinese Communists seemed to set a terrible

See page 190

KEY ISSUE

To what extent was the end of the Cold War in Europe the result of the policies of Mikhail Gorbachev?

example that threatened Communist regimes in Europe might copy. (The East German leader, Erich Honecker, discussed the possibility.) At Christmas, the Romanian dictator Ceauşescu was overthrown and murdered in a bloody revolution. There were outbursts of violence in Soviet Georgia and in the Baltic States.

In the event, Communism in East Central Europe died quickly and quietly. Perhaps the key decision was by the reformist Communist government in Hungary, opening the border with Austria and allowing hundreds of East Germans out into the West. Gorbachev visited East Berlin for the fortieth anniversary celebrations of the East German State and made it plain that there would be no support from the USSR if the Honecker regime tried the 'Tiananmen Square solution'. Soon afterwards, Honecker resigned. Ten days after that, the Berlin Wall was opened and the East German State melted away. In 1948–49, the Cold War had taken shape with one dramatic event in Berlin. Now, forty years later, another dramatic event in Berlin ended it.

A short time after the end of the Wall and the end of the Cold War, the Soviet Union itself disappeared. In August 1991, Gorbachev was saved from an attempted *coup* by hard-line Communists but the man who saved him, Boris Yeltsin, went on to take power himself and to transform the Soviet Union into the Russian Federation. The Cold War had begun in 1917 with the Bolshevik Revolution; it had always been, in part, an ideological struggle. Now, both the Soviet State and its Communist ideology were gone; so was the Cold War.

Since 1945, the world had been dominated by balance between the two superpowers. This relationship was much more stable than it appeared. The great peace settlement of 1919–20 did not lead to lasting peace, only to Fascism and war. The apparent nuclear tightrope of the Cold War provided Europe with fifty years of stability, peace and prosperity.

It is true there were many moments of real drama in the Cold War. McArthur nearly invaded China in 1951. John Foster Dulles considered the use of nuclear weapons to save Indochina in 1954. So did the Soviet leadership in the dispute with China in 1969–70. Both in Washington and in Moscow, sane and reasonable men thought nuclear catastrophe was all but certain in October 1962. In the 1960s Mao Zedong claimed that China would welcome, and win, a nuclear war. Even as late as 1983, the combination of the shooting down of KAL 007 and the *Able Archer* war scare had Moscow on full war alert. On both sides, flocks of birds were mistaken for incoming missiles.

In Paris in 1961, Khrushchev said to Kennedy, 'It would take only one miscalculation.' Kennedy told him angrily that nobody would let such a thing happen. The record of the Cold War proved him right. The next year, at the height of the Cuban Missile Crisis, Kennedy made his crucial TV broadcast. Afterwards he said to an aide, 'Well. That's it. As long as he doesn't foul it up.' Khrushchev didn't. For thirty years afterwards nobody else did either. (The first war in Europe since 1945, in the former Yugoslavia, happened after the end of the Cold War. It is

See pages 284–8

unlikely that the war in Yugoslavia would ever have happened without the collapse of the Soviet system.)

MAP 32
Post-1991 Europe

The collapse of the Soviet Empire in 1989–91 meant there was now only one superpower. Some observers claimed that the Cold War had been 'won' by the policies and values of the USA. One American historian, Francis Fukuyama, wrote of the 'End of History', arguing that all the big ideological and historical questions of the twentieth century had been resolved. He was almost certainly premature and over-optimistic. The end of the Cold War took away many of the certainties and safety-catches of post-war Europe. After 1991, it soon became apparent how many difficulties were involved in dealing with the legacy of the Cold War and especially with the resurgence of nationalism.

The Cold War was the legacy of Stalin and Hitler. The whole post-war era was moulded by the consequences of the Nazi–Soviet Pact and the World War which followed. The Cold War (or, as one Frenchman put it, the 'Hot Peace') was a temporary substitute for the peace settlement that never was. Between 1989 and 1991, the Second World War really came to an end; Hitler and Stalin were really dead and the world could move on.

6 ∽ BIBLIOGRAPHY

A clear and well-structured overview is *The Cold War* by H. Higgins (Heinemann, 3rd edition, 1993). A short and practical collection of source material, arranged in helpful outline chapters is *The Cold War* by E.G. Rayner (Hodder and Stoughton 'History at Source', 1987). An excellent handbook, full of detailed chronologies and well-organised information, is *The Longman Companion to the Cold War and Détente 1941–91* by J. Young (Longman, 1993). A comprehensive and detailed overview is provided in *The Cold War* by M. Walker (Fourth Estate, 1993). For an overall narrative, brilliantly illustrated but very American-oriented, see *Cold War* by J. Isaacs and T. Downing (Bantam, 1998). (This book accompanies the long series of television documentaries, *Cold War*, by Turner Original Productions, 1998).

On the early development of the Cold War, there is a useful and accessible collection of sources in *The Origins of the Cold War* by M. McCauley (Longman Seminar Studies, 1990) and a lively and readable chapter on 1945–61 in *People's Century, Vol. I* by G. Hodgson (BBC Books, 1996). The European background is covered in *Cold War Europe 1945–91* by J. Young (Arnold, 1995) and there is a comprehensive illustrated survey of 1917–89 in *Communism*, edited by G. Stern (Bantam, 1990). *The 'Times' Atlas of the Twentieth Century,* edited by R. Overy, also has good maps and other illustrative material.

The story of the satellite states is covered fully but from a very anti-Soviet standpoint in *The Fifty Years War* by P. Brogan (Bloomsbury, 1990). For specialised use, there are two books on early American policy: *Rise to Globalism* by S. Ambrose (Allen Lane, 1971) and *Shattered Peace* by D. Yergin (Penguin, 1980) and also an in-depth study, *Cold War to Détente 1945–85* by C. Brown and P. J. Mooney (Heinemann, 1986). Finally, *Russia: A History,* edited by G. Freeze (Oxford University Press, 1998) has accessible and up-to-date material based on recent Soviet archives. Similar but much more specialised material can be found in *Inside the Kremlin's Cold War* by V. Zubok and C. Pleshakov (Harvard University Press, 1996).

7 ∽ ESSAYS

A *Essay questions*

1. (a) What were the main sources of tension between East and West in the period 1945–49?
   (b) To what extent were these tensions 'merely the continuation of long-term tensions between 1917 and 1941'?
2. (a) Compare the gains made by Stalin in the Nazi–Soviet Pact with those made at the end of the war in 1945;
   (b) How valid is the view that 'Stalin's aims in 1939 and in 1945 were essentially defensive'?
3. (a) Outline the key stages in the development of East and West Germany in the period 1945–89;
   (b) With what justification has it been claimed that 'the key factor in the Cold War from 1945 to 1989 was the problem of Germany'?
4. (a) In what ways did the death of Stalin change the relationships between the superpowers after 1953?
   (b) Consider the view that 'Khrushchev's attempts to bring about peaceful co-existence deserve far more credit than they are usually given'.
5. In what ways and for what reasons did the Cold War attitudes and policies of the USA diverge from those of Western Europe after 1961?
6. Why, despite so many confrontations between the superpowers, was there no nuclear war in the period from the start of the Berlin Blockade in 1948 to the re-election of Ronald Reagan in 1984?

B *Planning essay answers*

PROBLEMS OF INTERPRETATION: THREE VIEWS OF THE ORIGINS OF THE COLD WAR

The introduction is probably the most important part of an essay answer. It should not be unduly long or complicated and should not be based on 'background'. An exam essay is an answer to a question. That answer should be based on an argument. The introductory paragraphs of an answer should set out the line of argument to be 'proved', with suitable evidence, later on. Sometimes, but not always, this might involve 'disproving' other possible arguments. The main requirement is to be decisive and not to fudge.

Consider these three possible introductions to a question on the origins of the Cold War: *To what extent was the Cold War the result of the deliberate policies of Joseph Stalin?*

(i)   Stalin was indeed the chief cause of the Cold War. Many factors were involved in causing the Cold War, including long-term ideological fixations going back to the beginnings of the Bolshevik state in 1917–24. There were many instances of Western policies being based on self-interest, or on misconceptions and failures to appreciate what terrible losses had been suffered by the Soviet people. But the key cause of the Cold War was in the deliberate political plan which Stalin followed, using the Red Army to create a Soviet Empire in East Central Europe. This plan was founded on the policies Stalin had set out long before the war. Victory in the war was to win back for Stalin the position he held after the 1939 pact with Hitler. The Cold War began when the Western powers belatedly realised what Stalin was up to.

(ii)   The idea that the Cold War was caused by aggressive Soviet expansion at the end of the Second World War is just a convenient excuse for the failures of policy by the Western allies. Stalin's aims were basically defensive, seeking to protect the USSR from the dangers which had nearly destroyed Soviet Russia in 1918–20 and again in 1941–43. Western policies, especially those of Harry Truman, ignored the interests and the sacrifices of the USSR and tried to bully Stalin into subservience by American military and economic power. As the American historian Stephen Cohen says, 'It took partners to create the Cold War.'

(iii)   George Kennan once said, 'The Cold War was nobody's fault but Hitler's.' It is pointless to blame the Cold War on the devious policies of Stalin or on the mistakes and self-interest of Churchill and Truman. The truth is that the Second World War turned Europe into a giant power vacuum. Into that vacuum, the new superpowers (who had not wanted to join the War until forced to in 1941) were unavoidably drawn. When American and Soviet armies met in the heart of a ruined Germany at Torgau in 1945, there was victory but no chance of peace. The Cold War was the result of Hitler's legacy.

Any of these three will work. Why not write your own, better, introduction?

ANALYSING A RANGE OF FACTORS

Essays covering a lengthy period can be difficult. The ideal balance between general ideas and specific information is not always easy to find. Consider the question: *Why was there no nuclear war between 1948 and 1984?*

The simple 'Why?' is not as simple as it seems. The odds are that there will be not one reason but several. Your answer will need to assess the relative importance of a variety of factors in connection with events over a number of years. Try to arrange a series of sub-questions as follows:

(i) What reasons were there to suppose that a nuclear war might happen at all? (The dangers of the arms race; one side using nuclear threats as 'blackmail' and miscalculating the other side's response? An accident, resulting from the complexity of modern weapons systems? A madman with his finger on the nuclear trigger? Mao Zedong believing that China's vast population would 'win' a nuclear exchange?)

(ii) What were the chief occasions when nuclear war nearly happened? (McArthur in Korea? John Foster Dulles in 1954? Cuba 1962? The Middle East in 1973? KAL 007 and *Able Archer* in 1983?)

(iii) What were the various factors which provided restraint? (Key personalities: Eisenhower? Truman? Kennedy? Khrushchev? Or the 'Balance of Terror'? – did nuclear weapons actually make the world a safer, not a more dangerous, place because Hiroshima and Nagasaki were awful, real-life warnings ideally placed at the end of a war, not a fatal error at the beginning of one?)

Is there one guiding idea, an 'above all' factor, which resolves this issue in your opinion? Or do you see it as the accumulation of several reasons?

Note: Remember to make up your mind before starting! A good conclusion is the idea you started with, not something tacked on at the end!

8 ᔐ DOCUMENTARY EXERCISE ON THE POTSDAM CONFERENCE, 1945

Study Sources A–F and answer the questions which follow.

In the course of twenty-five years, the Germans have twice invaded Russia via Poland. The British and American people have never experienced such invasions, which were terrible to endure, with results that will not be forgotten easily.

Germany was able to do this because Poland was always regarded as part of the *cordon sanitaire* [anti-Communist buffer-zone] round the Soviet Union. Previous European policy has always been that Polish governments must be hostile to Russia. As a result, Poland has been too weak to oppose Germany, or else has allowed the Germans to come through Poland to invade Russia. It is, therefore, a vital interest for the USSR that Poland should be both strong and friendly.

SOURCE A
Stalin sets out the Soviet position on Poland, in conversation with an American diplomat, before the conference.

SOURCE B
A Soviet view of the aims of the West from Khrushchev Remembers *by Nikita Khrushchev, 1970.*

The USA and Britain wanted to take advantage of the results of the war and impose their will not only on their enemy, Germany, but also on their ally, the Soviet Union, as well.

SOURCE C

The use of the Red Army to secure Soviet domination from Meeting at Potsdam *by American historian, Charles Mee, 1975.*

Stalin's technique for legitimising his position in Europe was straightforward enough. The Red Army moved in to fight the war. Behind the army, 'friendly' governments were established. Stalin then made a persuasive case to have these governments recognised. Then, when the army pulled back, these client governments would remain.

The technique worked in Romania, Poland and elsewhere. Now Stalin wished to move a little further and secure a slice of eastern Germany. For this, he used the Poles. The Poles had no 'right' to be in eastern Germany; Stalin's putting them there was extremely aggressive. But Stalin could, tenuously, justify it. At Yalta, the Big Three had agreed to the transfer of a large part of eastern Poland to the Russians – and to compensate Poland for this. So the Poles were to gain from Germany a chunk of territory to make up for what they had lost to Russia. To be certain he got what he wanted, Stalin moved the Poles in without waiting for a peace conference.

SOURCE D

Stalin is informed about the atomic bomb (successfully tested eight days earlier) at the Potsdam Conference, 24 July, recalled by Winston Churchill.

I was only a few yards away. I watched with close attention the momentous talk. I knew what the President was going to do. What was vital was to measure its effect upon Stalin. Truman casually mentioned to Stalin that the United States had a new weapon of unusual destructive force. Stalin showed no special interest. I was sure that Stalin had no idea of the significance of what he was being told, of the revolution in world affairs which was in progress. Later, as we were waiting for our cars, I found myself near Truman. 'How did it go?', I inquired.

'He never asked me a single question', Truman replied.

SOURCE E

Text of a letter to James Byrnes by President Truman, 5 January 1946.

At Potsdam, we were faced with an established fact. By circumstances, we were almost forced to agree to the Russian occupation of eastern Poland; and to Polish occupation of Germany east of the Oder river. There isn't a doubt in my mind that Russia intends to invade Turkey and to seize the Black Sea straits. Unless Russia is faced with an iron fist and strong language, another war is on the way. I don't think we should play compromise any longer. We should refuse to recognise Romania and Bulgaria. We should state our position on Iran in no uncertain terms and we should retain complete control of Japan. We should rehabilitate China and create a strong government there – the same for Korea. Then we should force a settlement of Russia's Lend–Lease debts. I'm tired of babying the Soviets.

At bottom of the Kremlin's view of world affairs is a traditional and instinctive Russian sense of insecurity. Russian rulers have always feared foreign penetration, or direct contact between the western world and their own, feared what would happen if Russians learned the truth about the world outside; or if foreigners learned the truth about the world within. The Kremlin seeks security only in patient but deadly struggle for total domination of rival power, never by compromises with it. Though impervious to reason, it is highly susceptible to the logic of force.

SOURCE F

USA diplomat, George Kennan, sets out the case for 'containment' in the 'Long Telegram', February 1946.

1. *Explain what Stalin meant by the word 'friendly' in Source A. (3 marks)*
2. *Using Source D and your own knowledge, explain the reasons why Stalin 'showed no special interest'. (3 marks)*
3. *How far do Sources A–F show Stalin's aims to be 'essentially defensive'? (6 marks)*
4. *Using your own knowledge and the evidence of these sources, discuss the validity of the view that Stalin had a deliberate plan in 1945 to dominate Eastern Europe. (8 marks)*

10 Social and Cultural Trends in Europe, 1945–95

INTRODUCTION

The Second World War was the catalyst for a 'social revolution' in Europe. During and after the war, there were massive shifts of population and also in attitudes. The impact of the war made 'Americanisation', 'Sovietisation', and 'Globalisation' key influences on the society and culture of Europe.

One important factor was the relative decline of European economic and political power. After 1945, it was the new Soviet and American superpowers who had predominance. With military and economic dominance, cultural dominance followed, taking different forms on either side of the Iron Curtain. For example, the society and culture of East and West Germany diverged markedly after 1945–49, even though the situation inherited from Hitler was almost identical. Another key factor was the process of 'decolonisation' and the growth of multicultural societies in Europe as a result of the inflow of immigrants from the former colonies. Because of these and countless other factors, patterns of popular culture and society were turned upside down.

To cover all these huge changes in depth would be beyond the scope of this book. It is also important to remember that worthwhile general conclusions about social and cultural trends are extremely difficult for historians to make. They run the risk of the over-simplification of complex topics. What this chapter does is to select certain themes and to set out some of the ways in which historians might go about explaining them and assessing their importance. Because of the nature of the topic and of the available study resources, Britain will figure prominently. At the end of the chapter, photographic source material and some sample essay questions provide an opportunity to build essay topics out of these wide-ranging themes.

It is the differences between the Europe of 1945 and the Europe of the 1990s which seem most obvious. The image of 1945 was, for example, much more black-and-white – in the cinema, in newspapers and advertising, even in the dress of people on the street. The sounds of 1945 were much quieter – a world without ever-present recorded music and in which streets were full of children playing (and twice a day masses of workers on bicycles) but almost devoid of traffic. Most adults, men and women, wore hats. In large parts of Europe, the emancipation of women was not even an issue. There was no such

KEY ISSUE

What aspects of culture and society changed? What stayed the same?

thing as a separate youth culture. Homosexuality was not only a taboo subject but also a crime. Social horizons were narrower. Mass tourism had not yet been invented. The influences of family, school and church were more clearly defined. The world seemed a smaller place. In Britain, for example, BBC radio held a media monopoly. The first 'national' television event was the coronation of 1953; commercial TV (and TV advertising) lay in the future.

Continuity, however, is just as important in history as change. In the Europe of fifty years ago, boys played football, mothers fell out with daughters, people watched films avidly, worried about their jobs, followed the latest fashions. Even when big changes did occur, they did not happen everywhere, nor at the same speed. There were huge variations in both the rate of change and its direction. Some of these variations were due to economic differences – social and cultural change tends to be an urban affair, depending on a certain degree of prosperity. Change happened in very different ways and much more slowly in southern Italy, for example, than in the urbanised north. Other variations arose from specific political conditions. Franco's Spain was very different from other parts of western Europe; almost all of Western Europe was very different from countries in the Soviet Bloc. There was also the influence of religion. Societies with strong traditional Catholic loyalties, such as Southern Ireland, Poland and Spain were less susceptible to new social and cultural trends, especially those affecting the family. It may be helpful to make a general differentiation between three loose categories:

(i)   the Iron Curtain countries;
(ii) the urbanised, prosperous areas of North West Europe;
(iii) the more rural and traditional areas of Southern Europe.

Here is Pécs, in Hungary, from Richard Bassett's *Guide to Central Europe*:

> From the Pannonia Hotel and the National Theatre, narrow streets lead to the cathedral square, with its delightful old pavilion cafés. Little seems to have changed here since the last century. Children play with hoops, cars are rare, and the ice-cream is rich and sugary.

This is a nice evocation of the days before the 'social revolution' which so changed Europe after 1945 – but Bassett was describing Pécs in 1986.

Why not collect from the older generation of your own family a range of reminiscences which reveal the differences between 'then' and 'now'?

1 ～ THE CAUSES OF CHANGE

There are countless aspects of social and cultural change in post-war Europe. The topics here are only an arbitrary selection – many important factors are not covered here but are worthy of attention. It should also be remembered that many of these trends applied particularly to Britain and certain parts of Western Europe. Different trends affected Eastern Europe – and it should be borne in mind that the impact of social trends is not uniform, nor does it happen everywhere at the same time:

- *Americanisation:* This was a trend which began well before 1945 but was vastly accelerated by the war. One obvious influence was the cinema, especially after the arrival of talking pictures at the end of the 1920s; but there were many others, from Ford motor cars to jazz. During the war, huge numbers of American servicemen were based in Europe, bringing with them the styles and sounds of the USA. Unlike 1918, many American troops remained in Europe and cemented these influences, especially in Britain and West Germany. The huge success immediately after the war of the Rodgers and Hammerstein musicals *Oklahoma!* And *South Pacific* is one example of the impact of American energy and optimism on war-torn Europe. From 1947 and the launch of the Marshall Plan, the penetration of the European economy by the power of American marketing proved unstoppable; seen in such varied products as Coca Cola, General Motors cars, popular entertainment and leisure wear. In the 1990s, one symbol was the spectacular impact of McDonalds chain restaurants in cities like Prague and St Petersburg;

See pages 387–8

- *Sovietisation:* The mirror image of Americanisation was the impact on Eastern and Central Europe after 1945 of Soviet domination. In the West, this was often seen as a purely negative factor, resulting in the denial of freedoms and the cutting of natural links with the west; but there was a genuine social and cultural agenda in the Soviet Bloc. Universal access to sporting and cultural activities and to higher education, heavy state sponsorship of the arts and subsidised public services, including transport, were all part of the system. Although this system was swept away in 1989–90, with many revelations about corruption, propaganda distortions, and the repressive measures involved, it was not long before deep concerns were being voiced about the loss of valued social and cultural benefits;

- *The Welfare State:* One area in which East and West were remarkably similar was in 'welfarism' and the provision of health care and other social benefits. Numerous diseases accepted as commonplace in 1945 – measles, whooping-cough, tuberculosis – were virtually eradicated. By the 1990s, the great majority of Europeans were living longer, healthier lives. (But, there are always exceptions. The death rate in the USSR actually increased during the 1980s!);

- As a result of these demographic changes, however, the rising costs of welfare provision became much larger, leading to painful political choices about levels of taxation and the arguments for 'privatisation'. This was a particular problem for the countries of East Central Europe, due to the suddenness with which the issues arose after 1989;

- *Mass education:* Two of the greatest social changes in post-war Europe were the advance of women and the emergence of a distinctive youth culture. (Both of these occurred at different times and in different ways in Eastern Europe.) The basis of all this was mass education. Before 1945, only a small minority had secondary education beyond the age of fifteen; by the 1990s, there were few young people entering full-time employment before eighteen and nearly half were in higher education. This was a social revolution, accelerated in the 1980s by the shrinking of old-style labour-intensive industries such as coal-mining, and by the spread of mechanisation. One key result of the emergence of a large, well-educated middle class was to create a massive new market in the cultural field, especially in the arts, newspapers, advertising and the media;

- *The mass media:* Cinema and television are discussed in more depth later in this chapter as an important part of popular culture; but the impact of the media in other fields was enormous. The impact of television on sport, for example, probably outweighed any other factor. TV advertising had a massive role in spreading social and cultural fashions and, perhaps most important of all, in extending 'globalisation' by bringing the mass marketing of multinational products even into the more remote parts of Europe;

- *The transport revolution:* Few things did as much to change Western Europe as mass car ownership and cheap air travel. From the 1950s, the motor car fundamentally changed the social and leisure activities of millions of people and transformed the urban environment. These new developments included housing, commuting, out-of-town shopping centres, motorways – and above all a shift away from the city. Between *c.*1850 and *c.*1950, the expanding city had been the hub of European society; in the post-war era, the population and vitality of many cities went into decline. One of the clearest signs of the impact of the car on Western society was the contrast with Eastern Europe before 1989. Cities like Prague became a magnet for millions of visitors precisely because they were lively places which had escaped the concrete jungle of flyovers and multi-storey car parks, and in which cheap public transport remained the basis of mass travel. Cheap air travel made possible the explosion of mass tourism. Package sunshine holidays, for example, changed the coastline of Spain forever. Mass participation in a previously élite activity like skiing had a similar impact on the mountains of Austria, France, Italy and Slovakia;

- *Multiculturalism:* After 1945, Europe became culturally diverse. The combined effects of the end of empire and the post-war economic prosperity drew hundreds of thousands of immigrants into Western Europe. In Britain, the arrival of the *Empire Windrush* in 1948 began a surge of immigration from Jamaica and the Caribbean, followed soon afterwards by many from the Indian sub-continent. In France, cities like Marseilles and Paris absorbed large numbers from North Africa and from French colonies south of the Sahara. In West Germany, the need for labour brought in thousands of *Gastarbeiter*, foreign workers mostly from South East Europe. One aspect of this was the prominence of ethnic restaurants and new trends in popular music; another was the rise of urban social tensions, especially in the case of 'second-generation' immigrant communities;

- *The post-war boom*: Behind almost all factors inducing change was prosperity. Mass ownership of cars, televisions, washing machines, mass travel, the welfare state and the rest could only be based on rising incomes. Before 1945, Europe had not only gone through the devastation of the war but also the great depression which preceded the war. What underpinned the 'social revolution' in Western Europe more than anything else was the long post-war boom which began with the Marshall Plan in 1947 and continued for the next thirty years. Even the Iron Curtain countries had their own version of long-term stability and relative economic recovery. Despite the oil-price crises of the 1970s and the recessions of the 1980s, the fact remained that the fifty years from 1945 were the longest period of peace and prosperity in the entire history of Europe.

> ### KEY ISSUE
>
> *In what ways and for what reasons did social and cultural developments in Eastern Europe differ from those in the West?*

2 ⤳ THE TIMESCALE OF CHANGE

A *Before 1945*

Even though 1945 was such an obvious break with the past, change in history is rarely as sudden as it seems. Many of the social and cultural developments of post-war European society had been coming for a long time. Some historians write in terms of a 'Thirty Years War' between 1914 and 1945 and suggest that the First World War did at least as much as the Second to break down the old cultural order and to let loose radical new trends. The Second World War was more an accelerator of change than a single, instantaneous cause. Key factors in this process included:

- The defeat of German power, begun in 1918 but not ended until 1945;
- The rise of the USA as a world power, begun in 1917 but delayed till 1945;
- The rise of the Soviet Union, begun in 1917 and victorious in 1945;
- The origins of the Cold War, matching the rise of Communism;
- Decolonisation, which seemed amazingly rapid after 1945 but which began with the shaking of European colonial empires in 1914–18;
- The legacy of the Fascist totalitarian regimes which were overthrown in 1945 but whose pre-war models remained influential in

such areas as economic planning, mass housing schemes and mass propaganda.

B *Post-war recovery, 1945–c.1960*

The immediate post-war period was shaped by the Cold War. The differences between Eastern and Western Europe became deeper and more permanent, cutting off 'westernised' societies like the Czechs. The Cold War institutionalised popular culture, as propaganda permeated almost everything produced for mass consumption – newspapers, the media, school textbooks. The trend was towards uniformity.

C *The Sixties 'Cultural Revolution', c.1958–c.1973*

In the 1960s, social and cultural patterns began to diversify. On both sides of the Iron Curtain, orthodox ideas were challenged, especially by the rise of a global youth culture and the consequences of the expansion of higher education. 1968 was a symbolic year, with the Prague Spring matching the 'events' of May in Paris. The 'spirit of 1968' mixed protest movements against nuclear weapons, or the Vietnam War, or the Stalinist system, with a fascination for new music and alternative lifestyles.

See pages 458–63

D *1968–c.1980*

In the 1970s, the cultural atmosphere of Western Europe was affected by the declining image of the USA and by the down-turn in the world economy. This was the decade of punk rock and urban terrorism; and what some commentators saw as a time of 'cultural pessimism' – the feeling that Western European civilisation was declining. In the Soviet Bloc, the Brezhnev regime tried hard to protect its youth from 'decadent' Western popular culture.

E *c.1980–95*

At the beginning of the 1980s, Western European society started to reflect the political swing towards the Right, as Thatcher and Kohl came to power and the Mitterand presidency abandoned its left-wing agenda. After 1985, the Soviet Bloc began to fall apart, bringing huge social and cultural changes at stunning speed. Sponsorship, television and corporate finance became key influences on sport and the arts. By the mid-1990s, the dominant trend was 'globalisation' and a seemingly unstoppable trend towards a uniform, multinational culture based on market forces.

3 ⌐ ASPECTS OF CHANGE

The following brief sections attempt to illustrate some aspects of those changes. They are not comprehensive – many other topics, from computers to contraception, from transport to terrorism, from supermarkets to soft drugs, might equally have deserved a mention – but they are intended to provide opportunities to relate general social and cultural themes to specific topics.

A *Buildings, motor cars and mass tourism*

One of the most obvious differences between Europe in 1995 and 1945 was in the built environment. In all forms of architecture, in roads, housing and in techniques of construction, modern developments transformed the outward appearance, and the life-styles, of large parts of the continent. Some of these transformations were gradual, as with the ever-increasing volume of traffic and its impact upon cities and upon road building. Some were local and sudden, such as the impact of mass tourism on previously isolated regions such as the Portuguese Algarve, or the Greek islands. Some were political, as with the housing schemes of Socialist planners; others were the uncontrolled results of the tide of post-war prosperity. Yet others were technological.

Many of these trends had begun before the war. Modernist architectural styles and mass housing schemes had developed in the 1920s, if not earlier. Most post-war architects were influenced by earlier pioneers of building in glass, steel and concrete, such as Le Corbusier, or the *Bauhaus* school in Weimar Germany. A considerable number of developments followed on directly from the centrally-planned mass building projects of the Fascist dictatorships in Mussolini's Italy, Vichy France or Nazi Germany. As one example, the colossal holiday complex at Prora, on the Baltic Sea, built by the Nazi *Strength Through Joy* organisation in the 1930s was a prototype for the massive hotel building, which covered the coasts of Spain thirty years later. The huge construction projects in Eastern Europe after 1945 were simply continuing with the 'Stalinist model' of the pre-war Soviet Union.

The war, however, brought a tremendous acceleration of change. The main reason was the sheer scale of destruction. The course of the war, above all the effects of area bombing, flattened whole cities. There was an urgent need to clear the ruins and to rehouse the millions who were homeless. How this was done varied. In some cases, as in Dresden, cities were left scarred by war damage for decades. In others, like Warsaw, the original city was recreated, almost brick by brick. In some, like Plymouth, Coventry and Kassel, a new and different modern city centre was built on the ruins of the old.

Not only buildings changed, but also people. Massive population transfers in 1945 made German cities into Polish ones, like Breslau, or Soviet ones, like Konigsberg. The entire Jewish culture which had been such an important part of the life of East Central Europe was gone forever.

The main influence in the 1940s was massive public building projects. The mood of the time was favourable to Socialist planning, not only in the Soviet Bloc but also in Britain, France and West Germany. It became a common saying that 'the planners finished what Hitler started', as pre-war buildings were cleared away and large new residential blocks mushroomed. Once the immediate post-war reconstruction was over, the process was continued by big slum clearance schemes and the growth of 'overspill' satellite towns built on greenfield sites, such as Speke near Liverpool, Vitrolles near Marseilles, or countless 'new town' developments in Eastern Europe. One of the great disappointments of the post-war era, on both sides of the Iron Curtain, was how many of these big new urban projects, launched with such high expectations, became centres of serious social problems from the 1970s.

In Western Europe, post-war prosperity and its side effects produced even bigger changes than the bombers or the planners. There was a mass movement of workers into areas of economic growth. The explosion of mass car ownership led to the inexorable growth of commuting, suburban housing and road building. The visible effects were motorways, multi-storey car parks and edge-of-town shopping centres such as the *Auchan* hypermarkets in France. The deeper effects included a drift of population and economic activity away from the city to the suburbs and fundamental changes in city life, affecting department stores, public transport, places of entertainment. These effects were not uniform. Many cities in Eastern Europe remained little changed, because they were less prosperous and because of rigid social controls. 'Americanisation' was most notable in Britain and West Germany.

Matching the growth of car ownership was the impact of mass tourism. Before the war, and in the generation which followed it, mass holidays meant the seaside resort, the holiday camp or the youth hostel. In the 1960s, the effects of the post-war boom and the technical development of larger aircraft made possible the cheap package holiday. As a result, huge areas of Europe, previously poor and neglected, became the centres of hotel building and the tourist economy. The first and most famous example was Spain, but the trend brought dramatic changes all over Europe: on the coasts of Greece and Yugoslavia and in

KEY ISSUE

What was the social impact of mass housing schemes in post-war Europe?

TABLE 46
Car ownership in Europe, 1990 (in millions)

Britain	24m
France	27m
Germany	33m
Italy	31m
USSR	16m
(Japan	56m)

See page 246

	Share of total employment (%)	Share of exports of goods and services
Austria	13.9	17.6
France	4.8	6.1
Germany	6.5	2.0
Greece	10.0	23.4
Portugal	5.6	15.5
Spain	9.1	19.9

TABLE 47
The importance of tourism in national economies, 1993

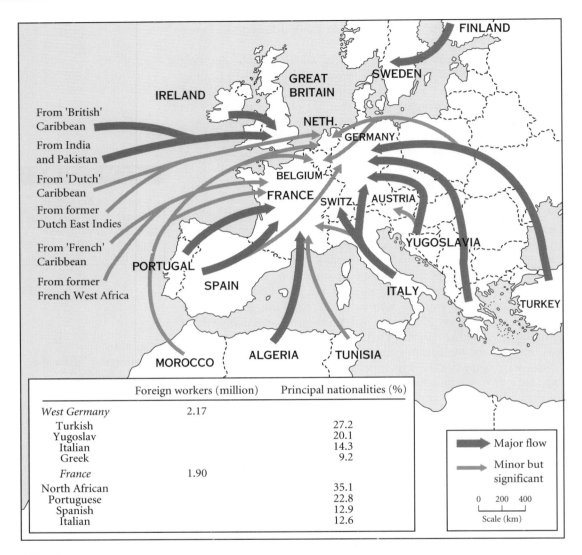

MAP 33
Migration of labour in Western Europe, 1945–73

	Foreign workers (million)	Principal nationalities (%)
West Germany	2.17	
Turkish		27.2
Yugoslav		20.1
Italian		14.3
Greek		9.2
France	1.90	
North African		35.1
Portuguese		22.8
Spanish		12.9
Italian		12.6

Legend:
— Major flow
— Minor but significant

0 200 400
Scale (km)

TABLE 48

Tourism in East Central Europe, 1994. Nights stayed by international visitors (in millions)

Czech Republic	17.1 m
Croatia	2.3 m
Hungary	21.4 m
Poland	18.8 m
Romania	2.8 m

the ski resorts of Austria and France. There were also tourist pressures on Europe's capital cities. In London and Paris, Rome and Vienna, the sheer weight of people threatened to overwhelm the main tourist attractions and to intensify the strain on public transport.

One of the marks of the importance of these changes was the suddenness of their impact on Eastern Europe after 1989. Cities such as Prague had been largely insulated from the side-effects of the motor car and of post-war affluence. In the 1990s, mass tourism arrived suddenly and was regarded as economically vital; millions of tourists were attracted by the very fact that so much of East Central Europe was

PICTURE 45
Post-war housing under construction in the Gorbals, Glasgow, in the late 1950s

PICTURE 46
The landscape of mass tourism – high-rise beach hotels

See page 465

KEY ISSUE

What were the social and cultural effects, both harmful and beneficial, of mass travel and tourism?

'unspoiled'. On both sides of the old Iron Curtain, the problems of protecting architectural and cultural treasures from overcrowding, pollution, consumerism and the sheer weight of the tourist millions became more and more urgent and difficult.

B *Cinema*

THE LEGACY OF THE PAST

The 1930s was the original great age of cinema. Although of little merit in itself, *The Jazz Singer*, the first feature film with sound, made in 1927, is one of the landmarks of the twentieth century, the beginning of a social and cultural revolution which changed the world. Sound films came on the scene at a significant time, when the USA had become a world economic power. Cinema was a key factor in the 'Americanisation' of Europe. It was also of enormous importance as a form of escapism from the miseries of the Great Depression. Arriving just in time for the rise of Stalin and Hitler, sound films were the ultimate propaganda weapon of the 1930s and of the Second World War.

A notable feature of sound films in the 1930s is how quickly the techniques were perfected. New film genres developed, swiftly becoming brilliantly successful, both within the USA and throughout Europe. There was the western, the musical, the gangster film, the cartoon, the 'screwball comedy', the romantic melodrama, the historical or propaganda epic. In one year, 1939, three classic films showed the grip that Hollywood had on the world's imagination: the Walt Disney cartoon feature (and Goebbels' favourite film) *Snow White and the Seven Dwarfs*; the Judy Garland musical, *The Wizard of Oz*; and the Technicolor epic drama *Gone With the Wind*.

The impact of cinema in the 1930s was not exclusively American. First, Hollywood itself was extremely European, being dominated by a relatively small group of leading studios, all founded by recent European immigrants, almost all of them Jewish. After 1933, this European influence was reinforced by a constant inflow of actors, directors, composers and writers, many, though not all, refugees from Hitler. They included both exiled Jews, like the directors Billy Wilder, Fritz Lang, Ernest Lubitsch, and also those enhancing their careers, such as Marlene Dietrich and Errol Flynn.

Second, not all films came from Hollywood. European cinema was important in its own right. In Britain and in France, the cinema provided popular and distinctive film styles. In Weimar Germany there was a well-established cinema with a big international reputation. This was then badly damaged by the rise of the Nazis. Many talented artists left Germany and Nazi cinema became famous for its blatant propaganda, especially for Leni Riefenstahl's documentary epics, *Triumph of the Will* and *Olympiad*. The propaganda film was an even more blatant aspect of Soviet cinema, most famously those by the founding father of propaganda films, Sergei Eisenstein, in epics like

Alexander Nevsky, but also in the trite and obvious type which Sheila Fitzpatrick has summed up as *'Boy-meets-Girl-meets-Tractor'.*

Cinema, alongside radio, was already the biggest single form of popular culture in the world in the 1930s, and the most powerful single weapon in influencing fashions and attitudes. In all countries, cinema was a vital way of keeping up morale in the Second World War. British, American and Soviet film makers showed that they were as expert as the Nazis at manipulating film and radio for propaganda purposes.

THE POST-WAR ERA

By 1945, the techniques of film making and the culture of film going were at a peak. In war-damaged Europe, the hunger for normality and the need for escapism meant that audiences were huge. Inevitably, cinema became an important part of the Cold War. Films in Eastern Europe were overwhelmingly state-controlled, based on a diet of war epics, 'social realism' dramas, and 'educational' documentaries. In the West, 1950s films were much more diverse, but tended to be politically 'safe', or outright anti-Communist. 'McCarthyism' affected Hollywood perhaps more than any part of American life. To some extent this also influenced films in Europe. The West German film industry was 'de-Nazified' and pro-Western, for obvious reasons. In Britain and the USA, a huge number of films were devoted to the War, often reinforcing ideas of patriotism and the Anglo–American alliance.

War attitudes were very prominent in newsreels and documentaries, which were extremely influential in the days before mass television ownership. The techniques of realistic documentary films, perfected during the war, influenced feature dramas. In the European cinema, especially in post-Fascist Italy, there were a number of films in the so-called 'new realism' movement, using documentary techniques to support gritty dramas, often against a war-torn background. Two highly influential directors were Roberto Rossellini, who made *Rome – Open City* and *Germany Year Zero,* and Vittorio de Sica. French directors like Henri Clouzot also used the semi-documentary techniques to thrilling effect.

The cinema of the 1950s has been described as 'The Great Escape'. The cultural mood was conformist. The impact of the Cold War and McCarthyism pushed American film makers into 'safe' genres, such as traditional westerns or musicals and romantic comedies, often set in European locations, such as *An American in Paris* and *Gigi.* In Britain, there was a flood of war films, such as *The Dam Busters, Reach For The Sky,* and *The Cruel Sea.* In continental Europe, the war evoked ambivalent attitudes and war films were rare; but several new directors established reputations for 'serious' films, such as the Swedish director Ingmar Bergman, whose best-known work was *The Seventh Seal* (1956). Both in Hollywood and in Europe the cinema was thriving. Foreign-language films were widely shown in European countries, usually sub-titled in France and Britain, often 'dubbed' in West Germany.

By 1960, however, cinema audiences in the West had dropped dramatically, to one-third of the 1950 peak. This was partly because the

KEY ISSUE

What was the impact of the Second World War on the post-war European cinema?

See page 395

TABLE 49
Films reflecting Western Cold War attitudes

The Iron Curtain	(1948)
I Married A Communist	(1950)
Red Danube	(1950)
Big Jim McLain	(1952)
The Third Man	(1949)

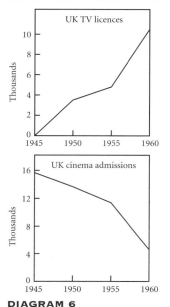

DIAGRAM 6
TV licences and cinema attendances, 1945–60

post-war boom in cinema-going was bound to slacken; but the chief reason was the effect of 1950s prosperity and, especially, of television. In a surprisingly short space of time, television undermined cinema as the standard mass entertainment. It was cheaper and easier to produce the programmes. TV also reached so many people so easily that it created cult followings much more readily than cinema and was a godsend to advertisers. Car ownership and the move to the suburbs loosened the hold of the city on mass entertainment. Numerous film stars shifted into television shows as part of the process, with Lucille Ball a prime example. Small local cinemas began to close by the hundred.

The growth of television meant that films had to change: sometimes bigger and more spectacular in *Cinemascope* or 3-D, sometimes more daring and original. The driving urge was to make films something that television could not do. Two staple film genres, the musical and the western, changed almost out of recognition. There was also a reaction in Europe, where film-makers saw themselves being 'swamped' by American influences and tried to fight back with their own distinctive style. This was especially true in the 1960s.

THE 'NEW WAVE'

The 1960s was the decade of youth and of a shift to the Left, tinged with anti-Americanism. This was the period of the 'New Wave' in France, of the rush of ambitious films by the new Italian directors, Federico Fellini, Luchino Visconti and Franco Zeffirelli, and of a number of gritty 'life-from-below' films in Britain, such as *Saturday Night and Sunday Morning* and *Room At The Top*. Comedies tended to be more cynical and satirical. In fighting back against television, there was an emphasis on big-screen epics and a trend towards more daring and explicit treatment of sex and violence. As the Cold War thawed, spy thrillers became more complex, with villains on both sides. Films were regarded as an art form, not merely mainstream entertainment, and were reviewed in the Sunday supplements. (This trend should not be exaggerated. In Britain, the top box-office successes of the 1960s were the James Bond films, starting with *Dr No* in 1962, and the *Carry On* comedies. The biggest earner of the decade was *The Sound Of Music*.)

The big development of this period was the French '*Nouvelle Vogue*', or New Wave. This rebellion against traditional, 'commercial', film styles began with *Le Beau Serge* by Claude Chabrol in 1958 and was carried on by a series of like-minded young directors, especially François Truffaut with *Quatre-Cent Coups* (*400 Blows*) and *Jules et Jim*, Alain Resnais with *Hiroshima Mon Amour* and *Last Year at Marienbad* and Jean-Luc Godard's *A Bout de Souffle* (*Breathless*). New Wave films often showed foreign influences (particularly admiration for Alfred Hitchcock) but were able to develop a distinctive, mysterious, French flavour. French cinema continued to keep a separate identity more successfully than anywhere else in Western Europe, though Italian cinema flourished for a time through the work of Fellini, Zeffirelli, Visconti and Michelangelo Antonioni.

KEY ISSUE

How many small businesses in your area are located in buildings which used to be local cinemas?

TABLE 50

'Anti-establishment' British films from the late 1950s

Look Back in Anger	(1958)
Room at the Top	(1958)
Saturday Night and Sunday Morning	(1960)
This Sporting Life	(1963)
The Ipcress File	(1965)

TABLE 51

Some key Italian films

La Dolce Vita, Fellini	(1960)
L'Aventura, Antonioni	(1960)
Romeo and Juliet, Zeffirelli	(1965)
The Leopard, Visconti	(1963)
Death in Venice, Visconti	(1971)

Cinema in Eastern Europe also showed more freedom and adventure, in parallel to the New Wave. In the 1950s, a number of new and original directors emerged in Poland. Between 1954 and 1958, Andrzej Wajda made a trilogy of films about Warsaw during the Second World War: *A Generation; Kanal; Ashes and Diamonds*. Wajda was followed by a younger generation of directors led by Roman Polanski who made his name in Poland with *Knife in the Water* and then moved to Hollywood to make *Rosemary's Baby* and *Chinatown*. Later, a wave of adventurous and individual films came from Czechoslovakia, mirroring the 'Prague Spring', such as Milos Forman's *Peter and Paula* (1964) and Jiri Menzel's *Closely Watched Trains* (1966). Like Polanski, Forman later moved to Hollywood. After the 1960s, however, cinema in Britain and Europe found it more and more difficult to resist American dominance of the market; or the impact of television.

See pages 167–8

KEY ISSUE

What does a study of European films in the 1960s reveal about the social and cultural trends of the time?

THE MODERN ERA

Hollywood was notably affected by the loss of national self-confidence following the Vietnam War. Spy thrillers became either complete spoofs or complex paranoid conspiracies. The western genre first went radical with anti-heroic, 'pro-Indian' films like *Little Big Man* (1970) and *Ulzana's Raid* (1972) and then virtually ceased to exist. The 1970s was a bad decade for heroes. It was also a bad decade for audiences. Fewer films were made and more cinemas closed. The emergence of the video-cassette and the video rental shop threatened to kill cinema dead.

In the USSR, the 'Khrushchev Thaw' produced a surge in the number and popularity of films after the tight controls of Stalin's last years. From 1954, Soviet films were less monumental and propagandistic, more concerned with 'real life' – such as *Serezha*, a moving story of childhood (1960) and the 'human' war films *Ballad of a Soldier*, and *The Fate of a Man*, both made in 1959. From 1964, Soviet cinema reflected the cultural conservatism of the new, post-Khrushchev regime – what Richard Stites calls 'Brezhnev's culture wars'. *Goskino*, the State Committee on Cinema, monitored all aspects of film production. The 'tsars' of *Goskino*, Alexei Romanov and Filipp Ermash, clamped down hard on film directors' freedom. Sex was out. Socialist realism was in. The Cold War political thriller made a comeback.

Cinema in the 'Brezhnev era' was also affected by a big rise in the influence of television but, compared with the West, cinema audiences declined only slightly, from 4.6 billion per year to 4.1 billion. The most popular films were escapist comedies and, especially, crime films. Films with approved political content and 'art' films were seldom popular. Most films side-stepped political issues altogether but one of the best and most popular films of the period, *Scarecrow*, daringly and blatantly attacked collective tyranny against the individual. Made in 1984, it hinted at the end of an era.

In the West, film started to make a recovery in the 1980s, as the film industry adapted to the factors which endangered it. One example of this was cooperation with television. Many films were joint-funded and

TABLE 52
Film production in Europe, 1945–95

Number of feature films produced	
Britain	1777
Czechoslovakia	2666
France	4446
Germany	3686
Hungary	778
Italy	3338
Poland	915
Spain	1816
Sweden	1176
Yugoslavia	1118

designed for cinema release first and then later televising – one award-winning British example was *Mona Lisa;* another was *Chariots of Fire.* Out-of-town shopping centres opened 'multiplex' cinemas, offering easy access by car and a choice of up-to-date films. There was special emphasis on the big 'special effects' film which outshone anything TV could offer. This was combined with a deliberate marketing of films for the new, affluent youth market. George Lucas and Steven Spielberg produced, in quick succession, *Star Wars, Raiders of the Lost Ark,* and *Back to the Future.* Such films and innumerable imitations were aimed at an essentially teenage audience. They developed special effects to a high degree. They set the fashion for endless sequels and for ancillary marketing of books, T-shirts and games associated with a film. In *Talking Pictures*, Barry Norman writes of 'the end of films for grown-ups'. Production costs escalated, pushing most of the European film industry into smaller and more specialised projects, leaving the blockbusters to Hollywood.

In 1995, the American dominance of cinema-going in Western Europe was as strong as ever, but cinema held a different place in society than it had in 1945. It could no longer automatically dominate the visual arts but had to compete with video, multiple television channels, CD-Roms and computer games. On the other hand, films were also kept alive by television, because TV schedules could never have been filled without them. Films such as *Breathless* and *Casablanca* became familiar to each new generation through repeated TV showings. Cinema was both part of the present and part of the past. Universities put on courses of film and media studies. Newspapers devoted pages to criticism of new releases and cinema remained important to the cultural history of Europe and its response to American influences.

KEY ISSUE

In what ways did the cinema bring about the further 'American-isation' of Europe after 1970?

C *The mass media*

TELEVISION

Television was still in its infancy in 1945. The technology had existed before the war (coverage of the 1936 Berlin Olympics, for example) but was far too expensive for mass television ownership. The post-war era, with its prosperity and suburbanisation, was ideally suited to the expansion of television in Western Europe. Television developed more slowly in the Soviet Bloc but, by the 1970s, had become as vital a part of everyday life as it was in the West.

Television, like Hollywood films, was part of the process of 'Americanisation'. The big USA networks, CBS, NBC, and ABC, set the pace in television production and much of their output was exported. TV westerns, such as *Gunsmoke*, or *The Lone Ranger*, police thrillers, quiz shows and comedy programmes became familiar to British and European audiences. Television was also an outlet for repeated showings of old films, most of them American. Many programmes produced in Europe copied staple American TV styles.

Against this trend, in most European countries the emphasis was on 'official' public broadcasting, In the Soviet Bloc, this meant complete State control. In Britain, it meant a national public broadcasting service, not directly under government control. The BBC, following the principles of public service laid down by Lord Reith from 1922, was well established in radio and enhanced its standing and worldwide reputation during the war. The BBC, financed by a licence fee, became a hybrid system mixing mass audience programmes in sport and light entertainment with its traditional role in news, national events and non-fiction programming. Two events in 1953, the 'Matthews Cup Final' and the Coronation of Elizabeth II, were landmarks in making TV the focus of the national consciousness in the way radio had been during the war.

From 1955, the BBC faced competition from ITV. This so-called 'duopoly' between the BBC and the private sector was extended by the arrival of BBC2 in 1968 and of Channel Four in 1976. Competition had significant effects on both sectors. The BBC frequently popularised its programmes in the battle for ratings, while the regulators of the ITV companies and Channel Four came under pressure to maintain standards and limit the amount of advertising. In the 1980s, 'terrestrial' television faced new competition from the wider range of channels and aggressive marketing of satellite and cable TV.

In France, more than in Britain, television was under close State control, following a pattern already established by the Vichy authorities from 1943. After the Liberation, this became RTF (*Radio-diffusion Television Française*), a civil service department controlling all broadcasting and reporting to the Ministry of Information. Television in France developed slowly before 1958, with fewer than one million TV sets in the country. Under the presidency of Charles de Gaulle, television gained a much more prominent role in national life, partly because de Gaulle himself was so aware of its political importance and used the televised speech to the nation frequently and to great effect.

The system was semi-privatised and renamed ORTF, (or *l'Office de RTF*). A second channel was opened but French television programming remained under heavy government influence. TV coverage of the 'events' of May 1968 led to political interference and an ORTF strike. In 1971, the brilliant but controversial TV documentary on the years of occupation, *The Sorrow and the Pity*, was banned. It was not shown in France until 1980.

French television remained an overall State monopoly until 1981, when the arrival of François Mitterand led to the Moinot Report, which proposed greater independence from government control. In 1986 a new private network, *Le Cinq*, was introduced. In most countries, the trend was towards privatisation and new technologies. Spain after 1975 was another interesting example of a closely-controlled system, *TVE* (TV Spain) being forced to accept diversification of channels and competition from the private sector.

In Germany, television inevitably reflected the Cold War. In the DDR, close State control mirrored the rest of the Soviet Bloc. One of

TABLE 53

Relative popularity of watching TV and going out in France, 1974

	1967	1973
Watching TV every evening	51.1%	65.1%
Going out at least once a week	10.8%	16.5%

See page 62

KEY ISSUE

In what ways and to what extent was television in Britain and Europe affected by government controls?

TABLE 54

Ownership of TV sets in Italy, 1974

	1965	1973
% of families owning TV sets	49%	92%

See page 228

the most striking programmes on East German television was *The Black Channel,* which consisted entirely of extracts from West German programmes, edited to fit the anti-western propaganda spoken by the East German commentator. In West Germany, the influence of the occupying powers ensured that television was closely regulated by regional councils, based on cities like Cologne, Hamburg and Munich, in order to keep central government out of the system. ARD, the regional network, was the only channel until 1981. Even when a second channel, ZDF, opened, its use of advertising was very restricted. As in other countries, however, video, cable and satellite had a growing impact; and big multimedia concerns in Germany like Bertelsmann and Springer formed consortia with European partners to exploit the expanding electronic media.

The impact of satellite television was another challenge to the national networks. The arrival of CNN, offering continuous news, was a significant factor, notably in its high-profile coverage of the Gulf War in 1991. Control of television, mass newspapers and aggressive bidding for the right to screen sports events made men like Axel Springer in Germany and Rupert Murdoch in Britain extremely powerful; often in ways which the networks, and national governments, found it hard to deal with. One spectacular example of the power of the integrated sports and media empire was Silvio Berlusconi who used his interests in Italian television and the media and his ownership of the giant football club AC Milan as the basis of a new political movement, *Forza Italia.* In 1994, this sports, media and political empire provided the platform for Berlusconi's successful bid to become Prime Minister.

The social and cultural influence of television was enormous. Wherever there was affluence, television ownership shot up. Wherever there were more TV sets, or more alternative channels, more people watched for more hours in the week. Everywhere, television became the main source of news and popular culture and was the chief battleground of politics. It fundamentally altered the nature of radio, of cinema, of newspapers, of advertising and of sport. It both reflected attitudes and helped to change them; for example, in the language and accents of television presenters, and in the acceptability of various patterns of sexual behaviour or political comment. Television both encouraged the growth of 'Americanisation' and did much to block it.

There was both continuity and change. Some popular genres of the 1950s, like the live variety show or westerns, virtually died out. Others, like the soap opera, the police thriller, the game show or the medical drama, went from strength to strength. Two examples from the 1950s illustrate this. *Coronation Street* became a permanent part of ITV schedules, spawning countless imitations. *Emergency Ward Ten* was a forerunner of similar programmes, not only of *Casualty* forty years later in Britain, but almost everywhere else. Examples of such imitations included soap operas such as *Lindenstrasse* and *Verbotene Liebe* (*Forbidden Love*) and the police thriller *Tatort* in West Germany, and the political puppet satire show *Les Guignols d'Info* in France.

Two important, if uneven, general trends were a steady drift towards more populist and more 'democratic' presentation and a steady loosening of the censorship of issues concerning 'bad' language, explicit sex and violence, or 'difficult' social issues. Even during the conservative Brezhnev era, these trends were beginning to influence styles of TV presentation in Eastern Europe and the USSR; after 1989 the speed of change was dramatic. In parts of the Eastern Bloc, despite extensive jamming, it was difficult to prevent western TV programmes from being picked up in the East. This was a particular problem for East Germany and helped to mould events in 1989.

By the 1980s, in Western Europe at least, so-called 'terrestrial' television had probably reached saturation point. There was no more time available to expand the hours of transmission or the hours people could watch. This, as much as technology or marketing, was the reason for greater diversification of channels and programmes aimed at specialist audiences. The role of the TV networks had been eroded, probably permanently. After 1989, similar pressures began to affect the State monopolies in the former Soviet Bloc.

RADIO AND THE PRESS

Several factors affected the nature of radio broadcasting and the press in Western Europe after 1945:

- *New technology:* in radio, cheap and portable receivers (the first mass-produced transistor radio was marketed in 1954, the Sony 'Walkman' in 1974); in the press, computers and the end of 'hot metal' printing. One result of this was a serious loss of influence for the print unions;
- *Global commercial factors:* especially the growth of multinational and multimedia 'empires' going beyond national boundaries;
- *The affluent mass youth market:* especially the explosion in demand for popular music, and the impact of advertising;
- *Diversification:* the relaxing of government controls and the emergence of new and varied outlets, especially local, commercial and 'pirate' radio;
- *Liberalisation:* changes in social and cultural attitudes towards what was acceptable or not in language or topics for discussion. In publishing, this was reflected in the style and marketing of 'tabloid' newspapers; in radio, it was reflected by the image of chat show hosts and 'disc jockeys'.

In the Soviet Bloc, radio was still the most important medium for news and entertainment, at least until the mass ownership of TV sets in the 1950s and 70s. It was also under rigid State control. Music in the USSR, for example, was extremely 'official'. The music the regime preferred to hear on the airwaves was patriotic mass songs by Soviet choirs, or 'approved' folk music. The softening of attitudes towards the West after 1954 brought a flood of western popular music to Soviet radio and three of the most popular star performers of the Khrushchev–Brezhnev era were Alla Pugacheva, Alexander Galich and

Vladimir Vysotsky, all of them at least slightly 'western' in style. In Brezhnev's time, they were seen as subversive by the authorities – in 1971, Galich was arrested for 'anti-Soviet activities'. 75 per cent of all records sold in the USSR were *estrada* – pop music. In the 1980s, well before the end of the Wall, pop music was already a key outlet for dissent and self-expression.

In the West, radio had to deal with the impact of television. Newspapers could not compete with the speed and immediacy of TV news, especially after the arrival of colour television in the 1960s, and of all-day coverage by CNN satellite news in the 1980s. Increasingly, newspapers switched the emphasis from news to comment; either serious in-depth analysis like the *Suddeutscher Zeitung* or *Le Monde*, or populist and sensationalist like *Bild* or *The Sun*.

Television led to the closure of magazines famous for their photo-journalism, such as *Life*, or *Picture Post*. Later, the development of newspaper colour supplements, financed by advertising, brought a revival in photo-journalism.

Radio kept its place in news reporting, by two contrasting styles. One continued the serious radio journalism which had developed during the war, often discussing issues at more length than on television news. The other mixed very frequent but very brief reports with sport and popular music programmes. Radio also exploited the increased mobility of modern life, targeting, for example, the specialised audience at breakfast time, commuters in their cars, or the late-night listener.

Another direct effect of television was that it increasingly dominated the content of newspapers. By the 1980s, western 'tabloid' newspapers relied to a high degree upon television celebrities for sensationalist front-page stories. Sports pages gave less attention to the events of matches or tournaments and devoted more space to quotations and interviews from the participants, often reacting to televised material. Two contradictory tendencies emerged by the late 1980s: on the one hand, a freer, less restricted system with an ever-increasing variety of newspapers and radio channels; on the other hand, an ever-greater concentration of ownership of press, radio and television in the hands of a small number of large international media corporations.

D *Sport*

Sport was an important feature of European society long before 1945. It was in the late nineteenth century that most traditional sports took shape: the first modern Olympic games in 1896, professional soccer in Britain in 1888, cricket test matches from 1878. The origins of most modern games lay in urbanisation. It was in industrial Britain that much organised sport began and from Britain that it spread, often 'exported' by British coaches to other parts of Europe and the world. Sport became part of the urban scene. Thousands played. Thousands watched. Even more thousands eagerly followed the reports in the press and, later, on radio. Industrialists and town councils provided sports facilities; in poorer areas the street was the playing-field. Sport became a major aspect of school life, of youth clubs and church groups, and of community identity. Many historic rivalries, in Glasgow, Liverpool, Madrid, Milan, go back well before 1914.

These rivalries were not always purely sporting ones. They could be complicated by sectarian divisions, as was notoriously the case in Glasgow, or by issues of class, or region. One of the most passionate of all rivalries was between Real Madrid and Barcelona, a match sometimes seen as a virtual replay of the Catalonian struggle against Franco in the Spanish Civil War. In the 1930s, sport became even more closely entwined with politics and nationalism. The first soccer World Cups to be held in Europe, in 1934 and 1938, were both won by Italy. The successes of the *Azurri* were inevitably milked by Mussolini's regime for their propaganda value. Stalin's USSR, like all totalitarian regimes, used sport as an image of national will and team spirit. In 1936 'Hitler's Olympics' in Berlin became a byword for the manipulation of sport for political purposes.

Even an individual sport like boxing was not immune. The Nazi regime made the utmost propaganda use of the success of the German boxer Max Schmeling. His world title fight in 1937 with the black American boxer, Joe Louis, was portrayed as an all-out battle between the 'Aryan' Schmeling and the 'degenerate' Louis.

Sport was also an important form of escapism. In the Depression Thirties, sport, together with cinema, was one of the few outlets for leisure and entertainment. When war came in 1939, most sport was immediately closed down. But governments soon realised the importance of sport for national morale. In Britain, for example, unofficial international soccer matches were organised, drawing huge crowds. By the end of the war in 1945, sport was at the heart of popular culture and there was a hunger for it, both as entertainment and as a sign of normal life being resumed. In the late 1940s Britain, for example, sport drew huge audiences which have never been matched since. Events such as Wimbledon, 'Ashes' cricket tests, the FA Cup Final, became national institutions.

East of the Iron Curtain, sport became part of the social benefits provided by Communist regimes and a badge of national and ideological success. Talented youngsters were identified at an early age and provided with intensive training. The USSR and other Soviet Bloc teams virtually monopolised international competition in sports such as gymnastics and ice-skating. Sports stars became privileged celebrities: the Czech distance runner Emil Zatopek in the 1950s, the Soviet ice-hockey 'Golden Goalie' Vladislav Tretyak in the 1980s. Sports teams were often controlled by State organisations: teams named *Red Star*, or *Dynamo* showed their links to the army – *CSKA* Sofia was the team of Ceauşescu's secret police. In the 1970s, sport was promoted with extra energy as part of Brezhnev's 'culture wars' against youthful hedonism and western decadence. Soviet Bloc policies in sport had some outstanding successes and many athletes made it to the top who might never have done so in the West. On the other hand, many felt

> ## KEY ISSUE
>
> *In what ways, and why, was sport an important part of popular culture in Europe in the years after the Second World War?*

constrained within the regimented system and many suffered lasting damage from the abuse of drugs and stimulants. The more rebellious simply opted out.

At first, sport was a useful light relief from the hardships of war-torn Europe. Then in the 1950s, it was affected by important new developments, especially television. In Britain, the 'Matthews' cup final of 1953 is often cited as the first event to be shared by the entire nation through its TV sets; the Rome Olympics of 1960 had a similar universal impact. The BBC set a trend with *Grandstand* and *Match of the Day*. Then there was the trend to European integration. The EEC was formed out of the Messina conference of 1955 and the 1957 Treaty of Rome: it is no coincidence that the European Champions Cup (proposed by the French magazine *l'Equipe*) began in 1955–56 and the Inter-Cities Fairs Cup in 1960. Such competitions needed another new trend: floodlighting. The floodlit, televised midweek evening match became a feature of the 1950s and has stayed so ever since, changing the face of most outdoor spectator sports in the process.

As with so many European issues, Britain was uncertain about following the 'continentals', either in patterns of play or even whether or not to join in. British teams did not enter the World Cup until 1950; the first English champions to qualify for the European Cup – Chelsea – were forbidden to enter. The 1956 champions, Manchester United, only took part by defying the Football Association.

While some post-war trends strengthened the place of sport in society, others undermined some traditional sports. The 1950s was the beginning of the age of affluence and above all the age of the motor car. The impact of the motor car was to lead to the diversification of sport and leisure. The working week no longer included Saturday mornings; the 'weekend' became open to shopping, caravanning and individua-listic activities, from golf to sailing to DIY. Sport also became more intensive, more professional. It ceased to be practical to be an amateur cricketer or golfer, or to be an Olympic athlete in your spare time. Cricket abandoned amateurism in 1964. The first 'open' Wimbledon tennis championships were held in 1968. By the time of the Munich Olympic Games in 1972, most gold medals were being won by full-time athletes from the Soviet Bloc, or by those backed by sponsorships and sports scholarships from the USA.

The victories of the Eastern Bloc athletes raised concern over the issue of performance-enhancing drugs in sport. This was widely rumoured throughout the 1970s, especially in respect of field events, where journalists suggested that the sisters Irina and Tamara Press should have been in the Soviet Union's men's team rather than the women's. Only after the Ben Johnson case in the 1988 Olympics, and, above all, after the revelations about sports science in East Germany when the archives of the GDR were opened after the end of the Wall, did the full extent of the problem come into the open. It also became clear how extensively drugs were being used by athletes in the West.

At the time, the full extent of the problem was not realised, even by those closely involved. The British sprinter, Kathy Cook, much admired her East German rival, the great Marita Koch. Cook knew many East Germans were on drugs but was sure Koch wasn't. It was disillusioning to discover in 1990 that Koch had been part of the drugs programme like everyone else.

Then there was the power of money. One aspect of the American-isation of European sport was the emergence of the sporting personality whose earnings were maximised by agents, first in tennis (with a separate professional circuit) and then golf (where Arnold Palmer was a role model for sporting superstars). This then spread into team sports. In England, for example, soccer players, however famous, had always stayed with one club because there was little point in moving when the maximum wage (£20 per week) was the same everywhere. An exceptional few, led by the Welsh international John Charles, became well-paid stars in Italy but more typical was Ray Wilson, widely regarded as the best left-back in the world. Wilson stayed with his unfashionable local team, Huddersfield, until he was twenty-eight, travelling to home matches by tram and walking along Leeds Road with the home supporters, carrying his boots in a brown paper bag.

The maximum wage only came to an end in England in 1961–62, after a long legal battle waged by Jimmy Hill and the newly formed player's union, the PFA.

Elsewhere in Europe, the highly-paid star already existed. In Italy, clubs like Inter-Milan and Juventus (funded by the car giant, Fiat) were paying huge sums to foreign imports. In Spain, Real Madrid won the first five European Cups with a team assembled from the best players from Europe and South America. Real Madrid's successes were heavily promoted by the Franco regime. The team became associated with the victory of the centre over the regions in Spain. As a result, many Spanish liberals prevented their sons from having anything at all to do with football, either playing or watching. This trend continued after 1975.

THREE GENERATIONS: LOFTHOUSE; PUSKAS; GULLIT

PROFILE

Nat Lofthouse was the perfect model of the sportsman in post-war Britain. Although an England international and a record-breaking goalscorer, he played his whole career for one club, Bolton Wanderers. Lofthouse expressed no regret at being too early for the high rewards gained by a later generation of soccer stars. He never forgot that signing for Bolton at the age of fifteen made him a footballer instead of a miner. In later life, he recalled his first pay packet, including the signing-on fee:

£10. Two white fivers. I put them on the kitchen table. I'd never seen so much money in one place. My dad earned less than £3 per week on the coal wagons. When he saw the money, he thought I'd pinched it.

Lofthouse was a household name. He starred in two FA Cup Finals, and was known as the 'Lion of Vienna' after scoring twice in a famous England victory in Austria; but he never earned more than £20 per week.

Ferenc Puskas was originally as classic an example of the 1950s as Lofthouse. Typical of the Eastern Bloc approach, he was nominally an officer in the Hungarian Army – and thus known as 'the galloping major'. He played for the army team, Honved, symbolising the role of sport in projecting the 'socialist model'. He captained Hungary in the 1954 World Cup, having already become famous by leading Hungary in a devastating 6–3 victory at Wembley which destroyed English illusions of supremacy. (To underline the message, Hungary won 7–1 in Budapest the following year.) Then, after the 1956 Budapest Rising, Puskas joined the flood of refugees westwards into Austria. The great Hungarian team broke up; Hungarian soccer never recovered. Puskas arrived in Spain, now a perfect example of the modern sporting mercenary. He became, along with the great Argentinian Alfredo di Stefano, one of the twin stars of the all-conquering Real Madrid team of the 1950s, best remembered for his part in the most famous of all European cup finals when more than 100 000 packed Hampden Park in Glasgow to see Real defeat Eintracht Frankfurt 7–3, Puskas scoring four. He played for Spain and ended his career as manager of teams in Canada and in Greece.

Puskas spanned two different sides of the Iron Curtain and also two different generations in his career. The reason why the 1960 Hampden Park match remained more famous than the 7–1 demolition of England, or the 1954 World Cup in Switzerland, is television, which did not bring soccer to a universal audience until the World Cup in Sweden in 1958. Puskas was one of the forerunners of the many star performers who left the Eastern Bloc to pursue a 'capitalist' career in the West. Others included the dancer Rudolf Nureyev and the tennis players Ivan Lendl and Martina Navratilova.

Ruud Gullit was the ultimate modern football star; he never knew the 1950s game in which Lofthouse played out his career and from which Puskas escaped. Unlike the one-club Lofthouse, Gullit played in Holland, Italy, Germany and England, acquiring enormous financial rewards and fluency in four languages in the process. Born in Surinam, he also broke through race barriers and was one of an articulate, self-confident group of black players in the Dutch national team. Much in demand for his opinions and as a fashion model, many managers found him difficult to handle because his name and reputation were bigger than their own. At the end of his playing career, he moved smoothly into football management with Chelsea and even more smoothly into media work for the BBC. Gullit, the multi-lingual millionaire, showed how far sport and society had changed since the days of the 'Lion of Vienna'.

Following the trends established in the 1960s, sport continued to enlarge its role in society. The salaries and transfer fees of athletes and players rose and kept on rising. (The first 'million-pound' player in Britain was Trevor Francis in 1979; Alan Shearer moved to Newcastle for £15 million in 1996.) Sporting stars became media celebrities, as the coverage of sport expanded and changed. By the early 1990s, satellite television provided live sport on an almost 24-hour basis and had a

PICTURE 47
Nat Lofthouse: the miner

PICTURE 48
*Wilf Mannion of
Middlesborough and
England goes back to his
roots*

PICTURE 49
*Blackpool 4, Bolton 3;
Wembley, 1953*

huge influence on how sport was financed, or even when it was scheduled. Specialist sport publications emerged, such as the French sports paper *l'Equipe* and the German soccer magazine *Kicker*. Sporting events such as the *Tour de France*, which used to be local or specialised, became familiar and truly international. Sponsorship and television rights made some sports richer from off-pitch activities than from live attendances. Sport became more fashionable: in journalism and conversation and, literally, in the sale of expensive leisure wear. In the process, sport moved away from its working-class, masculine origins. The audiences of the 1990s were richer, better-dressed and remarkably more female than those of forty years before.

Not all the changes were those of growth and success. Sport continued to be plagued by politics. From 1968 to 1991, sport in Europe and worldwide was affected by the struggle against apartheid in South Africa. The South African cricket tour of England in 1970 was cancelled under the threat of violent protest action. There were many other confrontations in the struggle against *apartheid*. The 1972 Olympics in Munich could never have happened at all without delicate negotiations between East and West Germany; and there was a gun battle at the airport after Palestinian terrorists had attacked Israeli athletes. The 1980 Moscow Olympics were boycotted by the USA following the Soviet invasion of Afghanistan; the 1984 Olympics in Los Angeles were hit by a Soviet boycott in retaliation. The very successful 1992 Olympics in Barcelona could never have happened without the political transformation of Spain after the death of Franco.

Changing patterns of leisure and education meant that the flow of talent into certain sports was reduced. Several sports, like soccer, became all-year sports. Other sports, like tennis in Sweden, moved indoors, becoming popular and accessible in countries where they had scarcely been played before. In the 1970s, golf was 'Europeanised' by stars like Severiano Ballesteros and Bernhard Langer. From 1981, Ryder Cup teams included European players.

Other controversial issues became important, especially hooliganism and racism. Like so many other issues, this can be traced to the affluent 1960s, when the new phenomenon of the large group of travelling supporters emerged. In England in the 1970s, there was fighting in and near football grounds. The first international event to be marred by serious trouble was the European Nations Cup in Italy in 1980. This trend was to reach crisis proportions with the Heysel disaster of 1985, when thirty-nine people died in disturbances at the Liverpool–Juventus European Cup final in Brussels, and with the even worse incidents when more than fifty died in the Bradford City fire and when ninety-five died in the Hillsborough disaster of 1989. This led to massive changes in the nature and policing of crowds and upon stadium design. Big sporting occasions became a major matter of public safety. It was also yet another example of problems going beyond national borders, as major sports events required planning and international police cooperation years in advance. Hooliganism was interrelated with several social issues outside sport: greater affluence and ease of travel,

> **KEY ISSUE**
>
> *In what ways did television affect the place of sport in European society?*

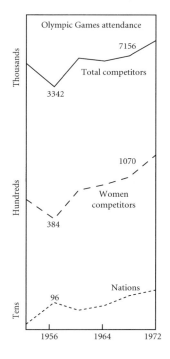

DIAGRAM 7

The expansion of the Olympic Games, 1956–72

increased consumption of alcohol, racism and the exploitation of sport by right-wing political extremists.

In some ways, the impact of sport proved beneficial. Black sporting stars became role models, as with Gary Sobers in English cricket, or the Portuguese star of the 1966 World Cup, Eusebio. One of the effects of decolonisation was the inflow of sporting talent from former colonies like Jamaica or Mozambique. Many black sportsmen, however, experienced discrimination as a bar to their progress, both at the top and at the lower levels. Racist chanting remained a feature of soccer crowds in Italy, Britain and elsewhere; and this was frequently linked with far-right politics. In Britain, the neo-Nazi *Combat 18* (meaning AH, the first and eighth letters of the alphabet) was closely linked to 'skinhead' soccer supporters. In France, the *Front National* made similar inroads; after the end of the Wall, there were particularly severe problems in the former East Germany.

In measuring social or cultural change, the question should always be: how much changed, and how much stayed the same? Many things plainly show continuity. Sporting stars of the 1940s, such as Denis Compton, were attractive to advertisers, just like the great French skier Jean-Claude Killy in the 1960s, or a modern-day Ruud Gullit. All over Europe, in any decade, boys put coats down in the park to make a goal. In the 1990s, as in the 1950s, boys of all ages hung on to radio commentaries or newspaper coverage of their team, and productivity went up in moments of triumph or gave way to absenteeism after a defeat.

But many images changed dramatically over fifty years. In much of Europe, the game in the street had virtually died out, killed by affluence and by the all-pervasive motor car. Teenage sporting millionaires emerged who would have been incredible to a tennis star of the amateur era, or to a soccer player who remembered the maximum wage. The 1990s sports audience, saturated with television coverage on a multitude of channels, sitting in all-seater stadia, dressed in fashionable leisure wear, a substantial minority of them women and girls, was far removed from the sporting crowds of the 1940s.

KEY ISSUE

Why did sport become so much associated with problems of public order in Europe between c.1970 and c.1995?

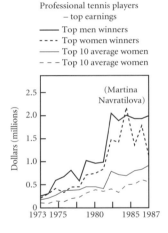

Professional tennis players – top earnings

—— Top men winners
- - - - Top women winners
—— Top 10 average women
– – – Top 10 average women

DIAGRAM 8
Earnings in professional tennis, 1973–87

E *The advance of women*

The role of women in society had been changing well before the Second World War, even since before 1914. Voting rights for women, access to higher education and female employment were well advanced by the 1920s. It is nevertheless true that the war did much to accelerate these developments. In the 1960s the generation of women born after the war set out on what has been described as a 'gender revolution'.

As with many aspects of social change, this revolution did not happen everywhere at the same time, or the same speed. There were big differences between the modern, urbanised societies of Northern and Western Europe such as Britain, West Germany and Scandinavia, compared with more traditional societies elsewhere. The role of women remained very different, for example, in Northern Italy compared with the South. Such differences often reflected economic factors; or the impact of university education; or the influence of religion; or political factors. In the Soviet Bloc there was a contradiction. Officially, Socialist teaching was committed to equality and women in the USSR had equal rights since the Revolution; during the war, women had played front-line roles. After 1945, many women in Eastern Europe did better than those in the West in matters such as access to education and State provision of child care. On the other hand, Communist society remained conservative and hierarchical. Few women rose high in the party élites.

The impact of the Second World War, like the First, brought women into new roles and responsibilities. In the process, attitudes and behaviour changed. In the suburbanised 1950s in Western Europe, however, there was a return to conventional attitudes, strongly reinforced by cultural stereotyping in television, magazines and the cinema. At the end of the war, surveys showed that four out of five women wished to keep their jobs but most found themselves being replaced by men as the armies demobilised. Conventional jobs for

PICTURE 50
'Rubble women', Berlin 1945

women were relatively unskilled and poorly paid – as telephone receptionists, shop assistants, textile workers. Better-educated women became librarians, nurses or teachers. Such jobs were rarely seen as careers, more an interval before the natural destination of marriage. It was difficult for wives to be legally or financially independent.

The apparent social consensus of the 1950s, however, was not as deeply rooted as it seemed. A number of factors combined to undermine traditional attitudes to women and family. One was the fact that the war had had much deeper effects than was outwardly visible. In Germany, the bitter, often disillusioning experiences of war and defeat seriously undermined pre-war perceptions. The Nazi era had already discredited ultra-traditional views of the place of women in society. Then, as Germany fell apart in 1944–45, women became self-reliant to an unheard-of degree.

Other factors accelerated the changes in the perceptions and roles of women in Western society. Increased access to higher education meant

ANALYSIS

War and liberation

In her memoirs *The Road Ahead*, Christabel Bielenberg described an encounter with Berlin's '*Trummerfrauen*' ('Rubble Women') in 1946:

As we sat there puffing away in the half-light, watched over by the towering ruins, I was able to listen to some of the stories they had to tell. None of them seemed really young any more and the tales they told were grimly repetitive. The long trek westwards, driven from their homes, husbands dead or missing, children lost, and then those days and nights in Berlin, the howling shells, the seething flames, as they prayed in vain that the Allies would arrive before the Russians. Lastly, the violation, some not once, not twice, but many times.

The day was not yet over for my companions: some had to fetch children from those who looked after them during the day, others had to join long queues for food. They had learned the value of teamwork in the survival game. The driver and the conductor and most of the passengers on the rickety old tram which picked me up were also women. It occurred to me that during the time we had laughed and talked together, hardly any mention had been made of the male sex. After six years of war, these women had carried on scrimping and saving, foraging for food, managing to keep their families alive and the remains of their homes intact. Could it be that they had discovered that they could do so quite successfully on their own?

increasing pressure for women to gain access to the professions. Changes in industry, away from heavy manual labour and towards machines and computers, made many more jobs available to women; where traditional industries closed, such as coal mining, many women suddenly became the main earners of a family. The contraceptive pill, first sold in the USA in 1960, involved a major change in the relationships between men and women. The affluence of the post-war boom opened up new opportunities both in work and leisure.

Such trends and ideas led to an organised 'feminist movement', reflected in books like Betty Friedan's *The Feminine Mystique and* Germaine Greer's *The Female Eunuch,* and to broader general changes in expectations and behaviour. Many female students in France, who had previously accepted the traditional view of women's place in society, changed their attitude completely after being involved in the student demonstrations in Paris in May 1968. In England in 1969 there was a big rally demanding equal pay for equal work. Some of this was class-based. The motives of many middle-class women in fighting for employment rights was often not economic but the desire for self-fulfilment. Feminists often had a degree of affluence and of education which meant the ability to make a choice. For many poorer women, there was often no choice at all.

Although the advance of women was often legal and institutional, fighting battles to open closed shops and to outlaw discrimination, there was perhaps an even more important shift in role models and cultural stereotypes. The 'ideal woman' shown in TV advertising in the 1950s was very different from the equivalent forty years later. In many European countries, programmes such as the American TV police series *Cagney and Lacey* popularised a new, assertive female role in what had previously been an exclusively male-dominated environment. Similar role models emerged in the news media and in sports reporting; though some commentators suggested that women were selected more to reinforce traditional stereotypes than to change them.

Marriage changed in many urban communities. Sexual behaviour became more open and the divorce rate increased. Trends were slower in some parts of Europe than others but the same general patterns emerged in the end.

The revolution in the 'permissive Sixties' was probably less sudden and extreme than many journalists and politicians of the time assumed. Pre-marital sex was hardly a new invention. What was new was the openness with which female sexual behaviour was discussed and portrayed in popular music, films and women's magazines. The French magazine *Elle* announced:

> In 946, women did not have 'lovers'. At least, the use of the word was banned in magazines aimed at women. In 1966, *Elle* has no fear of instructing women on 'how to succeed in your sex life'. The same is true of *Marie-Claire* and other magazines.

KEY ISSUE

In what ways did the experiences of the Second World War and its aftermath change attitudes of, and towards, women?

See page 460

The trend towards equality and self-expression for women and girls was part of the 'generation gap' and led to important social change and to controversies involving politics, religion and the law. Such issues included sex education, contraception, the legalisation of divorce and abortion.

One key example of how even conservative society strongly influenced by religion was not immune from change was Italy. Divorce became legal in Italy in 1970, the sale of contraceptives was legalised in 1971, followed by abortion law reform in 1978. The divorce law reform was only confirmed in a national referendum in 1974 after a long and bitter campaign by the combined forces of the Catholic Church and the Christian Democrat Party. It was a sign of the extent of social change that the vote, 59 per cent to 41, was so decisive. There were similar controversies, with a similar eventual outcome, in the Irish Republic. After long years of repression in Spain, divorce was legalised in 1981, though the government split over the issue. Abortion was legalised in 1985.

The advances made by women created new social and political problems. By the late 1980s, many politicians in many countries were openly expressing concern about the rise of the single mother. In 1950, people living alone made up 6 per cent of British households; by 1991 it was over 25 per cent. Child care became an important social and political issue, with increasingly widespread social acceptance of the idea of the working mother, often in conflict with continuing

PROFILE

THE CASE OF MARIE-CLAIRE

In France in 1972, the case of Marie-Claire Chevalier became a national sensation. Marie-Claire, a young girl living in a depressed suburb of Paris, Bobigny, became pregnant at sixteen, had a 'back-street' abortion which went wrong and was then rushed to a clinic where she was treated successfully. Her unmarried mother could not pay for this treatment and in any case abortion was against the law. The result was that first Marie-Claire and then her mother were put on trial, defended by a young woman barrister, Gisele Halimi. There was vocal support for the Chevaliers from radical feminists. The case attracted huge media attention and sparked a national debate which revealed how much public opinion had shifted on women's issues. Marie-Claire was acquitted. Her mother and the amateur abortionist, though technically found guilty, were given light sentences, immediately suspended. One French newspaper stated, 'The law against abortion has become null and void.' In 1975, the old 1920 abortion law was replaced. The case of Marie-Claire was a notable landmark in the social history of France.

traditional attitudes. As with many aspects of society, television both reflected the changes in the status of women and helped to promote those changes. In all countries, popular soap operas such as the BBC's *EastEnders,* or the German series *Lindenstrasse,* took up issues like working mothers, single parents, or sexual harassment at work. In all countries, television advertising reinforced perceptions of the 'new woman'.

By 1995, these fundamental changes in the roles of women in society still had some way to go. For thousands of women in Britain and Europe, however, there was, by 1995, a degree of independence and

PICTURE 51
Advertising poster for the Soviet film Little Vera, *1988*

sexual equality which had been unthinkable forty years before. In the words of one woman working as a chemical processor:

> It never occurred to me in the 1950s that I could do what the men were doing, that I could make the kind of money they were making. And it all came about because the doors were opened by the activists of their day.

F *'1968': Youth*

From the mid-1950s, one of the most notable changes in the society of post-war Europe was the emergence of a distinct youth culture; sometimes termed 'the rise of the teenager'. This affected, and was affected by, mass education, affluence and the exploitation of a new mass youth market in entertainment, fashion and popular music, and changing attitudes to sexual behaviour.

Of many changes in education, perhaps the most important was the widening of access to universities and other forms of higher education, which took place all over Europe, on both sides of the Iron Curtain. This reflected economic issues as the European economy became less labour-intensive and more mechanised and managerial but it was also important for social and political reasons, especially in and after the 1960s.

Mass expansion of higher education had a major impact on the expectations and status of women. It helped to produce a vocal and politically-aware student population capable of influencing politics, such as the 'events' of May 1968 in France, the Red Army Faction in West Germany, or widespread protests in Europe against the war in Vietnam. In the Soviet Bloc, the successful provision of education was one of the factors which produced the pressures for reform in the 1980s. All over Europe, education also helped to produce a mass audience for what had previously been the culture reserved for the élite – opera, serious drama, 'broadsheet' newspapers – and changed the nature of left-wing politics, which became much less 'working-class' and much more in the hands of graduates of law, politics, or the social sciences.

After the Second World War, education was a key factor in 'welfarism' and the widespread improvements in social provision. There was a massive programme of school building. In countries such as Hungary and Switzerland, there was a general political consensus about educational priorities. In other countries, above all in Britain, this post-war consensus did not last and education became a divisive issue. There were recurrent conflicts between the public and private sector, selective or comprehensive schools, formal or 'progressive' teaching methods. In France, there was a particular controversy over *laicite* and the issue of church schools. Despite local and national variations, there were clear general trends. All over Europe, young people spent more years in the educational system. In 1945, it was quite usual to enter the world of work at fourteen. By the 1990s, the overwhelming majority stayed at school until eighteen and most went on to some form of further training or higher education.

Outside education, various social and cultural factors changed the lives of young people and led to the emergence of a universal youth culture. This reached beyond political or religious differences. In the 1980s, despite strenuous efforts by the authorities to prevent it, 'jeans and pop music' undermined all efforts at the social control of youth in the Soviet Bloc. Similarly, in Catholic and Francoist Spain, the same social revolution ultimately took place as elsewhere in liberal Western Europe.

In the early years after the Second World War, patterns of entertainment and youth activity were much less affluent and much less individualistic. For one thing, there was much less leisure time available. Evenings stopped before midnight with the last performance at the cinema, or the last tram home. Much leisure time was not self-organised but part of school or family life. There was no equivalent to the personal stereo, no separate youth fashions, nor the disposable incomes had such things existed. Even watching television tended to be a family affair. Youthful leisure was generally group-based: team sports, youth clubs, church organisations, scouts or Young Pioneers. From the late 1950s, these patterns loosened and the identification of youth culture with anarchic freedom and popular music began. For the social historian, Arthur Marwick, the emergence of this youth culture in the period between *c.*1958 and *c.*1974 was a 'cultural revolution', producing a wider gap between the generations than at any previous time.

Many influences were American: through the cinema, through rock and roll and Elvis Presley, through the counter-culture music personified by Bob Dylan. (A side-effect of the American and British influence through popular music was the spread of English as the universal language of the new youth culture.) One of the features of the popularity of pop music, however, was its homegrown quality. The huge impact of the Beatles from 1962, or the Rolling Stones from 1963, or the many rock bands which proliferated in Eastern Europe in the 1980s was closely related to the local and youthful origins of the performers – music by youth as well as music for youth.

Although jeans and pop music were the most obvious examples of the power of the youth market, it had a great impact elsewhere. Television was affected both through advertising and through programming, not least in the phenomenon of soap operas designed for teenage audiences. Similarly, cinema found that many of its biggest box-office successes were films with appeal to youth. By the 1980s, youth culture was almost universal. The defining year of this 'revolution' was 1968, when specific student issues, awareness of radical politics, sexual freedoms, soft drugs and a general rebellion of youth mixed, briefly, with mainstream politics and produced a wave of upheavals in the USA, France, Italy, Britain and Eastern Europe. The

See page 429

TABLE 55
Students in post-school education, 1992

Britain	25%
France	40%
Germany	33%
Italy	31%
Norway	43%
Poland	22%

ANALYSIS

The global youth culture

In *The Age of Extremes*, the historian Eric Hobsbawm wrote:

> Through records and tapes, through good old radio, through the world distribution of images, through the personal contacts of international youth tourism, through the international network of the universities, through the force of fashion in a consumer society, a global youth culture came into being.

> Could it have emerged in any earlier period? Almost certainly not. It required the lengthening of full-time education and the vast expansion of the universities. It required those adolescents entering employment to have far more independent spending power, due to prosperity and full employment. It required urban concentrations of relatively well-paid girls, able to spend in the youth market. It also required the disruptive effects of the Second World War to create an enormous 'generation gap'.

political importance was overrated at the time and did not last. The cultural and behavioural effects did.

Student radicalism, partly political and partly about specific student grievances, had already flared up in 1967: in West Germany, led by Rudi Dutschke, and in Italy, starting at the *Cattolica* in Milan and then spreading to other universities. This unrest in Italy broke out into violent disturbances between police and students, culminating in the 'Battle of the *Valle Giulia*' in Rome. In the same month, March 1968, large-scale protests began at Nanterre University in Paris. 25 000 took part in a demonstration in London against the Vietnam War. An attempt to assassinate Rudi Dutschke raised the temperature of student protest to boiling point. In April, Italian workers took part in joint demonstrations with the students. Later in the year, French workers sided with the students in much the same way. 1968 was not only a time of upheaval in Western Europe. Youth protest was a significant factor in the 'Prague Spring', especially after the Dubček regime abolished press censorship. In the USA, the assassination of Martin Luther King intensified student protests – 700 were arrested at Columbia University.

See pages 77–9

The 'events' of May in France, therefore, were not the first nor the only outbreak of youth revolt but they went nearer than anywhere else to 'revolution'. Violent clashes between police and students escalated into long-running street battles and a major political crisis that rocked the foundations of de Gaulle's presidency. In the process, student activist leaders such as Daniel Cohn-Bendit ('Danny the Red') became household names.

In the summer of 1968, the focus shifted to back to the USA, with the assassination of Robert Kennedy and serious violence at the Democratic Convention in Chicago. Race riots in Watts, a district of Los Angeles, added to the tension. These American events were linked to affairs in Europe by the universal factors of student radicalism and the campaign against the war in Vietnam. In August, the crushing of the 'Prague Spring' by Warsaw Pact tanks brought youth protesters out onto the streets again. Swedish students tried to storm the Soviet embassy in Stockholm.

1968 was infectious. In the USA in September, there were protest marches for women's rights and against the Vietnam War. In Mexico City in October, on the eve of the Mexico Olympics, twenty-five students were killed when police fired on protesters. At the Games, American sprinters turned their gold medal ceremony into a Black Power demonstration. Nearly 100 000 joined an anti-war protest that ended in violent confrontation with police in Grosvenor Square. Anti-Soviet demonstrations took place in Prague. Before the end of the year, there were disturbances in Pakistan, Greece, and Spain. In Northern Ireland, a young Catholic activist, John Hume, came to the forefront of a campaign for civil rights. In Italy in December, one million went on strike as workers sided with youth protesters after police shootings in Sicily.

There were many diverse factors behind the 'revolt of youth' in 1968. There was a genuine political element, involving left-wing politics, anti-war protests and the campaign for civil rights. Che Guevara became a

TIMELINE
1968

May 1967	Radical student activism in West Germany
Nov	Serious unrest in Italian universities
March 1968	'Battle of the *Valle Guilla*' in Rome
	Nanterre university protests
	London demonstration against Vietnam War
	Attempted assassination of Rudi Dutschke
April	Demonstrations by students and workers in Italy
	Abolition of press censorship by Dubček regime
	Assassination of Martin Luther King
May	(3rd) Student/police violence in Paris
	(10th) 'Night of the Barricades' in Paris
	(29th) 'Disappearance' of President de Gaulle
	(30th) Mass rally by Gaullists
June	Assassination of Robert Kennedy
Aug	Race riots in Watts, Los Angeles
	Soviet invasion of Czechoslovakia
	Violence at Chicago Democratic Convention
Oct	Student occupation of LSE
Jan 1969	Death of Jan Palach
Feb	Violence between police and students in Rome
April	Resignation of President de Gaulle
Aug	Woodstock music festival

PICTURE 52
1968: Paris

TABLE 56
Youth unemployment in Western Europe, 1995, as % of total unemployed

Italy	39.4
Spain	37.3
Portugal	33.6
Britain	30.2
The Netherlands	29.4

cult figure for European youth. There was the 'generation gap' and rebellion against traditionalist approaches to education. There was sheer high spirits and youthful self-expression, shown in anarchic posters and graffiti, and in provocative popular music. Mick Jagger wrote *Street Fighting Man* in 1968 and saw it banned by the BBC. There were issues of sex and gender, both in demands for women's rights and in flamboyant displays of sexual behaviour. The CND movement was enlivened by the slogan 'Make love, not war'.

Though the special excitement of 1968 faded away, the place of youth in European society had been fundamentally changed.

The events of 1968–69 led in many directions. One was a surge in the movement for women's rights. Another was a swing towards radicalism and anti-establishment attitudes in the arts and entertainment. The daring musical *Hair* opened in 1969; the first transmission of *Monty Python's Flying Circus* took place in 1969. There was also a period of much more violent political protest. 1968–69 paved the way for the Red

PICTURE 53
1968: Prague

Army Faction ('Baader-Meinhof Gang') in West Germany, and for the Red Brigade in Italy.

In the 1980s and 1990s, political radicalism largely disappeared from the universities. Student protest became focused on special issues such as the environment, or animal rights. Youth culture moved more into consumerism and the disco scene; though there was also widespread concern over rising levels of youth unemployment and the social problems associated with it. After the end of the Wall in 1989, youth culture in Eastern Europe conformed rapidly to the Western model and the 'cultural revolution' became universal.

G *'1989': Cultural revolution in Eastern Europe*

The social and cultural differences between Eastern and Western Europe should not be exaggerated. Despite all the ideological and political pressures of the years of division, the people of the Soviet Bloc shared an enormous range of interests and activities with the people of Western Europe: skating and swimming, films and football, cycling and chess, dancing and digging allotments, watching television or else just 'going out'. Even so, life in the East was different in many important respects. Indoctrination and government control of information did have considerable effect on trends in entertainment. Leisure activities were more communal. Eastern Europe avoided many of the 'Americanising' tendencies that post-war affluence brought into the West, not least in the impact of the motor car. In the Brezhnev era, many young people resented these restrictions; the dramatic events of 1989 were a watershed, marking the sudden inrush of Western life-styles.

As so often in history, this was not quite as sudden as it seemed. Social and cultural changes had been visible for years, since well before the arrival of Mikhail Gorbachev in 1985. By then, society was already very urbanised. The fad for clothes and records with Western labels began long before *perestroika*. Popular novels appeared with lurid treatment of themes such as hard-currency prostitutes (*Intergirl*, 1988), or corrupt Stalinist bureaucrats (*The Reporter*, 1988). Newspapers such as *Moscow News* suddenly adopted a more direct and informal style of writing. Soviet cinema started churning out films featuring rock musicians (*Assa*, 1988), gang fights and explicit sex scenes (*Little Vera*, 1988). The shocking new films were popular; *Little Vera* sold fifty million tickets in three months. Similar trends affected Eastern Europe. Way-out rock bands became especially popular in Poland.

The authorities still attempted to prevent or restrict access to 'western decadence'. Western TV was jammed. The *Stasi* in East Germany monitored, and arrested, young people who tried to attend rock concerts in the West. Conservative commentators furiously attacked the 'moral degeneration' of youth. But even official organisations bent with the wind of change. In 1986, the main Soviet news programme, *Time*, was completely revamped and given slick, American-style presenters. Music video made a big impact on television; so did aerobics. Rock began to displace classical music as background to TV news or drama. There was a wave of TV adverts, video shops, rock groups. The impact of the political upheavals of 1989–91, therefore, was to accelerate and dramatise something which was already happening.

Society in the East had never been as monolithic as its enemies claimed, or as the Brezhnevites hoped. After 1989, however, diversity ran riot. Prague acquired numerous noisy discos. At the border crossings between the Czech Republic and Germany, hundreds of garden gnomes appeared, for sale to visiting Germans. Nearby were the mini-skirted young Czech girls who were the real target of the visitors, and for whom the gnomes were the cover story.

In Warsaw and Cracow, cafés and jazz bands took over town squares. This trend had begun some time earlier in Budapest; Hungary had been moving quietly towards a western-style consumer economy since 1968.

This rush to 'westernise' was not uniformly welcomed. The revelations of State corruption were painful. The realisation of the full extent of the gap in living standards was often disillusioning. Problems of price inflation and unemployment hit hard. The boom in tourism brought in hard currency but it also forced many people out of their apartments in the city because rents shot too high. There were problems with petty crime that had not existed before 1989. Western visitors to Prague in 1991 experienced a fascinating, post-Communist city amateurishly experimenting with tourism. By 1995, the same city had higher prices, less innocence, and many more police patrolling Wenceslaus Square at night. There was resentment against garish and exploitative Western capitalism. One unpleasant side effect was an upsurge in far-Right, neo-Nazi gangs, and in race-prejudice against 'Turks' in the former East Germany, for example, or against gypsies in Slovakia.

This process of economic, social and cultural adjustment was exciting and confusing, sometimes full of optimism, sometimes demoralising. It was more difficult for Russia, which had 'lost an empire', than for the former satellite States which had gained independence. In Russia, the end of the command economy was particularly painful and abrupt: by 1995, many working in key state enterprises, such as miners and nurses, were being paid late or not at all. In Moscow and St Petersburg, organised crime operated 'market forces' with more apparent success than legitimate business. In the Soviet Far East, Gorbachev was giving an enthusiastic speech on *perestroika*, when someone shouted 'What do you eat with it?'

For many, the disintegration of the old social and cultural patterns was a bewildering, negative experience, For others, it was over-whelmingly positive, indicating 'spontaneity, freedom, competition, individualism, – a market place of ideas, feelings, talent and energy'. According to Richard Stites,

Young people are stretching out to embrace the global culture, shouting an angry and ironic farewell to the mass culture their parents and grandparents once enjoyed.

From a wider view, according to Richard Bessel:

It is tempting but wrong to discuss the history of Eastern and Western Europe in separate categories – the one developed, the other backward; the one capitalist, the other socialist. If there has been such a thing as European society in the second half of the twentieth century, then Eastern Europe has been as big a part of it as the West. Virtually all important social and cultural trends were played out in Eastern as much as in Western Europe. The socialist experiment imposed on Eastern Europe reflected many of the same desires which motivated people in the western part of the continent. At the end of the twentieth century, the democratisation of culture and society means that Eastern and Western Europe are more alike – and that Europe as a whole is more like the rest of the world.

The 1990s, then, marked the end of the 'years of division'. The 'Brezhnev culture wars' had been won and lost. But history, above all cultural and social history, never allows neat and tidy endings. As the millenium approached, the safest assumption for historians was that nine out of ten predictions about the society and culture of Europe in the twenty-first century, whether full of optimism or full of doom, would probably turn out to be wildly wrong.

CULTURAL LANDMARKS, 1945–95

	Sport, Media and Cinema	Miscellaneous
1945	Last film of the Third Reich: *Kolberg* (Veit Harlan)	Start of United Nations
1946	*Germany Year Zero* (Rossellini)	Churchill's 'Iron Curtain' speech
1947	£7 minimum wage in English football	The Marshall Plan
1948	First post-war Olympic Games in London	Birth of the long-playing record
1949	Cold War cinema: *The Third Man* (Carol Reed)	End of the Berlin Blockade
1950	England first entered World Cup	First colour TV transmissions
1951	First *Goon Show* on BBC radio	Festival of Britain
1952	USSR competed in Olympics for first time	Crick and Watson discovered DNA
1953	England 3 Hungary 6 at Wembley	Coronation of Elizabeth II televised
1954	Roger Bannister, first four-minute mile;	First 'jumbo jet': Boeing 707
1955	Launch of the European Cup	Mass-produced transistor radio
1956	Eurovision song contest televised; *Kanal* (Andrej Wajda)	Budapest rising and Suez crisis
1957	Althea Gibson the first black Wimbledon champion	Launch of first *Sputnik*
1958	Munich airport tragedy	Clashes between 'Mods' and 'Rockers'
1959	'New Wave': *400 Blows* (Truffaut); *Breathless* (Godard)	Khrushchev's tour of USA
1960	Real Madrid's fifth European Cup; *La Dolce Vita* (Fellini)	Birth of mini-skirt in London
1961	*Last Year at Marienbad* (Resnais); *Jules et Jim* (Truffaut)	Yuri Gagarin space flight
1962	*Love Me Do* (The Beatles); *That Was The Week That Was* (BBC)	Cuban Missile Crisis
1963	*Dr Strangelove* (Stanley Kubrick)	Assassination of President Kennedy
1964	Start of the pirate station, *Radio Caroline*	First 'Oscar' for a black actor
1965	MBEs awarded to the Beatles	Ban on TV advertising of tobacco in UK
1966	Soccer World Cup in England; start of *Star Trek*	Escalation of war in Vietnam
1967	*Belle du Jour* (Luis Bunuel)	Decriminalisation of homosexuality in UK
1968	England cricket tour of S. Africa cancelled	Student rebellion in Paris; 'Prague Spring'
1969	*Monty Python's Flying Circus* (BBC TV)	First man on the Moon
1970	*The Conformist* (Bernardo Bertolucci)	Divorce made legal in Italy
1971	*Death in Venice* (Visconti); *Le Chagrin et le Pitié* (M Ophuls)	First *Intel* microprocessor
1972	Munich Olympic Games marred by terrorism	Last issue of *Life*; first of *Cosmopolitan*
1973	180 arrests for soccer hooliganism in UK	OPEC oil-price crisis
1974	*Lacombe Lucien* (Louis Malle)	*Abba* won Eurovision song contest
1975	First Cricket World Cup	End of the Franco regime in Spain
1976	Start of TV serials *Dynasty* and *I Claudius*	Start of 'Punk' fashions

	Sport, Media and Cinema	*Miscellaneous*
1977	First woman rider in Grand National; *Star Wars*	Pompidou Centre opened in Paris
1978	Big impact of USA TV series *Holocaust* in Germany	Birth of first 'test-tube baby'
1979	Launch of the Sony 'Walkman'	Mrs Thatcher first woman Prime Minister in Britain
1980	Boycott of Moscow Olympics; *Death of a Princess* (ITV)	Success of *Solidarity* in Poland
1981	Ryder Cup team included European golfers	Foundation of CNN news network
1982	'Rap' music became popular in UK	Falklands War
1983	First athletics world championships	Madonna made underwear into outerwear
1984	Soviet boycott of Olympics; *Heimat* (Edgar Reitz)	Women's protest at Greenham Common
1985	Heysel Stadium disaster; *Back to the Future* (Spielberg)	AIDS declared an epidemic
1986	*The Sacrifice* (Tarkovsky)	Chernobyl nuclear disaster
1987	*The Last Emperor* (Bertolucci)	Loss of *Herald of Free Enterprise*
1988	Ben Johnson drugs scandal at Seoul Olympics	Bombing of Pan Am 103 at Lockerbie
1989	Hillsborough tragedy	End of Berlin Wall
1990	Record TV audience for World Cup in Italy	Unification of Germany recognised
1991	CNN coverage of the Gulf War	Collapse of USSR; civil war in Yugoslavia
1992	Barcelona Olympic Games	Maastricht Treaty
1993	Spielberg's *Schindler's List*	Completion of the Channel Tunnel
1994	Saturation TV coverage of OJ Simpson case	36 women priests ordained in UK
1995	Riot by England football fans in Dublin	Fiftieth anniversary of the end of the war

4 ↬ BIBLIOGRAPHY

The social and cultural history of Europe can be elusive. Many books in this field are aimed at a very American–British audience, so that developments in Europe, especially Eastern Europe, are difficult to research. They also tend to be related to a particular time and thus to go out of fashion (and out of print) quickly. Some otherwise useful books are prone to complexity, and make only brief references to specific examples. Even so, there is much of value to be gained from a wide range of sources: films and fiction; fashion and advertising in the Sunday supplements; biographies; and, best of all, photographic evidence, either from journalists or from family albums.

Useful books include general histories such as: *Age of Extremes: The History of the Short Twentieth Century* by E. Hobsbawm (Abacus, 1995) or *Europe In Our Time* by W. Lacqueur (Penguin, 1992). Though from a world perspective rather than a European one, *People's Century* (2 vols.) by G. Hodgson (BBC, 1996) has several fascinating and accessible chapters to match the equally accessible television series. There is lively and up-to-date material on France in *The Cambridge Illustrated History of France* by C. Jones (Cambridge University Press, 1994). The 'cultural revolution' in Britain, the USA, France and Italy, *c.*1958–*c.*1974 is covered in fascinating and wide-ranging detail in *The Sixties* by A. Marwick (Oxford University Press, 1998). There is a provocative and well-illustrated account of the events of 1968 throughout Europe in *1968: Marching in the Streets* by Tariq Ali and S. Watkins (Bloomsbury, 1998). Soviet Russia is covered interestingly in *Russian Popular Culture: Entertainment and Society in the Twentieth Century* by R. Stites

(Cambridge Soviet Paperbacks, 1996). Many economic and geographical issues are covered briefly and well in *The 'Times' Atlas of the Twentieth Century* edited by R. Overy (Times Books, 1996).

Century Road (BBC Learning Zone, 1998) offers excellent in-depth video material on English social history. Students should also make use of the pictorial evidence available in the large number of books of collected photographs, and of works of reference in book form and on CD-Rom.

On individual topics, there is excellent material on women in *A Century of Women* (Penguin, 1998); on radio and television in *BBC: 70 Years of Broadcasting* by John Cain (BBC Books, 1992) and *Television: An International History* edited by A. Smith (Oxford University Press, 1995); on sport in *Sport in Britain: A Social History* edited by T. Mason (Cambridge University Press, 1989); on football in *Champions of Europe* (Guinness Books, 1991) and *World Cup* (Penguin, 1998) both by B. Glanville, and *The Football League: The First 100 Years* by Bryon Butler (Colour Library Books, 1988); and on cinema in *The Long View: An International History of Cinema* by B. Wright (Paladin, 1976). (For individual films, *Halliwell's Film Guide* is a mine of useful information.)

5 ✍ ESSAYS

A *Essay questions*

1. (a) Outline some of the ways in which 'Americanisation' affected European society and popular culture after 1945;
   (b) Assess the importance of the impact of American influences upon *either* television *or* popular music in Europe.
2. (a) Explain the various factors which promoted changes in the role and status of women in Europe in the period 1945–*c.* 1980;
   (b) Explain the various factors which hindered or prevented such changes.
3. 'In the period *c.* 1945–*c.* 1980, most Europeans enjoyed improvements both in living standards and in quality of life.'
   (a) Outline in what ways this statement is justified;
   (b) Explain why these improvements occurred.
4. (a) Explain the reasons for the growth and popularity of television in Britain and Europe after 1945;
   (b) Analyse the impact of television upon any one of the following: cinema; radio; newspapers and magazines; sport.
5. How far does your study of history support the claim made by Arthur Marwick that, 'Between *c.*1958 and *c.*1973, there was a 'cultural revolution' in western Europe'?
   (You may choose to illustrate your answer with special reference to any one individual country.)

6. What conclusions can be reached about the society and history of Europe in the period 1945–95 by a study of any one or more of the following: cinema; radio; newspapers; education; music; sport; television?

7. Explain how the evidence about culture and society contained in the photographs on pages 435, 449–50, 453, 457, 462 and 463 in this book might be used to illustrate continuity and change in any *one* of the following: the urban environment; popular entertainment; the roles of women and girls; youth culture.

B *Planning an essay*

Examine the influences that have promoted social and cultural change in this period with special reference to one of the following: cinema; television; sport; newspapers and radio; education.

Q

1. What happened? What needs to be explained?
(a) What social and cultural trends took place between c.1929 and c.1980? Outline some of the developments which you regard as important, focusing attention on a few themes you will deal with later in the essay;
(b) Sum up the timescale – the key events (Second World War; 1968, etc.) that shaped some of these developments;
(c) Define and explain some of the exceptions to your broad general themes – the, differences which are due to political, religious and regional factors. (eg., totalitarian dictatorships in the 1930s; the Soviet Bloc after 1945; the North–South divide in Italy; Franco's Spain).
2. Theories and causes – the argument of the essay
(a) Choose a selection of 'most important' influences which have caused, or accelerated, social and cultural changes (e.g., Americanisation; the long post-war economic boom in Western Europe; expansion of higher education);
(b) Argue why some causes are, in your opinion, especially important. Link these points to your chosen aspect of society/culture (cinema, sport, etc.).
N.B. Many of the trends you have identified at the start will also be causes or influences (e.g., television; Americanisation; global youth culture; mass tourism). Be careful about which angle you approach from.

Q

3. *Illustrating your arguments through a special topic*
Choose which topic you want to specialise in. Collect specific evidence covering the whole timescale and relating to three countries (a good choice might be Britain, France or Italy, somewhere in Eastern Europe). Then use this evidence to 'prove' that what you wrote about the general themes earlier in your essay makes sense – either because your examples are typical, or because they are 'exceptions-which-prove-the-rule'.

4. *Conclusion*
Ensure your conclusion comes back to the general themes with which you began.

Conclusion

WHAT HAPPENED TO EUROPE IN THE 'YEARS OF DIVISION'?

The key issue was that Europe was indeed divided. For almost fifty years, the Iron Curtain marked a military, political, economic and psychological frontier. For many people, 'Europe' came to mean the handful of Western countries that made up the EEC. Other countries came to be regarded as separate and 'Eastern' when, in fact, they were in the heart of Central Europe. The great significance of the end of the 'Gorbachev Revolution' of 1989–91 is that it removed this artificial dividing line, enabling trade and tourism to bring cities like Prague and Budapest back into the European mainstream where they belonged. One of the aims of this book is to restore the idea of Europe in its widest sense – what de Gaulle called 'Europe from the Atlantic to the Urals'.

On either side of the Cold War divide, the history of Europe followed a rhythm of events already familiar from the chapters of this book. There was the colossal impact of the Second World War and of the political and social revolutions it brought about. There was the massive task of reconstruction out of the ruins of the War. There was the development of the 'Soviet model' in Eastern Europe, paralleled by the political development of Western Europe under the twin umbrellas of NATO and the EEC. In the West, there was 'the thirty glorious years' of the long post-war boom. On both sides of the Iron Curtain, there was the massive expansion of state intervention in education and welfare. From the 1960s, there was the development of the global youth culture and the enormous growth of international tourism. In the 1980s, there was the intensification of Cold War hostilities, followed by the sudden collapse of the Soviet Bloc. In the 1990s, there was the difficult adjustment to the post-Cold War world, with an alarming return to instability and war.

Between the end of the Second World War and the aftermath of the Cold War, huge changes can be measured. In 1945, few would have guessed that fifty years later historians might be speculating about the 'death of socialism'. Those who hoped that the defeat of Hitler meant that fascism and anti-semitism had been discredited forever would have been discouraged by their resurgence forty years later. In 1945, nobody had any idea how the work of Alan Turing and others on the use of 'intelligent machines' for wartime code-breaking would lead to the ever-expanding role of computers in modern society. Only a handful might have guessed at the extent of decolonisation after 1945, or of the globalisation of the economy, or of the extent to which cinema and radio would be overtaken by television.

As always in history, there was continuity as well as change; and many significant trends did not seem especially important at the time, only afterwards.

The following brief glimpses of the lives of three different women in three different parts of Europe may illustrate how the patterns of continuity and change during the 'years of division' appeared at the end of the 1990s:

● Antonella was a woman who lived all her life in the village in the Italian *Mezzogiorno* where she was born in 1919. She spent her entire childhood and youth under fascism. She married at twenty-one and started her family amid the chaos of war and civil war in 1940–46. A pious Catholic, she voted Christian Democrat in every election until 1994, when she decided to support the neo-fascist MSI. Antonella made her living mostly from piecework at home, sewing and finishing clothes for a local businessman. Her younger daughter married a lawyer from Milan and the two women often disagreed over family issues, voting on opposite sides in the 1974 referendum on divorce. Of her five sons, only one stayed in the village; three moved north in search of work and one worked for twenty-four years in Detroit before returning home to buy the local café. At the time of her eightieth birthday in 1999, most of the population of the village was elderly like herself.

● Ludmila was born in a village in the Ukraine in 1920. When she was twelve, all her family except one younger brother died in the great famine of 1933. Her home was destroyed in 1941, when her village was overrun by the Germans, and again in 1943, when it was liberated. She had one child but both her brother and her husband were killed fighting on the Eastern Front in 1944. After the war, she worked for many years as a clerk on a large collective farm and, later, as a school caretaker. Though very religious, Ludmila remained a firm believer in Communism and remembers 'crying for days' when Stalin died. Her son served in the Navy with the Black Sea Fleet and neither he nor Ludmila were enthusiastic when the Ukraine declared its independence from the USSR. At the time of her seventy-fifth birthday in 1995, Ludmila was a widow living on a very small state pension. She spent a lot of her time looking after the newly-rebuilt church near her village and made occasional bus trips to Kiev to sell home-grown vegetables.

● Jean was born in a city in the North of England in 1909. She worked as a sales assistant in a department store until she married at the age of twenty-six. Her three sons all graduated from university in the 1960s; two became teachers and one an officer in the Royal Navy, later seconded to work at NATO headquarters in Belgium. Jean was a full-time housewife and mother and never lived away from her home city; but by the time of her ninetieth birthday in 1999, her grandchildren illustrated the new social mobility of post-war Europe. Of four granddaughters, one was working full-time in Germany, one was teaching English in China, one was training to be a teacher and one was still at school. Of her three grandsons, one was working as an engineer on a contract in the Persian Gulf, one was graduating from university and one was taking a year out after A-levels to work in the USA.

Literally millions of other snapshot biographies could tell a similar story about the impact of war and about the kaleidoscope of change in European politics and society between 1945 and the 1990s. Such changes, however, do not stop, nor do they always appear in the same light. In 1991, with the end of the Cold War, there was much easy optimism about the 'peace dividend' and the spread of Western prosperity and stable democracy across the new Europe. When NATO forces were drawn into the war in Bosnia in 1995 and again into Kosovo in 1999, however, such optimism seemed very simplistic and premature. In retrospect, the 'years of division' seemed rather more attractive.

At the end of the 1990s, there were deep anxieties about the dangers of nationalism and further ethnic conflicts, especially those threatening to bring instability to the Balkans and to the former USSR. There were widespread uncertainties about the widening of the European Union, about the stability of the European economy and about how to keep on paying for state welfare when so much of the population was over sixty-five. There were concerns about 'global warming' and dangerous pollution of the environment. As the end of the millenium approached, it was fashionable for journalists to sum up the past and to speculate about the future. For historians, the safest assumption is that most of these predictions will turn out to be very wrong and that most of the important developments of the next fifty years will be a surprise. No crystal ball can safely tell us what the *Years of...* textbook about 1995–2045 will be called – or even if there will still be history students waiting to learn from it.

Glossary

Index